Netwo

CCNA 1 Companion Guide

KU-681-240

Wendell Odom

Tom Knott

Cisco Press

800 East 96th Street

Indianapolis, Indiana 46240 USA

Networking Basics
CCNA 1 Companion Guide

Wendell Odom • Tom Knott

Published by:
Cisco Press
800 East 96th Street
Indianapolis, IN 46240 USA

Printed in the United States of America 1 2 3 4 5 6 7 8 9 0

First Printing   March 2006

Library of Congress Cataloging-in-Publication Number: 2005934969

ISBN: 1-58713-164-1

Publisher
John Wait

Editor-in-Chief
John Kane

Cisco Representative
Anthony Wolfenden

Cisco Press Program Manager
Jeff Brady

Executive Editor
Mary Beth Ray

Production Manager
Patrick Kanouse

Development Editor
Dayna Isley

Senior Project Editor
San Dee Phillips

Copy Editors
Sheri Cain
Bill McManus

Technical Editors
Stephen Kalman
K Kirkendall

Editorial Assistant
Raina Han

Book and Cover Designer
Louisa Adair

Composition
Mark Shirar

Indexer
WordWise Publishing Services

Proofreader
Gayle Johnson

Trademark Acknowledgments

Warning and Disclaimer

This book is part of the Cisco Networking Academy® Program series from Cisco Press. The products in this series support and complement the Cisco Networking Academy Program curriculum. If you are using this book outside the Networking Academy program, then you are not preparing with a Cisco trained and authorized Networking Academy provider.

For information on the Cisco Networking Academy Program or to locate a Networking Academy, please visit www.cisco.com/edu.

Feedback Information

At Cisco Press, our goal is to create in-depth technical books of the highest quality and value. Each book is crafted with care and precision, undergoing rigorous development that involves the unique expertise of members from the professional technical community.

Readers' feedback is a natural continuation of this process. If you have any comments regarding how we could improve the quality of this book, or otherwise alter it to better suit your needs, you can contact us through e-mail at feedback@ciscopress.com. Please make sure to include the book title and ISBN in your message.

We greatly appreciate your assistance.

CISCO SYSTEMS

Corporate Headquarters
Cisco Systems, Inc.
170 West Tasman Drive
San Jose, CA 95134-1706
USA
www.cisco.com
Tel: 408 526-4000
      800 553-NETS (6387)
Fax: 408 526-4100

European Headquarters
Cisco Systems International BV
Haarlerbergpark
Haarlerbergweg 13-19
1101 CH Amsterdam
The Netherlands
www-europe.cisco.com
Tel: 31 0 20 357 1000
Fax: 31 0 20 357 1100

Americas Headquarters
Cisco Systems, Inc.
170 West Tasman Drive
San Jose, CA 95134-1706
USA
www.cisco.com
Tel: 408 526-7660
Fax: 408 527-0883

Asia Pacific Headquarters
Cisco Systems, Inc.
Capital Tower
168 Robinson Road
#22-01 to #29-01
Singapore 068912
www.cisco.com
Tel: +65 6317 7777
Fax: +65 6317 7799

Cisco Systems has more than 200 offices in the following countries and regions. Addresses, phone numbers, and fax numbers are listed on the **Cisco.com Web site at www.cisco.com/go/offices.**

Argentina • Australia • Austria • Belgium • Brazil • Bulgaria • Canada • Chile • China PRC • Colombia • Costa Rica • Croatia • Czech Republic
Denmark • Dubai, UAE • Finland • France • Germany • Greece • Hong Kong SAR • Hungary • India • Indonesia • Ireland • Israel • Italy
Japan • Korea • Luxembourg • Malaysia • Mexico • The Netherlands • New Zealand • Norway • Peru • Philippines • Poland • Portugal
Puerto Rico • Romania • Russia • Saudi Arabia • Scotland • Singapore • Slovakia • Slovenia • South Africa • Spain • Sweden
Switzerland • Taiwan • Thailand • Turkey • Ukraine • United Kingdom • United States • Venezuela • Vietnam • Zimbabwe

About the Authors

Wendell Odom, CCIE No. 1624, is a senior instructor with Skyline Advanced Technology Services (www.skyline-ats.com), where he teaches the QOS, CCIE, and CCNA courses. Wendell has worked in the networking arena for more than 20 years, with jobs in pre- and post-sales technical consulting, teaching, and course development. He has authored several Cisco Press books, including the best-selling *CCNA INTRO Exam Certification Guide* and *CCNA ICND Exam Certification Guide*, as well as the *QoS Exam Certification Guide*, *Computer Networking First-Step*, and *CCIE Routing and Switching Official Exam Certification Guide*.

Tom Knott is the Cisco Networking Academy instructor at Southeast Raleigh Magnet High School in North Carolina. He has taught all versions of the CCNA curriculum since v1.0 and also teaches Fundamentals of UNIX and Networking I classes. As a regional instructor, he also trains and supports local Cisco Academies.

About the Technical Reviewers

Stephen Kalman is a data security trainer. He is the author of *Web Security Field Guide* (published by Cisco Press), and he is the technical editor of more than 20 books, courses, and computer-based training (CBT) titles. In addition to those responsibilities, Stephen runs a consulting company, Esquire Micro Consultants, which specializes in network-security assessments and forensics. Stephen holds CISSP, CEH, CHFI, CCNA, CCSA (Checkpoint), A+, Network+, and Security+ certifications. He is also a member of the New York State Bar.

K Kirkendall is an instructor at Boise State University in Boise, Idaho, where he teaches Microsoft, Cisco, network security, and CompTIA courses. For the last six years, K has also worked as a member of the Cisco Assessment Development and Innovation Group, where he is a subject matter expert (SME) for the Cisco Networking Academy Assessment and Cisco certification team. K has a BA in business administration from St. Leo College, and he is working on a master's degree in information technology at University of Idaho. He has several industry certifications, including CCNP, CCDP, CCNA, CCDA, CCAI, MCP, CNA, A+, Network+, and Server+. K has a wonderful and understanding wife, Jeanine, and they have five wonderful children and three grandsons (Isaiah, Kadren, and Tyler) and one granddaughter (McKaila).

Acknowledgments

From Wendell Odom:

This book was very much a team effort from many people. Taking a few moments at the end of writing a book to acknowledge each person's efforts is one of the joys of the book-writing process. Simply put, the great team we've had on this book has made this book not only possible, but also we hope that this book will be what instructors and students of the Cisco Networking Academy Program want in a Companion Guide.

Tom Knott provided the most precious commodity for writing this book: his knowledge and insights into the Academy Program and the online curriculum. The bonus was that Tom was a rock of consistency with his parts of the book, and on advising me about how to approach this audience. Tom, thanks for the hard and excellent work.

Thanks to the technical editors, both of whom provided excellent feedback on the manuscript, including technical comments and comments about how to approach the topics for this audience. While I must take the blame for any remaining errors, both tech editors helped catch and remove the errors. Steve Kalman, who worked on several of my other books, gave his usual strong technical input as usual, as well as some great stories and analogies that helped the book. K also added valuable insights about the organization of the topics in each chapter—thanks for helping us keep working to sift through the countless competing trade-offs with this book.

I had the pleasure of asking for help from family on a few occasions with this book as well. First, Katie Reed (my niece) helped me understand how students learn about fractions and ratios in school today, which was particularly helpful because it has been more than a few years since I learned about them in school. Uncle Buck helped out by explaining a little more—okay, a lot more—about how electricity really works. To boot, it was fun to talk about this stuff with others in the family. Thanks for all the help!

Mary Beth Ray and I first discussed this book almost two years before publication. MB knew we would have an opportunity to essentially rewrite and improve these books for this edition, and she's kept her eye on the ball for the long duration of this project. MB, thanks for inviting Tom and me to work on the book, and working with us through the bumps and bruises to get there.

Dayna worked as the development editor, which means that she (as usual) got to work on the first cut of the chapters. And she volunteered for it to boot! Seriously, Dayna, thanks for volunteering; you made it a much better book. Your memory for how all the content interrelates is amazing; it's scary when someone knows what you've written twice as well as you do. The book's a ton better because of you.

We used a different process for this book compared to most Cisco Press books, including the ones I'd written before. As a result, I got to see a lot of the behind-the-scenes work that is normally hidden from me. I'm more convinced than ever that I have the easy part of the writing job, and the folks who follow me at Cisco Press have the hardest parts. Sheri and Bill, thanks for taking my attempts at writing and turning it into something truly clear. It's not easy work, but the improvement is dramatic, and it's all the more difficult when sharing duties to get us to the game on time. San Dee, thanks for picking up the ball for the production process, dancing with too many fish to fry, and all the other silly mixed metaphors while getting this thing ready for the printer. Sorry for pushing to see PDFs of the chapters, but I have stuff to do! And for the rest of the crew I still didn't work with directly much at all, thanks for making it all happen.

Of all the other times in which I've written a book (this one's number 10, counting each new edition), I've never felt more indebted to the most important members of my family: my God, my wife Kris, and my little girl Hannah. This book required a lot of work in a short time—six months from starting until crossing t's and dotting i's—and it took many sacrifices at home. I look forward to more quality time with all of you.

From Tom Knott:

I have enjoyed watching the Cisco Networking Academy Program change and grow over the years. I appreciate the opportunity to grow with it and the support from Cisco Systems in Research Triangle Park, NC. Thanks in particular to Joe Freddoso, Shel Adderly, and Ruth McCullers Lee.

I also wish to thank Susan Weatherly and Debi Hallman from the Cisco Networking Academy Program for the encouragement and support over the years. I couldn't have made it to this stage without you.

Wendell Odom, the principal author of this book, showed great patience in leading me through this creative process. He not only helped with explaining how a book goes from concept to paper, but he also took the time to answer my many technical questions. I feel this cooperative effort has made me a better instructor.

Lastly, I wish to thank Mary Beth Ray and the rest of the Cisco Press editors (Dayna Isley and San Dee Phillips) who guided us through this project. Your timely feedback made it possible to meet the deadlines. Mary Beth, thank you for offering me this opportunity. It was both educational and fun.

Dedications

For Hannah Grace.

—Wendell Odom

For Donna and Marissa.

—Tom Knott

Contents at a Glance

Introduction   xxii

Chapter 1   Introduction to Networking   1

Chapter 2   Networking Fundamentals   69

Chapter 3   Networking Media   123

Chapter 4   Cable Testing   165

Chapter 5   Cabling LANs and WANs   187

Chapter 6   Ethernet Fundamentals   235

Chapter 7   Ethernet Technologies   267

Chapter 8   Ethernet Switching   295

Chapter 9   TCP/IP Protocol Suite and IP Addressing   337

chapter 10   Routing Fundamentals and Subnets   391

chapter 11   TCP/IP Transport and Application Layers   453

Appendix A   Answers to Check Your Understanding and Challenge Questions   485

Appendix B   Decimal to Binary Conversion Table   511

Appendix C   Extra Practice   517

Glossary   531

Index   567

Contents

Introduction   xxii

Chapter 1   Introduction to Networking   1

Objectives   1

Key Terms   1

Connecting to Networks and the Internet   3

What's a Network?   3

A Small Network: Two PCs and One Cable   4

A Very Large Network: The Internet   4

Perspectives on Networks of Different Sizes   7

Network Components   7

Computer Hardware   7

Network Interface Cards   13

Network Cabling Basics   16

Networking Devices   17

Enterprise Networks and Home Internet Access   19

Enterprise Network Basics   19

Accessing an ISP Through a Phone Line and an Analog Modem   21

Accessing an ISP Through a Phone Line and a DSL Modem   23

Accessing an ISP Through a Cable TV Cable and a Cable Modem   24

TCP/IP Protocol Suite and TCP/IP Software   25

Networking Standards, Protocols, and the TCP/IP Protocol Suite   25

Using HTTP to Download a Web Page   26

TCP/IP Networking Model   28

TCP/IP Transport Layer and the TCP Protocol   29

TCP/IP Internet Layer and the Internet Protocol   30

Troubleshooting Basics for IP   34

Troubleshooting Tools   38

TCP/IP Wrap Up   45

Network Math   45

Bits and Bytes   45

Names and Abbreviations for Large Numbers of Bits and Bytes   45

Names for the Rate at Which a Network Sends Data   46

ASCII Alphanumeric Code   47

Decimal Numbering System: Base 10   48

Binary Numbering System: Base 2   49

Converting From 8-Bit Binary Numbers to Decimal Numbers   49

Converting from Decimal Numbers to 8-Bit Binary Numbers   51

Generic Decimal-to-8-Bit-Binary Conversion Process   51

Example 1 of the Generic Conversion Process: Decimal 235   52

Alternative Decimal-to-Binary Conversion Process   54

Example 2 of the Generic Conversion Process: Decimal 192   56

Converting IP Addresses Between Decimal and Binary   56

Converting Decimal IP Addresses to Binary IP Addresses   57

Converting Binary IP Addresses to Decimal IP Addresses   57

Using a Conversion Chart   58

Hexadecimal Numbering System: Base 16   59

Boolean or Binary Logic   60

IP Subnet Masks   61

Using Boolean Math with Subnets   62

Summary   63

Check Your Understanding   64

Challenge Questions and Activities   67

Chapter 2   Networking Fundamentals   69

Objectives   69

Key Terms   69

Networking Basics and Terminology   71

A Brief History of the Networking Universe   71

The Need for Networking Protocols and Standards   73

Ethernet LANs and LAN Devices   74

Ethernet Repeaters   75

Ethernet Hubs and 10BASE-T   76

Ethernet Bridges   78

Ethernet Frames   80

Unicast and Broadcast Ethernet Frames and Addresses   81

LAN Switches   82

Wide-Area Networks   83

Point-to-Point Leased Lines   83

Routers and Their Use with WANs   85

MANs and SANs   85

MANs   85

SANs   86

Virtual Private Networks   87

Intranet VPNs   89

Comparing Intranet VPNs to Extranet and Access VPNs   90

Network Topologies   91
   Physical Bus, Physical Star, and Logical Bus Topologies   91
   Ring Topologies   94
   Hierarchical and Extended Star Physical Topologies   95
   Mesh: Full and Partial   95

Bandwidth   97
   LAN and WAN Bandwidth   97
      Ethernet LAN Bandwidths   97
      WAN Bandwidths   98
   Throughput Versus Bandwidth   100
   Calculating Data Transfer Time   102
   Analog Bandwidth   103
   Planning for Bandwidth   104

The OSI and TCP/IP Networking Models   105
   OSI Model   106
      OSI Layers   107
      Functions of the OSI Layers   108
   TCP/IP Networking Model   110
      Encapsulation   111
      Segments, Packets, Frames, and PDUs   112
      De-encapsulation   113
      Layer Interactions   114

Summary   115

Check Your Understanding   118

Chapter 3   **Networking Media   123**

Objectives   123

Additional Topics of Interest   123

Key Terms   124

Copper Media   125
   Digital Transmission Using Copper Wires   125
      The Chemistry Behind Electricity: Atoms and Electrons   126
      Insulators, Conductors, and Semiconductors   129
      Electromagnetic Force (Voltage)   130
      Current   130
      Resistance, Impedance, and Attenuation   132
      Circuits   133
   Popular LAN Copper Cabling   134
      Coaxial Cable   136

STP Cable   137
UTP Cable   139

Optical Media   146

Comparing Fiber-Optic Cabling and Copper Cabling   146

Electromagnetic Spectrum   147

Fiber-Optic Cabling   149

Using Two Fibers—One for Each Direction   150
Fiber-Optic Cable Components   150
Multimode and Single-Mode Fiber   151

Wireless Media   152

Enterprise WLAN Components and Design   153

WLAN Organization and Standards   155

Summary   157

Check Your Understanding   159

Challenge Questions and Activities   162

Chapter 4   **Cable Testing   165**

Objectives   165

Additional Topics of Interest   165

Key Terms   166

Frequency-Based Cable Testing   167

Waves   167

Sine Waves and Square Waves   168

Analog and Digital Signals   169

Simple and Complex Analog Signals   169
Creating Digital Signals from Analog Signals   170

Signals and Noise   171

Signaling over Copper and Fiber-Optic Cabling   172

Copper Cabling Transmission Basics   172
Optical Cabling Transmission Basics   174

Attenuation and Insertion Loss on Copper Media   175

Sources of Noise on Copper Media   176

Types of Crosstalk   178

Cable Testing Standards   180

Summary   183

Check Your Understanding   185

Chapter 5   Cabling LANs and WANs   187

Objectives   187

Additional Topics of Interest   187

Key Terms   187

Cabling LANs   189

LAN Cabling Fundamentals   189
Ethernet LAN Physical Layer   190
Choosing Ethernet Types (Speeds) in the Campus   191
Ethernet LAN Media and Connectors   194
Picking UTP Cable Pinouts   196
Connecting Ethernet Networking Devices   200
Repeaters   200
Hubs   201
Bridges   203
Ethernet Switches   206
Wireless Communications and Wireless Access Points   209
Ethernet NICs   211
Using the LAN: Models for PC Communications   212
Peer-to-Peer Networking   213
Client/Server Networking   215

Cabling WANs   216

WAN Physical and Data Link Layers   217
Router Serial Interfaces   217
Cable, DSL, and ISDN   220
WAN Speeds   221
Choosing DCE and DTE Cables   222
Fixed and Modular Routers   224
Router Console Cabling   225

Summary   227

Check Your Understanding   229

Challenge Questions and Activities   232

Chapter 6   Ethernet Fundamentals   235

Objectives   235

Additional Topics of Interest   235

Key Terms   235

Ethernet Fundamentals   237
The History of Ethernet   237

The Names of Different IEEE Ethernet Types   238

IEEE Ethernet Standards and the OSI Model   240

    IEEE 802.3 Standards   240

    The IEEE 802.2 Logical Link Control Standard   240

    Comparing Ethernet Standards to the OSI Model   241

Ethernet Framing   242

    Encapsulating Packets Inside Ethernet Frames   243

    The Fields in the IEEE 802.3 Frame   244

    DIX Framing and IEEE Framing   246

The Format of MAC Addresses   247

Sending Frames over Different Types of Ethernet   247

LLC, SNAP, and Determining the Type of Protocol   248

    Additional Background on IEEE 802.2 Logical Link Control   249

    The IEEE SNAP Header   250

    The DIX and IEEE Type Field   250

Ethernet Operation   251

Rules Governing When a Device Can Transmit: CSMA/CD   251

    The CSMA/CD Algorithm   252

    CSMA/CD and Collisions on 10BASE-T LANs with Hubs   253

Full Duplex, Half Duplex, and Collision Domains   254

    Preventing Collisions with Switch Buffering   255

    Collision Domains and Full Duplex   256

Autonegotiation of Duplex and Speed   257

Deterministic and Nondeterministic Media Access   259

Summary   260

Check Your Understanding   262

Challenge Questions and Activities   265

Chapter 7   **Ethernet Technologies   267**

Objectives   267

Additional Topics of Interest   267

Key Terms   267

10- and 100-Mbps Ethernet   269

10-Mbps Ethernet   269

10BASE-T   272

    10BASE-T Wiring   272

    10BASE-T Design: Using Hubs, CSMA/CD, and Half Duplex   275

    10BASE-T Design: Using Switches   276

100-Mbps Ethernet   278
   100BASE-TX Ethernet   278
   Designing Ethernets with Two Speeds   280
   100BASE-FX   281

Gigabit Ethernet and Beyond   282
   1000BASE-X   283
   1000BASE-T   286
   Future of Ethernet   288

Summary   290

Check Your Understanding   292

Challenge Questions and Activities   294

Chapter 8   **Ethernet Switching   295**

Objectives   295

Key Terms   295

Ethernet Switch Operations   297
   Layer 2 Bridging and Switching Operations   297
     The Forwarding and Filtering Decision   298
     Learning CAM Table Entries and Flooding Unknown Unicasts   301
     Handling Unknown Unicasts   304
     Forwarding Broadcasts and Multicasts   304
   The Cisco Switch CAM   306
   Switch Internal Processing   307
     Latency   307
     Store-and-Forward Switching   308
     Cut-Through Switching   309
     Fragment-Free Switching   309
     Comparing the Internal Processing Paths   310
   Spanning Tree Protocol   310
     STP Blocking   312
     STP States   313
     Changing the CAM with the Listening and Learning States   314

LAN Design: Collision Domains and Broadcast Domains   317
   Collision Domains   318
     Large/Long Collision Domains   319
     Creating Many Small Collision Domains   321
     How Switches and Bridges Prevent Collisions   323
   Layer 2 Broadcast Domains   325
     Performance Impact of Broadcast and Broadcast Domains   326
     The Impact of Broadcasts and Multicasts Today   327

Identifying Networking Devices by OSI Layer 328

Data Flow Using Layer 1, Layer 2, and Layer 3 Devices 329

The Ambiguous Term Segment 331

Summary 331

Check Your Understanding 333

Challenge Questions and Activities 336

Chapter 9 **TCP/IP Protocol Suite and IP Addressing 337**

Objectives 337

Additional Topics of Interest 337

Key Terms 337

TCP/IP Model 339

TCP/IP Network Access (Network Interface) Layer 340

TCP/IP Internet Layer 341

Core Protocols of the Internet Layer 341
Basic IP Routing 342
IP Packets 343
How IP Routing Uses IP Addresses 344

TCP/IP Transport Layer 345

TCP/IP Application Layer 347

Perspectives on the TCP/IP and OSI Models 349

Perspectives on the Different TCP/IP Layers 350
TCP/IP Internetworks and the Network Layer Perspective 350
Network-Centric and Host-Centric Views of Networking Models 352

IP Addressing Fundamentals 353

Basic Facts About IP Addresses 353

Address Assignment and Address Classes 353

Three Key Rules for IP Address Assignment on LANs 355
Defining Class A, B, and C IP Networks 356
Analyzing the Structure of IP Addresses 358
Other Address Classes and the Entire IPv4 Address Space 359
IP Network Number and the Broadcast Address 361

Network Math 362

Using the Powers of 2 362
Calculating the Number of Hosts per Network 363
Number of Class A, B, and C Networks 363
Converting from Decimal to Binary: Large Numbers 364

Subnetting Basics   364

A Simple Subnetting Example   365

Differing Views of the Format of Subnetted IP Addresses   366

Subnet Masks   367

Ensuring Unique IP Addresses Throughout the Internet   368

*Original Internet Design: Unique Network Numbers for Each
    Enterprise Network   369*

The Problem of IPv4 Address Depletion   370

One Short-Term Solution: NAT and Private IP Networks   371

Private IP Networks   372

Long-Term Solution: IP Version 6 (IPv6)   372

Assigning and Mapping IP Addresses   373

Static IP Address Configuration   373

Dynamic IP Address Configuration Using DHCP   375

Comparing Static and DHCP Address Assignment   377

Using ARP and Proxy ARP on LANs   378

Using IP ARP on a Single LAN   378

Using IP ARP in Larger Networks   380

Proxy ARP   383

Summary   384

Check Your Understanding   386

Challenge Questions and Activities   389

Chapter 10   **Routing Fundamentals and Subnets   391**

Objectives   391

Key Terms   391

IP Routing (Forwarding)   393

A Brief History of Some Confounding Terms   394

Routing Between Two Connected LAN Subnets   395

IP-Centric Perspective   396

Network Access Layer Perspective   397

IP Routing: Host Perspective   398

Brief Review of Routing So Far   400

A Deeper Look at Routing   400

Details of Routing in a Single Router   401

Perspectives on WAN Routing   403

IP Routing: Working with Layer 2 Protocols   403

Importance of Layer 3-to-Layer 2 Mapping   404

Comparing Routing and Switching Logic   405

Comparing the Benefits of Routing and Switching   406

Important Characteristics of IP   407
    IP Is Unreliable   408
    IP Is Connectionless   408
Full IP Header   409

Routing Protocols   411

How Routers Learn IP Routes   411
    Learning Connected Routes   411
    Static Routes   412
    Basics of Learning Routes with Routing Protocols   413
Routing Protocol Features   414
    Using Metrics to Pick the Best Routes   414
    Interior and Exterior Routing Protocols   418
    Routing Protocol Algorithms   419
    Routing Protocol Updates   421
    Classless and Classful Routing Protocols   422
Comparing Routing Protocols   422

IP Subnetting   424

A Brief Review of Subnetting   424
Determining the Number of Required Subnets and the Resulting Subnet
   Mask   425
    Determining the Number of Subnets and Hosts   426
    Determining the Number of Subnet and Host Bits in the Mask   427
    Determining the Subnet Mask: Binary Version   429
    Determining the Subnet Mask: Shortcut Version   432
Determining the Subnet Numbers and Assignable IP Addresses in Each
   Subnet   434
    Terminology and Background   434
    Finding the Subnet Numbers—Binary   435
    Finding the Subnet Broadcast Address: Binary   438
    Finding the Range of Valid Addresses   438
    Finding Subnets and Broadcast Addresses Using Shortcuts   439
Determining the Subnet in Which a Host Resides   442
    Finding the Resident Subnet: Binary   443
    Finding the Resident Subnet: Shortcut   444

Summary   445

Check Your Understanding   447

Challenge Questions and Activities   451

Chapter 11   **TCP/IP Transport and Application Layers   453**

Objectives   453

Key Terms   453

The TCP/IP Transport Layer   455

  Flow Control and Windowing   456
    Flow Control Through Dynamic Sliding Windows   456
    Flow Control Through Withholding Acknowledgments   457
  Establishing and Terminating TCP Connections   458
  TCP Error Recovery (Reliability)   459
  Segmentation, Reassembly, and In-Order Delivery   461
  TCP and UDP Header Reference   462
  Identifying Application Processes Using Port Numbers   464
    Connection to Servers: Well-Known Ports   465
    Comparing Well-Known, Dynamic, and Registered Ports   467

The TCP/IP Application Layer   468

  Application Protocols Used by End Users   469
    Name Resolution Using DNS   469
    World Wide Web and HTTP   471
    E-Mail Protocols: SMTP and POP3   472
    File Transfer Protocol   474
  Application Protocols Often Used for Network Management   475
    TFTP   475
    SNMP   475
    Telnet   476
  Application Protocol Summary   477

Summary   478

Check Your Understanding   479

Challenge Questions and Activities   484

Appendix A   **Answers to Check Your Understanding and Challenge Questions
                 485**

Appendix B   **Decimal to Binary Conversion Table   511**

Appendix C   **Extra Practice   517**

Glossary   **531**

Index   **567**

Icons Used in This Book

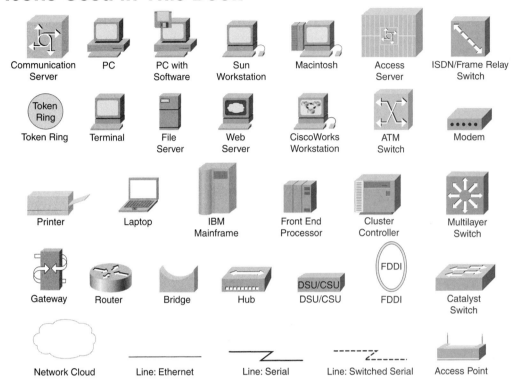

Command Syntax Conventions

The conventions used to present command syntax in this book are the same conventions used in the IOS Command Reference. The Command Reference describes these conventions as follows:

- **Boldface** indicates commands and keywords that are entered literally as shown. In actual configuration examples and output (not general command syntax), boldface indicates commands that the user manually inputs (such as a **show** command).

- *Italic* indicates arguments for which you supply actual values.

- Vertical bars (|) separate alternative, mutually exclusive elements.

- Square brackets [ ] indicate an optional element.

- Braces { } indicate a required choice.

- Braces within brackets [{ }] indicate a required choice within an optional element.

Introduction

The Cisco Networking Academy Program is a comprehensive e-learning program that provides students with Internet technology skills. A Networking Academy delivers web-based content, online assessment, student performance tracking, and hands-on labs to prepare students for industry-standard certifications. The CCNA curriculum includes four courses oriented around the topics on the CCNA certification exam.

Networking Basics CCNA 1 Companion Guide is the official supplemental textbook to be used with v3.1 of the CCNA 1 online curriculum of the Networking Academy. As a textbook, this book provides a ready reference to explain the same networking concepts, technologies, protocols, and devices as the online curriculum.

This book goes beyond previous editions of the Cisco Press *Companion Guides* by providing many alternate explanations and examples as compared with the course. You can use the online curriculum as directed by your instructor, and then also use this *Companion Guide's* alternate examples to help solidify your understanding of all the topics.

Goals of This Book

First and foremost, by providing a fresh, complementary perspective on the online content, this book helps you learn all the required materials of the first course in the Networking Academy CCNA curriculum. As a secondary goal, individuals who do not always have Internet access can use this text as a mobile replacement for the online curriculum. In those cases, you can read the appropriate sections of this book, as directed by your instructor, and learn the same material that appears in the online curriculum. Another secondary goal of this book is to serve as your offline study material to help prepare you for the CCNA exam.

Audience for This Book

This book's main audience is anyone taking the first CCNA course of the Networking Academy curriculum. Many Networking Academies use this textbook as a required tool in the course, while other Networking Academies recommend the *Companion Guides* as an additional source of study and practice materials.

This book's secondary audience includes people taking CCNA-related classes from professional training organizations and anyone wanting to read and learn about computer-networking basics.

Book Features

All the features for this edition of this book are either new or improved to facilitate your full understanding of the course material. The educational features focus on supporting topic coverage, readability, and practice of the course material.

Topic Coverage

The following features give you a thorough overview of the topics covered in each chapter so that you can make constructive use of your study time. Also see the section "A Word About the Scope of Topics in This Book" on the next page:

- **Objectives**—Listed at the beginning of each chapter, the objectives reference the *core* concepts covered in the chapter. The objectives match the objectives stated in the corresponding modules of the online curriculum; however, the question format in the *Companion Guide* encourages you to think about finding the answers as you read the chapter.

- **(New) Additional topics of interest**—Several chapters of this book contain topics that cover more details about previous topics or related topics that are less important to the chapter's primary focus. The list at the beginning of the chapter lets you know that additional coverage can be found on the accompanying CD-ROM.

- **(New) "How To"** —When this book covers a set of steps that you need to perform for certain tasks, this book gives the steps as a how-to list. When you are studying, the icon helps you easily refer to this feature as you skim through the book.

- **Notes, tips, cautions, and warnings**—Short sidebars in the margins point out interesting facts, time-saving methods, and important safety issues.

- **Chapter summaries**—At the end of each chapter is a summary of the chapter's key concepts. It provides a synopsis of the chapter and serves as a study aid.

Readability

The authors have completely rewritten the material so that it has a more conversational tone that follows a consistent and accessible reading level. In addition, the following features have been updated to assist your understanding of the networking vocabulary:

- **(New) Key terms**—Each chapter begins with a list of key terms, along with a page-number reference from the chapter. The terms are listed in the order in which they are explained in the chapter. This handy reference allows you to find a term, flip to the page where the term appears, and see the term used in context. The Glossary defines all the key terms.

- **(New) Glossary**—This book contains an all-new Glossary with more than 700 terms. The Glossary defines not only the key terms from the chapters, but also terms you might find helpful in working toward your CCNA certification.

Practice

Practice makes perfect. This new *Companion Guide* offers you ample opportunities to put what you learn into practice. You will find the following features valuable and effective in reinforcing the instruction you receive:

- **(New) Check Your Understanding questions and answer key**—Updated review questions are presented at the end of each chapter as a self-assessment tool. These questions match the style of questions you see on the online course assessments. Appendix A, "Answers to Check Your Understanding and Challenge Questions," provides an answer key to all the questions and explains each answer.

- **(New) Challenge questions and activities**—Additional—and more challenging—review questions and activities are presented at the end of most chapters. These questions are purposefully designed to be similar to the more complex styles of questions you might see on the CCNA exam. This section might also include activities to help prepare you for the exams. Appendix A provides the answers.

- **(New) Extra practice problems**—Appendix C, "Extra Practice," includes extra practice problems for some of the math-related topics in this book. You can access the answers at ciscopress.com after registering your book.

- **(New) Packet Tracer activities**—This book contains many activities to work with the Packet Tracer tool developed by Cisco Systems. Packet Tracer allows you to create networks, simulate how packets flow in the network, and use basic testing tools to determine whether the network would work. Version 3.2 of Packet Tracer is included on the accompanying CD-ROM. The various Packet Tracer configurations referred to throughout this book are accessible via ciscopress.com after registering your book. When you see this icon, you can use Packet Tracer with the listed configuration to perform a task suggested in this book.

- **Lab references**—This icon notes good places to stop and perform the related labs from the online curriculum. The supplementary book *Networking Basics CCNA 1 Labs and Study Guide* from Cisco Press (ISBN: 1-58713-165-X) contains all the labs from the curriculum plus additional challenge labs and study guide material.

A Word About the Scope of Topics in This Book

The CCNA 1 v3.1 course is chock-full of material to learn. The online curriculum offers an extensive introduction to networking. However, because the curriculum is taught in a range of different instructional settings—from high schools to universities—instructors choose what to cover to ensure their students' success.

This book's authors help instructors make these choices by prioritizing certain topics and putting less emphasis on other topics. This separation is based on directives from the Cisco

Networking Academy Program and instructor feedback in various academic settings. Rest assured, the full scope of the course topics in the curriculum is covered in this *Companion Guide*, either in the main text or on the accompanying CD-ROM.

The objectives in each chapter highlight the core topics that are covered. The section "Additional Topics of Interest," included at the beginning of some chapters, covers the material that is important for networkers to understand in the world today but that is not necessarily associated with the core course objectives. This material is found on the CD-ROM.

In addition, the authors have addressed a need for more information about real-world networks beyond the online course. So, the *Companion Guide* offers various examples and perspectives on networks in the real world and additional topics of interest to make you a better networker. We encourage you to take advantage of all the material, and yet we realize that you and your instructor have limited time to deliver and learn this material. We hope the segregation of the information simply helps you be more productive in focusing your time.

How This Book Is Organized

This book covers the major topic headings in the same sequence as the online curriculum for the CCNA 1 Cisco Networking Academy Program course. The online curriculum has 11 modules for CCNA 1, so this book has 11 chapters with the same names and numbers as the online course modules.

To make it easier to use this book as a companion to the course, inside each chapter, the major topic headings match the major sections of the online course modules. (Chapter 10 is an exception to this rule.) However, the *Companion Guide* presents many topics in slightly different order under each major heading. Additionally, the book typically uses different examples than the course and covers many topics in slightly greater depth than the online curriculum. As a result, students get more detailed explanations, a second set of examples, and different sequences of individual topics, all to aid the learning process. This new design, based on research into the needs of the Networking Academies, helps typical students lock in their understanding of all the course topics.

You can also use this book as an independent study source without being in a CCNA 1 class by reading the chapters in order.

Chapters and Topics

The book has 11 chapters and three appendixes. The chapters match the 11 modules of the online curriculum in number, name, and topics covered, as described in this list:

- **Chapter 1, "Introduction to Networking,"** defines networks and the Internet and discusses the basic components that comprise both. This chapter also introduces different number systems and the processes used to convert a number from one number system to another.

- **Chapter 2, "Networking Fundamentals,"** continues the process of introducing networking by explaining the meaning behind a wide range of networking terms. It also describes how the Open Systems Interconnection (OSI) reference model supports networking standards. In addition, this chapter describes the basic functions that occur at each layer of the OSI model.

- **Chapter 3, "Networking Media,"** is the first chapter that looks deeply at a small set of topics. It introduces the basics of electricity, which provides a foundation for understanding networking at the physical layer of the OSI model. This chapter also discusses different types of networking media that are used at the physical layer, including shielded twisted-pair (STP) cable, unshielded twisted-pair (UTP) cable, coaxial (coax) cable, and fiber-optic cable, as well as wireless media.

- **Chapter 4, "Cable Testing,"** continues the somewhat theoretical explanations from Chapter 3. This relatively short chapter focuses on UTP cabling, the technology and theories behind testing a cable, and the sources of noise that prevent a cable from passing data well.

- **Chapter 5, "Cabling LANs and WANs,"** describes the rationale and thought processes related to choosing the correct cables with which to build a local-area network (LAN). Although each LAN is unique, many design aspects are common to all LANs, so this chapter compares the options, including different kinds of cables, as well as the use of various LAN devices, such as hubs and switches. This chapter also covers wide-area network (WAN) cabling, including the choice of serial cables to connect routers to a WAN link, and console cables.

- **Chapter 6, "Ethernet Fundamentals,"** is the first of three consecutive chapters devoted to all things Ethernet. It covers the fundamental concepts of framing, Media Access Control (MAC) addresses, and how Ethernet LANs operate. It introduces many terms related to Ethernet, including collision domains and broadcast domains. Finally, this chapter describes segmentation and the devices used to create the network segments.

- **Chapter 7, "Ethernet Technologies,"** is a guided tour of all the popular Ethernet standards from the IEEE. To explain how each works, this chapter shows how hubs and switches work. It covers the common details of each, the speeds of the various standards, which use UTP, and which use fiber-optic cables.

- **Chapter 8, "Ethernet Switching,"** expands on the previous coverage of bridging and switching. It reviews and delves deeper into how switches work, both externally and internally. It also introduces the concept of the Spanning Tree Protocol (STP), which bridges and switches use to prevent frames from looping around a LAN. It also discusses the concepts of collision domains and broadcast domains in greater depth than previous chapters, comparing how each type of networking device might or might not create multiple collision domains or broadcast domains.

- **Chapter 9, "TCP/IP Protocol Suite and IP Addressing,"** is the first of three chapters that focus on topics related to the Transmission Control Protocol/Internet Protocol (TCP/IP) networking model. In particular, Chapter 9 introduces the TCP/IP model and IP addresses. This chapter ends with coverage of topics related to how a computer can be assigned an IP address.

- **Chapter 10, "Routing Fundamentals and Subnets,"** includes three major headings, each of which covers one of the three major functions of IP. This chapter begins with a discussion of IP routing, which is the logic routers use to forward IP packets. The second section explains the concept of routing protocols, which are protocols that help a router learn how it should route packets. Finally, the last section takes a more detailed look at IP addressing as compared with Chapter 9, specifically explaining how IP subnetting works.

- **Chapter 11, "TCP/IP Transport and Application Layers,"** concludes the core chapters of this book by examining the two higher layers of the TCP/IP networking model. This chapter compares the functions of TCP and User Datagram Protocol (UDP), as well as explaining how the most popular TCP/IP application protocols work.

This book also includes the following:

- **Appendix A, "Answers to Check Your Understanding and Challenge Questions,"** provides the answers to the Check Your Understanding questions that you find at the end of each chapter. It also includes answers for the challenge questions and activities that conclude most chapters.

- **Appendix B, "Binary/Decimal Conversion Chart,"** provides a table with decimal numbers 0 through 255 and their 8-bit binary equivalents. This chart can be useful when practicing subnetting.

- **Appendix C, "Extra Practice,"** provides various practice problems to reinforce processes and math formulas used to analyze many of the basic features of networking. The problems in this appendix are organized corresponding to the chapters in this book that explain the related process or formulas. You can find the answer key at ciscopress.com after registering your book.

- The **Glossary** provides a compiled list of all the key terms that appear throughout this book. The Glossary also defines other networking terms that you might find useful as you work toward your CCNA certification.

About the CD-ROM

The CD-ROM included with this book provides many useful tools:

- **Interactive media activities**—Activities from the online course that visually demonstrate some of the topics in the course. These tools can be particularly useful when your school's lab does not have the same cable or hardware or when you use this book for self-study.

- **Packet Tracer v3.2**—Included on the CD-ROM is the full version of Packet Tracer v3.2. Note that the configuration files this book references are available on ciscopress.com after registering your book. These files cover v3.2 and any subsequent releases of Packet Tracer. These configuration files match some of the examples from this book, as indicated by the icon, so you can load the configuration and watch the flow of packets in the same network.

- **Additional topics of interest**—Several chapters include a list at their beginning to let you know that the CD-ROM provides supplemental coverage of additional topics. The topics, provided on the CD-ROM, are beneficial to you becoming a well-rounded networker. (The free Adobe Acrobat Reader is needed to view these PDF files.)

About the Cisco Press Website for This Book

Cisco Press provides additional content that can be accessed by registering your individual book at the ciscopress.com website. Becoming a member and registering is free, and you then gain access to the following items and more:

- Answer key to the additional practice problems found in Appendix C

- All the Packet Tracer configuration files referred to within the *Companion Guide*

- Exclusive deals on other resources from Cisco Press

To register this book, go to www.ciscopress.com/bookstore/register.asp and enter the book's ISBN located on the back cover of this book. You'll then be prompted to log in or join ciscopress.com to continue registration.

After you register the book, a link to the supplemental content will be listed on your My Registered Books page.

About the CCNA Exam

The computing world has many different certifications available. Some of these certifications are sponsored by vendors and some by consortiums of different vendors. Regardless of the sponsor of the certifications, most IT professionals today recognize the need to become certified to prove their skills, prepare for new job searches, and learn new skills while at their existing job.

Over the years, the Cisco certification program has had a tremendous amount of success. The CCNA certification has become the most popular networking certification. Also, the CCIE certification has won numerous awards as the most prestigious certification in the computing industry. With well over 70 percent market share in the enterprise router and switch marketplace, having specific Cisco certifications on your resume is a great way to increase your chances of landing a new job, getting a promotion, or looking more qualified when representing your company on a consulting job.

How to Obtain Your CCNA Certification

Cisco Systems requires that you take one of two paths to get your CCNA certification. You can either take a single comprehensive exam or you can take two exams—with each exam covering a subset of the CCNA exam topics. Table I-1 lists these exams.

Table I-1 CCNA Exam Names and Numbers

Name	Exam	Comment
INTRO exam	640-821	Maps to Cisco Networking Academy Program CCNA 1 and 2
ICND exam	640-811	Maps to Cisco Networking Academy Program CCNA 3 and 4
CCNA exam	640-801	Covers all four courses

So, you could take the first two courses in the Academy Program, do some extra preparation for the exam, and take the INTRO exam. Then, you could take courses 3 and 4, prepare for the ICND exam, and break up your study. Alternately, you could take the CCNA exam at the end of all four courses.

How to Prepare to Pass the CCNA Exam(s)

The Cisco Networking Academy Program CCNA curriculum helps prepare you for CCNA certification by covering a superset of the topics on the CCNA exam. The four courses of the online curriculum, and the corresponding Cisco Press *Companion Guides*, cover many more introductory topics than the topics required for CCNA. The reason for this is that the curriculum is intended as a very first course in computing, not just networking. So, if you successfully complete all four semesters in the CCNA curriculum, you will learn the topics covered on the CCNA exam.

However, taking the CCNA curriculum does not mean that you will automatically pass the CCNA exam. In fact, Cisco purposefully attempts to make the CCNA exam questions prove that you know the material well by making you apply the concepts. The CCNA exam questions tend to be a fair amount more involved than the Cisco Networking Academy Program CCNA assessment questions. (For a deeper perspective on this point, refer to http://www.ciscopress.com/articles/article.asp?p=393075.) So, if you know all the concepts from the CCNA curriculum and *Companion Guides*, you have most all the factual knowledge you need for the exam. However, the exam requires that you apply that knowledge to different scenarios. So, many CCNA students need to study further to pass the exam(s).

Many resources exist to help you in your exam preparation. Some of these resources are books from Cisco Press, and some are other online resources. The following list details some of the key tools:

- *CCNA Certification Library* (ISBN: 1-58720-095-3), **by Wendell Odom**—This book covers the CCNA materials in more depth, with a large (more than 300) question bank of exam-realistic questions and many other tools to help in your study.

- *Cisco CCNA Network Simulator* (ISBN: 1-58720-131-3), **by Boson Software**—This software tool is a router/switch/network simulator that you can use to practice hands-on skills on Cisco routers and switches without having a real lab available.

- **Cisco CCNA Prep Center (http://www.cisco.com/go/prepcenter)**—A free online resource from Cisco Systems. (You need a Cisco.com account to access this site, but registration is free.) It has discussion boards, interviews with experts, sample questions, and other resources to aid in your CCNA exam preparation.

Don't forget to register your copy of this book at ciscopress.com to receive a special offer on Cisco Press books.

What's on the CCNA Exams

Like any test, everyone wants to know what's on the exam. Thankfully, Cisco Systems publishes a list of exam topics for each exam to give candidates a better idea of what's on the exam. Unfortunately, those exam topics do not provide as much detail as most people want to see. However, the exam topics are a good starting point. To see the exam topics for the CCNA exams, follow these steps:

Step 1   Go to http://www.cisco.com/go/ccna.

Step 2   Click the text for the exam about which you want more information.

Step 3   On the next window, click the Exam Topics link.

Beyond that, the CCNA curriculum covers what is arguably a superset of the CCNA exam topics. For example, this book's Chapters 3 and 4 cover many details about the physics behind how bits can be transmitted over a cable. None of the CCNA exam topics comes close to referring to these details. However, the CCNA exams do cover the vast majority of the topics that appear in the CCNA *Companion Guides*.

Some topics are certainly more important than others for the exams—topics that many people already know are more important. IP subnetting is probably the single most important topic because it is something that requires practice to master, and it can take time, and the exams are timed, of course. IP routing, LAN switching, and any hands-on skills covered in the curriculum are also important topics to know. Ironically, some of the topics that seem too basic to ever be on the exam just happen to be required to understand the more advanced topics. So, other than some of the extra details in Chapters 3 and 4 of this book, most of the rest of the topics in the curriculum and *Companion Guides* might be seen on the CCNA exam(s).

Note that with a typical CCNA exam having only 45–55 questions, your individual exam cannot possibly cover all the topics in the CCNA curriculum. The comments listed here refer to the possible topics for the exams.

CHAPTER 1

Introduction to Networking

Objectives

Upon completion of this chapter, you should be able to answer the following questions:

- What are the requirements for an Internet connection?

- What are the major components of a personal computer (PC)?

- What procedures are used to install and troubleshoot network interface cards (NICs) and modems?

- What basic testing procedures are used to test the Internet connection?

- What are the features of web browsers and plug-ins?

- What are the Base 2, Base 10, and Base 16 number systems?

- How do you perform 8-bit-binary-to-decimal and decimal-to-8-bit-binary conversions?

- How do you perform simple conversions between decimal, binary, and hexadecimal numbers?

- How are IP addresses and network masks represented in binary form?

- How are IP addresses and network masks represented in decimal form?

Key Terms

This chapter uses the following key terms. You can find the definitions in the Glossary:

Internet   page 4

enterprise network   page 4

Internet service provider (ISP)   page 6

personal computers (PCs)   page 7

central processing unit (CPU)   page 8

random-access memory (RAM)   page 9

disk drive   page 9

hard disk   page 9

input/output devices (I/O)   page 9

motherboard   page 9

memory chip   page 9

parallel port   page 10

serial port   page 10

mouse port   page 10

keyboard port   page 10

Universal Serial Bus (USB) port   page 10

expansion slots   page 10

network interface card (NIC)   page 11

video card   page 11

sound card   page 11

jack   page 14

local-area network (LAN)   page 14

continues

continued

Ethernet   page 14

plug-and-play   page 16

bits per second (bps)   page 17

networking devices   page 17

Media Access Control (MAC) address   page 19

servers   page 20

media   page 21

modems   page 22

digital subscriber line (DSL)   page 23

standards   page 25

protocols   page 25

Hypertext Transfer Protocol (HTTP)   page 25

Internet Protocol (IP)   page 25

protocol suite   page 25

Transmission Control Protocol/Internet Protocol (TCP/IP)
  page 25

web browser   page 26

web servers   page 26

binary digit (bit)   page 26

byte   page 26

plug-ins   page 28

Transmission Control Protocol (TCP)   page 28

IP address   page 31

dotted decimal   page 31

Universal Resource Locator (URL)   page 35

default gateway   page 37

ping   page 39

tracert   page 42

ASCII   page 47

decimal numbering (Base 10)   page 48

binary numbering (Base 2)   page 49

hexadecimal numbering (Base 16)   page 59

This chapter introduces the basic concepts and components of modern computer networks, including the basics of the TCP/IP protocol suite, upon which most modern networks are built. This chapter also covers some of the related binary, decimal, and hexadecimal math that is required to examine the details of how computer networks work. This chapter, along with Chapter 2, "Networking Fundamentals," provides an overview of many of the topics related to computer networking, introduces many terms, and provides a solid foundation before you get into more detailed subjects in later chapters.

Connecting to Networks and the Internet

The Networking Academy course that you are (likely) taking when using this book may be your first formal introduction to the world of computer networking. However, today, most people have grown up with networks and networking as part of the overall culture of the developed world. As a result, most people start this course and book with some opinions about what a network really is and what the Internet is. This section formally defines a network. It also defines the basic concepts and terms behind one special and important network: the Internet.

What's a Network?

To formally begin your networking journey, you need to start forming a more detailed and specific answer to the question "What's a network?" Assuming that you took the time and effort to register for the Cisco Networking Academy Program CCNA 1 course, which is a basic networking course, you probably already have some opinions about the answer to this question. This section begins to answer the question.

First, consider the following formal, but general, definition of a computer network:

> *A combination of computer hardware, cabling, network devices, and computer software used together to allow computers to communicate with each other.*

The goal of any computer network is to allow multiple computers to communicate. The type of communication can be as varied as the type of conversations you might have throughout the course of a day. For example, the communication might be a download of an MP3 audio file for your MP3 player; using a web browser to check your instructor's web page to see what assignments and tests might be coming up; checking the latest sports scores; using an instant-messaging service, such as AOL Instant Messenger (AIM), to send text messages to a friend; or writing an e-mail and sending it to a business associate.

This chapter starts the process of closely looking at the four networking components mentioned in the formal definition: computer hardware, computer software, cabling, and networking devices. Before you look at each component, however, it is helpful to think about some examples of networks.

A Small Network: Two PCs and One Cable

You can create a simple network with two computers and a cable. Although it's not a terribly impressive network, such a network does occasionally serve a good purpose in real life, as well as being useful for discussing networking and learning some basic skills in classroom labs. Figure 1-1 shows such a network.

Figure 1-1   A Two-PC, One-Cable Network

Figure 1-1 shows two computers, A and B, and a line that represents a networking cable. Implemented properly, this small network allows computers A and B to communicate. (That "implemented properly" phrase is simply a way to ignore the details you will learn over the coming months. More on that is covered in upcoming chapters.) This network certainly meets the formal definition for a computer network because multiple computers can communicate.

Although this network might seem small, small networks do have some useful purposes. For example, when you download a song to your PC and copy the song to an MP3 player over a cable, you have effectively created a small network. Another example of a small network is when two people with laptops attend the same meeting and use wireless to exchange files while sitting in the meeting.

A Very Large Network: The Internet

Consider a network that is the opposite of the simple network shown in Figure 1-1: the Internet. The Internet is somewhat challenging to define because it means many different things to so many people. From one perspective, the *Internet* is a very large, global network that allows almost every computer on the planet to communicate with the other computers on the planet. Not only is it a network in the formal sense, the communication it enables worldwide, across cultures and political boundaries, has fundamentally changed the world as we know it.

Under close examination, however, the Internet isn't a network at all. It's really a bunch of interconnected networks. In fact, that's how it got its name: Internet is short for *interconnected networks*. Figure 1-2 depicts part of the Internet.

All the pieces of Figure 1-2 create the Internet. First, on the left, two enterprise networks are shown: Retailer1 and Supplier1. The term *enterprise network* refers to a network built by one company, one government institution, one school system, or any other entity. In this case, these two companies hired network engineers to plan and implement a network that these companies' employees can use. At that point, the companies can carry on business communications between computers inside their respective companies.

Figure 1-2   Internet

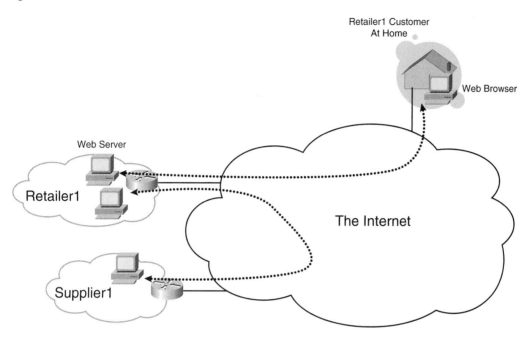

Besides communicating inside their respective companies, these two companies need to communicate with each other. Retailer1 needs to exchange information with its supplier, Supplier1. (For example, the retailer might simply need to order additional stock to fill its stores' shelves.) So, both Retailer1 and Supplier1 connect to the Internet, which allows the computers in the two companies to exchange information, such as orders and invoices, check on shipping and product availability, and the like.

Retailer1 also needs to communicate with its customers. Because Retailer1 sells consumer products, these consumers need to be able to get to Retailer1's website, which is located inside Retailer1's enterprise network. Therefore, Retailer1 has a second reason to connect to the Internet.

Next, potential customers also need to connect to the Internet. In Figure 1-2, the Retailer1 customer sits at home and uses a home computer and an Internet connection. After she's connected to the Internet, the customer can browse Retailer1's website, find products, order the products, pay via a credit card, and so on.

The Internet includes literally hundreds of thousands of enterprise networks, hundreds of millions of home users, and a mysterious cloud in the middle of Figure 1-2. When drawing figures of computer networks, if a portion of the network contains details that are not important to a particular discussion, that part of the network is typically represented as a cloud. Figure 1-2 is no exception. It shows the "Internet" as a big cloud without any details. Figure 1-3 removes the cloud, shows some details, and shows some other clouds.

Figure 1-3   Internet: A Closer Look

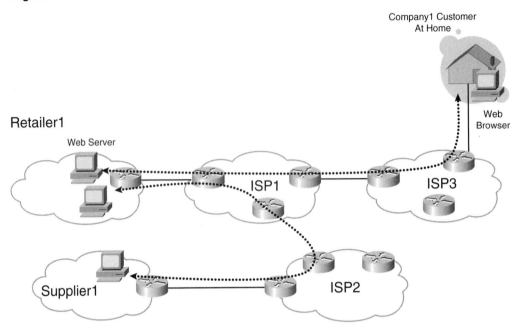

The core of the Internet is not one entity, but many. To create the Internet, a company called an *Internet service provider (ISP)* creates a network. An ISP then sells its services to businesses and individuals, with the most basic service being the ability for the customers' computers to send and receive data to and from any other computer on the Internet. To provide this basic overall service, an ISP must provide a customer with two things:

- A connection between an enterprise network, or a home user, and the ISP's network

- Connections between the ISP's network and every other part of the Internet

In Figure 1-3, three different ISPs supply a network connection to their respective customers. The home user, Retailer1, and Supplier1 each pay a fee, typically monthly, to their respective ISPs for the right to connect to that ISP. However, they do not pay money to the other two ISPs shown in the figure. For example, Retailer1 uses ISP1, so Retailer1 pays only ISP1 for its Internet service. Such agreements allow any company or individual to connect to an ISP, and it provides competition to keep prices more reasonable.

The ISPs must connect to each other so that they can forward traffic to all parts of the Internet. Figure 1-3 shows a direct line, which represents some networking cables, between two pairs of ISPs. The ISPs must have some path to each other so they can forward traffic between their respective customers, fulfilling their promise to connect their customers to the rest of the Internet.

ISPs do not need a direct connection to all other ISPs to meet the requirement of being able to reach all parts of the Internet. For example, ISP2 and ISP3 might need to send data between each other for some of their customers. To do so, they send it through ISP1. As long as some path exists so all ISPs can reach all other ISPs in the world by using one or more different ISPs, the requirement for complete connectivity to the Internet is accomplished.

Perspectives on Networks of Different Sizes

Comparing the simple network of Figure 1-1 with the Internet in Figure 1-3 shows how different networks can be, particularly in size. In fact, many individual enterprise networks connected to the Internet have more than 10,000 computers connected to them, in hundreds of locations. These types of enterprise networks are complex in and of themselves. Also, home users might have multiple computers connected to a home network that's connected to the Internet.

Interestingly, as you dig deeper into how networks work, you can see that many of the networking concepts covered in this class are used in small, medium, and large networks—even the Internet. Certainly, the larger the network, the more work and effort it takes to successfully implement the network. However, that complexity—and the requirement for more effort and work to successfully implement networks—is actually a good thing because it means more jobs, more variety in those jobs, and more opportunity.

Next, you closely look at some network components and begin to understand how network engineers can construct a network.

Note

Figure 1-3 shows several cylindrical icons that resemble hockey pucks. They represent a networking device called a router. Later chapters of this book, and major portions of the other three courses of the Networking Academy CCNA curriculum, expound upon the purpose and inner workings of routers.

Network Components

The people who create a computer network, referred to as network engineers, create networks by combining the four things mentioned in the formal definition of a network:

- Computer hardware (including NICs)
- Cables
- Networking devices
- Computer software

This section closely looks at the first three of these networking components. Networking software is covered later in this chapter in the section "TCP/IP Protocol Suite and TCP/IP Software."

Computer Hardware

Computers come in many shapes, sizes, and types. However, the vast majority of people use computers that are best categorized as personal computers. *Personal computers (PCs)* are computers that are specifically designed to be used by a single person at a time.

Although some knowledge of the basics of PCs is important for this course, you do not need detailed knowledge of PCs to do well in this course. If you are new to computers or if you want further background on PCs, take the HP IT Essentials I: PC Hardware and Software course or read the book *HP IT Essentials I: PC Hardware and Software Companion Guide* (published by Cisco Press).

The next several subsections cover the most commonly discussed PC components.

General Types of PC Components

From a basic perspective, a PC has the following components:

- **Processor (also called a *central processing unit [CPU]*)**—A computer processor, or CPU, acts as a computer's brain. A CPU's job is to process, or think about, what the computer is trying to do. (Figure 1-4 shows a picture of a CPU.) The CPU's job includes many things, such as the following:

  - Creating the image that is displayed on the computer's screen

  - Taking input from the keyboard or mouse

  - Sending data over a network

  - Processing data for software running on the computer

Figure 1-4   CPU

- **Microprocessor**—A silicon chip that contains a CPU. A typical PC has several micro-processors, including the main CPU.

- **Temporary memory (also called *random-access memory [RAM]*)**—The processor needs memory in which to work on things. RAM is the computer equivalent of the papers and notes you might keep on your desk when studying. The CPU can quickly and easily access the data stored in RAM, and that data typically pertains to something the PC is actively processing. Note that the contents of RAM are lost when the computer is powered off.

- **Read-only memory (ROM)**—ROM is a type of computer memory in which data has been prerecorded. After data has been written onto a ROM chip, it cannot be removed; it can only be read. (PCs can re-record information into another type of ROM, called electronically erasable programmable read-only memory [EEPROM]. The basic input/output system [BIOS] in most PCs is stored in EEPROM.)

- **Permanent memory (such as disks)**—Computers need long-term memory to store data that might be needed later, even after a computer is powered off. Permanent memory typically consists of a type of device called a *disk drive* or *hard disk*.

- *Input/output devices (I/O)*—To interact with humans, the computer must be able to know what the human wants it to do and provide the information to the human. Humans tell a computer what to do by manipulating an input device. For example, this occurs when the human types on the PC keyboard or moves/clicks with a mouse. For output, the computer uses a video display, audio speakers, and printers.

With these components, a PC can take input from the human, possibly gather data from the disk drives into RAM, process the data with the CPU, and provide the results through one of the output devices.

Motherboard

The PC *motherboard* holds many of the PC's most important components. The motherboard is a flat piece of plastic called a circuit board. Circuit board material is designed to be a good place to physically attach microprocessor chips, such as the CPU and RAM, and connect the components with wires and other hardware. The following list details some of the motherboard's individual components:

- **Printed circuit board (PCB)**—A thin plate on which chips (integrated circuits) and other electronic components are placed. Examples include the motherboard and various expansion adapters.

- **Transistor**—A device that amplifies a signal or opens and closes a circuit. Microprocessors can have millions of transistors.

- **Integrated circuit (IC)**—A device made of semiconductor material. It contains many transistors and performs a specific task. The primary IC on the motherboard is the CPU. ICs are often called chips.

- *Memory chips*—Another name for RAM, memory chips are Integrated circuits whose primary purpose is to be used to temporarily store information that is processed by the CPU.

- **Resistor**—An electrical component that is made of material that opposes the flow of electric current.

- **Capacitor**—An electronic component that stores energy in the form of an electrostatic field. It consists of two conducting metal plates separated by insulating material.

- **Connector**—A port or interface that a cable plugs into. Examples include serial, parallel, USB, and disk drive interfaces.

- **Light emitting diode (LED)**—A semiconductor device that emits light when a current passes through it. LEDs are commonly used as indicator lights.

- *Parallel port*—An interface that can transfer more than 1 bit at a time. It connects external devices, such as printers.

- *Serial port*—An interface used for serial communication in which only 1 bit is transmitted at a time. The serial port can connect to an external modem, plotter, or serial printer. It can also connect to networking devices, such as routers and switches, as a console connection.

- *Mouse port*—A port designed for connecting a mouse to a PC.

- *Keyboard port*—A port designed for connecting a keyboard to a PC.

- **Power connector**—A connector that allows a power cord to be connected to the computer to give electrical power to the motherboard and other computer components.

- *Universal Serial Bus (USB) port*—This interface lets peripheral devices, such as mice, modems, keyboards, scanners, and printers, be plugged and unplugged without resetting the system. PC manufacturers may one day quit building PCs with the older parallel and serial ports completely, instead using USB ports.

- **Firewire**—A serial bus interface standard that offers high-speed communications and real-time data services.

Expansion Slots and the PC Backplane

For various reasons, some parts of a computer cannot be easily attached to the motherboard. For example, disk drives are too large to attach directly to the motherboard. However, these devices still need to be accessible to the motherboard. So, the motherboard includes connectors that allow other parts, such as disk drives, to connect to the motherboard through a cable.

Other necessary computer components might be connected to the motherboard, or might not be connected, at the discretion of the PC's manufacturer. For example, the function provided by a NIC, which is important to networking, might be included on the motherboard of a PC, or it might not. (The upcoming section "Network Interface Cards" discusses NICs in more detail.)

To allow for additional functions besides what is provided on a particular PC's motherboard, PCs typically have the physical capability to accept expansion cards. These cards are built with the same general types of components as the motherboard: a circuit board, microprocessor chips, capacitors, and the like. However, these expansion cards typically fulfill a specific purpose. For example, if the motherboard does not include the same function as a NIC, a NIC can be added to the PC as an expansion card.

For expansion cards to useful, they must connect to the motherboard through the PC backplane. The backplane is part of the motherboard that is designed as a place to allow the connection of the expansion cards. The backplane also provides several standardized plastic connectors, called *expansion slots*, into which expansion cards can be inserted. By connecting expansion cards into the backplane, the cards and the motherboard can communicate. Figure 1-5 shows a motherboard with the expansion slots in the lower-right part of the figure (the white vertically oriented rectangles).

Note

Although a NIC is an optional component of a PC, because most consumers want network access, most every new PC sold today has an integrated NIC.

Note

Expansion cards are sometimes called expansion boards, or sometimes simply boards or cards.

Figure 1-5   PC Motherboard and Expansion Slots

Note

The term bus is used to refer to a PC's backplane.

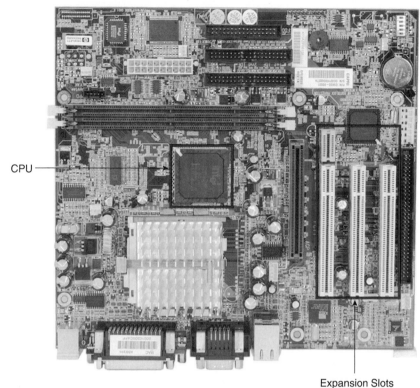

CPU

Expansion Slots

The following list identifies some of the more popular cards found in these expansion slots:

- *Network interface card (NIC)*—An expansion board that provides a network communication connection to and from a PC. Many newer desktop and laptop computers have an Ethernet NIC built into the motherboard. (Ethernet is the most popular type of local-area network [LAN] in use today.)

- *Video card*—A board that plugs into a PC to give it display capabilities. Video cards typically include onboard microprocessors and additional memory to speed up and enhance graphics display.

- *Sound card*—An expansion board that handles all sound functions.

Miscellaneous PC Components

This section completes this chapter's list of some of the PC's components. Specifically, it defines a few different types of permanent storage options and the system unit and power supply:

- **CD-ROM drive**—An optical drive that can read information from a CD-ROM. This can also be a compact disk read-write (CD-RW) drive, a digital video disk (DVD) drive, or a combination of all three in one drive.

- **Floppy disk drive**—A device that can read and write to floppy disks (see Figure 1-6).

Figure 1-6   Floppy Disk Drive

- **Hard disk drive**—A device that reads and writes data on a hard disk. This is the primary storage device in the computer.

- **System unit**—The main component of the PC system. It includes the case, chassis, power supply, microprocessor, main memory, bus, expansion cards, disk drives (floppy, CD hard disk, and so on), and ports. The system unit does not include the keyboard, the monitor, or any other external devices connected to the computer.

- **Power supply**—The component that supplies power to a computer by taking alternating current (AC) and converting it to 5 to 12 volts direct current (DC) to power the computer.

Desktop Versus Laptop

Laptop computers differ from desktop computers in that they can be easily transported and used. Laptops are generally smaller than desktops, with built-in video display and keyboard so that transporting it is convenient. In most cases, laptops weigh less than 10 pounds and have a battery that lasts several hours, so they can be used while traveling.

Laptop expansion slots are called *Personal Computer Memory Card International Association (PCMCIA)* slots or PC card slots. Devices such as NICs, modems, hard drives, and other useful devices, usually the size of a thick credit card, insert into the PC card slot. Figure 1-7 shows a PC card for a wireless LAN (WLAN).

Figure 1-7   PCMCIA Card

 Lab 1.1.2   PC Hardware

In this lab, you become familiar with the basic peripheral components of a PC system and their connections, including network attachments. You examine the internal PC configuration and identify major components. You also observe the boot process for the Windows operating system (OS) and use the Control Panel to find information about the PC hardware.

Network Interface Cards

For a PC to use a network, it must have some interface to the network cabling. PCs use network interface cards (NICs) to provide that interface. In fact, the name is somewhat self-descriptive: NICs are expansion cards that give a PC an interface to a network. Figure 1-8 shows a NIC.

Figure 1-8   Ethernet NIC

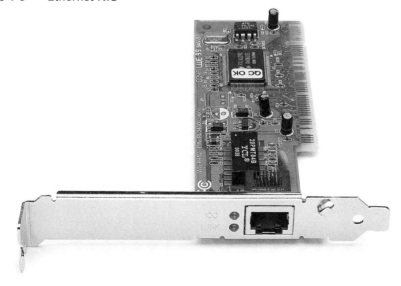

When installing the card in a PC, the part of the card on the right side of Figure 1-8, which slightly sticks out, is the part that is inserted into the expansion slots shown in Figure 1-5. The silver part at the bottom of the figure is the part that can be seen from the outside of the PC. This side has an opening, typically called either a socket or a *jack*, into which the networking cable can be inserted. (A jack is simply a hole, with a standard shape, into which a cable can be easily inserted.)

Figure 1-8 shows an Ethernet LAN NIC. The term *LAN* refers to a general type of network in which the distances between computers are relatively short—hence the phrase "local-area" in its name. Several types of LANs have been defined over the years, including Token Ring, Fiber Distributed Data Interface (FDDI), and *Ethernet*. Today, however, you are likely to use only Ethernet, in fact, the other two types of LANs have become so unpopular that it is difficult to find and purchase Token Ring or FDDI NICs.

When purchasing a NIC, consider the following features:

- **LAN protocol**—Ethernet, Token Ring, or FDDI. Today, Ethernet is used almost exclusively, and Token Ring and FDDI are seldom used. (Token Ring and FDDI are introduced briefly in Chapter 6, "Ethernet Fundamentals.")

- **Media supported**—Twisted pair, coaxial, wireless, or fiber optic.

- **Bus support on the computer**—PCI or Industry-Standard Architecture (ISA).

Finding an Ethernet NIC on Your PC

It might be an interesting exercise, at home or in the classroom, to look for an Ethernet NIC in your PC. To find one, look at the back of the PC where most of the connectors sit. Look for a jack, which is roughly rectangular in shape, like the dark rectangle on the side of the NIC shown in Figure 1-8. That's the socket into which the cable is inserted. The cable attached to the NIC typically has a connector called an RJ-45 connector (RJ means registered jack). (The cable's connector is simply the shaped plastic end of the cable.) The RJ-45 connector is shaped like the connector used on telephone cable for your home telephone, but it's just a little wider. Figure 1-9 shows the shape of the RJ-45 jack and connectors to help you in your search.

Note

The connector on your home telephone cable is called an RJ-11 connector.

Note that although a NIC can be inserted into a PC's expansion slot, many of the newer PCs sold today integrate the NIC's functions onto the motherboard. So, when you look on your PC's NIC, if you do not see the RJ-45 socket on any of the cards in the expansion slots, look at the other parts on the back of the computer; you might see the RJ-45 socket that's connected to the motherboard.

Figure 1-9   RJ-45 Jack and Connectors

Installing Ethernet NICs

These days, the physical installation of a NIC is relatively easy. The IT Essentials course covers the details in more depth, but the process is extremely similar for any expansion card:

Step 1 Shut down or power off the PC.

Step 2 Disconnect the power cord from the PC.

Step 3 Connect an antistatic strap to your wrist to protect the computer and NIC from your body's static electricity.

Step 4 Insert the NIC into the expansion slot.

Step 5 Reassemble the PC and turn it on.

After practicing a time or three, you should be able to easily insert the card. Figure 1-10 shows the physical installation.

Figure 1-10   Installing an Ethernet NIC

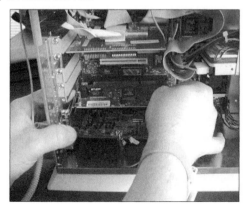

Besides the physical installation, the installer might or might not need skills relating to how to add hardware to the computer's OS, which is the software that controls the computer's actions. (For example, Windows XP and Linux are both computer OSs used on PCs.) Oftentimes today, you can physically install the NIC and turn the computer on, and the OS automatically adds the hardware. This process is called *plug-and-play*.

If the plug-and-play process does not work, a successful NIC installation might require you to examine and change software settings using the software that comes with the NIC. This might require knowledge of how the NIC is configured in the OS and how to use the NIC diagnostics. It might also require that you have the skills to resolve hardware resource conflicts. The IT Essentials course covers this knowledge and skill.

Network Cabling Basics

For networks to work, the computers must have the capability to take the bits sitting in RAM on one computer and somehow send a copy of those bits into RAM on the other computer. For the process to work, the computer typically asks the NIC to send the bits over the cable that is connected to the NIC. So, the NIC must be connected to some form of transmission medium over which it can send the bits to the other computer. This section introduces the concept of transmission medium by using a specific example: the small Ethernet network shown in Figure 1-1, which uses an electrical Ethernet cable.

As mentioned in this book's Introduction, the chapters generally cover a slightly broader range of topics than the online curriculum. The small amounts of extra coverage provide you with better context or different ways to think about the same concepts.

Occasionally, and particularly in this chapter, this book provides several pages of additional information on a few important topics. This section and the upcoming section "Networking Devices" are the first two sections in this chapter that take the discussions much deeper than what's given in the CCNA course. You might appreciate the additional depth at various points in your reading. However, if you or your instructor prefer to skip over these deeper bits of additional coverage, feel free to skip forward to the section "Enterprise Networks and Home Internet Access."

The topics in this section are covered in more depth in Chapters 3, 4, 5, and 7, and the topics in the section "Networking Devices" are covered to some degree in Chapters 2, 5, 8, 9, and 10.

Creating a Transmission Medium Using Cables

To send data—bits—to another computer, the computers can use some physical medium over which electricity can be sent. In this case, the physical medium is typically a set of copper wires because copper easily conducts electricity. Because copper wires are brittle, the wires are usually wrapped in a colored plastic coating to help prevent them from breaking. The plastic coating also helps provide some electrical insulation, which is a property discussed in detail in Chapter 3, "Networking Media."

The LAN cable connected to the NIC contains multiple copper wires. NICs tend to use more than one wire, with a typical Ethernet NIC using four wires. Additionally, the outer part of the cable, which is made of flexible plastic and other insulating materials, adds strength and protection to the combined wires. The cable keeps the set of wires together for convenient use and physically protects the wires.

For the simple network in Figure 1-1 to work (for example, for PC B to send bits to PC A), PC B needs to be able to send electricity to PC A. To do so, the copper wire inside the cable needs to be physically touching something inside the NICs on each end of the cable to have a path from PC B to PC A over which electricity can pass. Figure 1-11 shows the idea, with the NICs inside the PCs removed from the figure to more clearly show the details.

Figure 1-11   Connecting the Copper Conductors in a Cable to the NICs

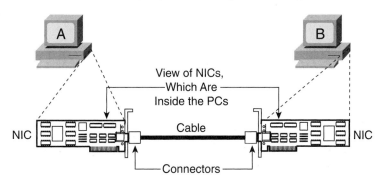

By connecting the NICs in the two PCs with the correct cable, the NICs now have a physical path between the two PCs over which electricity can flow. Now, they can use this electrical path to transmit bits.

The term *bits per second (bps)* often refers to the speed of network connections. Note that the unit is bits, not bytes. In real life, LANs typically run at much higher speeds, with a slow LAN transmitting at 10 million bits per second (megabits per second, or Mbps). The section "Names for the Rate at Which a Network Sends Data" describes the speeds at which bits can be sent over a networking cable.

Networking Devices

This chapter began with a formal definition of a network, which included components such as computer hardware and cabling. This chapter so far has described, in general terms, hardware and cabling. This section introduces the idea behind what the online curriculum calls *networking devices* and the role they play in creating networks. In particular, this section shows an example of a simple networking device called a LAN hub.

Companies create their LANs by connecting a cable between each computer and some networking device, oftentimes either a LAN hub or LAN switch. In turn, these devices connect to each other. Designed and engineered properly, each computer can use one cable to connect to only one networking device but still can communicate with many other computers.

The term networking device refers to a class of computer hardware devices that is designed for the specific purpose of building networks. Many types of networking devices exist, including two that are discussed throughout all four courses of the Networking Academy CCNA curriculum: switches and routers. For example, LANs can use one type of network device called a LAN hub (or simply hub). (The term hub comes from the idea of a wheel, in which the hub is in the middle and several spokes radiate from it.) A LAN hub has a large number of jacks (oftentimes, RJ-45 sockets) that connect the LAN cables attached to various PCs. By connecting each PC to the hub with a single cable, the network has an electrical transmission medium between each PC and the hub. When the hub receives electrical signals, it simply repeats those signals out all the other interfaces. Figure 1-12 shows an example of the cabling topology.

Figure 1-12   Small LAN with a Hub Network Device

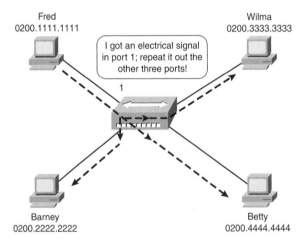

With a hub, the PCs need only a single NIC and a single cable that connects them to the hub. Figure 1-12 shows PC Fred transmitting data (shown as a dashed line), with the hub repeating the transmitted bits to each device connected to the hub. If another PC joins the network, the new PC simply needs a NIC with a cable that connects it to the hub; the existing devices require no changes.

A hub is just one example of a networking device that can be used to reach the main objective of networks: to allow multiple computers to communicate. LAN switches are another type of networking device similar to a LAN hub. A switch does the same work as a hub, but more efficiently, so today, switches are used more often than hubs. Also, routers (as shown in Figures 1-2 and 1-3) perform an important role. Routers can connect to wide-area networks (WANs), which provide a transmission medium across long distances. Chapter 2 closely looks at these networking devices, and later chapters further detail hubs, switches, and routers.

The behavior of a LAN using a hub also provides a good backdrop from which to cover a topic related to NICs—namely, the concept of an address for a NIC. The company that makes the NIC gives it a unique permanent address. The address is 48 bits long and is typically written in hexadecimal as 12 hexadecimal digits. (Each hexadecimal digit represents 4 bits.) When writing down these addresses, Cisco Systems tends to put two periods into the address to make it more readable. For example, in Figure 1-12, Fred has a NIC address of 020011111111, which is listed as 0200.1111.1111 on a Cisco product. The NIC address has many names besides NIC address. The most common name is *Media Access Control (MAC) address*.

When sending data, Fred adds a prefix to the data, including the MAC address of the intended recipient (for example, Barney). After the other three PCs receive the data, they use the destination MAC address to decide whether to process the data (Barney) or not (Wilma and Betty). (This is just one example of how NICs use their MAC addresses; you will learn about many other uses for MAC addresses before the end of this course.)

 You can view a simulation of the network operation in Figure 1-12 by using Packet Tracer. Download the sample Packet Tracer scenarios from your login at http://www.ciscopress.com/title/1587131641, and load scenario NA01-0112. For more information, refer to this book's Introduction.

Enterprise Networks and Home Internet Access

So far, this chapter has introduced three of the four main components of a computer network: computer hardware (including NICs), cables, and network devices. Today, most every enterprise has a network installed, with the devices using many of the concepts covered thus far. This section closely looks at enterprise networks and then examines a few of the technologies used to access the Internet.

Enterprise Network Basics

Enterprises vary in many ways. The network created and owned by the college, school, or training company at which you are taking this course mostly likely has a network. In fact, the PCs in the classroom might be connected to that network. If so, the PCs are actually part of the enterprise network that the school uses. An enterprise network is nothing more than a network created to support the activities of that enterprise, whether that activity is to make money, govern, or educate.

Enterprise networks can be large or small. Regardless of size, enterprise networks have many common requirements and features:

- They might have several physical locations that are too far away to use a LAN.

- The need to support many PCs for the people who use the enterprise network.

- The need to connect servers to the network. *Servers* have information that is useful and important for the enterprise's functions.

- Typically, the computer-support engineers work near one or a few of the network's main sites.

- The need for Internet access for most or all of the PCs in the enterprise.

To support such goals and requirements, an enterprise network might look like what's shown in Figure 1-13. The figure shows an enterprise with four sites: one main site and three other sites. This enterprise could be a small business, local government, or even a school with four campuses.

In Figure 1-13, Site 1 houses a server farm, which is a collection of servers located in the same location. The PCs throughout the enterprise network can access these servers through the enterprise network. For example, a PC at Site 2 is shown communicating with one of the servers (as noted with the dark dashed line). Note that each PC is connected to a networking device called a LAN switch; the switch allows local communications over a LAN. (Switches achieve the same goal as hubs, but more efficiently, as covered briefly in Chapter 2 and in more depth in Chapter 7, "Ethernet Technologies," and Chapter 8, "Ethernet Switching.") The routers (hockey-puck icons) connect to the LAN and the WAN, forwarding traffic to and from the WAN connection. (WAN connections are often represented by a crooked line, sometimes called a lightning bolt.)

Only the main site has a connection to the Internet through ISP1. Although only Site 1 has the connection, the PCs throughout the enterprise use the enterprise network to reach router R6, which then forwards traffic into the Internet through ISP1.

This design allows the users inside the enterprise to access the Internet, as well as users inside the Internet to access devices inside the enterprise. This enterprise-network design takes care of Internet connectivity for the entire enterprise. The next section covers the basics of Internet connectivity from the home.

Figure 1-13   Typical Enterprise Network

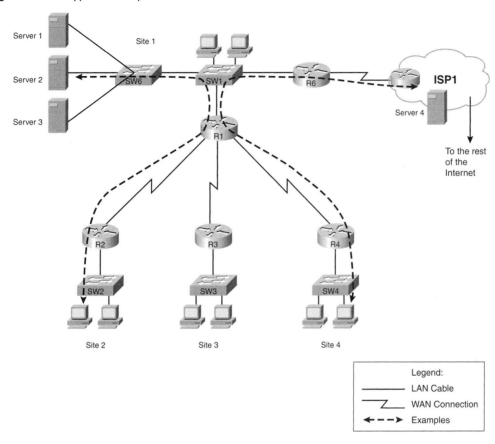

Accessing an ISP Through a Phone Line and an Analog Modem

As previously mentioned, many ISPs exist, with most vying for a share of the home Internet access market. As shown in Figure 1-2, to use the Internet from home, a PC must somehow connect to an ISP. These ISPs try to get your attention through marketing and advertising and want you to sign up with them to gain access to the Internet.

To access the Internet, a home PC needs to use some transmission medium. With LANs, the transmission medium is a cable that is relatively short, typically less than 100 meters in length. However, the distance between your house and the offices where the ISP keeps its networking devices might be long. Rather than install an expensive miles-long cable between your house and an ISP, only to have you change to a new ISP in two months, ISPs use *media* (plural of medium) that are already installed in your house—namely, a phone line or a cable TV cable. This section describes how telephone lines work with analog modems. You learn more about how networks use cable TV lines in the section "Accessing an ISP Through a Cable TV Cable and a Cable Modem," found later in this chapter.

When a phone call is placed, telephone companies essentially create an electrical circuit between two phones. When used to send and receive voice, the phones convert the sounds into an analog electrical signal by using a microphone built into the mouthpiece of the phone, sending that signal to the other phone. The receiving phone converts it back to sounds and plays it out a speaker built in to the phone's earpiece.

The analog electrical signal used by phones differs from digital electrical signals in that analog varies continuously, as shown in Figure 1-14.

Figure 1-14   Analog Electrical Signal

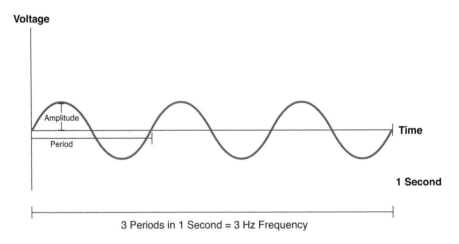

Figure 1-14 shows the voltage level on the y axis over time, with time on the x axis. In short, the voltage continuously varies from some positive to negative voltage (in other words, alternating current). Note that Figure 1-14 shows three complete cycles of the curve, beginning at the x axis, going up, down again, and back up to the x axis. The length of time it takes for one complete cycle to occur is called the *period*. The number of times that cycle occurs in 1 second is called the *frequency*. For example, the frequency shown in Figure 1-14 is 3 Hertz (Hz). (Hertz is a unit of measure that means "number of cycles per second.") Finally, the maximum (positive) and minimum (negative) voltage is called the *amplitude*.

Phone companies originally used analog electrical signals for voice traffic because analog signals look like voice waves as they travel through the air. Both electrical energy and sound waves vary in terms of frequency, amplitude, and so on. For example, the higher the frequency, the higher the pitch of the sound; the higher the amplitude, the louder the sound. An electrical signal sent by a phone is *analogous* to the sound waves; hence, the term *analog* describes this type of signal.

Computers can use **modems** to send data to each other by sending analog signals, such as the signal shown in Figure 1-14. Two computers can essentially place a phone call to one another by using their modems. The modems then send binary 0s and 1s to each other by varying, or modulating, the analog signal. For example, the modems might use a higher-frequency signal to mean 1 and a lower frequency to mean 0. From the phone company's perspective, however, it looks just like any other phone call because all the modems do is send the same kinds of analog electrical signals sent by a telephone.

Modems might exist as a built-in feature on the computer motherboard or as a separate internal expansion card. Modems might also be external to the PC, connecting to the PC via the PC's serial port. Such a modem is aptly named an external modem.

A Brief History of Remote Access

This section briefly reviews the history of modems and Internet access, even before the advent of the Internet. The idea of remote access to the Internet from home did not become a mainstream offering until the early 1990s. Before then, however, devices like modems were used for other purposes. The following list outlines the major events in the history of remote access:

1960s—Modems were used by dumb computer terminals to access large computers called mainframes.

1970s—Bulletin Board Systems (BBSs) allowed original PCs to access a server, let you post a message for others, and look at messages posted by others.

1980s—File transfers between computers became popular, as well as rudimentary interactive graphics.

1990s—Internet access through a modem became popular, with modem speeds rapidly increasing to 56 Kbps.

2000s—High-speed Internet access became more affordable and more popular.

The next two sections examine the high-speed Internet access methods that developed in the late 1990s, which are now mainstream technologies.

Accessing an ISP Through a Phone Line and a DSL Modem

Digital subscriber line (DSL) defines a much higher-speed method of using the same home phone lines that modems use. DSL differs from how modems work in many ways, such as the following:

- DSL uses digital electrical signals, not analog.

- Unlike modems, DSL allows a voice call to use the phone line simultaneously as DSL passes data.

- To not interfere with a concurrent voice call on the same phone line, DSL uses frequencies outside the range typically used for voice.

- DSL Internet service is "always on" in that no phone call or other effort must be made to access the Internet.

To use DSL, the home PC needs either an internal or external DSL modem or DSL router. Each of these devices understands, and uses DSL, but with slightly different features that are beyond the scope of the Networking Academy CCNA curriculum. Figure 1-15 shows a typical home installation with an external DSL router/modem.

Figure 1-15   Basic Operation of Modems

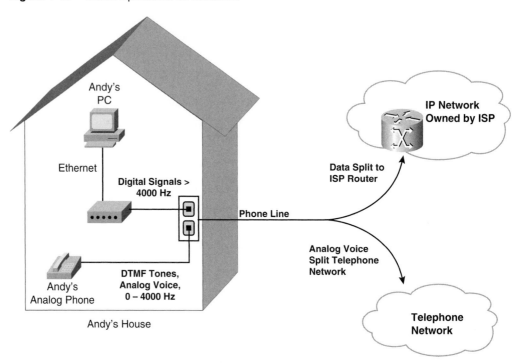

Figure 1-15 shows how both the normal phone and the DSL router connect, through a typical telephone line with an RJ-11 connector, to a phone socket. The local telephone company then splits out the voice to the telephone network and splits out the data to give to an ISP. In effect, the PC now has an electrical path between itself and the router, with the ability to send bits to and from that router. In turn, this access provides the PC with Internet connectivity.

Accessing an ISP Through a Cable TV Cable and a Cable Modem

Cable TV companies provide Internet access that, from a nontechnical perspective, is similar to DSL. The PC needs either an internal or external cable modem or a cable router. The cable modem/router connects to the CATV cable instead of the phone line. The cable modem sends and receives data to and from a router inside the cable TV company; at the same time, the CATV cable is still available for its primary purpose: TV. In other words, you can watch TV and switch channels all you want, while someone else in the house uses the Internet over the same CATV cable. Like DSL, the service is always on and doesn't require the user to do anything before beginning to use the Internet. Similar to DSL, it is fast, with download speeds well over 1 Mbps.

TCP/IP Protocol Suite and TCP/IP Software

The one network component that has not yet been covered in this chapter is software. Software provides the motivation and the reasons why a computer tries to communicate in the first place. You might build a network with computer hardware, NICs, modems, cables, and networking devices, but if no software exists, the computers do not attempt to communicate. Software provides that logic and that motivation for a computer to communicate.

You might have used computer software that, in turn, caused the computer to use the network. If you have ever opened a web browser to look at web pages or surf the web, you have used computer software that drives traffic across the network. In fact, because web browsers are so commonly used today, this section uses web browsers as examples.

Networking Standards, Protocols, and the TCP/IP Protocol Suite

For computer communications to be useful, the communication must follow a set of rules. Networking rules are formally defined by many different networking *standards* and networking *protocols*. Individually, a single networking standard or networking protocol defines the rules for a small part of what a network does. For example, an encoding scheme used by an Ethernet NIC would be a single standard. This section looks at a few networking protocols as examples, namely *Hypertext Transfer Protocol (HTTP)* and *Internet Protocol (IP)*.

Computers and network devices implement protocols mainly through computer software. For example, when you download a web page, the web browser uses HTTP, which the web-browser software implements. To deliver the data to and from the web server, the PC might use other protocols, such as the aforementioned IP. Today, most computer OSs implement IP, so IP is already built in to the OS and available for use.

Note

A computer OS is software that controls the computer hardware, providing a human interface to the computer. Windows XP and Linux are two examples of PC OSs.

For a network to work, all network components must use the same set of standards and protocols. Many options exist for standards and protocols to do the same (or similar) functions, so to help make sense of all that, a concept called a *protocol suite* or networking model was created. A protocol suite is a set of protocols through which, when a computer or networking device implements many of the protocols in the suite, the computers can communicate easily and effectively.

The *Transmission Control Protocol/Internet Protocol (TCP/IP)* protocol suite defines and collects a large set of networking standards and protocols that are used on most computers today. The concepts and protocols covered in this section, including HTTP and IP, are part of the TCP/IP protocol suite. Chapter 9, "TCP/IP Protocol Suite and IP Addressing," covers the TCP/IP protocol suite (also called the TCP/IP networking model) in depth.

Using HTTP to Download a Web Page

This section covers what might be a familiar topic: the use of a *web browser*. What is probably new is how web-browser software implements one of the many protocols inside the TCP/IP protocol suite (specifically, the HTTP protocol) to get the contents of a website from a web server. In case you're less familiar with web browsers and *web servers*, the next section briefly introduces these concepts.

Web Browsers and Web Servers

Web-browser software shows information in a window of a PC's video display. That information might be simple text, graphics, video, or animation. The browser can also play audio. Today, the most popular web-browser software comes from Microsoft, called Internet Explorer (IE). Netscape and Mozilla Firefox are two other popular web browsers.

A web server is software that distributes information from the web server to web browsers. For example, Cisco Systems has a website (www.cisco.com) that lists tons of information about its products and services. Cisco creates the website by placing the web pages on a server, installing web server software on that server, and telling the web server software to supply the web pages to any browsers that request the web pages.

Note that many people use the terms *website* and *web page* to refer to web-based content. The term website refers to a bunch of related content. For example, in the case of Cisco, if you spend time clicking different links in the browser after starting at www.cisco.com, everything you look at is part of the Cisco website. At any one point in time, however, you look at an individual web page.

Web browsers can display a large variety of content, but, in some cases, they also need help. For example, browsers can easily display text and graphics. For some functions, however, the browser relies on other software, with the browser placing the other software's display window inside its window. For example, a browser might not directly support the ability to show a video, but it might instead use software that plays a video. The Microsoft IE browser, for example, might use the Microsoft Windows Media Player (WMP) to show a video.

Downloading a Web Page

Computers store long-term data on disk drives in an object called a file. Computers, in their most basic form, work with *binary digits*, which people commonly abbreviate to *bits*. However, when describing computers, it is cumbersome to discuss and work with every little bit. So, computers combine 8 bits into a *byte* for a small amount of added convenience. The next step is to combine a set of bytes into a file. Computer files hold a set of related information. For example, a single computer file might hold a homework assignment you typed, a graphical image, a song that an MP3 player can play, a video, or any other single entity that computer software might want to manipulate or use.

When a web developer creates a web page, the result is a set of files stored on the web server. One or more files might hold the web page's text. Other files hold graphics (typically, one file per graphical image). Other files might hold audio that plays when you load the web page.

When a browser loads a new web page, the following sequence of events occurs:

1. The browser asks the server to send one file that has both instructions and displayable content.

2. The browser displays the contents of the file.

3. The browser also looks at the instructions inside the file, which might tell it to get more files from the web server.

4. The browser asks the server for the additional files.

5. The browser displays the additional content, as well as looking for additional instructions to download other files.

6. The browser continues to look for instructions to download other files that are part of the web page until all files are downloaded and displayed.

To actually request the files and to cause the files to be transferred from the server to the web browser, the browser and server both use HTTP. Figure 1-16 depicts the flow and logic of how the web browser transfers files.

Figure 1-16   HTTP Transfers Three Files

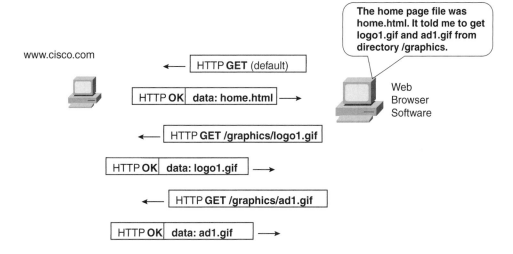

HTTP uses the concept of a *get request*. The HTTP get request identifies the file that the browser needs from the server. The server obliges and sends the file. In this case, the first file, called home.html, holds instructions telling the browser to ask for two more files.

Note

The term HTTP is derived from the first type of file supported by a web browser: a file with Hypertext Markup Language (HTML) text and instructions. Original web browsers needed to download HTML files exclusively and, to do so, they needed a protocol to transfer the HTML files. So, HTTP is derived from the idea of a protocol to transport hypertext.

Browser Plug-Ins

Browsers know how to display the information in HTML and other types of files. However, rather than having to understand how to display any and every type of content, oftentimes the browser uses another program to display some types of content. For example, browsers often use a program called Flash Player (www.macromedia.com) to display animations like what's shown in the online curriculum. For video or audio, browsers often use products such as QuickTime (www.quicktime.com), RealPlayer (www.real.com), or WMP (www.microsoft.com).

When a browser needs to use one of these programs, it typically displays the related information inside the browser window on the PC display screen. In effect, this additional program is "plugged in" to the browser window. As a result, many people refer to these programs as *plug-ins*.

Note

Flash Player from Macromedia is required before you can see all the content of the online course. It can be downloaded from www.macromedia.com.

 Lab 1.1.8   Web Browser Basics

In this lab, you learn how to use a web browser to access Internet sites, become familiar with the concept of a Universal Resource Locator (URL), and use a search engine to locate information on the Internet. You access selected websites to learn the definitions of networking terms and use hyperlinks to jump from a current website to other websites.

TCP/IP Networking Model

As previously mentioned, TCP/IP consists of a large number of protocols. In fact, the name TCP/IP refers to two of the more popular protocols inside TCP/IP: namely, *Transmission Control Protocol (TCP)* and Internet Protocol (IP). Because TCP/IP contains such a large volume of protocols, it is useful to think about the TCP/IP protocol suite by grouping its member protocols into categories called layers. Figure 1-17 shows the TCP/IP networking model and its component layers.

Figure 1-17   TCP/IP Networking Model and Protocols

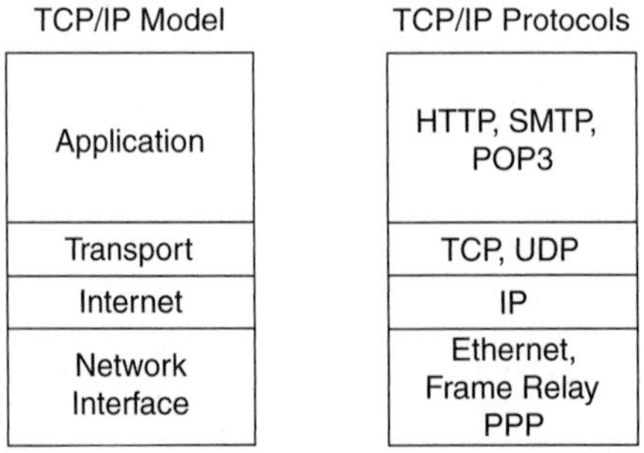

TCP/IP Model	TCP/IP Protocols
Application	HTTP, SMTP, POP3
Transport	TCP, UDP
Internet	IP
Network Interface	Ethernet, Frame Relay, PPP

The TCP/IP networking model, like other networking models, shows several layers on top of each other. Each layer implies a general category of service or function that the protocols at that layer perform. For example, the application layer provides services to applications. Web browsers are concerned with displaying information on the screen, but to do so, they ask for help from a TCP/IP application layer protocol (namely, HTTP).

Chapter 2 covers the details about networking models in general, referencing another popular networking model called the OSI reference model. Chapter 9 covers the details about the TCP/IP networking model.

> This chapter covers the most basic features of IP, TCP, IP routing, and IP subnetting; however, the online curriculum does not cover these topics until Modules 9 and 10. The book has included this additional coverage of these very practical parts of networking to balance the highly-theoretical coverage of the early chapters of this book. Also, many details in this section relate to the troubleshooting tools introduced in module 1 of the course.
>
> If you prefer to skip topics that are not mentioned in the online curriculum, skip forward to the section "Troubleshooting Basics for IP."

TCP/IP Transport Layer and the TCP Protocol

The TCP/IP transport layer is a group of protocols that provide services to application layer protocols. In fact, each layer of any networking model provides services to the layer just above it. This section describes one example of how a protocol at one layer provides a service to the adjacent higher layer by using the TCP and HTTP protocols in the example.

TCP happens to provide an important and popular service to many application protocols: the service of guaranteed delivery of data. Using HTTP (application layer) and TCP (transport layer, one layer below the application layer) as examples, consider the difference in logic used by the software on a web server:

- **HTTP**—I need to transfer files to another computer's web browser, but I do not have any way to recover data in case it gets lost.

- **TCP**—I have the capability to monitor transmitted data to determine whether the data arrived. If it gets lost, I can resend the data, which guarantees that all the data eventually arrives safely.

As you can see, the two protocols seem like they were made for each other. In fact, TCP predated HTTP by quite a few years, so when HTTP was created, the people who created HTTP simply decided to use TCP to perform guaranteed delivery of the data through TCP's error-recovery process. Figure 1-18 shows how the actual error-recovery process works.

Figure 1-18   Example of TCP Error Recovery

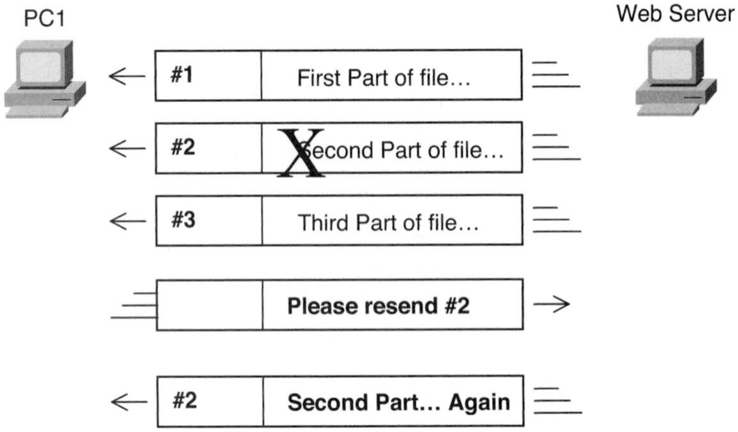

The TCP software, built in to the OS on the server, marks each packet with a *sequence number*, as Figure 1-18 shows. Because the second packet was lost, the PC on the left receives only the packets numbered 1 and 3. From that, the TCP software on the PC on the left—again, software built in to the OS on the PC—can surmise that packet 2 was lost somewhere along the way. To cause the server to resend the lost packet, PC1's TCP software sends a request to the server to resend packet 2, which it does.

The next section introduces IP, which provides the service of routing the packets from one computer to another.

TCP/IP Internet Layer and the Internet Protocol

The single most important protocol in the TCP/IP networking model is IP. It exists as part of the internet layer in the TCP/IP networking model. IP defines many things, but two features stand out by far as the most important. A large percentage of your work, thought, and learning in the Networking Academy CCNA classes somehow revolve around IP and its main two features:

- Routing
- Logical addressing

These features are linked in many ways, so they are best understood together. Although this chapter provides an introduction to networking, including networking software that implements TCP/IP, learning the basics of IP now helps provide some insight into where you will go in this class.

IP Addressing and Routing

Networks that use TCP/IP, which includes almost every network today, assign an *IP address* to each network interface. The IP address uniquely identifies that interface inside the network. After each network interface has a unique IP address, data can be sent from device to device by using these IP addresses, delivering the data to the one device that uses a particular IP address.

The preceding paragraph, although accurate, is relatively generic, so some concrete examples can help. IP addresses are 32-bit binary numbers. To make things easier on us humans, IP addresses might be written in *dotted-decimal* form. Dotted decimal means that the 32-bit number is represented by four decimal numbers separated by periods (dots). Each decimal number represents 8 bits. For example, the following line shows the same IP address in both binary form and dotted-decimal form:

> 00001010000000010000001000000011   10.1.2.3

Certainly, it is much easier to keep track of the dotted-decimal version of the IP address than the binary version of the same IP address. In this case, the decimal 10 represents the first 8 bits, the 1 represents the next 8 bits, and so on. For example, the 8-bit binary equivalent of decimal 10 is 00001010, which begins the 32-bit IP address just shown.

Now, consider the simple LAN shown in Figure 1-19. It has two PCs, each with an IP address.

Tip

The four decimal values inside an IP address each represent 8 bits. Most people use the term *octet* to refer to a single one of the four numbers inside an IP address. The decimal values must be between 0 and 255 and inclusive. Chapters 9 and 10 cover additional restrictions.

Figure 1-19   Single LAN with Two PCs and One Router

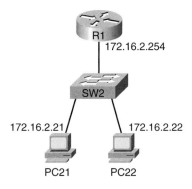

IP defines that each network interface that uses IP must have an IP address. In Figure 1-19, each PC has a single Ethernet LAN NIC. A NIC provides an interface to the network so the PCs can assign an IP address to the NIC. In fact, you can easily see the IP address assigned to a NIC on most any computer, if you know the details. On Microsoft Windows XP, for example, you can use the **ipconfig** command from a command prompt, as shown in Figure 1-20. Figure 1-20 shows the **ipconfig** command output from PC21 in Figure 1-19.

Figure 1-20   Sample **ipconfig** Output

```
C:\WINDOWS\system32\cmd.exe                                    - □ ×

C:\Documents and Settings\wodom>ipconfig

Windows IP Configuration

Ethernet adapter Local Area Connection:

        Connection-specific DNS Suffix  . :
        IP Address. . . . . . . . . . . . : 172.16.2.21
        Subnet Mask . . . . . . . . . . . : 255.255.255.0
        Default Gateway . . . . . . . . . : 172.16.2.254

C:\Documents and Settings\wodom>
```

Packet Tracer

The **ipconfig** command shown in Figure 1-20 can be performed using the Packet Tracer tool in Real-time mode. Feel free to experiment with the NA01-0112 configuration previously used in this chapter, and look at the IP addresses on Fred, Barney, Wilma, and Betty.

Using these IP addresses, the PCs can send each other packets of data. The packet includes end-user data and headers added by some other protocols, including the IP header added by the IP software on a computer. The IP header includes a source IP address and a destination IP address.

Lab 1.1.6   PC Network TCP/IP Configuration

In this lab, you learn the methods of discovering your computer's network connection, hostname, MAC (Layer 2) address, and network (Layer 3) address.

Note

IP addresses are considered to be logical addresses. The term logical is not meant to imply that other addresses are "illogical," but rather physical. For example, a MAC address is permanently associated with a single physical NIC, so a MAC address is a physical address. An IP address can be assigned to any PC, so IP addresses are not physical.

IP Address Organization: Subnets

Figure 1-21 adds a router and two switches to the network shown in Figure 1-19. In this network, the router is connected to three LANs, so it has three network interfaces, one connected to each LAN. Therefore, the router has an IP address for each interface because IP addresses uniquely identify interfaces used to connect to a network.

The IP addresses in Figure 1-21 must conform to certain rules. In this example, all IP addresses on the same LAN must use the same first three decimal numbers in their respective IP addresses. Figure 1-22 shows how the numbers are grouped.

Figure 1-21   Network with Three LANs Connected by One Router

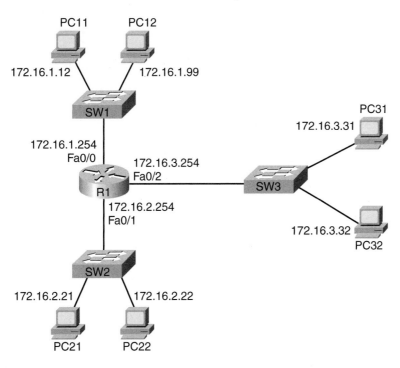

Figure 1-22   Grouping Effect of IP Addresses

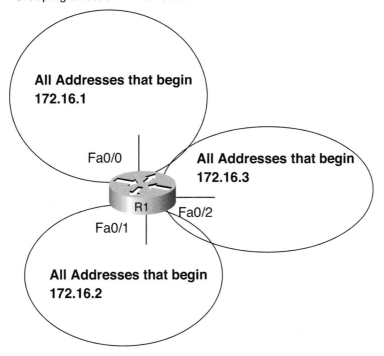

Figure 1-22 shows three separate IP subnets. A *subnet* is a group of IP addresses that share a common value for the beginning parts of the IP addresses in the subnet. Also, the members of a subnet must not be separated from each other by any routers. The three subnets in Figure 1-22 are loosely described as follows:

- All IP addresses beginning with 172.16.1
- All IP addresses beginning with 172.16.2
- All IP addresses beginning with 172.16.3

IP Routing with IP Routers

The rules about the IP addresses shown in Figure 1-22 allow for easy routing. The router keeps a table—called a routing table—that essentially lists all the groups of IP addresses that it can somehow reach and the interface out which it needs to send packets to reach those groups. For example, for Figure 1-22, router R1's routing table contains the equivalent of what's shown in Table 1-1.

Table 1-1   Pseudo-Routing Table on Router R1 in Figure 1-22

To Forward Packets Sent to Addresses That Begin With...	Send the Packets Out This Interface
172.16.1	Fa0/0
172.16.2	Fa0/1
172.16.3	Fa0/2

Note

Fa is short for Fast Ethernet, which is a type of Ethernet LAN that sends bits at 100 Mbps.

Armed with the information in Table 1-1, the router can receive data packets sent by any of the PCs in the network and make the correct decision about where to forward the packets.

Troubleshooting Basics for IP

Note

For those of you skipping the extra coverage of TCP, IP, IP subnetting, and IP routing, begin reading again at this heading.

Now that you know the very basics of IP addresses and routing, the rest of this section covers troubleshooting. Frankly, it is a bit ambitious to think about troubleshooting before covering more of the course. However, you can do some basic things that are both interesting and fun from any network-connected PC.

The online curriculum uses a how-to list, similar to the following one, that suggests general steps in how to approach problems when you troubleshoot:

How To

Step 1   Define the problem.

Step 2   Gather the facts.

Step 3   Identify possible solutions by doing the following:

1 Analyze the facts compared to the expected behavior of the network.

2 Determine possible root causes of the unexpected behavior.

3 Determine a set of actions that might solve the problem.

Step 4 Create an action plan to implement the solution you chose in Step 3.

Step 5 Implement the plan.

Step 6 Observe the results.

Step 7 Document the details.

Step 8 Introduce problems and troubleshoot.

One of the most valuable tools when troubleshooting any network is to have ready knowledge or references that describe how the network is supposed to work. The computers and network devices that comprise a network do attempt to follow the protocols, and these protocols define a series of steps that must be taken under certain conditions. If you know the steps that should occur, you can try to find the first step that is not working correctly and then look for reasons why that step failed.

This section describes some of the basics of IP addressing and routing, to complete the picture of what should happen, along with some tools that are useful for troubleshooting.

Name Resolution Using a Domain Name System Server

Although a basic understanding of IP addressing is useful at this point in the class, most computer users never even think about IP addresses. However, they do know the names of things that can be translated into IP addresses. For example, you might see an advertisement on TV or in a magazine that mentions a website. The ad might list something such as www.get-cisco-certified.com. You might open a web browser and plug that into the field called *Address* at the top of the browser, and the website suddenly appears. Or you might already be on some website and click something on the screen, and another website appears. When you do that, the browser's Address field changes because your clicking action causes the web browser to jump to another web address.

The correct term for the text placed into the Address field of a web browser is *Universal Resource Locator (URL)*. Many people simply call this a web address. The URL itself has some structure. For example, the following URL represents the web page from which you can look at all the Cisco Systems documentation:

http://www.cisco.com/univercd

By closely examining that URL, you can separate the URL into its components. First, the stuff before the double slash simply identifies the protocol to use, which, in this case, is the now-familiar HTTP protocol. The web server uses the stuff after the single slash to further identify the specific web page that the browser wants to see. The middle part of the URL—the part between the double slash and single slash—is called the hostname of the web server. When a PC user opens a browser and attempts to reach a URL, the following occur:

1. The PC finds the hostname inside the URL.

2. The PC requests name resolution from a Domain Name System (DNS) server to find the IP address of the server whose hostname is in the URL.

3. The DNS server supplies the IP address being used by the web server.

4. The PC can then send packets (like those containing HTTP get requests) to that IP address.

The overall process of asking a DNS server to supply the IP address associated with a name is called *name resolution*. Figure 1-23 shows an example of name resolution, with the steps in the preceding list referenced in the figure. (Chapter 9 covers DNS in more detail.)

Figure 1-23   DNS Resolution After Putting a URL into a Web Browser

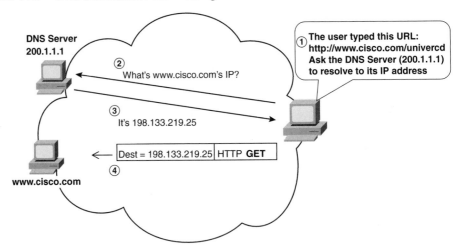

Although Figure 1-23 shows what happens when you browse the web, similar things happen with other protocols. For example, when you send an e-mail from your PC, your e-mail software sends the e-mail to an e-mail server. Your e-mail software is configured with a reference to the name of the e-mail server (for example, mail.skyline-ats.com). So, before sending an e-mail to the e-mail server, your PC must ask DNS to tell your computer the IP address of the e-mail server based on its name.

Default Gateway/Router

After it resolves a hostname into its corresponding IP address, a PC must next make a simple but important decision: Is the destination IP address on my same subnet or not? As previously mentioned, a subnet is a group of IP addresses that have the same beginning, or prefix, in their

IP addresses. All the hosts on the same LAN should be in the same subnet. Also, by definition, hosts on different subnets should be separated from each other by at least one router. So, for a PC connected to a LAN, its logical next step can be separated into the following statements:

- If the destination IP address is in my subnet, I do not need to send the packets to a router; I can send them directly over the LAN to the destination.

- If the destination IP address is in another subnet, at least one router exists between me and the destination. Routers are in charge of packet delivery, so I must send the packets to a router that is attached to the LAN.

To perform the second step in this list, a PC uses a concept called a *default gateway* (also known as a default router). A PC's default gateway is the IP address of a local router, one on the same subnet, to which the PC sends all packets destined for another subnet.

Figure 1-24 shows an example in which one host needs to send a packet to another host on the same subnet, and a second host needs to send a packet to another host in a different subnet.

Tip

When the first routers were created, they were called gateways. In fact, the first Cisco Systems commercial routers had a G (meaning gateway) in the name instead of an R. Although the industry has been using the term router instead of gateway for a long time, the concept described in this section is still more often called default gateway instead of default router. So, it's useful to remember both terms and know that they mean the same thing.

Figure 1-24   Sending Packets to the Same Subnet or Different Subnet

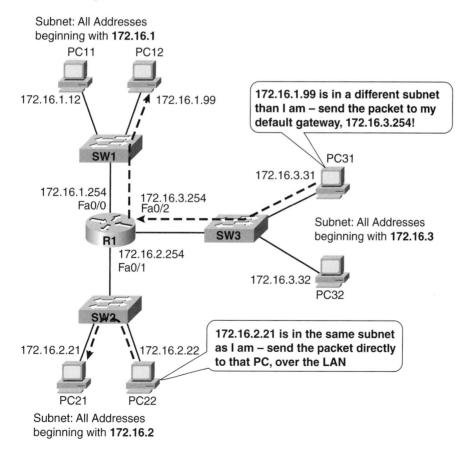

On PCs using Windows XP, the default gateway IP address is listed in the output of the **ipconfig** command. (Refer to Figure 1-20 for an example.) You can use any working PCs in the classroom to look at their default gateway IP addresses. You can also download the Packet Tracer configurations from www.ciscopress.com/title/1587131641 and then load the one named NA01-0124, which loads a configuration like the one shown in Figure 1-24. Then, you can use the **ipconfig** command on the PCs in the network and perform a simulation of the packets shown in Figure 1-24. Note that other OSs also have similar commands, such as **ifconfig** on Linux.

Troubleshooting Tools

When a user does something on his PC that makes the PC want to send data, a couple of things happen, in order, as described in the preceding section. This section and the next one describe a few basic troubleshooting steps. First, for reference, here are the first three basic steps that you will examine now. Other related steps will be covered after you get into more detail in the class:

1. When the user types/implies a name of another computer (for example, by choosing to go to a website with the name embedded in the URL), the PC asks DNS to resolve the name into an IP address.

2. After it knows the IP address, if the IP address of the other computer is local, the PC directly sends the packet to the other PC.

3. After it knows the IP address, if the IP address of the other computer is on another subnet, the computer sends the packet to its default gateway.

A reasonable methodology for troubleshooting is to somehow verify whether the PC can succeed at Step 1. If that succeeds, somehow verify if Step 2 is working, and so on. Most PC OSs include built-in tools that allow such testing, such as **nslookup, ping,** and **tracert**.

nslookup

You can use the **nslookup** command from a command prompt on many PC OSs, including Windows XP. The name stands for *Name Server Lookup*, which means that the command does the same sort of DNS request/lookup that would be done by a web browser when looking for a web server. Figure 1-25 shows sample output from **nslookup** on the PC in my office, looking for www.cisco.com. As you can see in Figure 1-25, www.cisco.com successfully resolved to IP address 198.133.219.25.

Figure 1-25   Sample nslookup Output

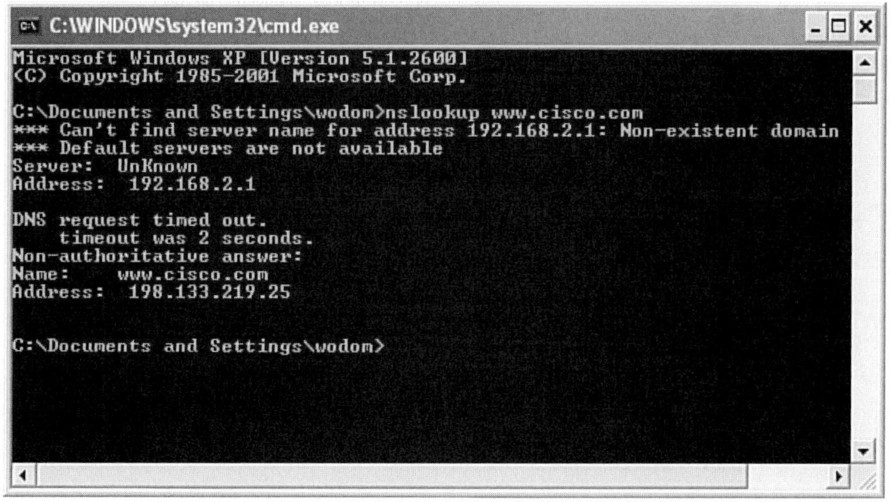

```
C:\WINDOWS\system32\cmd.exe                                    _ □ ×
Microsoft Windows XP [Version 5.1.2600]
(C) Copyright 1985-2001 Microsoft Corp.

C:\Documents and Settings\wodom>nslookup www.cisco.com
*** Can't find server name for address 192.168.2.1: Non-existent domain
*** Default servers are not available
Server:  UnKnown
Address:  192.168.2.1

DNS request timed out.
    timeout was 2 seconds.
Non-authoritative answer:
Name:    www.cisco.com
Address:  198.133.219.25


C:\Documents and Settings\wodom>
```

ping

The *ping* command tests a PC's capability to successfully send a packet to another IP address
and receive a response. The **ping** command sends a special packet, popularly called a *ping
request packet*, to the IP address listed after the **ping** command. Computers that implement
TCP/IP are required to support the capability to receive something loosely called a ping request
packet and send a *ping reply packet* back to the original sender. If the **ping** command receives
the ping reply packet, the command has verified that the two computers can send and receive
packets to and from each other.

Figure 1-26 shows sample **ping** command output from Packet Tracer. With the Packet Tracer
tool, you can simulate a **ping** command by using the Simulation tab and then clicking the PC.
Figure 1-26 shows PC22 pinging PC21 and PC31 pinging PC12, as shown in Figure 1-24.

Packet Tracer

You can perform the same command, using Packet Tracer, by opening file
NA01-0124, clicking the **Realtime** tab, double-clicking **PC22**, and issuing the
ping 172.16.2.21 command. Similarly, double-click **PC31** and issue the **ping
172.16.1.12** command to test the other route shown in Figure 1-24.

Figure 1-26   Sample Pings

Successful ping of PC21 from PC22

Successful ping of PC12 from PC31

The **ping** command can also test the capability of a PC to send packets to its default gateway. This step might be particularly useful to verify whether a PC can send packets to another subnet. Figure 1-27 shows a one-router, two-LAN network; however, this time, PC11 has the wrong default gateway configured. Because of this misconfiguration on PC11, PC11 cannot successfully send packets to hosts on other subnets. However, it can send packets to hosts on the same subnet because PC11 does not need to use its default gateway to reach other hosts. Figure 1-28 shows some of the steps involved in troubleshooting PC11 (this time from a screen shot using Packet Tracer).

As you can see from Figure 1-28, PC11 cannot even ping its default gateway. If a PC cannot ping its default gateway, it cannot successfully send packets through that default gateway, which means that it cannot send packets outside the local subnet.

 Packet Tracer   By loading Packet Tracer Configuration NA01-0124 and using real-time mode, you can duplicate the ping tests shown in Figure 1-28.

Figure 1-27   PC11 with a Misconfigured Default Gateway

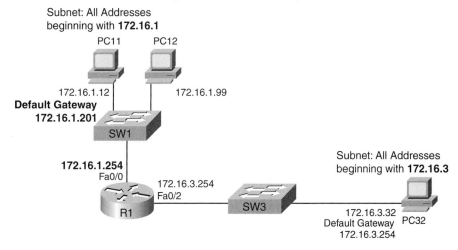

When you use the **ping** command to troubleshoot a problem, a simple sequence can be used to find out how far packets can be delivered into the network. For example, one step is to ping a PC's default gateway IP address, as previously mentioned. The following list summarizes the steps in the order that they are normally used:

 How To

Step 1 ping 127.0.0.1—Sends a ping down the software and backup. It simply tests the software on the local computer. (IP address 127.0.0.1 is called the loopback IP address. It is automatically configured every time TCP/IP is installed and is reserved for this self-test purpose.)

Step 2 ping the PC's own IP address—Tests whether the PC can use its own NIC.

Step 3 ping the default gateway—Tests connectivity over the LAN, whether the PC has referenced an IP address of some default gateway, and whether that default gateway's LAN interface is up and working.

Step 4 ping the destination computer—Tests the complete path between the PCs.

Figure 1-28   Troubleshooting PC11's Inability to Ping PC32

Successful ping of
PC12 (172.16.1.12)

Failed ping of
PC32 (172.16.3.32)
and
Failed ping of PC11's
default gateway
(172.16.1.201)

traceroute

The traceroute tool, typically pronounced "trace route," is found on many OSs and traces the route a packet takes through a network. The actual name of the command differs depending on the OS. In Microsoft OSs, the actual command name is *tracert*; on Cisco routers, Linux, and

UNIX, it is **traceroute**. Although you have been introduced to only the most basic parts of IP routing, it is good to know something about the **tracert** command when you begin your study of networking. You can actually learn much about routing just by experimenting with the **tracert** command on sample networks in the Packet Tracer tool and on real PCs attached to working networks.

tracert sends packets through the network to discover the IP addresses—and sometimes names—of the routers between one computer and another. For example, when PC31 pings PC12 from Figure 1-24, the command works, with the **tracert** command listing the IP addresses of any intermediate routers. Figure 1-29 shows this exact example.

Figure 1-29 shows two important lines of output from the **tracert** command. The first line lists the first router in the route: 172.16.3.254. This IP address is the router's IP address on the same LAN as PC31. In effect, this line of output means that PC31 first sends the packet to the router. The second line of output lists PC12's IP address of 172.16.1.12. This line means that PC12 itself was the next device that received the packet.

Figure 1-29   tracert on PC31 to PC12

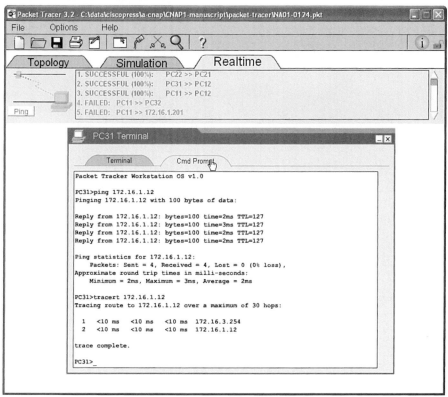

You can load the NA01-0124 configuration into Packet Tracer and repeat the example shown in Figure 1-29.

What's not listed in the output might be just as interesting. You know from Figure 1-24 that only one router is in the figure. The **tracert** command output confirms this fact. If there were three routers between PC31 and PC12, the **tracert** output would have listed a line of output for each router in the path as well as an ending line listing the IP address of the destination host.

If the DNS server is working correctly, **tracert** can also list the names of the devices. Packet Tracer does not have a DNS feature, so Figure 1-29 lists only the IP addresses. However, you can sit at a PC connected to the Internet, use the **tracert** command, and see many routers and their hostnames listed in a route. For example, Figure 1-30 shows a **tracert www.cisco.com** command issued on my desktop PC.

Figure 1-30   tracert from a PC to www.cisco.com

```
C:\WINDOWS\system32\cmd.exe                                          _ □ ×

Microsoft Windows XP [Version 5.1.2600]
(C) Copyright 1985-2001 Microsoft Corp.

C:\Documents and Settings\wodom>tracert www.cisco.com

Tracing route to www.cisco.com [198.133.219.25]
over a maximum of 30 hops:

  1     1 ms     1 ms     1 ms   192.168.2.1
  2     9 ms     9 ms    10 ms   10.52.0.1
  3     9 ms     9 ms     9 ms   srp9-0.mtgmoh1-rtr3.cinci.rr.com [24.29.0.129]
  4    20 ms    20 ms    19 ms   son0-0-1.ncntoh1-rtr0.neo.rr.com [65.25.128.233]

  5    81 ms    30 ms    29 ms   so-1-2-0-0.gar1.Chicago1.Level3.net [4.79.72.49]

  6    30 ms    30 ms    29 ms   ae-1-52.bbr2.Chicago1.Level3.net [4.68.101.33]
  7    86 ms    85 ms    85 ms   ae-0-0.bbr1.SanJose1.Level3.net [64.159.1.129]
  8    86 ms    86 ms    85 ms   as-1-0.bbr2.SanJose1.Level3.net [64.159.0.242]
  9    85 ms    86 ms    85 ms   p1-0.cisco.bbnplanet.net [4.0.26.14]
 10    86 ms    86 ms    87 ms   p1-0.cisco.bbnplanet.net [4.0.26.14]
 11    86 ms    85 ms    85 ms   sjce-dmzbb-gw1.cisco.com [128.107.239.53]
 12     *        86 ms     *     sjck-dmzdc-gw2.cisco.com [128.107.224.73]
 13     *         *        *     Request timed out.
 14     *         *        *     Request timed out.
 15    ^C
C:\Documents and Settings\wodom>
```

Tip

If the **tracert** command continues running and never completes, use the Ctrl-C key sequence to try and stop the command.

As you can see from the output listed in Figure 1-30, many routers sit between my PC and the server whose name is www.cisco.com. Also, the output shows that the command could not determine the last few routers, which are noted as asterisks in the last few lines of output.

Lab 1.1.7   Using ping and tracert from a Workstation

In this lab, you learn to use the TCP/IP **ping** and **tracert** commands to test connectivity in a network. In the process, you see name resolution occur.

Lab 1.1.9   Basic PC/Network Troubleshooting Process

In this lab, you apply the basic troubleshooting model to simple and common network problems. You also become familiar with the more common hardware and software problems.

TCP/IP Wrap Up

The preceding section covering TCP/IP introduced many concepts and answered several questions. However, it might also have created even more questions because, as in any introduction, many details were omitted. However, many of these questions are answered—even in the CCNA 1 course.

Some of the processes, concepts, and troubleshooting steps actually require some binary, decimal, and hexadecimal math. To prepare you for those upcoming topics, this chapter concludes with a section that covers these three numbering systems and how to convert between them.

Network Math

Understanding binary, decimal, and hexadecimal numbering systems is important to many aspects of working with computer networking and with computing in general. Binary numbering (Base 2) is necessary because it can represent the most basic operations on computers: operations that work with binary digits (called bits). Hexadecimal numbering (Base 16) is necessary because binary can be slightly difficult to work with, and hexadecimal numbering can easily represent those same binary numbers. Of course, the ability to work with decimal numbering (Base 10) is important because that's what we humans are accustomed to working with.

Bits and Bytes

At their most basic level, computers work with bits. Physically, these bits might exist in several states. For example, computer RAM (memory) consists of several chips, and the chips hold millions of little transistors. The transistors are components of a chip that can be placed into either an on or off state. The computer considers the off state to mean binary 0 and the on state to mean binary 1. Other parts of the computer might use other physical and electrical methods to store bits. (For example, a disk drive might store a magnetic charge onto the disk, with one type of magnetic charge meaning binary 0 and another meaning binary 1.)

Computers can also work with combinations of bits, the most common being an 8-bit byte. Some computers also use the term *word*, which refers to multiple bytes (typically, 4 bytes). The computer hardware might work with a byte at a time, a word at a time, or even a bit at a time, depending on what the computer hardware attempts to do.

Names and Abbreviations for Large Numbers of Bits and Bytes

Computers might process extremely large amounts of bits and bytes, so additional terms are needed to describe these large chunks of data—terms slightly more exact than *large chunk*, that is. Table 1-2 lists the terms and describes how many bits and bytes each term represents.

Table 1-2   Names and Units for Large Numbers of Bits and Bytes

Term	Number of Bits	Number of Bytes
Kilobit (Kb)	1000	125 (1/8th of 1000)
Kilobyte (KB)	8000 (8 * 1000)	1000
Megabit (Mb)	1,000,000	125,000 (1/8th of 1 million)
Megabyte (MB)	8,000,000 (8 * 1,000,000)	1,000,000
Gigabit (Gb)	1 billion	125 million (1/8th of 1 billion)
Gigabyte (GB)	8 billion (8 * 1 billion)	1 billion
Terabit (Tb)	1 trillion	125 billion (1/8th of 1 trillion)
Terabyte (TB)	8 trillion (8 * 1 trillion)	1 trillion

The abbreviations use a lowercase "b" when referring to bits and an uppercase "B" when referring to bytes. This convention is used throughout computing. Interestingly, when working with computing topics outside of networking, the terms that refer to bytes are used more often. However, networking usually refers to terms that refer to a number of bits.

Names for the Rate at Which a Network Sends Data

Networks transmit data from one device to another by using different transmission media. Depending on the media, and the type of device connected to the media, the device might send the data at a different rate. The names of these rates look similar to the names shown in Table 1-2, but in this case, the terms include the idea of some number per second. Table 1-3 lists the terms.

Table 1-3   Names and Units Transmission Rates

Term	Number of Bits per Second	Number of Bytes per Second
Kilobit per second (Kbps)	1000	125 (1/8th of 1000)
Kilobyte per second (KBps)	8000 (8 * 1000)	1000
Megabit per second (Mbps)	1,000,000	125,000 (1/8th of 1,000,000)
Megabyte per second (MBps)	8,000,000 (8 * 1,000,000)	1,000,000
Gigabit per second (Gbps)	1 billion	125 million (1/8th of 1 billion)
Gigabyte per second (GBps)	8 billion (8 * 1 billion)	1 billion
Terabit per second (Tbps)	1 trillion	125 billion (1/8th of 1 trillion)
Terabyte per second (TBps)	8 trillion (8 * 1 trillion)	1 trillion

When you download a file over the Internet, oftentimes a popup window appears that tells you the rate at which the file is being transferred. Note that when this happens, the units typically describe the number of bytes per second, not the number of bits per second. However, when an ISP sells its Internet access service, it typically describes the speed in bits per second (or Kbps or Mbps) because that is a measurement of the network's speed. You can test the speed of your Internet connection by opening a web browser and going to http://reviews.cnet.com/Bandwidth_meter/7004-7254_7-0.html.

ASCII Alphanumeric Code

Most of the networking discussion in the next few chapters revolves around bits and bytes. Some of those bits and bytes represent numbers; in fact, most of the rest of this section discusses the important math behind manipulating bits and bytes as numbers. However, before discussing the numbers, this section discusses how computers represent text.

Computers represent text by using bits and bytes. Because text does not represent any particular number, however, computers need a way to correlate a particular set of bits to mean the letter "a," another to mean the letter "A," another for "b," and so on. Such a convention is called alphanumeric code.

Today, the most popular alphanumeric code used by computers is *American Standard Code for Information Interchange (ASCII)*. For example, Table 1-4 shows a few capital letters and the 8-bit number that represents those letters on a computer.

Table 1-4   Sample ASCII Codes for Capital Letters A Through H

Letter	Binary ASCII Code	Decimal ASCII Code
A	01000001	65
B	01000010	66
C	01000011	67
D	01000100	68
E	01000101	69
F	01000110	70
G	01000111	71
H	01001000	72

Tip

The online course has an ASCII converter feature that allows you to type in any letter and see the ASCII equivalent (in decimal).

Table 1-4 shows the values as binary and decimal. Some of the upcoming sections describe how to convert any binary number, including ASCII binary codes, to decimal numbers for easier manipulation.

Decimal Numbering System: Base 10

Decimal numbering (Base 10) should be familiar because it's what you have been taught since early childhood. However, unless you love math, you probably have not thought about a few details because the concepts of decimal have become part of you. However, thinking about the following simple decimal concepts helps you better appreciate binary numbering, which is covered in the next section.

First, consider the number *235*, for example. The number itself is made up of three numerals: 2, 3, and 5. *Numerals* are simply symbols that represent a number. The decimal numbering system uses numerals 0 through 9. The word *digit* (short for *decimal digit*) is often used instead of *numeral*. For example, 3 is the second digit of the number 235.

What does the number 235 really mean? Well, if you say the equivalent in English, you say something like, "two-hundred thirty-five." To better appreciate how other numbering systems work, such as binary, consider a contrived and unusual expansion of the English-language version of 235:

Two 100s, three 10s, and five 1s

It's much easier to say "two-hundred thirty-five" than "two 100s, three 10s, and five 1s." However, they both basically mean the same thing. You could even think of it in mathematical terms:

$$(2 * 100) + (3 * 10) + (5 * 1) = 235$$

Both the contrived English phrasing and the mathematical formula describe the core meaning of a multidigit decimal number. Each individual decimal digit represents its own value multiplied by a value associated with that digit's position in the number. It's more obvious to see this in a table, such as Table 1-5.

Table 1-5   Decimal Numbering: 1s, 10s, and 100s Digits

Powers of 10	10^2	10^1	10^0
Value Associated with That Digit or Column	100	10	1
Digits	2	3	5

With decimal numbering, the right-most digit in a number represents a value of that digit times 1. That digit is called the *1s digit*. The second from the right represents the value of the digit times 10. That digit is called the *10s digit*. The third from the right represents a value of that digit times 100. That digit is called the *100s digit*. This same logic continues for larger numbers; each successive digit to the left has a value 10 times the digit to its right. In Table 1-5, the 5 means "5 times 1" because it's in the 1s column. Similarly, the single digit in the 10s column represents "3 times 10." Finally, the 2 in the 100s digit column means "2 times 100."

Because you have used it all your life, the math is probably so intuitive that you don't need to think about decimal numbering to this depth. In the next section, you see how binary numbering works on the same basic premise, but with just two numerals or digits.

Binary Numbering System: Base 2

Binary numbering (Base 2) represents numbers in a different way than decimal (Base 10). Both decimal and binary numbering use numerals or digits to represent the idea of a particular number. However, binary uses just two digits: 0 and 1.

Binary numbering works on the same general principles as decimal numbering, but with differences in the details. The best way to understand the similarities and differences is to look at a sample binary number. Binary is simply another way to write digits that represent a number. For each decimal number, you can write the same number in binary. For example, the following binary number is the equivalent of the decimal number 235:

   11101011

Similar to decimal, a multidigit binary number has assigned values for each digit in the number. Table 1-6 shows 11101011 with values assigned to each digit.

Table 1-6   Binary Numbering: 1s, 2s, 4s, 8s (and So On) Digits

	2^7	2^6	2^5	2^4	2^3	2^2	2^1	2^0
Powers of 2								
Value Associated with That Digit or Column	128	64	32	16	8	4	2	1
Number Itself	1	1	1	0	1	0	0	1

With decimal, the digits in a multidigit decimal number represent various powers of 10, with the right-most digit representing 10^0, which is 1. With binary, the digits represent powers of 2, with the right-most digit representing 2^0, which is also 1. As shown in Table 1-6, the right-most binary digit represent the number of 1s (2^0), the second from the right represents the number of 2s (2^1), the third from the right represents the number of 4s (2^2), and so on.

Table 1-6 shows the value associated with each digit (or column), with each being a consecutive power of 2, increasing from right to left. So, what does this mean? Well, just like the decimal number 235 means (2*100) + (3*10) + (5*1) = 235, the binary number 11101011 means the following, but written in all decimal numbers for clarity:

   (1 * 128) + (1 * 64) + (1 * 32) + (0 * 16) + (1 * 8) + (0 * 4) + (1 * 2) + (1 * 1) = 235 decimal

If you add up the numbers, you actually get 235 decimal. The number 235 (decimal) and 11101011 (binary) both represent the same number; they're just written in a different format.

Converting From 8-Bit Binary Numbers to Decimal Numbers

Many times in networking and computing, it is convenient to work with a number in both its decimal and binary form. To do that, you need to be able to convert between the two formats. This section describes how to convert from binary to decimal. (The next section after that describes how to convert from decimal to binary.)

In networking, the most frequent reason to convert numbers from decimal to binary relates to IP addresses. IP addresses are indeed 32-bit binary numbers, but they are frequently written in dotted-decimal notation. With dotted decimal, each decimal number represents an 8-bit binary number. So, this section focuses on examples that use 8-bit-long binary numbers.

Converting from binary to decimal is actually relatively straightforward, at least compared to converting from decimal to binary. In fact, you've actually already seen the math in the text following Table 1-6. To convert a binary number to decimal, you just have to think about the binary number in a table, such as Table 1-7, and apply what the table's numbers mean.

Table 1-7   An Example of Binary-to-Decimal Conversion: 10101101

Powers of 2	2^7	2^6	2^5	2^4	2^3	2^2	2^1	2^0
Value Associated with That Digit or Column	128	64	32	16	8	4	2	1
Number Itself	1	0	1	0	1	1	0	1

Table 1-7 looks exactly like Table 1-6, except the binary number itself is slightly different to show another example. To convert to decimal, you simply multiply each pair of numbers that are in the same column of the last two rows in the table and add the numbers from the results of each product. Table 1-8 repeats the same information shown in Table 1-7, but now the conversion process math is shown.

Table 1-8   Converting 10101101 to Decimal: Multiplying Each Column and Then Adding Them Together

Value Associated with That Digit or Column	128	64	32	16	8	4	2	1
Number Itself	1	0	1	0	1	1	0	1
Product of Two Numbers in Same Column	128	0	32	0	8	4	0	1
Sum of All Products	173							

The process is indeed simple as long as you remember all the powers of 2! When working with IP addressing, you need to memorize all the powers of 2 up through 2^8, or 256, as shown in the previous tables. The basic algorithm to convert binary to decimal can be summarized as follows:

Step 1   Write the powers of 2, in decimal, in the top row of a table, similar to Table 1-8.

Step 2   On the second line, write the binary number that is to be converted, lining up each binary digit under the powers of 2.

Step 3   Multiply each pair of numbers (the numbers in the same column).

Step 4   Add the eight products from Step 3.

Lab 1.2.6   Binary-to-Decimal Conversion

In this lab, you learn and practice the process of converting binary values to decimal values.

Tip

The online curriculum has a tool that gives you sample 8-bit binary numbers, asks you to provide the decimal equivalent, and then checks your answer.

Converting from Decimal Numbers to 8-Bit Binary Numbers

Converting from decimal to binary requires more effort and work compared with converting from binary to decimal. The generic process to perform the conversion has several steps. For this book's purposes, the conversion process is slightly simplified by assuming that the goal is to convert a decimal number to an 8-bit binary number. To ensure that 8 bits are enough, the only decimal values that can be converted are 0 through 255 (inclusive). Note that the only decimal values allowed as octets of an IP address are also 0 through 255.

Generic Decimal-to-8-Bit-Binary Conversion Process

This book shows a slightly different process than the online curriculum does for converting from decimal to binary. If you are happy and accustomed to the version described in the online course, you might want to skip to the section "Converting IP Addresses Between Decimal and Binary."

Begin by writing down eight powers of 2, starting with 128 on the left ending with 1 on the right (similar to Table 1-9). The blank lines below the powers of 2 are placeholders in which the binary digits will be recorded.

Table 1-9   Convenient Table for Converting Decimal to 8-Bit Binary

Power of 2	128	64	32	16	8	4	2	1
Binary Digits	___	___	___	___	___	___	___	___

Beginning with 128 and moving toward 1, repeat the following step eight times, once for each power of 2:

Step 1   If the decimal number is greater than or equal to the power of 2, do the following:

    a   Record a 1 as the binary digit underneath the power of 2.

    b   Subtract the power of 2 from the decimal number, which results in a number called the "remainder."

    c   Use the remainder for the next step/power of 2.

Step 2   If the decimal number is less than the power of 2, do the following:

    a   Record a 0 as the binary digit underneath the power of 2.

    b   Move to the next power of 2 and use the same remainder as in this step.

Example 1 of the Generic Conversion Process: Decimal 235

The first example shows how to convert decimal 235 to 8-bit binary. To begin, record the eight powers of 2, as shown in Table 1-9. Then, start with 128, and determine whether to use Step 1 or Step 2 of the algorithm based on where the decimal number is greater than or equal to 128.

In this case, it is clear that 235 => 128, so Step 1 in the algorithm is used. Record a binary 1 for the binary digit under 128. Then, calculate 235 – 128 = 107, and use this remainder in the next step. Table 1-10 shows the work in progress at this point.

Table 1-10   Results: Converting 235 After 128's Digit Is Found

Power of 2	128	64	32	16	8	4	2	1
Binary Digits	_1_	___	___	___	___	___	___	___

For the next step, the 64's digit is determined by using a remainder of 107. 107 => 64, so Step 1 is performed. Record a binary 1 for the binary digit under 64. Then, calculate 107 – 64 = 43, and use this remainder for the next digit to the right. Table 1-11 shows the results.

Table 1-11   Results: Converting 235 After 64's Digit Is Found

Power of 2	128	64	32	16	8	4	2	1
Binary Digits	_1_	_1_	___	___	___	___	___	___

For the next step, the 32's digit is determined by using a remainder of 43. 43 => 32, so Step 1 is performed. Record a binary 1 for the binary digit under 32. Then, calculate 43 – 32 = 11, and use this remainder for the next digit to the right. Table 1-12 shows the results.

Table 1-12   Results: Converting 235 After 32's Digit Is Found

Power of 2	128	64	32	16	8	4	2	1
Binary Digits	_1_	_1_	_1_	___	___	___	___	___

For the next step, the 16's digit is determined by using a remainder of 11. 11 < 16, so Step 2 is performed. Record a binary 0 for the binary digit under 16, and use the same remainder (11) for the next digit to the right. Table 1-13 shows the results.

Table 1-13   Results: Converting 235 After 16's Digit Is Found

Power of 2	128	64	32	16	8	4	2	1
Binary Digits	_1_	_1_	_1_	_0_	___	___	___	___

For the next step, the 8's digit is determined by again using a remainder of 11. 11 => 8, so Step 1 is performed. Record a binary 1 for the binary digit under 8. Then, calculate 11 – 8 = 3, and use this remainder for the next digit to the right. Table 1-14 shows the results.

Table 1-14   Results: Converting 235 After 8's Digit Is Found

Power of 2	128	64	32	16	8	4	2	1
Binary Digits	_1_	_1_	_1_	_0_	_1_	___	___	___

For the next step, the 4's digit is determined by using a remainder of 3. 3 < 4, so Step 2 is performed. Record a binary 0 for the binary digit under 4, and use the same remainder (3) for the next digit to the right. Table 1-15 shows the results.

Table 1-15   Results: Converting 235 After 4's Digit Is Found

Power of 2	128	64	32	16	8	4	2	1
Binary Digits	_1_	_1_	_1_	_0_	_1_	_0_	___	___

For the next step, the 2's digit is determined by again using a remainder of 3. 3 => 2, so Step 1 is performed. Record a binary 1 for the binary digit under 2. Then, calculate 3 – 2 = 1, and use this remainder for the next digit to the right. Table 1-16 shows the results.

Table 1-16 Results: Converting 235 After 2's Digit Is Found

Power of 2	128	64	32	16	8	4	2	1
Binary Digits	_1_	_1_	_1_	_0_	_1_	_1_	_0_	___

For the eighth and final step, the 1's digit is determined by using a remainder of 1. 1 => 2, so Step 1 is performed. Record a binary 1 for the binary digit under 1. No subtraction is needed here, but the remainder is always 0 at this point. Table 1-17 shows the final results.

Table 1-17 Results: Converting 235 After 1's Digit Is Found

Power of 2	128	64	32	16	8	4	2	1
Binary Digits	_1_	_1_	_1_	_0_	_1_	_1_	_0_	_1_

Alternative Decimal-to-Binary Conversion Process

The Networking Academy CCNA 1 curriculum describes another process for converting decimal to binary. Both are valid, as well as other methods your instructor might teach in class. The goal of all these tools is to help you learn how to convert decimal to binary; feel free to use any valid method that makes sense to you and results in the correct answer. The lab referenced here provides some extra decimal-to-binary conversion practice, using the process from the course in the explanation. For reference, Figure 1-31 repeats the flowchart for decimal-to-binary conversion, which is taken from the online curriculum.

Lab 1.2.5   Decimal-to-Binary Conversion

In this lab, you practice converting decimal values to binary values.

Figure 1-31   Decimal-to-Binary Conversion Steps Used in the Online Curriculum

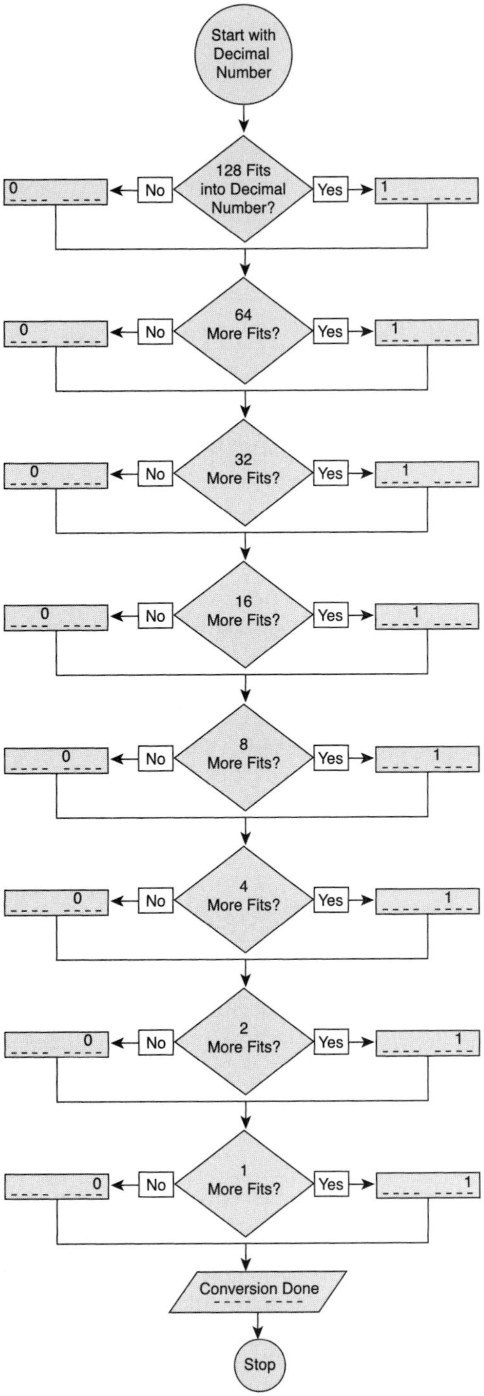

Example 2 of the Generic Conversion Process: Decimal 192

As you can see, the process is not particularly difficult at any one step, but it is laborious. Before leaving the process of converting decimal to its binary equivalent, however, this chapter includes one more example.

This example describes the steps taken to convert decimal 192 to its binary equivalent. Table 1-18 shows the binary equivalent, with each digit under the respective power of 2 that it represents (for easier reference).

Table 1-18   Results: Decimal 192 with Binary Equivalent

Power of 2	128	64	32	16	8	4	2	1
Binary Digits	_1_	_1_	_0_	_0_	_0_	_0_	_0_	_0_

Tip

The other popular decimal values when working with IP addressing are 0, 128, 192, 224, 240, 248, 252, 254, and 255. These numbers might be good values with which to practice the conversion process.

Tip

The online curriculum has a tool that gives you sample decimal numbers, asks you to provide the 8-bit binary equivalent, and then checks your answer.

The following list explains what happens at each step of the process, starting with the 128's digit:

Step 1   192 => 128, so the 128's digit is 1. 192 – 128 = 64, with 64 then being used for the comparisons for the 64's digit.

Step 2   64 => 64, so the 64's digit is 1. 64 – 64 = 0, with 0 then being used for the comparisons for the 32's digit.

Step 3   For the last six steps, the remainder (0) is always less than the power of 2. Therefore, record 0s for the remaining six digits.

This example shows how you can shorten the process once the remainder is 0. Essentially, once the remainder is 0, the rest of the binary digits are also 0.

Converting IP Addresses Between Decimal and Binary

IP addresses are 32-bit binary numbers, but because humans find it inconvenient to write 32-bit numbers, the addresses are written in dotted-decimal format. In dotted-decimal format, each octet has a decimal number between 0 and 255 (inclusive). Each decimal number represents 8 binary digits. So, to convert an IP address from decimal to binary (or vice versa), you must break down the problem into four different conversions between a decimal number and an 8-bit binary number.

By registering your book at the following website (www.ciscopress.com/title/1587131641) and navigating to the Extra Practice section, you can access multiple practice problems for all the conversion processes covered in this chapter. This Extra Practice section includes problems for conversions between binary, decimal, and hexadecimal, as well as conversions between binary and decimal IP addresses.

This section first describes how to convert dotted-decimal IP addresses to their binary equivalents, and then it describes the opposite.

Converting Decimal IP Addresses to Binary IP Addresses

You already read the math behind the conversion process between decimal and binary. To convert IP addresses, you simply need to follow a few additional rules:

Step 1   When converting a decimal IP address to binary, convert each of the four decimal numbers in the decimal IP address to an 8-bit number, which results in a total of 32 bits.

Step 2   Include leading 0s in the binary values; otherwise, the IP address will not have 32 bits.

Step 3   Form the 32-bit binary IP address by simply writing each of the four sets of 8 bits in order.

Note

This process asumes that the decimal conversion yields an 8-bit binary number, including any leading 0s.

The three-step process to convert a decimal IP address to its 32-bit binary equivalent simply requires that you convert each of the four decimal numbers, keeping any leading 0s, and combine the results into one long 32-bit binary number. For example, Table 1-19 shows a sample conversion of the IP address 100.235.2.2.

Table 1-19   Conversion of Decimal IP Address 100.235.2.2 to Binary

	1st Octet	2nd Octet	3rd Octet	4th Octet
Decimal Octet	100	235	2	2
Each Octet Converted to Binary (Step 1)	01100100	11101011	00000010	00000010
Resulting 32-Bit Number (Step 2)	01100100111010110000001000000010			

Table 1-19 begins with the decimal IP address in the first row and the results of each conversion step in the next two rows. The actual math for converting the decimal numbers (Step 1) is not shown, but you can refer to the previous section for examples using decimal 100 and 235. Step 2 just lists all 32 bits in succession. In real life, there is no need to actually write Step 3; you can just see the four sets of 8 bits in a row and think of it as a 32-bit number.

Converting Binary IP Addresses to Decimal IP Addresses

To convert a binary IP address to its decimal equivalent, you already know the 32-bit IP address. The process is relatively simple compared to converting decimal to binary:

Step 1   Separate the 32 bits into four groups of 8 bits (4 octets).

Step 2   Convert each binary octet to decimal.

Step 3   Insert a period between the four decimal numbers.

The algorithm can be shown with a sample binary value: 01100100111010110000000100000001. Table 1-20 organizes the bits into octets with 8 bits each.

Table 1-20   Conversion of Binary IP Address to Decimal

	1st Octet	2nd Octet	3rd Octet	4th Octet
Binary Value, Separated into Four Octets (Step 1)	01100100	11101011	00000001	00000 001
Each Octet Converted to Decimal (Step 2)	100	235	1	1
Decimal IP Address in Dotted-Decimal Format (Step 3)	100.235.1.1			

For some reason, many people trip up when completing the first step of this process. Whenever you convert a binary IP address to decimal, the conversion process must use four sets of 8 bits. Chapter 10 describes IP subnetting, for which you might work with parts of IP addresses that are not 8 bits in length. However, to convert binary and decimal IP addresses, you must always work with 8 bits at a time.

Using a Conversion Chart

You can always use a calculator to do the math of converting a decimal number to binary and vice versa. However, because IP addresses use only decimal numbers between 0 and 255, you can also use a binary/decimal conversion chart. A binary/decimal conversion chart simply lists decimal numbers and their binary equivalents. That way, you can look at the chart and find the numbers without doing all the math previously covered in this chapter. Appendix B, "Binary/Decimal Conversion Chart," contains a binary/decimal conversion chart.

For example, to convert 100.235.1.1 to binary, you can look in the chart and find the decimal number 100. Beside the number 100 is the 8-bit binary number 01100100. You can simply copy down those binary digits as the first 8 binary digits. Next, you find 235 in the chart, find the binary value beside it (namely, 11101011), write that down, and move to the next octet.

You can also use the chart to convert binary IP addresses to decimal by reversing this process.

Caution

The assessments for this course do not allow the use of calculators, nor do they provide sample tables like the ones shown in this chapter. You must practice the processes, particularly for converting IP addresses to and from decimal and binary, to prepare for these tests.

Hexadecimal Numbering System: Base 16

Hexadecimal numbering (Base 16), popularly called "hex," is another number system that is used frequently when working with computers because it can represent binary numbers in a more readable form. The computer performs computations in binary, but there are several instances in which a computer's binary output is expressed in hexadecimal form to make it easier to read. Each hex digit represents 4 bits, so the output is much smaller, which makes reading it much easier on the eyes.

The hexadecimal number system uses 16 symbols. Hex uses the same 10 numerals as decimal (0, 1, 2, 3, 4, 5, 6, 7, 8, and 9), plus six more. The additional symbols are the letters A, B, C, D, E, and F. The A represents the decimal number 10, B represents 11, C represents 12, D represents 13, E represents 14, and F represents 15, as shown in Table 1-21.

Table 1-21   Converting Between Hexadecimal Digits, Binary, and Decimal

Hexadecimal Digit	Binary Equivalent	Decimal Equivalent
0	0000	0
1	0001	1
2	0010	2
3	0011	3
4	0100	4
5	0101	5
6	0110	6
7	0111	7
8	1000	8
9	1001	9
A	1010	10
B	1011	11
C	1100	12
D	1101	13
E	1110	14
F	1111	15

In some parts of the computing world, converting between hexadecimal and decimal can be important. For networking, the most common conversion using hex is the conversion between hexadecimal and binary and vice versa. The conversion can be easily accomplished by simply using the information shown in Table 1-21.

Although hex-to-binary conversion is not required often in networking, occasionally, the need does arise when working with a Cisco router feature called the configuration register. Although the definition of what the configuration register does is not covered until the CCNA 2 course, the value, which is a four-digit hex number, can be manipulated. For example, most routers' configuration registers are set to hex 2102. However, individual bit values in the register have different meanings, so it is common to need to convert it to binary, as shown here:

0010000100000010

 Lab 1.2.8   Hexadecimal Conversions

This lab requires that you practice the process of converting hexadecimal numbers into binary and decimal numbers. Note that hex-to-decimal conversion is not covered in the online course, or this chapter, but the lab does cover the process.

Boolean or Binary Logic

Boolean math is a branch of mathematics created by George Boole. Boolean math creates a way to use math to analyze a large set of problems, including logic, electrical circuits, and certainly computing. Boolean math typically involves applying Boolean functions to 1 or 2 bits.

Two Boolean math operations are popular when performing IP subnetting calculations—namely, the Boolean AND and OR operations. Both functions take two different bits as input, and they provide a result of a single bit. Table 1-22 summarizes the AND and OR operations.

Table 1-22   Boolean AND and OR

First Bit	Second Bit	Results of an AND of These 2 Bits	Results of an OR of These 2 Bits
0	0	0	0
0	1	0	1
1	0	0	1
1	1	1	1

Although Table 1-22 shows the formal results, the logic of AND and OR can be simply phrased:

- A Boolean AND yields a 1 only if both bits are 1.

- A Boolean OR yields a 1 if at least one of the 2 bits is a 1.

In addition to the AND and OR, another Boolean function mentioned in the online course material is the NOT operation. This function takes a single bit as input and yields a result of the other bit. In other words, taking the NOT of 0 yields a 1, and the NOT of 1 yields a 0.

IP Subnet Masks

Chapter 10 shows how Boolean logic, particularly Boolean AND, can analyze and work with IP addresses. Some number of the first bits of the 32-bit IP addresses represents the group in which the IP address resides. These groups are called IP networks (or subnets). The number of these initial bits that represents the group (network or subnet) varies based on choices made by the people implementing the network. By considering IP address design concepts—which are covered in Chapters 9 and 10 and in other CCNA courses—a network engineer chooses the number of initial bits to use to identify a subnet.

After the engineer completes his analysis, he must tell the computers and networking devices how many initial bits have been chosen. To do so, the engineer uses a second 32-bit number called a *subnet mask*, which is a guide that determines how the IP address is interpreted. It indicates how many bits in the first part of the address identify the subnet. To do so, the mask lists several consecutive binary 1s and then all binary 0s. The number of initial binary 1s defines the number of initial bits that identify the subnet.

For example, earlier in this chapter, Figure 1-21 showed a sample internetwork, and Figure 1-22 showed the concept of subnets used in that internetwork. In Figure 1-22, a subnet mask of 255.255.255.0 was used. This mask, in binary, is as follows:

    11111111 11111111 11111111 00000000

With 24 initial binary 1s, this mask means that the first 24 bits of an IP address must be the same for all hosts in the same subnet. (Refer to Figure 1-22 to see this same logic in simple text.)

255.255.255.0 is just one example of a subnet mask. Many possible masks exist, but they must all begin with a number of binary 1s and then end in all binary 0s—the 1s and 0s cannot be mixed. Just for perspective, the following lines show two other popular and simple subnet masks:

    255.0.0.0   11111111 00000000 00000000 00000000

    255.255.0.0   11111111 11111111 00000000 00000000

The first of these masks means that all IP addresses must have their first 8 bits in common (first octet) to be in the same subnet. The second line means that all IP addresses in the same subnet must have their first 16 bits in common (first and second octets) to be in the same subnet.

Using Boolean Math with Subnets

IP uses a number called a subnet number to represent all IP addresses in the same subnet. A Boolean AND can find the subnet number. Although Chapter 10 covers this concept in more depth, Module 1 of the online curriculum introduces the concept, so it is introduced briefly in this chapter.

The following process allows you to find a subnet number, given an IP address and the subnet mask used with the IP address:

 Step 1   Convert the IP address and mask to binary. Write the IP address first and the subnet mask directly below it.

Step 2   Perform a bitwise Boolean AND of the two numbers.

Step 3   Convert the resulting 32-bit number, 8 bits at a time, back to decimal.

A bitwise Boolean AND means to take two equal-length binary numbers, AND the first bit of each number, AND the second bit of each number, then the third, and so on until all bits are ANDed together. Table 1-23 shows an example based on Figure 1-21 (IP address 172.16.2.21 and mask 255.255.255.0).

Table 1-23   Using a Bitwise Boolean AND to Find the Subnet Number

	1st Octet	2nd Octet	3rd Octet	4th Octet
IP Address 172.16.2.21 (Step 1)	10101100	00010000	00000010	00010101
Mask 255.255.255.0 (Step 1)	11111111	11111111	11111111	00000000
AND Result (Subnet Number [Step 2])	10101100	00010000	00000010	00000000
Decimal Subnet Number	172.16.2.0			

Summary

The online course points out that a connection to a computer network can be broken down into the physical connection, the logical connection, and the applications that interpret the data and display the information. This book further describes a network as computer hardware (for example, NICs and modems), software (for example, TCP/IP and web browsers), networking devices (for example, routers and switches), and network cabling.

TCP/IP software configuration includes an IP address, a subnet mask, and a default gateway. To test a connection, tools such as **ping** can verify whether packets can be delivered across a network. The **traceroute** command can also help isolate routing problems.

Access to the global TCP/IP, known as the Internet, requires some form of Internet access. This access can be gained using a modem, DSL, or cable modem. After connecting, a user can use applications, such as web browsers, which might use plug-ins, to view content held on servers in the Internet.

Computers recognize and process data using the binary (Base 2) numbering system. Often, the binary output of a computer is expressed in hexadecimal to make it easier to read. The ability to convert decimal numbers to binary numbers is valuable when converting dotted-decimal IP addresses to machine-readable binary format. Conversion of hexadecimal numbers to binary, and binary numbers to hexadecimal, is a common task when dealing with the configuration register in Cisco routers. The 32-bit binary addresses used on the Internet are referred to as IP addresses.

Boolean logic (a binary logic) allows two numbers to be compared and a choice generated based on the two numbers. Subnetting and wildcard masking use Boolean logic.

Check Your Understanding

Complete all the review questions listed here to test your understanding of the topics and concepts in this chapter. Answers are listed in Appendix A, "Answers to Check Your Understanding and Challenge Questions."

1. What is the function of a modem?

   A. Replace a LAN hub

   B. Allow two computers to communicate by connecting to the same modem

   C. Modulate a signal it sends and demodulate a signal it receives

   D. Demodulate a signal it sends and modulate a signal it receives

2. What is the main circuit board of a computer?

   A. PC subsystem

   B. Motherboard

   C. Backplane

   D. Computer memory

3. Select three popular web browsers.

   A. Mozilla Firefox

   B. Adobe Acrobat

   C. Internet Explorer

   D. Netscape

   E. Windows Media Player

4. What is a NIC?

   A. A WAN adapter

   B. A printed circuit board or adapter that provides LAN communication

   C. A card used only for Ethernet networks

   D. A standardized data link layer address

5. Which of the following is/are the resource(s) you need before you install a NIC?

   A. Knowledge of how the NIC is configured

   B. Knowledge of how to use the NIC diagnostics

   C. Ability to resolve hardware resource conflicts

   D. All answers provided are correct

6. Which number system is based on powers of 2?

   A. Octal

   B. Hexadecimal

   C. Binary

   D. ASCII

7. The terms and definitions in the following table are scrambled. Match the following terms with their definitions.

Term	Definition
Bit	Standard measurement of the rate at which data is transferred over a network connection
Byte	Approximately 8 million bits
kbps	Smallest unit of data in a computer
MB	Unit of measurement that describes the size of a data file, the amount of space on a disk or another storage medium, or the amount of data being transferred over a network

8. What is the largest decimal value that can be stored in 1 byte?

   A. 254

   B. 256

   C. 255

   D. 257

9. What is the decimal number 151 in binary?

   A. 10100111

   B. 10010111

   C. 10101011

   D. 10010011

10. What is the binary number 11011010 in decimal?

   A. 186.

   B. 202

   C. 218

   D. 222

11. What is the binary number 0010000100000000 in hexadecimal?

    A. 0x2100

    B. 0x2142

    C. 0x0082

    D. 0x0012

12. What is the hexadecimal number 0x2101 in binary?

    A. 0010 0001 0000 0001

    B. 0001 0000 0001 0010

    C. 0100 1000 0000 1000

    D. 1000 0000 1000 0100

13. Which of the following statements are true of **ping**? (Select the two best answers.)

    A. The **ping** command tests a device's network connectivity.

    B. **Ping** discovers the IP address of every router between two computers.

    C. The **ping 127.0.0.1** command verifies the operation of the TCP/IP stack.

    D. All of the answers are correct.

Challenge Questions and Activities

These activities require a deeper application of the concepts covered in this chapter, similar to how answering CCNA certification exam questions requires applying detailed concepts to a particular scenario.

The following two activities are difficult for this point in the class and, in some cases, have not yet been covered in the text. They are indeed meant to give you a challenging set of problems, ones that most readers are not yet able to fully answer. For those of you looking for an extra challenge, try the following exercises. By the end of the CCNA 1 course, if given enough time, you should be able to easily solve such problems.

Note

The network topologies shown in the Packet Tracer examples are not meant to show the same network topologies that appear in the online curriculum or the labs; instead, they purposefully use different topologies to show alternative examples.

Activity 1-1: Using Packet Tracer, load the *enterprise-working* configuration, which can be downloaded at www.ciscopress.com/title/1578131641. The configuration matches Figure 1-13. Characterize the subnets used in the design. For example, a LAN's subnet might be "All IP addresses that begin with 10."

Activity 1-2: Using Packet Tracer, load the *enterprise-broken-1* configuration, which can be downloaded at www.ciscopress.com/title/1578131641. The configuration matches Figure 1-13, except that some things were misconfigured on purpose. Test which PCs can **ping** other PCs. When a **ping** fails, work to discover the problem. Note that some problems might be caused by a problem that has not yet been fully explained at this point in this book; however, if you cannot solve them all, write what you can about the problems.

Networking Fundamentals

Objectives

Upon completion of this chapter, you should be able to answer the following questions:

- How did data networks develop?

- What are some common networking devices, and at what layer of the OSI model does each function?

- What are network protocols?

- What are the features of a LAN, WAN, MAN, and SAN?

- What are the functions, benefits, and technologies of VPNs?

- What are the differences between intranets and extranets?

- What are the diffreent network topologies and their advantages and disadvantages?

- What is the importance of bandwidth?

- What units are used to measure bandwidth?

- What analogy can be used to explain bandwidth?

- How is throughput different from bandwidth?

- How are data transfer rates calculated?

- What layered models are used to describe data communication?

- Why was the OSI reference model developed?

- What are the advantages of using a layered model?

- What are the seven layers of the OSI reference model?

- What are the four layers of the TCP/IP model?

- How are the OSI and TCP/IP models similar and different?

- What are the steps and PDUs in encapsulation and de-encapsulation?

Key Terms

This chapter uses the following key terms. You can find the definitions in the Glossary.

segment   page 74, 112

repeater   page 76

star topology   page 77

bus topology   page 77

hub   page 77

bridges   page 78

destination Media Access Control (MAC) address
  page 78

frame   page 80

LAN switches   page 82

link   page 84

metropolitan-area networks (MANs)   page 85

storage-area networks (SANs)   page 85

server farm   page 86

Virtual Private Networks (VPNs)   page 87

encrypt   page 89

continues

continued

intranet VPN   page 89

extranet VPN   page 90

access VPN   page 90

network topology   page 91

physical star topology   page 92

logical bus topology   page 92

ring topology   page 94

hierarchical physical topologies   page 95

full mesh   page 95

partial mesh   page 95

bandwidth   page 97

bits per second (bps)   page 97

throughput   page 100

network engineer   page 104

Open System Interconnection (OSI) model   page 105

TCP/IP model   page 108

network layer protocol   page 108

application layer   page 108

presentation layer   page 108

session layer   page 109

transport layer   page 109

network layer   page 109

data link layer   page 109

physical layer   page 109

encapsulation   page 111

de-encapsulation   page 111

packet   page 112

protocol data unit (PDU)   page 113

same layer interaction   page 114

adjacent layer interaction   page 114

The three major sections of this chapter take a closer look at networks and how they work, both in practice and in theory. The first section dives a little deeper into practical matters, particularly focusing on LANs and WANs, and the networking devices used to create LANs and WANs. The second section looks at how fast networks can transfer data and defines the terms *bandwidth* and *throughput*. The last major section examines the theory behind networking, particularly the TCP/IP and OSI networking models.

Networking Basics and Terminology

Computer networks provide a means for computers to share information. As a result of sharing the information, companies can operate their businesses more efficiently, governments can provide services to the general populace for less money, and schools can provide a better education for their students while keeping down costs.

Today's computing environments include many different types of networks. The most commonly known types of networks are called local-area networks (LANs) and wide-area networks (WANs). Many people know about LANs because they can see parts of the LAN—all you have to do is look at the back of a PC and see the LAN cable connecting the computer to a wall socket. LANs provide networking services within a relatively small geography, which is where the name "local" comes from. WANs connect LANs across a wide geography, hence the name "wide" in wide-area network.

Before getting into the basics of how different types of networks work today, the next few sections cover a bit of networking history and some of the reasons why today's networks use a wide variety of open networking standards.

A Brief History of the Networking Universe

The earliest commercial computers, called *mainframe computers*, were physically very large and required computer scientists to run them. Eventually, manufacturers created devices called *terminals*, which were devices with a display and a keyboard—and very little smarts. Terminals displayed on the screen whatever the user typed on the keyboard, with the computer reacting by running a program. The program might do some computations, gather more information to display, record information in a database, or any other computing function—and then display more information on the terminal screen for the user.

These terminals were originally located right next to the computer, but later, some of the earliest commercial networks were created so that users could have a terminal located in some other location and access the mainframe remotely. These types of networks began to become popular by the 1960s.

As more and more companies bought and used computers and networks, the prices of technology fell. By the late 1960s, minicomputers (called "minis") started to enter the marketplace. Minicomputers were essentially smaller cousins of the mainframes, less powerful but much less expensive. So, companies that could formerly simply not afford even a small mainframe could buy a minicomputer. Other companies could choose to own lots of minicomputers instead of one mainframe—creating a need for networks to connect minicomputers.

Finally, by the mid-1970s, the fist personal computers (PCs) were being built by researchers. By 1977, Apple announced an early personal computer called the Apple-II, a product that gained enough popularity to cause some attention from some of the existing larger computer companies of the time. By 1981, IBM, which held 70 to 80 percent of the worldwide computer sales dollars in the 1970s, announced its line of PCs.

The preceding paragraphs described very briefly the world of mainframes, minis, and PCs. For networking, the introduction and development of each class of computers meant some very specific things. First, WANs were needed to connect remote terminals to mainframes. Later, networks were needed to connect minicomputers as well as to provide remote terminal access to the minicomputers. Finally, the possibility of the mainstream acceptance of PCs, which could be affordably manufactured due to the invention of the microprocessor chip and other miniature computing technology, would drive the need for networks that could easily connect the PCs.

Table 2-1 lists some of the key dates and details of the brief history of computing, for reference.

Table 2-1   History of Computing

Time Period	Development
Early 1940s	Computers were large electromechanical devices that were prone to failure.
1947	The invention of the semiconductor transistor opened up many possibilities for making smaller, more reliable computers.
1950s	The integrated circuit was invented. It combined several—and then many, and now millions—of transistors on one small piece of semiconductor.
1960s	Mainframes with terminals were commonplace, and integrated circuits were widely used.
Late 1960s and 1970s	Smaller computers called minicomputers came into existence.
1977	Apple Computer introduced the microcomputer, also called the personal computer (PC).
1981	IBM introduced its first PC.
Mid-1980s	Computer users using standalone computers started sharing data (files) through the use of modems connected to another computer. This was called point-to-point or dialup communication.

The Need for Networking Protocols and Standards

As computers became very popular during the 1960s through the 1980s, networks also became popular. However, to create networks in those days, each vendor defined protocols and standards about how a network should work with its own products. Each vendor then created products that conformed to its own set of proprietary rules. If you wanted to use a network to connect computers from vendor X, you bought networking products from vendor X as well.

Although a vendor may have created standards and protocols, these standards were proprietary to that vendor because they were owned by a single company. For a period in the history of networking, proprietary standards had a positive effect. However, proprietary standards and protocols made it difficult for companies to try to offer new products that competed with the company owning a proprietary standard.

Eventually the networking world migrated away from the numerous proprietary networking protocols and standards instead choosing to begin to use open standards. Open standards are not owned by one company; instead, they are developed by a standards body, often with industry input, and the resulting standards are published in readily available documents. Open standards then allow much more competition, which speeds development of new products and drives down the cost. As a result, today's modern networks use components that (mostly) conform to open standards from different national or international standards bodies. Table 2-2 lists and describes the purpose of several popular standards organizations in the networking world.

Table 2-2   Popular Networking Standards Organizations

Standards Body	General Purpose
International Organization for Standardization (ISO)	An international standards body, comprised of delegates from each participating country, that develops a very wide range of international standards
Internet Engineering Task Force (IETF)	Develops the protocols of the TCP/IP networking model
Institute of Electrical and Electronic Engineers (IEEE)	An association of technical professionals that also develops a wide variety of standards, including LANs
American National Standards Institute (ANSI)	The organization legally responsible for choosing the standards considered appropriate in the United States
Telecommunications Industry Association (TIA)	A trade association that does many things, including the development of cabling standards
Electronic Industries Alliance (EIA)	A trade association that works closely with TIA on cabling standards
International Telecommunications Union (ITU)	An international standards organization, under the control of the United Nations, that develops worldwide telecommunications standards

Sifting through the different roles of the different standards bodies and the standards that they develop sometimes is difficult. Throughout the book, references are made to many of these standards bodies regarding a particular standard. For the topics covered in more depth in this book, the main standards bodies are TIA and EIA for cabling standards, IEEE for LAN standards, and IETF for TCP/IP standards.

The next section examines the basics of LANs, which use standards from the IEEE.

Ethernet LANs and LAN Devices

Note

Segment is a common networking term and has several different meanings. This chapter uses two of those meanings. The section "The Ambiguous Term Segment" in Chapter 8, "Ethernet Switching," covers all of the meanings.

Ethernet LANs originally used coaxial (coax) cable, similar to the cable used for cable TV. The cable has a copper wire in it, with insulation around the wire. To create an Ethernet, Ethernet network interface cards (NICs) would attach to a length of the right kind of coax cable, called a *segment*. Figure 2-1 shows a general example of how such an Ethernet was created, with some details left out to keep the discussion focused on the concepts.

Figure 2-1   Original Topology for 10BASE2 and 10BASE5 Ethernet

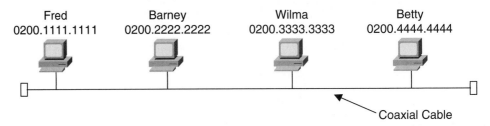

Figure 2-1 shows the basic topology of the original Ethernet, called 10BASE5, and its first successor, 10BASE2 Ethernet. Later chapters get into more detail, but these two early types of Ethernet had much in common. In particular, they both required a single medium created by the lengths of coaxial cable shown in Figure 2-1. Together, these cables created what was called an Ethernet segment. Because there was a single wire inside the cable, all NICs sent their data over the one wire, and all other NICs received the electrical signal. So, these types of Ethernet are said to be *broadcast* media, because any electrical signal sent by one device is received by all other devices.

Note

Figure 2-1 shows an example of a physical bus topology, covered in the later section "Network Topologies."

LANs like the one in Figure 2-1 have certain common characteristics:

- Limited to a relatively small geographic area
- Allows multiple devices access to high-speed media
- Administrative control rests within a single company
- Provides full-time connectivity
- Typically connects devices that are close together

10Base2 and 10BASE5 Ethernet LANs could be created using PCs, their NICs, and cables. As time went on, networking devices were introduced to the world of LANs. These devices performed a variety of functions, and will be covered in the upcoming sections. For reference, Figure 2-2 shows the icons used by Cisco to represent several common network devices. Note that the networking industry does not have standards for icons when drawing network diagrams, but for a Cisco-written course, the drawings use the icons shown here.

Figure 2-2   Cisco Networking Device Icons

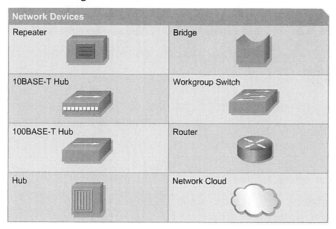

The following sections describe the subset of the LAN devices shown in Figure 2-2 that are used to build LANs:

- Ethernet repeaters
- Ethernet hubs and 10BASE-T
- Ethernet bridges
- Ethernet switches

The upcoming sections also describe some details of Ethernet frames and addresses, because those details must be understood before the functions of bridges and switches can be fully understood.

Ethernet Repeaters

The original types of Ethernet, like any other technology that transmits electrical signals over a wire, had distance limitations. The reasons are varied, but when an electrical signal is sent over a wire, the signal degrades. That means that a square waveform sent by a device will weaken and degrade by the time it reaches the other NICs on the LAN.

10BASE5 limited a single segment to 500 meters, and 10BASE2 limited a single segment to a little less than 200 meters (185 meters)—hence the 5 and 2 in their names. (The 10 stands for

10 Mbps.) To extend the distance of these LANs, the first Ethernet-specific networking device (historically speaking, that is) was called a *repeater*. A repeater had the following features:

- Typically had two ports for connecting to two different Ethernet segments

- Interpreted the incoming signal on one port as 0s and 1s

- Sent a regenerated clean signal out the other port

The term *repeater* was chosen, in short, because the device repeats what it hears in one port by sending the same signal out the other port. However, it does clean up the signal first. Figure 2-3 shows an example, with Fred and Barney now on a second segment, with a repeater between the two segments.

Figure 2-3   Repeated Ethernet Signal—Conceptual View

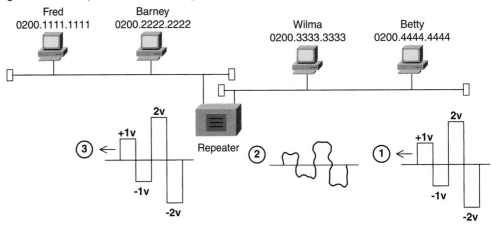

Note

Repeaters operate at Layer 1 of the OSI model because all the functions of a repeater relate to the physical (electrical) details of networking. The OSI model defines a structure of how networking products should work together, using seven numbered layers (1 through 7) to identify the layers. The last main section of this chapter covers OSI, its layers, and the meaning of phrases such as "operate at Layer 1."

The sequence shown in Figure 2-3 is as follows:

1. Betty sends a clean signal.

2. The signal degrades by the time it reaches the repeater.

3. The repeater regenerates a new clean signal that represents the same bits that Betty originally sent, and sends that clean signal out its other port.

Ethernet Hubs and 10BASE-T

10BASE2 and 10BASE5 were early Ethernet standards. Both standards had some problems, however, that led to the introduction of newer alternatives. For example, the coax cables were expensive and difficult to work with. Also, if the cable broke, everyone on the cable had problems, and the LAN was not usable.

To solve these and some other smaller issues, 10BASE-T was created. The 10 means that it still runs at 10 Mbps, and the *T* means twisted pair. 10BASE-T uses unshielded twisted-pair (UTP) cabling instead of coaxial cabling, which is much cheaper than coax cable, much easier to work with, and has a smaller diameter. UTP has become so popular, in fact, that most PCs in enterprise networks today use UTP cabling. (The UTP cables are typically terminated with RJ-45 connectors, which are shown in Figure 1-9 in Chapter 1.)

10BASE-T requires the use of a *star topology* rather than the *bus topology* used in 10BASE2 and 10BASE5. The older technology was called a "bus" because it looked like a bus route. A bus drives down a street, stopping at predetermined locations to drop off and take on new passengers. Similarly, 10BASE2 and 10BASE5 have a length of cable over which the electrical signals flow, with those signals being dropped off to each NIC, and with each NIC being able to send electrical signals onto the bus.

10BASE-T requires that each NIC be cabled to a *hub*. The shape of the cabling resembles a star, as shown in Figure 2-4. The left side shows the cabling of the PCs to the hub, and the right side shows a conceptual diagram of a star topology. (The star topology looks a little like a star, with the hub in this case being the center of the star, and the cables looking like light beams emanating from the star.)

Figure 2-4   10BASE-T with Hub—a Star Topology

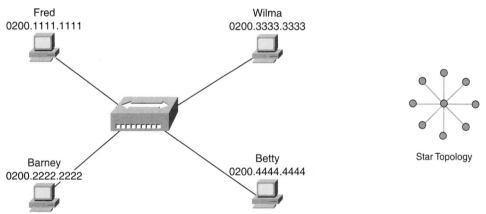

The hub, shown as the icon in the center of Figure 2-4, has two main objectives:

- Provides RJ-45 jacks so that UTP cables with RJ-45 connectors can be attached to the hub

- Repeats any incoming electrical signal on one port out all other ports on the hub

By combining both objectives, the hub has an electrical path to reach each NIC, and it has the ability to forward the regenerated signals, like a repeater, out all other ports. In fact, hubs were originally called *multiport repeaters*, because they performed the same electrical functions as a repeater, but they had lots of ports compared to the typically two-port repeaters of the early years of Ethernet.

Note

Because hubs perform the same general functions as repeaters—functions that relate to physical transmission—hubs also operate at Layer 1 of the OSI model. Again, the end of the chapter covers OSI.

Ethernet Bridges

While hubs provided some improvements over 10BASE2 and 10BASE5 Ethernet LANs, *bridges* provided a different set of improvements by adding some logic to the network. Hubs and repeaters simply react to the incoming signals, always regenerating and repeating the signals out all other ports. Bridges—another type of networking device—use programming logic to make more intelligent choices, meaning that a bridge reacts differently to different conditions.

The following list describes the basic steps in a bridge's forwarding logic:

1. Examine the incoming signal, interpret the signal as 0s and 1s, and find the *destination Media Access Control (MAC) address* listed in the frame.

2. If the destination MAC is reachable by that bridge via a different interface than the one on which the frame arrived, forward the frame using a clean regenerated signal. (This process is called *forwarding*.)

3. If the destination is reachable on the same interface in which the frame arrived, just discard the frame. (This process is called *filtering*.)

Note

The terms *interface* and *port* tend to be used synonymously when describing a physical LAN connector on a bridge, switch, repeater, or hub.

Figure 2-5 shows a simple design using a bridge. In their original form, bridges typically had two ports for the purpose of connecting two existing LANs. (You typically do not find any vendors selling bridges today; instead, they sell switches, which perform much better and are reasonably priced.)

Figure 2-5   A Bridge Making a Filtering Decision

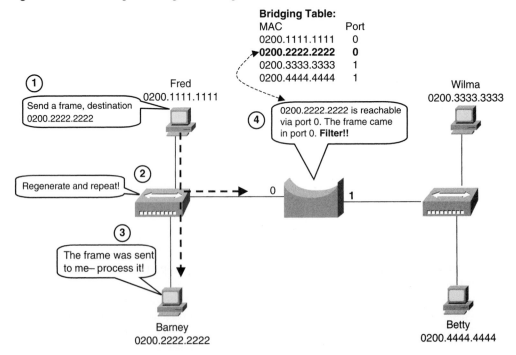

The following process explains the steps taken in Figure 2-5:

1. Fred sends an Ethernet frame, which is data prefaced with a destination MAC address of 0200.2222.2222, out his NIC.

2. The hub repeats the frame out both of its other ports.

3. Barney, whose NIC MAC address is 0200.2222.2222, receives the electrical signal, decides that it is meant for him, and processes the received data.

4. The bridge receives the signal in its port 0 and looks at the destination MAC address of 0200.2222.2222. The bridge's table says that 0200.2222.2222 is reachable out port 0, which is the same port in which the frame was received. So, the bridge does not need to forward the frame.

This example shows a couple of particularly good side effects of the bridge's operation. First, Betty and Wilma do not receive Fred's frame, so they have less work to do. More importantly, Wilma and Betty could send data to each other at the same time as Fred and Barney are sending data to each other—essentially expanding the capacity of the LAN to forward traffic. In fact, if Fred and Barney were to send data only to each other, and Wilma and Betty were to send data only to each other, the network in Figure 2-5 would actually support a total of 20 Mbps, because each of the two LANS has 10 Mbps of bandwidth.

If you load Packet Tracer configuration NA01-0205, you can run a simulation that shows the example of Figure 2-5, as well as upcoming Figure 2-6. From real-time mode, you can view the bridge table. Note that in simulation mode, a red X over a device means that it received the data but discarded it; a green check mark means it received the data and processed it; having neither means the data never made it to that device.

Figure 2-6 shows an example in which the bridge forwards a frame. In this case, Fred sends a frame to 0200.3333.3333, which is Wilma's MAC address. The following list explains each step in Figure 2-6 in more detail. Note that the first two steps are identical to the corresponding steps in Figure 2-5:

1. Fred sends an Ethernet frame, which is data prefaced with a destination MAC address of 0200.3333.3333, out his NIC.

2. The hub repeats the frame out both of its other ports.

3. Barney receives the electrical signal and decides not to process the frame because the destination MAC address of the frame is not Barney's MAC address.

4. The bridge receives the signal in its port 0 and looks at the destination MAC address of 0200.3333.3333. The bridge's table says that 0200.3333.3333 is reachable out port 1, which is a different port from the incoming port. So, the bridge forwards the frame.

5. The repeater on the right repeats the signal out all interfaces.

6. Wilma receives and processes the frame, while Betty receives and ignores the frame, because the destination MAC address of the frame is Wilma's MAC address.

Figure 2-6   A Bridge Making a Forwarding Decision

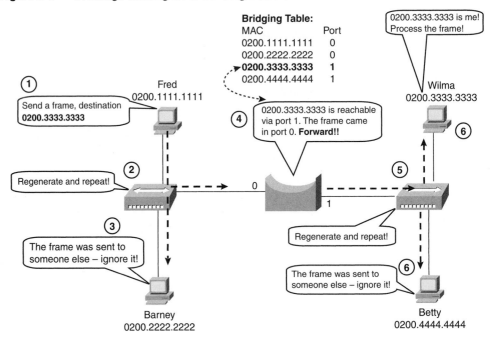

Ethernet Frames

This chapter has used the term *frame* a couple of times now, but without a specific definition. The term *Ethernet frame* refers to the data sent by an Ethernet NIC or interface. The first bits sent by a NIC are the Ethernet header, which holds overhead bytes useful for Ethernet operation—for instance, the destination MAC address is an important part of the Ethernet header. An Ethernet frame also includes headers from other protocols, like IP, as well as end-user data. It also includes a trailer, as shown in Figure 2-7.

Figure 2-7 does not show all the details (Chapter 6, "Ethernet Fundamentals," covers the details), but for now, keep in mind that Ethernet interfaces send and receive Ethernet frames as electrical signals; the frames include a header; and the header includes the sender's MAC address (called the source MAC address) and the intended recipient's MAC address (called the destination MAC address).

Figure 2-7   Conceptual View of an Ethernet Frame

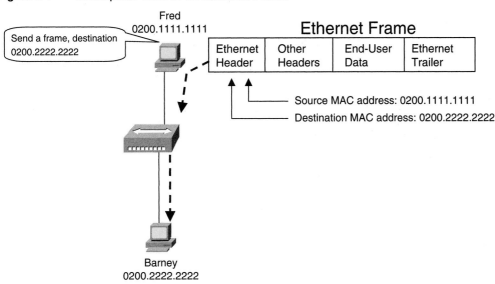

Unicast and Broadcast Ethernet Frames and Addresses

Before the introduction of bridges—in other words, with 10BASE2, 10BASE5, and 10BASE-T using only hubs—the LAN acted as a broadcast medium. Every frame sent by a NIC on those types of LANs went to every other NIC on the LAN. With the introduction of bridges, however, the rules changed, because the bridge filters frames, as shown earlier in Figure 2-5.

The term *unicast MAC address* refers to the MAC addresses referenced so far in this book. These MAC addresses identify a single NIC or Ethernet interface. MAC addresses burned into NICs are unicast MAC addresses. For example, the addresses used in Figure 2-5 (0200.2222.2222—Barney) and Figure 2-6 (0200.3333.3333—Wilma) are both unicast addresses, because they each identify a single PC's NIC.

Note

Frames sent with a unicast destination address are called *unicast frames*; frames sent to the broadcast destination address are aptly called *broadcast frames*.

In some cases, a computer attached to a LAN needs to send a frame that really does go to all devices attached to the LAN. To send data to all devices on the LAN, a computer needs to send the Ethernet frame with a special destination MAC address, called the *broadcast address*. The Ethernet broadcast address is FFFF.FFFF.FFFF. When a bridge receives a frame destined for the Ethernet broadcast MAC address, the bridge forwards the frame out all interfaces so that all devices receive the frame. Not only that, each PC or other computer receiving the broadcast must process the broadcast.

If you load the NA01-0205 configuration into Packet Tracer, use simulation mode, and run scenario 4, you will see an example of the process of Fred from Figure 2-5 sending a broadcast.

LAN Switches

Figures 2-5 and 2-6 depict sample LANs that might have been popular back in the early 1990s. By the mid-1990s, a new class of LAN devices began to emerge—*LAN switches*. The first LAN switches combined the functions of hubs and bridges, with today's LAN switches being generations beyond those basic functions. However, even with today's more sophisticated features, switches perform the same general functions:

- Like a hub, a switch provides a large number of ports/jacks into which cables can be connected, forming a physical star topology of cabling.

- Like both hubs and bridges, when forwarding a frame, the switch regenerates a clean square-wave electrical signal.

- Like bridges, a switch uses the same forwarding/filtering logic on a per-port basis.

Figure 2-8 shows a sample network, again with the same familiar PCs, but this time with a switch icon in the middle. The example shows Fred's frame sent to Barney (0200.2222.2222), with the switch forwarding the frame on port 2, and not on ports 3 and 4.

Figure 2-8   A Switch Making a Forwarding Decision

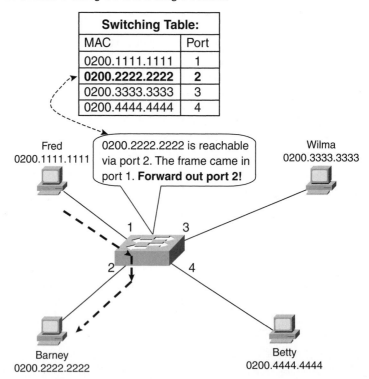

While a switch's forwarding and filtering logic works the same way as a bridge's, often the table of MAC addresses and ports is called a switching table rather than a bridging table. With Cisco switches, the table is also often called a Content Addressable Memory (CAM) table, as covered in more detail in Chapter 8.

 If you load the NA01-0209 configuration into Packet Tracer, use simulation mode, and run scenario 0, you will see an example of the process of Fred from Figure 2-8 sending a frame to Barney.

Note

Switches act like bridges, examining MAC addresses in frames. These addresses are defined by Ethernet standards that match OSI Layer 2, meaning that switches and bridges are often called Layer 2 devices.

Wide-Area Networks

Wide-area networks (WANs) get their name from the fact that they often cover a large distance, or wide geographic area. However, the more telling point about WANs is that they provide connectivity between locations for which only a few select companies have the right-of-way to run cables. For example, an enterprise network may need a WAN connection for sites only 1 mile away from each other if the company does not own the land between the sites. Certain LAN technologies could be used for a few dozen miles, assuming that the company had the right-of-way to run the cable.

Ultimately, WANs provide network connectivity between sites, typically connecting the LANs at those sites. The WAN connectivity comes in many types, some of which will be covered in more depth in later semesters of the CCNA curriculum. For perspective, the following list includes the most typically used WAN technologies:

- Modems (asynchronous dialup)
- Integrated Services Digital Network (ISDN)
- Digital subscriber line (DSL)
- Frame Relay
- T1 or E1 leased lines—T1, E1, T3, E3, and so on
- Synchronous Optical Network (SONET)—synchronous transport signal Level 1 (STS-1) (optical carrier [OC]-1), STS-3 (OC-3), and so on

The following WAN sections provide a general overview of a point-to-point WAN link and how routers are good devices to use for forwarding data over WANs.

Point-to-Point Leased Lines

A *point-to-point leased line* is a transmission medium that extends between two locations, with the medium being created by technology owned by another company. The term *leased line* means that the line (meaning cable) is owned by someone else (a service provider), and you can lease it for some period of time. For example, if a company has sites in Atlanta and Cincinnati, it would be ridiculous for it to attempt to install a cable between the two sites. So, the company leases the equivalent of a cable between the two sites from a WAN service provider. These service providers are often also telephone companies (telcos)—in fact, in some parts of the world, telcos are government-approved monopolies, so the only place to get a leased line is from the local telco.

Note

Many networking professionals use the term *link*, which is short to write and say, rather than something like "point-to-point WAN leased line."

Many alternate names exist for the term *leased line*. One name, *leased circuit*, refers to the fact that in telco terminology, when someone picks up the phone and calls someone, the telco creates a telephone circuit—a path through the telco's network that allows the analog voice to flow. With that same terminology, a leased line is like a permanent phone call between devices—a phone call that happens to be between computers, using digital instead of analog signals. The term *point-to-point leased line* is also often used, because the circuit is between two points. Often, the term **link** is used, because a WAN leased line connects, or *links*, two sites. For similar reasons, the terms WAN link and WAN connection are also used.

Figure 2-9 shows a drawing of a typical enterprise WAN. The leased lines are shown with a lightning-bolt line style.

Note

The round icons like the one labeled R1 are router icons.

Figure 2-9   Drawing of a Typical Enterprise WAN

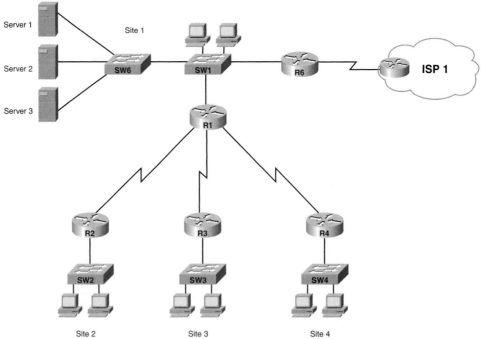

Routers and Their Use with WANs

Routers implement the IP protocol, including IP routing and addressing logic, for the purpose of routing packets from one destination to another. Although the details of how IP routing works have not yet been covered in class, they will be, and in quite a bit of detail. However, in the meantime, you can get a good appreciation for why routers work well with LANs just by considering the following general logic used by a router:

- Routers perform a basic but very important forwarding process in which they receive data, in the form of packets, and then forward the packets toward the destination.

- Routers can send and receive traffic on most any kind of physical networking media.

Focus on the fact that routers can connect to most any type of networking media. As a result, routers make the perfect networking device with which to connect a LAN with a WAN, because LANs and WANs are, by definition, different types of media. Chapter 9, "TCP/IP Protocol Suite and IP Addressing," and Chapter 10, "Routing Fundamentals and Subnets," cover routers and routing in more depth, and the topics in CCNA semester 2, "Routing and Routing Basics," are almost entirely devoted to how routers work.

Note

Routers perform forwarding logic based on the destination IP address of a packet. Because IP closely matches OSI Layer 3, routers are considered to be OSI Layer 3 devices.

MANs and SANs

This section briefly introduces two other types of networks besides LANs and WANs—namely, *metropolitan-area networks (MANs)* and *storage-area networks (SANs)*.

MANs

MANs cover a medium-sized geography—essentially in between the geographic size of a typical LAN and WAN. MANs today are often created by service providers, because they have more direct access to run the cables required to create the network. For example, a service provider may create a very high-speed, city-wide MAN. Because the network is limited to a metropolitan area, the cables used to create it are shorter, and they require much less expense—especially when installing the cables. So, the service provider may be able to offer very high-speed MAN services to its customers for a more reasonable price than for a comparable WAN. Figure 2-10 shows an example.

The optical media between the MAN routers may run at speeds as high as 10 Gbps or even 40 Gbps. With this design, instead of a point-to-point leased-line WAN between the four customer sites—requiring a total of six leased lines to connect each customer router directly to the other—each customer site can connect to one of the routers on the MAN. If the four customer sites are spread over a large metropolitan area, they may still be only a few miles from one of the MAN routers. The MAN routers can then forward the packets between sites.

Figure 2-10   High-Speed City-Wide MAN

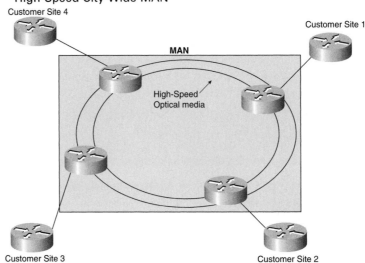

SANs

LANs, MANs, and WANs all have the same overall goal—to allow computers to communicate. Storage-area networks (SANs), however, do not share that goal. Instead, SANs allow computers to communicate with storage devices.

On the average PC, the storage devices, particularly the disk drives, sit inside the PC. However, when you build a large *server farm*, or have many computers that need to access the same data, it is often better to locate the disk drives and related hardware outside of the computers that need access to the data. To access and record data on those disk drives, the computers use a network between themselves and the disks. Such a network is called a SAN.

For example, when you use a web browser to look at books on www.amazon.com, you might enter a search term, in response to which the Amazon web server looks in a database of books. That database is stored on disk drives. However, have you ever considered how big a server would be needed by a company running a website as popular as Amazon? For such a site, Amazon has tens or hundreds of servers, all needing the same data. So, companies like Amazon use a SAN, as shown in Figure 2-11.

When you go to www.amazon.com, you connect to one of many web servers (as shown in Figure 2-11 with a dashed line between a PC and a server). Then, when you ask Amazon to search for a book, the server uses the SAN to look at the data in the database. Once the server has retrieved the information, it can send the data back to your web browser over the WAN/LAN.

The following list summarizes the features of SANs:

- **Performance**—SANs allow concurrent access of disk or tape arrays by two or more servers at high speeds. This provides enhanced system performance.

- **Availability**—SANs are commonly used to back up data to offsite locations, often up to and exceeding 10 km (6.2 miles) away. This allows for much greater systems availability.

- **Scalability**—A SAN can use a variety of technologies. This allows easy relocation of backup data, operations, file migration, and data replication between systems.

Figure 2-11   Typical SAN Used by Server Farm

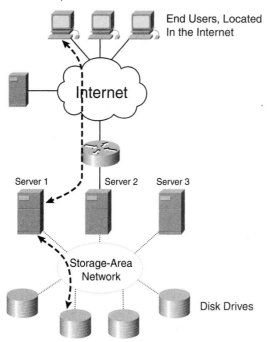

Virtual Private Networks

With the emergence of the Internet, companies have an interesting alternative to traditional WAN connections—to use the Internet to send packets between sites, rather than pay a service provider for WAN circuits. However, a company that wants to use the Internet for WAN connectivity typically also wants to keep those communications private. So, the companies use the Internet, along with a class of technology called *Virtual Private Networks (VPNs)*. This section explains the concepts behind using VPNs.

For example, imagine that a company has built the WAN shown earlier in Figure 2-9. Instead of that enterprise network, with WAN links to each of the three remote sites, the company could replace the WAN with the network shown in Figure 2-12.

Figure 2-12   Using the Internet as a WAN Alternative

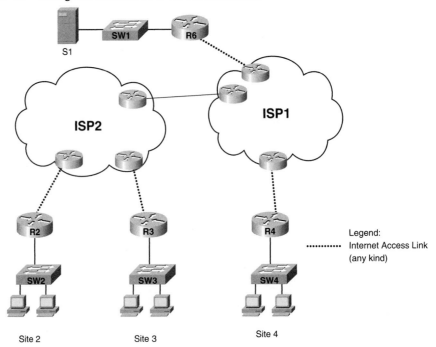

With this alternative design, the routers owned by Retailer1 can still send and receive packets, which is the whole point of having the WAN in the first place. In Figure 2-12, each site has an Internet access link, which preferably would use a higher-speed, always-on access technology such as DSL or cable, which you learned about in Chapter 1, "Introduction to Networking." The access links could use traditional WAN technologies, however, such as a leased line or Frame Relay. Regardless of the method of accessing an ISP, once each site is connected to the Internet, the Retailer1 routers can send and receive packets at that point.

This design is often less expensive than the traditional WAN alternatives, like the design shown earlier in Figure 2-9. However, this design using the Internet has a few negatives. First, packets between sites must compete with other Internet traffic for bandwidth, so the delay for getting packets through this network may be slightly longer than with traditional WAN links. More importantly, this design is much less secure than traditional WAN links. With traditional WAN links, for a hacker to break in and get a copy of the data going over the WAN links, the hacker has to physically get access to the wires supplied by the telco. When using the Internet, as in Figure 2-12, hackers can sit in their homes and attempt to access all the devices inside the Internet, with countless opportunities to somehow get copies of the packets—and steal the information inside those packets.

The next sections describe three types of VPNs: intranet, extranet, and access.

Intranet VPNs

VPN technology allows the design of Figure 2-12, while protecting the traffic from hackers. To do so, VPNs *encrypt* packets before they leave for the Internet. Encryption means that the packet, along with a secret number called an encryption key, is fed into a complicated mathematical function. The resulting value, called an *encrypted packet*, is transmitted through the Internet. Even if a hacker manages to somehow get copies of these packets, he could not easily read them. If the hacker has a lot of really fast computers, he might decrypt the packet eventually—after days or months of computing time—and then still not even be sure the decryption has worked correctly. And to really do any harm, the hacker would need to decrypt lots of packets. In other words, it is simply not practical for the hacker to break the encryption.

Figure 2-13 shows how VPN technology can be used to create an *intranet VPN*. In this design, the routers that connect to the various Internet access links encrypt the packets before sending them into the Internet, and decrypt them as they exit the Internet. In fact, Cisco sells models of routers that are optimized as VPN routers, as well as add-on hardware that performs the encryption work, because encryption requires a large amount of computing power. This design is called an intranet VPN because it includes only devices inside a single organization, with the prefix "intra" meaning "inside."

Figure 2-13   Intranet VPN

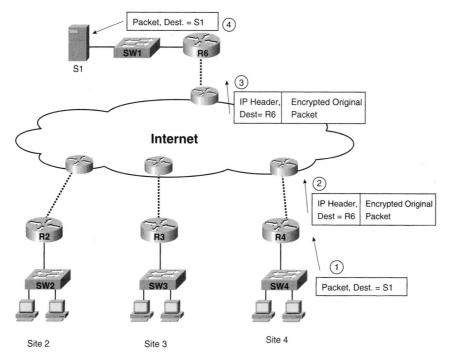

Note

The LAN at the main site at the top of Figure 2-13 is unchanged compared to Figure 2-9; however, the details of the LAN are omitted from Figure 2-13 to make it less cluttered.

The following list explains the steps shown for a typical packet in Figure 2-13:

1. A PC needs to send a packet to a server, in this case server S1, so the computer creates a packet with a destination IP address of S1's IP address. The PC then sends the packet to its default gateway (R4).

2. R4 encrypts the packet and places a new IP header in front of the encrypted packet. The new IP header is required so that the Internet's routers can forward the packet. Note that the destination address is R6, the router that will decrypt the packet.

3. Routers inside the Internet route the packet to R6 based on the new IP header added by R4.

4. R6 decrypts the original packet and discards the IP header that was used to get the packet over the Internet. As a result, R6 is now holding a packet whose destination IP address is the IP address of S1. So, R6 forwards the packet to server S1.

Comparing Intranet VPNs to Extranet and Access VPNs

VPNs use encryption technology to keep information private as it passes over the Internet. However, depending on how VPN technology is used, it is called either an intranet, *extranet*, or *access VPN*:

- **Intranet VPN**—A VPN between sites of a single organization

- **Extranet VPN**—A VPN between sites of different organizations

- **Access VPN**—A VPN between individual users and an enterprise network, allowing someone to work from home or while traveling

Figure 2-14 shows both an access VPN and an extranet VPN. Supplier1 and Retailer1 use an extranet VPN so that Retailer1 can order more products from Supplier1. The access VPN allows employees of Retailer1 to remotely access computers in the Retailer1 enterprise network, but do so without risking a hacker finding out sensitive information.

Figure 2-14   Retailer1's Extranet and Access VPNs

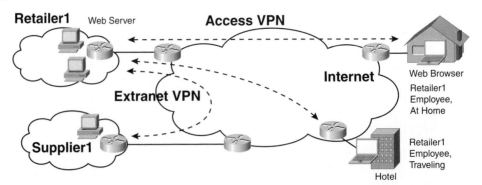

Network Topologies

Many options exist for the design of computer networks. During the design process, most engineers draw diagrams of the network, for planning purposes, future troubleshooting, and so that everyone can know about the design of the network. The network drawings typically show the computer hardware, networking devices, and cabling. Some drawings may ignore the physical cabling, instead focusing on the routing details in a network, which is a logical function (with logical meaning "not physical" in this case).

While many design options exist, most designs follow one of a handful of general network design topologies. A single *network topology* is a general characterization of what the network design looks like on a network drawing. This section covers the different network topologies and shows some more-typical network designs that happen to use those topologies.

Figure 2-15 shows the most popular physical network topologies.

Figure 2-15   Physical Network Topologies

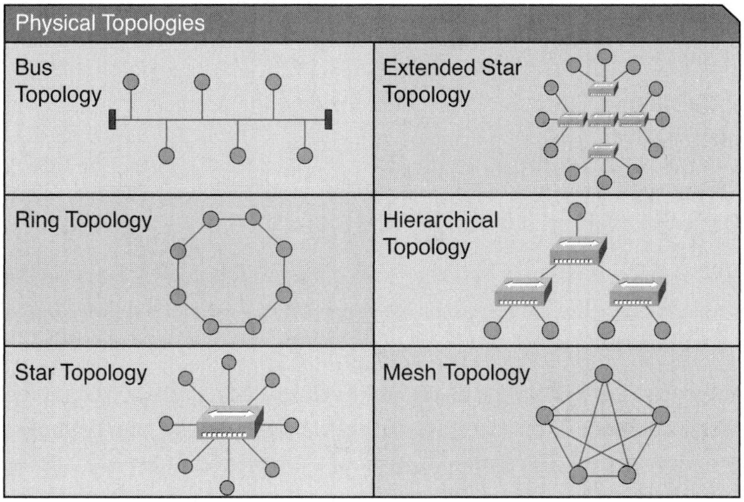

Physical Bus, Physical Star, and Logical Bus Topologies

10BASE2 and 10BASE5 Ethernet networks, as shown earlier in Figure 2-1, use a bus topology. Physical bus topologies are characterized by cabling that runs from device to device. It is called a "bus" in part because the drawings look like a street, with the bus stops located where PCs connect to the cable segment. Of particular note, a frame sent by one device on the bus is physically received by all devices on the bus, much like a real bus going to every bus stop on the street.

10BASE-T Ethernet networks with a hub, as shown in Figure 2-4, use a *physical star topology*. While the topology may not look exactly like a star, the idea is that the device at the center (a hub in Figure 2-4) is the star itself, with the cables being like the light rays emanating from the star.

10BASE-T networks that use hubs also use what is called a *logical bus topology*. The term "logical" refers to how the network operates, as opposed to where the cables run. With 10BASE-T, the hub operates the network by repeating an incoming signal on all other ports (except the incoming port). As a result, when one device sends an electrical signal, all other devices attached to the hub receive a copy of the same (regenerated) electrical signal—which is the same thing that happens on a physical bus. So, the operational logic used by a hub results in the same behavior as a physical bus, hence the name "logical bus." In fact, when 10BASE-T hubs were first introduced, it was quite common to describe 10BASE-T as "a physical star but a logical bus."

While 10BASE-T is an example of a logical topology, a more formal definition of the difference between physical and logical topologies can help:

- **Physical topology**—The topology is determined by the physical layout of the cabling and transmission media.

- **Logical topology**—The topology is determined by the media access control logic and how the devices collectively send traffic over the network.

Due to their differences, it is much easier to draw physical topologies, because they match the cabling. The features of a logical topology are not visible, so understanding logical topologies takes a little more effort.

Most modern Ethernet networks in a single building use a design that does not look a lot like a star topology at first glance, but it does use the same principles as a star. Assuming the building has hundreds of devices, possibly on multiple floors, a typical campus LAN design calls for inexpensive switches to be placed in different wiring closets near groups of users. The end-user PCs connect to these inexpensive access switches. Then, the access switches in turn connect to a distribution switch, which allows communications between all PCs in the building. Figure 2-16 shows the general idea.

The left side of Figure 2-16 shows the same network as the right, but the left side is purposefully drawn so that it looks more like the star topology shown in Figure 2-15. The right side of the figure shows how a network diagram of this network would be drawn today.

Whereas Figure 2-16 shows how a modern design uses the star physical topology, Figure 2-17 shows a typical complete design of a building LAN today. Note that a second distribution switch has been added, and all access switches connect to both distribution layer switches. With this design, one of the distribution layer switches could fail, and the network would still work.

Figure 2-16   Typical Modern LAN and Its Similarities to a Star Topology

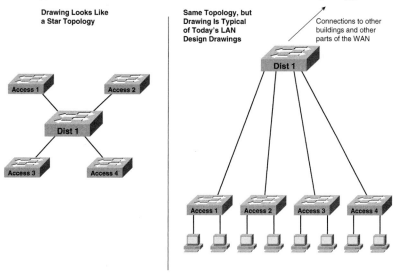

Figure 2-17   Typical Modern LAN Design for a Single Building

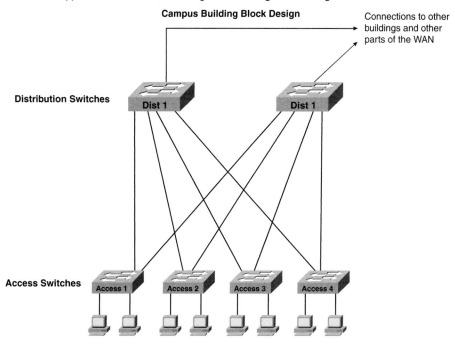

Ring Topologies

A physical *ring topology* connects networking devices and computers by installing a cable from the first device to the second device, from the second device to the third, the third device to the fourth, and so on, until the last device connects back to the first device. Figure 2-15 included a representation of a physical ring topology, showing the devices as circles. Ring topologies transmit the data around the ring, so each device can decide if the data was sent to it. If so, it can process the data, but if not, it just forwards the data so that it keeps going around the ring. Also, the devices on ring topologies clean up the electrical signal each time they transmit the data to the next device, so ring topologies have less of a need for repeaters.

Ring topologies may use a single ring or dual rings. With two rings, the second ring may be used for additional bandwidth, but more often it is used to protect against failures of the first ring. For example, MANs may support hundreds of high-speed (and high-revenue) customers—so the service provider wants to make sure the MAN does not fail. Figure 2-18 shows a dual-ring MAN in which one of the cables has been cut by a road construction crew. In this case, R1 and R2 notice the failure and loop the working parts of each ring together to form one complete working ring.

Figure 2-18   Typical MAN Dual Ring with Dynamic Packet Transport Failover

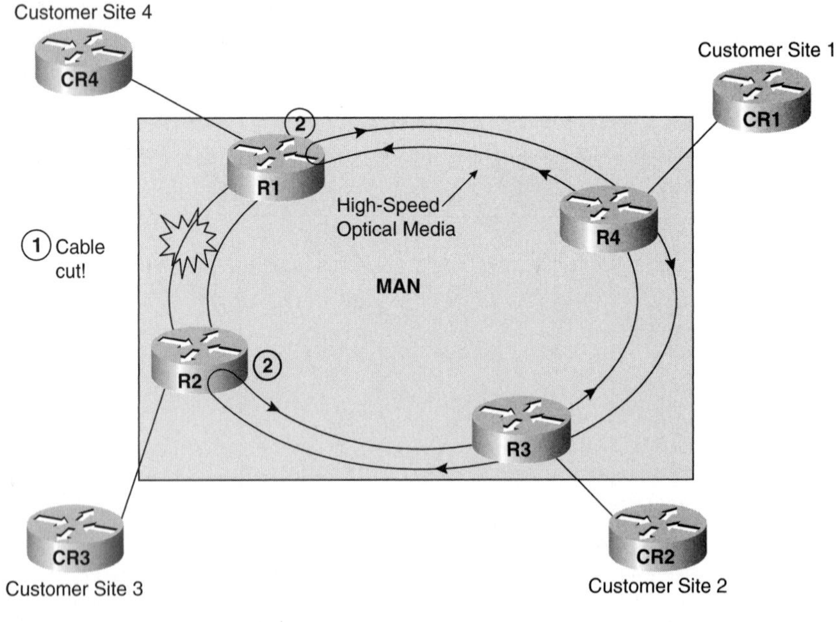

When a problem occurs on one of the cables, R1 and R2 can sense the problem and loop the cables to fix the problem, as shown in these steps:

1. R1 and R2 each detect that the cable between them has been cut.

2. R1 and R2 loop the primary ring to the backup ring using circuitry inside each router.

As a result, R1, R2, R3, and R4 still have one working ring, allowing the ring design to continue to work.

Hierarchical and Extended Star Physical Topologies

Hierarchical physical topologies and extended star topologies consist of a central device or site that connects to several other sites, much like a star topology. Then, the other sites also connect to several other sites, themselves appearing to be the center of a star topology. However, instead of drawing such designs radiating out from the center, they tend to be drawn as shown in Figure 2-19.

Figure 2-19   Hierarchical Network Design

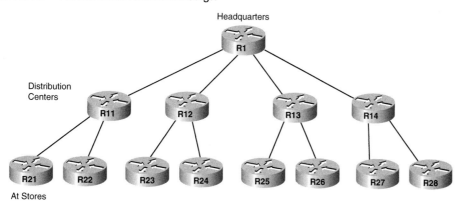

Note

The online curriculum suggests that the only difference between extended star and hierarchical topologies is that the devices at the central point in the hierarchy are controlling the traffic in the topology, which is not true of extended star topologies.

The topology shows one router at the top, with links to routers at four regional locations labeled as distribution centers. The routers at the regional locations connect to other remote sites, labeled as stores in the figure. Together, they form a hierarchy.

Extended star topologies have the same overall features as a hierarchical topology, but they are not drawn in a hierarchy. Instead, one part of the network is at the center of the diagram, with other parts of the network shown as radiating out from the center.

Many retail and banking companies use a hierarchical design like Figure 2-19. These companies have a main headquarters, but they also have regional centers. For instance, grocery store chains need geographically dispersed warehouses, typically at least one near each major population center at which they have stores, so that they can deliver goods to the local stores. The network might mimic that design, with a router at the main site, one router at each distribution center, and then a router at each store, as shown in Figure 2-19.

Note

The price of WAN links is often impacted by the distance between sites. So, a design like Figure 2-19, used instead of just running WAN links from the central site to each store, may be much more cost-effective.

Mesh: Full and Partial

The terms *full mesh* and *partial mesh* refer to both physical and logical topologies, most often with regard to WAN topologies. To appreciate when each might be most useful, consider the following two scenarios that describe different business models. First, a company has four divisions that need to share information directly. Computers in each division send data to computers in each other division. So, it makes sense for each division to have a direct WAN connection between the divisions.

Now consider another company that has one central site, with many small branch offices. The computers at the branch offices communicate with the servers at the central site, with little or no need to communicate with the computers at other branches. In that case, paying a service provider for a WAN link between branches would be a waste of money.

These two scenarios describe two classic cases for using a full mesh of WAN links versus a partial mesh. In a full mesh, all sites have a direct link to all others. In a partial mesh, some pairs of sites do not connect directly. Figure 2-20 shows both, with the left side showing the full mesh used to connect the four divisions of one company, and the right side showing the partial mesh of the company with branch offices.

Figure 2-20   Full and Partial Mesh—Physical

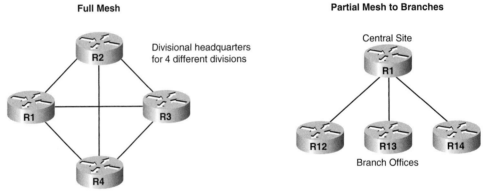

Note

Frame Relay is covered in the Networking Academy CCNA 4 course.

A WAN technology called Frame Relay frequently uses the terms full mesh and partial mesh, but with Frame Relay, these are logical meshes. Frame Relay has been a hugely popular WAN technology since the early 1990s, although it is starting to wane in popularity as newer technologies gain market acceptance. With Frame Relay, each router uses a relatively short physical WAN link to connect to a device inside a Frame Relay network—a device generically called a Frame Relay switch. That link provides the physical connection. Then, the Frame Relay service provider creates permanent virtual circuits (PVCs) between each pair of sites between which that customer wants to send data directly. PVCs cost money, so if you do not need to send data directly between sites very often, you do not need to add a PVC between those sites.

Bandwidth

In networking, the term *bandwidth* refers to the number of bits per second that can be sent by a device across a particular transmission medium. For example, the original 10BASE-T Ethernet specification allows 10 Mbps to be sent over UTP cabling. The term bandwidth may seem a bit odd when essentially it refers to the speed of bits going over a link, but the term comes from the world of analog electricity instead of the digital world typically used for networking.

An analogy for the first two of these concepts can be made with highways and cars. In this analogy, a road is like the cabling and the cars are like the network equipment. Imagine there is a brand-new section of highway that allows a car to be safely driven at 200 miles per hour (mph), assuming the road is completely clear. You own a Ferrari that can go 200 mph, and I still own my 10-year-old Honda, which could maybe do 100 mph downhill. If the police cleared the highway for us, you could drive 200 mph, but I could only go maybe 100 mph. Later, if we were both driving down a narrow, bumpy, pothole-filled road, we both might be relegated to driving only 30 to 40 mph. Similarly, networking cables can allow certain maximum speeds under the right conditions, but the networking devices might or might not run at the maximum speed.

Regardless of the type of cabling or the reasons why the bandwidth is limited to a certain rate, the amount of bandwidth is typically referenced as a number of *bits per second (bps)*, or another multiple of bits per second. Table 2-3 lists the popular units for bandwidth.

Table 2-3   Names and Units of Digital Bandwidth

Term	Number of Bits Per Second
Bits per second (bps)	1
Kilobits per second (kbps)	1 thousand
Megabits per second (Mbps)	1 million
Gigabits per second (Gbps)	1 billion
Terabits per second (Tbps)	1 trillion

LAN and WAN Bandwidth

The majority of networking links used today are LAN or WAN links. This section examines the most typical bandwidth settings used on typical networks today.

Ethernet LAN Bandwidths

In networking, the actual speed used on a given link is limited by three factors: the cabling, the cable length, and the speed at which the networking devices on the ends of the cable can try to send data. This point becomes more obvious when you look at a portion of Table 2-4, which lists the bandwidth settings for different variations of LANs. Ethernet standards call for the use of Category 5 (Cat 5) UTP cabling, for speeds of 10 Mbps, 100 Mbps, and even 1000 Mbps.

Note

The term micron is an abbreviation of micrometer, which is 1/1,000,000th of 1 meter (10^{-6} meters).

Note

Many of the standards and media types in Table 2-4 have not yet been covered in the class; the table is listed here for reference regarding different bandwidths.

The cable can go faster even, but the speed is dependent on the hardware on the end of the cable in these cases.

Note that Table 2-4 lists several variations of LAN standards and cables. The distance restriction applies to a single cable, when used by devices that conform to the listed standard. The information in Table 2-4 is covered in much more detail in Chapter 7, "Ethernet Technologies."

Table 2-4   Bandwidths for Various Ethernet Standards and Cables

Speed	LAN Standard	Cable	Maximum Distance
10 Mbps	10BASE2 Ethernet	50-ohm coaxial cable; thin	185 m
10 Mbps	10BASE5 Ethernet	50-ohm coaxial cable; thick	500 m
10 Mbps	10BASE-T	Cat-5 UTP	100 m
100 Mbps	100BASE-TX	Cat-5 UTP	100 m
1000 Mbps	1000BASE-TX	Cat-5e UTP	100 m
100 Mbps	100BASE-FX	Multimode optical fiber (62.5/125 micron)	2000 m
1000 Mbps	1000BASE-SX	Multimode optical fiber (62.5/125 micron)	220 m
1000 Mbps	1000BASE-SX	Multimode optical fiber (50/125 micron)	550 m
1000 Mbps	1000BASE-LX	Single-mode optical fiber (9/125 micron)	5000 m

WAN Bandwidths

WAN bandwidths vary significantly, as do LAN bandwidths. The engineers who design and build the service provider's network need to worry about such details as cable-length restrictions and which devices will be required to create a WAN service that is useful to the ISP's customers. The customers, mainly enterprise networks, need to worry about things like how fast the WAN link is, how much it costs, and the type of technology used. The type of technology dictates the type of networking device that the enterprise network needs to connect to each WAN link.

Table 2-5 lists several of the standard WAN services, the speeds, and comments on their typical use. Portions of the table refer to WAN links that are part of the telecommunication carrier (T-carrier) system. In the T-carrier system, used in the United States and several other parts of the world, the most basic unit of WAN transmission speed is a 64-Kbps WAN link called a Digital Signal level 0 (DS0). (The speed is 64 Kbps because that is the bandwidth needed for sending voice over a telco network in digital form.) The rest of the T-carrier system uses links that are a multiple of 64 Kbps (plus overhead). For example, a T1 (also called a DS1) is 24 DS0s, with some overhead; a T3 (DS3) is 28 T1s, with some overhead.

Table 2-5 WAN Bandwidth Standards

WAN Service	Typical User	Bandwidth
Modem using analog phone line	Individuals at home	56 Kbps
DSL	Individuals, home networks, small business sites for VPNs	128 kbps to 6.1 Mbps
ISDN BRI	Individuals, dial backup for businesses	128 kbps
ISDN PRI	Dial backup for businesses	1.536 Mbps (U.S.), 1.920 Mbps (Europe)
Frame Relay	Pervasive use by many businesses	U.S.: 56 kbps to 44.736 Mbps Europe: 56 Kbps to 34.368 Mbps
Subrate T1/E1	Businesses, smaller remote sites	Multiples of 64 Kbps (one or more DS0s), up to T1 or E1 speeds
T1 (U.S.)	Enterprise WANs, Internet access for business	Raw speed 1.544 Mbps, 1.536 available for data
E1 (Europe)	Enterprise WANs, Internet access for business	Raw speed 2.048 Mbps, 1.920 Mbps available for data
T3 (U.S.)	Enterprise Internet access, telcos, ISPs	44.736 Mbps (28 T1s plus overhead)
E3 (Europe)	Enterprise Internet access, telcos, ISPs	34.064 Mbps (16 E1s plus overhead)
STS-1 (OC-1)	Enterprise Internet access, telcos, ISPs	51.84 Mbps
STS-3 (OC-3)	Telcos and ISP backbones	155.520 Mbps
STS-12 (OC-12)	Telcos and ISP backbones	622.08 Mbps
STS-48 (OC-48)	Telcos and ISP backbones	2.5 Gbps
STS-192 (OC-192)	Telcos and ISP backbones	10 Gbps

Table 2-5 also includes several links that are part of the Synchronous Optical Network (SONET) standard. SONET, which was originally defined a few decades later than the T-carrier system, uses a basic unit of 51.84 Mbps called an optical carrier 1 (OC-1) or synchronous transport signal Level 1 (STS-1). The rest of the SONET speeds are multiples of this base speed. SONET assumes the use of fiber-optic cables, which use strands of glass over which light can be sent to encode bits. The combination of fiber-optic cables and networking devices that use lasers to send light over the cable results in networks that can support very high speeds and cable lengths over 100 km.

Throughput Versus Bandwidth

Bandwidth refers to how fast a device can send data over a single cable. As such, network planners definitely need to know the bandwidth of each link to be able to monitor usage and plan for upgrading the links to run faster.

The term *throughput* refers to how many bits are actually transferred between two computers. There are two key points to consider when comparing throughput to bandwidth:

- The throughput rate may vary over time based on the current conditions in the network, whereas bandwidth does not change over time.

- Bandwidth defines the speed of a single link, and throughput refers to the speed of data transfer between two computers—computers may be, and typically are, separated by several networking devices and several cables.

Figure 2-21 shows a typical enterprise network with its Internet connection. Throughput could be measured for two PCs that are currently downloading files from a server in the Internet.

Figure 2-21   Two Examples of Throughput

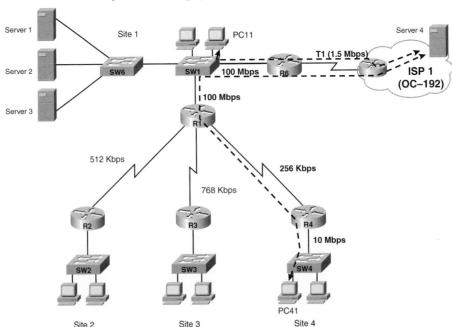

Throughput defines the actual measured bits per second that one computer can send to another at a particular time. So, between PC11 and Server4, you could download a file, notice the time required to download the file, and do some math to see the rate at which the file was downloaded.

Even though throughput defines the real current speed of data transfer from one computer to another, some basic analysis and math can be used to determine the theoretical maximum throughput based on the constraining link bandwidth in the path between the two endpoints. That is a lot of concept in one sentence, so examples definitely are in order. In Figure 2-21, the slowest link between PC11 and the server is the T1 Internet access link (1.5 Mbps). So, you reasonably assume that the best you could possibly get is 1.5 Mbps of throughput. For PC41, the best throughput would be 256 Kbps, because that is the constraining bandwidth in its path.

The online course uses analogies between bandwidth and water pipes. For example, a 2-foot-wide water main might run past your neighborhood. A 1-foot wide pipe may connect to it and run past everyone's house on your street. However, if you have a 4-inch pipe between the pipe at your street and your house, there is only so much water you can get out of your water spigots at home. You should be able to get all the water you want, but it just takes longer than it would if you had a big water pipe connected to your house.

Another way to think of bandwidth and throughput is "Bandwidth is what you pay for, and throughput is what you get." For example, you might pay for DSL service to an ISP, which the ISP rates at 1 Mbps. However, if you download files during the busy hours of the Internet, you may get only 100 Kbps.

Many factors besides the constraining bandwidth impact the actual throughput at any one point in time. For example, prime time for the Internet in the United States is between about 6 p.m. and midnight Eastern Time, the hours during which most people are home and accessing the Internet. During those times, the actual speeds for file downloads and response time for web browsing will be slower than, say, 6 a.m. on the East Coast. It is basically the same idea as rush hour on the highway system—when you drive during rush hour, you just don't get places as fast.

Many other factors impact actual throughput, including, but not limited to, the following:

- The the network devices in the route being used

- The type of data being transferred

- Protocols used to transfer the data

- The topology of the network

- The congestion level in the network, which is impacted by the number of concurrent users and the overall amount of data being sent

- The speed and current workload of the two computers that are communicating

- The time of day, which typically implies the number of active concurrent users of the network

Calculating Data Transfer Time

One way to get a perspective on throughput is to calculate how long it takes to transfer a file between two computers. The online curriculum calls such a calculation the data transfer time calculation. Two types of calculations are suggested by the online course: one that provides a theoretical maximum, based on the constraining link speed between the two computers, and one based on the actual throughput between the two computers at some point in time, which is likely to be lower. Figure 2-22 shows the details of the two calculations.

Figure 2-22   Data Transfer Time Calculations

Best Download $T = \dfrac{S}{BW}$	Typical Download $T = \dfrac{S}{P}$
BW =	Maximum theoretical bandwidth of the "slowest link" between the source host and the destination host (measured in bits per second).
P =	Actual throughput at the moment of transfer (measured in bits per second).
T =	Time for file transfer to occur (measured in seconds).
S =	File size in bits.

Although Figure 2-22 summarizes the details nicely, real examples definitely help. Using Figure 2-21's network as an example, Table 2-6 shows four different examples of calculating data transfer time. The first two examples are for PC11 and PC41 downloading a 1-MB file from the server on the Internet, Server4. These first two examples use the respective constraining link speeds, calculating the theoretical best data transfer time, as noted with the BW variable per Figure 2-22. The second two examples are identical to the first two, except that both assume a practical throughput value of one-half the constraining bandwidth.

Table 2-6   Four Examples of Calculating the Data Transfer Time

PC to Which File Is Downloaded	Variable BW: Constraining Bandwidth	Variable P: Real Throughput	Download Time
PC11	1.5 Mbps	—	$T = 8{,}000{,}000/1{,}500{,}000 = 5.3$ seconds
PC41	256 Kbps	—	$T = 8{,}000{,}000/256{,}000 = 31.25$ seconds
PC11	—	750 Kbps	$T = 8{,}000{,}000/750{,}000 = 10.6$ seconds
PC41	—	128 Kbps	$T = 8{,}000{,}000/128{,}000 = 62.5$ seconds

Although the math is not particularly difficult, there are a few problematic issues with this kind of calculation. First, many people forget to make the units match. For instance, the formula shows 8,000,000 for the file size, because the file is 1 MB, which is 8 million bits. Because the speeds in the formula (BW and P) are in bits per second, the file size must also be shown in bits to get the correct answer.

The other problem relates to picking a reasonable real throughput number. It is difficult to predict actual throughput in real life. However, you can run experiments and use tools to determine actual throughput at any one point in time. Many websites provide free throughput testing tools as well, including one from CNET.com: http://reviews.cnet.com/Bandwidth_meter/7004-7254_7-0.html (the same URL mentioned in Chapter 1).

You can access data transfer time practice problems by registering your book at the following website and navigating to the "Extra Practice" section: http://www.ciscopress.com/title/1587131641.

Analog Bandwidth

In the analog world, a number of consecutive frequencies—called *a band of frequencies* or *frequency band*—defined how much information could be sent with an analog signal. The wider (larger) the band of analog frequencies, the more information that could be sent—hence, the name *bandwidth* was born. When digital transmission came along later, even though the range of frequencies does not impact the speed, the term bandwidth remained as the term used to describe the speed of bits across a link.

Analog transmission requires a set frequency band to achieve its goals. For example, Chapter 1 mentioned the basic operation of a home telephone, which is a good example of how analog bandwidth works. A telephone converts the sounds into an analog electrical signal by using a microphone built into the mouthpiece of the phone. The phone then sends that analog electrical signal out the phone line. The receiving phone converts it back to sounds and plays it out a speaker built in to the earpiece of the phone. The phone companies use these analog signals because they look like the actual sound waves that go through the air.

Figure 2-23 shows a 3-hertz (3 Hz) signal, because the waveform repeats three times in 1 second. Using analog terminology, that means the signal has a frequency of 3 Hz. When a device sends an electrical signal that includes a range of consecutive frequencies, instead of just the single frequency shown in Figure 2-23, the device is using a band of frequencies. Analog bandwidth refers to the range, or width, of frequencies sent over the medium. For example, a telephone sends voice using a 4000-Hz analog bandwidth, with frequencies from 1 through 4000 Hz. However, all sounds that can be heard by humans—for instance, music, with many notes lower and higher than a human voice can create—uses frequencies from 0 to 20,000 Hz. So, FM radio stations actually use a band of about 200,000 Hz, again using more than is required to overcome some technical problems with transmission.

Tip

When you download a file over the Internet, often a popup window appears that tells you the rate at which the file is being transferred. When this happens, the units typically describe the number of bytes per second, not the number of bits per second. You can then calculate the actual real throughput in bits per second by just multiplying the number in that window by 8 to convert from bytes per second to bits per second.

Figure 2-23   Analog Electrical Signal

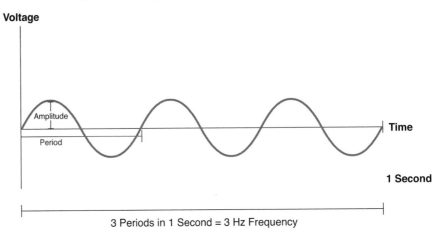

3 Periods in 1 Second = 3 Hz Frequency

Note

Although it is important to understand analog bandwidth, most of the discussions and coverage in this book relate to digital bandwidth.

One of the biggest negatives with analog transmission is the requirement for a minimum bandwidth range to be effective. If the telco could use a range of only 2000 frequencies instead of 4000, many sounds simply could not be passed over the phone line—making the phone pretty much useless. Without all the required bandwidth, FM radio stations might be able to play commercials, but when a song with high notes were played, all the high notes would be missing. Digital transmissions overcome such issues because using faster and faster speeds is not dependent on having wider and wider frequency bands.

Planning for Bandwidth

Network engineers plan, design, and implement networks while paying a lot of attention to the bandwidths of the various links in the network. They then use network management tools to gather utilization statistics, recording overall utilization numbers, as well as statistics showing the busiest few minutes on each link. By gathering these statistics and reviewing them, engineers can see which links tend to be congested more than others, make design changes, or simply replace a link with a faster one.

Why go to all the trouble? First, neither WAN nor LAN bandwidth is free. Service providers charge monthly for their WAN services. Many network managers' budgets for enterprise networks have recurring WAN costs that run into the 30 to 40 percent range of their overall budgets. Additionally, LAN links cost money, but not as much as WAN links. The main cost for LANs is the cost of the networking devices and their ports. For instance, you may have Cat-5 UTP run from each wiring closet to each desktop, so you decide that all PCs should get a new 1-Gbps NIC. However, doing so would cost $20 to 30 per PC. Plus, the switches in the wiring closet would probably need to be replaced. Additionally, there would be a significant labor cost to open every PC to install a new NIC. Regardless of whether it is a LAN or a WAN, the bandwidth is not infinite, and it costs real money and time to upgrade, so engineers need to monitor utilization of the links and plan for prudent use of money and time to upgrade links where needed.

Another reason network engineers typically monitor utilization is that the hunger for bandwidth grows continually. Twenty years ago, a T1 WAN (1.5 Mbps) link was typically used only between major WAN sites, and it was not cheap. That link might have supported hundreds of concurrent users. Now the average high-speed Internet connection goes that fast, or even faster—and that is just for a home user or two. Ten years ago, campus LANs used 100-Mbps Ethernet for backbone links between switches. Today, backbone links are created with multiple 1-Gbps links, or 10-Gbps links, with most every individual user PC using 100 Mbps. Many other examples exist, but, simply put, the need for bandwidth will continually grow for a long time—hence the continual need to measure and manage the bandwidth capacity in a network.

The online curriculum summarizes some of the key points in this section of the book with a list of four reasons why bandwidth is important:

- **Bandwidth is finite**—Although the bandwidth of an affordable network connection may grow over time, there is a limit.

- **Bandwidth is not free**—As mentioned in this section, WAN providers typically impose monthly charges for bandwidth, and LANs, where all the components are owned, still cost money to buy, install, and manage.

- **Network engineers need to plan for bandwidth**—The planning helps to make sure the network has enough capacity to support the users of the network.

- **Bandwidth demand is ever-increasing**—Throughout the history of networking, the demand for bandwidth has never decreased, but has always increased.

The OSI and TCP/IP Networking Models

Networking models define a related set of standards and protocols that, when used together, allows the creation of a working, effective network. This final major section of the chapter covers two commonly referenced networking models—the *Open Systems Interconnection (OSI) model* and the *TCP/IP model*.

As computers became very popular during the 1960s through the 1980s, networks also became popular. However, to create networks in those days, each vendor defined protocols about how a network should work with its own products. Each vendor then created products that conformed to its own set of proprietary rules. If you wanted to use a network to connect computers from vendor X, you bought networking products from vendor X as well. In fact, many vendors had so many protocols that they created formal but proprietary networking models for their set of protocols. (*Proprietary* simply means that the protocols were owned by that company, as opposed to being created by an independent, unbiased standards body.)

By the late 1980s, networking had become widely accepted in the marketplace, but networking was very messy because of the various proprietary networking models from many vendors. For example, IBM had significant market share in the mainframe market, so if you had a PC on your desk, and you used the mainframe, your PC had to support the proprietary protocols defined by IBM, called Systems Network Architecture (SNA). If you owned a DEC mini and an IBM mainframe, and you needed to connect the two via a network, you had to buy a device (called a gateway) that converted between IBM's SNA and DEC's equivalent, called DEC Networking (DECnet). Worse yet, if you had an Apple Macintosh (Mac) PC, you might need to support lots of proprietary protocols. For example, you might use Apple's AppleTalk proprietary networking model to talk to other Apple computers, Novell's NetWare proprietary model to share files with other users of a Novell file server, SNA so you could log in to the mainframe, and DECnet so you could use the DEC mini. It sounds messy, and it was.

Although it all worked, there were problems. The problem was not that the SNA networking mode was bad, or that the DECnet networking model was bad, and so on—in fact, the vendors documented the protocols and created networking models with which to separate functions, which was good. The problem was that proprietary networking models reduced competition, and there were too many networking models. What was needed was a single networking model that all computers would use. So, the OSI model was born.

OSI Model

The goal of the OSI model was to be the one open networking model that all vendors would implement to overcome the difficulties and inefficiencies with using multiple proprietary networking models. OSI was developed through a well-respected international standards body called the International Organization for Standardization (ISO). OSI was officially introduced in 1984, with protocols being added to it for the next 10-plus years.

The OSI model was a good idea because it provided all the normal benefits of a well considered networking model, plus it was open. The term *open networking model* refers to networking models developed by a standards body, which means that all vendors have equal access to the protocols and rules for building products. Most vendors through the late 1980s and into the early 1990s worked toward the eventual adoption of OSI as the preferred networking model to use, because they could all see the benefit of better interoperability between their products. The U.S. government provided some economic reasons to develop OSI by mandating that vendors support OSI by a certain date, or the U.S. government would not buy their products.

Even before OSI was really ready for use on computers in real working networks, many vendors and networking professionals started using terminology from OSI to describe the myriad other proprietary networking standards. As you might imagine, just keeping terminology straight when a PC runs four proprietary networking protocols could be quite daunting. Using OSI terminology allowed networking professionals to hold meaningful conversations about different networking models, but with a common set of terms, making those conversations a little easier.

It sounds like OSI saved the world of networking, and it probably would have if another open networking model had not come along and become more widely accepted. Because of TCP/IP's wide acceptance, vendors eventually put aside their OSI development efforts, and the U.S. government removed its mandate that all products support OSI. Today, it is rare to find a computer that implements the OSI model as its model for networking.

So why do we even bother mentioning OSI? Well, OSI's terminology is still used throughout the world of networking. So, to be able to talk the talk, you need to learn the terms, particularly those related to the OSI layers.

OSI Layers

All networking models break networking standards and protocols into layers. Each layer defines a general set of functions, with individual standards and protocols being part of one layer or another. By defining the general networking functions in layers, many benefits may be gained, including the following:

- Allows better standardization of different components

- Opens up competition in the market by allowing multiple vendors to create products that meet the functions of a particular layer

- Standardizes network components to allow multiple-vendor development and support

- Provides standardized interfaces between different layers, allowing companies to focus on developing products that implement some layers, and still work with products from other companies that implement adjacent layers

- Prevents changes in one layer from affecting the other layers so that they can be developed more quickly

- Breaks network communication into smaller component, to make learning easier

Like all networking models, the OSI model uses a set of layers that separate its many standards and protocols into different categories. The OSI reference model has seven layers, as shown in Figure 2-24.

Figure 2-24   OSI Reference Model Layers

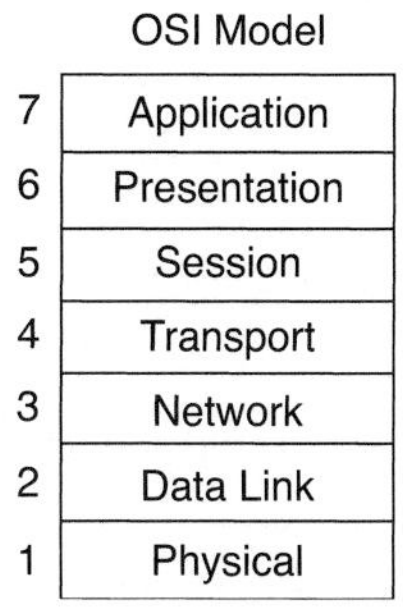

OSI Model

7	Application
6	Presentation
5	Session
4	Transport
3	Network
2	Data Link
1	Physical

When discussing protocols and standards, the names and numbers for the OSI layers in Figure 2-24 are typically used—even if they are different from the networking model that actually defines the protocol. (Remember, the OSI terminology gave networking professionals a common set of terms, and even after the OSI model failed to win market share, we still use its terminology.) For instance, TCP/IP's IP protocol defines routing and logical addressing. These same types of functions are defined by OSI Layer 3, the OSI network layer. So, the correct way to describe IP, using OSI terminology, would be to call IP a "Layer 3 protocol" or a "*network layer protocol*"—even though IP sits at the second layer of the TCP/IP networking model, called the internet layer.

Memorizing the names and numbers of the OSI layers is important, and it is something that all networking professional need to know. A couple of mnemonic phrases can help you remember the first letters of the layers. For example, the first letters of the following phrases match the first letters of the names of the OSI model, starting from the bottom of the model and going to the top:

- Please Do Not Take Sausage Pizzas Away
- Pew! Dead Ninja Turtles Smell Pretty Awful

The following mnemonic starts at the top of the model and moves downward:

- All People Seem To Need Data Processing

Functions of the OSI Layers

Networking professionals need to know the general types of functions defined at each layer of the OSI model to categorize other protocols as being at a particular layer. For instance, the text already mentioned that IP is described as a Layer 3 protocol, meaning OSI Layer 3. This section summarizes the OSI protocol layers' features.

Table 2-7 lists the seven OSI layers, with some comments about the types of functions defined at each layer.

Table 2-7   Descriptions of the OSI Layers

Layer	Description
7	The *application layer* is the OSI layer that provides services to the end-user's applications. It differs from the other layers in that it does not provide services to any other OSI layer; instead, it provides services only to applications outside the OSI model. Examples of Layer 7 applications include Telnet and HTTP.
6	The *presentation layer* ensures that the information that the application layer of one system sends out can be read by the application layer of another system. If necessary, the presentation layer translates among multiple data formats by using a

common format. One of the more important tasks of this layer is encryption and decryption. The common Layer 6 graphic standards are PICT, TIFF, and JPEG. Examples of Layer 6 standards that guide the presentation of sound and movies are MIDI and MPEG.

5	As its name implies, the *session layer* establishes, manages, and terminates sessions between two communicating hosts. The session layer provides a service to the presentation layer by synchronizing the dialog between the two hosts' presentation layers and manages their data exchange. Examples of Layer 5 protocols are the X Window System and AppleTalk Session Protocol (ASP).
4	The *transport layer* segments data given to it by the session layer into smaller chunks, because the network has restrictions on the size of a single packet sent over the network. This layer also defines error-recovery services. Examples of Layer 4 protocols are Transmission Control Protocol (TCP), User Datagram Protocol (UDP), and Sequenced Packet Exchange (SPX).
3	The *network layer* is a complex layer that provides connectivity and path selection between two host systems that might be located on geographically separated networks. Additionally, the network layer is concerned with logical addressing. Examples of Layer 3 protocols are Internet Protocol (IP) and Internetwork Packet Exchange (IPX).
2	The *data link layer* provides transit of data across a physical link by defining the rules about how the physical link is used. To do so, the data link layer is concerned with physical (as opposed to logical) addressing, network topology, network access, and error notification. Examples of Layer 2 protocols include Ethernet, Token Ring, PPP, and Frame Relay.
1	The *physical layer* defines the electrical, mechanical, procedural, and functional specifications for activating, maintaining, and deactivating the physical link between end systems. Such characteristics as voltage levels, timing of voltage changes, physical data rates, maximum transmission distances, physical connectors, and other similar attributes are defined by physical layer specifications.

Note

The online curriculum states that the OSI data link layer provides reliable communications and flow control. In networking, the word "reliable" typically really means "error recovery." Some older data link protocols provide these functions, but most data link layer protocols used today do not provide either reliability or flow control.

Table 2-7 lists a lot of concepts, and many people who are new to networking struggle with such lists. If that is the case for you, do not be too concerned. As you work through the different standards and protocols in this course, the book will refer to these by their OSI layer. After you understand several networking protocols more completely, you will better appreciate what the OSI layers really do. For example, the text earlier in this chapter characterized several networking devices based on the OSI layer most important to what each device does. Table 2-8 summarizes those devices and their OSI layer.

Table 2-8   Descriptions of the OSI Layers

Device	OSI Layer	Typical Spoken Phrases
Repeater	1	"It's a Layer 1 device"
Hub	1	"It's a Layer 1 device"
Bridge	2	"It's a Layer 2 device"
Switch	2	"It's a Layer 2 device"
Router	3	"It's a Layer 3 device"

Also note that most Cisco products focus on functions defined by the lower four layers of the OSI model. So, by the end of the first semester, you should begin to form a reasonable opinion about what devices and protocols work at each of the lower four layers. The upper three layers tend to focus on services about the application—in fact, the upper three layers' features totally concentrate on what happens to the computers that are the endpoints of some communication. However, the bottom four layers must consider issues about the networking cables and devices that sit between the two computers.

TCP/IP Networking Model

The TCP/IP networking model defines or references the set of networking standards and protocols used to build most networks today. TCP/IP began as part of a research project for the U.S. Department of Defense (DoD) in the 1970s, but the structure of the model remains the same today. Over the years, many new protocols have been added, and others changed. Compared to OSI, TCP/IP is the other major open networking model, and it happens to be the one that gained widespread marketplace acceptance.

Figure 2-25 shows two versions of the TCP/IP networking model. The version on the left shows the actual model, whereas the model on the right shows a popularly used alternative model. The difference lies in the bottom of the model, where the official model uses a single layer called the network access layer, and the alternate model instead uses the equivalent two layers of the OSI model.

Both versions of the TCP/IP model have layer numbers as well, starting with 1 at the bottom of the model diagrams. However, because everyone uses the OSI layer numbers when describing protocols, no one cares much about the TCP/IP layer numbers. Regardless of which version of the TCP/IP model a particular document references, the TCP/IP networking model has all the same benefits of other networking models, but when describing it, the OSI model's terms are used.

Figure 2-25   TCP/IP Reference Model Layers

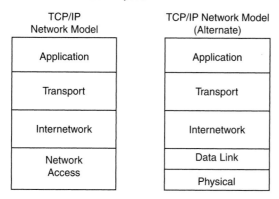

Encapsulation

All networking models use a concept and practice called *encapsulation* and *de-encapsulation*. This section looks at both using TCP/IP, and then it describes the same process with OSI.

Consider a person at a PC using a web browser and the web server to which the PC connects. The user might type in a URL (web address) in the browser and ask the server for a web page. The web server responds by sending the files that comprise the web page. To send that web page, the server must use the encapsulation process, as shown in Figure 2-26.

Figure 2-26   Five-Step TCP/IP Encapsulation Process

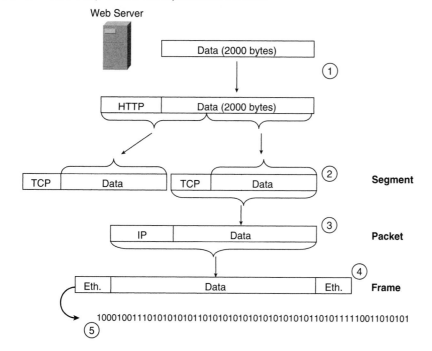

Figure 2-26 depicts the following process, starting with the rectangles near the top of the figure, going down:

1. The application software (a web server in this case) packages the contents of the web page along with any needed application headers. With web services, the HTTP protocol builds the header, including things like the name of the file that is being sent to the web browser. This process includes the application layer processing, which is typically implemented by the application software.

2. The transport layer software, which is TCP in this case, segments the data into chunks that are small enough to be accepted into the network. (The data created at Step 1 is too big to all be sent at once over the network; in this example, TCP creates two TCP segments.) TCP also adds a transport layer header to the data given to it from the application layer. (The data structure at this step, which includes the TCP header and data, is called a *segment*.)

3. The network layer software, IP in this case, adds a header for the purpose of supplying the destination logical address (the destination IP address in this case). The header also includes a source logical address (also an IP address) so that the computer receiving the data knows to whom to reply. With the destination IP address, the data can be routed to the end destination, be it on the same LAN or on the other side of the Internet. (The data structure at this step, which includes the IP header and data, is called a *packet*.)

4. The *network access* layer, specifically the part that more closely matches the OSI data link layer, adds another header, plus a trailer, to the data. Because this example uses an Ethernet NIC, this step adds an Ethernet header and trailer to the data. The header includes the destination MAC address, which is used for forwarding the data over the Ethernet. (The data structure at this step, which includes the Ethernet header, trailer, and data, is called a frame.)

5. The *network access* layer, specifically the part that matches the OSI physical layer, causes the bits to be physically transmitted over the medium.

This may seem like a lot of work, but these steps all have a separate but important role to play in making the communications work. For example, without the IP header, the routers between this PC and the e-mail server would not know how to route the packets.

Segments, Packets, Frames, and PDUs

Figure 2-26 also points out several terms that are very important when having discussions about the bits and bytes of networking. When discussing the entity at Step 2—the one with the transport layer header (TCP in the figure), those bytes are collectively called a *segment*. The entity at Step 3, with the network layer (IP) header, is called a *packet*. And, at the data link (OSI) or network access (TCP/IP) layer, the data that includes the data link header and trailer is called a frame.

Beyond those terms, OSI uses a more generic set of terms that relates back to the OSI layer in question. The base term is *protocol data unit (PDU)*, which refers to a set of data bytes that could be sent through a network. To describe the bytes that consist of the header for a particular layer, and its data, the term *Layer* x *PDU (LxPDU)* is used, with the x being the layer number. For example, an IP packet would be a Layer 3 PDU (abbreviated L3PDU) because it includes the Layer 3 header, and not the Layer 2 header, and IP is considered to be a Layer 3 protocol.

Table 2-9 lists the terms and definitions for easy reference.

Table 2-9   Frame, Packet, Segment, and LxPDU

TCP/IP Term	OSI Equivalent Term	Meaning
Frame	L2PDU	Data that could be sent through a network, with that data including the Layer 2 header and trailer, all headers from higher layers, and the end-user data.
Packet	L3PDU	Data that could be sent through a network, with that data including the Layer 3 header, all headers from higher layers, and the end-user data.
Segment	L4PDU	Data that could be sent through a network, with that data including the Layer 4 header, all headers from higher layers, and the end-user data.

De-encapsulation

De-encapsulation defines what happens once the bits are delivered to the destination computer. Essentially, each layer in the model performs a separate step to analyze the received headers and trailers. If everything looks acceptable, the computer eventually gives the data to the application.

Figure 2-27 shows an example of the de-encapsulation process. In this case, the web page that had been sent by the web server in the encapsulation example (Figure 2-26) has made it through the network and has been received by the PC that requested the web page.

Figure 2-27 depicts the following steps, which start when the electrical signal enters the NIC on the PC:

1. The network access layer, specifically the part that matches the OSI physical layer, interprets the incoming electrical signal as bits according to the correct Ethernet encoding scheme.

2. The network access layer, specifically the part that more closely matches the OSI data link layer, performs several tasks that analyze the contents of the Ethernet header and trailer. If all checks look good, the data field—which holds an IP packet—is extracted and handed to the next higher-layer protocol (IP).

3. The network layer software, IP in this case, looks at the IP header and makes several checks as well. Typically, at this point, everything looks fine, so the IP software extracts the contents of the data field—which holds a TCP segment—and hands it to the next higher-layer protocol (TCP).

4. The transport layer software (TCP) needs to analyze the header to perform several functions, including error recovery. Also, TCP needs to wait on the other TCP segment that comprised the data given to TCP by the application layer, back in Figure 2-26, so that TCP can reassemble the data into its original, in-order state. Once all segments are received and reassembled, TCP gives all the data to the application layer protocol, in this case HTTP.

5. The application layer protocol may also perform checks, finally giving the data to the application. The application, a web browser in this example, displays the data, reads any instructions for downloading other parts of the web page, and carries out any other appropriate functions for that application.

Figure 2-27   Five-Step TCP/IP De-encapsulation Process

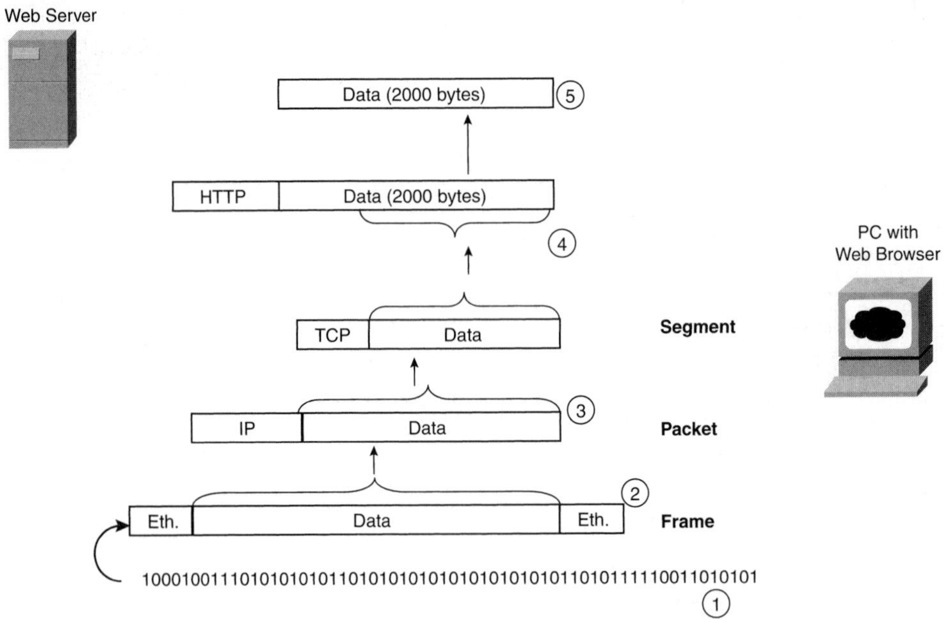

Layer Interactions

The final short section of this chapter highlights the definition of the terms *same layer interaction* and *adjacent layer interaction*. Although these two terms may sound a bit formal, the text has already explained the concepts—now you just need to know which concepts match these terms.

The term *same layer interaction* refers to how a protocol on one computer communicates with the same protocol on another computer. For example, when a user requests a web page with a browser, the browser creates an HTTP header that lists the name of the web page. The server, once it gets that request—which is held in the HTTP header—attempts to reply. So, the browser creates the HTTP header with an expectation that it will communicate something to the same layer on another computer.

Adjacent layer interaction was covered in Chapter 1, but because it is also mentioned briefly in the online curriculum for Chapter 2, a brief review is included here. When a protocol at one layer of a networking model provides a service to a protocol at the layer just above it, on the same computer, it is a case of adjacent layer interaction.

The terms and their meanings are summarized as follows:

- **Same layer interaction**—The creation of headers and possibly trailers, by a protocol at one networking layer on one computer, with the goal of communicating something to the same protocol, at the same layer, on some other computer.

- **Adjacent layer interaction**—On a single computer, the interaction of protocols that sit at adjacent layers of their networking model. This interaction includes the exchange of data during encapsulation and de-encapsulation, as well as how a protocol at a lower layer provides a service to a protocol at a higher layer.

Summary

Network devices, such as repeaters, hubs, bridges, switches, and routers, connect host devices together to allow them to communicate. Protocols provide a set of rules for communication between computers and those network devices.

The physical topology of a network is the actual layout of the wire or media. The logical topology defines how host devices access the media. The physical topologies that are commonly used are bus, ring, star, extended star, hierarchical, and mesh.

A local-area network (LAN) is designed to operate within a limited geographical area. LANs allow multiaccess to high-bandwidth media, control the network privately under local administration, provide full-time connectivity to local services, and connect physically adjacent devices.

A wide-area network (WAN) is designed to operate over a large geographical area. WANs allow access over serial interfaces operating at lower speeds, provide full- and part-time connectivity, and connect devices separated over wide areas.

A metropolitan-area network (MAN) is a network that spans a metropolitan area such as a city or suburban area.

A storage-area network (SAN) is a dedicated, high-performance network used to move data between servers and storage resources. A SAN provides enhanced system performance, is scalable, and has disaster tolerance built in.

A Virtual Private Network (VPN) is a private network that is constructed within a public network infrastructure. Three main types of VPNs are access, intranet, and extranet VPNs. Access VPNs provide mobile workers or small office/home office (SOHO) users with remote access to an intranet or extranet. Intranets are only available to users who have access privileges to the internal network of an organization. Extranets are designed to deliver applications and services that are intranet-based to external users or enterprises.

The number of bits that can be sent through a network connection in a given period of time is referred to as bandwidth. Network bandwidth is typically measured in thousands of bits per second (kbps), millions of bits per second (Mbps), billions of bits per second (Gbps), and trillions of bits per second (Tbps).

Throughput refers to the amount of data that can be sent between computers over a period of time. The throughput is limited by the slowest bandwidth link—the constraining bandwidth—between the two computers. One way to measure throughput is to calculate the time required to transfer a file between two computers. The data transfer time calculation can use the constraining bandwidth, which gives the theoretical fastest data transfer time, or some smaller speed, which includes many factors that slow down the amount of data that can flow through a network.

Analog bandwidth is a measure of how much of the electromagnetic spectrum is occupied by each signal. Digital bandwidth is simply measured in bits per second.

The concept of layers is used to describe communication from one computer to another. Dividing the network into layers provides the following advantages:

- Reduces complexity

- Standardizes interfaces

- Facilitates modular engineering

- Ensures interoperability

- Accelerates evolution

- Simplifies teaching and learning

Two such layered models are the Open System Interconnection (OSI) model and the TCP/IP networking model. The OSI reference model has seven numbered layers, each of which illustrates a particular network function: application, presentation, session, transport, network, data link, and physical. The TCP/IP model has the following four layers: application, transport, Internet, and network access.

Although some of the layers in the TCP/IP model have the same name as layers in the OSI model, the layers of the two models do not correspond exactly. The TCP/IP application layer is equivalent to the OSI application, presentation, and session layers. The TCP/IP model combines the OSI data link and physical layers into the network access layer.

No matter which model is applied, networks' layers perform the following five conversion steps to encapsulate and transmit data:

1. Images and text are converted to data.

2. The data is packaged into segments.

3. The data segment is encapsulated in a packet with the source and destination addresses.

4. The packet is encapsulated in a frame with the MAC address of the next directly connected device.

5. The frame is converted to a pattern of 1s and 0s (bits) for transmission on the media.

Check Your Understanding

Complete all the review questions listed here to test your understanding of the topics and concepts in this chapter. Answers are listed in Appendix A, "Answers to Check Your Understanding and Challenge Questions."

1. What is the name of the process that happens when a destination computer receives bits?

   A. Encapsulation

   B. De-encapsulation

   C. Segmentation

   D. Encoding

2. Using dialup modem connections, how many modems would it take to allow connections from ten individual computers to an ISP, assuming all 10 PCs were in the same building?

   A. One

   B. Five

   C. Ten

   D. Fifteen

3. What information is "burned in" to a network interface card?

   A. NIC

   B. MAC address

   C. Hub

   D. LAN

4. Which topology has all its nodes connected directly to one center point and has no other connections between nodes?

   A. Bus

   B. Ring

   C. Star

   D. Mesh

5. What do TIA and EIA stand for?

   A. Television Industry Association, Electronic Industries Association

   B. Telecommunications Industry Association, Electronic Industries Alliance

   C. Telecommunications Industry Alliance, Electronic Industries Association

   D. Téléphonique International Association, Elégraphique Industries Alliance

6. LANs are designed to do which of the following? (Select the two best answers.)

   A. Operate within a limited geographic area

   B. Allow many users to access high-bandwidth media

   C. Provide high-speed Internet access over a phone line

   D. Connect a traveling worker staying at a hotel to the corporate network

7. Which of the following statements best describes a WAN?

   A. It connects LANs that are separated by a large geographic area.

   B. It connects workstations, terminals, and other devices in a metropolitan area.

   C. It connects LANs within a large building.

   D. It connects workstations, terminals, and other devices within a small building.

8. Which of the following statements correctly describes a MAN?

   A. A MAN is a network that connects workstations, peripherals, terminals, and other devices in a single building.

   B. A MAN is a network that serves users across a broad geographic area. It often uses transmission devices provided by common carriers.

   C. A MAN is a network that spans a metropolitan area such as a city or suburban area.

   D. A MAN is a network that is interconnected by routers and other devices and that functions as a single network.

9. Which of the following is *not* one of the features of a SAN?

   A. SANs enable concurrent access of disk or tape arrays from multiple computers, providing enhanced system performance.

   B. SANs provide a reliable disaster recovery solution.

   C. SANs are scalable.

   D. SANs minimize system and data availability.

10. What service offers secure connectivity over a shared public network infrastructure?

   A. Internet

   B. Virtual Private Network

   C. Virtual Public Network

   D. WAN

11. What links enterprise headquarters, remote offices, and branch offices to an internal network over a shared infrastructure?

A. Access VPN

B. Intranet VPN

C. Extranet VPN

D. Internet VPN

12. Which of these answers best describes a network that connects multiple parties such as employees, customers, and partners?

A. The Internet

B. The extranet

C. The intranet

D. The LAN

13. Which of the following terms describes the wrapping of data as it moves down through layers?

A. Encoding

B. Encapsulation

C. De-encapsulation

D. Encrypting

14. The OSI model has how many layers?

A. Four

B. Five

C. Six

D. Seven

15. What is the OSI model?

A. A related set of standards and protocols that allows the creation of a working, effective network.

B. A nonproprietary set of rules created by an independent body.

C. A model that specifies how network functions occur at each layer.

D. All answers provided are correct.

16. Which of the following is the correct order of the OSI reference model layers, starting with Layer 1?

A. Physical, data link, transport, network, presentation, session, application

B. Physical, data link, network, transport, session, presentation, application

C. Physical, data link, network, session, transport, application, presentation

D. Physical, network, session, data link, transport, application, presentation

17. Which layer of the OSI model handles physical addressing, network topology, and network access?

A. The physical layer

B. The data link layer

C. The transport layer

D. The network layer

18. Which of the following best defines encapsulation?

A. Segmenting data so that it flows uninterrupted through the network

B. Compressing data so that it moves faster

C. Moving data in groups so that it stays together

D. Wrapping data in a particular protocol header

19. An e-mail message is sent from Host A to Host B on a LAN. Before this message can be sent, the data must be encapsulated. Which of the following best describes what happens next after a packet is constructed?

A. The packet is transmitted along the medium.

B. The packet is encapsulated into a frame.

C. The packet is segmented into frames.

D. The packet is converted to binary format.

20. In the TCP/IP model, which layer deals with reliability, flow control, and error correction?

A. Application

B. Transport

C. Internet

D. Network access

21. Repeaters can provide a simple solution for what problem?

A. Too many types of incompatible equipment on the network

B. Too much traffic on a network

C. Too-slow convergence rates

D. Too much distance between nodes

22. Which of the following is true of a bridge and its forwarding decisions?

   A. Bridges operate at OSI Layer 2 and use IP addresses to make decisions.

   B. Bridges operate at OSI Layer 3 and use IP addresses to make decisions.

   C. Bridges operate at OSI Layer 2 and use MAC addresses to make decisions.

   D. Bridges operate at OSI Layer 3 and use MAC addresses to make decisions.

23. Which of the following is true of a switch's function?

   A. Switches increase the size of collision domains.

   B. Switches combine the connectivity of a hub with the capability to filter or flood traffic based on the destination MAC address of the frame.

   C. Switches combine the connectivity of a hub with the traffic direction of a router.

   D. Switches perform Layer 4 path selection.

24. What does a router route?

   A. Layer 1 bits

   B. Layer 2 frames

   C. Layer 3 packets

   D. Layer 4 segments

25. Which of the following best describes encryption?

   A. A process for encoding data onto a medium

   B. A process for making data incomprehensible to anyone who is not authorized to view it

   C. Wrapping data in a header

   D. Token passing

CHAPTER 3

Networking Media

Objectives

Upon completion of this chapter, you should be able to answer the following questions:

- What are the electrical properties of conductors, semiconductors, and insulators?

- How are the concepts of voltage, resistance, impedance, current, and circuits related?

- What is attenuation?

- What are the specifications and performance of different cable types?

- What are the characteristics of coaxial cable, and what are its advantages and disadvantages when compared to other cable types?

- What are the characteristics of shielded twisted-pair (STP) cabling, and when is it appropriate for use?

- What are the characteristics of unshielded twisted-pair (UTP) cabling, and when is it appropriate for use?

- What are the characteristics of straight-through, crossover, and rollover cables? Where is each type used?

- What are the basic characteristics of fiber-optic cable?

- How does fiber-optic cable guide light for long distances?

- How are multimode and single-mode fiber similar? How are they different?

Additional Topics of Interest

Several chapters of this book contain additional coverage of previous topics or related topics that are secondary to the chapter's main goals. You can find the additional coverage on the CD-ROM accompanying this book. For this chapter, the following additional topics are covered:

- Ray model of light

- Reflection

- Refraction

- Total internal reflection

- Single-mode fiber

- Optical transmitters

- Optical receivers

- Connectors used with optical cabling

- Optical amplifiers and fiber patch panels

- Signals and noise in optical fibers

- Installation, care, and testing of optical fiber

- Basic wireless LAN (WLAN) operations

- Wireless authentication and association

- Radio wave and microwave spectrum

- Signals and noise on a WLAN

- Wireless security

Key Terms

This chapter uses the following key terms. You can find the definitions in the Glossary:

digital transmission   page 125

Coulomb's Law   page 127

electrical current   page 128

static electricity   page 128

electrostatic discharge (ESD)   page 128

insulators   page 129

conductors   page 129

semiconductors   page 130

electromotive force (EMF)   page 130

voltage   page 130

amp   page 130

direct current (DC)   page 131

alternating current (AC)   page 131

wattage   page 131

resistance   page 132

ohm   page 132

Ohm's law   page 132

impedance   page 132

attenuation   page 132

ground   page 134

Telecommunications Industry Association (TIA)
  page 134

Electronic Industries Alliance (EIA)   page 134

Thicknet   page 137

Thinnet   page 137

shielded twisted-pair (STP)   page 137

screened twisted-pair (ScTP)   page 138

unshielded twisted-pair (UTP)   page 139

registered jack 45 (RJ-45)   page 140

pinouts   page 140

straight-through cable   page 141

TIA/EIA-568-A   page 142

crossover cable   page 144

rollover cable   page 144

fiber-optic cabling   page 146

wavelength   page 148

frequency   page 148

multimode fiber   page 151

single-mode fiber   page 151

infrastructure mode   page 154

cell   page 154

associate   page 155

active scanning   page 155

Service Set Identifier (SSID)   page 155

passive scanning   page 155

beacon   page 155

Federal Communications Commission (FCC)   page 156

*carrier sense multiple access with collision avoidance
  (CSMA/CA)*   page 156

Direct Sequence Spread Spectrum (DSSS)   page 156

Orthogonal Frequency Division Multiplexing (OFDM)
  page 156

Wi-Fi   page 157

The first two chapters of this book described a wide range of networking topics, but they did not include a lot of details about any one topic. This chapter moves on from those two introductory chapters and delves deeper into the topic of *digital transmission*. Digital transmission is a general term that refers to how computing devices can take bits, which are binary digits, and transmit those bits from one device to another.

Digital transmission can be done in many ways. This chapter focuses on the three most common methods:

- By varying (modulating) an electrical signal as it passes over a wire that is typically made of copper

- By varying (modulating) the power of light as sent over a glass optical fiber

- By varying (modulating) the radio waves sent through space, which is commonly referred to as wireless communications

In each of these three types of digital transmission, the transmitting device uses a set of encoding rules to choose how to vary the transmitted signal, with those variations representing 0s and 1s. The receiver uses those same encoding rules to interpret the received signal back into 0s and 1s. As a result, the devices can send bits to each other.

This chapter begins by examining the copper wires and cables typically used in today's networks, including an introduction to the physics and chemistry behind basic electricity. Then, optical and wireless transmission are briefly covered.

Copper Media

Today's networks use several types of cables, but the most common type of cables use twisted pairs of copper wires. The first part of this section explains how electrical signals can be used to transmit bits across copper wires, focusing on the electrical and chemical characteristics of copper. The second part of this section then covers the details of copper cabling standards, focusing on the types of cabling and connectors most commonly used for networking cables today.

Digital Transmission Using Copper Wires

To understand the details of how digital transmission takes place, you must understand the basic concepts behind electricity. Interestingly, a deeper understanding of electricity requires knowledge of molecular chemistry and several concepts you might normally expect to see in an introductory physics class. This section begins with the chemistry details and moves on to the characteristics of electricity as it flows over a conductor, such as copper wire.

The Chemistry Behind Electricity: Atoms and Electrons

One of the most basic units of all matter in the universe is the atom. Each atom has several sub-atomic particles, each of which can have a positive, negative, or no electrical charge, as follows:

- **Protons**—Particles that have a mass equal to a neutron, and with a positive electrical charge

- **Neutrons**—Particles with a mass equal to a proton, but with no electrical charge

- **Electrons**—Particles that have negligible mass, but have a negative charge that is equal in strength to a proton's positive electrical charge

Each different type of atom, called an *element*, has a different number of protons. The periodic table of elements lists the different elements and their atomic numbers, which is the number of protons in one atom of each element. Figure 3-1 shows the periodic table.

Figure 3-1   Periodic Table of Elements

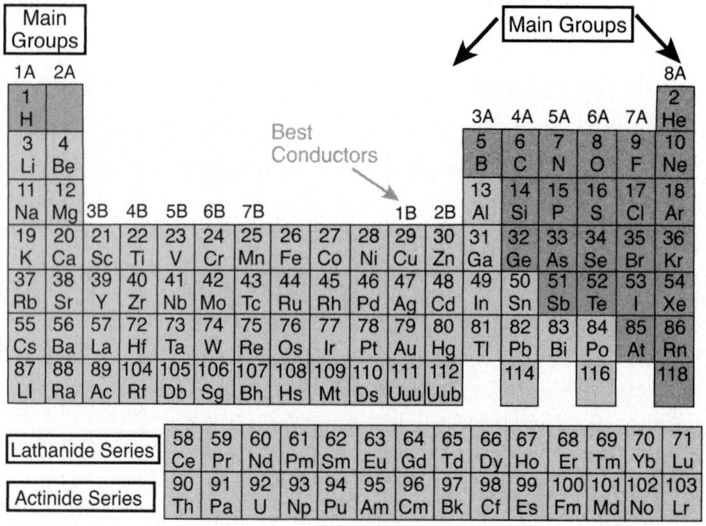

The periodic table lists the atomic number for each element. An atom of an element has an atomic number of (positively charged) protons and the same number of (negatively charged) electrons. For example, helium, which is found in the upper-right of the periodic table, has an atomic number of 2. So, a helium atom has two protons and two electrons. Also, helium's atomic weight (not shown in Figure 3-1) is 4; this number represents the total number of protons and neutrons in the atom. Based on an atomic weight of 4 and an atomic number of 2, a helium atom also has two neutrons. (Other atoms might have a different number of neutrons than protons.)

Each atom has a structure, with natural forces holding the atom in that structure. Atoms have a nucleus, which is composed of protons and neutrons, with the electrons orbiting the nucleus.

Because an atom has the same number of positively charged protons as it has negatively charged electrons, atoms have no net electrical charge. Figure 3-2 shows a helium atom's structure. It is based on a model created by Niels Bohr, a Danish physicist.

Figure 3-2   Bohr Model of a Helium Atom

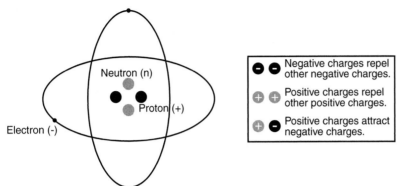

Figure 3-2 is not drawn to scale, but an analogy can give you a better sense of scale. If the protons and neutrons of this atom were the size of soccer balls in the middle of a soccer field, the electrons would be the size of cherries and would be orbiting near the outermost seats of the stadium. Given their relative size, electrons have little mass as compared to protons and neutrons. However, the negative electrical charge in an electron is the same strength as the positive charge in protons, so the net electrical charge in an atom is 0.

When electricity flows over a copper wire, the copper atoms change slightly. The next three sections explain the forces that keep an atom stable as shown in Figure 3-2, how electricity causes atoms to release electrons from their normal orbit, and how these free electrons create static electricity.

Forces That Keep Atoms Stable

The atom shown in Figure 3-2 can remain stable for long periods, with the protons and neutrons remaining in the exact relative location. Electrons move by orbiting the nucleus, but when an atom is stable, the electrons do not leave their orbits. Several different forces work to keep each atom stable, as described in this section.

Coulomb's Law defines one type of force in an atom; this law states that opposite charges attract and like charges repel. It also states that the strength of that repulsive force increases as the charges move closer to each other. The concept works exactly like magnets with the same magnetic charge. (The math shows that this repulsive force is inversely proportional to the square of the separation distance.) For example, the two protons inside a helium nucleus exert force against each other to push each other apart. Neutrons have no electrical charge, so they neither repel nor attract each other or protons.

Atomic nuclei remain together because another force acts to balance the repulsive electrical force between protons. In addition to Coulomb's Law, strong nuclear forces—forces that attract the matter inside the nucleus—also exist. You can think of these forces as microscopic gravity. Just as the Earth exerts a force on people so that they don't fly off the planet, the concentration of mass in the nucleus pulls the protons and neutrons together, which keeps the repulsive electrical force between the protons from causing the nucleus to fall apart.

Electrons experience two forces that balance each other out as well. Electrons generate centrifugal force from their motion orbiting around the nucleus. Centrifugal force is the outward force that is created when something moves in a circular motion. To see its effect, tie a ball to a string and swing it in a circle. Then, let go of the string to see the centrifugal force make the ball fly way out of its formerly circular path. To balance that force, the opposite electrical charges of protons and electrons attract these particles just enough to combat the centrifugal force. This process is much like the moon having centrifugal force away from the Earth because of its rotation around the Earth, but with the Earth's gravity pulling at the moon to prevent it from leaving orbit.

How Releasing Electrons Creates Electrical Current

Although the balancing forces of an atom's design are elegant and important, the ease with which these forces can be overcome is important for transmitting data using electricity. The forces that keep electrons in their orbits are weak—particularly weak in atoms of some elements, such as copper. Electrons in certain atoms, such as metals, can be pulled free from the atom. The ability to free electrons from their atoms brings us to the entire point of this review of atomic structure and chemistry:

> *Electrical current* can be made to flow over a metallic wire by making the atoms free their electrons.

The freed electrons move down the copper wire. More importantly, they cause the electrical charges to move down the wire at much faster speeds (around 70 percent of the speed of light in a vacuum). When one electron is freed, it exerts force on other atoms as it moves closer to them. That force causes other electrons to be freed while the original electron typically reattaches to some atom. This repeated process causes a wave of electrical energy, called electrical current, to pass over the wire.

A simple analogy can be made about electrical current by considering a rock thrown into a still pond. The rock splashes and creates a wave. The rock settles on the bottom of the pond and might not move for a long time. However, the wave created by the rock keeps spreading across the pond. Similarly, the electrons that leave an atom might not quickly propagate down the wire, but their effect—the electrical current—does propagate down the wire at speeds approaching the speed of light.

Electrostatic Discharge and Static Electricity

Sometimes, freed electrons do not reattach to an atom, which creates *static electricity*. If these free-floating static electrons have an opportunity to jump to a conductor, it can lead to *electrostatic discharge (ESD)*. For example, the human body is a conductor, so when you touch something that contains free electrons (static electricity), the electrons cause a current in your hand, and you receive a small electrical shock.

ESD might not harm people, but it can harm electronics. A static discharge can damage computer chips, data, or both. The logical circuitry of computer chips is extremely sensitive to ESD. You must take safety precautions before you work inside computers, routers, and similar devices.

 Lab 3.1.1   Safe Handling and Use of a Multimeter

In this lab, you learn how to use or handle a multimeter correctly.

Note

A multimeter is the generic name for an electrical testing device that can test for several electrical characteristics.

Insulators, Conductors, and Semiconductors

An atom that loses or gains an electron has a net positive or negative charge, depending on whether it now has more protons or electrons, respectively. Such atoms are called *ions*. Ions exert an electrical force on nearby atoms because of their net electrical charge. This force can cause a nearby atom to lose or gain electrons, which in turn makes that nearby atom an ion. In fact, it is this repetitive process that causes an electrical current to pass through a wire.

The electrical characteristics of any type of material relates to how easily an ion can be created. The more easily an atom can become an ion, the more easily it can be made to create an electrical current. Any material can be categorized by how easily it can pass an electrical current into one of the three types of materials listed in Table 3-1.

Table 3-1   Summary of the Three Main Types of Electrical Materials

Material	Definition	Examples
Insulator	Difficult for electrical current to flow	Plastic, paper, rubber, dry wood, air, pure water, and glass
Conductor	Easy for electrical current to flow	Copper, silver, gold, solder, water with ions, and the human body
Semiconductor	Electrical flow easily controlled	Carbon, germanium, gallium arsenide, and silicon

Note

Figure 3-1 points out a column in the periodic table that lists some of the best conductors. Because the human body is made of approximately 70 percent ionized water, it is also a conductor.

The atoms in *insulators* require a great deal of force to remove their electrons from orbit. This does not mean that electricity cannot flow, but that at an atomic level, the material has stronger forces that resist the release of electrons. Some electrical current can flow in insulators, but not much. On the other hand, the atoms in *conductors* have little force resisting the release of their electrons, which makes it much easier to create an electrical current.

Note

Silicon is common and can be found in sand, glass, and many types of rocks. The region around San Jose, California, is known as Silicon Valley because the computer industry, which depends on silicon micro-chips, started in that area.

The atoms in *semiconductors* can be precisely controlled as to when their electrons leave orbit. This fine level of control makes these substances particularly favorable materials from which to make electronics. In fact, the most important semiconductor is silicon (Si), which is used as the basic semiconductor for most kinds of microchips used in today's computers. Other examples from the same column of the periodic table include carbon and germanium (Ge). Gallium arsenide (GaAs), which is a molecule, is also a common semiconductor.

Electromagnetic Force (Voltage)

The physical world has forces that cause objects to move. For example, a river runs downhill because the Earth's gravity pulls the water down. Also, atmospheric pressure pushes on the air, which creates wind. The force that causes electrons to leave their orbit and create the wave of electrical current down a wire is called *electromotive force (EMF)*. Although the formal term is EMF, it is better known as *voltage*. EMF is created on a wire by two forces: a negative charge pushing electrons away from one end of the wire, and a positive charge pulling the negatively charged electrons toward the other end of the wire.

The amount of EMF, or voltage, can be measured only by looking at two points on the same (conducting) material. In fact, voltage is often described as the amount of power as measured between two points on a conductor. For example, if you attach a Fluke multimeter to two points on a wire, the multimeter can sense that the electrons are being pushed/pulled in a particular direction and with a particular force, thereby measuring the voltage. The amount of EMF is typically referenced as a number of volts. Just as steeper hills or higher pressures cause faster movement in water and air, higher voltage reflects a higher EMF. Voltage is represented by the letter V, and sometimes by the letter E (for electromotive force). The unit of measure for voltage is volt (V).

 Lab 3.1.2   Voltage Measurement

In this lab, you demonstrate the ability to measure voltage by using the multimeter.

Current

Electrical current is the flow of charges that is created when electrons move. When voltage (electrical force) is applied and a path for the current exists through some conducting material, electrons move from the negative terminal (which repels them) along the path to the positive terminal (which attracts them). Figure 3-3 shows the general idea of this concept.

The letter I represents current, as measured in units called amperes (*amps*). The current is described as the number of charges per second that pass by a point along a path. It can be thought of as the amount of electron traffic that flows past a particular point on a circuit. The more electrons that pass by any given point in a circuit, the higher the current.

Figure 3-3   Electrical Current

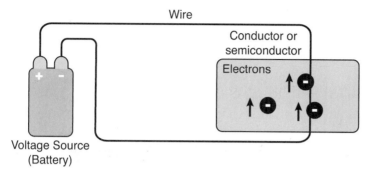

Types of Current

The current might always flow in one direction, as shown in Figure 3-3, or it might alternate directions. As a result, two main categories of electrical current exist:

- *Direct current (DC)*—The movement of electrons and current always flows in a single direction, from the negative terminal to the positive terminal. Figure 3-3, which uses a battery, shows an example of a DC circuit, with the electrons always flowing counterclockwise.

- *Alternating current (AC)*—the movement of electrons and current changes direction, because the terminals of the AC voltage source regularly change to negative and positive and back again. This change makes the direction of electron movement change, or alternate, with respect to time.

Power lines carry AC electricity because it can be delivered efficiently over long distances. DC can be found in flashlight batteries, car batteries, and as power for the microchips on the motherboard of a computer, where the power needs to go only a short distance.

Note

When an AC circuit reverses the flow of electrons, the current is said to have reversed polarity.

Creating Electrical Energy Using Voltage and Current

Electrical energy, or *wattage,* is defined as the ability to do work with electricity. To do the work, the electricity must have some power, or voltage, and the electricity must flow; in other words, there must be a current. So, electrical energy is actually the combination of current (measured in amps, which is the quantity of electrons past a given point) and voltage (measured in volts, which is the pressure or speed of electrons). The energy is measured as a number of watts (W), with wattage equal to voltage times amperage ($W = V * I$).

Electrical devices, such as light bulbs, electric motors, and computer power supplies, are rated in terms of watts, which is how much electrical energy they consume or produce. Given the wattage and knowledge of the voltage of a power outlet, you can calculate the required current. For example, a lamp in the U.S. might use a 60-watt light bulb, with the power outlet using the standard 110 volts. From that, the formula $W = V * I$ can be used, so $I = 60/110$ or about .55 amps of current for that single light bulb.

The role of current in the calculation of wattage can be seen by comparing static electricity and lightning. Both have very high voltages, but static electricity has very low current. However, lightning has high voltage and high current, and it can, of course, cause humans severe injury or death.

Resistance, Impedance, and Attenuation

Resistance is the property of a material that resists electron movement. Conductors have low resistance, which makes them good materials to use for electrical circuits. Insulators have high resistance, which makes them poor for passing electricity but good for other purposes, particularly for shielding in cables. The letter R represents resistance. The unit of measure for resistance is *ohm*, and it is represented by the Greek letter omega (Ω).

The relationship among voltage, resistance, and current is voltage (V) equals current (I) multiplied by resistance (R). In other words, V = I * R. This is *Ohm's law*, named after the scientist who explored these issues.

Current, voltage, and resistance are all important fundamental characteristics of an electrical circuit. Table 3-2 summarizes the terms used to refer to each characteristic, along with the unit of measurement for each.

Table 3-2   Electrical Characteristics and Units of Measurement

Electrical Characteristic	Abbreviation	Unit of Measurement	Abbreviation of Unit of Measurement
Current	I	Ampere	Amp, or A
Voltage	E or V	Volt	V
Resistance	R	Ohm	Ω

All materials have some amount of electrical resistance. AC circuits have additional forces besides electrical resistance that resist the flow of current and voltage. However, because the term *resistance* had already been defined, the term *impedance* is used to refer to the combined resisting force in an AC circuit. Impedance includes resistive forces in an AC circuit, including electrical resistance, plus a few other forces like capacitance and inductance. In short, resistance is the force that resists current in a DC circuit, and impedance (which includes resistance) is the force that resists current flow in an AC circuit.

Most people who implement networks do not sit around thinking about the resistance or impedance of a particular networking medium. However, they tend to consider the effects of *attenuation*. As an electrical current passes over a wire, the resistance and possibly impedance cause the signal to degrade. For example, Figure 2-3 in Chapter 2, "Networking Fundamentals," showed a clean square-wave graph of the electrical current as transmitted, with a much rougher and smaller current (signal) being received by the other device. The term attenuation refers to the reasons why a signal degrades as it passes over a medium. The attenuation of a signal, which resistance and impedance directly impact, is the main reason that each type of networking cable must be restricted to some maximum allowed length.

 Lab 3.1.3   Resistance Measurement

In this lab, you demonstrate the ability to measure resistance and continuity with the multimeter.

Circuits

Electrical circuits consist of conductive material through which an electrical current can flow. Figure 3-4 shows a simple circuit that is typical of a flashlight. The switch is like two ends of a single wire that can be opened (broken) and closed (shorted) to prevent or allow current, respectively.

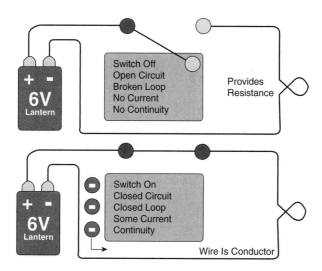

Figure 3-4   Serial Circuit: Flashlight

The top of Figure 3-4 illustrates the flashlight with its switch turned off. Moving the switch to the off position breaks the circuit's closed loop. Because no complete path for electron movement exists, no current can flow from the battery's negative terminal to its positive terminal. (Remember: The negative terminal repels the negatively charged electrons, and the positive terminal attracts them.)

The bottom of Figure 3-4 illustrates the flashlight with its switch turned on, which completes the circuit. Electrical current can then flow in a counterclockwise direction. The bulb converts some of the electrical energy to light and some to (wasted) heat. The bulb also adds to the resistance in the circuit.

An oscilloscope is an electronic device that is inserted into an electrical circuit and graphs the voltage levels over time. On an oscilloscope screen, the x-axis represents time, and the y-axis represents voltage. (Usually, two y-axis voltage inputs exist, so two circuits can be simultaneously observed and measured, and an easy comparison can be made.) Figure 3-5 shows an example of a graph that might be seen on an oscilloscope (in this case, showing an AC signal), which varies continuously from a positive to a negative voltage and back again over time.

Figure 3-5   AC as Graphed by an Oscilloscope

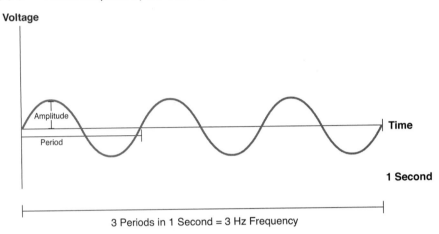

Finally, electricity naturally flows to the Earth, or *ground,* if a path exists. In effect, because the Earth can conduct electricity, the Earth can become part of an electrical circuit. When you install routers, switches, and other computing equipment, the installation instructions typically suggest connecting the equipment to ground. Grounding—the process of connecting the circuit to ground—protects the equipment from unexpected electrical currents because of a power surge. *Ground* typically means the zero-volt level (when making electrical measurements).

Note

Circuits may be parallel circuits or series circuits. The circuits shown in this chapter, and those used for digital transmission, are series circuits.

 Lab 3.1.5   Series Circuits

In this lab, you build and explore the basic properties of series circuits.

Popular LAN Copper Cabling

Although an understanding of the physics and chemistry behind electricity is useful background information, knowledge of cabling standards is more important to the typical jobs that today's network engineers perform. The previous explanations of electricity defined how electrical current flows over a wire, whereas cabling standards define the rules and requirements for each particular type of cable. The cables hold one or more copper wires, which, of course, conduct electricity, and can be used for encoding binary 0s and 1s as differing electrical signals.

The *Telecommunications Industry Association (TIA)* and the *Electronic Industries Alliance (EIA)* have jointly defined LAN cabling standards. The most popular standard is TIA/EIA-568-B, which defines commercial-building telecommunication cabling standards used in most LANs today. These standards define rules and requirements for unshielded twisted-pair (UTP) cabling and requirements for how to use the pins on the connectors on the ends of the cables.

The Institute of Electrical and Electronic Engineers (IEEE) defines LAN standards such as the IEEE 802.3 family of LAN standards, which defines all types of Ethernet. The IEEE standards define the requirements for LAN cabling by referring to the detailed work of other standards bodies, such as the TIA/EIA.

When reading the upcoming explanations of each type of networking cable, consider several points of comparison:

- What data transmission speeds can be achieved? The type of cable used imposes a limit to the speed at which data can pass over the cable.

- Will the transmissions be digital or analog? Digital and analog transmission might require different cable types.

- How far can a signal travel before attenuation becomes a concern? If the signal degrades, network devices might not be able to receive and interpret it. The distance the signal travels through the cable affects the signal's attenuation. Degradation is directly related to the distance the signal travels and the type of cable used.

IEEE 802.3 defines several Ethernet types that vary based on speed, the type of cabling supported, and the maximum cable length for a single cable. IEEE uses some names that imply the speed and type of cabling, as mentioned in Chapter 2. For a brief review, consider the following list, which shows the original three types of Ethernet LAN specifications approved by IEEE 802.3:

- 10BASE5

- 10BASE2

- 10BASE-T

Of these three types, the number in front defines the speed (10 meaning 10 Mbps). The word BASE refers to the baseband transmission techniques that Ethernet uses. Finally, the value after the word BASE refers to the cabling type. The 5 and 2 refer to coaxial cabling that can run 500 meters and (approximately) 200 meters, respectively. The T refers to UTP cabling.

Noise and attenuation restrict how far an electrical signal can travel over an Ethernet cable. For example, the original Ethernet type was 10BASE5, which used a thick coaxial cable. As defined, an Ethernet network interface card (NIC) can send an electrical signal for 500 meters over such a cable before attenuation and noise make the electrical signal unintelligible. It is much like when you try to talk to someone: The farther away he gets or the louder the surrounding area is, the more difficult it is to hear her.

The next few sections explain some details of coaxial cables, shielded twisted-pair (STP) cables, and UTP cables. More focus is given to UTP cables because, of the three types of cables, they are the most commonly used today.

Note

These Ethernet standards are listed in the order in which the IEEE introduced them. The 10BASE5and 10BASE2 names do not indicate the cabling type, but later standards, starting with 10BASE-T, include a code, like "T" in this case, to imply the type of cabling.

Note

The acronym STP also stands for Spanning Tree Protocol, which is covered in Chapter 8, "Ethernet Switching."

Coaxial Cable

Coaxial cable, as shown in Figure 3-6, consists of four main parts:

- Copper conductor
- Plastic insulation
- Braided copper shielding
- Outer jacket

Figure 3-6 Coaxial Cable

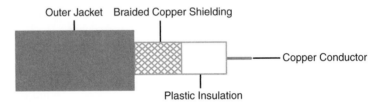

The solid copper conductor at the center of the cable provides the conductive electrical path over which electricity flows. By properly attaching the cable to Ethernet NICs, the NICs then have the capability to send electrical signals to each other. To send bits to each other, they simply vary the electrical signal by using a set of encoding rules. As long as the sender and receiver use the same set of encoding rules, they can send bits to each other as electrical signals.

Note

The electrical terms *shield* and *shielding* refer to a material that protects an electrical signal in one place from the effects of nearby electrical signals.

Although the copper conductor is important, the rest of the cable is also important. For example, the layer of flexible plastic insulation that surrounds the conductor helps reduce attenuation as the signal propagates through the conductor. It also reduces noise from outside sources, which Chapter 4, "Cabling Testing," covers in more detail. The braided copper shielding acts as additional shielding from outside noise and acts as a second conductive path for other purposes. Covering this shield is the outer jacket, which provides the cable with additional strength so that it does not break when it is pulled through the conduits.

Today's modern LANs no longer use 10BASE5 and 10BASE2, which are the only two IEEE Ethernet standards that call for coaxial cabling. However, from a theoretical perspective, coaxial cable has several advantages:

- Coaxial cable can run with fewer boosts from repeaters for longer distances between network nodes than either STP or UTP.
- Coaxial cable is less expensive than fiber-optic cable, although it is more expensive than UTP and STP.
- Coaxial technology is well known because it has been used in various types of data communication for many years. For example, coaxial cable is commonly used in homes to deliver cable-television signals and high-speed Internet access.

The IEEE moved away from thick coaxial cable toward thinner coaxial cable (10BASE2) and UTP cable (10BASE-T) to decrease cabling costs and ease the installation process. The relatively thick 10BASE5 cable, which is around .4 inches in diameter, was both heavy and difficult to bend. Although the cable had several benefits, such as allowing a single cable to be 500 meters, the installation cost and difficultly made it unwieldy. So, IEEE created 10BASE2, which uses a thinner coaxial cable (a little less than half the diameter of 10BASE5 cabling). Figure 3-7 shows the cables to a relatively close scale.

Figure 3-7   Coaxial Cables for Thicknet and Thinnet

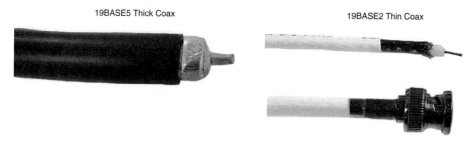

Because of the cable thickness, 10BASE5 and 10BASE2 became known as *Thicknet* and *Thinnet*. Because the thinner cable was cheaper to purchase and install, 10BASE2 also became known as *Cheapernet*.

STP Cable

Coaxial cables use a fairly large amount of shielding. The shielding provides a cleaner electrical current by reducing attenuation and noise, which allows for longer cabling lengths. However, shielding also contributes to the negative effects of coaxial cabling by making the cables more expensive, heavier, and difficult to bend when installing them.

As the IEEE improved its LAN standards, including other types of LANs besides Ethernet, it wanted to define standards that used lower-cost cabling that worked well. The two main categories of newer types of electrical cable were *shielded twisted-pair (STP)* and unshielded twisted-pair (UTP). As you can guess, STP cable includes shielding, and UTP does not. As a result, STP is more expensive than UTP and is slightly more difficult to install, but it has better electrical characteristics than UTP. In fact, when the IEEE first defined some LANs for use with UTP cabling, many industry observers wondered if UTP was good enough for use in a "real" LAN inside a company.

STP cable contains pairs of thin copper wires. The cable uses three types of insulation:

- Each single wire is covered in color-coded plastic insulation.

- Each pair of wires is twisted together with an insulator called a pair shield around them.

- All the wires in the cable (usually four pairs, but it can be two pairs) are covered by a shield called the overall shield.

Note

Twisting two wires together and sending the current in opposite directions reduces the effect of electrical interference. Today, most networking devices that use copper cabling use twisted pairs of wires.

Figure 3-8 shows an example of an STP cable.

Figure 3-8   STP Cable

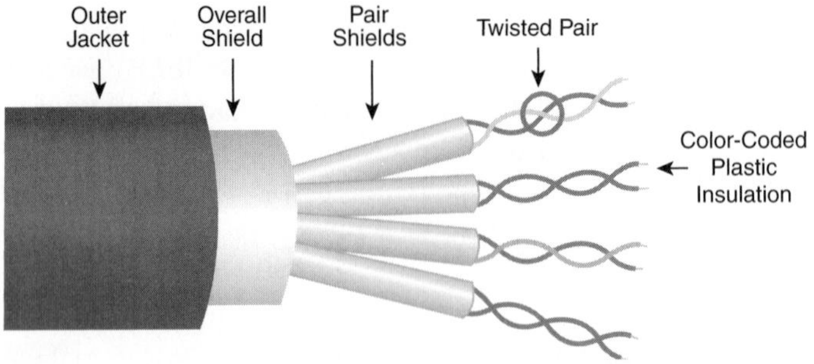

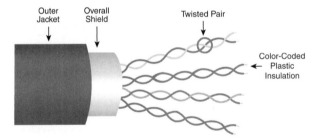

A cheaper variation of STP, called *screened twisted-pair (ScTP)*, can also be used. ScTP, also known as foil twisted-pair (FTP), simply leaves off the pair shields from an STP cable, as shown in Figure 3-9.

Figure 3-9   ScTP

Today, STP cabling—actual STP or ScTP—is a much less popular option than UTP. The biggest reason for STP being less popular is that UTP works well, and it is cheaper and easier to work with than STP. One of the reasons that STP cable is more difficult to install than UTP is that the metallic shielding must be grounded. If improperly installed, STP and ScTP become susceptible to noise problems because an ungrounded shield acts like an antenna and picks up unwanted signals. Also, STP and ScTP cable do not provide any significant cable-length advantages over UTP, with the older coaxial cable providing for medium distances, and fiber-optic cables supporting cable lengths of several kilometers.

STP does provide some benefits, however. Some physical locations simply have a large amount of electrical interference. In these installations, UTP cable might not work well, so STP provides a convenient and cost-effective solution. For example, the online curriculum suggests that STP is still somewhat popular in Europe.

UTP Cable

Unshielded twisted-pair (UTP) cable consists of pairs of thin copper wires that are twisted together and covered in color-coded plastic insulation. The wire pairs are then covered with a plastic outer jacket. Compared to STP cable, the pair shields and overall shield are simply missing. Figure 3-10 shows a UTP cable.

Figure 3-10   UTP Cable

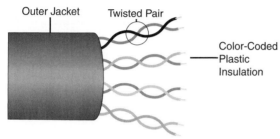

UTP cable has many advantages:

- It does not require grounding like STP cables do, so it is the easiest cable to add connectors to on the ends.

- Its relatively small diameter makes it more flexible, and as a result, it is easier to work with. The small diameter also means more UTP cable can fit into a conduit as compared with coaxial and STP cable.

- It supports the same data speeds as other copper media.

UTP's primary disadvantage is that it is more susceptible to electrical noise and interference than any other type of networking media. Because it has practically no shielding, the only real method UTP cables have to reduce interference is the cancellation effect that occurs by twisting together the pairs. (Interestingly, over time, UTP cables have improved by including more twists per meter of cable.) Also, compared with coaxial and fiber-optic cables, UTP cabling supports shorter cabling distances (typically, 100 meters when used for Ethernet LANs).

UTP cables have many important and useful characteristics. As a result, many variations of UTP cabling standards have been created. Additionally, the cables must have connectors added to the ends of the cable to make it convenient to connect the cable to routers, switches, and NICs. The next several sections cover the different UTP standards and the connectors. Several of the upcoming sections explain the details of UTP cable pinouts, which refers to which wires connect to certain parts of the connectors on the ends of the cables.

LAN UTP Cabling Standards

LANs were first created in the 1970s, with the first national and international LAN standards being produced in the 1980s. The 1990s saw Ethernet become the predominant LAN standard: beginning the 1990s at 10 Mbps, moving to 100 Mbps, and by the end of the decade, at 1000 Mbps (1 Gbps). The 2000s continue that trend with even faster Ethernet standards: 1-Gbps Ethernet NICs for PCs became affordable, and 10-Gbps Ethernet products came to the marketplace.

To create the faster and faster Ethernet standards, the standards bodies had to do plenty of engineering work, including work to create better cables that support these high speeds. Most of the engineering work relates to the effects of how electricity flows over the cables' wires. To support the various Ethernet standards, the TIA/EIA standardizes different categories of UTP cabling, as summarized in Table 3-3.

Table 3-3   TIA/EIA Cable Categories

UTP Cable Category	Purpose	Comments
Category 1	Telephones	Not suitable for data.
Category 2	Token Ring	Supports 4-Mbps Token Ring.
Category 3	Telephones and 10BASE-T	10BASE-T was created with a design goal of supporting the large installed base of Category 3 cable in the 1980s.
Category 4	Token Ring	Supports 16-Mbps Token Ring.
Category 5	Ethernet	Supports 10BASE-T and 100BASE-T.
Category 5e	Ethernet	Uses the same cable as Category 5, but with more stringent requirements on the connector and the cable testing. Supports Gigabit Ethernet.
Category 6	Ethernet	Officially supports 1-Gbps Ethernet, with work being done that could use Category 6 cable for 10-Gbps Ethernet.

Note

The electrical details that define what makes one cable meet one category and another be in a different category is beyond the scope of this book.

UTP Cable Pinouts

In addition to the cables' electrical characteristics, the TIA/EIA defines the connectors and pinouts that the cables use. When used for Ethernet, each UTP cable has a *registered jack 45 (RJ-45)* connector on the end of the cable. The connector has eight numbered slots into which the eight wires inside the cable need to be inserted when a connector is installed onto the end of the cable.

Using cabling terminology, the wires are called pins, and the numbered locations where the wires sit inside the connector are called *pinouts*. Depending on how the cable will be used, each wire needs to be placed into a particular pin slots on the RJ-45 connector on each end. A single wire can be connected into one pin slot on one end of the cable and into the same or a different pin slot on the other end of the cable. The pinout determines the pins used for each wire on each end of the cable.

Figure 3-11 shows an RJ-45 connector used by Ethernet for UTP cables. If you look closely, you can see most of the eight wires inside the cable sitting inside the transparent RJ-45 connector.

Figure 3-11   RJ-45 Connector

Note

Looking at the RJ-45 connector on the end of a real UTP cable shows better detail than what is shown in Figure 3-11. To get even more detail, look at an uncrimped RJ-45 connector. (An uncrimped connector has not yet been attached to the cable. A process called crimping attaches the connector to the end of the cable.)

The pins in the connector provide a precise point at which the copper wires in the cable connect to electrical contacts inside the connector. As a result, when the connectors on each end of a cable plug into a PC's Ethernet NIC and a port on a switch or hub, the NIC and switch/hub have completed electrical circuits between the two devices. The devices can then use the electrical circuits to send data to one another.

To make sense of the details about pinouts, you need to know a couple of key concepts that are true of 10- and 100-Mbps Ethernet options:

- Ethernet devices (at 10- and 100-Mbps Ethernet) use one pair of wires to transmit data.

- Ethernet devices (at 10- and 100-Mbps Ethernet) do not use the same pair to transmit and receive data, so two pairs of wires are needed (one for each direction of transmission).

Therefore, 10 and 100 Mbps Ethernet devices that use a UTP cable use two pairs of wires. The logic that they use when choosing how and when to use each pair determines the type of cabling pinouts required.

Note

Because the cable can have four pairs (eight wires), networking devices can have four separate electrical circuits available by using that single cable. Each wire pair creates a complete circuit over which electricity can flow.

Ethernet Straight-Through Cables and Pinouts

A typical cable between an end-user device and a LAN hub or switch uses a cable type called *straight-through cable*. To see why a straight-through cable works in these cases, consider the logic used by a typical PC NIC and a typical hub port, as shown in Figure 3-12. Figure 3-12 shows the wires inside the UTP cable, without any shielding, so that each pair's purpose is obvious. The figure also shows the PC NIC outside the PC to clarify where the cable connects.

Figure 3-12   Ethernet Straight-Through Cable Concept

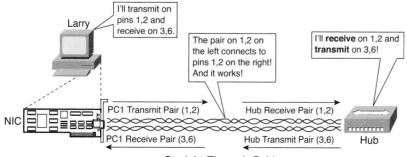

The PC's NIC uses the following logic:

- Send on the pair at pins 1 and 2 of the RJ-45 connector.

- Expect to receive electrical current on the pair of wires at pins 3 and 6.

LAN hubs and switches, knowing how NICs act, do just the opposite:

- Send on pins 3 and 6.

- Receive signals on pins 1 and 2.

To make it all work, the cable must be a straight-through cable, which is defined as follows:

The wire at a pin position on one end of the cable must be in the same pin position at the other end of the cable.

In other words, the wire at pin 1 must connect to pin 1 on the other end; the wire at pin 2 must connect to pin 2 on the other end; and so on. To create such a cable, any wire could connect to a pin location as long as it connected to the same one on the other end. However, the TIA/EIA defines two standards—TIA/EIA-568-A and TIA/EIA-568-B—to follow when deciding the pinouts of a cable (in other words, when deciding which wires go in which pin locations). Figure 3-13 shows the two TIA-standard pinouts for use with UTP cabling.

Figure 3-13   TIA-Standard Pinouts

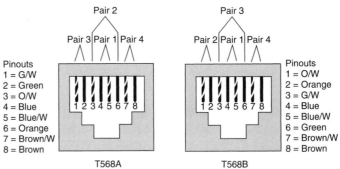

Table 3-4 lists the pinouts for the *TIA/EIA-568-A* standard, along with the typical colors used for each of the eight pin positions in the RJ-45 connector.

Table 3-4 TIA/EIA-568-A Pinouts

Pin Number	TIA/EIA-568-A Function	Wire Insulation Color	TIA/EIA-568-B Function	Wire Insulation Color
1	TD+	White/green	TD+	White/orange
2	TD-	Green	TD-	Orange
3	RD+	White/orange	RD+	White/green
4	Unused	Blue	Unused	Blue
5	Unused	White/blue	Unused	White/blue
6	RD-	Orange	RD-	Green
7	Unused	White/brown	Unused	White/brown
8	Unused	Brown	Unused	Brown

To create a straight-through cable, either the TIA/EIA-568-A or TIA/EIA-568-B standard pinouts can be used on the connectors on both ends of the cable.

Crossover-Cable Pinouts

In some cases, a LAN engineer needs to connect two devices that both want to send on the same pins. Figure 3-14 shows such an example (with two PCs). (Figure 3-14 shows the NICs outside each PC, and the wires inside the cable outside the cable's outer jacket, just to focus on how each wire pair is used.)

Figure 3-14 Need for Crossover Cables

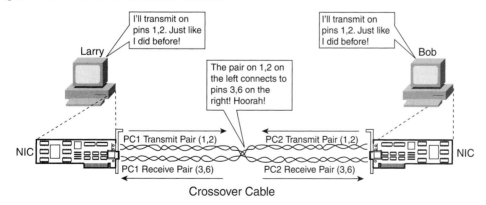

Both PC NICs send data on the pair at pins 1 and 2, and both expect to receive electrical signals on pins 3 and 6. So, the cable must connect a pair at pins 1 and 2 on one end of the cable and connect to pins 3 and 6, respectively, on the other end of the cable. This type of cable is called a *crossover cable*.

Figure 3-15 shows the pinouts for a crossover cable by using the TIA/EIA-568-B standard. Figure 3-15 shows how the two pairs typically used by Ethernet—the pair at pins 1 and 2, plus the pair at pins 3 and 6—are crossed. This figure also shows the pair at pins 4 and 5 being crossed to use pins 7 and 8 on the other end of the cable.

Figure 3-15   TIA/EIA-568-B Crossover Cable Pinouts

TIA/EIA-568-B Crossover Diagram

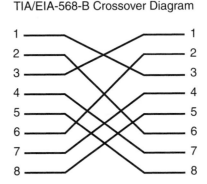

Console Connections and Rollover Cables

The final variation of UTP cable pinouts is called a *rollover cable*, which connects a wire to pin 1 on one end with pin 8 on the other end. Another wire connects to pin 2 on one end to pin 7 on the other end; another wire connects pins 3 and 6 on opposite ends; and so on.

Rollover cables are not used to create Ethernet LANs. Instead, they connect a PC's serial port to a console port on a Cisco router or switch. This physical connection allows the PC user to log in to the router or switch and enter commands. Figure 3-16 shows a connection from a PC to the console port of a switch using a rollover cable.

Figure 3-16   Rollover Cable and Adapter for Connecting to a PC Serial Port

Device with Console

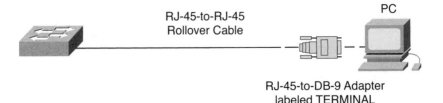

Figure 3-16 also shows an additional connector on the end of the cable. Most PC serial ports use a 9-pin or 25-pin connector, but a rollover cable typically has RJ-45 connectors on each

end. So, you must use an adapter, with an RJ-45 jack on one side, and a DB-9 or DB-25 plug on the other.

Choosing the Correct Cabling Pinouts

On a practical note, network engineers must know when to use a straight-through cable, crossover cable, or rollover cable. Knowing when to use a rollover is easy: Use it only when a PC connects to the console port of a networking device. For Ethernet cables, two key facts can help you know whether to use a straight-through cable or crossover cable:

- When connecting two devices that are similar in regard to which pins they use to transmit, use a crossover cable.

- When connecting two devices that differ in regard to which pins they use to transmit, use a straight-through cable.

For example, Figure 3-12 showed two devices that use a different pair to transmit data, so a straight-through cable is needed. Figure 3-14 showed two devices that use the same pair to transmit, so a crossover cable is needed. Of course, it helps to know which kinds of devices typically transmit on pins 1 and 2 and which transmit on pins 3 and 6. The following list details which devices use which pins to transmit data:

- **Pins 1 and 2**—PCs, routers, servers, and wireless access points' (APs') Ethernet ports

- **Pins 3 and 6**—Switches, hubs, and bridges

Some switches (commonly on products meant for home use) might have a port that transmits on pins 1 and 2. These ports are included in case two switches need to be connected; with this special port, the home user can use the same old straight-through cable to connect this port to a normal switch port that transmits on pins 3 and 6. This prevents the home user from needing to think about the concept of a crossover cable.

Note

Many Cisco switches have printed labels beside each port, such as 1x, 2x, and so on. The x means the transmit pins are reversed compared to a typical PC NIC, meaning the switch transmits on pins 3 and 6. Also, many modern switches can automatically detect when the wrong cable pin-out is used and swap the pairs internal to the switch.

Lab 3.1.9a   Communications Circuits

In this lab, you design, build, and test a simple communication system.

Lab 3.1.9b   Fluke Basic Cable Testing

In this lab, you use a simple cable tester to verify whether a straight-through or crossover cable is good or bad.

Lab 3.1.9c   Straight-Through Cable Construction

In this lab, you build a Category 5 or Category 5e UTP Ethernet network patch cable or patch cord and test the cable.

Lab 3.1.9d   Rollover Cable Construction

In this lab, you build a Category 5 or Category 5e UTP console rollover cable and test it for continuity and correct pinouts (the correct color of wire on the right pin).

Lab 3.1.9e   Crossover Cable Construction

In this lab, you build a Category 5 or Category 5e UTP Ethernet crossover cable to TIA/EIA-568-B and TIA/EIA-568-A standards. You also test the cable for good connections (continuity) and correct pinouts (correct wire on the right pin).

Lab 3.1.9f   UTP Cable Purchase

In this lab, you are introduced to the variety and prices of network cabling and components in the market. You will gather pricing information for UTP patch cables and bulk cable.

Optical Media

Networks use copper cabling and electricity to transmit bits from one device to another for many reasons. By the point in history at which networking first began to grow, scientists already had a good understanding of electricity and how it could be sent over wires, but research into optical transmission had not been developed as much. Later, researchers developed ways to use fiber-optic cables and infrared light to transmit data.

This section introduces *fiber-optic cabling*, which uses glass fibers to transmit light. The transmitter varies the light, and the receiver interprets the variations as binary 0s and 1s, much like an electrical transmitter varies the electrical signal on a UTP cable to send 0s and 1s to the receiver. However, this section defers the detailed discussion of the physics behind optical transmissions and cabling to the section "Additional Topics of Interest," which you can find on the CD-ROM accompanying this book.

Note

Fiber-optic cabling is also called fiber, fiber cabling, optical cabling, and fiber optics.

Comparing Fiber-Optic Cabling and Copper Cabling

In many cases, fiber-optic cabling can be used instead of copper cabling. However, the biggest downside is the expense. The cable itself is typically more expensive than copper cabling. Also, networking devices that use fiber optics are considerably more expensive than their electrical alternatives. Finally, fiber-optic cabling requires more skill to install, so the labor cost tends to be high. As a result, when either UTP cabling or fiber-optic cabling can be used, the most popular choice is to use UTP cabling.

Even with the cost difference, fiber-optic cabling is still a popular type of network cabling. Fiber-optic cabling simply works in some environments where copper cabling cannot. In some cases, either UTP or fiber-optic cabling could be used, but the benefits of fiber-optic cabling outweigh the cost difference. Here are some of the compelling reasons to prefer fiber-optic cabling in some cases:

- Fiber is not susceptible to lightning, electromagnetic interference (EMI), or radio frequency interference (RFI), and it does not generate EMI or RFI.

- Fiber has much greater bandwidth capabilities than other media.

- Fiber allows significantly greater transmission distances and excellent signal quality because the light energy on the fiber-optic cable attenuates much less than does electricity on copper cables.

- Fiber is more secure than other media because it is difficult to tap into a fiber and it is easy to detect someone placing a tap on a fiber.

- Current fiber transmitter and receiver technologies can be replaced by newer and faster devices without requiring fiber replacement.

- Sand, which is a plentiful substance, is the raw material from which fiber is made.

- Fiber-optic cabling has no electrical signals passing over the cable, so grounding is not an issue.

- The cable itself has a small diameter, which requires little space in a conduit.

- The cable itself is lightweight, which makes installation relatively easy.

- Fiber has better resistance to environmental factors, such as water, than copper wire.

- Lengths of fiber can be spliced for long cable runs.

Electromagnetic Spectrum

Light is pure energy. As pure energy, it can pass through many different media. For example, visible light can pass through the relative vacuum of space between the sun and the Earth, the atmosphere, a window, and many liquids.

Light can also be absorbed and reflected. For example, solar-power cells absorb the light from the sun and convert it into electrical power. The human body absorbs light from the sun, which makes us feel hot and gives us a suntan. Other material might reflect light—for example, by nature, mirrors reflect light. Also, people wear light-colored clothes in the summer because they reflect more light than dark-colored clothes, which makes people more comfortable.

Like most other forms of pure energy, light travels as a wave. Graphed over time, light energy looks like Figure 3-17. The x-axis uses a unit of time, and the y-axis graphs the light's power (or brightness).

Figure 3-17   Light Energy Over Time

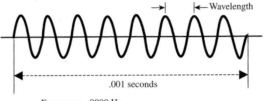

Light energy, and other forms of similar energy, can be described based on the characteristics of the graph in Figure 3-17. With light energy, the most common references are **wavelength** and *frequency*. Frequency is the number of times the repeating part of the graph occurs in 1 second. For example, in Figure 3-17, the cycle from the x-axis up, then below the x-axis, and back to the x-axis again happens eight times. If that complete cycle occurred 8000 times in 1 second, the light would have a frequency of 8000 Hertz.

The *wavelength* of a wave describes the length of one complete wave cycle. If you could some-how make the light stop where it sits in space and had instruments to measure an individual wave cycle, you could measure the length of a single repeating light wave. More practically, however, the wavelength can be calculated by using this formula: wavelength = speed of light / frequency.

Many forms of electromagnetic (EM) energy exist in the universe, including what humans know as visible light. The human eye is designed to see only a small portion of the wavelengths of EM energy. Other types of EM energy can be generated for the purpose of doing work. For example, X-rays are a form of EM energy, and so is the infrared energy that most TV remote controls use. All EM energy can be graphed as a waveform with a frequency and wavelength similar to Figure 3-17. Figure 3-18 shows the EM spectrum, which includes many different fre-quencies and wavelengths used by different kinds of EM energy.

The visible-light and infrared-light spectrums are the most important parts of Figure 3-18 for this book's purposes. Human eyes can sense visible light, which is EM energy with wave-lengths between 700 nanometers (nm) and about 400 nm. Different wavelengths inside this range appear to the human eye as different colors (for example, 700 nm looks like red, and 400 nm looks like violet).

Digital transmissions over optical cabling use the following different wavelengths in the infrared light range:

- 850 nm
- 1310 nm
- 1550 nm

These wavelengths were selected because they travel better through optical fiber than other wavelengths.

Note

Many references to optical transmission use the wave-length of the light, while references to wireless transmissions more often refer to the frequencies.

Note

A nanometer (nm) is one billionth of a meter (0.000000001 m) in length.

Figure 3-18   EM Spectrum

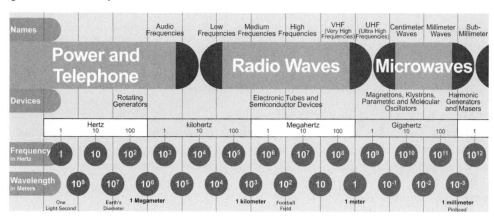

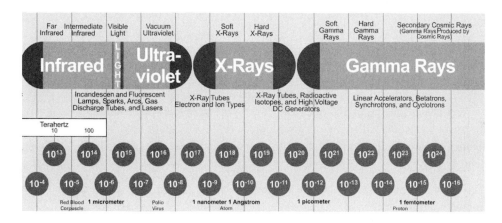

Fiber-Optic Cabling

Fiber-optic cables allow networking devices to send a modulated infrared light over a glass fiber in the middle of a cable. More plainly, one device shines a bright light that means a binary 1 and a dim light that means a binary 0. The receiving device watches the incoming light to record the incoming 1s and 0s.

Fiber-optic cables do not pass any electricity. Electricity and circuits on the transmitting computer take a set of bits and generate infrared light that represents the bits. The only type of energy signal that crosses the cable is the light itself. Because the physics behind the transmission of light differs so much from electricity, using fiber-optic cables has many benefits, including longer cable lengths and less susceptibility to interference.

The following sections explain the basics of fiber-optic cabling. First, the use of multiple fibers, one for each transmission direction, is explained. The next section describes the physical components of the cables. Finally, the differences between the two major types of fiber-optic cables—single-mode and multimode—are described.

Using Two Fibers—One for Each Direction

Just like most roads have at least two lanes—at least one lane for each direction—networking devices use a pair of fiber-optic cables—one for each transmission direction. On an individual fiber, light can travel in only one direction, so to achieve full-duplex communications, two separate cables are required. Figure 3-19 shows a typical pair of fiber-optic cables.

Figure 3-19   Duplex Fiber-Optic Cables

The cable marked Tx (for transmit) on each end connects to a part of a connector labeled Rx (for receive) on the other end. Essentially, a transmitter, typically a light-emitting diode (LED) or laser, transmits the light. The other end of that one cable must be connected to a receiver, which uses something called a p-intrinsic-n diode (PIN photodiode or simply photodiode). The photodiode senses the light's strength and wavelength and creates electrical charges that represent 0s and 1s.

When cables are pulled, multiple optical fibers are encased in the same larger cable. The most common multiples are 2, 4, 8, 12, 24, 48, and even more.

Fiber-Optic Cable Components

A single optical cable has five main components, as shown in Figure 3-20.

Figure 3-20   Five Elements of a Fiber-Optic Cable

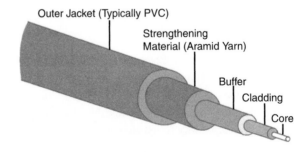

The cable components are described as follows:

- **Core**—Made of glass-like material called silicon dioxide (silica). The infrared light travels through the core.

- **Cladding**—Surrounds the core to reflect the light back into the core and prevent the light from escaping.

- **Buffer**—Surrounds the cladding to provide physical protection to the more fragile cladding and core.

- **Strengthening material**—Surrounds the buffer to prevent the fiber-optic cable from stretching when installers pull it. The material used is often Kevlar (generically called an aramid yarn), which is the same material used for bulletproof vests.

- **Outer jacket**—Surrounds the cable to protect the fiber from abrasion, solvents, and other contaminants. This outer jacket composition varies depending on the cable usage. The outer jackets of multimode optical cables are frequently orange.

Multimode and Single-Mode Fiber

One of the key benefits of fiber-optic cabling is allowing for longer cabling distance. The biggest negative is the expense, particularly for the equipment on the ends of the cable. Mainly because of these two competing, but important, features of fiber-optic cabling and optical transmission devices, standards bodies have defined two main branches of cabling and transmitters. For the cables, the two main categories are *multimode fiber* and *single-mode fiber*. For the transmitters, the main types are LEDs and lasers. Although not always true, generally speaking, the following are true:

> **Note**
>
> One notable exception to these general rules is Gigabit Ethernet, which does not use LEDs, it instead uses different types of lasers that vary in price and distance supported. See Chapter 7, "Ethernet Technologies," for more details.

- Less expensive LED transmitters are used with the relatively less expensive multimode cabling.

- More expensive laser transmitters are used with the more expensive single-mode cables.

- Single-mode cables, with laser transmitters, support significantly longer cabling distances than multimode using LEDs.

LEDs naturally emit light in many directions, while lasers emit light in a straight line. When networking devices use LEDs and fiber-optic cables, some of the light doesn't even make it into the cable. Other rays of light enter the cable at different angles, as shown in Figure 3-21.

The light rays that enter the multimode fiber can enter the core at different angles, as shown on the top of Figure 3-21. However, lasers can transmit the light down the center of the single-mode cable's core. Therefore, light can travel farther down a single-mode cable, supporting longer cabling distances.

Figure 3-21   Single-Mode Versus Multimode Fiber

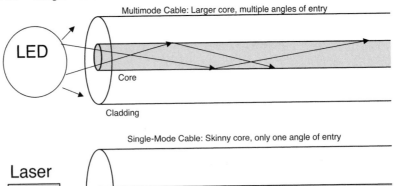

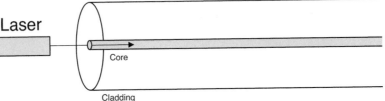

An analogy helps describe the light passing through a multimode cable. Imagine that you are at the mall with a friend. You want to go to the store at the other end of the mall, so you walk straight down the mall. Your friend likes to window-shop, so he walks to one side of the mall, then to the other, back and forth. As a result, you walk less distance and get to the store at the other end of the mall much faster than your friend, who walks a lot farther and takes more time. The light that keeps reflecting back and forth in a multimode fiber core takes a longer path, which requires more time, and more attenuation, than light that travels the center of the core.

Because multimode fiber allows light to enter the core at multiple angles, the core of a multimode cable must have a larger diameter than single-mode cables. Figure 3-22 shows a cross-section view of the four most common sizes of fiber-optic cables for networking. The cores are drawn to scale.

Figure 3-22   Comparing the Diameters of Fiber-Optic Cables

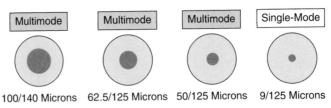

Wireless Media

Both electrical and fiber-optic transmissions require a cable. Electricity cannot simply pass through the air, so a conductor, such as a copper wire, is required. Infrared energy could pass through the air, but it doesn't go through solid materials well (things like walls, ceilings, and so on). So, fiber-optic cables act as a wave guide, which guides the infrared light to the other end of the cable, making fiber-optic transmissions possible.

The third major type of transmission media covered in this chapter is wireless transmission. Wireless transmission does not use a wire or cable of any kind; instead, it sends data through the air, or, more specifically, the space all around the computers and networking devices. Wireless communications use radio waves, which are just another frequency and wavelength of EM energy (refer to Figure 3-18). Although infrared waves or visible light waves cannot pass through solid materials well, radio waves can pass through some solid materials. Therefore, networking devices can send radio waves through space. Depending on the distances, volume of matter between the devices, and types of matter, the devices can communicate well.

This section covers the basics of wireless LAN (WLAN) communications. This chapter's "Additional Topics of Interest" section, which you can find on the CD-ROM, covers more of the technology details behind WLANs.

Enterprise WLAN Components and Design

To create a small enterprise's wired Ethernet LAN, you could use PCs with Ethernet NICs, and either a LAN hub or LAN switch. With today's enterprise WLANs, you need the following similar components:

- PCs with WLAN NICs
- Access points (APs), which act as a LAN hub for wireless devices

The PCs use their WLAN NICs to send and receive data with the wireless AP, which in turn allows communication with other devices. Figure 3-23 shows a Cisco Systems WLAN NIC on the left and an AP on the right.

Figure 3-23   Wireless NIC and AP

Of particular interest in Figure 3-23, notice the antennae that stick out of the NIC and AP. Just like radio stations use a large antenna to transmit music using radio waves, NICs and APs need antennae to transmit data using radio waves. Likewise, just like most car radios have antennae to receive the radio waves sent by the radio stations' antennae, the NIC and AP need antennae to receive the radio waves from other devices. For example, when the NIC needs to send data, it transmits radio waves, modulating the waves to imply 0s and 1s, by using an encoding scheme. The AP then receives the radio waves and interprets the received radio signal as 0s and 1s.

Note

The term *wired network* refers to any part of an internetwork that uses cables, regardless of whether the cables have copper wires or optical fibers in them. The term *wired* is used instead of *cabled* to contrast the terms *wired network* and *wireless network*.

From a design perspective, although WLANs provide the means for a device to send and receive without a cable, most of the servers with which it needs to communicate are on some wired network. Figure 3-24 shows a typical enterprise wireless design in *infrastructure mode*. In this mode, the LAN uses APs, with the PCs sending and receiving data to and from the AP. Figure 3-24 shows two APs that can then forward the traffic to and from the server farm in the wired part of the network.

Figure 3-24   Typical Enterprise WLAN Design

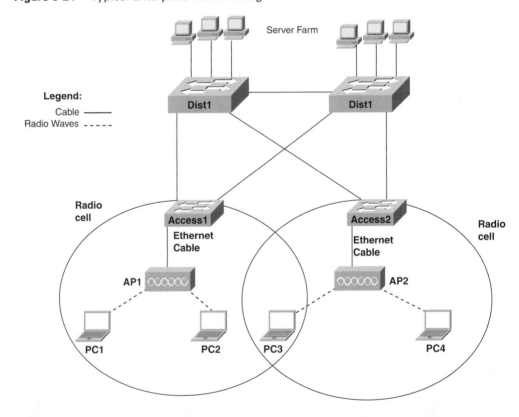

The circles represent each AP's radio *cell*, which is the range in which the APs can communicate with the wireless NICs. Depending on the structural composition of the location in which the AP is installed and the size and gain of the antennae, the size of the cell can range from a few dozen feet to 25 miles (around 40 kilometers). More commonly, the range is 300 to 500 feet (about 90 to 150 meters).

To install a WLAN that works with the existing LAN infrastructure, you need just a few components:

- At least one AP

- A straight-through cable to connect the AP to an existing LAN switch

- Wireless NICs in end-user devices so the devices can communicate with the APs

Most infrastructure WLAN designs use overlapping cells. (The online course suggests 20–30 percent overlap.) The overlapping cells each use slightly different frequencies, much like radio stations use slightly different frequencies. The overlapping cells have a few benefits. First, a mobile user can roam between the cells with only a brief interruption in WLAN connectivity (typically, less than a second). Additionally, devices in the overlapped cells (such as PC3 in Figure 3-24) can sense multiple APs and pick the best one based on the strength of the radio signal and the amount of radio noise.

Note

In Figure 3-24, the radio cells happen to cover the switches, but that's coincidental. LAN switches do not need to use wireless to send and receive data with the APs.

To choose which AP to use, a client needs to scan for the currently best AP and then *associate* with that AP. (The WLAN NIC typically considers the AP from which the NIC receives the strongest radio signal to be the currently best AP.) The scanning process can be either active or passive. *Active scanning* causes the wireless NIC to send a probe request. The probe request contains the *Service Set Identifier (SSID)* of the network the NIC wants to join. When an AP with the same SSID hears the probe, it responds, completing the association process.

NICs that use *passive scanning* do not initiate the scanning process by using probes. Instead, they passively listen for frames sent by the APs, called *beacon* management frames (beacons). When a NIC receives a beacon that contains the SSID of the network it wants to join, it attempts to associate with the AP.

Both active and passive scanning are a continuous process, which aids in the roaming process. The continual scanning allows a NIC to move around, automatically notice that it is in reach of another AP with better signal strength, and associate with that AP—all before getting out of the original AP's range. Nodes can associate or disassociate with APs as signal strength changes.

Besides the infrastructure WLANs discussed so far, any two wireless devices can form an ad-hoc WLAN network. To do so, the devices simply scan, find each other, and associate with each other. This allows easy and quick connects that allow the two devices to share data, but it is not secure.

WLAN Organization and Standards

Similar to wired Ethernet LANs, the IEEE also defines WLAN standards as part of its 802.11 committee. Similar to Ethernet LANs, several WLAN options exist at the physical layer, so the IEEE names the varying standards by placing a letter at the end of 802.11. Today, the most common standards are 802.11a, 802.11b, and 802.11g.

Radio waves, radio waves might interfere with other radio transmissions. Because of this potential interference, WLAN products must comply with governmental rules in the part of the world where the wireless devices are installed. For example, in the U.S., the *Federal Communications Commission (FCC)* sets standards for what radio frequencies can be used for WLANs, as well as restrictions on power. As you might imagine, not all countries agree on which wavelengths should be used for certain purposes, which makes it slightly more difficult to manufacture products for use in various parts of the world.

Note

802.11g is backward-compatible with 802.11b in part because of their use of the same frequency band.

Today, WLAN standards use two frequency bands: the 2.4-GHz band (802.11b and 802.11g) and the 5-GHz band (802.11a). The 2.4-GHz band is approved by almost every country for use by consumer electronic devices, including WLANs. These devices include many wireless phones that can be used in homes. The 802.11a standard uses the 5-GHz range, but the frequency band is not approved for use for WLANs in all countries, which makes worldwide acceptance of 802.11a more of a challenge.

Another important difference between the 802.11 standards relates to the rates of data transmission. For any WLAN cell, the devices all share the bandwidth. For example, in Figure 3-24, PC1, PC2, and AP1 share one cell, and PC3, PC4, and AP2 share another cell. Although the data rate might be one speed, the throughput—the amount of data that is actually transported over the cell—is typically much smaller. For example, 802.11b has a data rate of 11 Mbps but a throughput of around 2–4 Mbps.

Tip

WLAN devices can dynamically adjust to use slower data rates to ensure that the data is transmitted. Generally, the slower the data rate, the larger the cell. To get better reach in a single radio cell, lower the data rate.

Packet Tracer   Packet Tracer configuration NA01-0324 shows a simulation with wireless collisions. The configuration is similar to Figure 3-24.

Because each cell is shared, the devices must make an effort to give all devices a chance to send. 802.11 WLANs use a standard called *carrier sense multiple access with collision avoidance (CSMA/CA)*. The concept is similar to Ethernet's CSMA/CD, but the WLAN devices try to avoid collisions rather than detect them.

Another key difference between WLAN standards relates to the physical layer transmission standard. The original 802.11 standard defined two options:

Note

The details of how FHSS, DSSS, and OFDM work are beyond the scope of this course.

- Frequency Hopping Spread Spectrum (FHSS)

- *Direct Sequence Spread Spectrum (DSSS)*

Later standards used a new method called *Orthogonal Frequency Division Multiplexing (OFDM)*.

Table 3-5 lists the three commonly available options for 802.11 WLANs today.

Table 3-5   WLAN Standards

Standard	Spectrum Used	Maximum Data Rate	Physical Layer
802.11a	5 GHz	54 Mbps	OFDM
802.11b	2.4 GHz	11 Mbps	DSSS
802.11g	2.4 GHz	54 Mbps	OFDM

The Wi-Fi alliance (http://www.wi-fi.org) promotes many standards within the wireless arena. It also promotes the term *Wi-Fi* to refer to any of the IEEE 802.11 WLAN standards. Note that the online course defines this term to mean "DSSS systems that operate at 1, 2, 5.5, and 11 Mbps." Today, Wi-Fi more generally refers to all IEEE 802.11 standards.

Summary

Copper cable carries information using electrical current. The electrical specifications of a cable determine the kind of signal a particular cable can transmit, the speed at which the signal is transmitted, and the distance the signal travels.

When working with computer networks, an understanding of the following electrical concepts is helpful:

- **Voltage**—The pressure that moves electrons through a circuit from one place to another

- **Resistance**—Opposition to the flow of electrons, which is why a signal becomes degraded as it travels the conductor

- **Current**—Flow of charges created when electrons move

- **Circuits**—A closed loop through which an electrical current flows

Circuits must be composed of conducting materials and must have sources of voltage. Voltage causes current to flow, while resistance and impedance oppose it. A multimeter measures voltage, current, resistance, and other electrical quantities expressed in numeric form.

Different LAN standards define the use of coaxial cable, UTP cable, and STP cable, with UTP being most commonly used today. Twisted-pair cables often use RJ-45 connectors, with the wires using different pinouts depending on how the cable will be used. A straight-through cable pinout works when connecting unlike devices, such as a switch and a PC. A crossover cable pinout works when connecting similar devices, such as two switches. A rollover cable pinout works for connecting a PC to the console port of a router. Different pinouts are required because the transmit and receive pins are in different locations on each of these devices.

Optical fiber is the most frequently used medium for the longer, high-bandwidth, point-to-point transmissions required on LAN backbones and WANs. Networking devices send light energy over the optical cables to securely transmit large amounts of data over relatively long distances. An optical transmitter sends the light down the core of the cable with an optical receiver converting the light that arrives at the far end of the cable back to the original electrical signal. Optical transmissions typically use two cables—one for each direction.

Optical cables consist of five main parts. The light shines down the center of the cable, which is called the core. The cladding surrounds the core to reflect as much light as possible back into the core. A buffer surrounds the cladding to provide protection and strength. Outside of the buffer is an aramid yarn, which is typically made from Kevlar, for protection and to prevent the fiber cable from stretching when installers pull it. The final element is the outer jacket, which surrounds the cable to protect the fiber from abrasion, solvents, and other contaminants.

The laws of reflection and refraction are used to design fiber media that guides the light waves through the fiber with minimum energy and signal loss. After the rays enter the fiber's core, a light ray can follow only a limited number of optical paths through the fiber. These optical paths are called modes. If the diameter of the fiber's core is large enough that light can take many paths through the fiber, the fiber is called multimode fiber. Single-mode fiber has a much smaller core that allows only light rays to travel along one mode inside the fiber. Because of its design, single-mode fiber is capable of higher rates of data transmission and greater cable-run distances than multimode fiber.

A wireless network can consist of as few as two devices, with two PCs using their wireless NICs to form a small ad-hoc wireless network. Alternatively, an infrastructure mode topology can be set up by using an AP to act as a central hub for the WLAN.

Several IEEE 802.11 standards exist for wireless LANs. Of these, 802.11a and 802.11g use a 54 Mbps data rate, with 802.11b using an 11 Mbps data rate. IEEE 802.11a uses frequencies in the 5-GHz range, whereas 802.11b and 802.11g use the same 2.4-GHz frequency band.

Check Your Understanding

Complete all the review questions listed here to test your understanding of the topics and concepts in this chapter. Answers are listed in Appendix A, "Answers to Check Your Understanding and Challenge Questions."

1. Match the name of the type of matter with its property:

1. Conductor	A. Electrical flow is easily controlled.
2. Semiconductor	B. It's difficult for electrical current to flow.
3. Insulator	C. Electrical current flows easily.

   A. 1-C, 2-B, 3-A
   B. 1-A, 2-C, 3-B
   C. 1-B, 2-C, 3-A
   D. 1-C, 2-A, 3-B

2. What is attenuation as it relates to copper cabling?

   A. The increase in noise caused by outside interference, such as light fixtures or electric motors
   B. The weakening of a data signal caused by cable resistance and interference
   C. The force that causes like-charged objects to repel
   D. The decrease in a signal caused by decreased impedance

3. Match the following to their respective units of measure:

1. Voltage	A. Ohm
2. Current	B. Ampere
3. Resistance	C. Volt

   A. 1-C, 2-B, 3-A
   B. 1-B, 2-C, 3-A
   C. 1-A, 2-C, 3-B
   D. 1-C, 2-A, 3-B

4. Electrons flow in _____ loops called _____.

   A. open; voltage
   B. closed; voltage
   C. open; circuits
   D. closed; circuits

5. What is the maximum cable length for Ethernet over UTP?

   A. 185 meters

   B. 500 meters

   C. 10 meters

   D. 100 meters

6. How many pairs of wires are used in the TIA-EIA-568-B wiring standard?

   A. Two

   B. Four

   C. Six

   D. Eight

7. Category 5 and Category 6 UTP typically use which type of connector?

   A. STP

   B. BNC

   C. RJ-45

   D. RJ-11

8. What advantage does coaxial cable have over STP or UTP?

   A. Coaxial cable is capable of achieving 10 to 100 Mbps.

   B. Coaxial cable is inexpensive.

   C. Coaxial cable can run for a longer distance before a repeater must be installed.

   D. Coaxial cable takes less space to install.

9. What does twisting the wires do in a twisted-pair cable?

   A. It makes it thinner.

   B. It makes it less expensive.

   C. It reduces noise problems through the cancellation effect.

   D. It allows six pairs to fit in the space of four pairs.

10. What is the importance of the TIA/EIA standards?

   A. They provide a framework for the implementation of the OSI reference model.

   B. They provide guidelines for manufacturers to follow to enhance proprietary standards.

   C. They recommend UTP cable as the preferred medium for long runs between buildings.

   D. They provide guidelines used for LAN cabling, such as the 568-B standard.

11. How many fiber-optic strands are used in a full-duplex connection between two networking devices?

   A. One strand receives and transmits simultaneously.

   B. Two strands connect the two devices, one for sending in each direction.

   C. Four strands are used to achieve full duplex.

   D. Eight strands are used, which is similar to UTP using eight wires.

12. What is one advantage of using fiber-optic cable in networks?

   A. Fiber-optic cable is inexpensive.

   B. Fiber-optic cable is easy to install.

   C. Fiber-optic cable is an industry standard and is available at any electronics store.

   D. Fiber-optic cable is not susceptible to electromagnetic interference (EMI).

Challenge Questions and Activities

The questions and activities in this section require a deeper application of the concepts covered in this chapter. The questions listed here are similar in both difficulty and style to what you might see on a CCNA certification exam, whereas the activities are similar to the exams only in that they require applying detailed concepts to a particular scenario.

Use the following figure for the challenge question and Packet Tracer activity in this section.

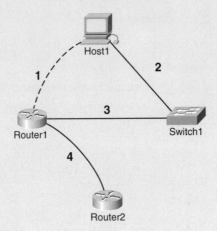

The following list describes the connections shown in the figure:

1. Serial port on Host1 to console port on Router1

2. Ethernet port on Switch1 to Ethernet port on Host1

3. Ethernet port on Router1 to Ethernet port on Switch1

4. Ethernet port on Router 1 to Ethernet port on Router2

1. Select the option that lists in order the cable type used for the numbered connections in this figure:

A. Rollover, straight-through, rollover, crossover

B. Crossover, straight-through, straight-through, rollover

C. Crossover, straight-through, straight-through, rollover

D. Rollover, straight-through, straight-through, crossover

Packet Tracer

Activity 3-1: Use the figure to create a Packet Tracer design by following these steps:

Step 1. Open Packet Tracer and select **Options** on the menu bar. Make sure that Simple Mode does not have a check mark beside it.

Step 2. Drag and drop two routers, a switch, and a PC to the drawing space. Arrange them as shown in the figure in the preceding challenge problem.

Step 3. Click the **Connect** icon. Select **Console** as the cable type. Then, select the PC and the **RS232** connection. Select the first router and choose the console connection.

Step 4. Click the **Connect** icon again. This time, use a copper straight-through connection from the first router to the switch, using the first copper Ethernet port on each end.

Step 5. Make a copper connection from the switch to the PC by using any available switch port.

Step 6. Make a connection from the first router to the second router by using a FastEthernet connection over copper. This is a crossover connection.

If all the connections are correctly configured, a green dot appears at each end of the cable.

For an additional challenge, follow these steps:

Step 1. Add IP addresses and establish connectivity from the PC to the second router. To do this, choose the **Options** pull-down menu and turn on Simple Mode.

Step 2. Click the first router and then select port 0/0. Give it an IP address of 192.168.1.1 and a subnet mask of 255.255.255.0. Then, click port 1/0. Give it an IP address of 192.168.2.1 and a subnet mask of 255.255.255.0.

Step 3. Click the second router. Click the port that has the green light. Give it an IP address of 192.168.2.2 and a subnet mask of 255.255.255.0.

Step 4. Click the PC. Set its default gateway to 192.168.1.1. Set its IP address to 192.168.1.2 and the subnet mask to 255.255.255.0.

Step 5. Now, the fun part! Select the **Realtime** tab at the top of the screen. Click the **Ping** button near the top left. Click the PC and then click the second (farthest away) router. The ping should be successful.

CHAPTER 4

Cable Testing

Objectives

Upon completion of this chapter, you should be able to answer the following questions:

- What terms (and their definitions) are used to describe waves?

- What are the differences between sine waves and square waves?

- What type of wave is a typical data signal?

- What effects do attenuation and impedance mismatch have on signal strength?

- How does the use of twisted copper wire pairs reduce noise?

- What is insertion loss?

- How do EMI and RFI affect fiber-optic and copper cabling?

- What are the three types of crosstalk?

- Why is a larger number of decibels (–30 dB) better than a smaller number (–10 dB) when measuring NEXT?

- What are the ten primary cable-testing parameters used to meet the TIA/EIA standards?

- What types of wiring faults can a wire-map test detect?

Additional Topics of Interest

Several chapters of this book contain additional coverage of previous topics or related topics that are secondary to the chapter's main goals. You can find the additional coverage on the CD-ROM accompanying this book. For this chapter, the following additional topics are covered:

- Exponents and logarithms

- Decibels

- Viewing signals in time and frequency

- Noise in time and frequency

- Bandwidth

- Other crosstalk testing parameters

- Time-based parameters

- Testing optical fiber

- A new standard: Category 6 UTP

Key Terms

This chapter uses the following key terms. You can find the definitions in the Glossary.

amplitude   page 167

frequency   page 167

period   page 167

square waves   page 168

analog signals   page 169

digital signals   page 169

insertion loss   page 176

noise   page 176

crosstalk   page 176

near-end crosstalk (NEXT)   page 178

far-end crosstalk (FEXT)   page 179

power sum near-end crosstalk (PSNEXT)   page 179

wire map   page 180

reversed-pair fault   page 181

split-pair wiring fault   page 182

transposed-pair wiring fault   page 182

This chapter covers several topics related to the testing of cables. The first section reviews important copper-cabling concepts and then provides more detail about the physics behind transmitting electrical signals over copper cabling. The second section discusses different factors, including noise and environment, that may negatively impact a cable's ability to pass a proper transmission signal. It also describes the cabling tests that you can use to identify such problems.

Frequency-Based Cable Testing

The electrical signals sent over networking cables operate at a predefined set of frequencies. The frequency, along with other characteristics, can be changed to send binary 0s and 1s. To test cables, cable-testing equipment sends electrical signals like those sent by the actual network devices, checking for common problems and noise.

To understand how the devices used for cable testing work, you need a little more information about the characteristics of electrical signals as they pass over the transmission medium. This section provides that additional information.

Waves

Energy, including electrical current, light, and radio signals, travels in waves. All these types of waves can be described with the same set of terms:

- *Amplitude*—The height of the wave, as measured in various units, including volts, power, and meters.

- *Frequency*—The number of new waves that arrive in 1 second, as measured in hertz

- *Period*—The amount of time between each wave, measured in seconds

Although few people sit at the beach measuring ocean waves, ocean waves have the same general attributes as waves of electrical energy. A calm ocean might have waves of only a foot or so in height (amplitude), whereas waves at Hawaii's North Shore might be 30 to 40 feet in height. Ocean waves may hit the shore more frequently during an incoming tide amidst a storm, and less frequently on a clear day when the tide is going out. A higher frequency also means that less time passes between waves, which means a shorter period.

Like ocean waves, electrical signals also have an amplitude, frequency, and period. The amplitude represents the voltage level. An AC voltage, frequently used in networking, continually varies from positive to negative and back again. As a result, the graph of the voltage over time shows a wave. The number of times a complete wave occurs in a second is called the frequency of the wave—just like with ocean waves.

Figure 4-1 shows a representation of the concepts of amplitude and period, with the frequency being 1/period.

Figure 4-1   Amplitude, Frequency, and Period

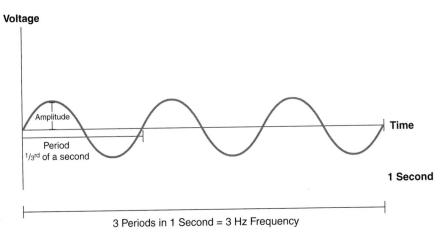

3 Periods in 1 Second = 3 Hz Frequency

Sine Waves and Square Waves

Sine waves, or sinusoids, are graphs of mathematical functions that have specific characteristics:

- **Periodic**—They repeat the same pattern at regular intervals.

- **Continuously varying**—No two adjacent points on the graph have the same y-axis or x-axis value.

Sine waves can be used to represent the behavior of many naturally occurring events and many man-made events. The graph can represent many different types of information on the y-axis, with the x-axis representing time. Anything whose value varies periodically over time can be shown as a sine wave. For example, the distance from the Earth to the sun varies as the Earth completes its yearly rotation, so a graph of the distance between the Earth and the sun, graphed over a year, is a sine wave. Also, when you ride a Ferris wheel, the distance between you and the ground varies over time, again being a sine wave. Likewise, the time of day that the sun rises, which changes slightly every day, can be graphed as a sine wave. More importantly for the course, sine waves can be used to represent an electrical, optical, or radio wave.

Networking devices typically use *square waves* instead of sine waves when transmitting data. Square waves are periodic, but their value does not change continuously over time, so a graph representing these waves shows right angles. A square wave's y-axis value—the amplitude— typically stays constant for a time period and then changes (almost) instantly to some other value. Figure 4-2 shows a sample square wave.

Figure 4-2   Digital Signals

Note

The term *pulse* is often used to refer to a single one of the rectangles in Figure 4-2.

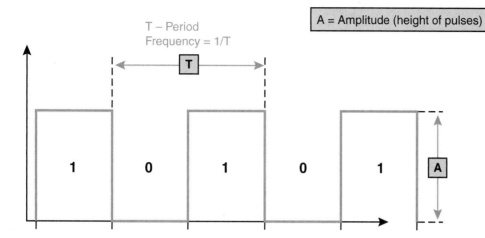

Square waves, like all waves, can be described in terms of amplitude, period, and frequency. Because square waves have a discrete value for some period of time, rather than changing continuously, they can be conveniently used for sending binary 0s and 1s. For example, Figure 4-2 implies a simple scheme in which a binary 1 could be represented by a high amplitude and a binary 0 could be represented by a low amplitude. The receiver simply would need to sample the incoming electrical signal and look at the voltage (amplitude) to decide if it is high (1) or low (0).

Analog and Digital Signals

Sine waves are called analog waves, or *analog signals*, because they are analogous to many naturally occurring phenomena. Square waves are called digital waves, or *digital signals*, because their primary purpose is to represent binary digits. As it turns out, digital signals can be created by creating a complex set of analog signals at the same time. This section provides a bit of background on the analog signals, and then it explains the concept of how to build a digital signal.

Simple and Complex Analog Signals

You can better appreciate electrical waves and their complexity by thinking about sound waves as well. Sound waves are also analog (sine) waves. As such, analog electrical signals can be used to represent sound waves. For example, a microphone takes the analog sound waves from the air and converts those waves into the equivalent analog electrical wave. Speakers receive the electrical analog wave over a cable and convert the electrical wave back to the equivalent sound waves.

First, consider a single-frequency sound wave, whose frequency can be detected by the human ear. For example, suppose a pianist plays middle C on a piano and a microphone picks up the sound. When the microphone converts the sound to electricity and sends it over a cable to a speaker, the speaker plays a single tone or sound. Using a tool such as an oscilloscope or spectrum analyzer, the electricity that represents the tone could be graphed, and it would look like a sine wave.

Next, consider someone playing a simple song on that same piano, with the microphone picking up the sound and playing it out the speaker. The human hears several tones, and the waves used to represent this sound are more complex than when the pianist simply plays middle C by itself. An oscilloscope or spectrum analyzer could graph each of the separate sine waves, one for each frequency.

Finally, imagine a sound system at a rock concert. The range of different sounds is enormous, and an oscilloscope would graph countless different individual sine waves.

Creating Digital Signals from Analog Signals

The complex sets of sounds described in the previous section—whether they were from a piano or a rock band—are sent over an electrical cable as one complex electrical signal. To test copper cables used for networking, testing tools can send a single waveform or multiple analog waveforms. The testing device can send multiple well-chosen waveforms that, when added together to form a more complex electrical signal, happen to closely approximate a square wave. Figure 4-3, which is a derivation of a figure from the course, represents the idea.

Figure 4-3   Adding Analog Waves to Approximate a Digital Test

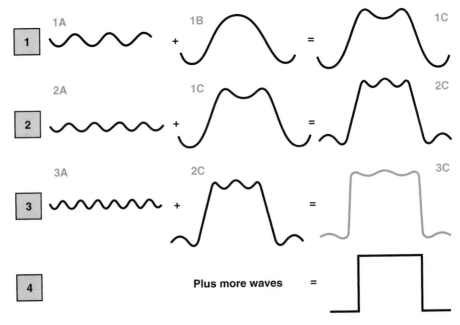

Figure 4-3 shows a progression by which sending two signals makes the resulting signal look more similar to a square wave; adding a third signal can make the resulting complex signal look even more like a square wave; and so on. The following list describes the corresponding four numbered rows in Figure 4-3:

1. The first two waves, labeled 1A and 1B, when sent over the wire, result in the waveform shown as 1C.

2. This row shows a third wave (2A) being added to the complex wave (1C) from the first row. The resulting waveform (2C) looks more similar to a square waveform.

3. This row shows a fourth wave (3A) being added to the complex wave (2C) from the second row. The resulting waveform (3C) looks even more like a square waveform.

4. The last step shows the eventual complex wave, which is a square wave, created by sending the right combination of analog signals.

By adding the right combination of analog waves, the testing gear can closely approximate a digital signal over the wire. This gives the testing tools a great deal of flexibility in how they test networking cables because the tools can easily change the combination of analog waves and approximate most any digital segment for testing purposes.

Now that the details of waves, waveforms, sine waves, and square waves are all fresh in your mind, the next section examines the signals that should go over the wires, the noise that can get in the way, and how cable testing can be used to minimize the problems.

Signals and Noise

Networking devices and network interface cards (NICs) send electrical and light energy over a cable to send bits to one another. Many factors can cause problems with the transmitted signal. Noise, which refers to any interference on the physical medium that makes it difficult for the receiver to detect the data signal, is one such factor. Copper cabling is relatively susceptible to many sources of noise, whereas optical cabling experiences very few effects from noise. Some level of noise on the medium is inevitable, but the noise level must be kept as low as possible to ensure good network performance. Just as it is difficult to carry on a conversation with someone when there is a lot of background noise, data signals may be difficult to understand when a lot of electrical noise exists.

In addition to noise, other factors that can cause the transmitted signal to degrade include the length of the cable, whether the proper grade of cabling is used, the quality of the installation of the connectors on the ends of the cable, and the speed of the LAN.

This section begins by looking at some of basic causes of signal interference. Following that, the text looks at noise, its sources, and how you can test cables to determine if too much noise is occurring.

Signaling over Copper and Fiber-Optic Cabling

Even without an unusual amount of noise, the electrical transmission of data faces many different kinds of possible problems. For example, one key to good network performance is to make sure the devices on either end of the cable have been electrically grounded. Why? Networking devices transmit bits on copper cable by varying the voltage. Voltage is a measurement of the *difference* in EMF between two points. So, the voltage level of a signal sent by one networking device is the difference in voltage between ground and the electricity sent over the wire. Similarly, when receiving a signal, and measuring the voltage, a device compares the incoming signal's voltage to ground. Thus, two networking devices need to use the same electrical ground so that they have the same reference point from which they measure the voltage on the wire.

Attenuation is another potential problem for both electrical and optical transmissions to overcome. Attenuation occurs any time an electrical signal crosses a copper cable, but too much attenuation makes the signal become unintelligible. LAN devices may represent binary 0s and 1s as differing voltage (amplitude) levels. Attenuation decreases the amplitude of a signal. As a result, the receiver may not be able to determine whether the transmitter sent a binary 0 or 1. Similarly, optical attenuation occurs as the power of the light decreases as it goes over the fiber-optic cabling.

Note

In the typical three-prong electrical plugs used with computing equipment, one of the prongs connects to electrical ground.

Finally, the faster the LAN, the less room for error. With the advancement to higher and higher bandwidths on LANs, the duration of time for which an electrical signal represents the next bit is very small. For example, at 10 Mbps, the electrical signal that represents a single bit is on the wire for 1/10,000,000 of 1 second. At 100 Mbps, that same bit would be on the wire for only 1/100,000,000 of 1 second. At 1 Gbps, it is even less time. These advances in speed make the receiver's job much more difficult, so the cable must be able to pass the signal with very little attenuation or degradation. One of the keys to dealing with this challenge of higher speeds is to ensure that new cable installations use the best available Category 5e or 6 UTP cables, with properly installed connectors on the ends of the cables.

The next two sections take a brief look at copper and optical cabling and how they deal with noise and interference.

Copper Cabling Transmission Basics

As covered in Chapter 3, "Networking Media," the copper wires used by networking devices sit inside either a shielded cable or an unshielded cable. Shielded cables protect a wire from noise outside the cable and, in some cases, from interference from other wires inside the cable.

Coaxial cable was one of the earliest forms of LAN cabling, although it is seldom used today. Coaxial cable consists of a solid copper wire in the center to conduct electricity and additional layers to provide strength and shielding. Around the copper wire is an insulating material, which is in turn surrounded by a braided conductive shielding. In LAN applications, the braided shielding is electrically grounded, protecting the inner conductor from external electrical noise. The shielding also helps eliminate signal loss by keeping the transmitted signal confined to the cable, which helps make coaxial cable less "noisy" than twisted pair. Coaxial cable is also more expensive. The need to ground the shielding and the bulky size of coaxial cable also make it more difficult to install than other types of copper cabling. Figure 4-4 shows the structure of a coaxial cable.

Figure 4-4   Coaxial Cable

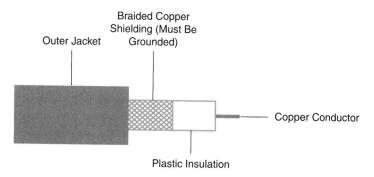

Shielded twisted-pair (STP) cable, as expected, also includes shielding, whereas unshielded twisted-pair (UTP) does not. STP provides three primary methods to maintain signal quality and reduce the effects of noise:

- The outer conductive shield protects the wires inside the cable from noise outside the cable. The outer shield must be electrically grounded.

- The inner foil pair shields protect each wire pair from noise generated by the other pairs.

- The twisting of the wire pairs combats several kinds of crosstalk, which is covered in more detail in the section "Sources of Noise on Copper Media."

Figure 4-5 shows an STP cable with its shielding.

Figure 4-5   Shielded Twisted-Pair Cable

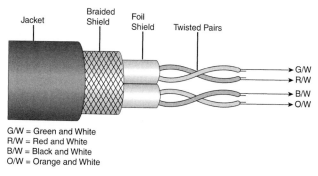

UTP contains no shielding and is the noisiest copper cabling, but it is the most frequently used because it is inexpensive and easier to install. Because UTP does not have shielding, the cable itself does not require grounding, making the process of adding connectors less difficult. However, a UTP cable's only real protection against noise is the twisting together of the pairs (see Figure 4-6), with more twists causing less interference.

Note

The term electromagnetic
interference (EMI) refers to
all energy that interferes with
the energy signal sent over
a transmission medium.

Figure 4-6   Unshielded Twisted-Pair Cable

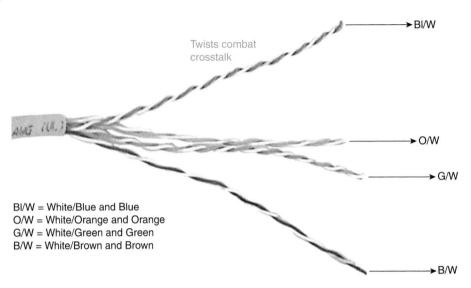

Bl/W = White/Blue and Blue
O/W = White/Orange and Orange
G/W = White/Green and Green
B/W = White/Brown and Brown

Note

One reason fiber-optic cables
support longer distances is
that the light attenuates less
than comparable electrical
signals, and the cable is
much less susceptible to
noise.

Optical Cabling Transmission Basics

Networking devices transmit light over fiber-optic cables, increasing and decreasing the intensity of light to represent binary 1s and 0s. The light passes through the core, with the cladding reflecting the light back into the core, which helps prevent attenuation of the light. The buffer prevents light from outside the cable entering the core. Also, the cable has no electrical component and no electrical signals, so it is totally immune to electrical noise. Figure 4-7 shows the components of a fiber-optic cable.

Figure 4-7   Fiber-Optic Cable Components

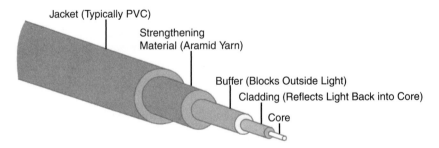

Optical transmission has many advantages over electrical transmissions over a copper cable. Light in an optical cable does not attenuate as quickly as an electrical signal on a copper wire, particularly when a laser is used to generate the light. Also, because optical cable does not have any electrical components, the cable does not have to be grounded. This makes optical cabling a good choice for links between buildings, because electrical ground may be different in the different buildings. Also, optical cabling is not susceptible to the effects of electromagnetic interference (EMI). With all of these advantages, optical cables could become even more popular in LAN environments, particularly if cabling and equipment prices decrease.

Attenuation and Insertion Loss on Copper Media

Attenuation in an electrical signal is simply a decrease in voltage as the signal crosses the wire. Even in a perfectly installed network, with all the best cables, connectors, and equipment, some attenuation will occur. In fact, LAN standards define maximum cable lengths in part because of attenuation of the signal. Graphically, an attenuated signal simply has a smaller amplitude, as shown in Figure 4-8.

Figure 4-8   Attenuation

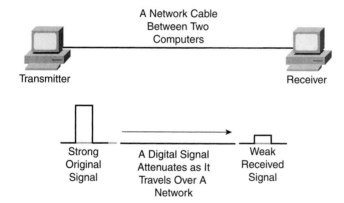

Attenuation is expressed in decibels (dB) using negative numbers. For example, –1 dB means the signal is down 1 dB, and –2 dB means the signal is down 2 dB. A "smaller" negative decibel value of –1 dB means less attenuation has occurred as compared with –2 dB. Note that "smaller" in this context refers to the absolute value of decibels; of course, –1 is actually greater than –2.

Attenuation can be caused by several factors:

- The resistance of the copper cable converts some of the signal's electrical energy to heat.

- Impedance in general, which can also be increased significantly by using defective connectors.

- Electrical energy is also lost when it leaks through the cable's insulation.

- The frequency of the signal, with higher frequencies attenuating more than lower frequencies.

Note

All of these causes of attenuation get worse with longer and longer cables. For example, more electricity is converted to heat in a longer cable than in a shorter cable.

The first two points in the list refer to the cable's electrical resistance and impedance. The term impedance refers to several electrical phenomena that resist the flow of electricity in an AC circuit—namely, resistance, inductance, and capacitance. Impedance is measured as a number of ohms, with the normal impedance of a Category 5 cable at 100 ohms.

Although some attenuation occurs simply due to the nature of electrical transmission, poorly installed connectors can cause significantly more attenuation. A poorly installed connector may have a different impedance value than the cable—a condition called *impedance discontinuity* or *impedance mismatch*. An impedance discontinuity at the receiving connector causes some of the signal to be reflected back down the wire, as opposed to the signal continuing in the same direction—resulting in some attenuation.

Note

The term jitter refers to slightly different concepts in other parts of networking, particularly with Voice over IP (VoIP).

Badly installed connectors on both ends of the cable can also cause an effect called *jitter*. The reflected signals on each end can be reflected on the other end, causing a ping-pong effect, or echoes. These echoes strike the receiver at different intervals, making it difficult for the receiver to accurately detect data values on the signal.

The combination of the effects of signal attenuation and impedance discontinuities on a communications link is called *insertion loss*. Proper network operation depends on constant characteristic impedance in all cables and connectors, meaning that there are no impedance discontinuities. With properly installed cables and connectors, attenuation should occur only due to the normal effects of impedance, with good network performance.

Sources of Noise on Copper Media

The term *noise* refers to any electrical energy on the transmission medium, besides the transmitted signal, that makes it more difficult for a receiver to interpret the data sent by the transmitter. Many sources can cause noise—for example, motors or fluorescent lights near a cable may cause electrical noise. Noise may also be caused by poor installation of connectors. Finally, noise may be caused by an effect called *crosstalk*, which is explained in some detail in this section.

Crosstalk is noise created on one wire as a result of current flowing over a nearby wire. To appreciate how that happens, you need to know the following basic laws from physics:

■ An electrical current passing through a wire creates a magnetic field outside the wire.

■ A magnetic field passing through an electrical conductor creates an electrical current in that conductor.

So, when a networking device sends a current down a wire, the current creates a magnetic field outside the wire. The magnetic field goes through the other nearby wires, possibly creating an electrical current in those other wires—in other words, causing crosstalk. In fact, if other cables are nearby, the magnetic field could create an electrical current in the wires inside those other cables as well. (Causing crosstalk in a nearby cable is called *alien crosstalk*.)

The laws of physics cannot be changed. However, standards bodies consider the problem of crosstalk when they define standards, and cable installers can combat the crosstalk problem as well. For example, in environments with lots of electrical noise, STP cabling can be used instead of UTP, because the shielding in the STP cabling significantly reduces crosstalk. Standards bodies can also define the use of a twisted pair of wires, instead of not twisting the wires together, because a twisted pair of wires helps cancel out the crosstalk. Also, cable installers can test the cables to identify cables that are susceptible to crosstalk and identify the problem, whether it is a poor connector or some nearby source of magnetic energy.

Understanding why a twisted pair reduces crosstalk requires more knowledge of basic physics. Ampere's rule states that if you hold a cable or wire in your right hand so that your thumb points in the direction of current flow, your four fingers point in the direction of the induced magnetic field. (The magnetic field is circular around the wire that creates it.) By using a pair of wires, and sending the same amount of current on each wire—but in different directions—the magnetic fields mostly overlap, but with the magnetic fields pushing in opposite directions, canceling each other out. The twisting effect helps make the fields overlap more exactly, with a higher number of twists per meter making the fields overlap even more, canceling more of the crosstalk.

Cable installers can cause crosstalk by untwisting the wires too much when installing a connector on the end of a cable. Figure 4-9 shows an example of a poorly installed connector on the left, and a properly installed connector on the right. To ensure reliable LAN communications, the untwisting of wire pairs must be kept to an absolute minimum. Today, many cabling vendors sell tools that make adding connectors to UTP cabling relatively easy to do without untwisting the wires very much.

Figure 4-9   RJ-45 Connector Vulnerable to Crosstalk

Bad Connector. Wires are
untwisted for too great a length.

Good Connector. Wires are untwisted
only to the extent necessary
to attach the connector.

Cable-testing instruments measure crosstalk by first applying a test signal to one wire pair. The cable tester then measures the amplitude of the unwanted crosstalk signals induced on the other wire pairs in the cable. Also note that higher transmission frequencies cause more crosstalk, so the tests typically use the highest frequencies to ensure that the cable meets the highest part of the cabling standards.

Types of Crosstalk

There are many types of crosstalk. The three most common types, which are explained in more detail in this section, are the following:

- Near-end crosstalk (NEXT)

- Far-end crosstalk (FEXT)

- Power sum near-end crosstalk (PSNEXT)

When a current on a wire causes crosstalk in another wire, the induced electrical current always flows in the opposite direction. For example, Figure 4-10 shows an example of crosstalk, specifically *near-end crosstalk (NEXT)*. The figure shows the intentional current on the lower of the two pairs, with the current flowing to the right. The current induced due to crosstalk, labeled NEXT, flows right to left.

Figure 4-10   Near-end Crosstalk

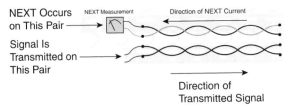

A cable-testing tool needs to be connected to only one end of the cable to be able to detect the amount of NEXT. The testing tool can transmit a test signal on one pair, and because the NEXT current comes back toward the testing device, the device can simply monitor the other wires. For example, in Figure 4-10, the testing tool could connect to the RJ-45 connector on the left, send an electrical signal on the lower pair, and measure the induced current on the upper pair. The amount of crosstalk is computed as the ratio in voltage amplitude between the test signal (on the lower pair in Figure 4-10) and the crosstalk-induced electrical signal on the other pair (the upper pair).

Tip

Traditionally, cable testers do not show the minus sign indicating the negative decibels for crosstalk measurements. So, you would interpret a reading of 30 versus 10 on a NEXT test to mean 30 is better than 10.

The amount of crosstalk is expressed as a negative value of decibels. As with attenuation, the words can get in the way, but a smaller number (a number with a higher absolute value) means less noise induced by crosstalk, and a larger number (a number with a lower absolute value) indicates more noise. For example, a NEXT reading of –30 dB, compared to a NEXT reading of –10 dB, means that the 30-dB test has less NEXT.

The TIA/EIA cabling standard requires that NEXT be measured from every pair to every other pair in a UTP link, and from both ends of the link. To shorten test times, some cable-testing instruments allow the user to test the NEXT performance of a link by using larger frequency step sizes than specified by the TIA/EIA standard. The resulting measurements might not comply with TIA/EIA-568-B and might overlook link faults. To verify proper link performance,

NEXT should be measured from both ends of the link with a high-quality testing instrument. This verification is also a requirement for complete compliance with high-speed cable specifications.

Although Figure 4-10 shows a basic example of NEXT, it does not specify what makes the crosstalk "near-end" versus "far-end." NEXT occurs when the crosstalk occurs near the source of the test signal—for instance, in Figure 4-10, NEXT would be crosstalk created near the left end of the cable. Crosstalk that occurs nearer to the other end of the cable from the transmitter is appropriately called *far-end crosstalk (FEXT)*. FEXT causes less noise than NEXT due to the following:

- The transmitted signal has attenuated by the time it reaches the other end of the wires, so the attenuated signal induces less current in the other wires.

- The induced FEXT has farther to travel to get back to the testing equipment, so the noise attenuates some as well.

Some types of Ethernet, particularly 10BASE-T and the huge installed based on 100BASE-T, use one pair of wires for transmitting data and one pair for receiving data. So, a cable test in which the testing equipment sends current down one pair, sensing NEXT on the other pair, is a good test. However, some later Ethernet standards, including 100BASE-T4 and 1000BASE-T (Gigabit Ethernet) transmit on all four wire pairs inside the cable. So, the traditional NEXT test does not properly test a cable's ability to support 100BASE-T4 and 1000BASE-T.

Note

With both NEXT and FEXT, the noise flows in a direction opposite to the test signal.

A test called *power sum near-end crosstalk (PSNEXT)*, shown in Figure 4-11, measures the cumulative effect of NEXT from all wire pairs in the cable. PSNEXT is not really a separate test; instead, it relies on the NEXT test. The testing device builds a PSNEXT test result of one pair by combining the NEXT results of sending a current down the other three pairs.

Figure 4-11   Power Sum Near-End Crosstalk (PSNEXT)

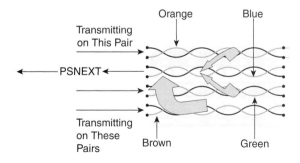

The combined effect of crosstalk from multiple simultaneous transmission sources can be detrimental to the signal. TIA/EIA-568-B certification now requires the PSNEXT test, in addition to other tests, as described in the next section.

Cable Testing Standards

The TIA/EIA-568-B standard specifies ten tests that a copper cable must pass if it is to be used for modern, high-speed Ethernet LANs. All cable links should be tested to the maximum rating that applies for the category of cable being installed. The following primary testing parameters must be verified for a cable link to meet TIA/EIA-568-B standards:

- **Wire map**—Tests cable pinouts.

- **Insertion loss**—Measures attenuation that occurs over the length of the cable.

- **NEXT**—Measures crosstalk that occurs on the end of the cable nearest to the transmitted signal.

- **PSNEXT**—A NEXT calculation that sums the NEXT on one pair when transmitting on all other pairs.

- **Equal-level far-end crosstalk (ELFEXT)**—A calculated value that provides a good number for comparing FEXT of different cables, regardless of their length.

- **Power sum equal-level far-end crosstalk (PSELFEXT)**—A calculation that combines ELFEXT when all wire pairs are used for simultaneous transmission.

- **Return loss**—A measurement of the loss of power in the signal (noise) reflected back to the transmitter.

- **Propagation delay**—The time required for the signal to pass from one end of the cable to the other.

- **Cable length**—A test that use Time Domain Reflectometer (TDR) to determine the length of the cable.

- **Delay skew**—A measurement of the difference in propagation delay over the fastest and slowest pairs in the cable.

This section does not cover the details of all of these tests, but it does introduce some of the concepts. This section focuses on the *wire-map* test, which tests the Ethernet cable pinouts described in Chapter 3. The Ethernet standard specifies that each of the pins on an RJ-45 connector has a particular purpose. For example, when connecting an Ethernet NIC to a switch, the cable should be a straight-through cable, which connects the wire at pin 1 on one end of the cable to pin 1 on the other end, pin 2 to pin 2, and so on.

To perform the wire map test, a testing device must be placed on both ends of the cable. Besides testing the pinouts, the testing device finds if an open circuit (a wire is broken or not attached properly to a connector) or short circuit (two wires are not protected by insulation and are touching) condition is present.

For reference, Figure 4-12 shows the wiring as defined by the TIA/EIA-568-A and TIA/EIA-568-B standards.

Figure 4-12   TIA/EIA-568-A and TIA/EIA-568-B Wire Pinouts

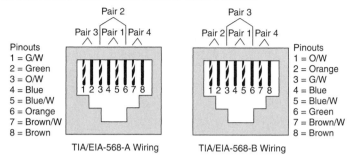

The wire map test can detect several different wiring faults, including the ***reversed-pair fault***, which occurs when the wires in a single pair have been reversed. For example, a straight-through cable calls for one pair to be connected to pins 1 and 2 on each end of the cable, but more specifically, the wire at pin 1 on one end must be connected to pin 1 at the other end, and the other wire in the pair must be connected to pin 2 at each end. If one of the wires is on pin 1 on one end and pin 2 on the other—and vice versa for the other wire in the same pair—the cable has a reversed-pair fault. Figure 4-13 shows this particular reversed-pair fault.

Figure 4-13   Reversed-Pair Wire Fault, Pins 1 and 2

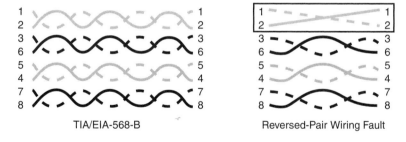

Figure 4-14 shows two other problems that can be identified with the wire map test. The wire map on the left shows an open condition, which means that a wire is not connected, and no current can flow. (Figure 4-14 shows the wire at pin 5 in an open state.) The wire map on the right shows a short, which in this case shows that the wires on pins 1 and 2 are touching and allowing current to pass between the wires. Both problems typically occur due to a faulty connector installation. The center wire map shows a wire map test that passes.

Two additional wire map tests identify the following common problems:

- Split-pair wiring fault

- Transposed-pair wiring fault

Note

Each of the three boxes in Figure 4-14 shows what the screen of the cable tester might look like when performing a wire-map test.

Figure 4-14   Cable Wire Map Problems

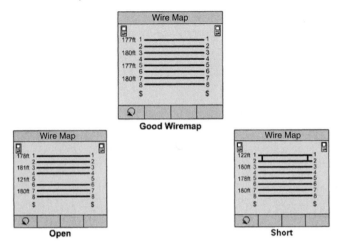

A *split-pair wiring fault* occurs when one wire from a pair is switched with one wire from a different pair at both ends. Look carefully at the pin numbers in Figure 4-15 to detect the wiring fault. A split-pair wiring fault means that the cable will be attempting to transmit data over wires that are not part of the same pair, so it will not work, and worse yet, it will cause unnecessary crosstalk.

A *transposed-pair wiring fault* occurs when a wire pair is connected to completely different pins at both ends. Of course, with a crossover cable, the cable purposefully transposes specific wire pairs. Better cable testers can detect valid crossover cable pinouts, which transpose pairs, as well as note when pairs are transposed in a way that does not match any useful cabling pinout. Some testers may incorrectly think that a valid crossover cable has a transposed-pair wiring fault because of the transposed wire pairs. Transposed pairs also occur when two different color codes on punch-down blocks (representing TIA/EIA-568-A and TIA/EIA-568-B) are used at different locations on the same link.

Figure 4-15 shows examples of split-pair and transposed-pair wiring faults.

Note

You can find more labs for this chapter in the "Additional Topics of Interest" section on the CD-ROM.

 Lab 4.2.9a   Fluke 620 Cable Tester: Wire Map

In this lab, you learn the wire-mapping features of a Fluke 620 LAN CableMeter or its equivalent.

Figure 4-15   Split-Pair and Transposed-Pair Wiring Faults

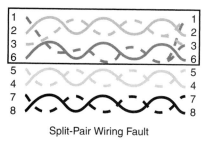

Split-Pair Wiring Fault

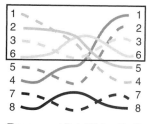

Transposed-Pair Wiring Fault

Summary

Text characters, words, pictures, video, or music can be represented as binary digits, or bits. These bits can be communicated over a network by using electrical voltage patterns on wires. The bits can also be converted to light waves or radio waves, and then back to voltage patterns.

The three main methods of transmitting data in a network are electricity, light, and radio. All three forms of energy flow in waves that are created by disturbances. All waves have similar attributes such as amplitude, (time) period, and frequency. Sine waves are periodic, continuously varying functions. Analog signals look like sine waves. Square waves are periodic functions whose values remain constant for a period of time and then change abruptly. Digital signals look like square waves.

Noise consists of the undesired signals in a communications system. Noise originates from other cables, radio frequency interference (RFI), and electromagnetic interference (EMI). On copper cable, the noise may interfere with the receiving device's ability to accurately interpret the received signal. Proper cable installation according to standards increases LAN reliability and performance.

Signal degradation occurs due to various factors, including attenuation, impedance mismatch, noise, and several types of crosstalk. Attenuation is the decrease in signal amplitude over the length of a link. Impedance is a measurement of resistance to the electrical signal. Cables and the connectors attached to the cables must have similar impedance values or else some of the signal may be reflected back from a connector. This is referred to as impedance mismatch or impedance discontinuity.

Crosstalk involves the transmission of signals from one wire to a nearby wire. There are three distinct types of crosstalk: near-end crosstalk (NEXT), far-end crosstalk (FEXT), and power sum near-end crosstalk (PSNEXT).

STP and UTP cable uses twisted pairs of wires to take advantage of the effects of crosstalk to minimize noise. Additionally, STP contains an outer conductive shield and inner foil shields that make it less susceptible to noise. Although UTP contains no shielding and is more susceptible to external noise, it is the most frequently used because it is inexpensive and easier to install.

Fiber-optic cable is used to transmit data signals by increasing and decreasing the intensity of light to represent binary 1s and 0s. The strength of a light signal does not attenuate as quickly as the strength of an electrical signal does over an identical-length cable. Optical signals are not affected by electrical noise, and optical fiber does not need to be grounded. Therefore, optical fiber is often used between buildings and between floors within a building.

The TIA/EIA-568-B standard specifies ten tests that a copper cable must pass to be used for modern, high-speed Ethernet LANs. Optical fiber must also be tested according to networking standards. Category 6 cable must meet more rigorous frequency testing standards than Category 5 cable.

You can find supplemental coverage of topics related to those described in this chapter on the CD-ROM in the "Additional Topics of Interest" section. The next chapter, covers more details about cabling LANs and WANs.

Check Your Understanding

Complete all the review questions listed here to test your understanding of the topics and concepts in this chapter. Answers are listed in Appendix A, "Answers to Check Your Understanding and Challenge Questions."

1. Which of the following is a characteristic of fiber-optic cable?

   A. It uses an intense incandescent light.

   B. Its core is made of highly reflective Kevlar.

   C. It relies on total internal cancellation to guide light for long distances.

   D. It is less susceptible to noise than other types of networking media.

2. Which of the following describes attenuation?

   A. A loss of signal strength

   B. An increase in signal amplitude

   C. The delay experienced during signal travel

   D. The time it takes a signal to reach its destination

3. Which of the following is a cause of crosstalk?

   A. Poorly terminated network cabling (wires untwisted too much)

   B. The loss of a signal's ground reference

   C. AC line noise coming from a nearby video monitor or hard disk drive

   D. FM radio signals, TV signals, various types of office equipment

4. Which of the following are tests specified by the TIA/EIA-568-B standard for copper cable? (Select three answers.)

   A. Signal harmonics

   B. Conductive response

   C. Wire map

   D. Signal absorption

   E. Insertion loss

   F. Propagation delay

5. What are three distinct kinds of crosstalk? (Select three answers.)

   A. NEXT

   B. FEXT

   C. ANEXT

   D. SPNEXT

   E. PSNEXT

6. What are two characteristics of sine waves? (Select two answers.)

    A. They have a y value that remains constant over time.

    B. They repeat the same pattern at regular intervals.

    C. They are continuously varying.

    D. They are generated by Ethernet NICs.

7. Which cable type is the cheapest to install?

    A. Coaxial

    B. Fiber-optic

    C. STP

    D. UTP

8. What can be discovered by using an Ethernet cable-testing device to do wire maps?

    A. Faulty serial circuits

    B. The location of a cabling run

    C. Information about the distance to a cabling fault

    D. Incorrect pinouts

9. Which standard specifies ten tests that copper cabling must pass to be used in a high-speed Ethernet LAN?

    A. IEEE 802.2B

    B. IEEE 802.3B

    C. IEEE-568-B

    D. TIA/EIA-568-B

10. Through wire testing, electrical interference and signal loss can be measured. Match the terms in the left column with the definitions in the right column.

Term	Definition
Near-end crosstalk	Decrease in signal amplitude over the length of a link
Far-end crosstalk	Crosstalk occurring farther away from the transmitter
Power sum near-end crosstalk	Measures the cumulative effect of NEXT
Attenuation	Crosstalk signal measured from the same end of the link
Insertion loss	Ensures that no open or short circuits exist in the cable
Wire map	Combination of impedance discontinuities on a communications link and signal attenuation

CHAPTER 5

Cabling LANs and WANs

Objectives

Upon completion of this chapter, you should be able to answer the following questions:

- What are the characteristics of Ethernet networks?

- What are the pinout requirements for straight-through, crossover, and rollover cables?

- What is a peer-to-peer network? How does it work?

- What are the functions, advantages, and disadvantages of client/server networks?

- What are the functions, advantages, and disadvantages of repeaters, hubs, bridges, switches, and wireless network components?

- What are the characteristics of router serial ports, their cables, and connectors?

- How are serial, ISDN, DSL, and cable modem WAN connections similar and different?

- How are DCE, DTE, and CSU/DSU devices connected in various WAN configurations?

Additional Topics of Interest

Several chapters contain additional coverage of previous topics or related topics that are secondary to the main goals of this chapter. You can find the additional coverage on the CD-ROM. For this chapter, the following additional topics are covered:

- Routers and ISDN BRI connections

- Routers and cable connections

- Routers and DSL connections

Key Terms

This chapter uses the following key terms. You can find the definitions in the Glossary:

end-user level page 191

workgroup level page 191

backbone level page 191

attachment user interface (AUI) page 195

Automatic Medium-independent Crossover (Auto-mdix) page 198

5-4-3 rule page 201

multiport repeaters page 202

concentrators page 202

electromagnetic (EM) page 209

infrared (IR) page 209

radio frequencies (RFs) page 209

spread spectrum page 210

access points (APs) page 210

client page 213

continues

continued

server   page 213

peer-to-peer model   page 213

client/server model   page 213

network operating system (NOS)   page 215

point-to-point WAN link   page 216

serial interface   page 217

serial cables   page 217

channel service unit/data service unit (CSU/DSU)
   page 218

telco   page 219

Integrated Services Digital Network (ISDN)   page 220

Basic Rate Interface (BRI)   page 220

B channels   page 220

D channel   page 220

cable modems   page 220

T/1 circuit   page 221

E/1 circuit   page 221

clocking   page 222

data communication equipment (DCE)   page 222

data terminal equipment (DTE)   page 222

HyperTerminal   page 226

auxiliary port (aux port)   page 227

Chapter 1, "Introduction to Networking," and Chapter 2, "Networking Fundamentals," provided an overview of networking. Chapter 3, "Networking Media," and Chapter 4, "Cable Testing," described many topics related to how bits can be transmitted over various cable types. These topics could easily be in a physics class. This chapter (and its corresponding course module) moves the course to more practical matters related to cabling. Although the details of the preceding chapters are important, they do not specifically tell you how to use cables to connect networking devices to create a network. This chapter focuses on how to connect local-area network (LAN) and wide-area network (WAN) devices. Along the way, the course includes several labs and, in most cases, you connect equipment in the classroom and make it work.

This chapter is separated into the two major categories of networks: LANs and WANs. Note that a few WAN topics are also included in the section "Additional Topics of Interest," which is available on the accompanying CD-ROM.

Cabling LANs

This section focuses on how to use cables to build a LAN. To create a LAN, cables must be used, but of course, they must be connected to something. So, the first part of this section focuses on the cables themselves, including explanations about how a network engineer chooses the correct cable type. This section then reviews the main devices used to build a LAN—repeaters, hubs, bridges, switches, and network interface cards (NICs)—and how those devices impact cable lengths and network installation. This section concludes by briefly comparing the two models of how PCs can use the LAN: peer-to-peer networking and client/server.

LAN Cabling Fundamentals

In this section, you'll learn about many aspects of LAN cabling, including the different LAN physical layer standards and the types of cables, connectors, and wiring pinouts used when connecting various devices. Before we get into the details, note that most network diagrams show Ethernet cables as a single ordinary straight line. In comparison, other LAN types, such as Token Ring and FDDI, are shown as circles, and WAN links are often shown as jagged lines, as shown in Figure 5-1.

Figure 5-1   Line Styles Used for Cables in Network Diagrams

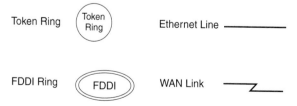

This section mainly focuses on unshielded twisted-pair (UTP) cabling because it is the most commonly used LAN cabling type. Unless otherwise stated, this chapter's figures use straight lines to specifically represent UTP cables.

Ethernet LAN Physical Layer

Each Ethernet LAN standard specifies the type of cabling required. For example, the earliest Ethernet standards used coaxial (coax) cabling, with today's standards using either twisted-pair (typically UTP) or fiber-optic cabling.

The IEEE separated Ethernet standards into IEEE 802.3 and IEEE 802.2. IEEE 802.2, which is called Logical Link Control (LLC), defines part of the OSI data link layer. The IEEE 802.3 standards define a part of the data link layer, which is called the Media Access Control (MAC) sublayer, plus all the physical details for each Ethernet type, including the cabling details. Figure 5-2 shows many of the Ethernet standards.

Figure 5-2   Comparing Popular Ethernet Standards to OSI

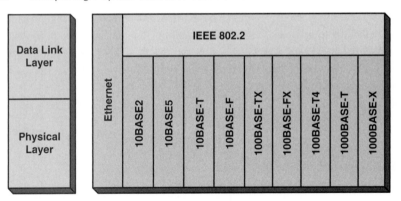

When building a LAN, a network engineer must pick the best type of cabling based on IEEE standards, such as the ones listed in Figure 5-2. For example, for a link between buildings, an engineer might choose to use a cable defined by the 1000BASE-X standard, which defines several options for Gigabit Ethernet using fiber-optic cables. When picking a cable type, the main considerations are as follows:

- Does the maximum allowed cable length meet the requirements for that cable segment?

- What is the cost of the cable?

- What is the cost of the equipment on the ends of the cable?

- Which cables support the different Ethernet speeds?

- How easy will it be to install the cable?

- How susceptible will the cable be to interference?

Although these points are important when selecting a cable type, one of the most important considerations is the speed of each Ethernet link, as described in the following section.

Choosing Ethernet Types (Speeds) in the Campus

Besides choosing the cable type, an engineer must consider the speed of the Ethernet types that are chosen for different parts of the LAN. During this process, an engineer must consider end users' needs and the connections between networking devices throughout the LAN and WAN. An engineer must also consider the type of equipment that is already installed and whether an increase in speed on some segments is worth the cost of buying new equipment.

For example, the vast majority of PCs that are already installed in networks today have 10/100 NICs, which means that the NICs can dynamically negotiate to use either 10BASE-T (10-Mbps) or 100BASE-TX (100-Mbps) Ethernet, each using the same UTP cable. So, a network engineer can easily pick UTP cabling and expect that the average end-user PC would use 10BASE-T or 100BASE-TX, with the vast majority autonegotiating to use 100BASE-TX Fast Ethernet. (The process of automatically negotiating the speed of the Ethernet link, as well as the duplex setting on the link, is called Ethernet autonegotiation.) However, today's newer PCs come with either a 1000BASE-T NIC or a 10/100/1000 autonegotiating NIC that runs at any of these three speeds. So, a network engineer whose network is installing many new PCs with 10/100/1000 autonegotiating NICs must then also consider whether it is worth the money to upgrade the LAN switches to support 1000-Mbps (1-Gbps) Ethernet.

The online course defines three terms that characterize the ways in which Ethernet links (cables) are used. Depending on the type, the course suggests the Ethernet speed used for each type of link. The terms are as follows:

- *End-user level*—Links (Ethernet cables) between a hub/switch and the end-user device (typically, a PC).

- *Workgroup level*—Links between the hub/switch that attach to end users' computers and other hubs/switches in the LAN core.

- *Backbone level*—Links between the hubs/switches in the LAN core. These switches do not have links to end-user devices; they connect only hubs/switches.

Figure 5-3 shows a sample campus LAN with these terms shown on the figure's left.

Table 5-1 lists the current online curriculum's point of view about the use of various Ethernet speeds and types on the three general link types.

Figure 5-3   Campus LAN with Online Curriculum's LAN Level Terms

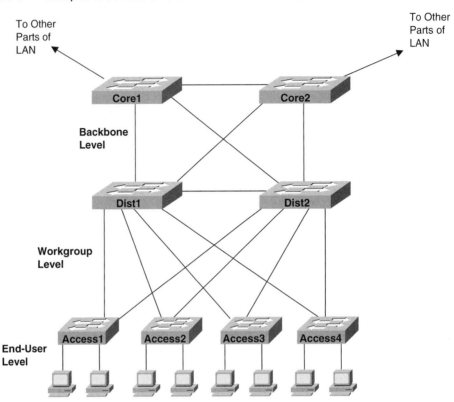

Table 5-1   Ethernet Types and Speeds Used on Various Link Types

Level	Is 10BASE-T Used?	Is 100BASE-TX Used?	Is 1000BASE-T Used?
End user	Yes	Yes	No
Workgroup	Yes, but not typically	Yes, typically	Seldom, for high-speed workgroups
Backbone	No	Yes, for lower traffic volumes	Yes, typically

Of course, it is useful to know what the course says are good practices, such as the information shown in Table 5-1. However, the problem with the information in any book or course about "what is typical"—particularly with Ethernet—is that the information changes over the years. In the past, 10-Mbps Ethernet links to each end-user PC were considered extremely fast, whereas in today's corporate world, most every PC uses 100 Mbps. In Table 5-1, 100 Mbps is suggested for typical workgroup links and 1-Gbps links for high-speed workgroups. However, reality has passed by that recommendation; 1-Gbps links are commonly used between workgroup switches and core switches. Also, most backbone links are multiples of 1 Gbps, with 10-Gbps Ethernet finally becoming more commonplace for backbone links in medium-to-large campus LANs. So, whenever you see recommendations like those shown in Table 5-1, keep in mind that, as with any networking technology, history shows that the speeds increase over time.

When discussing Ethernet speeds for various link types, you must be familiar with a few related terms. Cisco Systems publishes design recommendations for various networks, including campus LANs. These design recommendations use the terms shown in Figure 5-4.

Figure 5-4   Common Cisco LAN Design Terminology

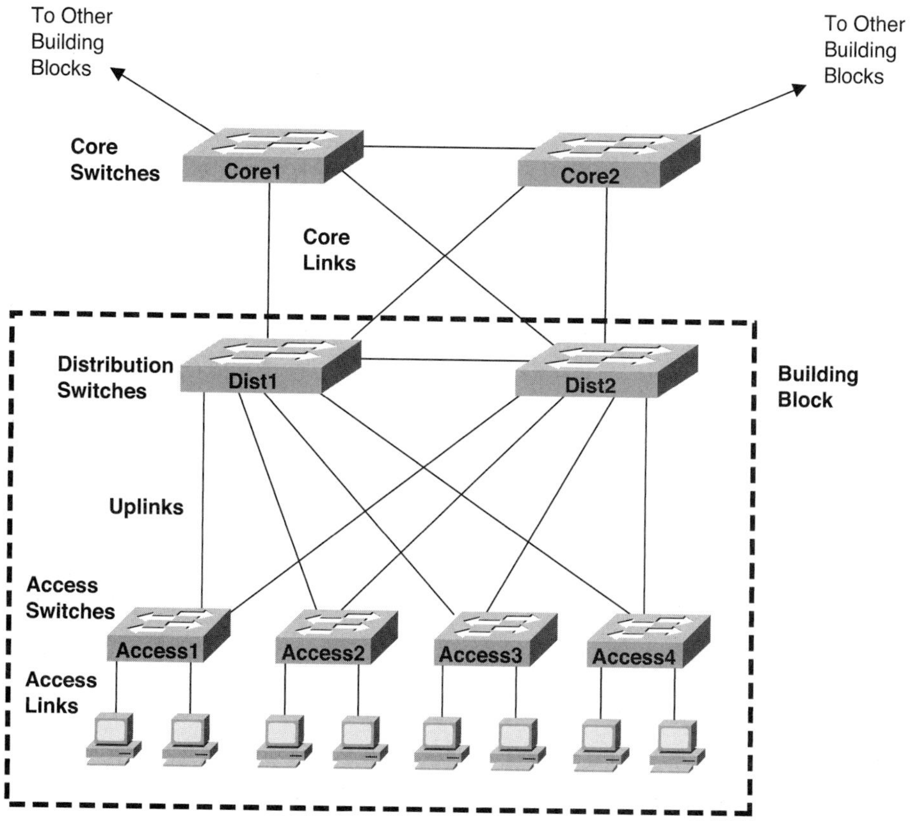

Cisco suggests the best way to build different types of networks, calling those suggestions "best practices." The components of the campus design model are as follows:

- **Access switches and links**—End-user devices connect to LAN switches, called access switches, with the Ethernet links called access links.

- **Distribution switches and uplinks**—A larger number of access switches in a single building then connect to a small number of switches, called distribution switches. The links from the access switches to the distribution switches are called uplinks.

- **Building block**—A single building's design, with access and distribution switches, is called a building block.

- **Core switches and links**—For larger campuses, each building block is then connected to a small number of typically very fast switches, called core switches, using Ethernet links referred to as core links.

Regardless of the set of terms used, keep in mind that, over the years, the typical speeds used for each link type will probably get faster and faster. Note that the CCNA 3 course covers these details in more depth.

Ethernet LAN Media and Connectors

As you've learned in this chapter, network engineers consider many factors when they choose the type of media to use when building a LAN. This section reviews the basics of such decisions and includes a reference for some of the key decision points.

When picking the media to use for different parts of a LAN, one of the main considerations is the maximum length of a single segment. For example, Figures 5-3 and 5-4 show several straight lines that presumably represent some type of Ethernet cable, but because the figures do not mention the lengths of the cables, the media type is unknown. Table 5-2 lists the various Ethernet standards, along with the type of media supported, cable lengths, and connector types.

Table 5-2   Ethernet Types, Media, and Segment Lengths

Ethernet Types	Media	Maximum Segment Length	Connector
10BASE2[*]	50-ohm coax (Thinnet)	185 m (606.94 feet)	British Naval Connector (BNC) or Bayonet Neill Concelman (BNC)
10BASE5[*]	50-ohm coax (Thicknet)	500 m (1640.4 feet)	Attachment unit interface (AUI)
10BASE-T	TIA/EIA Category 3, 4, 5 UTP, two pairs	100 m (328 feet)	ISO 8877 (RJ-45)
100BASE-TX	TIA/EIA Category 5 UTP, two pairs	100 m (328 feet)	ISO 8877 (RJ-45)
100BASE-FX	62.5/125-micron multimode fiber	400 m (1312.3 feet)	Duplex media interface connector (MIC), ST, or SC
1000BASE-CX	Shielded-twisted pair (STP)	25 m (82 feet)	ISO 8877 (RJ-45)

Ethernet Types	Media	Maximum Segment Length	Connector
1000BASE-T	TIA/EIA Category 5 UTP, four pairs	100 m (328 feet)	ISO 8877 (RJ-45)
1000BASE-SX	62.5/50-micron multimode fiber	275 m (853 feet) for 62.5 micron fiber; 550 m (1804.5 feet) for 50 micro fiber	SC
1000BASE-LX	62.5/50-micron multimode fiber; 9-micron single-mode fiber	440 m (1443.6 feet) for 62.5 micron fiber; 550 m (1804.5 feet) for 50 micro fiber; 3 to 10 km (1.86 to 6.2 miles) on single-mode fiber	SC

* Of the Ethernet types listed in this table, only 10BASE2 and 10BASE5 use a physical bus topology. The rest use a physical star topology.

Although Table 5-2 lists many details, most engineers simply remember the general distance limitations and then use a reference chart (such as Table 5-2) to remember each specific detail. An engineer must also consider the physical paths that the cables will use to run through a campus or building and the impact on the required cable length. For example, a cable might have to run from one end of the building to the other, then through a conduit that connects the floors of the building, and then horizontally to a wiring closet on another floor. Oftentimes, those paths are not the shortest way to get from one place to the other. So, the chart's details are important to the LAN planning process and the resulting choice of LAN media.

After the media types are selected, a network engineer must either order cables of specific lengths with specific connectors on the ends or make the cables. To make the cables, a raw spool of cable is used, and the engineer then cuts a length of cable and adds the connectors to the cable's ends. Figure 5-5 shows some of the popular connector types that Table 5-2 mentioned.

An engineer must also plan for the type of connector that the NICs and networking devices use. To support UTP cabling, most devices today use RJ-45 jacks, which are openings that accept the male RJ-45 connector (as shown in Figure 5-5). Some older NICs and networking devices use *attachment user interface (AUI)* connectors, which are similar to the drawing shown in Figure 5-5. In that case, the NIC or device must use a transceiver that has both an AUI interface and an RJ-45 jack, with the AUI side connected to the device, and the RJ-45 jack connected to the Ethernet cable.

Note

Ethernet transceivers transmit and receive Ethernet signals—in fact, the name *transceiver* is a shortened version of "transmitter/receiver."

Figure 5-5   Common LAN Cable Connectors

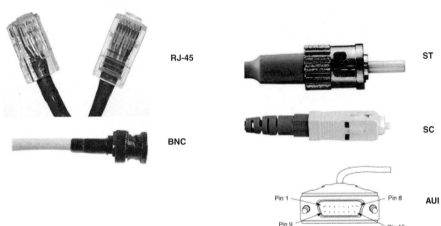

Picking UTP Cable Pinouts

So far, this chapter explained some of the thinking behind LAN installation. A network engineer estimates the length required for each cable and then picks the appropriate media after she considers all the related facts, which includes cabling and equipment cost, connectors, Ethernet speed requirements, and other factors. This section covers the final step in the process before the UTP cables can be installed: namely, cabling pinouts. This section reviews the concepts of UTP cabling pinouts, which Chapter 3 previously introduced.

The TIA/EIA-T568-A and TIA/EIA-T568-B standards define how each of the colored wires inside a UTP cable should be connected to RJ-45 connectors. For proper operation of a LAN link, each wire must be connected to the proper pin position on the connectors on each end of the cable. Figure 5-6 shows a reminder of the TIA/EIA-T568-A and TIA/EIA-T568-B cable pinouts for a single connector.

Figure 5-6   TIA/EIA-T568-A and TIA/EIA-T568-B Pinouts

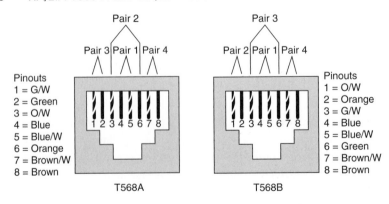

Figure 5-6 shows the pinouts for both standards. If you look at the end of a cable, you can typically see the colors of the wires on the end of the cable.

Each pair works together to create a circuit, which causes each of the wires to pass current in the opposite direction as compared with the other wire in the pair. So, for pair 1 with TIA/EIA-T568-A, the wire at pin 1 uses positive polarity, sending current down the wire, while pin 2 uses negative polarity, receiving current in the wire. Mainly as a historical reference to terms used in the original telephone networks, the wire using positive polarity is sometimes called a *tip*, and the wire using negative polarity is sometimes called a *ring*.

Pinouts of Straight-Through and Crossover Cables

Although having a TIA/EIA-T568-A and TIA/EIA-T568-B reference helps, to create *straight-through* and *crossover* cables, you must know how to connect the wires on the connectors on both ends of a cable. Simply put, the requirements are as follows:

- **Straight-through**—Use TIA/EIA-T568-B (or TIA/EIA-T568-A) on both ends of the cable.

- **Crossover (10BASE-T and 100BASE-TX)**—Use TIA/EIA-T568-A on one end and TIA/EIA-T568-B on the other. This swaps pair 1 and pair 2.

- **Crossover (1000BASE-T)**—Use TIA/EIA-T568-B on one end, and then swap the orange/green pairs (pairs 1 and 2) and the blue/brown pairs (pairs 3 and 4) on the other end.

The concept of a straight-through cable is relatively simple. The wire at pin 1 on one end connects to pin 1 on the other end, the wire at pin 2 on one end connects to pin 2 on the other end, and so on for all eight pins.

However, the 10BASE-T and 100BASE-TX crossover cable requires more thought. First, both of these Ethernet types use two pairs—one for transmission in each direction—and, specifically, the pin pairs 1 and 2 and 3 and 6. So, these two pairs must be swapped to create a crossover cable. Figure 5-7 shows the required pinouts to create the crossover cable.

Figure 5-7   10BASE-T and 100BASE-TX Crossover Cable

The orange wire pair and the green wire pair switch places on one end of the cable.

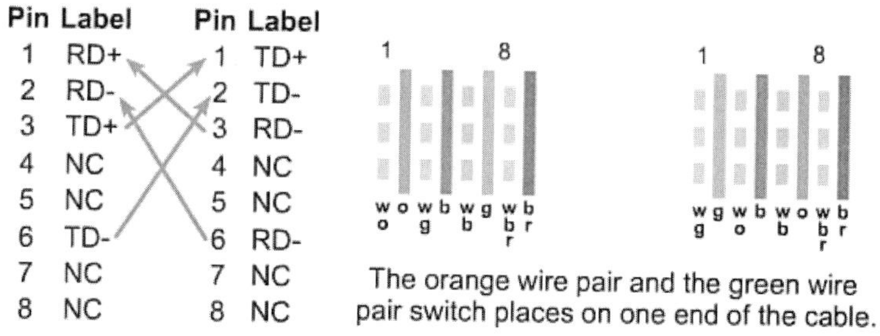

This crossover cable works well with 10BASE-T and 100BASE-TX because it swaps only the two pairs (orange and green pairs) used for transmitting data. However, because 1000BASE-T uses all four pairs for transmission, a correct 1000BASE-T crossover also needs to cross the other two pairs. Figure 5-8 shows an example of a crossover that works with 1000BASE-T.

Figure 5-8   1000BASE-T Crossover Cable

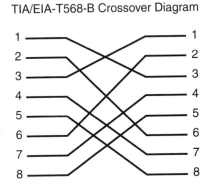

TIA/EIA-T568-B Crossover Diagram

Many products, including Cisco switches, use a feature called *Automatic Medium-independent Crossover (Auto-mdix)* to detect when a cable with the wrong pinouts connects two 1000BASE-T ports and to adjust so the cable works. So, in many cases, using a 1000BASE-T straight-through cable between two switches actually works in spite of the fact that the wrong cabling pinouts are used.

Choosing When to Use Straight-Through and Crossover Cables

For Ethernet cables, two key facts can help you know whether to use a straight-through cable or crossover cable:

- When connecting two devices that are alike in regards to which pins they use for transmitting, use a crossover cable.

- When connecting two devices that differ in regards to which pins they use for transmitting, use a straight-through cable.

To know which cable pinout to use, the first step is to know which pins each type of device uses to transmit. The following list details which devices transmit on the pair at pins 1 and 2 and which transmit using the pair at pins 3 and 6:

- **Pins 1 and 2**—PCs, routers, servers, wireless access points' (APs') Ethernet ports

- **Pins 3 and 6**—Switches, hubs, bridges, repeaters

For example, in Figures 5-3 and 5-4 (previously shown in this chapter), the links between the PCs and the switches would use straight-through cables, and the links between switches would

Note

This discussion of choosing between straight-through and crossover cables mainly applies to 10BASE-T and 100BASE-TX, which transmit on one pair in each direction.

use crossover cables. For your reference, the following list notes some of the more common uses for a straight-through cable:

- Switch to router

- Switch to PC or server

- Hub to PC or server

Also for your reference, the following list notes some of the more common uses for a crossover cable:

- Switch to switch

- Switch to hub

- Hub to hub

- Router to router

- PC to PC

- Router to PC

One of the potentially tricky parts of choosing the right cable when connecting switches is that some switch ports transmit on pins 1 and 2 instead of on pins 3 and 6. To show which ports use which pins, Cisco prints an X beside each port that uses pins 3 and 6 to refer to the fact that the port has already crossed over the wire pairs. So, when you connect two switch ports that have Xs, you need a crossover cable. However, when only one of the two ports has an X, you need a straight-through cable. Figure 5-9 illustrates both cases.

Figure 5-9   Determining Pinouts of Cisco Switch Ports

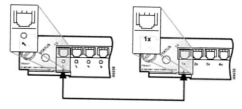

Use straight-through when only one port is designated with an "x".

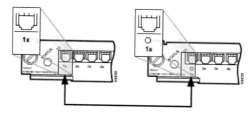

Use crossover cable when BOTH ports are designated with an "x"or neither port is designated with an "x".

Note

Some consumer switches, such as those from the Cisco Linksys division, label a port as an "uplink" port instead of marking it with an X. These ports also transmit on pins 1 and 2, which allows the home user to ignore the idea of crossover cables when she connects to a high-speed Internet service.

 Lab 5.1.5   RJ-45 Jack Punch Down

In this lab, you learn the correct process for terminating or punching down an RJ-45 jack. You also learn the correct procedure for installing the jack in a wall plate.

Now that this chapter has reviewed some of the facts about cabling and explained the things a network engineer must consider when choosing cables, the next section focuses on networking devices and how to connect cables to those devices.

Connecting Ethernet Networking Devices

When designing a LAN, network engineers must pay close attention to the distances between devices. Although some of that planning includes planning the length of individual cable segments, an engineer must also consider how networking devices impact the allowed length of multiple LAN cables used together. In addition to performing their basic functions, networking devices can extend the length of a LAN. For example, Figure 5-10 shows a simple 10BASE-T LAN in which two PCs connect to different 10BASE-T hubs, with two other hubs between the two PCs.

Figure 5-10   Maximum-Length 10BASE-T LAN with Hubs

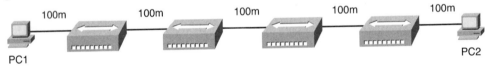

According to the 10BASE-T standard, the design shows the largest number of hubs (four) that can be in between two end-user devices. So, instead of using a single-mode optical cable to achieve the required distance, a network engineer has alternatives (as shown in Figure 5-10), such as simply using multiple different networking devices. This section reviews the most commonly used networking devices when building an Ethernet LAN.

Repeaters

Repeaters extend the distances over which Ethernet devices can effectively send data to each other. Cabling distances are limited in part because when an electrical signal is sent over a wire, the signal degrades. Repeaters may receive a degraded signal, but they always generate and send a new clean signal. To do this, a repeater receives a (possibly degraded) electrical signal in one port, creates a regenerated and retimed clean signal, and sends that new signal out the other port. Figure 5-11 shows an example; the signal sent by Betty, to Fred, is shown at the bottom of the figure.

Figure 5-11   Basic Function of a Repeater

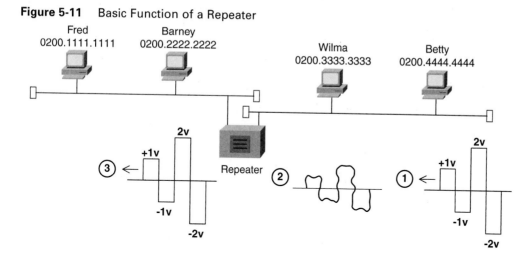

Repeaters cannot indefinitely extend a LAN. For 10BASE-T, the number of repeaters allowed between two end-user devices is limited by a rule called the *5-4-3 rule*. In short, there can be at most 5 cables and 4 repeaters between any two end-user devices. The 3 in the 5-4-3 rule refers to the fact that, of the 5 cables, only 3 can have end-user devices on them. Effectively, if Figure 5-10 had shown repeaters instead of hubs, it would show the maximum-length LAN per the 5-4-3 rule, with 5 cables and 4 repeaters. Such a design with 10BASE-T would allow for a distance of 500 between the two PCs.

Interestingly, regarding the use of repeaters, 100BASE-TX has even more restrictive rules than the 5-4-3 rule. For more information, refer to the section "Additional Topics of Interest" for Chapter 7, "Ethernet Technologies," which is located on the CD-ROM.

Hubs

The IEEE created 10BASE-T, along with the Ethernet hubs required to create 10BASE-T LANs, to overcome a couple of problems with the older Ethernet standards. First, the installation of the coax cable for 10BASE2 and 10BASE5 LANs was difficult, in part because of the bus topology. 10BASE-T was the first type of Ethernet to use a different physical cabling topology, called a star topology. The star topology uses a single cable to connect each new device to an Ethernet hub, making the installation of each new device more convenient. Additionally, working with the much thinner and flexible UTP cables made cable installation easier as well. Finally, the UTP cabling was much less expensive than coax cabling, helping to make Ethernet much more affordable for the average company.

However, 10BASE-T's UTP cables supported only a maximum single cable length of 100 m versus the longer distances of the 10BASE5 (500 m) and 10BASE2 (185 m) standards. To

Note

Most hubs have between four and 24 ports—oftentimes, a multiple of four ports—with the intent that devices in one small area can be connected to one hub, with the hub then connecting to other hubs or switches.

Note

Because they repeat any electrical signal, hubs and repeaters create a single *collision domain*. This term refers to a set of devices for which, if any two of the devices simultaneously send an Ethernet frame, the electrical signals overlap, destroying both frames. The reasons behind the 5-4-3 rule have to do with the timing related to a collision domain. (Chapter 6, "Ethernet Fundamentals," covers the concept of collision domains.)

Note

Fast Ethernet hubs must use even more restrictive rules than the 5-4-3 rule, as covered in the "Additional Topics of Interest" section for Chapter 7, located on the CD-ROM.

Note

The hubs described throughout this book are assumed to be either active or intelligent hubs, both of which regenerate electrical signals.

make up for the shorter cable lengths that UTP supported, 10BASE-T allowed the use of repeaters and hubs. 10BASE-T hubs originally had two main functions:

- Similar to repeaters, hubs receive electrical signals on one port, regenerate the signal, and send it out all other ports.

- Hubs contain multiple RJ-45 jacks to provide a place to connect UTP cables with RJ-45 connectors, which creates the physical star topology.

By combining both functions, the hub has an electrical path to reach each NIC and can forward the regenerated signals out all other ports (similar to a repeater). In fact, hubs were originally called *multiport repeaters* because the original repeaters typically had only two ports, and hubs had many more ports. Also, because hubs served as a central location for connecting end-user devices, they were also sometimes called *concentrators*.

Because hubs repeat any received electrical signal out all other ports (except the port in which the signal was received), an electrical signal sent by one device is forwarded to all other devices attached to the hub. Figure 5-12 shows an example.

Figure 5-12 10BASE-T with Hub Operation

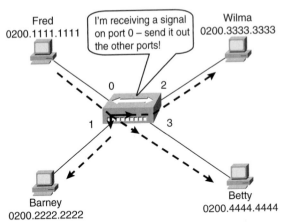

Packet Tracer configuration file NA01-0512 shows a network that matches Figure 5-12. The simulation tool allows you to see how two frames—one sent by Fred to Barney and one sent by Wilma to Betty—collide in both networks because of the single collision domain.

Hubs tend to fall into one of three basic categories—passive, active, or intelligent—depending on several distinctions. Table 5-3 lists the three types and contrasts them.

Table 5-3   Comparing the Three Types of Ethernet Hubs

Type	Repeats Signal?	Requires Power?	Supports Advanced Troubleshooting Features?
Passive	No	No	No
Active	Yes	Yes	No
Intelligent	Yes	Yes	Yes*

* Intelligent hubs support network management and diagnostic features that allow network engineers to log in to the hub to troubleshoot problems.

Both repeaters and hubs provide benefits when building a LAN. A repeater extends the LAN's length, while a hub both extends the length and provides a connection point to create a convenient physical star topology. However, creating LANs with repeaters and hubs leaves all the connected devices in a single collision domain. Additionally, the end-user devices on such a LAN must share the LAN bandwidth. For example, the LANs in Figures 5-10, 5-11, and 5-12, assuming they were using 10BASE-T, all shared 10 Mbps of bandwidth.

The next two sections describe bridges and switches, which provide similar benefits as repeaters and hubs, but with the added benefit of creating a larger number of smaller collision domains and adding to the amount of bandwidth available in a LAN.

Lab 5.1.7   Hub and NIC Purchase

In this lab, you become familiar with various network components and their prices. This lab specifically looks at Ethernet hubs and NICs.

Bridges

Bridges connect multiple LAN segments, forwarding traffic between the segments as needed. When forwarding the traffic, bridges act like repeaters in that they forward a regenerated electrical signal. Additionally, bridges provide some significant performance enhancements to LANs, which this section describes.

Unlike repeaters and hubs, bridges use logic to decide when to forward frames. The logic is based on Ethernet protocols that closely match OSI Layer 2, so bridges are considered to be Layer 2 devices. To decide when to forward frames—and when to not forward frames—bridges use the following logic:

1. Examine the incoming signal, interpret the signal as 0s and 1s, and find the destination MAC address listed in the frame.

2. If the destination MAC is reachable by that bridge via a different interface than the one on which the frame arrived, forward the frame using a clean regenerated signal. (This process is called *forwarding*.)

3. If the destination is reachable on the same interface in which the frame arrived, discard the frame. (This process is called *filtering*.)

Figures 5-13 and 5-14 show examples of a bridge's filtering and forwarding decision, respectively. Figure 5-13 shows a bridge receiving a frame, sent by Fred to Barney's destination MAC address, and the bridge choosing to not forward the frame.

Figure 5-13   Bridge Making Filtering Decision

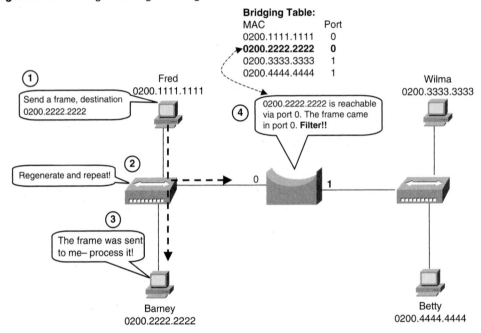

The following list explains the process shown in Figure 5-13:

1. Fred sends an Ethernet frame, which is data prefaced with a destination MAC address of 0200.2222.2222, out his NIC.

2. The hub repeats the frame out both of its other ports.

3. Barney receives the electrical signal, notices that the destination MAC address is his own MAC address, and processes the received data.

4. The bridge receives the signal in its port number 0 and looks at the destination MAC address of 0200.2222.2222. The bridge's table says that 0200.2222.2222 is reachable out port 0, which is the same port in which the frame was received. Therefore, the bridge does not need to forward the frame.

This example also provides a small insight into how bridges improve LAN performance. When the actions shown in Figure 5-13 occur, devices on the hub on the right—such as Betty and Wilma—could send frames at the same time. The bridge would not forward the frames, and no collisions would occur. So, the network shown in Figure 5-13 would actually support a total of 20 Mbps, because each of the two LANs has 10 Mbps of usable bandwidth.

Figure 5-14 shows an example of the same network as Figure 5-13, but this time, Fred sends a frame to Wilma. In this case, the bridge decides that it needs to forward the frame out port 1 to the right.

Figure 5-14   Bridge Making a Forwarding Decision

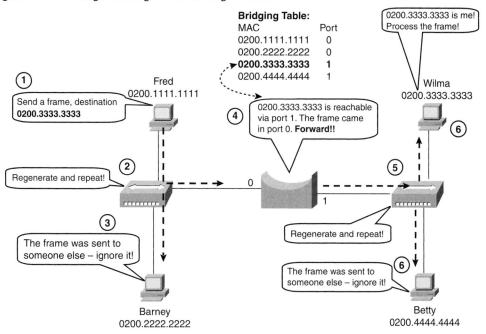

The following list explains each step in more detail. Note that the first two steps are identical to the steps shown in Figure 5-13:

1. Fred sends an Ethernet frame, which is data prefaced with a destination MAC address of 0200.3333.3333, out his NIC.

2. The hub repeats the frame out both of its other ports.

3. Barney receives the electrical signal and decides not to process the frame because the frame's destination MAC address is not his MAC address.

4. The bridge receives the signal in its port number 0 and looks at the destination MAC address of 0200.3333.3333. The bridge's table says that 0200.3333.3333 is reachable out port 1, which is a different port than the incoming port. Therefore, the bridge forwards the frame.

5. The hub on the right repeats the signal out all interfaces.

6. Wilma receives and processes the frame while Betty receives and ignores it because the destination MAC address of the frame is not Betty's MAC address.

Packet Tracer configuration NA01-0513 shows a network with the same topology as Figures 5-13 and 5-14. The simulation tool shows Figure 5-13's logic in Scenario 0 and Figure 5-14's logic in Scenario 3. Scenario 5 shows both LANs concurrently sending data. Note that Packet Tracer's simulation mode shows a red X over a device when the device received the data but discarded it, a green check mark means the device received the data and processed it, and having neither means the data never made it to that device.

Tip

The online curriculum's page about bridging includes a helpful animation that shows how one bridge forwards a frame and a second bridge filters the same frame.

Bridges separate LANs into different collision domains. For example, a frame sent by Fred will not collide with a frame sent by Wilma because the bridge stores the frames and waits until the LAN segments are not busy. This is the main reason why bridges create more bandwidth in a LAN.

The following list summarizes some of the key benefits of using bridges:

- Bridges have the benefit of a repeater because bridges always forward a regenerated signal.

- Bridges do not have to conform to the 5-4-3 rule as do 10BASE-T repeaters, so technically, you could build a long LAN by connecting a large number of bridges.

- Bridges create additional network bandwidth by separating LANs into multiple collision domains.

Bridges, however, have a few negatives. The actual bridge products that were formerly sold by vendors typically had only a few physical ports (typically, only two). So, bridges did not provide one of the key benefits of a hub, which is to provide a convenient device to connect the many PCs in a LAN. The next devices, LAN switches, bring all the features together.

Because switches do the same things as bridges, only much faster and with many more features, vendors such as Cisco Systems no longer sell Ethernet bridge products. The next section explains the basic functions of switches, with their forwarding, filtering, and address-learning features working just like bridges.

Ethernet Switches

In even their most basic form, LAN switches provide all the main benefits of repeaters, hubs, and bridges. Additionally, modern LAN switches provide a vast array of other features. In fact, today, most LANs use switches only because bridges no longer exist, switches run much faster than hubs but are roughly the same price, and LANs need repeaters only when extremely long cabling distances are required.

The basic functions of a switch are summarized as follows:

- Like a hub, a switch provides a large number of ports/jacks into which cables can be connected, forming a physical star topology of cabling.

- Like repeaters, hubs, and bridges, when forwarding a frame, the switch regenerates a clean square wave electrical signal.

- Like bridges, a switch uses the same forwarding/filtering logic on a per-port basis.

- Like bridges, switches separate a LAN into multiple collision domains, with each domain having separate bandwidth, thereby significantly increasing LAN bandwidth.

- Beyond the functions of bridges, hubs, and repeaters, switches offer many advanced features, like virtual LANs (VLANs), and much faster performance.

Figure 5-15 shows an example of a switch forwarding a frame based on its MAC address table. The same familiar PCs are used, with Fred sending a frame to Barney (0200.2222.2222). The switch forwards the frame on port 2 and not on ports 3 and 4.

Figure 5-15   Switch Making a Forwarding Decision

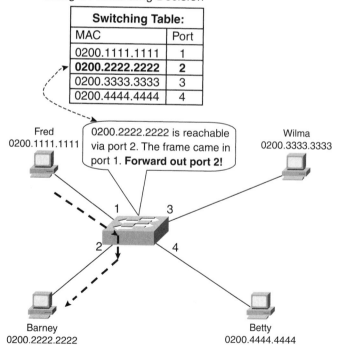

Although a switch's forwarding and filtering logic works the same way as a bridge, oftentimes, the table of MAC addresses and ports is called a *switching table* instead of a bridging table. With Cisco switches, the table is also oftentimes called a *Content Addressable Memory (CAM) table*. Besides using the completed CAM to make forwarding decisions, like bridges, switches also dynamically learn the entries in the CAM. Chapter 8 covers all these details.

Although Figure 5-15 shows the basics of how a switch, like a bridge, forwards frames based on the destination MAC address, it does not show one of the significant advantages of a switch. Switches place each switch port in a separate collision domain, which also means that each port has its own bandwidth. Figure 5-16 shows an example in which all four devices on a switch simultaneously send a frame, and all frames are delivered without collisions.

Figure 5-16   Switch with Four 100-Mbps Ports—400 Mbps

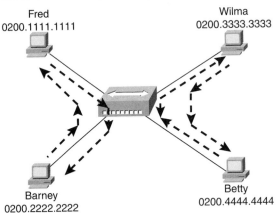

The switch allows all the devices to send at the same time without collisions. Switches prevent collisions by noticing when the switch could cause a collision. Instead of sending the frame and causing the collision, the switch temporarily stores the frame in a memory buffer. Then, the switch forwards the frame once a collision will not occur. Additionally, switches allow Ethernet links to use full-duplex logic in some cases, which means that both devices are on the end of an Ethernet cable. Chapter 6 covers full duplex in more detail, and Chapter 8 shows a more detailed example of how switches use buffering to prevent collisions.

Switches also create much more bandwidth than do hubs, bridges, and repeaters. If all the ports were using 100-Mbps speeds, the switch, just for these four ports, would have created 400 Mbps of bandwidth. The same design, using a hub, would have required the devices to share 100 Mbps.

 Packet Tracer   If you load the NA01-0516 configuration into Packet Tracer, use simulation mode, and run Scenario 0, you will see an example of the process of all four devices sending a frame at the same time, as shown in Figure 5-16.

 Lab 5.1.10   Purchasing LAN Switches

In this lab, you become familiar with various network components and their prices. This lab specifically looks at Ethernet switches and NICs.

Lab 5.1.13a   Building a Hub-Based Network

In this lab, you create a simple network between two PCs by using an Ethernet hub. You identify and locate the proper cables, configure workstation IP addresses, and test connectivity by using the **ping** command.

Lab 5.1.13b   Building a Switch-Based Network

In this lab, you create a simple network between two PCs by using an Ethernet switch. You identify and locate the proper cables, configure workstation IP addresses, and test connectivity by using the **ping** command.

Wireless Communications and Wireless Access Points

Chapter 3 introduced the concept of a wireless LAN (WLAN). This section discusses some more general concepts about wireless communication and then provides a brief review of WLAN access points (APs).

Wireless Communications Overview

Although today many people think the term "wireless" implies WLANs or Wi-Fi, many different types of wireless communication methods actually exist. Technically, wireless communications are any form of communication that does not use a cable or wire. Instead, most every type of wireless communication uses *electromagnetic (EM)* energy, such as radio waves, microwaves, or infrared (IR) light.

Many people choose to use wireless either because it is the only communications method that works in a particular situation or because it is convenient. However, in many cases, people use wireless because it allows for mobility. For example, the Space Shuttle, the Space Station, and the average commercial airplane use wireless communications because using a cable is impractical. Police and fire departments use wireless communications to allow their people to go to emergencies and always keep in touch.

Both *infrared (IR)* and *radio frequencies (RFs)* are popular for wireless communication today. IR and RF are simply different ranges, or spectrums, of EM energy, each with different characteristics. IR and RF are used for different types of communications because of their different characteristics. IR requires that the devices have a line-of-sight between each other; if some object or person is between the two devices, IR does not work. For example, most TV remote controls use IR, and if you can't see the TV from where you are sitting with the remote control, you cannot change the channel. However, IR can be used for applications in which all the devices sit in the same room. IR also uses cheaper components than RF.

RF has been popular for wireless communications for more than a century. Applications include radio stations on the AM and FM dials of your car stereo, communications between airplanes and air-traffic control, and communications within police and fire departments. Radio Frequencies

Note

Refer to Figure 3-18 (in Chapter 3) for a look at the range of EM spectrum (wavelengths) that can be used for wireless communication.

do not require a line of sight, and they can bounce off materials to reach a range of destinations. However, the range of Radio Frequencies is affected by distance, the amounts and types of materials between the sender and receiver, and, to some degree, weather. For example, your car radio might not work well after you drive into a parking deck because the parking deck has many steel rods inside the cement.

All wireless devices designed for two-way communication need a transmitter and a receiver. The transmitter generates and transmits the EM energy that represents a set of bits. The receiver senses the EM energy and decodes that energy back into the original bits. In products, both functions can be combined into a single physical component called a transceiver. With WLANs, the transceiver is often simply referred to as an antenna.

All the popular WLAN standards mentioned in Chapter 3 use RF spectrum. WLAN standards use a range or spread of frequencies, which is called *spread spectrum*, so that interference on one frequency does not impact the WLAN too much. The original 802.11 WLAN standards used a transmission method called *Frequency Hopping Spread Spectrum (FHSS)*; 802.11b followed this standard and used the *Direct Sequence Spread Spectrum (DSSS)* transmission method. (Both FHSS and DSSS are beyond the scope of the course.)

WLAN Review

This chapter has both reviewed and expanded the coverage of repeaters, hubs, bridges, and switches. Continuing that trend, this chapter's coverage of wireless communications would not be complete without a brief review of wireless *access points (APs)*.

WLAN APs have much in common with hubs and switches. Hubs and switches provide a centralized device to which end-user devices can connect. APs provide that same role for wireless end-user devices, with the obvious difference that no cabling is required. Like hubs and switches, APs have limitations on distance between the AP and end-user devices. Like hubs, APs create a shared medium, which means that the end users share the bandwidth available via the AP. Figure 5-17 shows a hub, switch, and AP connected to end-user devices.

When creating a network similar to that shown in Figure 5-17, the PC cards do not need networking cables at all; instead, they use their wireless NICs to transmit and receive data. The AP needs a cable to connect it to the rest of the network—typically, a straight-through UTP cable connecting it to a LAN switch, as shown in Figure 5-17.

Figure 5-17   AP, Switch, and Hub Used for End-User Device Access

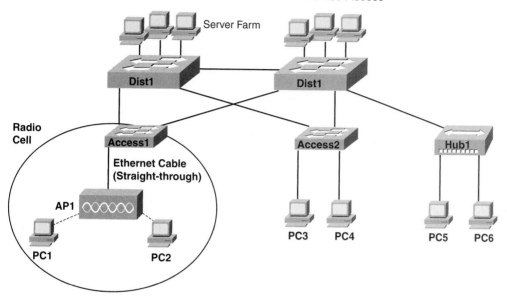

Ethernet NICs

Network interface cards (NICs) are PC expansion cards that create a way for a PC to connect to and use a LAN. To do that, the NIC must operate at both Layer 1 and Layer 2 of the OSI model. NICs operate at Layer 1 because they send and receive electrical signals over the attached cable by using a built-in Ethernet transceiver. NICs operate at Layer 2 in that they frame data inside a header and trailer, with the header including a Layer 2 address called the *Media Access Control (MAC) address*.

Typically, network diagrams do not even bother showing a PC's NIC as separate from a PC, partly because it is assumed that each computer has one, and partly because only the outside of the NIC is visible in real life. In most desktop PCs, the NIC either sits inside an expansion slot or is built into the motherboard. On laptops, the NIC might be built in or it might be in a small expansion slot (called a PC card slot) with the NIC being about the size of a credit card. Figure 5-18 shows a NIC that has not yet been installed into a PC card slot; Figure 5-19 shows the side of the NIC that would be visible from outside the computer after it is installed. This part includes the RJ-45 jack.

Figure 5-18   Ethernet NIC: Circuit Board Internal to the PC

Figure 5-19   Ethernet NIC: External Part with RJ-45 Connector

Today, most Ethernet NICs have an RJ-45 connector, but in some cases, the NIC's connector might not match the cabling. In those cases, the NIC can be replaced with another NIC that matches the cabling, the cable/connector can be changed, or a small device that converts from one connector to another can be used. For example, the Cisco 2500 series routers, which are no longer sold or supported by Cisco Systems, use an AUI connector for their Ethernet ports, with most UTP cables having an RJ-45 connector. To use the cable with an RJ-45 connector, a Cisco 2500 series router used an external transceiver that converted one type of signal or connector to another (for example, to connect a 15-pin AUI interface to an RJ-45 jack). Also, the use of an AUI connector means that the device does not have a built-in transceiver, so the external transceiver also provides this required and important function.

This concludes this chapter's coverage of LAN cables and devices. Before moving on to WAN cabling and devices, the next few sections examine how PCs use a LAN to communicate.

Note

Although Cisco no longer sells the 2500 series routers, they are still used and sold on Internet auction websites. Currently, available models of new Cisco routers typically use RJ-45 connectors for Ethernet ports.

Using the LAN: Models for PC Communications

Computers use networks to share information and resources. A network might be as simple as two PCs and a printer in someone's house, with the printer connected to one of the PCs. In that network, the PC with the printer could share the printer, which allows the other PC to print documents. Both computers typically have a disk drive with files on them, so both computers could share their files or information stored in databases. Whatever the specific reasons, networks exist to enable computers to share data and resources.

Networking uses the terms *client* and *server* to refer to whether a computer needs to use some resource on another computer or whether the computer provides the service. For example, the PC without a printer is a client that needs to use the printer, and the PC with the attached printer is the server because it provides print services.

The networking world has used many different strategies and designs for how computers share their resources. Although many different terms have been used to describe these strategies and designs, most of those specific designs fall into one of two different communication categories: the *peer-to-peer model* and the *client/server model*. The main differences can be summarized as follows:

- **Peer-to-peer**—A computer acts as a peer with other computers by acting as a client in some cases and as a server in other cases.

- **Client/server**—A computer acts as either a client or as a server.

The following two sections cover the details of each model.

Peer-to-Peer Networking

Computers in a peer-to-peer network act as equals, or peers, providing their services to each other. As a peer, each computer can take on the client function or the server function. For example, each of two PCs in the same house could allow the other PC access to all its files. PC A could copy a file from PC B, making PC A the client in that case. Later, when PC B copied a file from PC A, PC A would be the server.

To act as a server, a computer user must decide to share its resources with other peers on the network. A computer does not have to share all files and directories, printers, or any other resource. So, the computer's owner must make an effort to tell the computer what resources (files, printers, databases, and disk drives) can be shared. For example, Figure 5-20 shows a screen from a computer called Constellation, in which the computer user decides to share his My Documents folder.

Figure 5-20   PC Constellation Shares a Folder

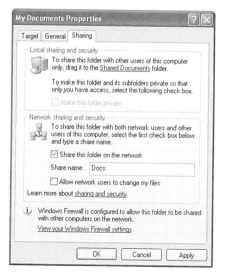

After PC Constellation is told to share its folder, other computers can see the folder and copy files to and from it. Figure 5-21 shows a screen image from another computer (not Constellation) in which the other computer can see the folder that PC Constellation shares. Note that the left side of the window lists \\Constellation as a reminder, with the \\ meaning that the data is on another computer whose name is Constellation.

Figure 5-21   Another PC Sees Constellation's Folder

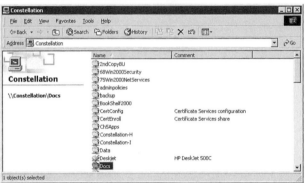

Peer-to-peer networks have several advantages over client/server networks. They are simple to install and require no special hardware or software because most modern desktop operating systems (OSs) provide support for peer-to-peer networking. Users control their own resources, which means that no network administrators are required; this saves the salary cost of having a network administrator.

However, peer-to-peer networks also have many disadvantages, particularly in larger networks. This makes the client/server model more popular in most companies. Peer-to-peer networking lacks any centralized security controls, relying on each end user to protect his PC—and the company's information assets. Individual users must back up their own systems to be able to recover from data loss in case of failures. When a computer acts as a server, that machine's user might experience reduced performance because the computer spends its time working on requests from other PCs. Peer-to-peer networks do not work well with more and more users. (The online course suggests that at most ten PCs be used in a single peer-to-peer network.) Because end users must perform the work, each end user needs to be trained on how to manage his own computers. In fact, this last point about end-user training might be the most significant reason why peer-to-peer networking is typically used only in homes today (because it is inexpensive); client/server networks are used in businesses.

 Lab 5.1.12   Building a Peer-to-Peer Network

In this lab, you create a simple peer-to-peer network between two PCs. You identify and locate the proper cable, configure workstation IP addresses, and test connectivity by using the **ping** command. You also share a folder on one PC and access it with the other PC.

Client/Server Networking

In a client/server network, the end-user computers all act as clients. Dedicated computers, called servers, provide all services—file sharing, database sharing, printers, and other resources. Figure 5-22 shows the basic idea behind a client/server network. On the left, three client workstations use a single server. (*Workstation* is just another generic word for computer.) On the right, the services are provided by multiple servers, which is common today. With multiple servers, one server might fail or be brought down for maintenance, and the end users do not know anything is happening.

Figure 5-22   Client/Server Networking Model

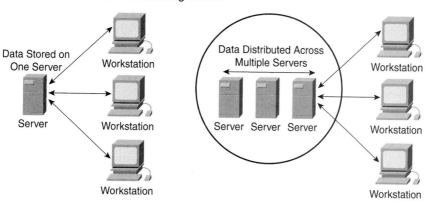

In the client/server model, the end-user PCs typically use less powerful and less expensive hardware and software. However, the servers, depending on expected use, typically use a more expensive *network operating system (NOS)* and hardware. The servers often typically need to be up and working all the time, and they need to provide services for a large number of users. Therefore, the NOS is required, with special features to support a server's unique requirements. Additionally, the hardware might need to be more powerful than a computer used by a single person.

The client/server model offers several benefits over peer-to-peer networks. One important advantage is centralized security. Before a client can access the server resources, the user must be identified and authorized to use the resource. You handle this authorization by assigning each user an account name and password. Each user is verified by an authentication service that acts as a sentry to guard access to the network. By centralizing user accounts, security, and access control, server-based networks simplify the work of network administration.

Another advantage for the client/server model is easy data backup. When users create data that is important to that company's business, the business has a need, and sometimes a legal obligation, to keep a copy of the data in case the server fails and cannot be repaired. With all the data stored in a centrally located server farm, data backup becomes more manageable.

Using servers does have some disadvantages. First, server hardware and software cost more than end-user PC hardware and software. Personnel costs can be higher because of a dedicated network administrator. Also, when a company cannot afford multiple servers, the server becomes a single point of failure; if the server fails, the network is essentially useless until the server works again.

Table 5-4 summarizes the main points of comparison between the peer-to-peer and client/server networking models.

Table 5-4   Comparing Peer-to-Peer and Client/Server Networking

Comparison Point	Peer-to-Peer	Client/Server
Requires a dedicated server	No	Yes
Requires a more expensive NOS	No	Yes
Requires a dedicated network administrator	No	Yes
End users must be trained and skilled in network administration	Yes	No
More secure	No	Yes
Easier to back up data	No	Yes
Scales well	No	Yes
Single point of failure	No	Yes[*]

[*] Client/server has only a single point of failure when a single server is used.

Cabling WANs

The Cisco Networking Academy Program CCNA curriculum covers the details of LANs in the CCNA 1 and CCNA 3 courses, with most of the detailed discussions about WANs being covered in the CCNA 4 course. However, it is important to understand the basics of WANs, particularly when you begin to learn about routers. This section builds on the coverage of WANs from Chapters 1 and 2, reviewing some concepts and focusing on the cabling routers use when they connect to WAN links.

As briefly mentioned in Chapter 1, routers are the best networking device to connect to a WAN. The reason for this is that the processes and logic used by routers do not change much at all for any kind of LAN or WAN interface. In fact, routers were purposefully designed to allow interconnection of a wide variety of LANs and WANs. For example, Figure 5-23 shows a simple internetwork with two LANs at two different sites, with a single *point-to-point WAN link* between the routers.

Figure 5-23   Simple Internetwork with Two Routers

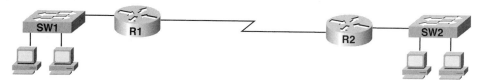

Note

The internetwork shown in Figure 5-23 resembles the internetwork used in many of the labs in the CCNA 2 course.

Figure 5-23 shows the WAN link with a jagged line, which is often called a lightning bolt because of its similarity to a cartoon-style lightning bolt. However, the figure ignores the cabling details. The majority of this section explains the details behind the WAN link. Along the way, a few details about other types of WAN links are covered, along with some information about connecting to a router's console.

WAN Physical and Data Link Layers

Routers can have both LAN and WAN interfaces, but the LAN interface cabling details are slightly more obvious. For example, if you need a router that has a Fast Ethernet interface, that router will likely have a familiar RJ-45 jack in it. You can plug in a UTP cable that has an RJ-45 connector on it. The router will always use Ethernet data-link rules on the interface and never try to use the interface as a Token Ring LAN or FDDI LAN interface. After you put a Fast Ethernet interface on a router, its OSI Layer 1 and 2 operation is completely Ethernet.

Some router WAN interfaces are like router Ethernet interfaces in that they use a single type of connector, and the router always uses a particular data-link protocol on that interface. However, in some cases, the router instead has a wide variety of physical interfaces and different data-link protocols. First, this section examines a traditional and flexible router WAN interface called a *serial interface*. Following that, three other types of WAN interfaces are briefly discussed: Integrated Services Digital Network (ISDN), digital subscriber line (DSL), and cable.

Router Serial Interfaces

Traditional router WAN interfaces are more flexible than router LAN interfaces. When you buy a router with a popular interface called a **serial interface**, the physical connector on the router is somewhat generic. Then, you can pick from among a large variety of cables to connect the serial port; however, the other end of the cable can have one of several different kinds of connectors, all different from the serial interface's connector on the router. Besides that, even after you select the right cable, you can configure the router to tell it to use one of several different OSI Layer 2 data-link protocols on the serial interface.

Note

The routers in Figure 5-23 would use serial interfaces for the WAN link.

Routers use serial cables to connect a router serial interface to another device called a channel service unit/data service unit (CSU/DSU). (More on CSU/DSUs in a few pages.) So, to select the right **serial cables** (cables that connect to router serial interfaces), a network engineer must first look at the router's serial interface to determine the type of serial interface connector. Figure 5-24 shows drawings of two of the more popular types of router serial interface connectors used today, but others also exist.

Figure 5-24 Different Connectors on Router WAN Interface Cards

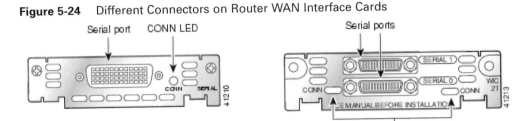

Figure 5-24 shows two small router components, called WAN interface cards (WICs), which can be installed into routers. The left side of the figure shows a card called a WIC-1T, with one serial interface that uses one style of physical connector. The right side of the figure shows a WIC-2T, with two serial interfaces, each of which uses a different but smaller connector. Note that each of the WICs are about 3 inches wide and 1 inch tall, and the actual serial connectors are much smaller.

The next step in selecting the right serial cable requires that you know what is on the other end of the cable that connects to a router's serial interface. Figure 5-25 shows slightly more detail of how cabling works with a WAN link. (Note that the lines are not drawn to scale.)

Figure 5-25 WAN Link with Serial Cables, CSU/DSUs, and the Telco Shown

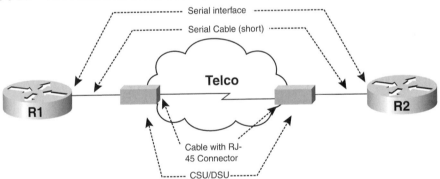

Many WAN links require a device called a *channel service unit/data service unit (CSU/DSU)*. The technical reasons are beyond the scope of this book, but knowing something about these devices is important to understanding cabling. First, the router's serial port must be connected to the CSU/DSU using a serial cable. CSU/DSU vendors sell different models of CSU/DSUs that have various physical connectors, each of which conforms to some cabling standard. So, to buy the right serial cable, you must first determine the type of connector on the router's serial interface and the type of connector on the CSU/DSU. Then, you can order a serial cable with the correct connector on each end.

Figure 5-26 shows a drawing of the connection between a router and a CSU/DSU; it shows the five different types of connectors that can be found on a CSU/DSU.

Figure 5-26   WAN Serial Cables Used with a Router

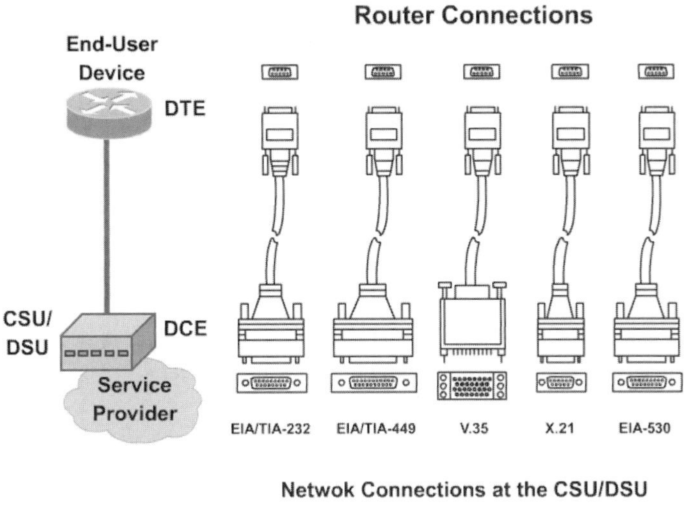

Figure 5-26 shows five cables. At the bottom of the cables, you see a view of what the ends of the cables look like. The number of "dots" represent the number of pins on the end of the cable. Note that each connector has a different shape or different number of pins.

The CSU/DSU also connects to another cable: the cable supplied by the *telco*. Referring to Figure 5-25, the center of the figure shows the line supplied by the telco. The telco happens to use RJ-45 connectors on the physical cable, but with different pinouts than Ethernet cables.

Although the explanations of serial interface cables can be a bit laborious, picking the right cables is usually straightforward. Most companies standardize so that all or most of their routers use the same kind of serial interface connector and use CSU/DSUs with the same connector. As a result, the engineers at that company do not have to think much about what serial cables to buy. Also, in some cases, CSU/DSUs and serial cables are not needed at all. Cisco Systems sells routers with serial interfaces that have the CSU/DSU built into the serial interface card. So, instead of the mess of picking the right serial cable, the line from the telco—with its familiar RJ-45 connector—plugs directly into the router's serial interface, which has an RJ-45 jack.

In addition to picking the right serial cables, a network engineer must also consider what WAN data-link protocol to use on each serial interface. Routers can be configured to use one of several options for WAN data-link protocols on each serial interface. For example, in Figure 5-23, either the default data-link protocol called High-Level Data Link Control (HDLC) or the Point-to-Point Protocol (PPP) can be used. In other cases, another popular protocol, called Frame Relay, can be used.

The options for WAN data-link protocols are completely independent of the physical cables chosen. Table 5-5 summarizes the options for the connectors on the CSU/DSU end of a serial cable, along with the three most popular options for serial data-link protocols.

Note

Telco is short for telephone company, which refers to the company from which a WAN link can be leased.

Note

"Configuring a router" means that you log on to the router and enter commands that tell the router how to act.

Table 5-5   OSI Layers 1 and 2 for Router Serial Links

OSI Layer	Options on Router Serial Interfaces
2	HDLC, PPP, Frame Relay
1	TIA/EIA-232, TIA/EIA-449, V.35, X.21, EIA-530

Cable, DSL, and ISDN

The telco provides the WAN links shown in Figure 5-23 by running a cable from its nearest office to the building where the router sits. That installation process costs extra money. Today, alternative technologies exist that use cables that are already installed in a home or building (specifically, the phone line and the CATV cable). This section briefly covers three such technologies that a router can use.

Integrated Services Digital Network (ISDN) allows a WAN connection to be dialed like a phone call. In other words, the WAN link does not have to be up and working all the time. Typically, a router uses ISDN when its permanent WAN link, like the one shown in Figure 5-23, fails for some reason. A router uses ISDN to do the equivalent of picking up the phone and calling the other router, which temporarily establishes a WAN link until the leased line comes up again.

Several varieties of ISDN lines exist, but an ISDN *Basic Rate Interface (BRI)* line is the one ISDN service that uses the already installed local phone line. A BRI allows two concurrent 64-Kbps WAN links called *B channels*. These links can dial the same other router to have more bandwidth, or two different routers can be called. BRIs also include a signaling channel, called the *D channel*, which controls the setup and teardown on the "calls" to another router.

Today, digital subscriber line (DSL) and *cable modems* are popular methods of high-speed Internet access. They can also be used for WAN connections for routers. DSL uses the local phone line, while cable modems, unsurprisingly, use the CATV coax cable.

ISDN, DSL, and cable all use variations of PPP for the data-link protocol, but they use different physical connectors for the cabling. Table 5-6 summarizes the cabling types and the connectors used for each WAN type.

Caution

ISDN BRI connectors on routers are RJ-45 jacks; however, connecting a BRI port to a non-ISDN device can harm the other device.

Table 5-6   ISDN, DSL, and Cable: Cables and Connectors

WAN Type	Medium/Cable	Connector
ISDN	Phone line	RJ-45
DSL	Phone line	RJ-11
Cable	CATV coax	F connector

Note that the F connector is the typical round connector on the end of a CATV cable, and the RJ-11 connector is the typical modular jack that common telephones use.

WAN Speeds

WAN links can run at a large variety of speeds. For example, leased lines might run as slow as 2400 bps. More typically, they run at some multiple of 64 Kbps up to 1.536 Mbps (24 * 64 Kbps). A single line from the phone company that runs at 1.536 Mbps is called a *T/1 circuit*. (The literal speed of a T/1 is 1.544 Mbps, but 8 Kbps is overhead, so the bandwidth available for the routers is 1.536 Mbps.)

Traditional WAN speeds do not stop at T/1 speeds, because even faster WAN links exist. For example, a WAN link can run at various multiples of T/1 speed, with a commonly used circuit called a T/3 circuit running at 28 times the speed of a T/1, for almost 43 Mbps of bandwidth. Also, another entire set of WAN speeds exists using Synchronous Optical Network (SONET), as briefly mentioned in Chapter 2. SONET uses fiber-optic cables, with the slowest speed being 51.84 Mbps. Many other speeds are simply multiples of that base 51.84 Mbps speed—with some exceeding 10 Gbps. Regardless of speed, remember that the line is leased, so the telco charges more money for faster links.

The length of the serial cables used between the routers and the CSU/DSUs is, in part, limited based on the speeds. Table 5-7 lists the various speeds supported and the maximum cabling lengths. Keep in mind that, although the length seems short at higher speeds, the cables need only to connect a router and a CSU/DSU, and these devices typically sit in the same room, oftentimes in the same equipment rack. So, the short maximum cable lengths are typically not a problem.

Note

An *E/1 circuit*, which is used in Europe and other parts of the world, combines 32 channels at 64 Kbps each for a rate of 2.048 Mbps.

Table 5-7   Serial Cable Lengths in Comparison to Speed

Data (bps)	Distance (Meters) TIA/EIA-232	Distance (Meters) TIA/EIA-449, V.35, X.21, EIA-530
2400	60	1250
4800	30	625
9600	15	312
19,200	15	156
38,400	15	78
115,200	3.7	—
T1 (1.544 Mbps)	—	15

ISDN BRI, DSL, and cable use existing cabling into a building. ISDN BRI links support 64 Kbps in each of the two B channels; that speed is unlikely to improve because of better competing technologies. DSL and cable support similar speeds into the multiple Mbps range, typically with slightly over 1 Mbps from the Internet service provider (ISP) toward the user. However, cable tends to run faster than DSL because of some engineering options not available to DSL; so, in most cases, CATV speeds tend to exceed DSL.

Lab 5.2.3a   Connecting Router LAN Interfaces

In this lab, you identify the Ethernet or Fast Ethernet interfaces on the router.

Lab 5.2.3b   Building a Basic Routed WAN

In this lab, you create a simple routed WAN with two PCs, two switches or hubs, and two routers.

Lab 5.2.3c   Troubleshooting Interconnected Devices

In this lab, you identify and correct networking problems related to cabling issues and workstation IP addressing issues.

Choosing DCE and DTE Cables

WAN links are often long, typically connecting sites that are tens, hundreds, or sometimes thousands of miles apart. So, the telco needs to provide a function called *clocking* or synchronization. The idea is that if a device sends bits at 1.544 Mbps on one end, the other end needs to ensure that it is sampling the incoming signal at exactly 1.544 Mbps. For that to work properly, each device must use a clock, sending or sampling the electrical signal every 1/1,544,000th of a second. That's a small time window. So, just in case one router's clock runs a bit slow or a bit fast, the WAN link needs a way to adjust or synchronize the clocks on both devices. It is slightly like watching a spy movie, when the spies stop to synchronize their watches so they are on the exact same time before they perform some amazing plan that is timed down to the second.

On a typical WAN link, the telco is in charge of synchronizing everyone's clock. The CSU/DSU monitors the clocking from the telco over the line from the telco. Then, the CSU/DSU tells the router the timing, which makes the router synchronize its clock as needed. Many people refer to this process as a master/slave relationship, with the CSU/DSU being a slave to the Telco's clocking, and the router slaving itself to the CSU/DSU's clock.

The world of networking uses the following terms to refer to whether a device is supplying the clock signal to another device or changing its clock to match another device:

- *Data communication equipment (DCE)*—A device that supplies clocking to another device

- *Data terminal equipment (DTE)*—A device that receives clocking from another device and adjusts its clock as needed

Figure 5-27 shows a typical WAN link with the routers listed as DTEs and the CSU/DSU on each end supplying clocking as DCEs.

Figure 5-27   DCE and DTE on a Typical WAN Link

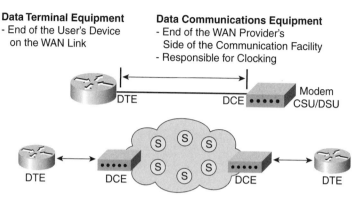

So far, the definitions of DCE and DTE have focused on the true but generic meanings of the terms. When buying Cisco WAN cables, however, each cable is available as a DTE cable or DCE cable, *depending on the router's role*. So, in Figure 5-27, you would pick the right serial cable that was a DTE cable that matched the router's serial connector and CSU/DSU connector on opposite ends.

In some cases, the router needs to act as the DCE, supplying the clocking function and requiring a DCE cable. Routers typically act as a DCE when two routers sit in a lab at the same location, and a network engineer wants to create a WAN link between the routers for testing. Rather than buying two CSU/DSUs and leasing a real WAN link, the engineer can cable the two routers together to create a point-to-point WAN link, as shown in Figure 5-28.

Figure 5-28   Router as DCE: Back-to-Back Serial Connection

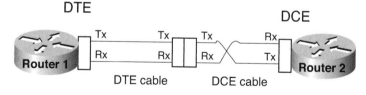

Figure 5-28 makes the cable look larger than life to make the point, but the two routers' serial interfaces are cabled together with two cables. One router (Router 2, in this case) uses a DCE cable, while the other router uses a DTE cable. When connecting the cables, the following occur:

■ The DCE cable swaps the transmit pin and receive pin on the cable, much like an Ethernet crossover cable swaps the transmit and receive pairs. (The telco does the swapping in a real WAN link.)

■ The use of the DCE cable makes it possible for the DCE router to provide clocking on the link.

Fixed and Modular Routers

One of the steps when installing a new WAN link is to determine the type of physical serial interface on a router. For some Cisco routers, all the physical interfaces are permanently installed in the router hardware, so after you buy the router, you know what physical interfaces are used. Other Cisco routers have card slots, which are similar in concept to PC expansion card slots, into which different cards can be inserted. So, the type of physical serial interface cannot be determined until the specific card is chosen.

Note

Typically, routers have their physical interfaces on the back of the router.

Cisco routers with only permanently installed physical interfaces are called fixed-function routers, and those with the capability to add and remove cards are called modular routers. Figure 5-29 shows the back of a fixed-function Cisco 2503 router. The figure illustrates the different components, but more importantly, there is no place on the back of router to somehow remove the interfaces.

Figure 5-29   Fixed-Function Cisco 2503 Router

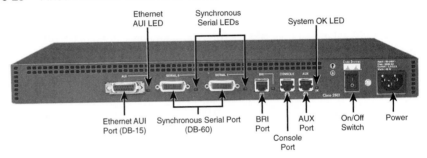

Much of the current Cisco router product line supports at least some modular interfaces. For example, the Cisco 1840 series routers include some fixed-function models and some modular router models. (You can browse to http://www.cisco.com/cdc_content_elements/flash/nextgen/webversion/portfolio/demo.htm?NO_NAV and, with some searching, find a 3D product tour of the modular Cisco 1841 router.) Figure 5-30 shows part of the 3D product demo. (Note that the headings on the left of Figure 5-30 can help you navigate to the right place on the web page to find the 3D tour.)

Figure 5-30 shows part of an 1841 router's back. In the top portion of the figure, on the left side, two fixed Fast Ethernet ports are shown. On the right, a high-speed WIC (HWIC) slot is shown. The HWIC in this part of the router can be removed with a screwdriver and replaced with other cards, such as the WIC-1T and WIC-2T (shown previously in Figure 5-24).

Cisco routers assign a unique number to each interface type so that network engineers can identify each interface. For example, the Cisco 2503 router in Figure 5-29 identifies the two serial interfaces as Serial0 and Serial1. Some models of routers use two numbers to identify ports; for example, the 1841 router in Figure 5-30 uses FastEthernet0/0 and FastEthernet0/1 as names of the two built-in Fast Ethernet interfaces. Some routers even use three numbers; for example, with a two-port serial card in an 1841 router, the serial interfaces might be called Serial0/1/0 and Serial0/1/1. The best way to know the names of the interfaces in a given router model is to turn it on and use commands such as **show ip interface brief**, which is covered in the CCNA 2 course, to list the interfaces by name.

Figure 5-30   Cisco 1841 Modular Router

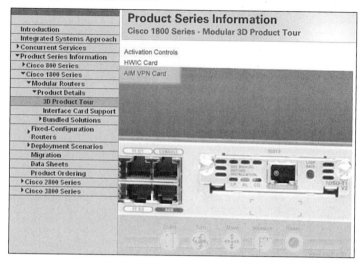

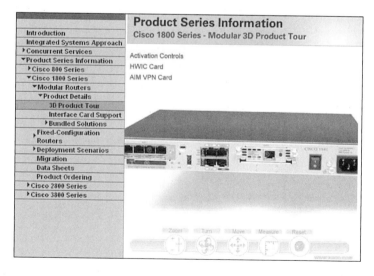

Router Console Cabling

This last short section of this chapter covers a topic that technically isn't a WAN or a LAN cabling topic. However, to gain access to the most common Cisco LAN and WAN devices today—switches and routers—you need to know about Cisco switch and router console ports and the cables used to connect to them.

To configure or troubleshoot a Cisco router or switch, follow these steps:

 Step 1   Connect a PC to the console port of the router or switch by using a rollover cable.

Step 2   Configure a terminal emulator on the PC with the proper settings.

Step 3   Log in to the router or switch by using the terminal emulator on the PC.

First, the PC must be connected to the router/switch console. To do so, Cisco supplies a rollover cable with RJ-45 connectors on each end. This cable does not use Ethernet crossover cable pinouts; instead, it maps pin 1 on one end to pin 8 on the other; pin 2 on one end to pin 7 on the other; pin 3 to pin 6; pin 4 to pin 5; and so on. Figure 5-31 shows an example of the cabling.

Figure 5-31   Console Cabling

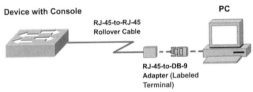

Note

Some newer PCs do not have a serial port with a DB-9 connector; instead, they use USB ports for serial communications. Adapters can be purchased to allow the cable to connect to a USB port instead.

Many PCs have a nine-pin connector, which is called a DB-9 connector, used for serial communications. This connector might be called a serial port (or sometimes a COM port). Most routers and switches have an RJ-45 jack for the console. So, to connect a router console port to a PC's COM port, the rollover cable, with two RJ-45 connectors, must use an adapter to convert from RJ-45 to DB-9, as shown in Figure 5-31. In fact, Cisco sometimes provides console cables that have a DB-9 connector on one end instead of requiring the adapter that converts from RJ-45 to DB-9.

Besides connecting the console rollover cable, a terminal emulator must be configured to use the proper settings. Some Microsoft OSs include a terminal emulator called *HyperTerminal*, which can be found under All Programs > Accessories > Communications on the Windows XP Start menu. The required settings are as follows:

- 9600 bps
- 8 data bits
- No parity
- 1 stop bit
- No flow control

Also, if the PC has more than one serial port, the emulator must be configured to use the correct serial port.

After connecting the cable and configuring the terminal emulator, the router or switch should respond if the user simply presses the Enter key on the keyboard. The details of what to do next are covered early in the CCNA 2 curriculum.

Although both routers and switches have a console port, routers also have an **auxiliary port** **(aux port)**, which is intended for remote out-of-band management of a router. A modem can be cabled to the aux port of a router, with a normal phone line connected to the modem. Then, a network engineer can sit at the PC at her desk and, by using a modem and normal phone line, call the modem connected to the router. Using a terminal emulator, the engineer can log in to the remote router. This allows the network engineer to access the remote router to troubleshoot problems, even when the network is broken and the router might not be accessible through the WAN links connected to the router. (*Out-of-band management* refers to the fact that the management traffic—the logging in to the remote router, in this case—uses some transmission medium besides the ones used for end-user traffic.)

Tip

The online curriculum includes a good interactive media activity that shows console cables and connectors under the heading "Setting Up Console Connections."

 Lab 5.2.7   Establishing a Console Connection to a Router or Switch

In this lab, you create a console connection from a PC to a router or switch by using the proper cable, and then you observe the user interface.

Summary

Ethernet is the most widely used LAN technology, and it can be implemented on various media. Ethernet technologies provide a variety of network speeds, from 10 Mbps to 10 Gigabit Ethernet, which can be applied to appropriate areas of a network. Media and connector requirements differ for various Ethernet implementations.

A NIC's connector must match the media. Coax cable typically needs a BNC connector, whereas fiber cabling typically uses ST, SC, or MT-RJ connectors. For twisted-pair cabling, the RJ-45 connector is typically used.

Twisted-pair cabling must use the correct pinout, or wire sequence, on each end of the cable for the LAN segment to work properly. A crossover cable pinout is required to connect two similar devices, such as two switches, whereas a straight-through cable connects different devices, such as connections between a switch and a PC. A rollover cable connects a PC to the console port of a router.

Repeaters regenerate and retime network signals and allow them to travel a longer distance on the media. Hubs act as multiport repeaters, also regenerating and retiming signals. Hubs also provide a central device to connect devices using a star topology; because of this feature, hubs are sometimes called concentrators.

Bridges and switches use logic at Layer 2 of the OSI model to decide when to forward frames and when to not forward (filter) frames. To do so, bridges and switches examine the destination

MAC address of the frame and compare the address with a list of MAC addresses and ports. Because the bridges and switches do not forward the frames unless it is necessary, they actually create LANs with more bandwidth than do hubs and repeaters, which greatly improves network performance.

LAN switches provide the same basic functions as a bridge, but with many advanced features. Typically, switches have a large number of ports that act as a concentration point, like a hub. Today's switches significantly outperform bridges, to the point where vendors such as Cisco Systems no longer sell bridge products. Switches also support a large variety of advanced features, including virtual LANs (VLANs).

A wireless network can be created with much less cabling than other networks, typically with wireless APs being connected via a cable to the rest of the wired LAN. The wireless devices use transmitters and receivers to convert bits to EM waves (transmitter) and convert them back to bits at the destination (receiver). The two most common wireless technologies used for networking are IR and RF.

Typically, computers use either a peer-to-peer model of communications or a client/server model. In both models, one computer acts as a client and issues a request for a service from another computer that acts as a server. For example, a client might want to print a document, but it does not have a printer. So, the client computer that wants to print the document can send the document to the server, which then prints the document. In a peer-to-peer network, networked computers act as equal partners, or peers, with each computer taking on the client or server function as needed. In a client/server arrangement, network services are located on a dedicated computer called a server, and end-user computers always act as clients.

Routers are responsible for routing data packets from source to destination computers. To do so, routers typically connect to a wide range of network media, including all types of Ethernet LANs, as well as many WAN media-like high-speed serial links: ISDN, DSL, and cable modems.

Each type of WAN connection requires some form of media and connector. When a router's serial interface is used, the cable type is determined based on the physical connector on the router's serial interface, as well as the physical interface on the CSU/DSU to be used on the link. Additionally, each serial cable is either a DTE or DCE cable, depending on which role the router plays (typically, DTE).

On any serial WAN link, a router acts as either DTE or DCE. The DCE provides synchronization and clocking, with the DTE adjusting its clock to match the DCE. Traditionally, a router acts as DTE, and the CSU/DSU acts as the DCE. However, cases arise when a router needs to be the DCE.

You can find supplemental coverage of topics related to those described in this chapter in the section "Additional Topics of Interest," which is located on the CD-ROM.

Check Your Understanding

Complete all the review questions listed here to test your understanding of the topics and concepts in this chapter. Answers are listed in Appendix A, "Answers to Check Your Understanding and Challenge Questions."

1. Which of the following is a characteristic of an Ethernet switch? (Pick two answers.)

    A. It filters based on the source MAC address.

    B. It creates separate broadcast domains.

    C. It functions like a high-speed multiport bridge.

    D. It filters based on the destination IP address.

2. Which type of cabling is the most appropriate choice for Ethernet connectivity from a switch to a workstation?

    A. Coax

    B. UTP

    C. Fiber-optic

    D. RJ-11

3. Comparing switches, hubs, repeaters, and bridges, which of these devices typically have multiple ports that provide a convenient connection point for end-user computers? (Select the two best answers.)

    A. Repeater

    B. Switch

    C. Bridge

    D. Hub

4. What is the name of the connector on an external transceiver used by some older networking devices that do not have RJ-45 connectors for Ethernet?

    A. NIC

    B. DCE/DTE

    C. CSU/DSU

    D. Attachment user interface (AUI)

5. For which of the following do you need to provide a crossover cable?

    A. Connecting a switch to a switch

    B. Connecting a switch to a router

    C. Connecting a workstation to a hub

    D. Connecting a workstation to a switch

6. From a wireless laptop's perspective, to which of the following is a wireless AP most similar?

   A. Hub

   B. Switch

   C. Router

   D. Bridge

7. Which device is best for connecting a LAN to a WAN?

   A. Hub

   B. Bridge

   C. Workgroup switch

   D. Router

8. What data-transmission method does a WAN use?

   A. Parallel

   B. Serial

   C. Single

   D. None of the answers are correct

9. Which of the following best describes a DCE device?

   A. User device at the end of a network

   B. Equipment that serves as the data source or destination

   C. Physical devices such as protocol translators and multiplexers

   D. Device that provides the clocking rate for a serial connection

10. Which of the following acts as a DTE in a typical WAN link between two sites that are located several hundred miles apart?

    A. ISP

    B. CSU/DSU

    C. Telco

    D. Business's on-premises router

11. When DSL is installed, what type of connection is used between the home computer and the ISP?

    A. Cable

    B. Telephone line

    C. ISDN

    D. DB-9

12. What type of connector connects a router and an external CSU/DSU?

    A. RJ-45

    B. RJ-11

    C. Serial

    D. Console

13. What type of cable connects a terminal and a console port?

    A. Straight-through

    B. Rollover

    C. Crossover

    D. Coax

Challenge Questions and Activities

These activities require a deeper application of the concepts covered in this chapter, similar to how answering CCNA certification exam questions requires applying detailed concepts to a particular scenario.

 Packet Tracer   **Activity 5-1:** Compare the differences of using a hub and a switch as the central device in a network.

Part One:

Step 1   Start Packet Tracer.

Step 2   Choose **Options** and make sure that there is a check mark beside Simple Mode.

Step 3   Drag and drop one hub onto the screen.

Step 4   Drag and drop four PCs around the hub.

Step 5   Click each PC and give it the address information from this table.

PC	Gateway	IP Address	Subnet Mask
PC0	192.168.1.254	192.168.1.10	255.255.255.0
PC1	192.168.1.254	192.168.1.11	255.255.255.0
PC2	192.168.1.254	192.168.1.12	255.255.255.0
PC3	192.168.1.254	192.168.1.13	255.255.255.0

Part Two:

Step 1   Connect each PC to the hub. Click **Connect**, click **PC0**, and then click the hub.

Step 2   Continue this process for each PC. If successful, all connections should have green dots at both ends.

Part Three:

Step 1   Select the **Simulation** tab at the top of the screen. Click the red plus sign (**+**) at the top of the screen. This creates a new packet. Click **PC0** to make it the source of the packet, and then click **PC2** to make it the destination.

Step 2   Click the red plus sign (**+**) to create another packet. Click **PC3** to make it the source of the packet, and then click **PC2** to make it the destination.

Step 3   Choose **Options** and make sure that the Animation and Sound options have a check mark beside them.

Step 4   Play the animation and notice the collisions.

Part Four:

Step 1   Click the **Topology** tab at the top of the screen.

Step 2   Select the **Remove** icon and delete the hub.

Step 3   Drag and drop a switch onto the screen.

Step 4   Connect the PCs to the switch.

Step 5   Select the **Simulation** tab at the top of the screen. Play the animation and notice what is different from the simulation where the hub was installed.

CHAPTER 6

Ethernet Fundamentals

Objectives

Upon completion of this chapter, you should be able to answer the following questions:

- What are the Ethernet IEEE naming standards?

- Ethernet operates at which layers of the OSI reference model?

- What are the basics of Ethernet technology?

- What is the 802.3 framing process and frame structure?

- What are the key fields of an Ethernet frame and their purposes?

- What is Media Access Control (MAC)?

- What is the CSMA/CD process?

- How are full duplex and the reduction of collision domains related?

- What is autonegotiation as relates to speed and duplex?

Additional Topics of Interest

Several chapters of this book contain additional coverage of earlier topics or related topics that are secondary to the main goals of the chapter. You can find the additional coverage on the CD-ROM accompanying this book. For this chapter, the following additional topics are covered:

- Ethernet timing

- Interface spacing

- Ethernet collisions

- Ethernet errors

Key Terms

This chapter uses the following key terms. You can find the definitions in the Glossary:

10BASE-T   page 239

100BASE-T   page 239

100BASE-FX   page 239

1000BASE-TX   page 239

baseband   page 239

broadband   page 239

IEEE 802.3   page 240

Logical Link Control (LLC)   page 241

framing   page 242

encapsulation   page 243

frame   page 243

destination MAC address   page 245

source MAC address   page 245

preamble   page 245

continues

continued

Start Frame Delimiter (SFD)   page 245

Frame Check Sequence (FCS)   page 245

cyclic redundancy check (CRC)   page 245

Type field   page 246

Length field   page 246

Media Access Control (MAC)   page 247

burned-in address (BIA)   page 247

Organizationally Unique Identifier (OUI)   page 247

CSMA/CD   page 251

collision   page 252

collision back-off timer   page 252

loopback circuit   page 254

half duplex   page 254

full duplex   page 255

buffering   page 255

autonegotiation   page 258

Fast Link Pulse (FLP)   page 258

nondeterministic   page 259

probabilistic   page 259

deterministic   page 259

token passing   page 259

This chapter begins a sequence of three chapters that focus entirely on topics related to Ethernet. The earlier chapters introduced some of the basics of Ethernet, as well as a fair amount of detail about the cables, and the related physics, of how Ethernet can transmit using different types of cables. This chapter focuses on the fundamental features of Ethernet and the rules they define about how an Ethernet should operate. Chapter 7, "Ethernet Technologies," covers more details about each different Ethernet standard, and Chapter 8, "Ethernet Switching," explains more details about how Ethernet LAN switches work.

The term *Ethernet* refers to many different LAN standards. This chapter begins by explaining a bit of the history of Ethernet, details that reveal why Ethernet has enjoyed a long life through the continual introduction of newer and more advanced variations of Ethernet. These standards have some similarities and some differences, but the common thread between them all is that they all use the same frame structure. The first section of the chapter reviews the basic terms used for various types of Ethernet and then covers the common details related to Ethernet frames, how they are used, and what each part of a frame means.

The second major section of the chapter explains several operational details of Ethernets, including the very important details of carrier sense multiple access with collision detection (CSMA/CD). These operational issues, like autonegotiation and duplex, apply to most every type of Ethernet in some way.

Ethernet Fundamentals

Interestingly, almost every chapter of the course and book so far mentions Ethernet in some way. This chapter begins the process of pulling those concepts together and filling in some of the details. This first section of the chapter is essentially a tour of the basics of Ethernet. It includes such topics as Ethernet history, the names of the different Ethernet standards, how Ethernet relates to the OSI model, Ethernet framing, and Ethernet MAC addresses.

The History of Ethernet

Ethernet was created primarily by Robert Metcalfe and others at Xerox in the early-to-mid-1970s. They later teamed with Digital Equipment Corporation (DEC, which was also known as Digital) and Intel to create some of the initial products and to publish a set of proprietary standards to which the three vendors agreed. Those standards and the products that used them became known as DIX Ethernet, with *DIX* referring to the first letter of each of the three cooperating companies. They continued development through a second version of the standard, which became known as DIX Version 2, or simply DIXv2, published in 1980. This standard defined protocols and the physical details of what became known as 10BASE5.

In the early 1980s, the IEEE took over the development of the standards with the blessings of the originally involved companies. The IEEE held the first meeting of its new LAN committee in February 1980. That committee, dubbed the 802 committee, was tasked with developing

IEEE standards for LANs. The 802 committee discovered the need for several different LAN standards, so it formed subcommittees. Specifically, it created the 802.3 subcommittee to work on Ethernet standards, and the 802.2 subcommittee to work on standards that applied to several types of LANs, including Ethernet and Token Ring. So, both the 802.2 and 802.3 standards relate in some way to Ethernet.

Since its inception, the 802.3 subcommittee has published standards for 10BASE5 (1980), 10BASE2 (1985), 10BASE-T (1990), Fast Ethernet (100 Mbps, 1995), Gigabit Ethernet (1 Gbps, 1998), and 10 Gigabit Ethernet (10 Gbps, 2002). While the progression is impressive, the more impressive feat may be that each new type of Ethernet supports the same basic Ethernet frame. The common framing throughout all types of IEEE Ethernet, plus other features in common among all Ethernet types, has helped make Ethernet a success today. By using common framing, the Ethernet family remains very simple, particularly once you understand one type of Ethernet. Ethernet has been very successful as a result of the common framing standards as well as other reasons:

- Ethernet is relatively simple.

- Adding a new type of Ethernet is easy, because many people already understand other types of Ethernet.

- Ethernet is reliable, with many well-tested components and protocols being used for newer types of Ethernet.

- Ethernet is inexpensive, with new types of Ethernet typically experiencing rapid price reductions within a few years of their introduction.

The next section takes a closer look at the names of the various types of Ethernet.

The Names of Different IEEE Ethernet Types

The IEEE has continued to improve Ethernet over the years, adding new options for different speeds and cabling in particular. These changes include supporting media with longer cabling distances as well, even to the point of making Ethernet a viable option for short WAN and MAN connections. This section covers the basics of the different types of Ethernet, the standards that define them, and how those standards compare to the OSI model.

Ethernet standards differ in two main respects:

- Speed

- Type of cabling supported

For example, Gigabit Ethernet supports different standards that use unshielded twisted-pair (UTP) copper and fiber-optic cabling. Because these two types of transmission media differ so much, the IEEE defines Gigabit Ethernet over fiber in one standard and Gigabit Ethernet over UTP cabling in another standard.

The IEEE uses two styles of names to refer to the different Ethernet standards. One style simply uses the name of the IEEE subcommittee that performed the work to define the standard. For instance, the fiber Gigabit Ethernet standard is called IEEE 802.3z because the 802.3z subcommittee developed the standard.

However, many people use the other style of name more commonly—that is, names that actually identify the speed and something about the cabling type. For example, names like *10BASE-T*, *100BASE-TX*, *100BASE-FX*, and *1000BASE-T* identify the speed, with *T* and *F* referring to twisted-pair cabling and fiber-optic cabling, respectively. These commonly used Ethernet names list the basic differentiating features of each type of Ethernet, as follows:

- **Speed**—The speed of the standard is listed in megabits per second (Mbps) before the word BASE.

- **Baseband transmission**—All current Ethernet standards use baseband transmission, hence the word BASE in the middle of the names.

- **Cabling**—The text after the word BASE identifies the type of cabling; for example, *T* stands for twisted pair.

For example, 10BASE-T simply means a 10-Mbps transmission rate using a baseband signal and twisted-pair (copper) media.

Although the concepts of speed and cabling should be familiar by this point in the course, the concept of baseband transmission was not covered in earlier chapters. *Baseband* transmission means that a single frequency is used to encode bits over the medium. The term "band" is simply short for "bandwidth," and in the analog world, bandwidth refers to a range of consecutive frequencies. The term "base" refers to the use of a single base frequency. (Knowing the origins of the term helps some people and hinders others—just remember that it uses a single frequency.)

One of the reasons the term *baseband* is used at all relates to early, now-obsolete versions of Ethernet. These other technologies used a method call *broadband*, which means that a broad range of frequency bands was used to send signals. The common Ethernet names needed to include some information about whether baseband or broadband transmissions were used, so the Ethernet names included either BASE or BROAD in the name. For example, 10BROAD36 is an old Ethernet standard that used broadband transmission.

One common example of broadband transmission is FM radio. A radio station that is at 104.7 on the dial transmits at a broad range of frequencies surrounding 104.7 million hertz (megahertz, or MHz). The actual transmission covers 200 kHz (kilohertz)—in other words, a range of 200,000 different frequencies. Of course, many other radio stations can also transmit at the same time; to do so, they must use other frequency bands.

Note

Today, the term broadband often refers to fast Internet access, such as digital subscriber line (DSL) and cable, regardless of what kind of physical signaling and frequencies are used. As it turns out, both DSL and cable do technically use broadband transmission techniques, but overuse of the term broadband in advertising has made it widely perceived as synonymous with "high speed."

IEEE Ethernet Standards and the OSI Model

As mentioned earlier, in the section "The History of Ethernet," people at Xerox invented Ethernet and then teamed with Intel and Digital to develop products and publish vendor standards for Ethernet. In 1980, development of Ethernet standards was handed over to the IEEE. This section examines some of the details about IEEE Ethernet standards and how these standards relate to the OSI model.

IEEE 802.3 Standards

The *IEEE 802.3* subcommittee began its life in 1980 with the process of standardizing the only type of Ethernet that existed at the time: 10BASE5 Ethernet. The IEEE 802.3 subcommittee used the work and documents provided by Xerox as the basis for its work, creating an 802.3 standard that matched the DIXv2 standard in most ways. (The one big exception was the difference in framing, which is covered in the section "Ethernet Framing" later in this chapter.)

The 802.3 subcommittee's role kept growing due to the need to further develop and expand Ethernet. As a result, the 802.3 subcommittee itself has additional subcommittees, most often used to spearhead the development of each new supplement to the Ethernet standard. As a result, there are many Ethernet standards, all named after their subcommittee names, defining additional variations of Ethernet.

The many different 802.3 standards that define different types of Ethernet concern themselves with several details of Ethernet operations, including the following:

- Physical transmission details, including cables, connectors, encoding, and speeds

- Media access issues, such as the carrier sense multiple access collision detect (CSMA/CD) algorithm used by NICs to determine when they are allowed to send data over the medium

- Errors during transmission, discovered using the 802.3 trailer's Frame Check Sequence (FCS) field

- MAC addresses, their format, and their location in the 802.3 header

- The ability of NICs to synchronize to the incoming signal by providing a Preamble and Start Frame Delimiter (SFD)

Most of the functions defined in this list happen to be implemented through the IEEE 802.3 Ethernet frame, which is covered later in this chapter in the section "Encapsulating Packets Inside Ethernet Frames." So, most of the new and different work for each new type of Ethernet relates to the physical layer details—how to transmit the bits over a particular cable and have it work without causing any problems.

The IEEE 802.2 Logical Link Control Standard

When the IEEE 802 committee first created its subcommittees in the early 1980s, it created five subcommittees, which are listed in Table 6-1.

Table 6-1   Original IEEE 802 Subcommittees

Subcommittee	Purpose
802.1	LAN management and control functions
802.2	Functions common to several LAN types, originally 802.3, 802.4, and 802.5
802.3	Ethernet LANs
802.4	Token bus LANs
802.5	Token Ring LANs

The 802.1 and 802.2 subcommittees had responsibility for LAN features that could be used for all three types of LANs defined by the other three subcommittees. For example, what today is known as the Spanning Tree Protocol (STP), used by Ethernet switches to control the use of redundant paths in an Ethernet, is a control function; it was defined by an 802.1 standard because the IEEE envisioned STP as a feature that could be used by all types of LANs.

The original focus of the 802.2 subcommittee was to standardize any feature that spanned all three of the early LAN standards as defined by the 802.3, 802.4, and 802.5 subcommittees. The 802.2 subcommittee determined that all three LAN types needed to somehow control the LAN, using a set of logic and rules. So, the standard was named *Logical Link Control*, or LLC.

The online curriculum mostly ignores the topic of the 802.2 LLC standard because the need for 802.2 has decreased due to other developments. However, a basic knowledge of 802.2 can be useful for building networks today, so additional coverage of 802.2 LLC is included in this chapter under the heading "Additional Background on IEEE 802.2 Logical Link Control."

Comparing Ethernet Standards to the OSI Model

The OSI model's lower two layers map to the functions defined in the IEEE Ethernet standards, as shown in Figure 6-1.

Figure 6-1   Comparing OSI and Ethernet Standards

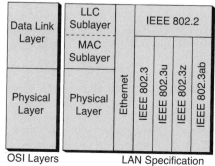

Figure 6-1 points out several details about the IEEE Ethernet standards. First, each new type of Ethernet defines some physical layer standards and details of the data link layer. Figure 6-1 shows several of the 802.3 supplements that define different types of Ethernet. For example, it shows 802.3ab, which is the name of the subcommittee and the name of the IEEE standard for Gigabit Ethernet over UTP cabling. 802.3z defines Gigabit Ethernet over fiber, and 802.3u defines Fast Ethernet, which is 100-Mbps Ethernet, over UTP cabling. All of these standards define the details of physical transmission over some medium, so they match the OSI physical layer.

The IEEE 802.3 standard defines many physical layer details, as well as the lower half of the data link layer, called Media Access Control (MAC). 802.3 includes the MAC protocol to perform several functions that physical layer (Layer 1) standards cannot. The following list describes the differences in functionality:

- Layer 1 standards cannot communicate with upper-layer protocols, but the MAC protocol can communicate with higher layers.

- Layer 1 standards cannot identify other computers, so MAC defines physical addressing in the form of MAC addresses.

- Layer 1 standards define how to send bits but cannot interpret their meaning, so MAC standards define framing.

- Layer 1 standards cannot manage the process of which device can send at what time, so the MAC protocol defines CSMA/CD.

Ethernet Framing

The term *framing* refers to two things:

- The process of encapsulating data inside a header and possibly a trailer

- The meaning given to the bits inside those headers and trailers

Although the definition of framing is formal, the concept is relatively straightforward. When a computer sends bits over a cable, it sends them for a specific purpose—to get some other computer to receive those bits and process the data. Framing defines the meaning of the transmitted bits.

An easy analogy can be drawn between framing and sending a letter. After you write the letter, it needs to be put into an envelope, because the post office will not send a piece of paper by itself. Additionally, the address must be written on the envelope, and in a particular place, with a postage stamp in a different place. So, to send the letter, you must put something around the letter (an envelope) and put the right information onto that envelope.

Ethernet framing works with the same general ideas. Like an envelope, the NIC adds an Ethernet header and trailer around the Layer 3 protocol data unit (L3PDU) to encapsulate the data. (As a quick reminder, an L3PDU, as covered in Chapter 2, includes the header and data for a Layer 3 protocol but does not include the headers and trailers of lower layers.) Like the address and stamp, the header and trailer must have the properly formatted information, because otherwise the frame will not be delivered correctly over the LAN.

The Ethernet standards define many functions at both Layer 1 and Layer 2 of the OSI model. The physical transmission details vary for each of the many types of Ethernet. However, all the different IEEE Ethernet standards use the same framing.

Encapsulating Packets Inside Ethernet Frames

The best way to get a real sense of the process of framing data, and the fields inside the frame's header and trailer, is to look at a real frame. Figure 6-2 shows an example of the encapsulation process, by which Ethernet, which works at OSI Layers 1 and 2, takes the L3PDU (for instance, an IP packet) and places the L3PDU behind an Ethernet header. That process is generically called *encapsulation*, and sometimes is called framing. The term *frame* refers to the resulting bits that include the Ethernet header and trailer.

Figure 6-2   Ethernet Encapsulation and the IEEE 802.3 Frame

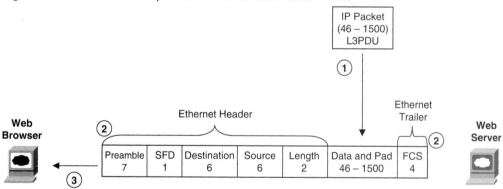

First, focus on the encapsulation process, ignoring the specific words inside the header and trailer for now. A protocol just above Ethernet in the OSI model, like IP, needs to send some data. The first step in the process shows an IP packet that needs to be sent by the web server back to the web browser on the left. To send this IP packet over an Ethernet LAN, the following process (as listed in the figure) occurs:

1. The IP software gives the IP packet to the Ethernet software.

2. The Ethernet software encapsulates the IP packet (L3PDU) between an Ethernet header and trailer.

3. The Ethernet NIC on the web server physically transmits the bits that comprise the frame over an Ethernet LAN.

Note

Sometimes students confuse the terms encapsulation and encoding, but they are indeed different concepts. Encoding refers to the process of how a device varies the electrical signal or light signal to transmit a 0 or 1 over some medium.

The Fields in the IEEE 802.3 Frame

The Ethernet header and trailer include several specific pieces of data that are used in some way for the purposes of the Ethernet protocol. Each piece of information is called a field, with each field having a specific name and purpose. Figure 6-3 shows the framing of three different styles of Ethernet frame.

Figure 6-3   Three Styles of Ethernet Framing

DIX

Preamble 8	Destination 6	Source 6	**Type 2**	Data and Pad 46 – 1500	FCS 4

IEEE 802.3 (Original)

Preamble 7	SFD 1	Destination 6	Source 6	**Length 2**	Data and Pad 46 – 1500	FCS 4

IEEE 802.3 (Revised 1997)

Preamble 7	SFD 1	Destination 6	Source 6	**Length/ Type 2**	Data and Pad 46 – 1500	FCS 4

The framing shown in Figure 6-3 names the fields inside the header and trailer. In other words, the header and trailer contain a defined number of bytes, and within each, different sets of bytes have different meanings. For example, the Destination field holds the 6-byte MAC address to which a frame should be delivered. Table 6-2 lists the names of the fields in the IEEE 802.3 Ethernet header and briefly defines each field's purpose.

Table 6-2   IEEE 802.3 Ethernet Header

Field	Length of Field (Bytes)	Purpose
Preamble	7	Synchronization
Start Frame Delimiter (SFD)	1	Signifies that the next byte begins the Destination MAC field
Destination MAC Address	6	Identifies the intended recipient of this frame
Source MAC Address	6	Identifies the sender of this frame
Length	2	Defines the length of the frame's data field (either Length or Type is present, but not both)

Field	Length of Field (Bytes)	Purpose
Type	2	Defines the type of protocol listed inside the frame (either Length or Type is present, but not both)
Data and Pad[1]	46—1500	Holds data from a higher layer, typically an L3PDU (generic), or with TCP/IP, an IP packet
Frame Check Sequence (FCS)	4	Provides a method for the receiving NIC to determine if the frame experienced transmission errors and, if so, to discard the frame

[1] If the packet is less than 46 bytes, extra bytes, called padding, are added so that the field is 46 bytes. Padding is added because the data field must be at least 46 bytes in length.

Many of the fields have an obvious purpose, as covered in earlier topics in the book. For example, the *Destination MAC Address* field allows a switch to determine how to forward the frame. Also, when a computer receives an Ethernet frame, the computer can look at the destination MAC address, compare that value to its own MAC address, and decide whether the frame is meant for it or some other device.

The *Source MAC Address* field identifies the sending NIC or interface, which allows the receiving NIC or interface to know the address of the device that sent the frame. It is also very useful to the process that bridges and switches use to build their bridging and switching tables.

The *Preamble* and *Start Frame Delimiter (SFD)* work together to allow synchronization of the transmitted signal. Ethernet devices (at 10 and 100 Mbps speeds) do not transmit a signal when idle. So, to let all NICs and interfaces get ready to receive a frame, the frame needs to have a few bytes that mean nothing more than "Pay attention; you are about to get a frame." The Preamble and SFD together fulfill that role.

The *Frame Check Sequence (FCS)* allows the receiving NIC or interface to decide if the frame had an error. To make this decision, the sending NIC uses some polynomial math, called a *cyclic redundancy check (CRC)*, with the frame (beginning with the destination MAC address field) as input. The sender puts the results of that CRC formula into the FCS field. The receiver then receives the frame and runs the same CRC math on the received frame. If the results match the FCS field in the received frame, the frame had no errors. If they do not match, the receiver believes the frame had an error and thus discards the frame.

DIX Framing and IEEE Framing

When the IEEE created the framing standards for Ethernet, it changed the framing slightly compared to the DIXv2 specification. Figure 6-3, earlier in this chapter, showed the original DIX framing at the top of the figure, the original IEEE Ethernet framing in the middle, and the current IEEE Ethernet framing at the bottom.

The DIX frame has two main differences with the original 802.3 standard framing. DIX did not use the term SFD, instead simply calling the entire first 8 bytes, which are used for synchronization, the Preamble. There is no functional difference between the DIX and IEEE 802.3 frames in the first 8 bytes, other than the names used to describe these bytes.

The other difference is the DIXv2 *Type field* versus the IEEE *Length field*. The DIXv2 Type field identifies the contents of the data field in the frame. Xerox kept a list of 2-byte values, called protocol numbers, that identified each unique protocol. Any vendor could register with Xerox to be assigned a number for one or more of its protocols—protocols it wanted to be allowed to send over an Ethernet LAN. Later, the IEEE took over managing the list of protocol numbers and the protocol that each number implied.

The protocol numbers are very important to the de-encapsulation process. For example, when a NIC receives a frame, it will eventually want to de-encapsulate the data from the Ethernet frames and give the data to the right software on that receiving computer. The Type field identifies the type of data—for example, an IP packet, or an L3PDU of some other protocol. Without the knowledge listed in the Type field, the receiving computer would not know to which software to give the data.

The 2-byte IEEE Length field occupies the exact same position in the frame as does the DIX Type field. This field lists a number that identifies the length of the data field in bytes. To perform the function of the original DIX Type field, the IEEE originally relied upon a couple of other headers that followed the 802.3 field.

Note

The additional headers used by the IEEE include the 802.2 LLC header, covered in the "LLC, SNAP, and Determining the Type of Protocol" section later in this chapter.

Interestingly, the IEEE planned the Ethernet standards so that the older DIXv2 frames and the original IEEE frames could coexist on a LAN. By doing so, the IEEE allowed an easy migration from existing DIXv2-compliant NICs and networking devices to IEEE-standard devices that used IEEE framing. To allow devices to identify which frame type is used for a particular frame, the IEEE did not assign protocol type numbers below 1536 (hexadecimal 600). The maximum allowed length of the data field is 1500 bytes. So, a device can simply look at the 2 bytes after the Source MAC Address field and know that the frame uses a Type field if the number is 1536 (decimal) or higher, meaning that the frame is a DIXv2 frame. If the value of the 2-byte field after the source MAC address is less than 1536, the device can determine that the frame has a length field and that the frame is an IEEE 802.3 frame.

In 1997, the IEEE updated 802.3 to officially accept yet a third small variation on these two types of frames, as shown at the bottom of Figure 6-3. This new standard essentially makes the original DIX framing an IEEE standard, allowing the 2 bytes after the Source MAC Address field to be used as a Type field (value 1536 or more) or a Length field (value less than 1536). Formally, the IEEE names this 2-byte field the Length/Type field.

The Format of MAC Addresses

Media Access Control (MAC) addresses are 6-byte hexadecimal (hex) numbers that are used to identify NICs and other Ethernet interfaces that connect to a LAN. Each NIC has a ***burned-in address (BIA)***, which is a permanent unicast MAC address assigned to the card. The term BIA simply refers to a MAC address, with emphasis on its being the MAC address that was permanently assigned to a NIC or interface at the time of manufacture.

The IEEE developed a set of requirements for BIAs that ensures that each Ethernet BIA is unique among all other BIAs in the world. To do that, the IEEE defined rules about how BIAs are assigned and defined the structure of a MAC address. MAC addresses are 6 bytes long, with the first half and second half used for different purposes, as shown in Figure 6-4.

Figure 6-4   Structure of a MAC Address

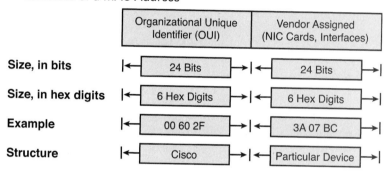

The structure allows the IEEE to impose rules upon the vendors that create Ethernet products. First, before a vendor is legally allowed to sell Ethernet NICs or other devices with Ethernet interfaces (such as switches or routers), the vendor must register with the IEEE. At registration, the IEEE assigns a 3-byte code, called the *Organizationally Unique Identifier (OUI)*, to that vendor. Then, the IEEE requires that the vendor follow these two rules with regard to the BIAs assigned to its products:

- All BIAs assigned to NICs or other networking devices must use that vendor's assigned OUI as the first 3 bytes of the BIA.

- All BIAs with the same OUI as the first 3 bytes must be assigned a unique value in the last 3 bytes.

By following these two rules, one vendor will never create a BIA that is the same as another vendor's BIA. As a result, the world should have globally unique BIAs.

Sending Frames over Different Types of Ethernet

As mentioned earlier in the chapter, in the "IEEE Ethernet Standards and the OSI Model" section, many Ethernet standards exist, varying in terms of bandwidth (speed), media supported, and other features. However, each type of Ethernet uses the exact same framing. The use of the same framing allows the following to occur in a campus LAN:

> An Ethernet frame can be sent by a device on one type of Ethernet, and can go over different links using different types of Ethernet, with no problems—because they all use the same framing.

By using the same framing for all new types of Ethernet, the IEEE has enabled companies to slowly migrate to newer types of Ethernet and keep some computers on the older style of Ethernet during the migration. For example, Figure 6-5 shows a campus LAN, with each highlighted link using a different style of Ethernet.

Figure 6-5   Sample Campus LAN with Different Types of Ethernet

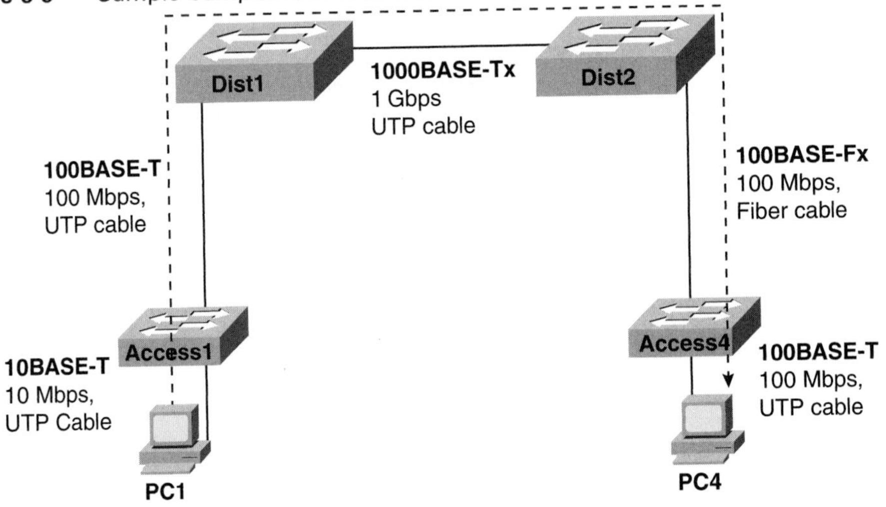

PC1 and PC2 can exchange data all they want. When they do, the frames sometimes go over copper wires, and sometimes over fiber-optic cables. Sometimes the frames are transmitted at 10 Mbps, sometimes at 100 Mbps, and other times at 1 Gbps. As long as the LAN is connected with working Ethernet segments, the fact that all types of Ethernets use the same frames allows these frames to be sent over all types of Ethernet without any trouble.

LLC, SNAP, and Determining the Type of Protocol

The online curriculum makes only minor references to the 802.2 LLC standard. The use of 802.2 LLC headers has decreased over time, particularly with the IEEE 802.3 standard allowing the use of a Type field instead of the Length field, as shown earlier in Figure 6-3. However, a basic knowledge of 802.2 can be useful for building networks today, so some coverage is included here.

Keep in mind that this section covers materials not covered in the online curriculum. If you or your instructor prefers to skip over these deeper bits of additional coverage, feel free to skip to the section "Ethernet Operation" later in this chapter.

Additional Background on IEEE 802.2 Logical Link Control

The original focus of the 802.2 subcommittee was to standardize any feature that spanned all three of the early LAN standards: 802.3 Ethernet, 802.4 Token Bus, and 802.5 Token Ring. The 802.2 subcommittee determined that all three LAN types needed to somehow control the LAN, using a set of logic and rules. So, the subcommittee was named "Logical Link Control," or LLC.

The term "link" in LLC has traditionally been used to refer to the concept of how two devices communicate over a transmission medium. For instance, two devices on either end of a WAN leased line were said to be "linked"; someone might ask whether "the link is up," meaning not only is the leased line functional, but are the two devices succeeding at using the transmission medium. The term LLC was adapted from that general usage of the term link, because the 802.2 subcommittee defines details that ensure that when two devices attempt to communicate using the medium, they communicate correctly.

After the dust settled, the 802.2 had defined two main categories of functions. To accomplish these functions, the 802.2 subcommittee created its own header, called the 802.2 header. The two base features are the abilities to do the following:

- Identify the type of data inside the frame's data field

- Control the transmissions between two devices on a LAN, specifically to perform error recovery when frames are lost

The second of these functions typically is not used today, but the first function is still used in production networks. The de-encapsulation process, described in Chapter 2, "Networking Fundamentals," needs to know what data is in the frame's data field. For example, the Ethernet frame may have an IP packet in the data field, or the data field could contain something else. In the old days, many other Layer 3 protocols could have been inside the frame; that is still possible today, although many networks use TCP/IP as the only OSI Layer 3 protocol. Today, other variations of content in an Ethernet frame, mostly related to advanced IP features, could be in the frame's data field. Regardless, there needs to be some way to determine what is in the data part of the frame for the receiving device to know what to do with the data.

The original IEEE 802.3 Ethernet standards relied on the work of the 802.2 subcommittee to solve this problem of identifying the type of data. The 802.2 subcommittee defined a field in the 802.2 LLC header called the Destination Service Access Point (DSAP). (The concept is identical to the DIXv2 Type field mentioned earlier in the chapter in the section "DIX Framing and IEEE Framing.") This field holds a number that identifies the contents of the data. The IEEE maintains a list of DSAP values and the corresponding protocol implied by each DSAP value.

To conform to IEEE standards, the IEEE 802 committee originally required that an 802.2 header must follow each 802.3 (and 802.4 and 802.5) frame header. As a result, a standard 802.3 frame always has a DSAP field in the 802.2 header, as shown in Figure 6-6.

Figure 6-6   IEEE 802.3 and 802.2 Headers

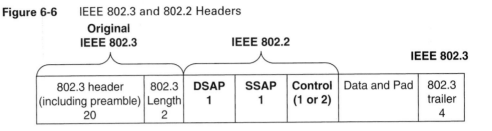

The IEEE SNAP Header

The original DIX Ethernet header had a 2-byte Protocol Type field that identified the contents of the data field in an Ethernet frame. The IEEE 802.2 subcommittee made the unfortunate choice of defining the 802.2 DSAP field as a single byte. This choice, plus a couple of other choices that meant only 6 bits of the DSAP byte could actually be used to identify the protocol inside the frame's data field, meant that the DSAP field did not allow enough different protocol type values. Worse yet, the IEEE ran out of valid DSAP values before a value was assigned to IP! So, the IEEE needed a Type field that was 2 bytes long. However, changing the DSAP values for existing products from a 1-byte field to a 2-byte field would have been too disruptive.

The original solution to this problem was to use an optional header called the Subnetwork Access Protocol (SNAP) header. The header includes an OUI field, which is mostly unused, and a 2-byte protocol Type field. The IEEE maintains a list of SNAP types and their corresponding protocols—in fact, it is the exact same set of numbers still maintained for use as the DIXv2 Type field and the IEEE 802.3 standard Type field.

The DIX and IEEE Type Field

This chapter's story of the Type fields for Ethernet is finally coming to a close. Figure 6-7 shows three different frame formats with the different Type fields, in the chronological order of their addition to the Ethernet family. Each example shows framing with an IP packet inside the data portion of the frame.

Figure 6-7 shows numbers to the left of the frames, which correspond to the following explanations:

1. The original DIX frame format, with a 2-byte Type field. This framing was first used in the 1970s.

2. The IEEE standard for framing, with SNAP header. This framing was introduced in the mid-1980s (802.3 and 802.2 headers) and 1988 (SNAP header part).

3. The new revised IEEE standard for framing, with a Length/Type field. When the Length/Type field is less than 1536, it is a Length field, with an 802.2 header following; when it has a value of 1536 (decimal) or more, it is a Type field and identifies what follows the 802.3 header. The IEEE approved this framing in 1997.

Figure 6-7   Ethernet Framing with Variations on the Type Field

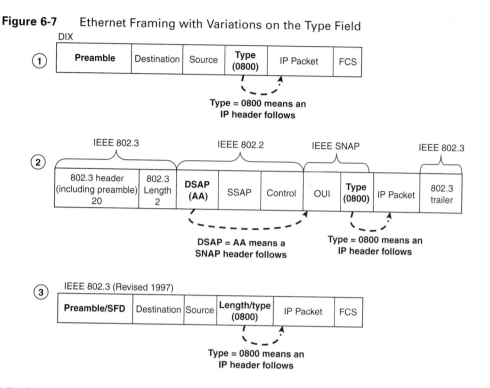

Note

In the IEEE-standard frame, the DSAP value of hex AA means that a SNAP header follows. The SNAP Type and DIX/IEEE Type fields of hex 0800 mean that the data holds an IP packet.

All of these frame formats can be used on Ethernet LANs today. Keep in mind that some network analyzers, such as the Ethereal software tool, may refer to a frame similar to the bottom one in Figure 6-7 and call it a DIXv2 frame, even though it follows the latest 802.3 standard.

Ethernet Operation

When you get in your car to go somewhere, you cannot simply drive as fast as you want, ignore all road signs, never stop, and expect to get where you are going without running into someone, or them running into you. As much as it might be nice to ignore the traffic laws sometimes, getting places safely is ultimately more important than the delay while sitting at traffic lights, or waiting until it is safe to cross a road.

Ethernet LANs have the same kinds of rules about how the LAN segments can be used. The 802.3 MAC standards define these rules. In fact, it is these rules that give true meaning to the term Media Access Control, because the rules do indeed control how Ethernet devices access the LAN media. This section covers several topics related to Ethernet media access control.

Rules Governing When a Device Can Transmit: CSMA/CD

The CSMA/CD algorithm defines the rules that Ethernet NICs must follow to access an Ethernet LAN. The best way to understand *CSMA/CD* is to focus on the original Ethernet standards of 10BASE5 and 10BASE2, both of which use a physical bus topology. With a bus topology, only one device can send at one time. If multiple devices attempt to send at the same time, their electrical signals would overlap and be added together. The resulting single electrical signal does not represent the original bits of either frame or, in some cases, may not represent any bits at all due to illegal voltage levels. Such an occurrence, when two Ethernet devices send at the same time, causing their electrical signals to overlap, is called a *collision*.

The CSMA/CD Algorithm

The ethernet MAC standard suggests the following general CSMA/CD rules for how Ethernet devices should send data:

> Wait until the LAN is unused, and then send the frame. However, listen to detect whether the frame being sent collided with another frame. If no collisions occurred, the frame must have made it across the LAN. If a collision did occur, wait, and try to send the frame again.

This one statement summarizes the general idea behind the CSMA/CD algorithm. Note that with the CSMA/CD algorithm, collisions are not necessarily a bad thing, in that they are expected. However, the more often collisions occur, the worse the performance of the LAN. The following list outlines a more complete description of the CSMA/CD algorithm:

1. A device listens until the LAN is silent. The LAN is silent—in other words, there is no electrical signal on the cable—when no device is currently sending data.

2. The device sends its frame.

3. The transmitting device listens for collisions while it is still transmitting the frame.

4. If no collisions occurred, the process is complete. If a collision does occur, the following steps are taken.

5. All devices whose transmitted frames collided send a jamming signal. The jamming signals, typically 32 bits of consecutive 1s and 0s, ensure that all devices notice that a collision occurred.

6. All devices whose frame collided set independent semirandom *collision back-off timers*. Each device cannot attempt to send its respective frame again until that timer expires.

Figure 6-8 shows a conceptual example of the CSMA/CD process, with four steps shown top to bottom in the figure. The process in Figure 6-8 is as follows:

1. Both PCs sense that the LAN is not busy, because no stations are currently sending data. (This action corresponds to the phrase "carrier sense" in CSMA/CD, because the devices listen for the presence of the carrier signal or carrier frequency.)

2. Both PC A and PC D send at the same time. (This action corresponds to the phrase "multiple access" in CSMA/CD, because multiple devices can attempt to access the LAN at one time.)

3. The collision occurs.

4. PC A and PC D detect the electrical effects of the collision—a step termed collision detection in the full name of CSMA/CD. They both send a jamming signal, set a back-off timer, and wait before trying to resend their respective frames.

Figure 6-8 Origins of the Name CSMA/CD

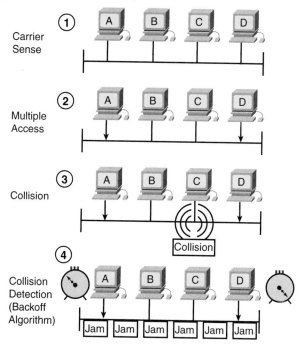

CSMA/CD and Collisions on 10BASE-T LANs with Hubs

With only a single wire inside a coax cable used for 10BASE2 and 10BASE5, the concept of collisions is a little easier to imagine. However, with 10BASE-T, using a hub, collisions can still occur, but the collision process is not quite as obvious. 10BASE-T networks use UTP cabling, which has both a transmit pair and a receive pair. At first glance it does not appear that a sending device, sending the data on its transmit pair, would be able to sense a collision with a frame being received on its receive pair. However, the other devices in the network can easily sense a collision, as shown in Figure 6-9.

Figure 6-9 Detecting Collisions with 10BASE-T on Nontransmitting Devices

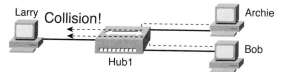

Hubs operate at Layer 1, simply repeating all received signals out all ports (except the port in which the signal was received). In Figure 6-9, the hub receives both frames and repeats both out Larry's port, so Larry easily recognizes a collision. However, Bob and Archie, who sent the frames, do not seem to notice, but they need to realize a collision occurred so that they can set back-off timers and resend the data.

10BASE-T NICs use a *loopback circuit* on the NIC to be able to recognize collisions. The loopback circuit simply takes the signal sent out a NIC's transmit wire pair and loops it back onto the receive pair, right on the card. Figure 6-10 shows the idea, with the NIC shown as a large rectangle to have space to represent the concept. Note that the figure shows how Bob will recognize a collision, rather than both Bob and Archie, just to reduce clutter.

Figure 6-10   Detecting Collisions with 10BASE-T on Transmitting Devices

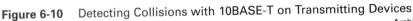
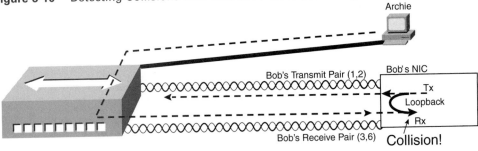

Figure 6-10 shows the insides of Bob's UTP cable, with both the transmit and receive twisted pair shown. Bob sends his frame out his transmit pair, and Bob's NIC also loops back that transmitted signal onto where the NIC receives the incoming signal on Bob's receive pair. The hub, when receiving the frame from Archie, repeats the signal out Bob's port, so Bob also receives Archie's signal. When the two signals combine—Bob's looped signal and the received signal from the hub—the result is an overlapped electrical signal that looks like a collision.

Full Duplex, Half Duplex, and Collision Domains

CSMA/CD has been a vital part of Ethernet for a long time. However, CSMA/CD causes throughput over an Ethernet to degrade as the LAN gets busier. Also, the fact that devices must have their frames collide, wait, send again, possibly collide again, and so on, does impact network performance to varying degrees. (The term *collision waste* refers to the degradation in Ethernet performance due to collisions.)

Ethernet LAN performance was also restricted to some degree because Ethernet NICs must use logic called *half duplex.* Duplex refers to the fact that the NIC can handle traffic in dual directions: transmitted and received. The term "half" refers to the fact that with CSMA/CD, the NIC restricts itself to use only half of those two directions at once—in other words, the NIC can only send, or only receive, at a given point in time. Remember, the very first step of CSMA/CD essentially means "do not send if you are currently receiving," which imposes half-duplex logic.

To improve Ethernet LAN performance, Ethernet standards advanced to the point that, in some cases, collisions cannot occur, making CSMA/CD unnecessary, and allowing for the use of *full duplex* logic. Full duplex means that a NIC can send and receive at the same time. This section covers the reasoning that explains why CSMA/CD may not be needed in some cases, which then allows a NIC to use full duplex.

Preventing Collisions with Switch Buffering

Switches prevent collisions by buffering frames. The process of buffering frames is demonstrated in the example shown in Figure 6-11. The figure shows a LAN with four PCs attached to a switch. Three of the PCs send a frame at the same time, all destined for Fred's MAC address. The switch, instead of forwarding the frames out the same port at the same time, causing a collision, holds two of the frames in memory—a process called *buffering*.

Figure 6-11   Switch Buffering Example

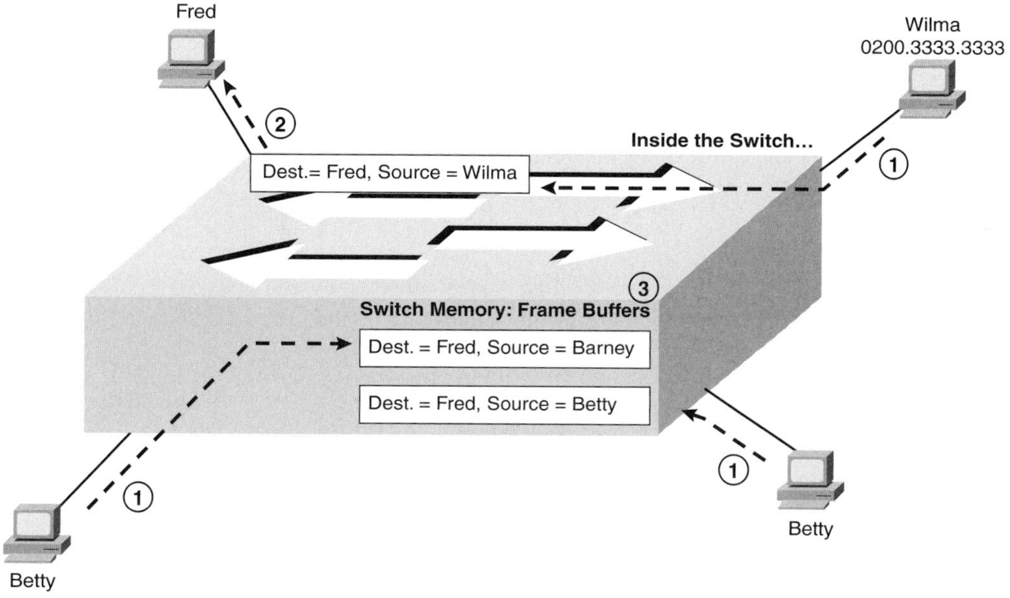

Figure 6-11 shows the following process:

1. Barney, Betty, and Wilma each send a frame, destined for Fred, at the same time.

2. The switch forwards Wilma's frame and buffers the other two in memory.

3. When finished sending Wilma's frame, the switch gets another frame to send, for instance, Barney's frame.

Collision Domains and Full Duplex

Due to switch buffering, each port of a switch is considered to create its own collision domain. The term collision domain refers to the set of Ethernet devices whose frames could possibly collide. Figure 6-12 shows a familiar simple LAN, with four PCs attached and the collision domains marked.

Figure 6-12   Collision Domains with a Switch

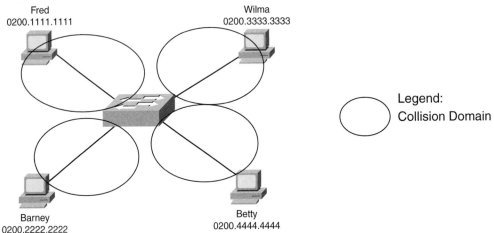

The main point about collision domains is that a frame in one collision domain does not cause collisions in another collision domain. A switch's buffering process prevents those collisions.

Full-duplex logic can be used in parts of a LAN topology that meet certain restrictions. In fact, Figure 6-12 would allow full duplex to be used on all four of the PC NICs shown in the figure. The rule for when full duplex may be used is as follows:

> Full duplex may be used in collision domains that have only two NICs or Ethernet interfaces attached.

For example, because each collision domain in Figure 6-12 has one NIC and one switch interface, the switch port and the NIC in each case can use full duplex. For perspective, keep in mind that the cable has both a transmit path and a receive path, so the frames cannot physically collide. The switch does not attempt to send two frames at a time, due to its buffering logic. So, full duplex is allowed on each segment in Figure 6-12.

When full duplex is enabled, the following occur:

- The NICs/interfaces allow themselves to send and receive at the same time.

- CSMA/CD is no longer needed, because there is no possibility of a collision. So, enabling full duplex also disables CSMA/CD.

- Because CSMA/CD is disabled, the NIC disables its loopback logic, because the loopback logic is used specifically to detect collisions—collisions that cannot occur in this case.

Do not confuse the definition of the requirements for full duplex to mean "full duplex can be used if a switch is being used." That is simply not the case. For example, Figure 6-13 shows an alternative LAN design, with a switch and a hub on the left, and the same design on the right but with two switches. On the left, one collision domain includes a hub and two PCs, meaning that collision domain includes a switch interface, two PC NICs, and three interfaces on the hub. So, that collision domain has more than two NICs or interfaces in it, meaning that collisions can occur and full duplex cannot be properly used.

Note

When a device either manually or through autonegotiation uses full duplex, it by definition also disables its CSMA/CD logic and disables its loopback circuit.

Figure 6-13   Switches and Hubs: Case That Does Not Allow Full Duplex

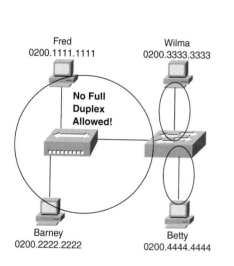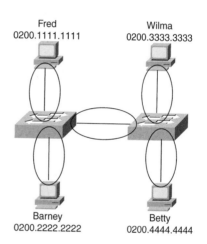

Legend:

Collision Domain

With the hub on the left side of Figure 6-13, one collision domain includes the hub, a switch port, Fred, and Barney—certainly more than two Ethernet ports. So, the requirement for full duplex is not met in that case. However, the network on the right shows only collision domains with two Ethernet ports, so full duplex could be used in each case.

Autonegotiation of Duplex and Speed

Ethernet supports a wide variety of speeds and two duplex options. (Note that for 1000-Mbps [Gigabit] speeds and slower, both duplex options are allowed; for higher speeds, only full

Note

To learn more detailed information about NLPs, FLP bursts, and the autonegotiation process, go to Chapter 6's Additional Topics of Interest file on the CD-ROM accompanying this book and search for the section "The Ethernet Autonegotiation Processes."

Note

The devices only claim to support full duplex if they think that the requirements for full duplex are met.

Note

Many Cisco switches can detect the correct speed even when the NIC on the other end of the link has disabled autonegotiation.

Note

If a NIC disables autonegotiation and sets the duplex to full, the switch ends up using half duplex. The link typically still works, but with poor performance.

duplex is allowed.) Because so many options exist, the IEEE standards include a process by which Ethernet NICs and switch ports can automatically negotiate the speed and the duplex settings. This process is named ***autonegotiation***.

To autonegotiate, Ethernet NICs and switch ports exchange information about their capabilities. Many PCs today have NICs called 10/100 NICs because they support both 10-Mbps and 100-Mbps speeds. Other NICs might support only 1000 Mbps, or support only some other speed. Others might even support 10, 100, and 1000 Mbps (1 Gbps) speeds. So, the devices on each end of the cable—often a NIC and a switch port—need to tell each other what each is capable of doing, through an Ethernet autonegotiation process called a capabilities exchange.

Autonegotiation, defined in IEEE 802.3X, uses a feature called ***Fast Link Pulse (FLP)*** bursts to exchange capabilities. FLP bursts are a series of Network Link Pulses (NLPs) that allow the devices on each end of an Ethernet cable—devices referred to as link partners by the autonegotiation process—to send each other a set of bits. These bits do not look like a normal frame because they are sent via the NLP signals, so the devices do not attempt to process them as a normal frame, and they cannot be forwarded anywhere else.

The FLPs contain bits that describe all the capabilities of the Ethernet NIC or interface. Once the devices have exchanged their capabilities, the two devices decide to use the lowest common capability supported by both devices. As you might guess, they pick the fastest speed that both support, and they also pick full duplex over half duplex. The following list describes the order of choices for autonegotiation, starting with the most preferred and going to the least preferred:

- 1000 Mbps, full duplex

- 1000 Mbps, half duplex

- 100 Mbps, full duplex

- 100 Mbps, half duplex

- 10 Mbps, full duplex

- 10 Mbps, half duplex

Speed and duplex may be manually configured or autonegotiated. If one link partner disables autonegotiation and manually sets the speed and duplex, and the other link partner attempts autonegotiation, the two devices may end up using different speed or duplex settings. With a speed mismatch, the link will not work at all. With a duplex mismatch, the link may work, but with excessive collisions.

Autonegotiation works well over copper media, but autonegotiation is not supported on Ethernet interfaces that use fiber. Thankfully, the need for autonegotiation does not exist on fiber media because fiber Ethernet links are typically used for connections between switches. The speed and duplex would normally be configured on trunks between switches.

Deterministic and Nondeterministic Media Access

This section describes a concept that probably mattered more when many LAN standards were available and competing for market share in the 1980s and early-to-mid-1990s. However, this topic does provide an interesting perspective for future developments in the world of networking, as well as a brief historical perspective.

The Ethernet MAC process, controlled by CSMA/CD, is a ***nondeterministic*** process. The term nondeterministic in this case means that the number of times a single device is allowed to use the LAN, or the amount of LAN bandwidth a device can use, cannot be determined ahead of time. The reason why it cannot be accurately predicted is that CSMA/CD does not guarantee each device any specific right to send frames. A PC could listen, hear nothing, send, collide, and back off—with another device then sending in the meantime. This device could keep colliding each time. Statistically speaking, with Ethernet and CSMA/CD, it is possible for a device to go several seconds without being able to send a frame.

Mathematics can give a probability of how much access and bandwidth would be available to a single Ethernet device, under certain conditions. However, that would simply be a probability of getting that much bandwidth. So, nondeterministic media access, like CSMA/CD with Ethernet, is sometimes also called ***probabilistic***.

Deterministic media access, on the other hand, means that mathematics can accurately predict the bandwidth allowed to the devices on the LAN, under some assumed conditions. Two formerly popular LAN standards, Token Ring (IEEE 802.5) and Fiber Distributed Data Interchange (FDDI, ANSI X3T9.5), are deterministic. Both use a ***token-passing*** mechanism and a logical ring topology. (FDDI uses a physical ring as well, often a dual ring for redundancy, whereas Token Ring uses a physical star topology but a logical ring.) The token-passing mechanism for both works basically as shown in Figure 6-14, which shows the following process:

1. A token enters PC1; that token has a bit set that means the ring is free, and anyone who receives this token can claim the right to send a frame.

2. PC1, which needs to send a frame, claims the right to send a frame by marking the token as "busy."

3. PC1 forwards its frame around the ring, preceded by the busy token.

4. PC2 receives the busy token and frame; although PC2 wants to send a frame, it cannot do so right now.

Figure 6-14   Token Passing in Token Ring

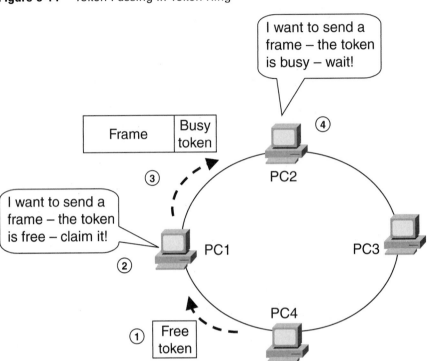

One of the keys to seeing why this process is deterministic lies in a later step. The frame always takes one complete trip around the ring. Then, the sending station, in this case PC1, removes the frame. The key next step is that PC1 must then send a free token—it cannot send another frame. That way, the next downstream neighbor gets a chance to send a frame. (In some cases, a device can send a limited number of frames in a row, but it must give others a chance to send.) If all devices wanted to send a frame, they would each get a chance, in the same order as they are shown in the ring. The result of this process is that the performance of the LAN for a single device can be predicted (determined), making it a deterministic LAN media access process.

Summary

Ethernet is a family of LAN technologies that includes 10 Mbps Ethernet, Fast Ethernet, and Gigabit Ethernet. When Ethernet needs to be expanded to add a new medium or capability, the IEEE issues a new supplement to the 802.3 standard. The new supplements are given a one- or two-letter designation, such as 802.3u. Ethernet relies on baseband signaling, which uses the entire bandwidth of the transmission medium.

IEEE 802.3 Ethernet operates at two layers of the OSI model: the lower half of the data link layer, known as the MAC sublayer, and the physical layer. IEEE 802.2 Logical Link Control defines Ethernet's operational details in the rest of the data link layer. Ethernet at Layer 1 involves interfacing with media, signals, bit streams that travel on the media, components that put signals on media, and various physical topologies. Layer 1 bits need structure, so OSI Layer 2 frames, as defined by the 802.3 MAC sublayer, define the framing standards.

All types of IEEE-standard Ethernet use the same frame structure. The fields in an Ethernet frame, in order, are as follows:

- Preamble

- Start Frame Delimiter (SFD)

- Destination Address

- Source Address

- Length or Type

- Data and Pad

- Frame Check Sequence (FCS)

The Address fields of the Ethernet frame contain Layer 2, or MAC, addresses for the source and destination.

All frames are susceptible to errors from a variety of sources. The FCS field of an Ethernet frame contains a number that is calculated by the source node based on the data in the frame. At the destination, it is recalculated and compared to determine that the data received is complete and error-free.

Ethernet allows the use of the carrier sense multiple access with collision detection (CSMA/CD) algorithm to manage access to the Ethernet shared medium. CSMA/CD manages the link, but it is a nondeterministic media access control algorithm. Other MAC algorithms, including the token-passing methods used by Token Ring and FDDI, are deterministic.

With CSMA/CD, a NIC waits for an absence of a signal on the media and then starts transmitting. If two or more nodes transmit at the same time, a collision occurs. If a collision is detected, the nodes wait a random amount of time and retransmit.

Autonegotiation detects the speed and duplex mode, half duplex or full duplex, of the device on the other end of the wire and adjusts to match those settings.

You can find supplemental coverage of topics related to those described in this chapter on the CD-ROM in the "Additional Topics of Interest" section. The next chapter, Chapter 7, covers more details about the various Ethernet standards.

Check Your Understanding

Complete all the review questions listed here to test your understanding of the topics and concepts in this chapter. Answers are listed in Appendix A, "Answers to Check Your Understanding and Challenge Questions."

1. Which of the following is *not* one of the recognized IEEE 802.2 or 802.3 sublayers?

A. Media Access Control

B. Data Link Control

C. Logical Link Control

D. None of the other answers is correct.

2. Which layers of the OSI model map to the IEEE 802.3 standard?

A. 2 and 3

B. 1 and 2

C. 3 and 4

D. 1 and 3

3. What are the two base features of LLC?

A. The ability to identify the type of data inside the data field of the frame

B. The ability to verify valid MAC addresses

C. The ability to control how a token is passed

D. The ability to control the transmissions between two devices on a LAN, specifically to perform error recovery when frames are lost

4. What do the first six hexadecimal numbers in a MAC address represent?

A. The whole MAC address

B. Organizationally Unique Identifier

C. Interface Unique Identifier

D. None of the other answers is correct.

5. MAC addresses are how many bits in length?

A. 12

B. 24

C. 48

D. 64

6. What is the name of the access method used in Ethernet that explains how Ethernet works?

   A. TCP/IP

   B. CSMA/CD

   C. CMDA/CS

   D. CSMA/CA

7. Where does the MAC address reside in a computer?

   A. Transceiver

   B. Computer BIOS

   C. NIC

   D. CMOS

8. Which of the following statements best describes communication between two devices on an Ethernet LAN?

   A. The source device encapsulates data in a frame with the destination MAC address of the destination device and then transmits it. Everyone on the LAN may see it, but the devices with nonmatching addresses otherwise ignore the frame.

   B. The source encapsulates the data and places a destination MAC address in the frame. It puts the frame on the LAN, where only the device with the matching address can check the Address field.

   C. The destination device encapsulates data in a frame with the destination MAC address of the source device and puts it on the LAN. The device with the matching address removes the frame.

   D. Each device on the LAN receives the frame and passes it up to the computer, where software decides whether to keep or discard the frame.

9. Which functions are associated with Ethernet framing?

   A. Identifies which computers are communicating with one another.

   B. Signals when communication between individual computers begins and when it ends.

   C. Flags corrupted frames.

   D. All of the other answers are correct.

10. Media Access Control refers to what?

   A. The state in which a NIC has captured the networking medium and is ready to transmit

   B. Rules that govern media capture and release

   C. Rules that determine which computer in a shared-medium environment is allowed to transmit the data

   D. A formal byte sequence that has been transmitted

11. What process does a receiving device use to determine if a frame has been "damaged" during transmission?

    A. The 802.2 LLC header always includes a value that determines if a frame had an error; if an error occurs, the receiver always asks the sender to retransmit the frame.

    B. The CRC is calculated and compared to the value in the FCS.

    C. The source and destination MAC addresses are verified.

    D. An algorithm is run that checks the SFD against the EOF delimiter.

12. In an Ethernet or IEEE 802.3 LAN, when do collisions occur?

    A. When one node places a frame on a network without informing the other nodes

    B. When two stations listen for traffic, hear none, and transmit simultaneously

    C. When two network nodes send frames to a node that no longer is broadcasting

    D. When jitter is detected and traffic is disrupted during normal transmission

13. Which is an important Layer 2 data link layer function?

    A. Logical Link Control

    B. Addressing

    C. Media Access Control

    D. All of the other answers are correct.

14. Which is true of a deterministic MAC protocol?

    A. It defines collisions and specifies what to do about them.

    B. It allows the hub to determine the number of users active at any one time.

    C. The minimum amount of access to the medium by a given device can be determined (mathematically).

    D. It allows the use of a "talking stick" by network administrators to control the media access of any users considered "troublemakers."

Challenge Questions and Activities

These questions require a deeper application of the concepts covered in this chapter and are similar to the style of questions you might see on a CCNA certification exam.

1. A network has two 100-Mbps hubs, each connected to the same 100-Mbps switch. Which of the following statements are true? (Select two.)

    A. Hubs cannot be connected to switches because they are not compatible with IEEE 802.1q.

    B. Computers that connect directly to the 100-Mbps switch via full duplex will not use CSMA/CD.

    C. The links between the hubs and the switch must be full duplex.

    D. Computers that connect to the 100-Mbps hubs and use autonegotiation will choose half duplex.

2. What field is in an IEEE 802.3 frame but is not part of a DIX frame?

    A. Destination MAC Address

    B. Source MAC Address

    C. SFD

    D. FCS

 Activity 6-1: Use Ethereal (or another protocol analyzer) to capture a few dozen packets. Click individual packets until you find an Ethernet II (DIXv2) frame and an IEEE Ethernet 802.3 frame.

Expand the Ethernet II frame information for each and look for any terms you may recognize from this chapter. Which of these two types of frames also includes an LLC section?

CHAPTER 7

Ethernet Technologies

Objectives

Upon completion of this chapter, you should be able to answer the following questions:

- What are characteristics of the different types of 10-Mbps Ethernet?

- What are the 10BASE-T wiring parameters?

- What factors affect Ethernet timing limits?

- What are the different types of 100-Mbps Ethernet and their characteristics?

- How did Ethernet evolve?

- What are the Media Access Control (MAC) methods, frame formats, and transmission process of Gigabit Ethernet?

- What pinouts and media are used with Gigabit Ethernet?

- How are Gigabit and 10-Gigabit Ethernet similar and different?

- What are the basic architectural considerations of Gigabit and 10-Gigabit Ethernet?

Additional Topics of Interest

Several chapters contain topics that cover more details about previous topics or related topics that are a bit tangential to the primary focus of the chapter. The additional coverage can be found on the CD-ROM. For this chapter, the following additional topics are covered:

- 10BASE5

- 10BASE2

- 100BASE-FX

- Repeaters and hubs with Fast and Gigabit Ethernet

- 10-Gigabit Ethernet

- Ethernet encoding

Key Terms

This chapter uses the following key terms. You can find the definitions in the Glossary:

10BASE5   page 269

10BASE2   page 269

asynchronous transmission   page 271

10BASE-T   page 272

IEEE 802.3x   page 272

straight-through cable   page 273

continues

continued

TIA/EIA 568A   page 274

crossover cable   page 274

5-4-3-2-1 rule   page 276

IEEE 802.3i   page 277

100BASE-TX IEEE 802.3u   page 278

Fast Ethernet   page 278

backbone links   page 280

redundancy   page 280

Gigabit Ethernet   page 282

GigE   page 282

IEEE 802.3z   page 282

1000BASE-X   page 283

1000BASE-SX   page 283

1000BASE-LX   page 283

transmitter   page 285

detector   page 285

1000BASE-T   page 286

IEEE 802.3ab   page 287

IEEE 802.3ae   page 289

Metro Ethernet   page 289

Chapter 6, "Ethernet Fundamentals," introduced the concept of the Ethernet family of standards. This chapter continues that theme by going deeper into several Ethernet technologies. This chapter begins with a section covering the Ethernet technologies that are more likely to be used by the average end-user device today—namely, several different standards for 10 Mbps and 100 Mbps. The second section covers 1000-Mbps Ethernet.

10- and 100-Mbps Ethernet

Today, the most commonly used Ethernet technologies in enterprise local-area networks (LANs) are variations of Ethernet that run at 10 Mbps, 100 Mbps, and 1000 Mbps (1 Gbps). 100 Mbps is easily the most popular today, at least in terms of the absolute number of network interface cards (NICs) using a particular Ethernet speed. This section, which basically spans the first half of this chapter, focuses on the Ethernet variations at these speeds, which you are most likely to encounter in an enterprise LAN—at least today.

Interestingly, if you look at the history of Ethernet over the past 30 years, the speeds keep getting faster, the variety of media that can be used keeps getting larger, and the distances supported over a single cable keep expanding—all while the price per port on switches keeps decreasing. If history is any indication, by the next edition of this book, or for sure by the edition after that, this section will instead cover 100 Mbps, 1 Gbps, and 10 Gbps as the mainstream Ethernet technologies and will ignore all variations of 10 Mbps as being too old to matter. Also, the other Cisco Networking Academy Program CCNA Companion Guides for later courses—the ones that cover wide-area network (WAN) technology in more depth—will need to cover Ethernet as a metropolitan-area network (MAN) and WAN technology. Ethernet has a long and successful history, and it has a bright future.

10-Mbps Ethernet

Previous parts of the online course and this book introduced the 10-Mbps Ethernet standards to various degrees. This section lists and explains a few details about the standards for each type of 10-Mbps Ethernet, briefly reviewing a few topics that have already been covered, and introducing a few new concepts.

The three 10-Mbps Ethernet standards are *10BASE5*, *10BASE2*, and 10BASE-T. 10BASE2 and 10BASE5 have each been around for more than 20 years and have been replaced by more modern Ethernet alternatives. 10BASE-T's use is waning over time, but it can still be found in many networks. Table 7-1 lists some of the key details about each standard.

Table 7-1   Comparing 10-Mbps Ethernet Options

Type	Other Name	Cabling	Maximum Length of One Cable, No Repeaters	IEEE Standard	Year IEEE Released Standard
10BASE5	Thicknet	Thick coaxial	500 m	802.3	1980
10BASE2	Thinnet	Thin coaxial	185 m	802.3a	1985
10BASE-T	—	UTP twisted pair	100 m	802.3i	1990

The 10 Mbps IEEE 802.3 standards cover all of Open System Interconnection (OSI) Layer 1 (physical layer) and a part of OSI Layer 2. The part of 802.3 that corresponds to the lower half of the OSI Layer 2 is called the Media Access Control (MAC) sublayer. Another IEEE protocol, which is called IEEE 802.2 Logical Link Control (LLC), defines the upper sublayer of the OSI Layer 2 for Ethernet. Figure 7-1 shows the relationship of the standards with the OSI layers.

Figure 7-1   Ethernet Standards and the OSI Layers

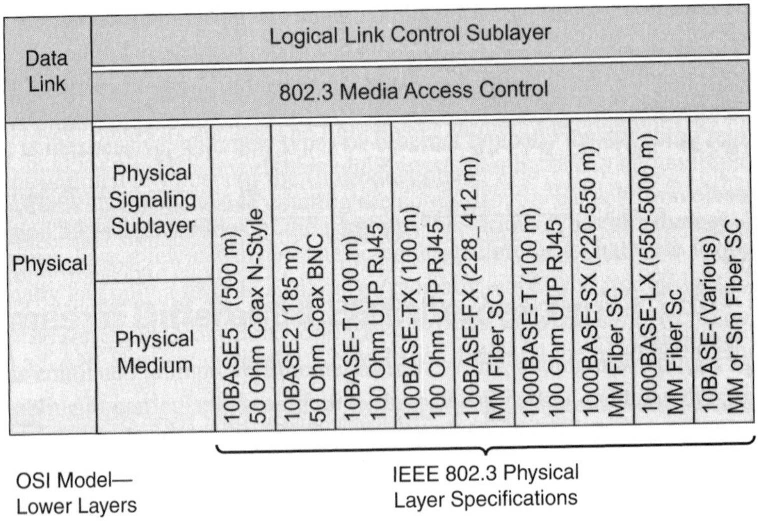

Figure 7-1 represents the fact that 10BASE5, 10BASE2, and 10BASE-T all use different physical layer specifications because they differ in many ways regarding the physical layer functions. Although that is true, all three standards share many common features, many of which you learned about in previous chapters.

For example, the term *Ethernet timing* refers to several sometimes-related parameters about how much time certain events can take on an Ethernet. Chapter 6's section "Additional Topics of Interest," which you can find on the CD-ROM, covers many concepts related to Ethernet timing. All three types of 10-Mbps Ethernet share the same settings for these timing-related features of Ethernet, which are repeated in Table 7-2 for your reference.

Table 7-2   Common Ethernet Timing Settings for 10-Mbps Ethernet Standards

Parameter	Value
Bit-time	100 nanoseconds (ns)
Slot time	512 bit-times (51.2 microseconds)
Interframe spacing	96 bits
Collision attempt limit	16
Collision backoff limit	10
Collision jam size	32 bits
Maximum untagged frame size	1518 octets
Minimum frame size	512 bits (64 bytes)

Note

Historically, some Networking Academies ignore the details of Ethernet timing as listed in Table 7-2. It might be useful to ask your instructor whether such topics are considered important in your particular Networking Academy. Regardless, these details are included for your reference.

Chapter 6 also covered the details of Ethernet framing. As a reminder, Figure 7-2 shows an example of the three variations of Ethernet frames, as covered in Chapter 6, "Ethernet Fundamentals." All three types of frames are allowed on any of the types of 10-Mbps Ethernets.

Figure 7-2   Ethernet Framing Review

DIX

Preamble 8	Destination 6	Source 6	Type 2	Data & Pad 46 - 1500	FCS 4

IEEE 802.3 (Original)

Preamble 7	SFD 1	Destination 6	Source 6	Length 2	Data & Pad 46 - 1500	FCS 4

IEEE 802.3 (Revised 1997)

Preamble 7	SFD 1	Destination 6	Source 6	Length/ Type 2	Data & Pad 46 - 1500	FCS 4

Note

Refer to Figure 6-7 in Chapter 6, and the text surrounding it, for more information on the other headers used with the 802.3 header.

All three 10-Mbps Ethernet options use a logical bus topology and *asynchronous transmission* logic. The term asynchronous transmission means that the Ethernet devices do not send any electrical signals when idle; in fact, long periods can pass without any electrical signals on the wires. The term asynchronous refers to the fact that the receivers must synchronize themselves to the sender each time some device sends a frame. In fact, the Preamble and Start Frame Delimiter (SFD) header fields were created specifically to allow receivers to see a long set of signal transitions that occur when sending alternating binary 1s and 0s. With asynchronous transmission, all three 10-Mbps Ethernet standards use the preamble and SFD to ensure that all receivers have synchronized themselves to the incoming signal before receiving the first important part of the header (namely, the Destination Address field).

Ethernet timing and framing are just two common parts of Ethernet among all three 10-Mbps Ethernet options. The following list mentions other key features that are identical across all three 10-Mbps Ethernet options:

- Shared medium
- Carrier sense multiple access collision detect (CSMA/CD) algorithm and half-duplex operation
- Design rules about the number of repeaters or hubs used between two end-user devices
- Timing parameters
- Frame format
- Logical bus topology
- Asynchronous transmission (with silence between frames)

The "Additional Topics of Interest" document for Chapter 7, which can be found on this book's CD-ROM, covers these features in more detail.

10BASE-T

Although it is similar to 10BASE5 and 10BASE2 in many ways, the *10BASE-T* standard represents a major departure from the physical bus topology of its older cousins. The IEEE approved the 10BASE-T standard in 1990, 10 years after approving the original IEEE 10BASE5 standard. 10BASE-T represented some significant advancements in technology, particularly the use of a physical star topology as well as using UTP cabling. The star topology uses a hub at the center with a cable from the hub to a single device.

Another major difference between 10BASE-T and the other 10-Mbps Ethernet options arose with the advent of the IEEE standard for full duplex in 1997 (*IEEE 802.3x*). The full-duplex standard defines how two devices connected via a single Ethernet cable, with two transmission paths that connected two Ethernet devices (like a cable between a 10BASE-T switch and a PC), to both send at the same time. This simple addition significantly increases 10BASE-T performance.

This section looks at the star cabling topology and the cables themselves that are used for 10BASE-T. It also revisits the CSMA/CD discussions from Chapter 6, but only to address some design issues when building 10BASE-T networks with hubs. Finally, the last part of this section covers design rules when using 10BASE-T switches.

10BASE-T Wiring

10BASE-T supports Category 3 (Cat3), Category 5 (Cat5), and Category 5e (Cat5e) unshielded twisted-pair (UTP) cabling. The support for Cat3 UTP is more of a historical fact because, when 10BASE-T was created, a large amount of Cat3 cabling was already installed to support telephones. Supporting Cat3 made economic sense because companies avoided running additional cable. However, from its inception, 10BASE-T worked better on Cat5 cabling; the IEEE intended for the new 10BASE-T installations to use Cat5 cabling because of its better quality. Today, new installations must definitely install Cat5e cabling and connectors to allow an easier future migration to Gigabit Ethernet, which requires Cat5e for its UTP-based standards.

10BASE-T defines the use of two twisted pairs inside the UTP cable: one for transmitting and one for receiving. Figure 7-3 shows a conceptual view of 10BASE-T operation using two twisted pairs.

Note

Cisco LAN switches, like most other LAN switches, typically act like hubs with regards to wiring.

Figure 7-3   Using a Straight-Through UTP Cable

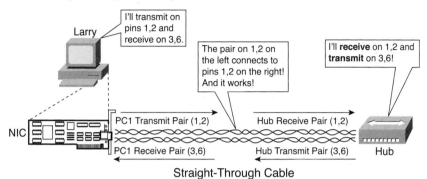

Figure 7-3 shows the idea behind a straight-through cable and the logic required on the hub to support it. First, the *straight-through cable* connects the wire at pin 1 on one end of the cable with pin 1 on the other end, pin 2 with pin 2, and so on. So, the PC's NIC uses the twisted pair attached to pins 1 and 2 for transmitting and the pair on pins 3 and 6 for receiving. To make it work correctly, the hub does the opposite: It receives data on the pair attached to pins 1 and 2 and transmits on the pair at pins 3 and 6.

To make a straight-through cable, the wires on each end of the cable must be crimped to an RJ-45 connector using the same wiring standard on both ends of the cable. Figure 7-4 shows an RJ-45 connector and the two TIA-standard pinouts for use with UTP cabling.

Figure 7-4   TIA-Standard Pinouts

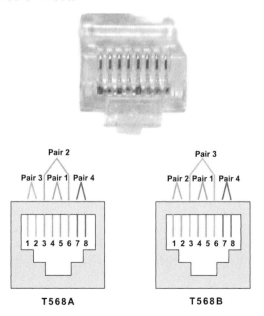

Table 7-3 lists the pinouts for the *TIA/EIA 568A* standard and the typical colors used for each of the eight pin positions in the RJ-45 connector.

Table 7-3   TIA/EIA 568A Pinouts

Pin Number	T568A Function	Wire Insulation Color
1	TD+	White/orange
2	TD–	Orange
3	RD+	White/green
4	Unused	Blue
5	Unused	White/blue
6	RD–	Green
7	Unused	White/brown
8	Unused	Brown

Hubs and switches are often connected to each other for the purpose of forwarding data between them. Such a connection requires a *crossover cable* to connect the pair used by each device to transmit (pins 3 and 6) to the other device's receive pair (pins 1 and 2). The same crossover cable is also required when connecting two PCs' NICs with a single cable. Figure 7-5 shows an example with two PCs.

Figure 7-5   10BASE-T Crossover Cable

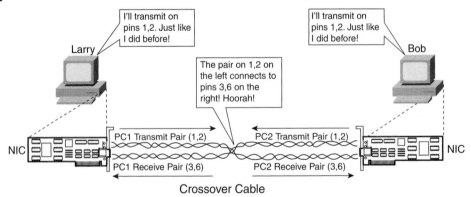

When building a network, one of the more important practical tasks is choosing whether a straight-through cable or crossover cable is needed. Simply put, when connecting a centralized LAN device, such as a hub or switch, to an end-user device, such as a PC, use a straight-through cable. When connecting two similar devices, such as two PCs, two switches, or a switch and a hub, use a crossover cable.

10BASE-T Design: Using Hubs, CSMA/CD, and Half Duplex

Although 10BASE-T wiring certainly differs from its predecessors 10BASE2 and 10BASE5; all three use the CSMA/CD algorithm to avoid and recover from collisions. 10BASE2 and 10BASE5 must have CSMA/CD in all cases because their physical topology—a shared physical bus—passes the electrical signal sent by one device over the entire cable. The devices on the LAN can attempt to send at the same time, which causes a collision.

10BASE-T requires CSMA/CD when using hubs, but it does not require CSMA/CD in many cases (but not all) when using switches. This section focuses on 10BASE-T implementation rules when hubs are used. The next section focuses on the rules when switches are used, specifying when CSMA/CD is and is not needed.

The key design rule for 10BASE5, 10BASE2, and 10BASE-T using hubs is called the 5-4-3 rule. The rule is simply this:

> Between any two devices on a LAN, there can be at most:
>
> - Five cable segments
> - Four hubs
> - Three LAN segments with devices attached to them

Figure 7-6 shows a sample network in which two devices are separated by the maximum of five segments and four hubs. Only two LAN segments are populated with end-user devices in this figure.

Figure 7-6   Example of a Long Delay for Hearing a Collision

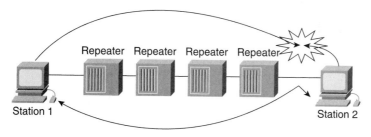

The 5-4-3 rule makes sure that CSMA/CD works correctly by ensuring that a collision can be heard in a reasonable amount of time. In Figure 7-6, when station 1 sends a frame, that frame might get all the way to a few meters from station 2 before station 2 decides to send a frame. Station 2 listens and, hearing silence, begins to send a frame. So, they each send frames, and the frames collide. Then, for station 2 to know that a collision occurred, the electrical results of that collision, called a *collision fragment*, must propagate back over the LAN to station 1.

The delay for the electricity to get to the collision point and then back again is impacted by distance, cabling type, and any repeaters or hubs in the path. Each repeater or hub adds some

Note

Ethernet interfaces on routers act like PCs in regards to cabling. So, when connecting a router's Ethernet interface to a hub or switch, use a straight-through cable.

Note

In the *5-4-3-2-1 rule*, which expands on the definition of the 5-4-3 rule, the 2 represents the number of segments that cannot have any end-user devices attached, and the 1 indicates that the entire network is a single collision domain.

Note

Some hub and switch products are called stackable hubs or switches. A single set of stackable hubs often counts as one hub or repeater for the 5-4-3 rule.

delay when it forwards a signal. The more hubs in between the sending device and the other end of the LAN, the more delay a single frame experiences. All 10-Mbps Ethernet standards require that a frame be able to go from one end of the LAN to the other, and back, in 50 microseconds. By limiting the number of hubs, the 5-4-3 rule helps meet that 50-microsecond round-trip delay requirement.

Frankly, today, most enterprises would not build a new network out of 10BASE-T hubs. Switches work much better, and the prices are reasonable. Before closing the subject of design with 10BASE-T hubs, however, consider the alternative design shown in Figure 7-7, which shows a single collision domain with many 10BASE-T hubs. However, no two devices have more than two hubs between them, so the design easily meets the 5-4-3 rule requirements.

Figure 7-7   Good Design Practices with 10BASE-T Hubs

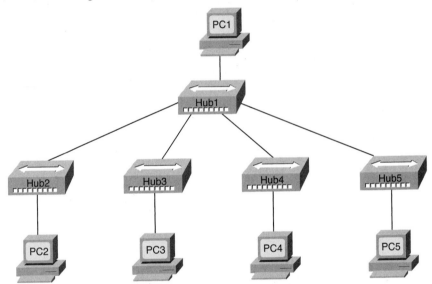

10BASE-T Design: Using Switches

The exclusive use of 10BASE-T switches, instead of hubs, removes the 5-4-3 rule's design restrictions. The 5-4-3 rule's core purpose relates to round-trip time in long collision domains. However, with switches (or bridges), each interface is in a separate collision domain. In 10BASE-T LANs that use only switches, each interface creates a small collision domain with only itself and one device on the other end of the cable. With switches, the collision domains are small, as shown in Figure 7-8.

Figure 7-8   Using Switches to Create Many Smaller Collision Domains

Note

Installing 20 LAN switches in a row, as implied in Figure 7-8, is probably not the best overall design choice, but it would work.

Figure 7-8 shows a LAN similar to Figure 7-7, but with switches instead of hubs. The 5-4-3 design rule applies to each collision domain and, in this design, each collision domain is at most a single 100 meter cable. As a result, the design could literally connect 20 switches in a row, and it would work just fine because the 5-4-3 rule does not apply to the entire network, just each collision domain.

The IEEE 802.3x full-duplex standard, released in 1997, created yet another important design and performance feature for 10BASE-T. The original 10BASE-T specification, *IEEE 802.3i*, did not allow 10BASE-T to use full-duplex logic at all. For example, in Figure 7-8, the switches create many collision domains, but without full duplex, every single link must use CSMA/CD logic, and only one device can send over a single link at any one time. With the introduction of full duplex in 802.3x, full duplex was then allowed on 10BASE-T, but only under these restrictions:

- Ethernet switches/bridges must be used (no hubs or repeaters).

- Only two Ethernet interfaces can be in the same collision domain.

For example, all the Ethernet segments in Figure 7-8 can use full duplex because each collision domain has either one PC and one switch interface or two switch interfaces.

Note

Refer to Chapter 6, Figure 6-13, and the related text for a review of full duplex and collision domains.

Full duplex more than doubles the bandwidth that is available with 10BASE-T as compared to half duplex. First, the devices on either end of the cable can both send at the same time, essentially doubling the bandwidth by allowing for 10 Mbps of bandwidth in each direction (for a total of 20 Mbps). Additionally, full duplex means that CSMA/CD has been disabled on that segment, so collisions cannot occur. Therefore, all the time wasted while collisions occur (while waiting for a chance to send and so on, called collision waste) does not happen on full-duplex links.

For now, this concludes the coverage of 10-Mbps Ethernet options. The section "Additional Topics of Interest," which you can find on the CD-ROM, has more coverage of the details of 10BASE2 and 10BASE5, as well as coverage of the line-encoding scheme used for all three 10-Mbps Ethernet types.

Lab 7.1.2   Waveform Decoding

In this lab, you integrate knowledge of networking media; OSI Layers 1, 2, and 3; and Ethernet by decoding a digital waveform of an Ethernet frame.

100-Mbps Ethernet

The IEEE standardized 10BASE-T in 1990. At that time, many companies were still migrating from dumb computer terminals to PCs and still adding LANs to their networks. 10BASE-T offered a LAN standard that included the least expensive NICs and the least expensive cabling, as compared with other types of LANs. Additionally, many vendors competed with Ethernet products, which drove prices down considerably. 10BASE-T flourished.

By the early 1990s, the Internet had started to become more than a researchers' network. The Internet itself grew at more than 10 percent *per month* throughout the 1990s. The 1990s saw the Internet grow from a network that was only truly understood by geeks to one of the more significant economic events of the past 100 years.

The boom of PCs on the desktop, all connected to LANs, plus the Internet revolution, conspired to create an environment in which 10 Mbps to the desktop was simply not enough bandwidth. At the same time, LAN backbones also needed upgrading. As a result, the IEEE announced several 100-Mbps Ethernet standards. This section examines the two 100-Mbps standards that had the most impact in the marketplace: 100BASE-TX and 100BASE-FX.

100BASE-TX Ethernet

The IEEE introduced *100BASE-TX IEEE 802.3u*, one of the early members of the 100-Mbps *Fast Ethernet* family, in 1995. The IEEE had previously introduced 100BASE-T, which supported Cat3 cabling. However, for a myriad of reasons, 100BASE-TX, which specifies Cat5 cabling, became more popular.

Compared with 10BASE-T, 100BASE-TX has many identical features. Here are some of the better-known equivalent features:

Note

100BASE-TX refers to a specific IEEE standard (802.3u), and the term Fast Ethernet typically refers to any of the IEEE Ethernet standards that run at 100 Mbps.

- Supports CSMA/CD and half duplex

- Supports autonegotiation today (the autonegotiation standard came out after 100BASE-TX)

- Uses the same Cat5/5e cabling

- Uses the same single cable length restriction (100 m)

- Uses the same Ethernet frame format

- Uses most of the same timing parameters

- Uses the same pinouts on the RJ-45 connectors

- Can disable CSMA/CD and instead use full duplex under the same conditions (per IEEE 802.3x)

The differences between 10BASE-T and 100BASE-TX relate to the physical layer. 100BASE-TX transmits data at 100 Mbps, which is 10 times faster than 10BASE-T. It also uses synchronous transmission, which means that 100BASE-TX always sends some bits, even when it is idle. When no data frames need to be sent, 100BASE-TX NICs continuously send something called an idle frame. So, unlike 10BASE-T, 100BASE-TX always has an electrical signal on the wire. (When using CSMA/CD, instead of listening for silence, a 100BASE-TX NIC listens for idle frames and considers that to mean that the segment is idle.)

The Ethernet timing parameters of 100BASE-TX mostly follow the same standards as 10BASE-T. However, a few of the settings differ as a direct result of the speed. For example, the bit-time is 1/10th of the bit-time of 10BASE-T (100 nsec) because 100BASE-T is 10 times faster. Also, the slot time is still 512 bit-times, but with a single bit-time being smaller, the actual slot time is also 1/10th of the value used by 10BASE-T. Table 7-4 lists the parameters related to timing commonly used among all variations of Fast Ethernet.

Table 7-4   Common Ethernet Timing Settings for 100-Mbps Ethernet Standards

Parameter	Value
Bit-time	**10 nsec**
Slot time	512 bit-times (**5.12** microseconds)
Interframe spacing	96 bits
Collision attempt limit	16
Collision backoff limit	10
Collision jam size	32 bits
Maximum untagged frame size	1518 octets
Minimum frame size	512 bits (64 bytes)

When Fast Ethernet first came into the market, vendors offered various Fast Ethernet hubs, bridges, and switches. However, Fast Ethernet's design restrictions when using hubs were even more strict than the 5-4-3 rules for 10BASE-T. By this time, many engineers preferred to stay away from hubs altogether, given the design restrictions and poorer overall performance because of collisions. However, when Fast Ethernet products first hit the market, the price differences between Fast Ethernet hubs and switches tended to be significant enough so that some designs used 100-Mbps hubs, some used switches, and some used both. (Some vendors, including Cisco Systems, created devices that essentially had multiple hubs inside one product, connected to each other with an internal switch, to provide a compromise between price, performance, and design flexibility.)

Note

The section "Additional Topics of Interest," which you can find on the CD-ROM, provides more details on the encoding methods that 100BASE-TX uses and other Ethernet standards.

Note

If your Networking Academy does not cover the Ethernet timing topics in Chapter 6, ask your instructor whether you need to study the timing-related parameters shown in Table 7-4.

Note

The section "Additional Topics of Interest," which you can find on the CD-ROM, covers 100BASE-T designs with hubs (under the heading, "Repeaters and Hubs with Fast Ethernet").

Designing Ethernets with Two Speeds

The IEEE introduced autonegotiation as part of the 802.3u Fast Ethernet standard. As covered in Chapter 6, autonegotiation allows an Ethernet NIC or interface to send fast link pulses (FLPs) to exchange its capabilities with the device on the other end of the cable. This feature enabled an entirely new type of Ethernet product: NICs and switch ports that could use either 10 or 100 Mbps and either half or full duplex.

Figure 7-9 shows a simple Fast Ethernet design that first became common soon after the introduction of Fast Ethernet. Interestingly, today, many LANs continue to have similar designs, although the connection between switches is more likely to use Gigabit Ethernet. The design shows two switches connected by a 100BASE-TX link with several end-user PCs connected to 10/100 ports.

Figure 7-9   Typical 10/100 Ethernet Design

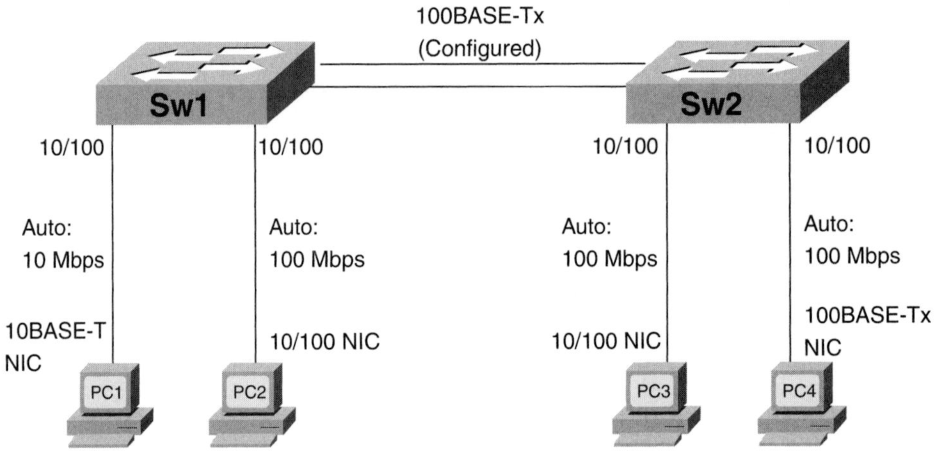

This design points out the strengths of using autonegotiation and provides a backdrop from which to discuss practical matters about network implementation. The PCs have various NICs:

- One NIC that supports only 10 Mbps (PC1)

- Two NICs that support 10 or 100 Mbps (PC2 and PC3)

- One NIC that supports only 100 Mbps (PC4)

From a practical perspective, network engineers can simply install the 10/100 switches, connect the cables, and let the end users decide when to upgrade their NICs from the older 10BASE-T NICs. Even if the network engineers perform the NIC upgrades for users, the migration does not have to happen over one weekend.

Figure 7-9 also shows two 10BASE-TX links between switches. Links between switches are often called trunks (and sometimes called *backbone links*). Networks often use two trunks for *redundancy*; therefore, if one link fails, connectivity is still maintained through the other link.

The design shown in Figure 7-9 does not allow the use of hubs instead of switches. Whenever an Ethernet device needs to support different speeds, the device must act like a switch or bridge. A hub, which acts as a Layer 1 repeater, cannot adapt between speeds. This fact provided another reason for companies to install switches, not hubs, when migrating from a 10-Mbps-only Ethernet LAN to one that used Fast Ethernet and 10/100 NICs.

100BASE-FX

The design shown in Figure 7-9 works well, as long as none of the Ethernet segments need to be more than 100 meters in length. However, many LAN designs predating the 1995 release of Fast Ethernet needed to connect LANs over distances longer than 100 meters. Oftentimes, these LANs existed inside a campus or office complex. The office-complex owners allowed their tenants to install fiber-optic cables under the ground between buildings, which allowed the LANs in the different buildings to be connected.

By the time 100BASE-FX was standardized, another type of LAN called Fiber Distributed Data Interface (FDDI) had become popular to connect distant LANs. FDDI allowed for the longer cabling distances provided by optical fiber and a robust 100 Mbps speed. Before the introduction of 100BASE-FX, a LAN design between buildings might have looked like what's shown in Figure 7-10.

Note

The design shown in Figure 7-9 uses only one of the backbone trunks at a time by default because of the operation of Spanning Tree Protocol (STP). (Chapter 8, "Ethernet Switching," covers STP.) However, by configuring a feature called *EtherChannel*, the links can be used simultaneously. (EtherChannel is not covered in the current Networking Academy CCNA curriculum.)

Figure 7-10   Backbone Design Using FDDI

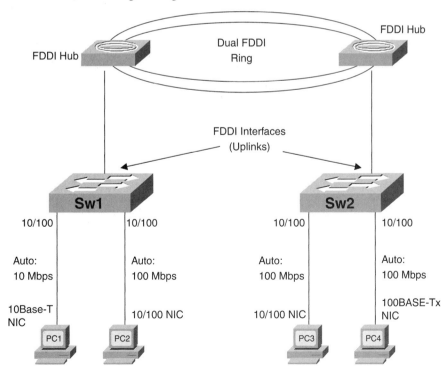

Another technology called Asynchronous Transfer Mode (ATM), which is meant for both the LAN and WAN, also became popular by the mid-1990s. Essentially, it would take the place of the FDDI equipment shown in Figure 7-10 (with the Ethernet switches having ATM interfaces). However, forwarding Ethernet frames over FDDI or ATM LANs caused some inefficiencies and required extra hardware (at more expense), but they both provided a working solution.

With the introduction of 100BASE-FX, also as part of the IEEE 802.3u standard, the IEEE provided a standard that allowed the same speed as FDDI, with similar cabling distances, but without the inefficiencies of using multiple types of LANs. In effect, 100BASE-FX allowed Ethernet to compete with FDDI and ATM as a backbone technology, with designs like Figure 7-9, but with the backbone links being 100BASE-FX to meet the distance requirements between buildings.

100BASE-FX did not catch on in the market as much as 100BASE-TX, which was wildly popular. Essentially, many companies with existing FDDI backbones did not see enough benefit in 100BASE-FX to spend money to migrate to it. Others migrated to ATM, which allowed for higher speeds (typically, 155 Mbps or 622 Mbps in the mid-1990s). In short, the competition for 100BASE-FX was greater, so although 100BASE-FX was used, it was not pervasive.

100BASE-FX's future in the marketplace essentially died with the introduction of the 1000-Mbps fiber Ethernet standards, at least after reasonably priced equipment became available.

Gigabit Ethernet and Beyond

Gigabit Ethernet was the next major evolution in the Ethernet family. It runs at 1 Gigabit per second (1 Gbps), although many documents and products list the speed as 1000 Mbps for easy comparison to 10-Mbps and 100-Mbps Ethernet variations.

GigE, as Gigabit Ethernet is commonly called, began with *IEEE 802.3z*, which introduced Gigabit Ethernet over fiber. The UTP-based IEEE 802.3ab standard, which required some significant leaps in engineering, came later (in 1999). Both standards define the use of the same familiar Ethernet framing and many of the same timing parameters as the older Ethernet family members. The significance of using the same framing cannot be emphasized enough, because it allowed a simple, familiar, and now faster (and eventually cheaper) technology in the LAN. Gigabit Ethernet essentially completed the job of removing other competing LAN technologies, such as FDDI and ATM, from the enterprise LAN.

Table 7-5 lists the common timing parameters among all Gigabit Ethernet variations. Most settings are equivalent to the earlier Ethernet standards, except for the obvious change in some values because of the faster speed. The one exception is that the slot time, which is used only when CSMA/CD and half duplex are used, was increased from 512 bit-times (which is the standard for 10-Mbps and 100-Mbps Ethernet) to 4096 bit-times. (In Table 7-5, the differences are shown in bold.)

Table 7-5   Common Ethernet Timing Settings for 1000-Mbps Ethernet Standards

Parameter	Value
Bit-time	**1 nsec**
Slot time	**4096 bit-times (4.096 microseconds)**
Interframe spacing	96 bits
Collision attempt limit	16
Collision backoff limit	10
Collision jam size	32 bits
Maximum untagged frame size	1518 octets
Minimum frame size	512 bits (64 bytes)

The next section explains the two commercially popular fiber-based Ethernet standards—1000BASE-LX and 1000BASE-SX—followed by coverage of the copper standard, 1000BASE-T.

1000BASE-X

The term *1000BASE-X* refers to three separate Gigabit Ethernet standards, all of which use fiber-optic cabling. The two standards that became commercially popular, *1000BASE-SX* and *1000BASE-LX*, differ mainly in terms of their purposes: short distances (SX) and long distances (LX). Table 7-6 lists the key differences between the two standards.

Table 7-6   Comparing 1000BASE-SX and 1000BASE-LX

Standard	Cable Type	Maximum Cable Length	Transmitter	Wavelengths
1000BASE-SX	Multimode fiber	220 m	Laser	Short, typically 850 nm
1000BASE-LX	Single-mode fiber	5000 m	Laser	Long, typically 1310 nm

The 1000BASE-X standards provide several key advantages compared to using 1000BASE-T with copper. The following list details a few of the more important advantages of 1000BASE-X over 1000BASE-T:

- Noise immunity, because optical fibers do not experience interference from nearby radiation.

- Because 1000BASE-X is not electrical, no grounding or potential electrical problems exist.

- Provides various options for different types of cabling, connectors, and price points.

- Cabling distance allows a more widely dispersed Ethernet LAN.

Note

Figure 7-11 notes the 1000BASE-CX standard, which was not widely installed. It was designed for use between switches inside wiring closets.

One of the more significant advantages of 1000BASE-X over 1000BASE-T is the cabling distance. Figure 7-11 compares the cabling distance for a single cable.

Figure 7-11   Comparing Maximum Cabling Distances: 1000BASE-X and 1000BASE-T

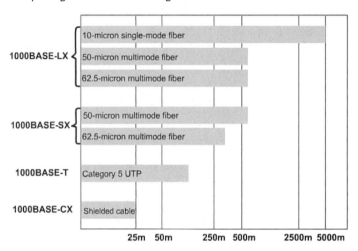

Note

1000BASE-ZX, which is another IEEE 802.3z standard, supports links up to 70 km. Cisco Systems also sells 1000BASE-LX equipment that supports 10 km.

At the time of its introduction in 1998, 1000BASE-X represented a great option for backbone links between switches in a dispersed campus network. In fact, by 1998, many enterprises had moved away from FDDI, using either multiple 100-Mbps Ethernet links (100BASE-FX) or ATM for backbone links. (ATM could use Synchronous Optical Network [SONET] technology, which uses speeds that are multiples of 51.84 Mbps.) By 1998, reasonably priced ATM components for backbone links would run 155 Mbps—or even 622 Mbps—with higher speeds available. With 1000BASE-X, longer backbones could be built, and with the ability to use multiple parallel active Gigabit links (up to eight) in a single Gigabit EtherChannel, backbone links could run at multiples of 1 Gbps. Figure 7-12 shows an example.

Figure 7-12   Backbone with Two 1000BASE-X Links

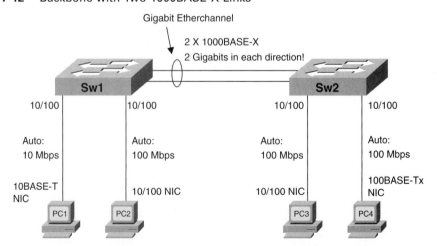

Most backbone designs between switches use at least two parallel links, as shown in Figure 7-12. If the cables exit the building and run underground between buildings in a campus, the cables can run through different conduits to minimize the chance of cutting all cables when someone digs near the conduit. Also, Cisco created a proprietary technology called EtherChannel, which allows up to eight parallel Fast Ethernet or Gigabit Ethernet links to combine so that all are active at once. So, compared to ATM, the hardware required to create a 2-Gbps full-duplex backbone connection quickly became cheaper than ATM alternatives, making Gigabit Ethernet a hugely popular choice as a backbone technology. Today, many enterprise networks use Gigabit links for trunks (often, multiple links in an EtherChannel) with 10/100 interfaces connected to the end-user population.

For 1000BASE-SX and 1000BASE-LX, the cabling types differ to some degree, but the cable layout is the same. Both use two fiber strands—one for transmission in each direction. The concept is similar to copper Ethernet standards, which use a single twisted pair for transmission in each direction. The cables typically use either an SC connector or an MT-RJ connector, which has the same size and shape as an RJ-45 connector. Figures 7-13 and 7-14 show the connectors.

Figure 7-13   SC Connector

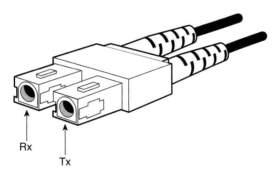

Figure 7-14   MT-RJ Connector

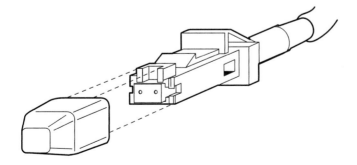

The small circles on the end of each connector represent the end of the actual fibers. For communications to work, the *transmitter* on one end of a fiber must connect to the *detector*

(receiver) on the other end. So, every fiber Ethernet cable must essentially act like a crossover UTP cable in concept, as shown in Figure 7-15.

Figure 7-15   Matching Transmitter with Receiver on 1000BASE-X

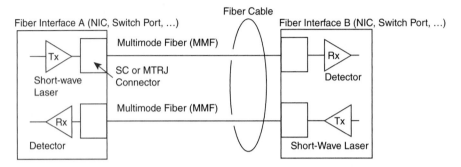

Figure 7-15 shows a single fiber cable with two individual fiber strands. The strand connected to the transmitter (Tx) on one side is connected to the detector (Rx) on the other. The figure shows multimode fiber (MMF) with (less expensive) short-wave lasers as transmitters, which indicates 1000BASE-SX. The cabling concept works the same with 1000BASE-LX, with (more expensive) long-wave lasers as transmitters and single-mode fiber (SMF) cabling. To transmit bits, all the light is transmitted at a particular frequency, with the power of the light (brightness) determining if a bit is a 0 or a 1. Depending on the type of transmitted signal, different wavelengths of light can be used (refer to Figure 7-11).

1000BASE-T

The IEEE standardized fiber-based 1000BASE-X Ethernet more quickly than the 1999 release of the *1000BASE-T* copper UTP-based Gigabit Ethernet standard. The primary original motivation for Gigabit Ethernet was to provide a fast backbone technology that supported single buildings (1000BASE-SX) or large campuses (1000BASE-LX), with faster speeds, with a technology completely compatible with earlier Ethernet standards. 1000BASE-X did just that and was well received in the market. 1000BASE-X also came first because the engineering required to transmit at 1 Gbps over fiber had already been worked out, particularly because of the large amounts of earlier work with SONET and another technology called *Fibre Channel*. On the other hand, 1000BASE-T required some amazing engineering to find a way to transmit data at Gigabit speeds over copper cabling; therefore, the 1000BASE-T standard required much more work than 1000BASE-X.

Released in 1999, *IEEE 802.3ab*, also called 1000BASE-T, defines the Gigabit Ethernet standard for using copper UTP cabling. 1000BASE-T uses four-pair Cat5e cabling, not Cat5. Not coincidentally, most installed Cat5 cabling can be re-terminated and made to pass a Cat5e cable test. The IEEE designed 1000BASE-T expecting that, with some additional work to re-terminate existing Cat5 cables, 1000BASE-T could use existing wiring.

To run at 1 Gbps over UTP cabling, the engineers who developed 1000BASE-T used what might seem like a magician's trick to anyone without an electrical engineering degree. Briefly, 1000BASE-T sends 125 million different electrical symbols, per second, over the wire, using methods similar to 100BASE-Tx. (You can read more about 100BASE-TX encoding in the section "100BASE-TX PMD Line Encoding" in the "Additional Topics of Interest" document for this chapter, which can be found on the CD-ROM.) The 1000BASE-T designers created a way to send 2 bits in each electrical signal (called a symbol) so that 250 Mbps can be sent over a single pair. Then, the standard states that all four pairs need to be used for transmitting. The standard includes a way to simultaneously both send and receive over each pair without causing collisions. So, 1000BASE-T transmits twice as many bits per second (250 Mbps) as 100BASE-TX (125 Mbps) over a twisted pair, and it does that on all four pairs to reach 1 Gbps in each direction.

Although the electrical details of 1000BASE-T transmission might be fascinating for electrical engineers, most people ignore the details and accept that it works just fine. However, the concept of simultaneous two-way transmission over the same twisted pairs gives many engineers a reason to doubt, especially knowing that 1000BASE-T (and other Gigabit Ethernet standards) supports CSMA/CD. However, when 1000BASE-T interfaces use half duplex and CSMA/CD, the NICs and interfaces simply use logic that notices when actual frames are being received, and if so, the NIC does not send. Also, they notice collisions not through the physical effects of colliding frames, because the technology does not create such collisions. Instead, collisions are noticed through this logic: If a NIC sends a frame and begins to receive one as well, a collision is assumed.

From a practical perspective, Gigabit Ethernet does not use CSMA/CD and half duplex by choice. In reality, to need to use CSMA/CD and half duplex, the equivalent of a Gigabit Ethernet hub needs to exist, and no one sells them. Instead, vendors sell switches with Gigabit interfaces; each switch port creates a different collision domain with only two interfaces in each domain, which allows Gigabit Ethernet to simply not use CSMA/CD. So, although the Gigabit Ethernet standards do support CSMA/CD and half duplex, they are unlikely to be used in an actual production network. In fact, Ethernet standards that are faster than Gigabit Ethernet do not even bother to support half duplex and CSMA/CD.

1000BASE-T cabling uses four pairs. For connections between a NIC and a switch, a straight-through cable pinout is required. Table 7-7 lists the names of the pins for a 1000BASE-T straight-through cable.

Note

1000BASE-T defines a function that Cisco Systems calls Automatic Medium-independent Crossover (Auto-mdix). This feature allows switches to detect if a straight-through cable is mistakenly used between switches and then reverse the interface's logic to make the cable work correctly.

Table 7-7   1000BASE-T Straight-Through Cable Pin Lead Names

Pin	Number Signal	Wire Insulation Color
1	BI_DA+ (bidirectional data, positive going)	White/orange
2	BI_DA– (bidirectional data, negative going)	Orange
3	BI_DB+ (bidirectional data, positive going)	White/green
4	BI_DC+ (bidirectional data, positive going)	Blue
5	BI_DC– (bidirectional data, negative going)	White/blue
6	BI_DB– (bidirectional data, negative going)	Green
7	BI_DD+ (bidirectional data, positive going)	White/brown
8	BI_DD– (bidirectional data, negative going)	Brown

Switch-to-switch or NIC-to-NIC connections require a form of crossover cable. Note that, as with 10BASE-T and 100BASE-TX crossover cables, the pair at pins 1 and 2 and the pair at pins 3 and 6 are crossed. For 1000BASE-T, the other two pairs are also crossed.

Lab 7.1.9a   Introduction to Fluke Network Inspector

In this lab, you learn how to use the Fluke Network Inspector (NI) to discover and analyze network devices within a broadcast domain.

Lab 7.1.9b   Introduction to Fluke Protocol Inspector

In this lab, you learn how to use the Fluke Network Protocol Inspector to analyze network traffic and data frames.

Future of Ethernet

Ethernet has a bright future in the enterprise LAN. 10-, 100-, and 1000-Mbps Ethernet has a stronghold on the LAN installations of most enterprise LANs. On the end-user side of the LAN switch infrastructure, most companies' next major upgrade to their LAN switching hardware includes many 10/100/1000 ports to support end users, with many PC manufacturers either including 1000BASE-T interfaces on the motherboard or, better yet, 10/100/1000 autonegotiating interfaces. The migration of using 1 Gbps to the desktop has begun.

For the enterprise LAN backbone, many installations already run multiple 1-Gbps links as an EtherChannel between switches, which provides multiples of 1 Gbps between switches. Additionally, a fiber and copper (using twin-ax cable) standard for 10 Gigabit Ethernet have been approved by the IEEE, with products now available from vendors such as Cisco. Historically, Ethernet prices have fallen drastically within the first two or three years after the introduction of each new Ethernet standard, so LANs with 1 Gbps to most desktops, and multiple 10-Gbps interfaces between switches to form a backbone, seem likely within the next few years.

The introduction of the fiber-based 10 Gigabit Ethernet standard (10GBASE-X, defined in *IEEE 802.3ae* in 2002), with the capability to use a single segment of up to 40 km in length, opens up an entirely new world to the Ethernet family. Service providers can use 10 Gigabit Ethernet to build their high-speed networks. Also, with the longer distances for 1000BASE-LX, service providers can use Gigabit Ethernet to connect to customer locations. For example, Figure 7-16 shows a typical MAN, built by a service provider, with 10 Gigabit links between its sites inside a city.

Figure 7-16   Service Provider MAN with 10 Gigabit and 1 Gigabit Ethernet

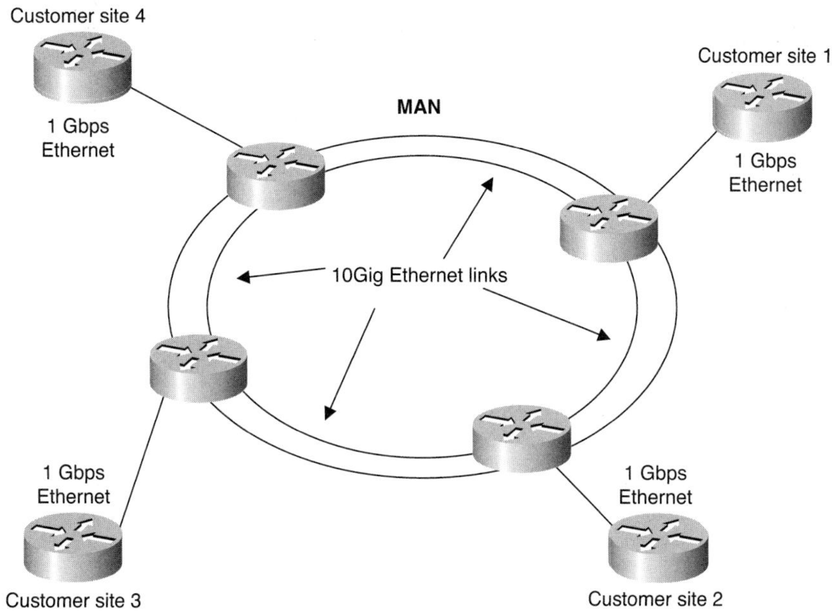

Today, many service providers offer services like the service shown in Figure 7-16. The industry uses the term *Metro Ethernet* for such designs, particularly because the familiar Ethernet frame is used throughout the WAN.

Networking media continues to expand to use faster speeds. Current LAN limits are generally at the following levels:

- **Copper**—Up to 1000 Mbps (probably more)
- **Wireless**—Up to 100 Mbps (probably more)
- **Optical**—Up to 10 Gbps (soon to be more)

Copper and wireless media have more difficulties in reaching higher speeds than optical media. For copper and wireless media, the limits are based on the frequencies that can be passed over the media. For optical networks, the frequency bandwidth should not be a constraint in the foreseeable future. Instead, the constraints relate to building better transmitters and receivers, as well as the fiber-cable manufacturing process. Also, other technologies have preceded Ethernet by attempting digital transmission over optical cable at speeds higher than 10 Gbps, which speeds the development of faster speeds for optical Ethernet. Ethernet will most likely continue to expand in the foreseeable future. Work has already begun on 40 Gbps, 100 Gbps, and even 160 Gbps.

Although the future might be unpredictable, Ethernet will certainly play an important and central role in building networks for many years to come.

Summary

Ethernet has increased in speed 1000 times, from 10 Mbps to 10,000 Mbps, in less than a decade. All Ethernet forms share a similar frame structure, and this leads to excellent interoperability. Most Ethernet copper connections are now switched full duplex. 10GigE and faster were exclusively optical fiber-based technologies, but with some work also being performed on 10GigE copper standards.

10BASE5, 10BASE2, and 10BASE-T Ethernet are considered legacy Ethernet technologies. The four common features of Legacy Ethernet are timing parameters, frame format, transmission process, and the 5-4-3 basic design rule. The 5-4-3 design rule states that a single LAN (10BASE2, 10BASE5, or 10BASE-T with hubs) can have only five segments, four repeaters, and three segments occupied between any two devices on the LAN.

10BASE-T, using twisted-pair copper wire, was introduced in 1990. Because it used multiple wires, 10BASE-T offered the option of full-duplex signaling. 10BASE-T carries 10 Mbps of traffic in half-duplex mode and 20 Mbps in full-duplex mode.

10BASE-T links can have unrepeated distances up to 100 m. Beyond that, network devices, such as repeaters, hubs, bridges, and switches, extend the scope of the LAN. With the advent of switches and full duplex, the four-repeater rule is not required. You can indefinitely extend the LAN by daisy-chaining switches. Each switch-to-switch connection, with a maximum length of 100 m, is essentially a point-to-point connection without the media contention or timing issues of using repeaters and hubs.

100-Mbps Ethernet, also known as Fast Ethernet, can be implemented using twisted-pair copper wire, as in 100BASE-TX, or fiber media, as in 100BASE-FX. 100-Mbps Ethernet forms can transmit 200 Mbps in full duplex.

Because the higher-frequency signals used in Fast Ethernet are more susceptible to noise, 100-Mbps Ethernet uses two separate encoding steps to enhance signal integrity.

The fiber versions of Gigabit Ethernet, 1000BASE-SX and 1000BASE-LX, offer the following advantages: noise immunity, small size, and increased unrepeated distances and bandwidth. The IEEE 802.3 standard recommends that Gigabit Ethernet over fiber be the preferred backbone technology.

You can find supplemental coverage related to topics described in this chapter on the CD-ROM in the "Additional Topics of Interest" section. Chapter 8 covers how Ethernet switches work.

Check Your Understanding

Complete all the review questions listed here to test your understanding of the topics and concepts in this chapter. Answers are listed in Appendix A, "Answers to Check Your Understanding and Challenge Questions."

1. What is the purpose of the 5-4-3 design rule?

   A. Provide time for CSMA/CD to work in a 100BASE-T full-duplex network

   B. Ensure that CSMA/CD works correctly by making sure that collisions are heard in a reasonable amount of time

   C. Provide five LAN segments for hosts

   D. Provide four LAN segments for hosts

2. What is the maximum distance for Thicknet Ethernet without using a repeater?

   A. 185 m (606.95 ft)

   B. 250 m (820.2 ft)

   C. 500 m (1640.4 ft)

   D. 800 m (2624.64 ft)

3. 10-Mbps Ethernet operates within the timing limits offered by a series of no more than _____ segments separated by no more than _____ repeaters.

   A. Three, two

   B. Four, three

   C. Five, four

   D. Six, five

4. Fast Ethernet supports up to what transfer rate?

   A. 5 Mbps

   B. 10 Mbps

   C. 100 Mbps

   D. 1000 Mbps

5. Identify two Gigabit Ethernet over fiber cable specifications.

   A. 1000BASE-TX

   B. 1000BASE-FX

   C. 1000BASE-SX

   D. 1000BASE-LX

   E. 1000BASE-GX

6. What transmitter and cable type are used for 1000BASE-SX

   A. Long-wave laser over SMF and MMF

   B. Electrical transmitter using Category 5 UTP copper wiring

   C. Electrical transmitter using balanced, shielded, 150-ohm, two-pair STP copper cable

   D. Short-wave laser over MMF

7. What is the best choice for network backbones on large campuses?

   A. 100BASE-T

   B. 1000BASE-LX

   C. 1000BASE-SX

   D. 1000BASE-CX

8. What is the IEEE standard for 10GigE?

   A. 802.3z

   B. 802.3u

   C. 802.3ae

   D. 803.3

9. Although 1000BASE-T standards support CSMA/CD and half duplex, why are you unlikely to see them on a network?

   A. This requires the use of 1000BASE-T hubs, and no one sells them.

   B. 100BASE-T is still adequate for network backbones.

   C. The 5-4-3 rule prevents implementation in large networks.

   D. The collisions slow down network throughput to unacceptable rates.

10. What is the maximum transmission distance supported by 1000BASE-SX Ethernet?

   A. 82 m

   B. 100 m

   C. 220 m

   D. 500 m

   E. 5000 m

Challenge Questions and Activities

These activities require a deeper application of the concepts covered in this chapter, similar ro how answering CCNA certification exam questions require applying detailed concepts to a particular scenario.

Activity 7-1: Describe the progression of Ethernet standards, beginning with 10BASE5, through 10GigE, including the general order in which the standards were approved, their common names (for example, 10BASE-T), the type of media, and the transmission rate.

Activity 7-2: This chapter mentions using straight-through and crossover cables in a network. Where is each type of cable used?

CHAPTER 8

Ethernet Switching

Objectives

Upon completion of this chapter, you should be able to answer the following questions:

- How do bridges and LAN switches operate?

- What is latency?

- What are the differences among common switching methods such as cut-through switching, store-and-forward switching, and fragment-free switching?

- What are the functions and features of the Spanning Tree Protocol (STP)?

- What is the difference between a collision domain and a broadcast domain?

- Which Layer 1, 2, and 3 devices create collision domains and broadcast domains?

- What is a Content Addressable Memory (CAM) table, and how is it used?

- How does data flow through a network, and how do broadcasts cause problems with the flow?

- What is network segmentation, and which devices create segments?

Key Terms

This chapter uses the following key terms. You can find the definitions in the Glossary.

application-specific integrated circuits (ASICs) page 298

forwarding   page 299

filtering   page 299

bridging table   page 299

switching table   page 299

MAC address table   page 299

Content Addressable Memory (CAM) table   page 299

unknown unicast frame   page 304

broadcast frames   page 304

multicast frames   page 304

latency   page 307

propagation delay   page 307

queuing delay   page 308

store-and-forward switching   page 308

asymmetric switching   page 308

cut-through switching   page 309

symmetric switching   page 309

fragment-free switching   page 309

trunk   page 310

continues

continued

broadcast storm   page 312

Spanning Tree Protocol (STP)   page 312

blocking state   page 312

forwarding state   page 314

disabled state   page 314

Bridge Protocol Data Units (BPDUs)   page 315

Spanning Tree Algorithm (STA)   page 315

IEEE 802.1D   page 315

listening state   page 315

learning state   page 315

STP topology   page 315

collision domain   page 318

shared bandwidth   page 319

shared media   page 319

round-trip time   page 320

segmentation   page 321

switched LAN   page 323

switched bandwidth   page 323

microsegmentation   page 323

segment   page 323

queuing   page 323

broadcast domain   page 325

Layer 1 devices   page 329

Layer 2 devices   page 329

Layer 3 devices   page 329

data flow   page 329

This chapter contains the book's final detailed explanations about Ethernet for this book and the CCNA 1 course. The first section of the chapter focuses on switch operations, reviewing many concepts covered earlier in the course. This coverage includes the detailed external and internal logic of how a switch forwards frames. The first section also introduces the Spanning Tree Protocol (STP) for the first and only time in this book.

The second half of the chapter, comprising the section "LAN Design: Collision Domains and Broadcast Domains," focuses more on some issues related to LAN design. This section completes the explanation of the concept of a collision domain and introduces the concept of a broadcast domain. To do so, this section compares the operation of repeaters, hubs, bridges, switches, and even routers, and how they either do or do not create multiple collision domains and broadcast domains.

Ethernet Switch Operations

This section covers some familiar concepts, plus many new concepts, all related to how a bridge or switch makes a decision of how and where to forward Ethernet frames. To begin, this section reviews the bridging and switching logic that has already been introduced in this book—namely, the forward/filtering decision made by any LAN bridge or switch. It goes on to explain how a switch learns the entry in its switching table, as well as how a switch or bridge decides to forward broadcast and multicast frames.

Switches use some interesting processes internally to achieve the high speeds and low latency for forwarding Ethernet frames today. Part of this section explains the internal processing logic used by switches.

Finally, this section covers the Spanning Tree Protocol (STP), which helps a switch prevent a frame from being forwarded around a LAN continuously.

Layer 2 Bridging and Switching Operations

Two of the earliest LAN networking devices were repeaters and hubs. These devices worked well, at least in the context of the technology available at the time. These devices essentially allowed multiple LAN segments to be connected into larger LAN segments, extending the length of the LAN segment, within certain design rules such as the 10BASE-T 5-4-3 design rule.

As time went on, it became apparent that a totally different kind of LAN forwarding device was needed. As a result, vendors created LAN bridges. These networking devices forwarded Ethernet frames based on the destination MAC address. Such work required that the bridge be aware of Ethernet framing and MAC addresses defined in IEEE 802.3, which is an OSI Layer 2 standard. Bridges also extended LAN distances, but without some of the negative effects of repeaters and hubs, particularly for larger LANs. However, LAN bridges were actually typically much more expensive than repeaters and hubs, because most bridges were PCs running software that performed the bridging, whereas hubs and repeaters just required some basic electronics. Bridges also typically had only two Ethernet interfaces, whereas hubs typically had many more.

Although bridges were useful, they could be improved upon. The next major step for a LAN-specific forwarding device was called a LAN switch. Switches essentially do the exact same things as bridges. However, LAN switches appeared on the marketplace after chip technology had evolved to the point at which the actual work done by the switch could be done with chips, instead of using software on a general-purpose PC. (Many of these chips are called *application-specific integrated circuits (ASICs)*). So, switches could support lots of interfaces, in a much smaller space, plus do the same work as bridges—and, most importantly, do it much faster. In fact, when the networking world transitioned bridges to the new, faster switches, many people referred to switches as "bridges on steroids."

When switch prices began to fall after years of being available from vendors, bridges pretty much disappeared from the market. However, because bridges and switches perform similar functions, in the same general way, much of what is covered in this chapter applies equally to bridges and switches. The text will point out the cases in which a particular section applies only to switches. The section "Switch Internal Processing" describes specific switch features that do not apply to bridges, mainly because vendors quit developing new bridge products once switches became reasonably priced.

The Forwarding and Filtering Decision

Hubs and repeaters simply react to the incoming signals, always regenerating and repeating the signals out all other ports. They make no decisions and require no programming logic—they simply receive, regenerate, and send the regenerated signal out all ports (except the one in which the signal was received). Bridges and switches use programming logic to make more intelligent choices, meaning that a bridge reacts differently to different conditions.

Note

The CCNA 1 course covers bridges and switches to point out the similarities and differences, but many vendors, including Cisco, have not offered products called a "bridge" for a number of years.

Bridges and switches differ in how they work internally, but that is mainly a result of the fact that bridges were popular over ten years ago, and switches use current technology. Bridges typically implemented their logic in software, whereas switches implement their logic in hardware. As a result, switches tend to run much faster than bridges, with the ability to forward many more frames than a bridge. For example, Cisco makes switches that can forward hundreds of millions of Ethernet frames per second.

Regardless of how fast bridges and switches do their work, both types of devices use the same forwarding and filtering logic, which works as follows:

1. Examine the incoming signal, and interpret the signal as 0s and 1s. (This function uses OSI Layer 1 standards.)

2. Interpret the received bits based on Ethernet framing rules, and find the destination MAC address listed in the frame. (This function relies on headers defined as part of the 802.3 MAC sublayer, which matches OSI Layer 2.)

3. Examine a table that lists MAC addresses and corresponding bridge/switch interfaces. The interface identifies the bridge/switch interface out which the frame should be forwarded.

Find the entry matching the destination MAC address of the frame:

a. If the frame came in a different interface from the one listed in the table, forward the frame, using a clean regenerated signal. (This process is called *forwarding*.)

b. If the frame came in the same interface as the one listed in the table, discard the frame. (This process is called *filtering*.)

The bridging/switching algorithm is purposefully very simple. The original bridges were PCs with two NICs and some bridging software—PCs with far less memory and computing power than the average MP3 player today. Requiring such a device to attempt to perform a complex algorithm on thousands of frames per second would have easily overwhelmed the hardware, so bridging logic was purposefully kept as simple as possible.

The next few pages describe the basic filtering and forwarding decision logic used by both bridges and switches.

> **Note**
>
> The words *interface* and *port* are used interchangeably when referring to the physical LAN interfaces on a bridge or switch. The longer, equivalent terms *switch port* and *switch interface* are also used often.

Scenario 1: Bridge Filtering Decision

Bridges and switches forward or filter frames based on the contents of a table. Several terms refer to this table, including **bridging table**, **switching table**, **MAC address table**, and *forwarding table*. Also, Cisco calls this same table a **Content Addressable Memory (CAM) table**, because Cisco switches use a special type of memory called CAM to store the table. Figure 8-1 shows how a bridge uses its CAM to make a filtering decision.

> **Note**
>
> Instead of using the term "the CAM table," many people simply say or write "the CAM" for short, a practice used in this book.

Figure 8-1   A Bridge Filtering Decision Based on the CAM

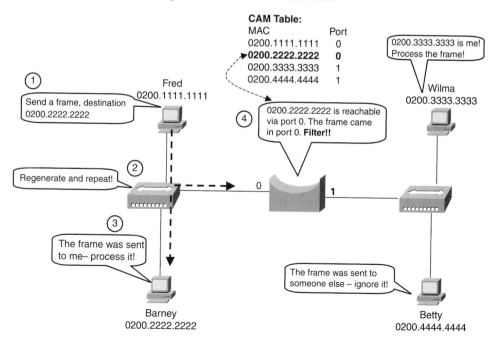

The following process explains the corresponding steps shown in Figure 8-1:

1. Fred sends an Ethernet frame with a destination MAC address of 0200.2222.2222.

2. The hub repeats the frame out both of its other ports.

3. Barney receives the electrical signal and decides it is meant for him because the destination MAC address is his NIC's MAC address. So, Barney processes the received data.

4. The bridge receives the signal in its port number 0 and looks at the destination MAC address of 0200.2222.2222. The bridge's table says that 0200.2222.2222 is reachable out port 0, which is the same port in which the frame was received. So, the bridge does not need to forward the frame and thus filters the frame by simply discarding it.

Scenario 2: Bridge Forwarding Decision

Figure 8-2 shows the same network as Figure 8-1, but in this case, Fred sends a frame to 0200.3333.3333, which is Wilma's MAC address. The bridge needs to forward the frame, because the frame enters the bridge's left-side interface, with Wilma being reachable on the bridge's right-side interface.

Figure 8-2 A Bridge Forwarding Decision Based on the CAM

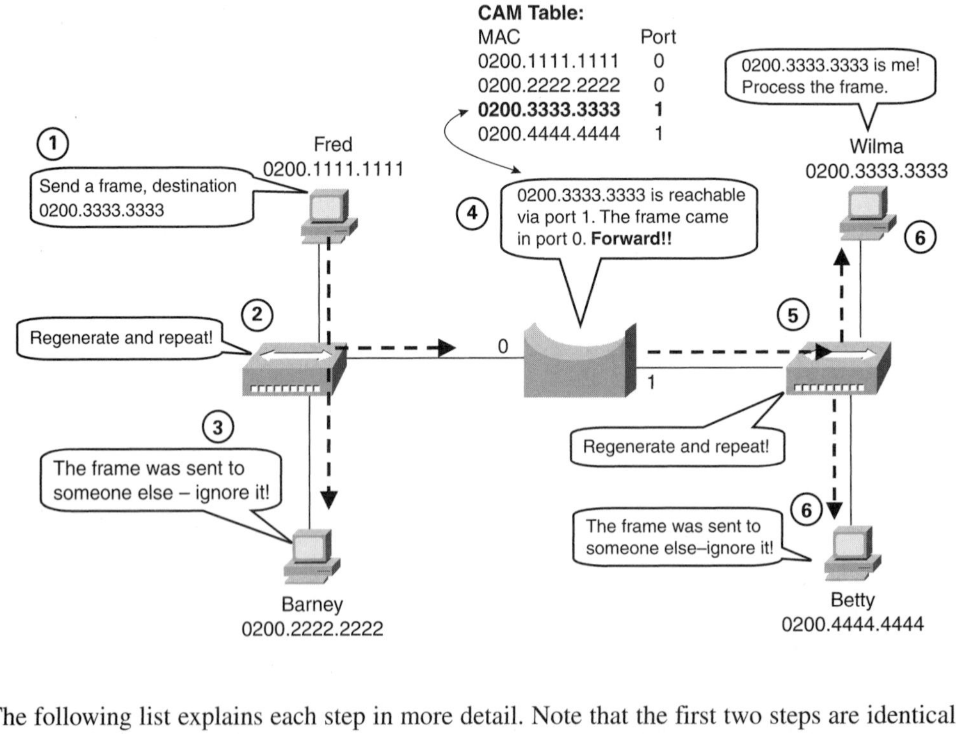

The following list explains each step in more detail. Note that the first two steps are identical to the corresponding steps in Figure 8-1, other than the different destination address of the frame.

1. Fred sends an Ethernet frame with a destination MAC address 0200.3333.3333.

2. The hub repeats the frame out both of its other ports.

3. Barney receives the electrical signal, and decides not to process the frame because the destination MAC address of the frame is not Barney's MAC address.

4. The bridge receives the signal in its port number 0, and looks at the destination MAC address of 0200.3333.3333. The bridge's CAM holds an entry that says 0200.3333.3333 is reachable out the bridge's port 1, which is a different port from the incoming port (port 0). So, the bridge forwards the frame.

5. The repeater on the right repeats the signal out all interfaces.

6. Wilma receives and processes the frame, while Betty receives and ignores the frame, because the destination MAC address of the frame is Wilma's MAC address.

By loading Packet Tracer configuration file NA01-0802, you can use the simulation tool to show the exact same flows shown in Figure 8-1 (scenario 1) and Figure 8-2 (scenario 2). Also, in real-time mode, double-clicking the bridge displays the bridging table.

Learning CAM Table Entries and Flooding Unknown Unicasts

Switches (and bridges) must dynamically learn the entries in the CAM. In most cases, when a switch first powers up, the CAM is empty. This process implies a couple of questions:

- How does a switch learn the entries to add to its CAM?

- What logic does a switch use when the CAM does not have an entry that matches a MAC address?

This section answers the first question, and the next section answers the second question. To learn CAM table entries, bridges and switches use the following logic:

1. Examine incoming frames, noting the source MAC address of the frame and the interface in which the frame was received.

2. Add that source MAC address and corresponding incoming interface to the table.

Figure 8-3 shows an example with an empty CAM to start, with a CAM entry for Fred's MAC address being built after Fred sends a frame.

Figure 8-3   Learning CAM Table Entries: One Switch

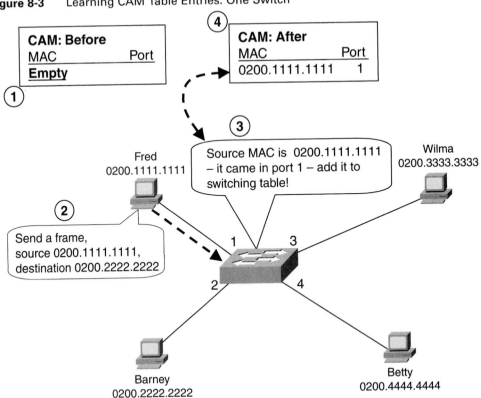

The following steps correspond to the steps in Figure 8-3:

1. The switch's CAM is empty.

2. Fred sends a frame, source MAC address 0200.1111.1111, destination MAC address 0200.2222.2222 (Barney).

3. The switch notes the source MAC address of the received frame and notes the incoming interface (port 1).

4. The switch adds that new MAC/port mapping to the CAM.

By using this process, the switch now knows how to forward frames to Fred's MAC address (0200.1111.1111). The next time the switch receives a frame destined for Fred's MAC address—which may be very soon, assuming that Barney replies—the switch will have an entry that it can use for forwarding the frame to Fred.

Figure 8-3 shows the switch learning a single entry for the switching table. However, the process happens every time a frame is received. That means that as soon as all four PCs in Figure 8-3 send a single frame, the switch's CAM will be complete, at least for this small LAN. Also, if someone were to move a PC to another port off the switch, the switch would update the CAM as soon as that moved PC sends another frame.

The CAM typically has a limited size, often 1024 or 4096 entries in Cisco switches. Because most LANs are far smaller than 1024 devices, this limitation is not severe. However, for good housekeeping, switches typically keep a timer for each entry. If the switch does not receive any frames with a particular source MAC address for a long time (typically hours), the switch times out the CAM entry by removing it. If the device later sends another frame, the switch adds the entry back to the CAM.

Figure 8-4 shows a second example of learning CAM entries. In this case, the figure shows two switches connected via a trunk. Focus on the fact that both switches act independently to add their own CAM entries; there is no attempt to communicate with each other. Each switch simply reacts to the frames it receives.

Figure 8-4   Learning CAM Table Entries: Two Switches

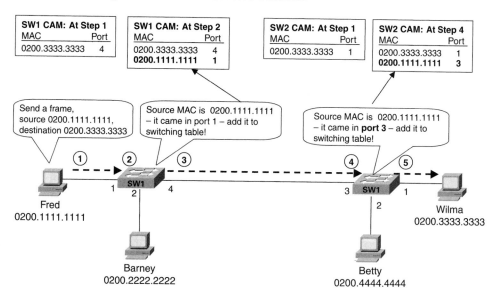

The example of Figure 8-4 begins with both switches' CAMs having an entry for Wilma's MAC address (0200.3333.3333). SW1's CAM references SW1's interface 4, which means that SW1 will forward frames sent to 0200.3333.3333 out the trunk to SW2. At the beginning of the example, SW2's CAM lists MAC address 0200.3333.3333 with interface 1, meaning that SW2 forwards frames sent to 0200.3333.3333 directly to Wilma. The arrows in the figure show where the frame is forwarded.

The purpose of presenting Figure 8-4, however, is to show how each switch independently adds entries to its CAMs. The following list outlines the logic of how each switch adds a CAM entry for Fred's MAC address (2000.1111.1111), with the corresponding steps shown circled in Figure 8-4:

1. Fred sends a frame, source 0200.1111.1111, destination 0200.3333.3333 (Wilma).

2. SW1 looks at the source MAC address of the frame, notes the incoming interface (1), and adds that entry to SW1's CAM.

3. SW1 forwards the frame out its port 4, per SW1's current CAM entry.

4. SW2 looks at the source MAC address of the received frame, notes the incoming interface (3), and adds that entry to SW2's CAM.

5. SW2 forwards the frame out its port 1, per SW2's current CAM entry.

Handling Unknown Unicasts

Switches typically learn the CAM entries for all working devices on the LAN, at least as soon as those devices start sending data over the LAN. However, there will be instances in which a switch receives a frame and the destination MAC address of the frame is not in that switch's CAM. The switch still needs to make a forwarding decision for the frame.

The term *unknown unicast frame* refers to a frame for which a switch does not have the frame's destination MAC address in the CAM. When processing an unknown unicast frame (often simply called an *unknown unicast*, leaving off "frame"), the switch floods the frame. Formally, switch (or bridge) flooding is defined as follows:

> The process of forwarding a frame out all ports except the port in which the frame was received.

Figure 8-5 shows an example in which a switch receives an unknown unicast frame, flooding the frame at Step 5.

Forwarding Broadcasts and Multicasts

So far, this chapter has discussed how switches forward unicast frames. By definition, a unicast frame has a destination MAC address of a single NIC or Ethernet interface. However, Ethernet also uses two other classes of frames, called *broadcast frames* and *multicast frames*. (The terms *broadcast* and *multicast* are also often used, again leaving off "frame.") These types of frames can be generally defined as follows:

- **Broadcast frames**—Frames sent to a destination MAC address of FFFF.FFFF.FFFF. Such frames should be delivered to all devices on the same LAN.

- **Multicast frames**—Frames sent to one of a range of multicast MAC addresses. The most popular Ethernet multicast addresses begin with 0100.5E or 0100.5F, because these multicast MAC addresses are used for IP multicasting. Such frames should be delivered to multiple devices on the LAN, but not necessarily to all devices.

Figure 8-5   Flooding Unknown Unicasts

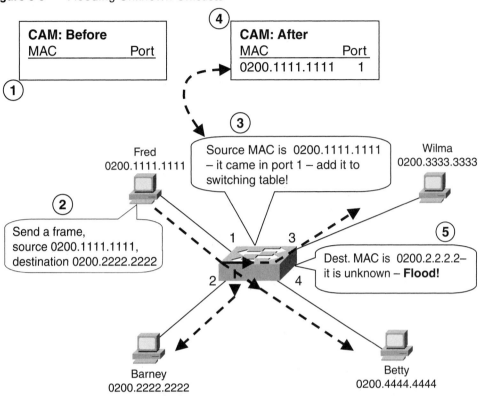

Some switches process broadcasts and multicasts in the same way, and some do not. First, for broadcasts, switches use the following forwarding logic:

Flood broadcasts out all interfaces except the interface in which the frame arrived.

For example, a broadcast sent by Fred would be forwarded like the unicast example shown in Figure 8-5.

Ethernet multicast addresses provide a way for a subset of the devices on the LAN to receive certain frames. For example, streaming audio and video applications may use IP multicast. A company CEO might hold a company-wide videoconference, with the conference's video and audio sent over the network. When the video and audio pass over the LAN, the data can pass as multicast Ethernet frames. Those dutiful employees at their PCs, listening to and watching the videoconference, need to receive and process the multicast frames. The PCs used by the other employees who are not interested in listening to the CEO's message do not need to receive the same multicast frames.

Switches differ slightly in how they forward LAN multicasts. On some low-end switches, particularly those meant for home use, the switches simply flood multicasts just like broadcasts. On other, higher-end switches, such as most of the current Cisco switch product line that is sold to Enterprise customers, the switches use one or more of several switch features that allow the switches to forward multicasts more efficiently, without having to flood the frames.

Note

Cisco creates some switch products with businesses in mind and others with home use in mind. The business switches, which this book refers to as Enterprise switches or Enterprise-class switches, tend to be more expensive and larger and have more software features, such as the multicast optimizations covered here.

Figure 8-6 shows two similar LANs. On the left, the switch does not have any multicast optimization features, so it floods a multicast sent by Fred. On the right, the switch does support multicast optimization features. In this case, Barney and Wilma want to receive Fred's multicast frames, but Betty does not.

Figure 8-6   Different Forwarding Behavior for Multicasts

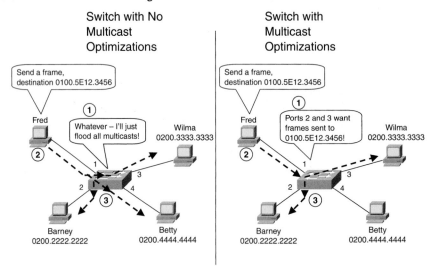

Note

Multicast optimization features are not covered in the Academy CCNA curriculum. If you want to read more about these features, however, go to http://www.cisco.com and search for IGMP snooping, RGMP, and CGMP.

In both halves of Figure 8-6, Step 1 shows the anticipated thought process of each switch. At Step 2, Fred sends a multicast frame to 0100.5E12.3456. Step 3 shows flooding on the left, and efficient forwarding only to Barney on the right.

 Packet Tracer   Packet Tracer configuration file NA01-0806 shows a network like Figure 8-6. Simulation scenario 1 shows the case on the left of the figure, in which the switch floods a multicast.

The Cisco Switch CAM

All switches (and bridges) use some table that lists MAC address and the port/interface through which each MAC address can be reached. The generic terms for this table include bridging table, switching table, forwarding table, and MAC address table.

Cisco calls this table the CAM table or, more frequently, simply the CAM. CAM stands for Content Addressable Memory, which is a special type of memory that is used for many applications, not just for switches. Generically speaking, CAM is a type of memory chip that has some great properties for table lookup.

First, for perspective, consider how a human looks something up in a list, a list of 500 last names, for example. If the list is not sorted, the human would have to read the entire list, probably from top to bottom. If the list were alphabetized, the human brain could easily scan to find the right first letter and then quickly find the name.

Computers frequently need to find information in lists. If you're taking a full set of computer science courses along with this course, you will likely spend some time learning about different ways that computers can efficiently search lists. However, searching lists takes time. If a computer searches a list sequentially, the time required to find an entry may vary; if the term being sought is the first entry, finding it will take much less time than if the term is the last entry. Simply put, searching through lists takes some amount of time for the computer, and some search algorithms vary in how long it takes to find an entry.

When searches need to occur a lot—such as twice for every frame received on a LAN switch, and for hundreds of thousands, or millions, of frames per second—the search process needs to be very efficient and take very little time. To meet those requirements, the switch may require either a very powerful (and more expensive) CPU, or a way to spend almost no effort when doing a search of the table. CAM provides that very fast and relatively inexpensive solution for performing searches of tables.

CAM allows for a hardware-based search of a table. Cisco switches use CAM to store the MAC address table. When the switch wants to search for a MAC address in the table, the switch inputs the MAC address into the CAM, and the CAM instantly outputs the table entry. The table lookup process occurs quickly, every time, regardless of table size. CAM allows Cisco switches to perform low-latency forwarding of frames, without requiring fast and expensive CPU chips.

Switch Internal Processing

The amount of time required to look up the source MAC address (for adding CAM entries) and the destination MAC address (for the forwarding decision) in the CAM impacts how long the switch takes to forward a frame. However, the use of CAM makes that process short enough and, more importantly, consistent enough that it does not have a noticeable effect on how long a switch takes to forward a frame. This section covers a few topics related to the time a switch takes to forward a frame through a network, including the time required as the frame passes through the switches themselves.

Latency

In networking, the term *latency* refers to how long it takes for a frame or packet to progress through the network from one device to another. Some factors that affect latency cannot be improved—for example, electricity requires a certain amount of time to go from one end of the cable to another. That type of latency is called *propagation delay*. Other types of latency may vary based on network conditions—for example, a switch may receive a frame that needs to be forwarded out port 1, but 20 other frames may already be sitting in memory buffers awaiting their chance to exit port 1 as well. This kind of delay is typically called *queuing delay* because it is delay caused by having to wait in a queue until the frame gets its turn to leave the switch. Certainly, the time required for the CAM table lookup of the destination MAC address also consumes time, although that particular step is practically insignificant. The online curriculum also lists a set of factors that impact latency, copied here for convenience:

- Media delays may be caused by the finite speed that signals can travel through the physical media (propogation delay).

- Circuit delays may be caused by the electronics that process the signal along the path.

- Software delays may be caused by the decisions that software must make to implement switching and protocols.

- Delays may be caused by the content of the frame and the location of the frame switching decisions. For example, a device cannot route a frame to a destination until the destination MAC address has been read.

One of the factors that impacts latency is the internal processing path of the forwarding device. Cisco switches collectively support three major variations of this internal processing, discussed next, each of which has some good and bad features. Note that not all switches support all three methods.

Store-and-Forward Switching

Store-and-forward switching means that a switch must receive the entire frame, storing it in memory, before forwarding the frame. Although that process may seem obvious, consider that the switch just needs to know the destination MAC address to make a forwarding decision. The Destination MAC comes right after the Preamble/Start Frame Delimiter (SFD) in an Ethernet frame, so the switch has all the information that it needs to make a forwarding decision as soon as the destination MAC address of the frame has been received. However, with store-and-forward switching, the switch first receives and stores the entire frame before forwarding the frame.

Store-and-forward switching has several advantages, including the following:

- The Frame Check Sequence (FCS) field is at the end of the frame. Store-and-forward switching allows the switch to receive the frame, check the FCS field, and, if an error exists, discard the frame. By doing so, the switch does not forward in-error frames.

- By waiting for the entire frame, the switch can check for a rare error in which the 802.3 Length field does not match the actual frame's Data field length.

- To forward between ports running at different speeds—called *asymmetric switching*—store-and-forward switching must be used (instead of the other two options—cut-through switching and fragment-free switching—which you learn about in the following sections).

Interestingly, the main disadvantage of store-and-forward switching is that it causes more latency than the other two switching methods. However, at higher Ethernet speeds, the amount of added latency becomes very small. (The next section points out more details when comparing store-and-forward switching to cut-through switching.)

Cut-Through Switching

Cut-through switching takes advantage of the fact that the destination MAC address is located at the beginning of the Ethernet frame. With cut-through switching, the switch immediately makes the forwarding decision after finding the destination MAC address in a newly received frame. Because CAM table lookup is so fast, the switch knows out which port it should forward the frame even before the rest of the 802.3 header has been received. Instead of waiting for the entire frame to be received, the switch simply starts forwarding the frame.

Cut-through switching makes sense for one primary reason: each frame has less latency, because the switch can forward the frame before receiving the entire frame. Interestingly, this improved latency benefit is greater at slower speeds. For example, consider a 1250-byte frame, which is 10,000 bits long. At 10 Mbps (10,000,000 bps), it takes the switch 10,000/10,000,000 seconds (or 1 ms, or 1000 microseconds) to receive the entire frame. By using cut-through switching instead of store-and-forward switching, the frame's latency can be reduced by most of that 1000 microseconds. At 100 Mbps, that same-sized frame takes only 100 microseconds to be received, so cut-through switching can only save, at most, almost 100 microseconds. At gigabit speed, cut-through switching's savings becomes even smaller, saving at most 10 microsecond per frame.

Cut-through switching has several negatives as well:

- It cannot check the FCS, so it may forward errored frames.

- It forwards before some legitimate collisions have occurred, meaning it may forward useless frames that are actually fragments resulting from a collision.

- It only works with *symmetric switching*, which is switching when both the input and output port are the same speed. It does not work with asymmetric switching because of the speed mismatch.

Fragment-Free Switching

Cut-through switching has one interesting side effect: it is too fast. In an Ethernet LAN that matches the correct design guidelines, collisions should occur while a frame's first 64 bytes is being transmitted. Cut-through switching often begins forwarding a frame before receiving the first 64 bytes. So, cut-through switching could actually forward some collision fragments, which of course could not possibly be a legitimate frame.

Fragment-free switching is a third forwarding option in Cisco switches. It is like cut-through switching, but instead of going as fast as possible, it waits until it has received 64 bytes before forwarding the frame. That ensures that the switch does not forward frames that have collided as normal, within the first 64 bytes of the frame.

Comparing the Internal Processing Paths

Table 8-1 summarizes the three switch internal processing paths, along with the key points of each.

Table 8-1   Cisco Enterprise Switch—Internal Processing Paths

Processing Path	Positives	Negatives
Store-and-forward	■ Allows for FCS and length check ■ Allows asymmetric switching	■ Highest latency compared to other methods
Cut-through that	■ Lowest latency	■ Forwards frames that do not pass FCS or do not meet Length field check ■ Cannot work with asymmetric switching ■ Can forward normal collision fragments ■ Benefits are smaller at higher speeds
Fragment-free	■ Low latency ■ Does not forward normally collided frames	■ Forwards frames that do not pass FCS or that do not meet Length field check ■ Cannot work with asymmetric switching Benefits are smaller at higher speeds

Spanning Tree Protocol

Most Enterprise LAN designs include redundant physical paths. If one trunk were to fail, or a card in the switch were to fail, another path would be available, and the users would still be able to access the network. (The term *trunk* is often used to refer to a link between two switches; the term backbone link may also be used, but it is less popular today.) For example, Figure 8-7 shows a typical Enterprise LAN design for a single building. The number of access switches would vary, depending on how many end-user devices exist, but each access switch typically uses trunks to two different distribution switches. In this design, one of the distribution switches could fail, and the end users connected to the access switches would still have a physical path to use to reach the rest of the network.

Redundant LAN designs like Figure 8-7 also introduce the possibility of frames that continually loop around the LAN. The switches and bridges in a LAN may cause frames to loop due to the logic they use to forward unknown unicast and broadcast frames. Figure 8-8 shows a slightly simpler but still redundant LAN, with three switches and three PCs. In the figure, PC1 sends a broadcast that loops around the LAN.

Figure 8-7   Typical Enterprise LAN Building Design, with Redundancy

Note

Cisco Enterprise LAN switches have STP enabled by default.

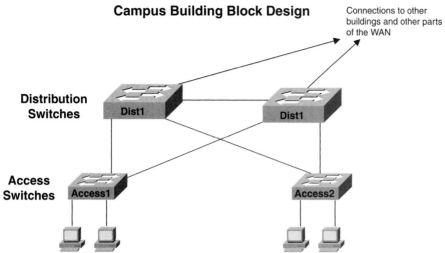

Campus Building Block Design

Figure 8-8   The Problem That STP Solves: Switching Loops

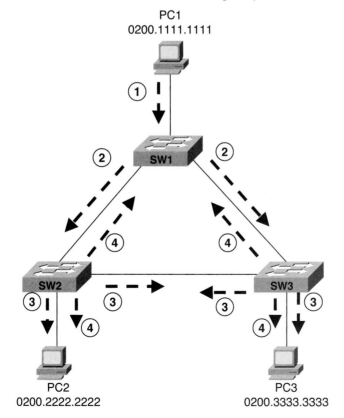

In Figure 8-8, PC1 sends a broadcast, but it ends up looping around the LAN in both directions. Copies of PC1's broadcast are represented as dashed lines. Although fewer than ten dashed lines appear in the figure, in the time you've spent reading this paragraph, the number of broadcasts in a real network could have numbered into the thousands. The following list outlines what happens at each step identified in Figure 8-8. Keep in mind that a switch's forwarding logic for broadcasts is to flood the frame out all ports, except the incoming port.

1. PC1 sends one broadcast frame.

2. SW1 floods the frame out both ports 2 and 3.

3. SW2 floods the broadcast it got from SW1 out ports 2 and 3 around the same time, SW3 floods the broadcast it got from SW1 out its ports 2 and 3. At this point, PC2 and PC3 have received one copy of the broadcast.

4. SW2 floods the copy of the broadcast it received from SW3. SW3 also floods the copy of the broadcast it received from SW2. PC2 and PC3 both receive their second copy of the broadcast.

As you might imagine, this process continues for a very long time—in fact, if the switches or links do not fail, this process would continue to the point that no other traffic could be sent over the LAN, causing what is known as a *broadcast storm*.

Ethernet LAN designs with physical redundancy require the use of the *Spanning Tree Protocol (STP)* to prevent frames from looping around a LAN. STP is a protocol that causes switches (or bridges) to dynamically choose to use only a subset of the interfaces in the LAN so that frames cannot loop. The following sections explain how STP prevents switching loops and describe the various states in which STP can function.

STP Blocking

STP solves the looping problem by making some switch ports simply quit forwarding or receiving frames. In effect, STP breaks the loop by preventing frames from leaving or entering one or more interfaces. An interface that STP causes to not process traffic is considered to be in an STP *blocking state*. Figure 8-9 shows the same network as in Figure 8-8, but this time with STP implemented. In Figure 8-9, PC1 again sends a broadcast, but STP has caused SW3 to put one interface in a blocking state, thereby preventing loops.

With SW3's port 1 in a blocking state, SW3 physically receives the frame from SW1 at Step 2, but SW3 simply ignores the frame. Similarly, when SW3 needs to flood a frame, it chooses to not flood the frame out port 1, again because it is in a blocking state. As a result, in this network, no frames can loop. (The other steps shown in the figure simply show normal forwarding logic for broadcasts.)

Figure 8-9 STP Solves the Problem: SW3 Port 1 Blocks

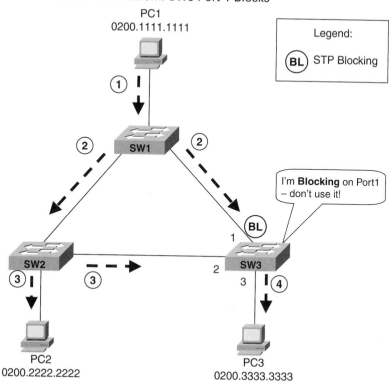

Figure 8-9 shows a broadcast from PC1 being delivered to all devices in the LAN, but it also shows that the broadcast no longer loops. This behavior is part of the formal definition of STP, which can be summarized as follows:

STP causes switches (and/or bridges) to dynamically choose a subset of ports to place in a blocking state. The other states remain in a forwarding state, a state in which the interfaces can forward traffic. STP chooses the interfaces on which to block to create only one active path between any two devices.

Stated a little differently, STP causes the LAN to use particular paths through the network, while the rest remain idle and unused. For example, in Figure 8-9, the link between SW1 and SW3 remains unused.

STP States

In addition to blocking state, STP uses other interface states to do its work. Three of these states are considered to be stable states, meaning that an interface could stay in that STP state for hours, days, or even weeks at a time. Two of the states are considered to be transitory, because an interface stays in these states for only a few seconds. Table 8-2 lists the states, along with a brief definition.

Table 8-2   IEEE 802.1D STP Interface States

State	Stable or Transitory	Definition
Blocking	Stable	The interface does not process received frames or send frames out this interface.
Forwarding	Stable	The interface forwards and receives frames normally.
Disabled	Stable	The interface has failed or has been administratively disabled. No frames are received or forwarded on the interface, and it is not a current candidate to be placed into a forwarding state.
Listening	Transitory	Used as an interim state while a switch waits for its CAM entries to time out. The switch does not forward frames in this state.
Learning	Transitory	Used as an interim state while a switch learns new CAM entries based on newly received frames. The switch does not forward frames in this state.

The forwarding and blocking states are the most common states, because each physically working interface settles and stabilizes into one of these two states. Failed interfaces, or interfaces that the network engineer disables on purpose, stabilize into a *disabled* state. For example, in Figure 8-9, one interface (SW3's port 1) has stabilized as blocking, and the rest of the interfaces are in a forwarding state.

STP uses the listening and learning states as part of a process to solve a problem with the switches' CAMs. When some switch interfaces change from forwarding to blocking, or blocking to forwarding, some entries in the switches' CAMs may not be valid any more. The next section describes how STP reacts to changes in a LAN topology, converges to a new stable STP topology, and how the listening and learning states are used by STP to help ensure that the CAM tables change as needed.

Changing the CAM with the Listening and Learning States

To appreciate the STP listening and learning states, you need to understand the contents of some switches' CAM tables when STP is stable, and then consider what has to change in the switches' CAMs when the topology changes. The topology could change when a trunk between two switches fails, or when a new trunk comes up. But the key to understanding these two states is to understand how the switches' CAMs must change when the topology of the LAN changes. For example, Figure 8-10 shows a sample LAN topology like Figure 8-9, but this time with the STP states listed and each switch's CAMs listed.

Figure 8-10   Stable STP Topology and Switch CAMs in a Three-Switch Network

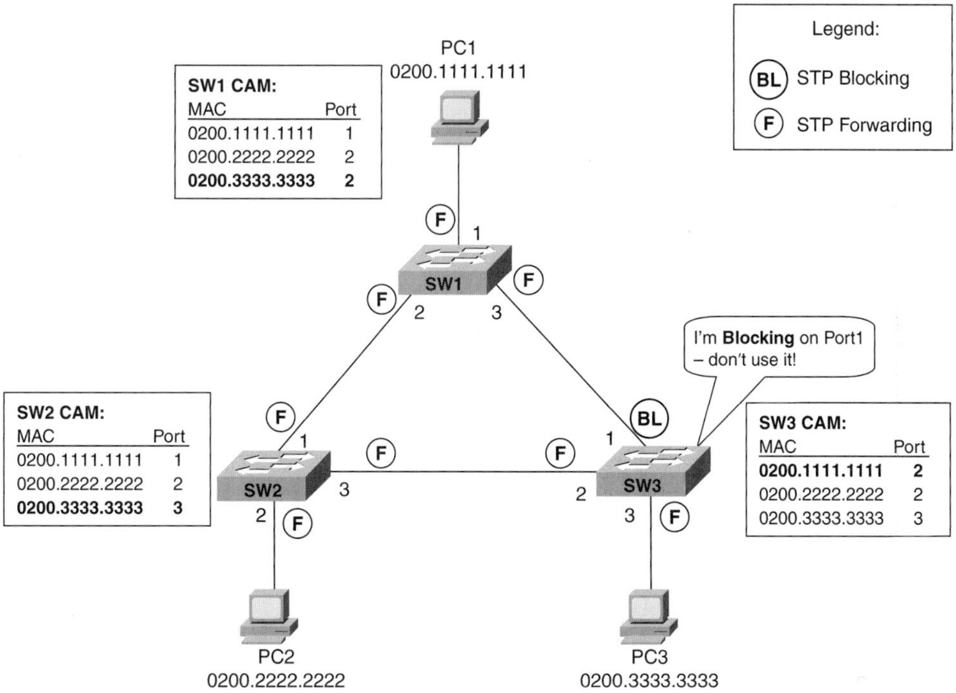

First, note the stable STP states of blocking and forwarding. All ports forward, except for SW3's port 1. As a result, the operation of this network acts just like the network in Figure 8-9.

Next, examine the CAMs on each switch, particularly SW1 and SW3. Because the SW1–SW3 trunk does not pass any traffic, neither switch could have possibly learned any MAC addresses from frames received on that trunk. Note that SW1 does not list port 3 in its CAM entries, and SW3 does not list its port 1 in its CAM. Frames sent from PC1 to PC3, or vice versa, would take the long path through SW2 according to the current STP topology and CAM table entries.

STP determines the STP topology shown in Figure 8-10 by creating and sending STP *bridge protocol data units (BPDUs)* to each other. BPDUs, along with the *Spanning Tree Algorithm (STA)*, are defined in the *IEEE 802.1D* standard. The switches send BPDUs to each other, using the distributed STA logic to the topology information learned via the BPDUs. This process results in each switch deciding which interfaces should forward and which ones should block.

STP uses the *listening* and *learning* states when it needs to transition to a new STP topology. The term *STP topology* simply refers to the topology of the network when each interface is in one of the three stable STP states. STP remains in the stable topology until something changes—for instance, a switch fails, an interface fails, a new switch is added, or the engineer administratively disables an interface.

When STP determines that the STP topology needs to change, two things need to happen:

- Some interfaces need to change to a new stable state. For example, a failed interface might change from forwarding to disabled, or a formerly blocking interface might need to change to a forwarding state.

- The CAM tables may need to change. So, the switches time out the CAM table entries to allow new entries to be learned.

STP uses the listening and learning states as interim states when transitioning an interface from blocking to forwarding. The reason for these interim states is to allow time for two events:

- For the switches' CAM table entries to time out (during the listening state)

- For the switches to relearn the MAC addresses and the (possibly different) interfaces used to reach each MAC address (during the learning state)

These two steps cause the switches to have an accurate CAM table before they forward any frames, preventing temporary loops.

The best way to understand listening and learning states is to use an example, shown in Figure 8-11. In the figure, the following occur:

1. SW2's port 3 (the trunk to SW3) fails.

2. SW2's port 3 and SW3's port 2 (each end of the failed trunk) change to a disabled state.

3. SW3's formerly blocking port 1 needs to change to a forwarding state; to do so, it moves first to a listening state and then to a learning state.

4. Many CAM table entries need to change to list different port numbers. The figure shows the results after the STP topology has stabilized. The remainder of this section then describes the function of the interim transitory listening and learning states.

Figure 8-11 lists in bold the changed CAM table entries (as compared with the other STP topology in Figure 8-10). For example, SW3 now has two CAM entries that refer to the newly forwarding port 1. To allow this to happen, port 1 moves into the listening and then learning state, and then into the forwarding (stable) state, as follows:

1. **Listening state**—STP changes the interface from blocking to listening. The listening state, default 15 seconds, allows time for the CAM table entries on the switches to time out. (The switches time out the entries based on a 15-second timer by default.)

Note

In some cases, a switch might wait 20 seconds (default) before moving an interface from the blocking state into the listening state, as shown in Figure 8-11. In such cases, STP convergence would take 50 seconds—20 seconds in the initial waiting period, and 15 seconds each in the listening and learning states.

Figure 8-11   A New STP Topology After a Failure

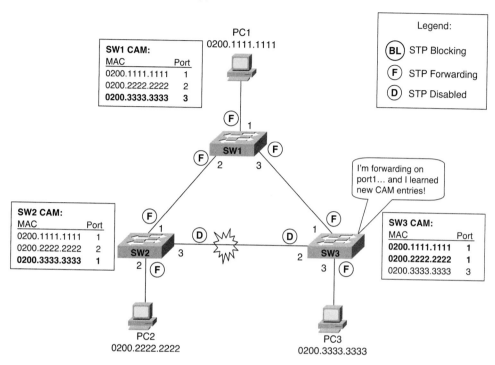

2. **Learning state**—STP changes the state from listening to learning. The learning state, also used for 15 seconds by default, allows time for a switch to learn new CAM entries for frames coming in the interface. However, the switch does not forward frames based on these entries yet to prevent looping frames.

3. **Forwarding state**—STP transitions the port from learning to forwarding state.

By following this process, STP can ensure that looping frames do not occur, even when the topology is changing. Without these interim steps, some switches may be using old CAM entries and some may be using new ones, and loops could occur.

Note

While switches learn CAM entries on an interface in a learning state, some switch's CAM tables might not be filled completely until the interfaces reach a forwarding state.

LAN Design: Collision Domains and Broadcast Domains

When building an Ethernet LAN, five main types of networking devices can be used to connect the various cables: repeaters, hubs, bridges, switches, and routers. These networking devices have different impacts of two interesting concepts: which devices can send frames that could possibly collide with each other, and which computers will receive a broadcast frame sent by another device. This section covers two main topics, collision domains and broadcast domains, which are based on these two concepts, respectively.

Collision domains were covered in Chapter 6, "Ethernet Fundamentals," and Chapter 7, "Ethernet Technologies". This chapter collects those thoughts into one large section while pointing out some of the reasons why a small set of large collision domains is bad, whereas a large set of small collision domains is good. This section goes on to cover the concept of broadcast domains, which has not been covered in any depth so far in the course or book.

Collision Domains

This section covers collision domain concepts and examples and explains how collision domains are created by different devices. The end of this section explains some of the reasons why modern network designs attempt to reduce the size of each collision domain.

The term *collision domain* can be formally defined as follows:

> A set of LAN interfaces (including NICs and network device interfaces) for which a frame sent out any two of these interfaces, at the same time, would cause a collision.

The formal definition is accurate, but as with most things in networking, examples definitely help. Figure 8-12 shows a sample LAN design using one 10BASE-T hub. Hubs repeat incoming electrical signals out all other ports, as quickly as they can. Hubs also do not consider CSMA/CD logic, which means that hubs do not listen and wait for silence before repeating a signal. So, any frames sent simultaneously by two of the PCs in Figure 8-12 will collide. As a result, the network has a single collision domain.

Figure 8-12   One Collision Domain with One 10BASE-T Hub

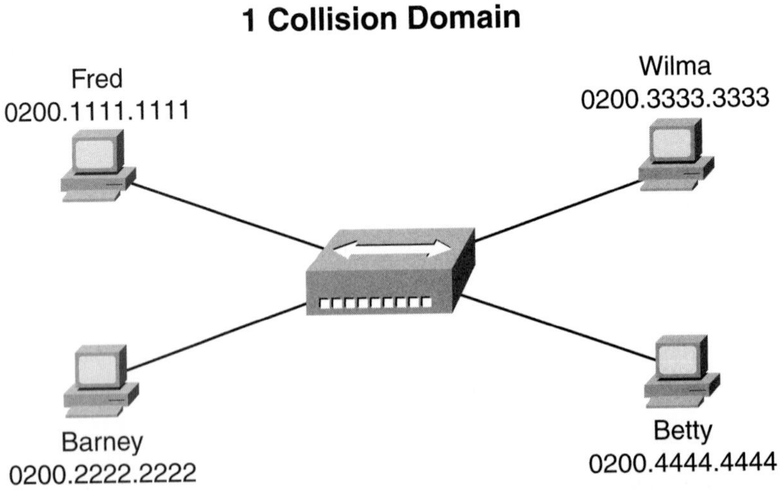

1 Collision Domain

Fred
0200.1111.1111

Wilma
0200.3333.3333

Barney
0200.2222.2222

Betty
0200.4444.4444

The bandwidth in a single collision domain must be shared. In other words, even though a LAN might have many PCs with 10-Mbps NICs, the collective devices must share access to the LAN, because they all must use CSMA/CD, which allows only one of them to send at a time.

The terms *shared bandwidth* and *shared media* refer to the fact that the devices share the same media and bandwidth. For example, in Figure 8-12, the theoretical maximum throughput for the combined devices on the LAN is 10 Mbps.

Large/Long Collision Domains

As covered in Chapter 7, several cabling restrictions exist for the size of a single collision domain that is using CSMA/CD. For example, the 5-4-3 rule (also called the 5-4-3-2-1 rule), used for 10BASE-T networks, implies the following requirements:

- 5 segments of network media.

- 4 repeaters or hubs, at most, between any two end-user devices.

- 3 links at most, between each two end-user devices, may have end-user devices connected to them.

- If 5 segments exist between two end-user devices, 2 segments must not have any end-user devices connected to them.

- 1 large collision domain.

Figure 8-13 shows a very large 10BASE-T collision domain that meets the 5-4-3-2-1 design rule.

Figure 8-13   One Collision Domain with Multiple 10BASE-T Hubs

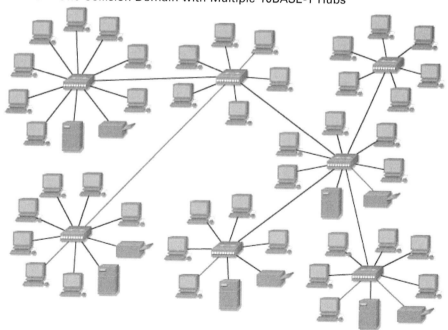

Figure 8-13 does indeed use at most four hubs between any two devices. Also, the links between the hubs have only the two hubs attached to them, so the "2 links with no hosts"

Note

The online curriculum specifically defines the term *shared media* to refer to physical media that is physically shared, such as a 10BASE2 or 10BASE5 bus. It also uses the term *extended shared media* to refer to that same kind of network when it is extended using repeaters. Either of these types refer to networks that consist of a single collision domain.

requirement is met. (The "3" and "2" parts of the 5-4-3-2-1 rule required special attention with 10BASE5 and 10BASE2, but with 10BASE-T hubs, those requirements are met almost accidentally with the links between pairs of hubs.)

The restrictions of the 5-4-3-2-1 rule for 10BASE-T, and the even tighter restrictions on collision domains with 100-Mbps and Gigabit Ethernet, are required due to the *round-trip time* of the collision domain. With a minimum frame size of 64 bytes (512 bits), a 10BASE-T NIC can send the bits in a minimum-sized frame in 512/10,000,000 of 1 second, or 51.2 microseconds. With the typical delays introduced by repeaters, hubs, NICs, and signal propagation, 10BASE-T networks that conform to the 5-4-3-2-1 rule easily meet the requirement for an under 51.2-microsecond round-trip time.

Although reviewing the 5-4-3-2-1 rule may be interesting, the more important part of this discussion for purposes of this chapter relates to the single collision domain shown in Figure 8-13. The details regarding the large single collision domain shown in that figure cannot be overstressed, especially the following:

- Within one collision domain, all the devices share the 10 Mbps of bandwidth.

- Within one collision domain, a (practically) simultaneous transmission of a frame by two or more PCs results in a collision.

The four PCs in Figure 8-12 share 10 Mbps of bandwidth, but that may not seem like a big deal. In Figure 8-13, lots of devices share the same collision domain, meaning that they all share the same 10 Mbps of bandwidth. What if 100 devices share a 10-Mbps LAN, similar to the one depicted in Figure 8-13? In theory, each PC on the LAN would get 1/100th of the LAN bandwidth on average—that would be roughly 100 Kbps. That is basically the same speed as low-speed Internet access today, per PC. Worse yet, Ethernet performance, when CSMA/CD is used, degrades severely under higher loads. The reason? With more devices, spread over more distances, the LAN has to send many more frames. The more frames, the more collisions. With more collisions comes much more wasted time because the stations have to resend the frames. Eventually, under enough load, a LAN may even become unusable.

A classic graph, a version of which is shown in Figure 8-14, compares the number of collisions on an Ethernet LAN with the utilization of the LAN as measured in megabits per second. Although other factors impact the graph, the version shown in Figure 8-14 includes the numbers most typically quoted. Essentially, once an Ethernet LAN reaches about 30 to 40 percent utilization, the number of collisions increases dramatically—and the LAN performance degrades dramatically. Simply put, as the LAN becomes more and more highly utilized, the overall performance degrades due to the wasted effort of colliding frames.

The number of devices connected to the same collision domain has a large impact on LAN utilization. For example, in a single collision domain using 10BASE-T, with 100 PCs, assuming that 35 percent utilization is the most that the network engineer would like to see, the 100 devices would be sharing 3.5 Mbps. That means each PC could get only about 35 Kbps of bandwidth (on average) before the LAN would degrade. The network engineer, however, can't control the LAN to prevent it from becoming overutilized and performing poorly.

Figure 8-14   Higher LAN Utilization Resulting in Much Higher Percentage of Collisions

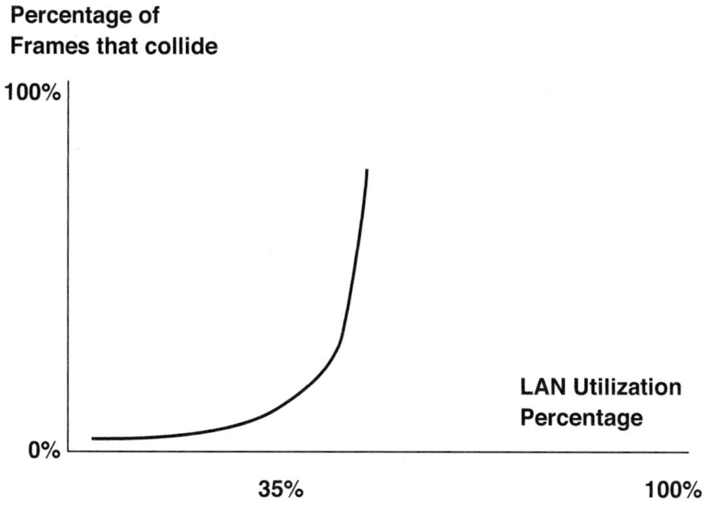

To summarize, large collision domains should not be used, for the following reasons:

- **Shared bandwidth**—All devices in the same collision domain share that bandwidth, meaning that, as the collision domain grows, the amount of bandwidth available to each end-user device, on average, is smaller.

- **Higher utilization**—The more devices in a single collision domain, the better the chance of driving utilization higher, resulting in varying degrees of worsening LAN performance.

A better solution is to break up a collision domain into many smaller collision domains, using bridges and switches, as described in the next section.

Creating Many Small Collision Domains

Using LANs with many small collision domains significantly reduces the negative effects of large collision domains. To see why, consider Figure 8-15, which shows two LANs cleverly named LAN 1 and LAN 2.

The process of breaking the LAN into multiple collision domains is called *segmentation*. Switches, bridges, and routers can be used to segment LANs into multiple collision domains. In the figure, switches have been used to segment the LANs into three collision domains on the left and five collision domains on the right. Each switch interface connects to a separate collision domain.

Figure 8-15   Two LANs with Many Small Collision Domains

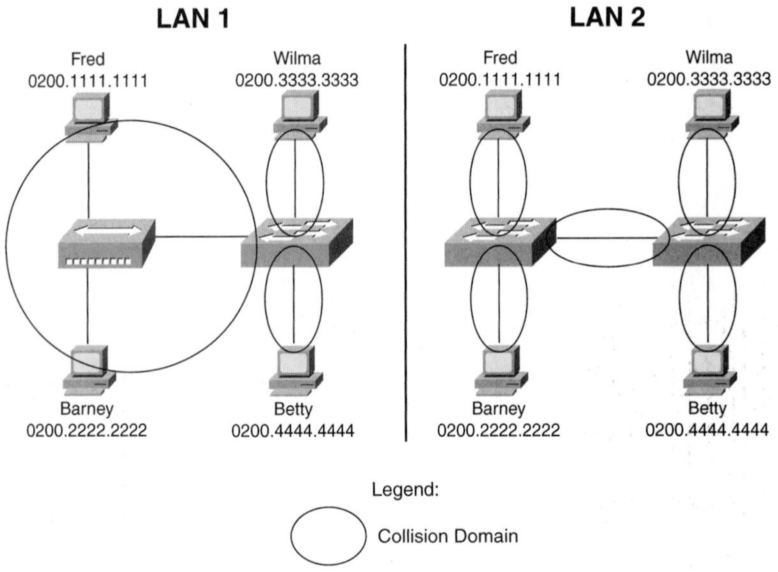

LAN 1   **LAN 2**

Fred
0200.1111.1111

Wilma
0200.3333.3333

Fred
0200.1111.1111

Wilma
0200.3333.3333

Barney
0200.2222.2222

Betty
0200.4444.4444

Barney
0200.2222.2222

Betty
0200.4444.4444

Legend:

Collision Domain

The benefits of segmenting LANs into multiple collision domains—some obvious and some not—are as follows (assume all links are 10 Mbps):

- Design rules, such as the 10-Mbps 5-4-3-2-1 rule, apply to each individual collision domain. With a much smaller part of the LAN in each collision domain, meeting rules such as the 5-4-3-2-1 rule is easier to achieve.

- With smaller collision domains, reaching the (around) 35 percent LAN utilization mark, at which point LAN performance with CSMA/CD degrades, is statistically less likely.

- Each collision domain shares its bandwidth with the devices inside the same collision domain, but each collision domain gets its own bandwidth. LAN 1 in Figure 8-15 actually has 3 × 10 Mbps of bandwidth, or 30 Mbps, whereas LAN 2 has 5 × 10 Mbps of bandwidth, or 50 Mbps.

Packet Tracer Packet Tracer configuration file NA01-0815 uses the network shown in Figure 8-15, with two simulations. (The simulations may be chosen in simulation mode by using the scenario pull-down near the top of the window.) The first scenario shows a hub always repeating frames, causing frames to collide. The second scenario shows frames passing over each of the three collision domains at the same time, demonstrating the increased bandwidth provided by multiple collision domains.

The terms *switched LAN* and *switched bandwidth* refer to the effect of using switches, as noted in the last point in the previous list. Switched bandwidth refers to the fact that each switch port creates more bandwidth, because each switch port connects to a different collision domain. For instance, if you compare a LAN with 24 devices connected to the same 10BASE-T hub, the LAN has a shared bandwidth of 10 Mbps. Take the same devices, and connect them to a 24-port 10BASE-T switch, and the LAN has a switched bandwidth of 24 × 10 Mbps, or 240 Mbps.

LAN 2 in Figure 8-15 uses only two switches, with no repeaters or hubs. In this case, the switch creates five collision domains, four of which have only one switch port and one PC NIC. Such designs are said to be using a process called *microsegmentation*, which refers to a practice of putting a single end-user device off each switch port (instead of a hub or repeater). With microsegmentation, collision domains consist of the switch port and one other device.

Microsegments—LAN segments with a switch port and one other device—meet the requirements to allow full duplex. Creating collision domains that allow full duplex creates yet another advantage for using many small collision domains. Again assuming 10 Mbps on each LAN (just for consistency), by implementing full duplex on the links in LAN 2 of Figure 8-15, each link gets 10 Mbps in each direction, for a total of 20 Mbps per microsegment. Additionally, the degraded performance shown in the graph in Figure 8-14 does not occur, because collisions simply do not occur once full duplex is used. So, each segment gets 10 Mbps in both directions, with no concerns about whether high LAN utilization will degrade performance of the LAN.

For perspective, a 10BASE-T hub with 24 ports has 10 Mbps shared among all 24 devices. A 24 port 10BASE-T switch, with one device off each port, can support full duplex on each port. As a result, that LAN has a theoretical bandwidth of 24 × 20 Mbps, or 480 Mbps, without performance problems under loads much higher than 35 percent.

To summarize, the main benefits of using many small collision domains, created by using bridges or switches, are as follows:

- Collision domain length design rules, such as the 10-Mbps 5-4-3-2-1 rule, apply to a much smaller part of the LAN, making the 5-4-3-2-1 rule easier to achieve.

- Small collision domains reduce the probability of LAN overutilization, because there are fewer devices.

- Each collision domain gets its own separate switched bandwidth, instead of having to use shared bandwidth, creating more available bandwidth in a LAN.

- With the smallest collision domain of two interfaces/NICs, full duplex can be enabled. This doubles the bandwidth in each full-duplex collision domain and removes any concerns about performance degradation when the collision domain reaches high utilization.

How Switches and Bridges Prevent Collisions

Switches reduce or even prevent collisions by *buffering* or *queuing* frames. The process of buffering frames can be easily seen in Figure 8-16, which shows the same LAN as LAN 2 in

Note

The term *segment* often refers to the same concept as a collision domain, although segment is an ambiguous term in the world of networking, as you learn later, in the section "The Ambiguous Term Segment."

Note

The term *point-to-point* can be used to refer to a cable, with both a transmit and receive path, that connects two interfaces or NICs. Microsegments use point-to-point LAN links.

Figure 8-15, but in this example, three other PCs send Fred a frame at the same time. The switch, instead of forwarding the frames out Fred's switch port at the same time, causing a collision, holds two of the frames in memory—a process called buffering or queuing.

Figure 8-16   Switch Buffering Example

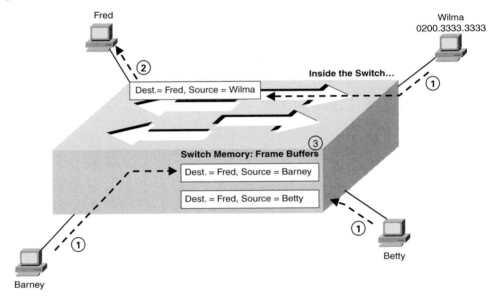

Figure 8-16 illustrates the following process:

1. Barney, Betty, and Wilma each send a frame, destined for Fred, at the same time.

2. The switch forwards Wilma's frame and buffers the other two in memory.

3. When it is finished sending Wilma's frame, the switch gets another frame to send—for instance, Barney's frame.

Repeaters and hubs, on the other hand, do not perform buffering—they simply repeat the bits. For example, if a hub were used instead of a switch in Figure 8-16, collisions would have occurred.

 Packet Tracer   Packet Tracer configuration file NA01-08-shared-switched has extensive scenarios with three topologies side by side. Each scenario shows the same attempted frame flows and the effects of collisions in that scenario.

Bridges, switches, and routers all buffer frames or packets. They also consider CSMA/CD rules when forwarding frames, first listening for a silent LAN before sending (assuming CSMA/CD has not been disabled by the enabling of full duplex). As a result, all three of these types of devices separate LANs into different collision domains.

Layer 2 Broadcast Domains

Another term that relates to what happens when frames flow through a LAN is *broadcast domain*. Formally, a broadcast domain is defined as follows:

> The set of LAN interfaces (including NICs and network device interfaces) for which a broadcast frame sent by any one device will be forwarded to all the other interfaces in that same broadcast domain.

From early coverage in this chapter, you know that bridges and switches forward broadcasts. Hubs and repeaters forward broadcasts as well, because they do not even think about whether the electrical signal is a broadcast frame—they just regenerate and repeat the electrical signals. In short, repeaters, hubs, bridges, and switches all forward broadcasts, meaning that they do not separate a LAN into different broadcast domains.

Figure 8-17 shows a sample LAN with six switches, a router, and two broadcast domains. As it turns out, of the five network devices covered in the CCNA 1 course, only routers stop the flow of broadcasts. Note that in Figure 8-17, the broadcast domain on the left floods a broadcast, but the router does not flood that broadcast to the broadcast domain on the right.

Note

Appendix C, "Extra Practice," has practice exercises in the section "Chapter 8 Exercises" that ask you to identify the collision domains, broadcast domains, and places where full duplex may be used.

Figure 8-17   One Router Creating Two Broadcast Domains

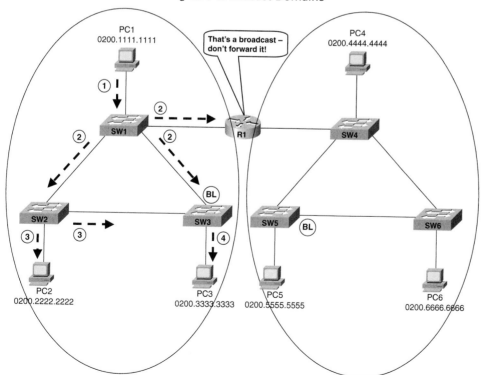

Packet Tracer	By loading Packet Tracer configuration file NA01-0817, you can see the effects of a router on LAN broadcasts.

Performance Impact of Broadcast and Broadcast Domains

Network engineers try to limit the size of broadcast domains when creating LANs today. Many reasons exist for thinking about the size of a broadcast domain when designing a LAN, but the main reason covered in the course has to do with the performance impact of broadcast and multicast frames.

To appreciate the impact of broadcast and multicast frames, you must understand a distinction about what a PC NIC can and cannot do. NICs can recognize the destination MAC address of an incoming frame and determine whether it is a unicast. If it is a unicast, the NIC can decide either to give the frame to the CPU (when the destination MAC address is that NIC's MAC address) or to silently discard the frame (when the destination MAC address is not that NIC's MAC address).

However, a NIC cannot determine if its computer needs to process multicasts and broadcasts. The information needed to make that decision is available only to the CPU. So, the NIC is obligated to give the frame to the CPU—even if the last 8 million broadcasts were not needed by the CPU. Figure 8-18 illustrates this process.

Figure 8-18   NIC Giving Broadcasts and Multicasts to the CPU

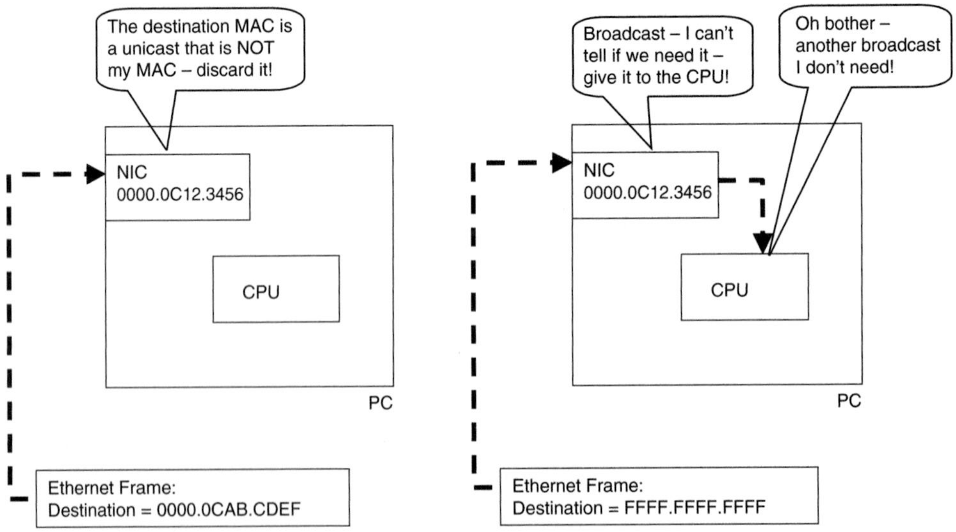

Broadcasts and multicasts can become voluminous enough to waste a lot of CPU capacity. Figure 8-19 shows a graph from the online course that shows the results of a rather old test of the impact of broadcasts. In the test, once the LAN had 1000 broadcasts per second, the CPU

on a (then) rather powerful workstation was reduced to 80 percent of its normal capacity to perform work.

Figure 8-19 More Broadcasts, Less CPU Capacity for End-User Work

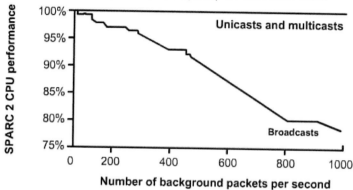

A 20 percent reduction in overall CPU performance is certainly enough to matter—and that would occur for all similar computers on that same LAN. But 1000 broadcasts per second seems like a lot, and it is. In the old days, LANs supported a large variety of vendor-proprietary networking models in addition to TCP/IP. Some of these networking models tended to use broadcasts quite a bit. Also, with some older LAN technologies, some design advantages could be gained by creating very large broadcast domains, but with a downside of consuming more CPU with more broadcasts. (Typically, when comparing two broadcast domains, a broadcast domain with twice as many devices as the other broadcast domain has roughly twice as many broadcasts, if all other factors are equal.) So, in the past, some LANs experienced very high numbers of broadcasts, similar to the 1000 per second referenced in Figure 8-19.

The Impact of Broadcasts and Multicasts Today

Today, the biggest risk of wasting CPU relates more to multicasts than to broadcasts. Switches by default flood multicasts just like broadcasts. As more and more IP multicast applications emerge—such as desktop video streaming—more and more LAN multicasts occur.

The volume of these multicast frames can make the volume of broadcasts in networks of the mid-1990s pale in comparison. To prevent the waste of CPU, today's Enterprise LAN engineers should enable multicast optimization tools in switches to prevent the switches from flooding the multicasts to every device in the LAN. (The section "Forwarding Broadcasts and Multicasts," earlier in this chapter, reviewed the basic concepts of multicast forwarding in a switch.)

The CCNA 1 course uses two examples of broadcasts in a LAN: Routing Information Protocol (RIP) broadcasts and Address Resolution Protocol (ARP) broadcasts. Although neither type of broadcast occurs in enough volume to cause problems in today's networks, both types of broadcasts have caused problems in some cases in the past. Understanding these examples, then, may help you better understand how broadcasts affect today's networks.

ARP sends requests to find some information. These ARP requests are LAN broadcasts and are common and very important in LANs today. (ARP is covered in depth in Chapter 9, "TCP/IP Protocol Suite and IP Addressing.") However, the number of ARP broadcasts sent by an individual PC in practice is relatively low, most often far less than one per minute. All computers that support TCP/IP use ARP, but then they remember the information they gain from ARP—meaning that the computers do not need to repeat their ARP broadcasts very often. Even in the 2000-device broadcast domain suggested in the CCNA 1 course, in practice, ARPs would not constitute a significant number of broadcasts.

The other example from the course, referring to RIP, represents a significant concern in years past. Routing Information Protocol (RIP) is an IP routing protocol typically used by routers. In the past, UNIX workstations, which are computers using the UNIX operating system, also ran RIP, because these workstations often could and did act as routers as well. Many used RIP by default, so many people would install new UNIX workstations and not even be aware that they were sending RIP broadcasts. So, some broadcast domains might have had hundreds of RIP broadcasts per second in extreme cases.

Today, however, RIP is typically disabled by default on UNIX workstations. Most enterprises' routers do not use RIP at all. Also, current LAN designs consider a broadcast domain of a few hundred to be very large. All of these factors combine to mean that RIP should not create a significant enough number of broadcasts to impact CPU performance today.

Identifying Networking Devices by OSI Layer

Network engineers should be able to identify both collision domains and broadcast domains and describe the effects of devices being in the same collision domain or broadcast domain. Also, engineers should know which kinds of networking devices separate a LAN into different collision domains and broadcast domains. Table 8-3 lists the five key networking devices covered in this course and whether that device separates a LAN into separate collision domains or broadcast domains.

Table 8-3   Whether Devices Create Separate Collision Domains and Broadcast Domains

Device	Highest Layer at Which It Operates	Separates LAN into Multiple Collision Domains on Each Interface	Separates LAN into Multiple Broadcast Domains on Each Interface
Repeater	1	No	No
Hub	1	No	No
Bridge	2	Yes	No
Switch	2	Yes	No
Router	3	Yes	Yes

The second column in the table refers to the highest OSI layer used by the networking device when doing its work. For example, repeaters and hubs consider only the physical characteristics of the electrical signals, so they use only Layer 1. Thus, hubs and repeaters are considered to be *Layer 1 devices*. Switches and bridges send and receive electrical signals, but they also consider framing, looking at the fields in the 802.3 MAC header—all defined at the OSI data link layer, Layer 2. Thus, bridges and switches are considered to be *Layer 2 devices*. Finally, routers can physically send and receive on Ethernet interfaces, understand Ethernet Layer 2 framing, and make routing decisions based on the Layer 3 IP header. As a result, routers are considered to be *Layer 3 devices*.

Figure 8-20 shows a sample network using a Layer 1 device (hub), a Layer 2 device (switch), and a Layer 3 device (router). The figure shows the location of the broadcast domains and collision domains in the network.

Figure 8-20   Sample Network with Collision Domains and Broadcast Domains Shown

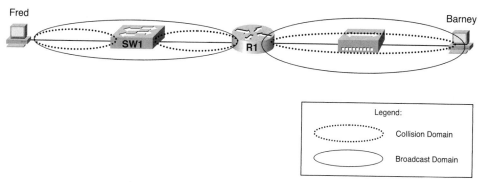

Although the location of the broadcast domains and collision domains in Figure 8-20 should be a little more obvious after reading this chapter, practice never hurts. Appendix C has a few extra practice problems that show different sample network diagrams, asking you to identify the collision domains, broadcast domains, and which links can use full duplex.

Data Flow Using Layer 1, Layer 2, and Layer 3 Devices

The Figure 8-20 network provides a good backdrop to define the topic called *data flow* by the online curriculum. The data flow process focuses on the OSI layers that a device considers when data passes through the device. Layer 1, Layer 2, and Layer 3 devices need to think about the bottom one, two, and three OSI layers, respectively, as part of that process. Many Cisco documents and classes use a figure similar to Figure 8-21 to describe data flow, network devices, and the OSI layers used by each.

Figure 8-21   Data Flow with Layer 1, Layer 2, and Layer 3 Devices

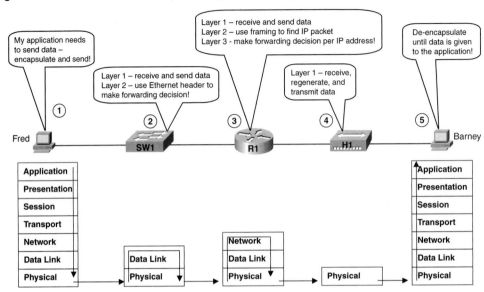

The bottom of Figure 8-21 shows representations of the OSI layers used by each of the computers and network devices shown in the figure. For example, the figure shows the bottom two layers of the OSI model—physical and data link—below the switch icon, because the switch performs functions of both Layers 1 and 2. The specific steps listed in Figure 8-21 are as follows:

1. Fred's application needs to send data, so Fred uses software and hardware at all layers in the OSI model to encapsulate the data and send the data out Fred's Ethernet NIC.

2. SW1, a Layer 2 device, needs to process the received frame based on Layer 1 and Layer 2:

   a. Layer 1: Decoding the received electricity into bits, and later encoding bits as electricity for transmission

   b. Layer 2: Using 802.3 Ethernet framing for many things, such as finding the destination MAC address to make a forwarding decision

3. Router R1, a Layer 3 device, needs to process the received frame based on Layers 1 through 3:

   a. Layer 1: Decoding the received electricity into bits, and later encoding bits as electricity for transmission

   b. Layer 2: Using 802.3 Ethernet framing for many things, such as checking the FCS to make sure the frame did not have any errors

   c. Layer 3: Looking at the destination IP address in the packet header to make a forwarding decision

4. Hub H1, a Layer 1 device, needs to simply receive the electrical signal, regenerate a nice square waveform, and send that regenerated waveform—all Layer 1 functions.

5. Barney receives the incoming electrical signal and de-encapsulates the data until it can finally give the end-user data to the application.

The Ambiguous Term *Segment*

The term *segment* has many meanings in the world of networking. Even inside the world of Ethernet LANs, the term has been used to mean different things to different people over different time periods. For example, the course suggests the following three main uses of the term segment:

- **LAN concepts**—A segment is a collision domain, which is a section of a LAN that is bounded by bridges, routers, or switches.

- **LAN (physical)**—In a LAN using a bus topology, a segment is a continuous electrical circuit that is often connected to other such segments with repeaters.

- **TCP**—When used with the TCP protocol, the term segment (verb) refers to the work TCP does to accept a large piece of data from an application and break it into smaller pieces. Again with TCP, used as a noun, segment refers to one of those smaller pieces of data.

Additionally, many people refer to a LAN segment and really mean "broadcast domain." So, when using the term segment in conversation or when reading, particularly when discussing LANs, be careful to note the exact meaning of the word.

Summary

Bridges and switches work the same way with regard to basic forwarding, learning, flooding, and STP. They build their forwarding tables by examining the source MAC addresses of incoming frames. Bridges and switches make forwarding and filtering decisions by looking at the destination MAC address of each frame as compared with the bridging/switching table. They flood unknown unicast frames, which are frames for which no matching entry exists in the bridging/switching table. Finally, bridges and switches flood broadcasts, and they flood multicasts unless some multicast optimization features have been enabled.

Switches differ from bridges in that they use much more powerful hardware, plus they have many other advanced features. (Most of the advanced features are not covered in this book or the course.) Switches use special memory called Content Addressable Memory (CAM) to hold the switching table. The CAM allows switches to find a MAC address, and its associated port, quickly every time, regardless of the length of the CAM table.

Latency is defined as the time that passes while a frame or packet is sent through a network. Propagation delay—the time it takes the electrical or optical energy to pass over the cable—contributes to latency.

The internal processing path used by a switch also impacts the latency experienced by Ethernet frames. The three internal processing path options are cut-through switching, store-and-forward switching, and fragment-free switching. Cut-through switching provides the lowest latency of the three options, but it does not do error checking and can sometimes forward collision fragments that are useless. Store-and-forward switching creates the most latency, because it must receive the entire frame before sending the frame out the destination port, but this method allows a check of the FCS, and it is the only working option when asymmetric switching (switching between ports of different speeds) is used. The third option, fragment-free switching, works like cut-through switching except that it waits until 64 bytes of the frame are received before sending the frame, which enables it to detect normal collisions.

Switches and bridges use the Spanning Tree Protocol (STP) to identify and block redundant paths through the network. The result is a logical hierarchical path through the network with no loops.

A collision domain with a single device connected to a switch port is called a microsegment. Microsegments use a single twisted-pair cable, allowing both interfaces to send and receive at the same time without causing a collision—thereby allowing full duplex. Because collisions can no longer occur, CSMA/CD is disabled.

Placing a large number of computers in the same collision domain increases demand on the available bandwidth, resulting in an increased probability of collisions. Breaking a large collision domain into numerous smaller collision domains can help reduce the probability of collisions while adding bandwidth to the network. Separating LAN segments by putting bridges and switches between them creates additional collision domains, one per switch port and bridge port.

Broadcast domains consist of a set of devices in which if one device sends a LAN broadcast, all other devices receive the broadcast. Layer 2 devices do not separate a LAN into multiple broadcast domains, but Layer 3 devices (routers) do.

Check Your Understanding

Complete all the review questions listed here to test your understanding of the topics and concepts in this chapter. Answers are listed in Appendix A, "Answers to Check Your Understanding and Challenge Questions."

1. Which of the following is *not* a feature of microsegmentation?

   A. Collision domains consist of the switch port and one other device.

   B. It allows for full-duplex connections.

   C. It increases the capacity of each workstation connected to the network.

   D. It increases collisions.

2. LAN switches use which of the following to make the forwarding decision?

   A. IP address

   B. MAC address

   C. Network address

   D. Host address

3. Which of the following is a feature of full-duplex transmission?

   A. It allows two devices to send and receive data simultaneously over a single Ethernet cable.

   B. It doubles bandwidth between nodes.

   C. It provides collision-free transmission.

   D. All answers provided are correct.

4. What are the three common types of switching methods?

   A. STP, CRC, and FCS

   B. Fragment-free, store-and-forward, and cut-out

   C. Store-and-forward, cut-through, and fragment-free

   D. Asymmetrical, symmetrical, and fragment-check

5. The Spanning Tree Protocol allows which of the following?

   A. Bridges to communicate Layer 3 information

   B. A redundant Layer 2 network path, without suffering the effects of loops in the network

   C. Static network paths for loop prevention

   D. None of the answers provided is correct

6. Which of the following is *not* one of the STP port states?

   A. Blocking

   B. Learning

   C. Listening

   d. Transmitting

7. Which of the following is true concerning a bridge and its forwarding decisions?

   A. Bridges operate at OSI Layer 2 and use IP addresses to make decisions.

   B. Bridges operate at OSI Layer 3 and use IP addresses to make decisions.

   C. Bridges operate at OSI Layer 2 and use MAC addresses to make decisions.

   D. Bridges operate at OSI Layer 3 and use MAC addresses to make decisions.

8. Which of the following are features of bridges? (Select three answers.)

   A. They operate at Layer 2 of the OSI model.

   B. They are more intelligent than hubs.

   C. They do not make any forwarding decisions.

   D. They build and maintain address tables.

9. Which of the following statements is true of microsegmentation?

   A. Each workstation gets its own dedicated segment.

   B. All the workstations are grouped as one segment.

   C. Microsegmentation increases the number of collisions on a network.

   D. None of the answers provided is correct.

10. Which of the following is true of LAN switches?

    A. They repair network fragments known as microsegments.

    B. They are very high-speed multiport bridges.

    C. Lower bandwidth makes up for higher latency.

    D. Attached hosts require a new NIC in order to be connected to a switch.

11. What is the name for a set of LAN interfaces (including NICs and network device interfaces) for which a frame sent out any two of these interfaces at the same time would cause a collision?

    A. Collision domain

    B. Network domain

    C. Broadcast domain

    D. Network segment

12. Using repeaters does which of the following to the size of a collision domain?

    A. Reduces

    B. Has no effect on

    C. Extends

    D. None of the answers provided is correct

13. The process of using complex networking devices, such as bridges, switches, and routers, to break up collision domains is known as which of the following?

    A. Sectioning

    B. Segmentation

    C. Collision domain reduction

    D. None of the answers provided is correct

Challenge Questions and Activities

These questions require a deeper application of the concepts covered in this chapter and are similar to the style of questions you might see on a CCNA certification exam.

The network design has one router, two switches, four hubs, and eight hosts. The following questions refer to this network.

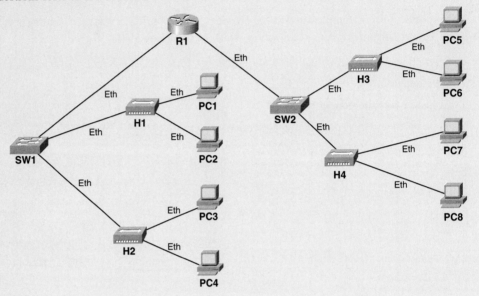

1. How many collision domains are in this network?

   A. One

   B. Two

   C. Three

   D. Four

   E. Five

   F. Six

2. How many broadcast domains are in this network?

   A. One

   B. Two

   C. Three

   D. Four

   E. Five

   F. Six

CHAPTER 9

TCP/IP Protocol Suite and IP Addressing

Objectives

Upon completion of this chapter, you should be able to answer the following questions:

- Why was the Internet developed, and how does TCP/IP help the Internet meet its design goals?

- What are the four TCP/IP layers?

- What are the functions of each layer of the TCP/IP model?

- How does the TCP/IP model compare to the OSI model?

- What are the function and structure of an IP address?

- What is the difference between public and private IP addresses?

- What is a static assignment of an IP address?

- How do static and dynamic addressing differ, and when is each used?

- How does DHCP do dynamic addressing?

- Why is subnetting necessary?

- What is ARP, and how does it work between devices on the same LAN?

- How does a router handle an ARP request for a device that is on a different network from that of the device making the ARP request?

Additional Topics of Interest

Several chapters of this book contain additional coverage of earlier topics or related topics that are secondary to the main goals of the chapter. You can find the additional coverage on the CD-ROM accompanying this book. For this chapter, the following additional topics are covered:

- RARP

- BOOTP

Key Terms

This chapter uses the following key terms. You can find the definitions in the Glossary.

Internet Activities Board (IAB)   page 340

Internet Engineering Task Force (IETF)   page 340

Requests For Comments (RFCs)   page 340

network access layer   page 340

host   page 340

internet layer   page 341

Internet Protocol (IP)   page 341

IP routing   page 342

packet   page 343

directly connected networks   page 345

continues

continued

next-hop router   page 345

transport layer   page 345

internetwork   page 351

Internet   page 352

IP version 4 (IPv4)   page 353

octet   page 353

IP network   page 355

unicast IP address   page 356

network part   page 356

host part   page 356

Class D   page 359

Class E   page 359

loopback IP address   page 360

IP network numbers   page 361

network ID   page 361

network address   page 361

network broadcast address   page 361

host address   page 362

subnetting   page 365

subnets   page 365

subnet broadcast address   page 365

subnet mask   page 368

Internet Assigned Numbers Authority (IANA)   page 369

American Registry for Internet Numbers (ARIN)   page 369

public IP addresses   page 370

IPv4 address depletion   page 370

Network Address Translation (NAT)   page 371

private IP addresses   page 372

IP version 6 (IPv6)   page 372

Dynamic Host Configuration Protocol (DHCP)   page 375

Address Resolution Protocol (ARP)   page 378

ARP request   page 380

ARP broadcast   page 380

ARP reply   page 380

ARP table   page 380

proxy ARP   page 383

This chapter changes the focus of this course from LANs to TCP/IP, the IP protocol, and routers. Most end-user devices in enterprise networks today connect to LANs. However, the computers on these LANs need to communicate with each other, and to do that, they typically use protocols from the TCP/IP model. One of the most important parts of TCP/IP, the Internet Protocol (IP), defines many of the details about how computers can and should communicate using TCP/IP.

This chapter contains three sections. The first section reviews the TCP/IP networking model, its different layers, and some perspectives on how they are used. The second major section takes the first deep look at IP addressing. Understanding IP addressing will be one of the most important parts of the CCNA courses for anyone wanting a career in networking. The final section covers the actual mechanics of IP address assignment and another key part of the TCP/IP internet layer, Address Resolution Protocol (ARP).

TCP/IP Model

Chapter 2, "Networking Fundamentals," covered the basics of networking models—specifically, the OSI and TCP/IP models. This first major section reviews those concepts and takes the coverage of TCP/IP a little deeper.

Networking models separate the details of how to create networks in many smaller sets of focused standards. By breaking the details into smaller parts, a vendor can create a particular product by focusing on only one part of the networking puzzle. For example, one company can write an e-mail software package, Cisco can build routers, another company can worry about making Ethernet NICs, and yet another company can make good cables. Each of these products focuses on the functions defined at one part of the TCP/IP model, but working together, they create a usable working network.

TCP/IP was first developed as part of a contract from the U.S. Department of Defense (DoD). From that original work, the TCP/IP networking model (formerly called the DoD model) was created, defining a networking model for TCP/IP. Figure 9-1 shows a classic comparison of the TCP/IP and OSI networking models.

Figure 9-1   TCP/IP and OSI Networking Models Compared

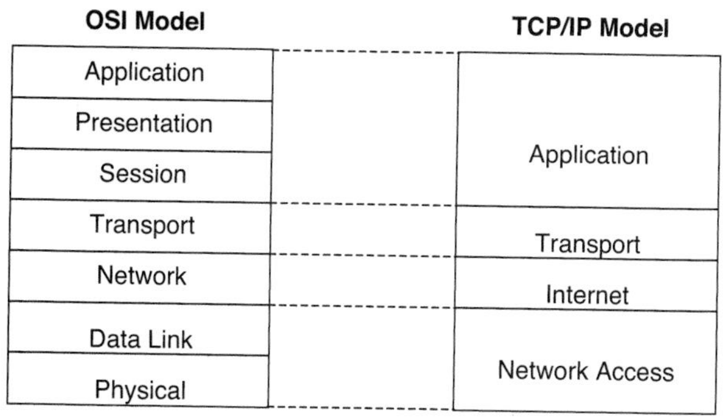

OSI Model		TCP/IP Model
Application		Application
Presentation		
Session		
Transport		Transport
Network		Internet
Data Link		Network Access
Physical		

Tip

You can find copies of RFCs at many websites for free. Some even make interesting reading, like RFC 1118, "The Hitchhiker's Guide to the Internet." See http://www.rfc-editor.org to locate a specific RFC.

TCP/IP is an open standard. Committees under the direction of the *Internet Architecture Board (IAB)* and the *Internet Engineering Task Force (IETF)* define TCP/IP standards. These organizations essentially play the same roles for TCP/IP as the IEEE does for Ethernet standards. IETF and its volunteer members research and create individual protocols in the TCP/IP model. Today, many of the volunteers represent vendors that have a vested interest in a particular protocol, but anyone with interest can participate. The documents that describe a particular standard or protocol are called *Requests For Comments (RFCs)*.

Next comes a description of the layers of the TCP/IP model, with some specific example protocols at each layer.

TCP/IP Network Access (Network Interface) Layer

The TCP/IP *network access layer* defines how computers and networking devices should access a physical medium to send bits to another computer or networking device. These functions essentially match OSI Layers 1 and 2.

Note

The term *host* in TCP/IP terminology means any computer that uses TCP/IP.

Interestingly, the TCP/IP model does not actually define any network access layer standards—instead, the model refers to other well-defined networking standards. For example, the TCP/IP model defines Ethernet as an approved standard to be used at the network access layer. The IETF actually purposefully avoids defining OSI Layer 1 and 2 standards because many other standards bodies already work on these details. Instead, the IETF works to make sure each new type of physical network can be well supported by TCP/IP as a network access layer protocol, allowing TCP/IP to grow and support newer (and typically faster) physical networks.

Figure 9-2 shows a diagram of the TCP/IP model, with some of the specific network access layer standards referenced.

Figure 9-2   Standards at the TCP/IP Network Access Layer

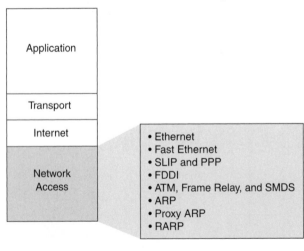

Of particular importance in Figure 9-2, note that ARP, proxy ARP, and RARP are mentioned. As covered later in this chapter in the section titled "Using ARP and Proxy ARP on LANs," these protocols work mainly at TCP/IP's internet layer (OSI network layer), but they provide an interface to the network access layer. The rest of the listed protocols are true Layer 1 and 2 protocols that can be used to send data from one host to another.

Also note that many texts use the term *network interface layer* instead of network access layer. Cisco courses, including the Academy curriculum, use the term network access layer most often. Also, because the OSI model's physical and data link layers correlate to the TCP/IP network access layer, many people consider the TCP/IP model to have five layers by splitting the network access layer into two layers—physical and data link—to match the OSI model.

TCP/IP Internet Layer

The TCP/IP *internet layer* defines how to deliver data from one host to another. That statement may sound a lot like the description of what a network access layer protocol like Ethernet does. However, unlike Ethernet and other network access standards, the internet layer defines how to send data over multiple different physical networks, including any variety of supported LAN, MAN, and WAN media. In contrast, network access standards like Ethernet just define how to send data over one particular type of physical network.

The internet layer achieves this ability to send data over any type of physical network by purposefully separating its logic from the underlying physical networking details. This allows hosts and networking devices, mainly routers, to use the same processes and logic regardless of the underlying physical networks being used. An analogy can be made to a car taking a trip. The car might be driven on city streets, secondary roads, and large highways. It might have to stop at traffic signals, or it might travel on highways with no traffic signals. The driver may change how she drives based on the type of road—going slower or faster, stopping a lot or not—but she still is just driving the car. In this analogy, the internet layer defines the equivalent of driving a car, with a few details included for rules about how to send packets on particular types of physical media.

Core Protocols of the Internet Layer

The TCP/IP internet layer defines several protocols, with the most prominent being the *Internet Protocol (IP)*. However, several other protocols also play key, although smaller, roles. Table 9-1 lists the main internet layer protocols and their functions.

Table 9-1   Four Key Internet Layer Protocols

Protocol	Description
Internet Protocol (IP)	Defines routing, logical IP addressing, the format of IP headers and packets, and interfaces.
Address Resolution Protocol (ARP)	Defines the process by which an IP host dynamically learns the mapping between another host's IP address and its MAC address.
Internet Control Message Protocol (ICMP)	Defines messaging used to manage and control IP—for example, the **ping** command uses ICMP messages.
Reverse Address Resolution Protocol (RARP)	Mostly unused today. Provides a rudimentary method for IP address assignment.

Of these protocols, IP certainly defines the most important and vital parts of the TCP/IP network layer. The next several pages focus on the features of IP.

Basic IP Routing

The IP protocol defines a process called *IP routing*, or simply routing. Although Chapter 10, "Routing Fundamentals and Subnets," covers IP routing in depth, a basic understanding of routing is helpful for understanding the basics of IP addressing covered in this chapter.

IP routing defines how to forward data, in the form of IP packets, from one host to another. The routing process allows the packets to be sent over a large variety of physical networks. Figure 9-3 shows a simple example, with the routing logic presented in the message balloons.

Figure 9-3   Basic TCP/IP Routing

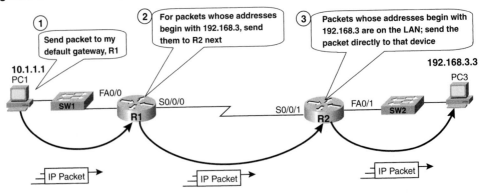

Figure 9-3 highlights the IP routing logic used by three devices to route a packet from PC1 to PC3. Their logic is summarized in the following matching steps:

1. PC1 realizes that it needs help to send the packet to 192.168.3.3. Knowing that 192.168.3.3 is not on the same LAN (more details later in the section titled "IP Addressing Fundamentals"), PC1 sends the IP packet to a router (R1).

2. Router R1 knows how to forward packets to reach all the destinations shown in the figure. In this case, R1 sends the IP packet to R2.

3. Router R2 knows that all addresses that begin with 192.168.3 are attached to the same Ethernet to which R2 is attached. So, R2 just sends the IP packet inside a frame addressed to PC3's MAC address, knowing that the LAN can forward that frame directly to PC3.

Note

Historically, the term *packet switching* has been used to refer to the same general process as routing.

None of the routing logic in this simple example mentions the specifics of the two Ethernet LANs or the leased line between the routers. To a great degree, the IP routing process ignores these details of the underlying physical networks. Of course, those details are needed and useful—for instance, the packet cannot get across the LAN without some understanding of Ethernet and the existence of the physical Ethernet LANs. However, when thinking about IP routing, most of the discussion and explanations can ignore the OSI Layer 1 and 2 details.

IP Packets

IP routing defines how hosts and routers forward data, in the form of IP packets, from one host to another. An IP packet is simply the header defined by the IP protocol, along with any higher-layer protocol headers and the end-user data. Figure 9-4 shows the general idea.

Figure 9-4   IP Packet Format

IP Packet - Basic Format

IP Header	TCP/IP Transport and Application Layer Headers	End-user Data

To build such a packet, a host's network layer must be given data from the next higher layer— for example, TCP. For that to happen, the application layer must be given data by an application. For instance, if the user of PC1 opens a web browser enters in the URL http://www.cisco.com, the browser forms a Hypertext Transfer Protocol (HTTP) request, builds an HTTP header, and gives that to TCP. TCP adds its header and gives that combined data (called a segment) to IP. IP then adds its header, creating the packet shown in Figure 9-4.

Conspicuously missing from Figure 9-4 are the data link header and trailer. In networking, the term *packet* specifically refers to data that includes the OSI Layer 3 equivalent header, plus any later headers, and end-user data, specifically omitting the data link header and trailer details.

Note

Some texts use the term *datagram* instead of *packet*.

How IP Routing Uses IP Addresses

IP defines both the rules for routing packets and the rules for IP addressing. Both functions work together to create efficient IP routing. To see why, consider Figure 9-5, which shows the same basic internetwork as in Figure 9-3.

Figure 9-5   Routing Logic Using Routing Tables

All Addresses begin with 10   All Addresses begin 172.20   All addresses begin 192.168.3

10.1.1.1   192.168.3.3
PC1   PC3

FA0/0   S0/0/0   FA0/1
10.1.1.251 R1   S0/0/1   R2   192.168.3.252
            172.20.1.251   172.20.1.252

R1's Routing Table Group	Output Interface	Next-hop Router
Starts with 10	FA0/0	connected
Starts with 172.20	S0/0/1	connected
Starts with 192.168.3	S0/0/0	R2

R2's Routing Table Group	Output Interface	Next-hop Router
Starts with 10	S0/0/1	R1
Starts with 172.20	S0/0/1	connected
Starts with 192.168.3	Fa0/1	connected

IP addresses must be assigned according to rules that group IP addresses. Figure 9-5 shows three separate physical networks, each circled, with a statement of the IP addresses that can be used inside each circle. These groups of IP addresses, which are called IP networks, must be together to allow efficient routing. (Later sections of this chapter cover the details of how IP addresses are grouped.)

Packet Tracer   Packet Tracer configuration file NA01-0905 has a working configuration that matches Figure 9-5. In real-time mode, you can view the routing table as depicted by Packet Tracer by double-clicking the router icons.

Routers use IP routing tables to tell them out which interfaces to forward packets. Figure 9-5 shows sample IP routing tables for each router. Note that the routing tables each list only three entries—one for each of the three IP networks. By requiring IP addresses on the same LAN to use the same identical value in the first parts of the actual addresses, routing can be performed without requiring large IP routing tables.

If the designers of the IP protocol had not required the grouping of IP addresses into IP networks, the resulting routing tables would have been a *huge* mess. If IP used an alternative structure in which IP addresses were not grouped, routers would need one entry in their routing tables for each IP address in existence, instead of one entry for each large group. For example, in Figure 9-5, if both LANs have 500 hosts attached, the routers would each have to have 1000 entries in their routing tables. Although most routers could handle a routing table with 1000 entries, imagine routers in the middle of the Internet, with hundreds of millions of hosts connected to the Internet. These routers need to route lots of packets per second—often on the order of millions—and would need to look up the IP addresses in a routing table with several hundred million entries, which is way too much work for even the most expensive routers today. So, IP addressing was created from its inception to allow routing tables to list groups of IP addresses in a single entry, allowing routing tables to stay relatively small.

The routes used by a router differ slightly depending on whether a router connects to the IP network or whether a router must use other routers to reach the IP network. The IP networks to which a router directly attaches or connects are called *directly connected networks*. Routers learn routes to directly connected networks easily. Routers can also forward packets to IP networks to which a router is not directly connected. To do so, a router forwards packets to another router, called the *next-hop router*. For example, R1's route to reach IP addresses beginning with 192.168.3 is through R2, so that route lists R2 as the next-hop router. Routes for directly connected networks do not have a next-hop router, because there is no need to send those packets to another router.

To summarize, IP routing relies on the organization of IP addresses into groups to allow efficient routing. The basic rules that achieve that efficient routing are as follows:

- IP addresses for hosts on the same physical network must have the same value in the first part of the addresses.

- Routers can scale their routing tables because routers need only one entry for each group—each *IP* network—by referencing that first in-common part of the IP addresses.

Keeping the previous two points in mind when learning about IP addressing can help explain why IP addressing works as it does. For now, though, this chapter continues with its more theoretical look at the TCP/IP protocol.

TCP/IP Transport Layer

The TCP/IP *transport layer* focuses on the needs of the end-user host and the applications running on it. The transport layer also mostly ignores the underlying IP network, much like the IP routing process tends to ignore the underlying physical networks.

For example, Figure 9-6 shows two PCs' perspective of the transport layer. PC1 needs to send a 1-MB file to PC2. PC1's and PC2's transport layer protocols know that IP routing exists between them, but their actions do not change whether the IP network is a single LAN or the entire Internet. Because they ignore the details, diagrams that focus on the TCP/IP transport layer simply show the IP network as a cloud.

Figure 9-6   Transport Layer Perspective

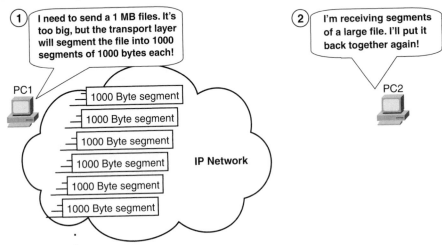

Figure 9-6 illustrates one of the main features of the transport layer, called *segmentation*. Applications ask the transport layer to send large chunks of data, but the underlying network imposes limits on the size of the data. For example, Ethernet allows only 1500 bytes in the Data field, which has to hold the entire IP packet. The end-user data inside a TCP segment's data field is then typically at most 1460 bytes, because the IP and TCP headers are each 20 bytes long. The TCP/IP transport layer takes a large chunk of data from the application layer, segments the data into sizes that are legal for sending through the network, and sends them.

An easy analogy can be made between the transport layer and how the average person uses the postal system. People send letters through the postal system regularly, but they generally do not care much about what trucks, planes, trains, and boats are used to deliver their letters. They might care about how much time delivery takes, and that the postal service seldom loses the letters, but the delivery details are unimportant. Similarly, transport layer protocols on host computers use the IP network, but they do not consider the details to be all that interesting or important.

TCP/IP includes two main options for transport layer protocols:

- Transmission Control Protocol (TCP)

- User Datagram Protocol (UDP)

Both are covered in more detail in Chapter 11, "TCP/IP Transport and Application Layers." Both protocols define some level of detail about how to get data from one computer's application process to another computer's application process. Both TCP and UDP ignore the underlying IP network for the most part.

Of course, two protocols would not be needed if they did everything the same. TCP provides several extra functions over and beyond what UDP provides. However, TCP pays a price: more overhead and typically less speed than UDP. Table 9-2 lists and describes the functions of both TCP and UDP.

Table 9-2   Comparing TCP and UDP

Transport Layer Feature	Description	TCP	UDP
Segmentation of data	Breaking large chunks of data into network-legal sizes, called segments, before sending	Yes	No
Multiplexing using port numbers	Identifying the application process that needs the data on each computer, not just the computers themselves	Yes	Yes
Error recovery	Monitoring for lost segments and resending them	Yes	No
In-order delivery of data	Monitoring received segments and putting them back in the correct order before giving the data to the application	Yes	No
Flow control	Monitoring network performance and causing the sending computer to slow down to avoid congestion in the network	Yes	No

Unfortunately, the functions of the transport layer can be difficult to grasp without going into more detail. Chapter 1, "Introduction to Networking," showed a brief example of transport layer error recovery using TCP, in the section "TCP/IP Transport Layer and the TCP Protocol." Figure 9-6 in this chapter showed a function performed by TCP—namely, the segmentation of data into sizes allowed to be transmitted in the network. Chapter 11 goes into more detail about each of the functions in Table 9-2.

TCP/IP Application Layer

The TCP/IP application layer protocols provide services to applications. Many people confuse the application layer with the applications themselves. Although applications do directly use an application layer protocol, the applications are different from the application layer protocol.

For example, a web browser is an application that displays text, graphics, and video, and sometimes plays audio for an end user. To do all of these things, the browser must request and transfer many files from a web server. To use the network to transfer files, the web browser uses HTTP. Generally, the application provides the user interface, and the application protocol performs the actual underlying communications required by the application.

Figure 9-7 shows a representation of some of the application layer protocols.

Figure 9-7   Application Layer Protocols

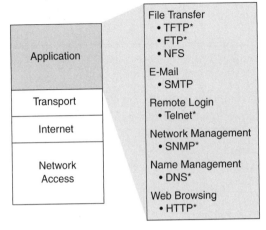

* These application protocols are used by many hosts, but they are also used when managing, controlling, and
accessing routers.

Table 9-3 explains the application layer protocols listed in Figure 9-7.

Table 9-3   Application Layer Protocols

Protocol	Description	Transport Layer Protocol
Hypertext Transfer Protocol (HTTP)	Defines the commands, headers, and processes by which web servers and web browsers transfer files.	TCP
Trivial File Transfer Protocol (TFTP)	A very simple protocol, implemented using a very small amount of software, that allows file transfer.	UDP
File Transfer Protocol (FTP)	A very robust protocol used for transferring files.	TCP
Network File System (NFS)	A distributed file system protocol suite developed by Sun Microsystems that allows remote file access across a network.	UDP
Simple Mail Transfer Protocol (SMTP)	Defines the process by which e-mail may be forwarded and then held for later retrieval by the intended recipient.	TCP
Terminal Emulation (Telnet)	Defines the protocols used to allow a user on one computer to remotely access another computer, enter commands, and have those commands be executed on the other computer. It is popularly used by network engineers to remotely access routers and switches.	TCP

Table 9-3   Application Layer Protocols *(continued)*

Protocol	Description	Transport Layer Protocol
Simple Network Management Protocol (SNMP)	An application protocol that typically is not used by end users; instead, it is used by the network management software and actual networking devices to allow a network engineer to monitor and troubleshoot network problems.	UDP
Domain Name System (DNS)	A protocol that defines how a computer may refer to another computer by name, send a request that lists that name, and receive a reply that lists that name's corresponding IP address.	UDP
Dynamic Host Configuration Protocol (DHCP)	A protocol used to dynamically assign IP addresses to hosts.	UDP

Chapter 11 briefly covers additional information about many of these application protocols.

Perspectives on the TCP/IP and OSI Models

Now that you have been reminded of a few details about both the TCP/IP model and the OSI model, this section closes out the more theoretical coverage of these models. In particular, this section takes a broader view of these networking models, the kinds of things they do, and the perspectives held by the different layers of the models.

First, it is important to note, and to memorize, which TCP/IP layers match which OSI layers. All networking professionals should know these details because almost every bit of literature about networking refers to the layers. In particular, the TCP/IP layers are referenced by name and their equivalent OSI layer numbers; the OSI layers are referenced by their names and numbers as well.

Keep in mind, though, that TCP/IP layers are almost never referenced by their own layer numbers. In fact, most often, TCP/IP protocols are listed with the equivalent OSI layer number—for example, IP would be called a Layer 3 protocol. (See the Chapter 2 section "The OSI Layers" for more perspectives on the referencing of TCP/IP protocols based on OSI layers.) Table 9-4 lists the details.

Table 9-4   Summary of the TCP/IP and OSI Models' Layers

TCP/IP Layer*	Name	OSI Layer(s)	OSI Layer Name(s)
4	Application	5–7	Application (7), presentation (6), and session (5)
3	Transport	4	Transport
2	Internet	3	Network
1	Network access	1–2	Data link (2) and physical (1)

* The TCP/IP layer numbers are practically never referenced.

Perspectives on the Different TCP/IP Layers

Layered networking models provide many benefits. One benefit is that models enable courses and books to discuss, describe, and draw figures about networks while focusing on the details of a particular layer. The most obvious perspective on a network is a physical (Layer1) diagram of what the cabling looks like, mainly because it relates to something that can be seen and built in a lab. However, as mentioned earlier, in the section "Basic IP Routing," when explaining IP routing, the details of the underlying physical network may not be part of the discussion. So, Figure 9-8 shows three variations on how a LAN might be drawn:

- Top: The details of the Ethernet topology matter.

- Middle: The details of the Ethernet topology do not matter, but the fact that the network is an Ethernet does matter.

- Bottom: The details, and whether or not the network is an Ethernet, do not matter.

The first type of diagram (top) shows the cabling details, but the other two obscure the details. The middle diagram's style looks like a drawing of a 10BASE5 Ethernet LAN, because this style has been used to generically represent an Ethernet for a long time. The bottom diagram obscures all details, implying that they are unimportant to the discussion.

TCP/IP Internetworks and the Network Layer Perspective

The TCP/IP internet layer (OSI network layer, Layer 3) defines the details of routing and logical addressing. Often, instead of showing the underlying physical networks, as was shown in Figure 9-5, the details are hidden by clouds, as shown in Figure 9-9.

Figure 9-8   Three Variations on Drawing an Ethernet

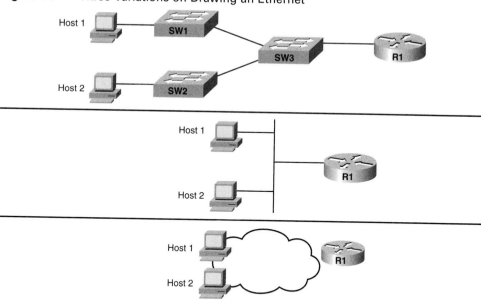

Figure 9-9   Diagram of a Network, Layer 3 Perspective

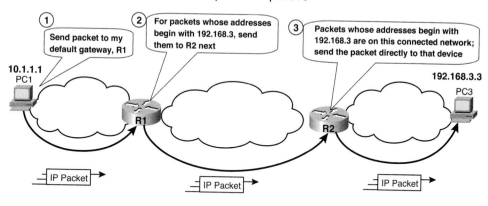

Figure 9-9 also happens to provide a perfect example of the term *internetwork*. If each cloud represents some unspecified physical network, routers R1 and R2 could be considered to connect multiple networks. The term internetwork refers to multiple physical networks that are connected by routers. In fact, the term internetwork is simply a shortened form of the phrase "interconnected networks."

Because the term *network* may become overused in the world of networking, and because IP addressing has a specific meaning for the phrase "IP network," the term internetwork will be used to refer specifically to networks such as the one shown in Figure 9-9, with routers connecting multiple physical networks into an internetwork.

It is also easy to confuse the term *Internet* and internetwork. The proper noun Internet refers to a very specific internetwork, introduced in Chapter 1, that connects practically every company and hundreds of millions of individuals. An internetwork is any IP network that uses routers to connect individual LANs, MANs, and WANs. Also, the term internet, as a common noun (not capitalized), refers to a layer of the TCP/IP model.

The routing examples shown earlier in Figures 9-3 and 9-5 show examples of internetworks. The course mentions several attributes of an internetwork:

- It must be scalable in the number of networks and computers attached.

- It must be able to handle the transport of data across vast distances, including entire-Earth and near-Earth space.

- It must be flexible to account for constant technological innovations.

- It must adjust to dynamic conditions on the network.

- It must be cost-effective.

- It must be a system that permits anytime, anywhere data communications to anyone.

Network-Centric and Host-Centric Views of Networking Models

To wrap up this discussion of different perspectives on the functions of the TCP/IP layers, consider for a moment how TCP/IP's bottom two layers—matching OSI Layers 1 to 3—differ from TCP/IP's two upper layers—matching OSI Layers 4 to 7. The lower layers concern themselves with the delivery of data between the hosts, whereas the upper layers concern themselves with functions on the host computers, mostly ignoring the details of delivery between the hosts. Using the postal service analogy again, the bottom parts of TCP/IP act like the employees and equipment inside the postal system, working to make sure that all the mail is picked up and delivered correctly. The upper layers act like the general populace that uses the postal system, assuming that the postal system is there and it works.

Figure 9-10 shows a classic diagram (appearing in various forms throughout the history of TCP/IP) that depicts the network- and host-centric layers of the TCP/IP and OSI models.

Figure 9-10   Network-centric and Host-centric Views of OSI and TCP/IP Models

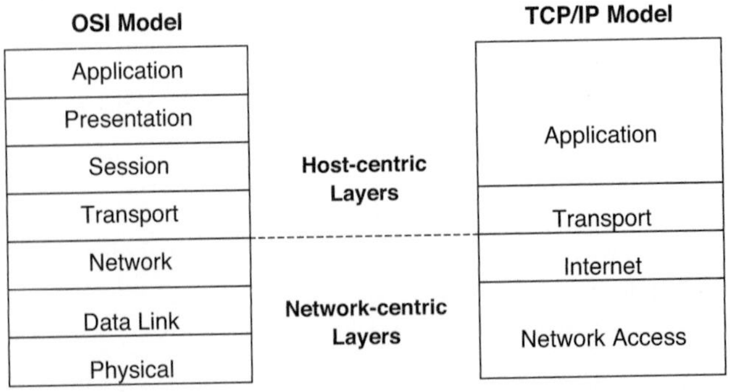

Next, the chapter turns from theoretical to practical networking, with a detailed look at IP addressing.

IP Addressing Fundamentals

The IP protocol has begun what will probably be a decades-long migration from the older version of IP *(IP version 4, or IPv4)* to IP version 6 (IPv6). An experimental IP version 5 was never fully developed. To prevent confusion, the next version after version 5 was numbered version 6. This section focuses on IPv4 addresses, with a brief mention of IPv6 addresses.

Basic Facts About IP Addresses

IPv4 addresses can be explained using two different views of the structure of the addresses: classful IP addressing and classless IP addressing. Cisco Networking Academy courses CCNA 1 and 2 stick to the classful view of IP addressing, with CCNA 3 then going on to explain classless IP addressing. So, throughout this book, all views of IPv4 addresses will be classful.

IP addresses must conform to the following rules:

- They must be unique inside a particular internetwork.

- They are 32-bit numbers—for example, 00001010000000010000001000000011.

- They are typically written, entered, and displayed as dotted-decimal numbers—for example, 10.1.2.3.

- Each decimal number in a dotted-decimal IP address represents 8 bits of the IP address.

- Each of the four decimal values in an IP address is between 0 and 255, inclusive, because 8 bits can represent decimal values 0 through 255.

Each decimal number in an IP address is often called an *octet*; the origin of the term relates to the fact that it represents eight binary digits.

Note

The term *dotted quad* is also used to refer to the format of an IP address.

Address Assignment and Address Classes

To truly understand IP addressing, you need to understand the rules by which IP addresses can be chosen for a device. These rules were introduced earlier in the chapter in the section "How IP Routing Uses IP Addresses," which showed how IP addresses must be grouped into IP networks to allow routers to keep a relatively short routing table. To begin, examine Figure 9-11, which shows a small LAN, with several PCs, and the IP addresses assigned to the LAN NICs.

Figure 9-11   Simple IP Network with Three PCs

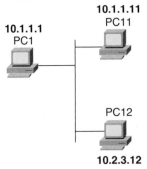

The IP addresses assigned to the computers happen to all start with a first octet of 10. In fact, to conform to IP addressing rules, all the PCs on the same LAN must use the same value for the first part of their IP addresses—in this case, a first octet of 10.

IP addresses are assigned to network interfaces rather than to entire computers. Because most PCs simply have a single physical network interface—such as a single Ethernet NIC—most people think that the IP addresses are assigned to the computer. For example, compare the two screenshots shown in Figure 9-12. The figure shows **ipconfig** command output from two different PCs. The first PC has a single network interface, which happens to be an Ethernet NIC. The second PC (a laptop PC) has an Ethernet NIC and a wireless LAN card. On the laptop, **ipconfig** lists separate IP address information for each interface.

Figure 9-12   ipconfig Listing an IP Address per Network Interface

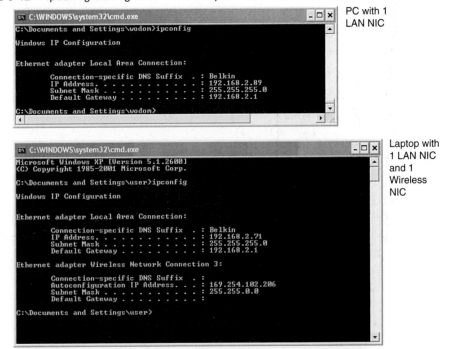

Many examples and figures in this chapter also show routers with multiple interfaces, and therefore multiple IP addresses. For example, Figure 9-5 showed multiple IP addresses on the two routers.

Three Key Rules for IP Address Assignment on LANs

IP addresses should be assigned based on some rules about which IP addresses can be used on the same LAN and which IP addresses can be used on different LANs. The following list details the three key rules of IP address assignment:

- Devices on the same LAN should use IP addresses in the same group; the group is called an *IP network*.

- Devices on different LANs that are separated by at least one router should use IP addresses in different IP networks (in other words, different groups).

- IP addresses must be unique inside the same internetwork.

To appreciate these three rules, consider a scenario based on Figure 9-11. A new computer is attached to the LAN in the figure. What must be true about the new IP address assigned to the new computer's Ethernet NIC? According to the third rule, the new IP address must not be used by the other three computers—namely, it cannot be 10.1.1.1, 10.1.1.11, or 10.2.3.12.

This chapter has not yet defined enough information to fully appreciate the first two rules. So, Figure 9-13 shows an example from which the first two rules can be explained. According to the rules, the hosts on each LAN should be in a different IP network.

Figure 9-13   Three LANs, Three IP Networks

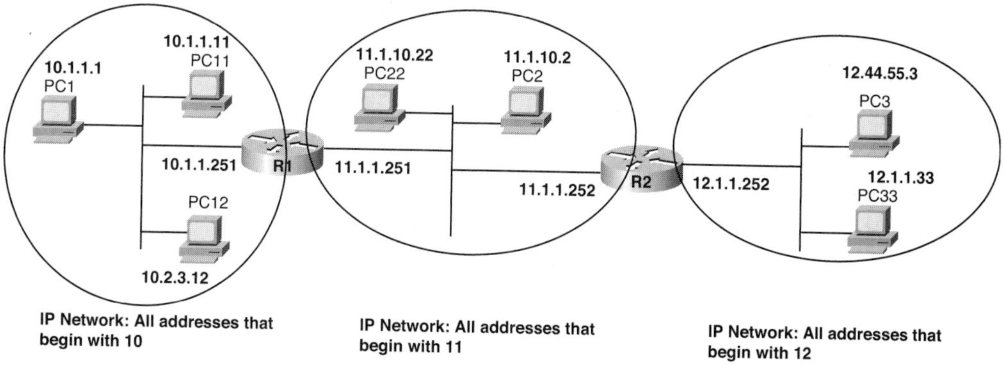

Figure 9-13 shows three physical networks, separated by two routers. According to the first IP addressing rule, the hosts on a single one of these LANs need to be in the same IP network. The three networks can be loosely characterized as follows:

- All IP addresses that begin with 10

- All IP addresses that begin with 11

- All IP addresses that begin with 12

The second rule states that devices on different LANs should use IP addresses in different IP networks. For example, PC22's IP address could not begin with 10, because the IP addresses of the hosts on the left-side Ethernet begin with 10. And, of course, every host must use a unique IP address, which they do.

 Load Packet Tracer configuration file NA01-0913-broken for a sample configuration that resembles Figure 9-13 but has several IP addresses being assigned incorrectly. You can look at the configuration or use pings to test, find the problems, and then fix the problems. (Nothing needs to be changed or fixed on the routers.) Configuration file NA01-0913 can also be loaded, which shows a working version of the network in Figure 9-13.

Both routers in Figure 9-13 have two IP addresses listed, because IP addresses are assigned to each interface. Also note that the router interfaces must conform to the IP addressing rules as well, so R1's IP address on its left interface must begin with 10, and its IP address on the right interface must begin with 11. By attaching an interface to each IP network, the router connects to multiple IP networks, creating an internetwork.

Defining Class A, B, and C IP Networks

This chapter so far has purposefully given general descriptions of IP networks, using phrases like "all addresses that begin with 10." This section explains the IP addressing rules more specifically, using more exact terminology and examples.

The term *unicast IP address* refers to an IP address that can be assigned to a single interface. All the examples in the chapter so far have shown unicast IP addresses. The term unicast refers to the fact that the address is used by a single host interface.

IPv4 defines three classes of unicast IP addresses. The class is determined by the value of the first octet of the address, as listed in Table 9-5.

Tip

The details in Table 9-5 are very important in the world of TCP/IP, and should be memorized.

Table 9-5   Classful IP Address Classes Based on First Octet

Range of Values in First Octet (Inclusive)	Class	Length of Network Part	Length of Host Part
1–126	A	1 octet	3 octets
128–191	B	2 octets	2 octets
192–223	C	3 octets	1 octet

The class of an address defines its structure, which includes two parts: a *network part* and a *host part*. The combined network and host parts of the address comprise the entire 4-byte (32-bit) IP address. Depending on the class of the address, the network part is either 1, 2, or 3 octets long, with the host part comprising the remaining octets. Figure 9-14 points out the details visually.

Figure 9-14   Network and Host Parts of Classful Addresses—No Subnetting

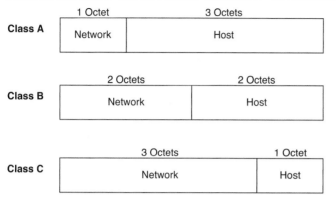

Using the information in Table 9-5, along with Figure 9-14, you can look at any unicast IP address and determine its class and structure—specifically, the size of the network and host parts of the address. For example, the following list details how the LAN on the left in Figure 9-13 would be analyzed based on the information in Table 9-5 and Figure 9-14:

- The addresses all begin with 10 in the first octet, making them Class A addresses (see Table 9-5 for details on how to identify the class of the address).

- Per Table 9-5, Class A addresses have a 1-octet network part.

- Per Table 9-5, Class A addresses have a 3 octet host part.

Similarly, the other two LANs could be analyzed to determine that they also use Class A addresses, and that the networks consist of the addresses that begin with 11 (middle LAN) and 12 (right-side LAN).

Finally, to pull all these concepts together, consider the following general definition of an IP network:

> An IP network consists of all unicast IP addresses for which the network part's value is the same value.

Remembering the three key rules for IP address assignment, all IP addresses on the same LAN must be in the same IP network. With the formal definition of an IP network in mind, now you know that the IP addresses in a single IP network must have the same value in the network part of their addresses, as was shown in Figure 9-13.

The example of Figure 9-13 shows only Class A networks. However, other classes of networks can be easily used as well. For example, Figure 9-15 shows a sample internetwork that uses one Class A, one Class B, and one Class C network.

Figure 9-15 Three LANs, Three IP Networks

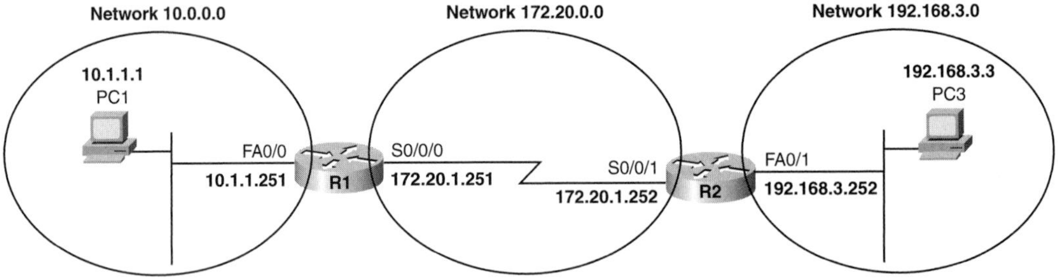

The figure shows the LAN on the right using addresses that begin with 192, meaning that those addresses are in a Class C network. As a Class C network, the first 3 octets (192.168.3) must be in common among all IP addresses. Similarly, the WAN link between the routers uses Class B addresses that begin with 172.20, because Class B addresses must have their first 2 octets in common.

(This example shows the most basic use of IP networks. If you have some experience with IP addressing, you may see this example and wonder how it relates to what you have seen outside class. This example gives the basics, with later parts of this chapter, Chapter 10, and the remaining CCNA courses providing even more detail and other options.)

Note

Most instructors agree that you must master the ability to analyze the structure of an IP address before moving on to subnetting. If the sample practice problem coming next does not make sense, please ask your instructor questions.

Analyzing the Structure of IP Addresses

The concepts related to looking at an address, determining its class, remembering how many network octets exist, and listing the value of those octets in statements like "all hosts that begin with…" are very important. Mastering these details requires practice.

Table 9-6 shows a completed example of the kinds of practice problems listed in Appendix C, "Extra Practice". In the appendix, your job would be to complete the grayed parts of Table 9-6.

Table 9-6 Answer Table for Practice Problems for Class A, B, C Network Analysis

IP Address	Class (A, B, or C)	Size of Network Part	Size of Host Part	Value of Network Part	Value of Host Part
10.1.1.1	A	1	3	10	1.1.1
172.22.3.4	B	2	2	172.22	3.4
192.168.55.66	C	3	1	192.168.55	66

All the answers in this case can be supplied by following this process:

How To

Step 1 Compare the first octet of the IP address to the ranges listed in Table 9-5, noting if that first octet implies Class A, B, or C. Record the type in the table.

Step 2 From Table 9-5, note the number of network and host bytes, and record those in the answer table.

Step 3 In the "Value of Network Part" column, write down the value of the first 1, 2, or 3 octets of the IP address, based on the number of octets listed in the "Size of Network Part" column.

Step 4 In the last column, write down the remaining octets of the IP address.

Note

Appendix C provides practice problems related to IP addressing. Work through those problems now until you can look at any unicast IP address and think of its structure without referring to your notes.

Other Address Classes and the Entire IPv4 Address Space

You may have noticed when looking at the list of first octets for Class A, B, and C addresses in Table 9-5 that the table covered only values 0 through 223 in the first octet. So, 224 through 255 were not mentioned. This section defines the rest of the IPv4 address space, which includes addresses that use these higher values in the first octet.

IPv4 uses *Class D* IP addresses to multicast packets to a dynamically changing set of hosts. With IP multicast, a host can send a packet to a multicast destination IP address and expect that many hosts will receive a copy of the packet. To make that happen, the routers make copies of the original packet, forwarding the copies throughout the internetwork so that all hosts that care to receive the packet get a copy.

Note

The term *IPv4 address space* refers to all numerically possible IPv4 addresses, starting at 0.0.0.0 and going through 255.255.255.255.

For example, the president of a company may be making a speech to employees. Those employees could start a desktop video application and watch the speech. One copy of each video packet could be sent from the president's location, with the network replicating the packet and sending it to any locations that need it. If there are certain sites in the company at which no one is watching the video, the packets would not be replicated and sent to those sites.

IP reserves the rest of the IP address space, called *Class E* addresses, for research purposes. Table 9-7 lists the five official classes of IPv4 addresses, along with some key pieces of information about the addresses.

Table 9-7   IPv4 Address Classes A Through E

Class	First Octet	Initial Bits That Identify It as This Class	Description
A	1–126	0	Unicast IP addresses
B	128–191	10	Unicast IP addresses
C	192–223	110	Unicast IP addresses
D	224–239	1110	Multicast IP addresses
E	240–255	1111	Experimental use

All the information in Table 9-7 has been mentioned before, except for the information in the third column. The third column points out the bit pattern that begins each class of IP address. For example, all Class A addresses begin with binary 0, and Class B addresses always begin with 10. As a result, computers can easily determine the class based on these bits. Humans could easily determine the class by simply memorizing the information in the first two columns. For the purposes of the CCNA exams and working with networking as a career, you should definitely memorize the information in this table.

You may have also noticed that the values of 0 and 127 are not listed in the "First Octet" column of Table 9-7. Addresses that begin with 0 and 127 have been permanently reserved for some special purposes. For example, the IP address 127.0.0.1, called the *loopback IP address*, can be used to test software. A packet sent to address 127.0.0.1 should be encapsulated by a computer down to the IP layer, and then de-encapsulated as if the packet had just been received. This process allows applications to test their ability to ask for services from the higher layers of TCP/IP, but to be able to test even without a working physical network connection. Network 0.0.0.0 has been reserved for historical reasons.

Figure 9-16 shows a graphical view of how much of the IP address space is assigned to each class. The graph shows the entire IPv4 address space as a pie chart, with the amounts used by the five classes shown as slices of the pie chart.

Figure 9-16   Relative Sizes of the IPv4 Address Classes

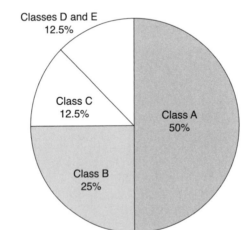

When IP addressing and Class A, B, and C networks were first created, the IP addressing designers gave 50 percent of the address space to Class A networks. Class B networks were given half of what was left, or 25% of the address space. Class C networks were given half of what was left at that point, or 12.5% of the address space, leaving 12.5 percent of the address space available for future assignment. When Class D was created years later, RFCs defined half of what was left for Class D, so Class D addresses got 6.25 percent of the available address space. Class E addresses then got the remaining 6.25 percent.

IP Network Number and the Broadcast Address

So far in this chapter, IP networks have been referred to with phrases such as "all IP addresses that begin with 10." However, computers, particularly routers, need a more concise way to refer to specific IP networks. So, IP defines a number that represents each IP network. These numbers are referred to as *IP network numbers*. (The terms *network ID* and *network address* are also used.) The following statement formally defines IP network numbers:

> An IP network number is a dotted-decimal number that represents a particular IP network. This number has the same value for the network part as do the other IP addresses in the same IP network, and 0s in the host octets.

For example, Figure 9-17 shows a revised version of Figure 9-13, but with the formal terminology shown. It includes references to the IP network numbers 10.0.0.0, 11.0.0.0, and 12.0.0.0. It also lists common phrasing used when speaking; for example, "This is IP network 10" might be spoken instead of "This is IP network 10-dot-0-dot-0-dot-0."

Figure 9-17   Correct Convention for Classful Network Numbers

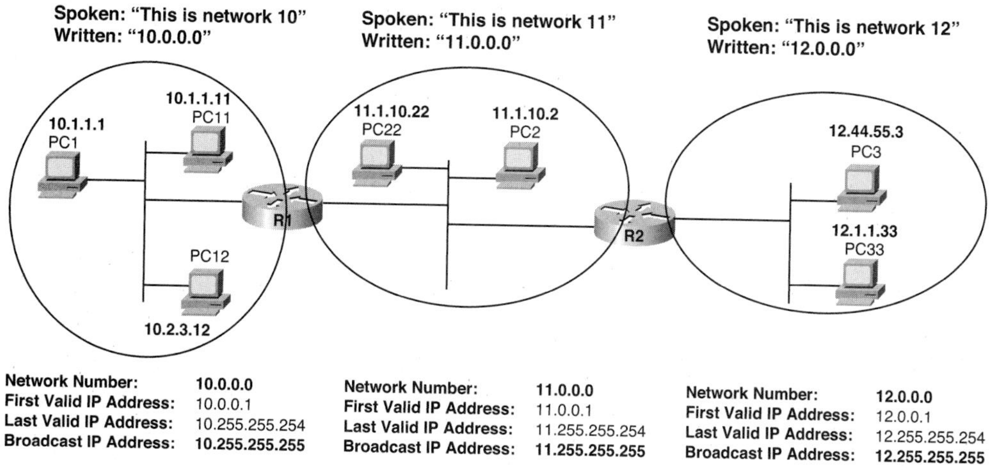

IP addressing rules specify that two numbers in each network should be reserved for special purposes. These reserved values cannot be assigned as a unicast address to any host interface. The network number for each network is one of the reserved values—for example, you could not configure a PC with an address of 10.0.0.0, because that is the network number. (Most OSs would reject your attempt to use 10.0.0.0 as an address on an interface.) The second reserved number is called the *network broadcast address*, defined as follows:

> An IP network broadcast address is a dotted-decimal number that, when a packet is sent with this address as the destination IP address, the packet should be sent to every host in that classful network. This number has the same value for the network part as do the other IP addresses in the network, and binary 1s for the host part. Because the host part is 3, 2 or 1 octets long, the decimal value of the network broadcast addresses end with 3, 2, or 1 octets of 255.

Numerically, the network number is the very smallest numeric value in a network, and the network broadcast address is the very largest numeric value in the network. By definition, the network number has the same value in the network part as all the other addresses in the same IP network, but all binary 0s in the host part. Also by definition, the broadcast address has all binary 1s in the host part.

All numbers between the network number and broadcast address are the IP addresses that can be assigned to interfaces in that network. The term *host address* is often used to refer to an assignable IP address in an IP network, specifically to imply that the address is not one of the two reserved numbers in each network.

Network Math

Before moving on to cover the basics of subnetting, this section covers a few details ofg networking math. Chapter 1 covered many details of converting between decimal and 8-bit binary. Chapter 1 also included details of converting IP addresses between their decimal and binary equivalents. If those details are not fresh in your memory, you should consider working through more of those kinds of problems, at least before the next chapter's more detailed coverage of IP subnetting.

Using the Powers of 2

Anyone working in a technical job in any part of the computing world will likely come across the powers of 2 as a regular part of their job. Table 9-8 lists the powers of 2, from 2^0 up to 2^{15}, and their corresponding values.

Table 9-8   The Powers of 2, 2^0 through 2^{15}

2^0	2^1	2^2	2^3	2^4	2^5	2^6	2^7	2^8	2^9	2^{10}	2^{11}	2^{12}	2^{13}	2^{14}	2^{15}
1	2	4	8	16	32	64	128	256	512	1024	2048	4096	8192	16384	32768

Memorizing the entire table is not vital, but memorizing the powers of 2 up through 2^{10} is practical because you will refer to these numbers often. However, it may be practical to simply keep a short reference handy; through repetitious use, you will naturally memorize the lower numbers in the list.

Networking, particularly IP addressing, uses the powers of 2 to describe how many items can be numbered using a certain number of bits. For example, if you had a bunch of items to which you needed to assign a number, and you had only 1 bit, how many different items could you number? Well, only two, using the binary numbers 0 and 1. If you had 2 bits with which to number them, you could number four items, with binary numbers 00, 01, 10, and 11. With 3 bits, you could number eight items, using 000, 001, 010, 011, 100, 101, 110, and 111.

The following statement summarizes the rule for how to identify the number of items that can be uniquely numbered using n bits. Simply put:

The number of things that can be uniquely numbered using n bits is 2^n.

Calculating the Number of Hosts per Network

With IP addressing, you can use the powers of 2 to determine the number of hosts in a single network. For example, Class A network 10.0.0.0 includes addresses 10.0.0.1, 10.0.0.2, 10.1.1.1, 10.255.43.98, and lots of others. It would be impractical to write down all the possible IP addresses in Class A network 10 and count them.

To calculate the number of hosts in a single network, you must first find out the number of host bits, and then calculate 2 to that power. For example, Class A network 10.0.0.0 has a 1-octet network part and a 3-octet host part, like all other Class A networks. So, there are 3 octets' worth of bits—24 bits—with which to number different IP addresses in network 10.0.0.0. As a result, there are (seemingly) 2^{24}, or 16,777,216, host IP addresses in network 10.0.0.0.

The other small twist to the math is that each network has two reserved numbers: the network number and the broadcast address. In the case of network 10.0.0.0, the numbers are 10.0.0.0 (the network number) and 10.255.255.255 (the broadcast address). So, when calculating the number of hosts per network, the formalized formula is as follows:

$$2^{\text{number-of-host-bits}} - 2$$

Table 9-9 lists the number of hosts per network for Class A, B, and C networks.

Table 9-9   Number of Hosts in Each Class A, B, and C Network

Class	Size of Host Field (Bytes)	Size of Host Field (Bits)	Number of Hosts per Network
A	3	24	$2^{24} - 2 = 16,777,214$
B	2	16	$2^{16} - 2 = 65,534$
C	1	8	$2^8 - 2 = 254$

Number of Class A, B, and C Networks

Although it is not needed very often, the same math used to calculate the number of host addresses per network can be applied to calculate the number of unique Class A, B, and C networks. However, this math also has a small twist or two. For example, consider the Class A networks. Each has a 1-octet network field. From the math you learned in the previous section, you might think that 2^8, or $2^8 - 2$ (which considers the reserved networks 0.0.0.0 and 127.0.0.0), might give the right number of Class A networks. However, both are wrong.

The reason that those two formulas do not give the correct number of Class A IP networks is that all Class A networks begin with a binary 0. In effect, the first bit of the 8-bit network field is fixed at binary 0. So, the number of Class A network is actually $2^7 - 2$, because only 7 bits of that first octet can vary from Class A network number to network number.

The same logic applies to calculating the number of Class B and C networks, except that there are not two reserved network numbers. Table 9-10 summarizes the numbers, along with the fixed bits and number of bits that feed into the formula.

Table 9-10   Number of Different Class A, B, and C Networks

Class	Size of Network Field (Bytes)	Size of Network Field (Bits)	Number of "Fixed" Bits at Beginning	Number of Network Bits That Vary	Number of Networks
A	1	8	1	7	$2^7 - 2 = 126$
B	2	16	2	14	$2^{14} = 16,192$
C	3	24	3	21	$2^{21} = 2,097,152$

Converting from Decimal to Binary: Large Numbers

The last bit of math mentioned in this section relates to the decimal-to-binary and binary-to-decimal conversion steps listed back in Chapter 1. In Chapter 1, all the examples used decimal numbers between 0 and 255, inclusive, and 8-bit binary numbers. The reason for using just 8-bit numbers is that these are the numbers you work with when working with IP addressing. It makes sense to practice math based on what you will use in real life.

To represent decimal numbers larger than 255 in binary on a computer, the computer needs to use more than 1 byte to hold the number. For example, the number 5432 in decimal is 1010100110110 in binary. To store that in memory, computers typically use 2 bytes and leading 0s, as follows: 0000101010010110110.

The same math in Chapter 1 can be used to convert between decimal and binary for larger numbers. However, the practical use of these conversion processes for this class is limited to 8-bit numbers.

Subnetting Basics

Before jumping into the concept of subnetting, it is helpful to review a few facts and rules covered so far. First, IP address assignment rules (so far) state that hosts on the same LAN should be in the same IP network, and that hosts in a different LAN should be in different IP networks. Figure 9-7, several pages back, shows those concepts.

Now, consider the fact that a single Class A network has over 16 million available host IP addresses. Can you imagine a LAN needing to support 16 million hosts? In real networks,

LANs of a few hundred hosts are common, but LANs with a few thousand devices are less common. So, there is a huge number of wasted IP addresses.

The process of **subnetting** allows the network designer to subdivide a classful IP network into smaller groups, called **subnets**. You can think of the term subnet as meaning "subdivided network." Then, the subnets can be used exactly like IP networks. For reference, the same IP address assignment rules covered earlier—the rules that explain which IP addresses must be in the same or different IP networks—are repeated next. However, the rules have been changed to replace the phrase "IP network" with "IP subnet":

- Devices on the same LAN should use IP addresses in the same group; the group is called an *IP subnet*.

- Devices on different LANs that are separated by at least one router should use IP addresses in different IP subnets (in other words, different groups).

- IP addresses in an internetwork should be unique.

Additionally, more formal definitions of subnet and subnet number sound a lot like the definitions of network and network number:

- **Subnet**—A group of IP addresses that all have the same value in the first part of the address

- **Subnet number**—A dotted-decimal number that represents a particular IP subnet

Essentially, the term *subnet* refers to the concept of what a subnet is, and the term *subnet number* refers to the number that computers use to reference a particular subnet.

A Simple Subnetting Example

As usual, a simple but specific example can help clarify a concept. Figure 9-18 shows the same three-LAN internetwork used in Figure 9-17. In Figure 9-17, which shows the topology without subnetting, three IP networks were needed. With subnetting, three subnets of one IP network can be used instead. Figure 9-18 uses Class A network 10.0.0.0, broken into three subnets, as follows:

- IP addresses beginning with 10.1.1

- IP addresses beginning with 10.1.2

- IP addresses beginning with 10.1.3

The results of the design are very similar to Figure 9-17, with some small but important differences. The first 3 octets, instead of just the first octet, must be the same for host IP addresses on the same LAN. As a result, each group (subnet) is relatively small—but not too small: each LAN has a subnet that contains 254 assignable IP addresses. Each subnet has a subnet number to represent the subnet, akin to an IP network number. Each subnet also has a **subnet broadcast address**, sometimes called a *directed broadcast address*—again akin to the network broadcast address. And as with IP network numbers and broadcast addresses, the IP subnet number and broadcast address cannot be assigned to a host as a unicast IP address.

Figure 9-18   Sample Internetwork Using Subnetting

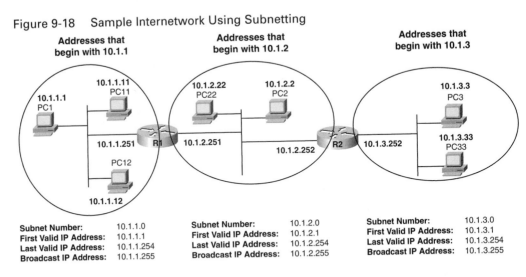

Subnet Number:	10.1.1.0
First Valid IP Address:	10.1.1.1
Last Valid IP Address:	10.1.1.254
Broadcast IP Address:	10.1.1.255

Subnet Number:	10.1.2.0
First Valid IP Address:	10.1.2.1
Last Valid IP Address:	10.1.2.254
Broadcast IP Address:	10.1.2.255

Subnet Number:	10.1.3.0
First Valid IP Address:	10.1.3.1
Last Valid IP Address:	10.1.3.254
Broadcast IP Address:	10.1.3.255

This example purposefully uses one of the simpler examples of IP subnetting. Subnetting can be much more difficult to work with than this example, but the concepts behind subnetting are the same—taking a larger group of IP addresses, such as an entire IP network, and subdividing it into smaller, more usable chunks.

Packet Tracer configurations NA01-0918 and NA010-0918-broken serve the same purpose as the similarly named Packet Tracer configurations for Figure 9-13. You can use either the working configuration for experimentation or the broken configuration to test your troubleshooting skills by using the **ping** command to find configuration errors. (Note that the routers are configured correctly.)

Differing Views of the Format of Subnetted IP Addresses

The example shown in Figure 9-18 depicts the rule that host IP addresses on the same LAN must have the same first 3 octets. To most people, that means the address still looks like it has two parts—the part in common among hosts on the same LAN, and the part that is unique on that LAN. As a result, many people think of subnetted IP addresses as having two parts—a subnet part and a host part, similar in concept to having a network and host part when not using subnetting. However, IP formally defines three parts in the structure of an IP address when subnetting:

■ Network part

■ Subnet part

■ Host part

Figure 9-19 shows three different views of the structure of the subnetted addresses in Figure 9-18.

Figure 9-19   Format of Subnetted IPv4 Addresses in Figure 9-18

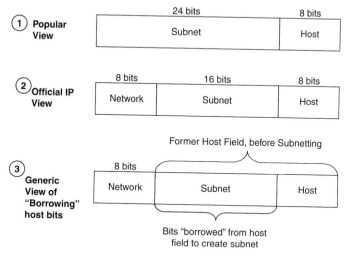

The following comments relate to the diagrams labeled 1, 2, and 3 in Figure 9-19:

1. This diagram shows a popular but inexact view of subnetting. The example requires the first 3 octets to be the same value in a subnet, with the first 3 octets being the first 24 bits. So, the popular view is that the first 3 octets, or first 24 bits, make up the subnet part of the address, and the last octet (the last 8 bits) is the host part.

2. This diagram shows the exact definition of the structure of a subnetted IP address according to the IP protocol. It shows a three-part address, with a network, subnet, and host part. The network part in this case is 8 bits because the addresses are Class A addresses—in other words, the length of the network part is based on Class A, B, and C rules. Because the design calls for the first 3 octets to be in common, and the first octet is the network part, the second and third octets, totaling 16 bits, comprise the subnet part of the address.

3. The last diagram shows the concept of borrowing bits. When subnetting, the size of the network part does not change. So, to create space for the subnet part, some of the host bits are borrowed, or lent, or taken, to form the subnet part of the address. But the size of the network part stays the same, based on the rules for Class A, B, and C networks.

Subnet Masks

The example of subnetting covered in the last few pages uses a Class A network, with subnetting rules that mean that the first 3 octets of the addresses have to be the same for hosts in the same subnet. However, subnetting allows the network engineer to choose a size for the subnet part of the addresses. So, while this example used a 1-octet network part, 2-octet subnet part, and 1-octet host part, other examples may use different settings. However, there are other rules to consider, all of which are covered in Chapter 10.

Computers need a way to numerically represent the concepts of the structure of an IP address as shown in Figure 9-19. IP defines a number called the *subnet mask*, or simply mask, exactly for that purpose. While the details are not important yet, the subnet mask identifies the combined network/subnet part and the host part. Then, the Class A, B, and C rules can be used to decide where the network and subnet parts are in an address.

For example, in Figures 9-18 and 9-19, a subnet mask of 255.255.255.0 would have been used. This mask means the following:

- The network and subnet parts are the first 3 octets, because the mask has 255 in each of those octets.

- The host part is the last octet, because the mask has a 0 in that octet.

To find all three parts of the address, you then simply need to decide how much of the combined network/subnet part is the network part and how much is the subnet part. To do that, just consider the class rules, where Class A's network part is 1 octet, Class B's network part is 2 octets, and Class C's network part is 3 octets.

For example, the IP address 10.1.2.3, with mask 255.255.255.0, can be analyzed as follows:

- Using the mask, the network and subnet part together is 3 octets, with a value of 10.1.2, and the host part is 1 octet, with a value of 3.

- Using class rules, the network part is 1 octet, namely 10. So, the subnet part is 2 octets, with a value of 1.2 in this case.

When Class A, B, and C networks are not subnetted, they are said to use default masks or default subnet masks. These default values imply the two parts of an unsubnetted IP address: the network and host parts. The actual default masks are 255.0.0.0 (Class A), 255.255.0.0 (Class B), and 255.255.255.0 (Class C).

So, why present all of these details about the structure of an IP address? Well, most any technical networking job requires that you be able to look at an IP address, and a subnet mask, and determine the structure of the IP address. After completing the next short section, you may want to go to the Appendix C section for Chapter 9 and complete some of the subnetting exercises.

 Lab 9.2.7   IP Addressing Basics

The purpose of this lab is to name the five different classes of IP addresses and to describe the characteristics and use of the different IP address classes.

Ensuring Unique IP Addresses Throughout the Internet

The IP address assignment rules in this chapter so far have described how to assign IP addresses inside one enterprise network. One of these rules is that each IP address must be unique;

otherwise, routers would not know to which host they should deliver a packet that is sent to a duplicated IP address.

This section takes the discussion of unique IP addresses one rather large step further. To make the Internet work, the original design called for unique IP addresses on every host that ever needed to use the Internet. Yes, that means that a unique IP addresses would be needed on essentially every computer on the planet.

Unique IP addresses on all computers, worldwide, sounds like a big goal—but similar things had already been accomplished before TCP/IP came around. Most significantly, the world's combined telephone companies had agreed to telephone number assignment rules that would allow all phone lines to have a unique phone number. Because of that agreement, every phone line and cell phone today has a unique telephone number. This section explains how the original design of the Internet attempted to achieve the same general goal as the telephone network. This section also explains a few details about how these original design goals have changed today.

Original Internet Design: Unique Network Numbers for Each Enterprise Network

Ensuring unique IP addresses throughout the Internet required thought, rules, and people to administer the process of assigning IP addresses. The administrative authority has been given to several organizations over the years, mostly not-for-profit organizations. Currently, the *Internet Assigned Numbers Authority (IANA)* (http://www.iana.org) has the ultimate authority. IANA distributes the authority to assign registered unique IP addresses to IANA member organizations in different parts of the world. For example, IANA has given the *American Registry for Internet Numbers (ARIN)* the authority and responsibility to assign IP addresses in the United States.

Note

Although the IANA member organizations typically perform the IP address assignment, and other organizations have administered this process in the past, the rest of this section simply refers to IANA.

IANA followed key rules that allowed it to ensure unique IP addresses throughout the Internet. Basically, IANA assigned entire Class A, B, or C IP network numbers to companies. Then, the companies used subnetting to create smaller subnets and assigned individual IP addresses from those subnets. However, each company could use only IP addresses in its assigned networks.

The process by which IANA assigns IP addresses can be summarized as follows:

1. IANA assigned unique Class A, B, or C network numbers to companies (or other organizations) that asked for a network number. These networks are considered to be registered IP networks.

2. IANA looked at each request, assigning one (or more) Class A, B, or C networks, depending on the size of the company and the size of its network.

3. To ensure unique IP network numbers on the Internet, IANA never assigned the same Class A, B, or C network to more than one company.

4. Inside a company, the network engineers would subnet and assign the IP addresses any way they wanted, as long as they used only addresses inside their company's registered IP network.

A company following this process ended up with one or more registered IP networks, which meant that the company had registered with IANA to be the only company in the world to use that IP network number—at least when connecting to the Internet. Figure 9-20 shows the concept of the worldwide Internet when following these rules.

Note

Addresses inside registered IP network numbers, which are legal for use in packets sent through the Internet, are called *public IP addresses*.

Figure 9-20   Unique IP Networks for Each Company Attached to the Internet

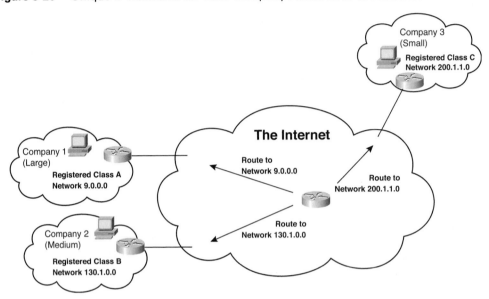

Assuming IANA did its job right, these rules ensured that no two companies or organizations used the same registered Class A, B, or C network numbers. Inside a company, IP addresses could be accidentally duplicated, but it was up to the enterprise network engineers to resolve those problems and use unique addresses. Also, when enterprises made such mistakes, it harmed only hosts inside that company and did not harm other hosts on the Internet.

The Problem of IPv4 Address Depletion

When assigning IP network numbers, IANA would consider the size of the company's network as detailed on the application form. Large companies got Class A network numbers, medium-sized companies got Class B network numbers, and small companies got Class C network numbers. However, the IPv4 IP address was just too small. Eventually, all 126 Class A networks were assigned. By the early 1990s, it appeared that all the Class B networks would be assigned in the near future as well, mainly due to the rapid growth of the Internet. This phenomenon became known as *IPv4 address depletion*, and something had to be done about it to allow the rapid expansion of the Internet to continue.

The IETF took both a short-term and long-term approach to preventing IPv4 address depletion. The short-term attack included several tools for IPv4. One tool, called classless interdomain routing (CIDR), is not covered until the CCNA 3 course. The other tool, called *Network Address Translation (NAT)*, or sometimes *Port Address Translation (PAT)*, is covered in more detail in the CCNA 4 course. However, to gain appreciation of the IPv4 address depletion problem and solutions here in the CCNA 1 course, you need to know just a little about NAT.

One Short-Term Solution: NAT and Private IP Networks

NAT allows a company to use just a few registered IP addresses instead of an entire registered Class A, B, or C network. The details of how NAT works are not covered in this course, but it is useful to understand a few NAT concepts.

With NAT, hosts inside the corporate network may use any IP addresses, but typically, IP addresses called private IP addresses are used. However, hosts on the Internet think that the hosts using the private addresses are using valid, IANA-assigned, registered, and globally unique IP addresses. Figure 9-21 shows the general idea. In this case, four hosts inside Company 1's enterprise network are connected to the web server. However, on the Internet, all the hosts appear to be using a single IP address—one of the registered IP addresses from IANA.

Figure 9-21   Effects of NAT with Private IP Networks

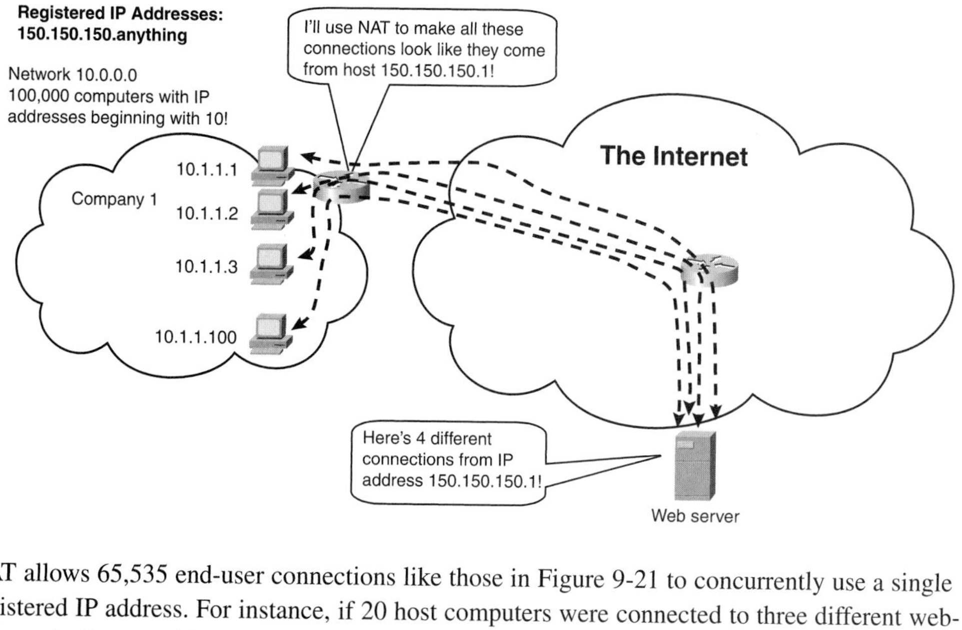

NAT allows 65,535 end-user connections like those in Figure 9-21 to concurrently use a single registered IP address. For instance, if 20 host computers were connected to three different websites each, they would collectively have created at least 60 connections. As a result, each company needs only a small number of IP addresses registered by IANA, each able to support over 65,000 concurrent connections. Usually, even a medium-sized company can get by with five to ten IP addresses instead of a whole Class B network, and small companies can get by with one registered IP address instead of a whole Class C network.

Private IP Networks

NAT takes advantage of some special reserved IP network numbers called private IP networks. (Addresses inside private IP networks are called *private IP addresses*.) NAT works best if the IP addresses used inside a company are not part of a network registered with IANA. RFC 1918, "Address Allocation for Private Internets," defines a set of private networks. IANA purposefully will never assign registered IP network numbers to these private networks.

IETF's original intent in defining private IP network numbers was that they be used by internetworks that would never connect to the Internet. For example, in the early days of the Internet, many companies had no interest in connecting to the Internet, either because they feared the security risks or because they were short-sighted. Additionally, many lab networks inside companies need the flexibility of being separated from the corporate network.

NAT expanded the use of private IP network numbers to internetworks that do connect to the Internet. As covered in the preceding section, NAT helps prevent IPv4 address depletion, and NAT works best when companies also use private IP networks.

Table 9-11 lists the private IP network numbers as defined by RFC 1918.

Note

If you were to go into most any company or home-based network today and look at the IP addresses used on the computers in that network, they likely would be from one of the private IP networks listed in Table 9-11.

Table 9-11   Private IP Networks per RFC 1918

Class	Range of Network Numbers	Total Number of Networks
A	10.0.0.0	1
B	172.16.0.0–172.31.0.0	16
C	192.168.0.0–192.168.255.0	256

In short, most companies today use private IP networks, along with NAT, which allows each company to need a lot fewer registered public IP addresses, and prevents IPv4 address depletion.

Long-Term Solution: IP Version 6 (IPv6)

NAT and other short-term solutions to the IPv4 address depletion problem worked, and worked well. Currently, almost 15 years after the initial work to find a solution to the IPv4 address depletion problem, most of the Internet is still using IPv4.

The long-term solution calls for a whole new version of the IP protocol, called *IP version 6 (IPv6)*. IPv6 has many new features as compared with IPv4, including a 128-bit IP address. As a result, there are 3.4×10^{38} (give or take a few) IPv6 IP addresses. The number is staggering—it is almost 10^{30} IP addresses for each person on the planet. Thus, IPv6 will not run out of unique addresses for many years, if ever.

Figure 9-22 shows a comparison of IPv4 and IPv6 addresses. The bottom part of the figure shows a binary IPv6 address, which has 16 sets of 8 bits to show the 128-bit binary IPv6 address. IPv6 addresses are typically written in hexadecimal, with eight sets of four hexadecimal digits, with the sets of four digits separated by colons.

Figure 9-22   Comparing IPv4 and IPv6 Addresses

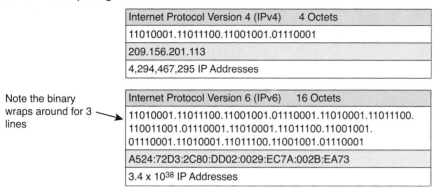

Internet Protocol Version 4 (IPv4)   4 Octets
11010001.11011100.11001001.01110001
209.156.201.113
4,294,467,295 IP Addresses

Note the binary wraps around for 3 lines →

Internet Protocol Version 6 (IPv6)   16 Octets
11010001.11011100.11001001.01110001.11010001.11011100. 110011001.01110001.11010001.11011100.11001001. 01110001.11010001.11011100.11001001.01110001
A524:72D3:2C80:DD02:0029:EC7A:002B:EA73
3.4 x 10^{38} IP Addresses

Assigning and Mapping IP Addresses

The original design of the Internet required that each IP address must be unique. To ensure that each network interface on all computers on the planet used unique IP addresses, each company should request and be assigned one or more class A, B, or C network numbers. No two companies are assigned the same network numbers. Then, if each company uses only IP addresses from its assigned network numbers, the Internet, which connects all these companies, can ensure that the IP addresses are unique.

Although it is important to know what IP addresses should be assigned to computer interfaces, that process is mainly a planning process. Once the IP addressing scheme has been planned, the engineer must be able to assign IP addresses to computer interfaces. This section covers the two popular methods of assigning IP addresses to host computer interfaces today: static configuration, and dynamic configuration using Dynamic Host Configuration Protocol (DHCP).

Beyond IP address assignment, it is also important to know how hosts can send packets to other hosts based on the underlying network access layer, which does the work of the OSI data link (Layer 2) and physical (Layer 1) layers. The end of this section describes some of the most important details of how IP uses the underlying protocols and physical networks.

Note

Today, a function called Network Address Translation (NAT), as covered in the CCNA 3 course, allows IP addresses to be duplicated by multiple companies, while allowing the Internet to work.

Static IP Address Configuration

Static IP address configuration simply means that the user or network administrator enters the IP address of the computer in the appropriate place for that operating system. Along with the IP address, the computer needs to know some related information; Table 9-12 lists the typically configured items.

Table 9-12   IP Address and Related Static Configuration Options

Item	Description
IP address	The IP address to be used by this computer.
Subnet mask	A dotted-decimal number that helps define the structure of the IP address, specifically the size of the host part of the address.
Default gateway (default router) IP address	The IP address of a router on the same local subnet. When sending packets to hosts on other subnets, this device sends the packets to the default router.
DNS server IP address	The IP address of the server that handles requests to supply the IP address that corresponds to specific host names.

Figure 9-23 shows the same familiar three-LAN network, but this time with suggested configuration values for PC1.

Figure 9-23   Four Key Static Configuration Items

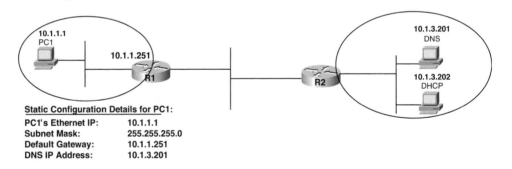

First, consider the subnet mask of 255.255.255.0, which defines the structure of the IP address. This mask means that the first 3 octets (24 bits) comprise the network and subnet parts of the address, and the last octet comprises the host part.

The term *default gateway*, also called *default router*, refers to some basic routing logic mentioned briefly a few times earlier in the chapter. When PC1 wants to send a packet to a host in another subnet, PC1 should send the packet to a router—in this case, router R1. To do so, PC1 needs to know R1's IP address of its interface on PC1's subnet. So, PC1 simply needs to know the IP address to which it should send packets that need to be forwarded to other subnets—in this case, 10.1.1.251.

Finally, as mentioned in Chapter 1, users tend to use DNS names instead of IP addresses, but computers must then translate the names into the corresponding IP addresses. Typically, name resolution occurs using a DNS server. So, PC1 needs to have the DNS server IP address configured. (Often, multiple DNS IP addresses are configured, because multiple DNS servers are used in case one of them fails.)

The configuration steps differ from OS to OS. Figure 9-24 shows the configuration screen on Windows XP, configured with the details shown in Figure 9-23.

Figure 9-24   Windows XP Static IP Configuration

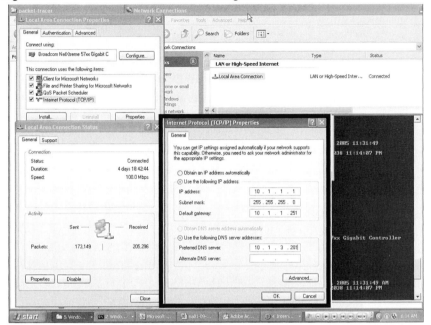

Dynamic IP Address Configuration Using DHCP

Dynamic IP address assignment has long been a goal of TCP/IP. In the early days, a protocol called Reverse Address Resolution Protocol (RARP) was used. Later, a much more robust protocol called Boot Protocol (BOOTP) was developed. Finally, *Dynamic Host Configuration Protocol (DHCP)* expanded BOOTP, becoming today's standard for dynamic IP address assignment.

DHCP allows a host that does not have a static IP address configured on an interface to send a request to a DHCP server. The server then sends back a DHCP reply. The DHCP reply includes an IP address that can be used by that host. In addition to supplying the IP address, the DHCP server supplies all the other information mentioned in the preceding section: the mask, default gateway, and DNS server IP addresses. DHCP can also supply other information. In fact, as a protocol, it is designed to be flexible and expandable, so as new requirements and features need to be dynamically learned, DHCP can still be used, without the need for a new protocol. DHCP's flexibility has allowed it to remain a popularly used protocol in almost every enterprise network in the world.

Figure 9-25 shows the same internetwork as shown in Figure 9-23, but in this case, PC1 uses DHCP instead of static configuration. The PC whose IP address is 10.1.3.202 acts as the DHCP server.

Note

RARP and BOOTP are briefly covered in the "Additional Topics of Interest" section for this chapter, which you can find on the CD-ROM accompanying this book.

Note

DHCP servers are DHCP software, installed on any computer with an IP address. In production environments, the software is usually on a server with redundant power supplies, located in a data center, for better availability.

Figure 9-25   PC1 and DHCP Server Information: Before Address Assignment

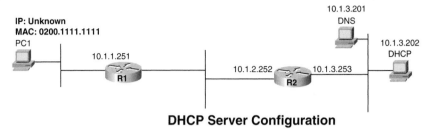

DHCP Server Configuration

Subnet:	Allowed to be Assigned:	Mask	Def. GW	DNS
10.1.1.0	**10.1.1.1 – 10.1.1.200**	255.255.255.0	10.1.1.251	10.1.3.201
10.1.2.0	10.1.2.1 – 10.1.2.200	255.255.255.0	10.1.2.252	10.1.3.201
10.1.3.0	10.1.3.1 – 10.1.3.150	255.255.255.0	10.1.3.253	10.1.3.201

Current Address Leases:

MAC	IP
None	None

Figure 9-25 shows the state of the DHCP process before any IP addresses are assigned. The server must be told for which subnets it should assign IP addresses, as well as the range of addresses it can assign. For example, it can assign addresses 10.1.1.1–10.1.1.200 in subnet 10.1.1.0, but by implication it cannot assign addresses 10.1.1.201–10.1.1.254. Such logic is typical, because some IP addresses in each subnet need to be reserved for static assignment. Also, note that for each subnet, the configuration includes the other three key items that each host needs to know: the mask, default gateway, and DNS IP address(es).

To obtain an IP address, the PC must act as a DHCP client. A DHCP client sends a DHCP message, called a DHCP request, asking for an appropriate IP address, plus the rest of the key details. The DHCP server replies with a DHCP Acknowledgment (DHCP ACK, sometimes called a DHCP reply), which includes the IP that should be used. Figure 9-26 shows the overall details.

Figure 9-26   DHCP Client Request and DHCP Server Acknowledgment

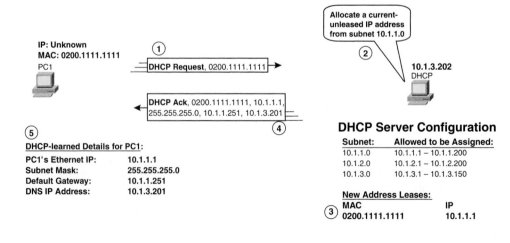

Figure 9-26 denotes the various logic steps with circled numbers, explained as follows:

1. PC1 sends a DHCP request. The request includes PC1's MAC address, which will be used to uniquely identify PC1 from other DHCP clients. The message is both an Ethernet broadcast and an IP broadcast (MAC address FFFF.FFFF.FFFF and IP address 255.255.255.255.)

2. The DHCP server receives the request and decides to allocate a currently unused address in subnet 10.1.1.0.

3. The DHCP server makes a note of the assigned IP address (10.1.1.1) and the MAC address of PC1 (0200.1111.1111) so it server does not allocate that same IP address to another host.

4. The DHCP server sends the DHCP ACK back to PC1. It includes PC1's IP address, mask, default gateway, and DNS IP address. The message is a subnet broadcast, meaning that it is forwarded to PC1's subnet, and then sent as a broadcast on PC1's subnet.

5. PC1 processes the received DHCP ACK.

An address assigned by a DHCP server is considered to be leased. The DHCP lease has an expiration period, after which the host will need to request a new IP address. Most DHCP clients simply renew their lease of the IP address before it expires. If the lease does expire, and a PC requests a new lease of an IP address, the server typically assigns the same IP address again, unless it has already been assigned to another host.

Comparing Static and DHCP Address Assignment

DHCP provides significant benefits to the average enterprise network:

- When companies move employees and their PCs, the PCs can be installed in the new offices, send a DHCP request, and be up and running—with no intervention from network support personnel.

- Laptop computers can be moved all over a network, to another company's network, to home offices, to hotel rooms, and so on, and use DHCP to obtain an IP address that works on each network as the situation dictates.

- The DHCP server can keep statistics of the usage of IP addresses, so network engineers can monitor when subnets may be getting crowded or are running out of IP addresses.

- DHCP overcomes one of the largest negatives of static configuration: when a computer is removed from a subnet, DHCP reclaims the IP address once the lease expires so that another host can use the IP address.

Using DHCP makes a lot of sense for the average end-user host, but using static IP address assignment makes sense in several other cases. For example, server IP addresses need to stay the same, so most are statically assigned. Likewise, IP addresses used by routers and switches need to stay the same, so these are typically statically assigned. Finally, environments in which end-user hosts do not move often can make good use of static IP address assignment.

Lab 9.3.5   DHCP Client Setup

The purpose of this lab is to introduce Dynamic Host Configuration Protocol (DHCP) and the process for setting up a network computer as a DHCP client to use DHCP services.

Using ARP and Proxy ARP on LANs

When hosts have been assigned IP addresses, they will likely start sending IP packets to some other hosts. For an IP host to send an IP packet over a LAN, the sending host must know the Ethernet MAC address of another device on the LAN. Hosts typically learn this vital information by using the *Address Resolution Protocol (ARP)*, which is described in the next few pages. In particular, the next short section focuses on how to use ARP on a single LAN, followed by how ARP works on larger internetworks.

Using IP ARP on a Single LAN

Figure 9-27 shows two perspectives on how PC1 makes decisions when it sends an IP packet to another host on the same LAN. The top of the figure shows the IP-centric perspective, which ignores the underlying LAN; the lower part of the figure shows the additional detail required for PC1 to forward the packet over the LAN.

Figure 9-27   Two Perspectives on Forwarding a Packet

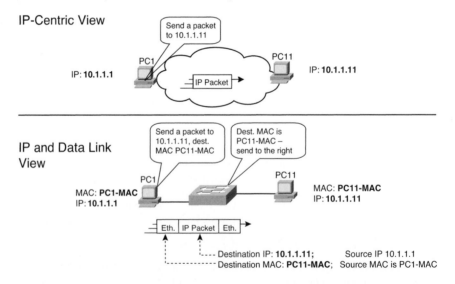

To forward the packet, PC1 must encapsulate the packet inside an Ethernet frame. The resulting frame has four addresses that must be known by PC1 and put into the headers before the whole process will work. The four addresses are the source and destination MAC addresses and the source and destination IP addresses.

As it turns out, the first time that PC1 needs to send data to PC2, PC1 knows all the addresses except the destination MAC address. PC1 knows its own MAC address because it is burned into the NIC. PC1 knows its own IP address due to configuration or DHCP. PC1 knows the destination IP address either because the human entered the IP address or, more likely, because the human entered a DNS name and PC1 has already resolved the name into an IP address. The only missing address, then, is the destination MAC address, which in this case should be PC11's MAC address.

To be able to build the frame shown at the bottom of Figure 9-27, PC1 needs to know the MAC address used by host 10.1.1.11 (PC11). Using common networking terminology, PC1 needs to map the destination IP address to its MAC address. This correlation between another host's IP address and its MAC address is generally called *mapping* information, in this case specifically mapping Layer 3 addresses to Layer 2 addresses.

The people who invented the IP protocol could have required that PC1 keep a manually entered list of possible destination IP addresses and their corresponding MAC addresses. However, no one would want to bother keeping up with such a list. Instead, a whole new network layer protocol, ARP, was created to dynamically solve this specific problem. Figure 9-28 shows the ARP process by which PC1 would learn PC11's MAC address.

Figure 9-28 Example of the ARP Process

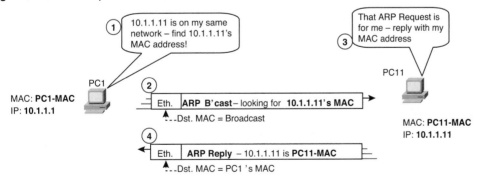

Note

Figure 9-28 does not show an IP header in the ARP messages because ARP messages do not use IP at all; ARP is considered another protocol that is part of TCP/IP's internet layer.

Steps 1 and 3 in Figure 9-28 briefly explain PC1's and PC11's logic, respectively, when using ARP. Steps 2 and 4 show the main concepts inside two typical ARP messages. The steps are as follows:

1. PC1 knows it needs to send an IP packet to PC11, whose IP address is 10.1.1.11. Because 10.1.1.11 is in the same network as PC1, PC1 decides it should try to find PC11's MAC address. To do so, it uses ARP.

2. PC1 sends an ***ARP request***, which is also called an ***ARP broadcast*** because it is sent as a LAN broadcast to MAC address FFFF.FFFF.FFFF. The ARP request acts as a question, asking the host whose IP address is in the message (10.1.1.11 in this case) to reply with its MAC address.
3. PC11, after getting the request, sees its own IP address (10.1.1.11) in the request. So, PC11 creates an ***ARP reply***, which includes PC11's IP and MAC addresses. The other hosts on the same LAN receive the ARP broadcast but do not reply.
4. PC11 sends the ARP reply as a LAN unicast to PC1's MAC address.

From this point forward, PC1 can send packets to PC11 without the need for more ARPs. Each IP host, including routers, keeps the information learned by ARP in a table called an ***ARP table*** or ARP cache. So, when a host needs to encapsulate an IP packet in an Ethernet frame, and the host needs to know the right destination MAC address, it first checks its ARP table. If the entry is still there, the device already knows the correct MAC address. If not, it needs to send an ARP request to find the MAC address.

You can view the ARP cache on any PC running a Microsoft OS by using the **arp –a** command. The **arp –d** * command empties the ARP cache, so any packets sent after that require a new ARP request to be issued. Figure 9-29 shows a screen capture of the PC **arp** command, showing an ARP cache, the clearing of the cache, a **ping** command (which in turn causes an ARP request), and the new ARP cache entry.

Note

ARP cache entries time out after a period in which no frames are sent to that MAC address.

Note

Packet Tracer supports the **arp –a** command as well, but not the **arp –d** * command.

Note

If you begin a packet capture with Ethereal or any other network analyzer, and then perform the steps shown in Figure 9-29, the capture will show the contents of the ARP broadcast and ARP reply as shown in Figure 9-28.

Figure 9-29 ARP Cache on a PC

```
C:\WINDOWS\system32\cmd.exe
C:\Documents and Settings\wodom>arp -a

Interface: 192.168.2.89 --- 0x2
  Internet Address      Physical Address      Type
  192.168.2.1           00-30-bd-c1-41-a0     dynamic
  192.168.2.71          00-00-e2-87-5f-09     dynamic

C:\Documents and Settings\wodom>arp -d *

C:\Documents and Settings\wodom>arp -a
No ARP Entries Found

C:\Documents and Settings\wodom>ping www.cisco.com

Pinging www.cisco.com [198.133.219.25] with 32 bytes of data:

Reply from 198.133.219.25: bytes=32 time=88ms TTL=117
Reply from 198.133.219.25: bytes=32 time=86ms TTL=117
Reply from 198.133.219.25: bytes=32 time=85ms TTL=117

Ping statistics for 198.133.219.25:
    Packets: Sent = 3, Received = 3, Lost = 0 (0% loss),
Approximate round trip times in milli-seconds:
    Minimum = 85ms, Maximum = 88ms, Average = 86ms
Control-C
^C
C:\Documents and Settings\wodom>arp -a

Interface: 192.168.2.89 --- 0x2
  Internet Address      Physical Address      Type
  192.168.2.1           00-30-bd-c1-41-a0     dynamic

C:\Documents and Settings\wodom>_
```

Using IP ARP in Larger Networks

To fully appreciate how ARP is used when one host wants to communicate with a host in another network or subnet, you need a little deeper knowledge of data encapsulation. Figure 9-30 shows a simple two-LAN network in which PC1 sends a packet to PC3.

Figure 9-30 IP Routing Logic, Including Data Link Perspective

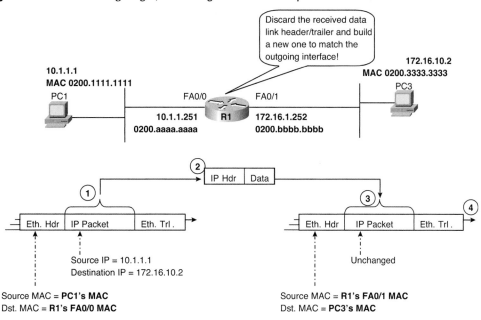

Figure 9-30 focuses on the IP packet and the Ethernet headers used on either side of the router. Referring to the circled numbers in Figure 9-30, the important details of this particular example are as follows:

1. PC1 sends an IP packet to its default gateway (R1, 10.1.1.251) by sending the packet inside an Ethernet frame. The Ethernet frame's destination MAC address is R1's MAC address.

2. R1, after receiving the frame, discards the Ethernet header and trailer, because they are no longer needed.

3. Before forwarding the IP packet out interface FA0/1, R1 encapsulates the IP packet into a new Ethernet frame. The Ethernet frame has a new Ethernet header and trailer. The new header's destination MAC is PC3's MAC address.

4. R1 forwards the Ethernet frame out interface FA0/1. The IP packet has no substantive changes to it, but it is encapsulated inside a new Ethernet header and trailer.

 Packet Tracer configuration file NA01-0930 has a topology that matches Figure 9-30. By using the simulation tool, you can watch a packet go from left to right, with the MAC and IP addresses shown at each step.

In effect, routers use the network access layer protocols—the equivalent of the OSI data link and physical layers—to deliver IP packets to the next router or host that needs to receive the packet. A close analogy is the postal service. Its job is to deliver letters to many postal addresses. To do so, it uses small and large trucks, planes, trains, boats, whatever—but the goal is to deliver letters. However, no single truck, plane, or boat takes the letter from a person's house all the way to the other person's house. Likewise a router uses whatever physical networks it has available, but its goal is to deliver IP packets. Routers use the various physical networks to move the packets to the next router or host.

Now, to see how ARP is used when PC1 wants to talk to PC3, consider the host logic used when routing a packet. That logic has two branches:

- If the destination IP address is on my same network/subnet, send the packet directly to that host.

- If the destination IP address is not on my same network/subnet, send the packet to my default router.

Figure 9-28 showed an example of the first branch in logic. PC1 sent a packet to PC11 (10.1.1.11), which was in the same IP network; to do so, PC1 sent the packet inside a frame, with the frame addressed specifically to PC11.

For the second branch in logic, needed when PC1 sends packets to PC3 (172.16.10.2), PC1 must send the packet to its default gateway. To do that, PC1 must ARP to find its default gateway's MAC address. Figure 9-31 shows just that example.

Figure 9-31   Host Logic: Sending a Packet to Another Subnet by Using a Default Gateway

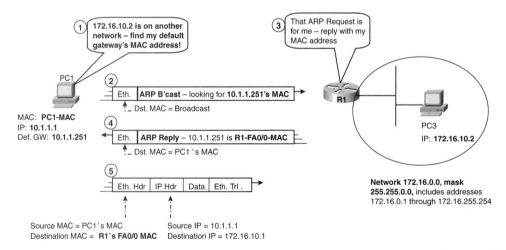

When any host computer decides to send a packet to another network or subnet, it knows that it needs help from a router. So, it sends the packet to its default gateway router, as shown in

Figure 9-31. To do that, the host must know the default gateway's MAC address, so it uses ARP to learn that MAC address.

To test the behavior described in this section, find a PC, identify one other IP address in the same subnet, and pick a website on the Internet (for instance, http://www.cisco.com). Then, use an **arp –d *** command to clear the ARP cache on the PC. After you **ping** the other host in the same subnet, entering an **arp –a** command should list that host. After you open a web browser to http://www.cisco.com or another website, entering the **arp –a** command should list the default gateway.

Lab 9.3.7   Workstation ARP

The purpose of this lab is to introduce Address Resolution Protocol (ARP) and the **arp –a** workstation command.

Proxy ARP

This final section of ARP coverage focuses on a variation of ARP called *proxy ARP*, which is no longer used very often. Proxy ARP can be used when a host has an incorrect subnet mask, which then impacts its thought process of when a host should send an ARP for a local host, and when a host should send an ARP to find the default gateway. To see what this all means, consider Figure 9-32, which shows a classic case in which proxy ARP is required. In this case, PC1 wants to send a packet to PC4, IP address 10.1.2.2.

Figure 9-32   The Need for Proxy ARP

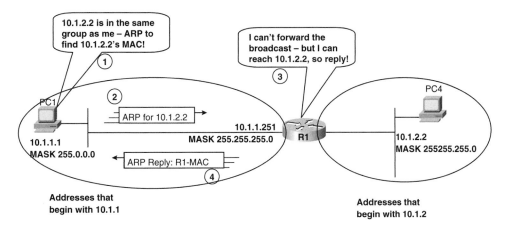

Focusing for a moment on Step 1 in Figure 9-32, PC1 has been configured with an incorrect subnet mask of 255.0.0.0 and thus mistakenly thinks that all IP addresses that begin with 10 are on its LAN. The intended configuration was probably a mask of 255.255.255.0, which would have meant that all hosts whose IP addresses begin with 10.1.1 would be on the LAN.

Note

When an ARP entry has been learned, the entry refreshes each time it is used. For example, each time PC1 in Figure 9-31 sends a packet to R1's MAC address, the ARP table entry on PC1 resets a timer to 0. So, as long as a host keeps sending frames to a MAC address listed in its ARP cache, the entry stays in the ARP cache. After a time period in which the ARP cache entry is not used, the host removes it. (The length of time is dependent on the OS, typically a few hours.) After the ARP cache entry has been removed, the host needs to send another ARP request the next time it needs to send a packet to that same IP address.

Now on to Step 2. Because of PC1's incorrect subnet mask, PC1 thinks that 10.1.2.2 should be on the same LAN. So, PC1 does not think it needs to send packets through any routers, but rather thinks that it should be able to send them directly to PC4—so PC1 sends an ARP request.

Step 3 shows why the router decides to send a proxy ARP reply, and Step 4 shows the actual proxy ARP reply. First, routers do not forward LAN broadcasts, so R1 simply cannot forward the ARP request of Step 2. R1 knows that this ARP broadcast cannot possibly reach 10.1.2.2. Beyond that, R1 has a route by which it could forward the packet to 10.1.2.2. So, router R1 sends an ARP reply—called a proxy ARP reply in this case—listing R1's MAC address in the reply. Essentially, R1 takes the place of, or acts as a proxy for, the true destination host 10.1.2.2.

At the end of this whole process, PC1 is unaware that R1 actually replied to the ARP instead of the real host, 10.1.2.2. It does not matter, because now when PC1 sends IP packets to 10.1.2.2, it sends them inside Ethernet frames addressed to R1's MAC address—the exact same thing that would have happened if PC1's mask had been configured correctly. R1 then forwards the packets correctly to PC4.

Summary

The TCP/IP reference model has four layers:

- **Application layer**—Provides services to applications, typically data presentation and general structure for making requests of the underlying network. Corresponds to OSI Layers 5, 6, and 7.

- **Transport layer**—Provides many features, including the ability to connect an application process on one computer with an application process on another computer. Corresponds to OSI Layer 4.

- **Internet layer**—Provides logical addressing and routing services. Corresponds to OSI Layer 3.

- **Network access layer**—Defines the physical medium and the access rules for using it. Corresponds to OSI Layers 1 and 2.

Routers forward IP packets based on the destination IP address in the packet header. To allow efficient routing, IP addresses must be assigned to individual computers—called hosts—based on rules that group IP addresses numerically.

IPv4 addresses are 32 bits long. They are usually written as dotted-decimal numbers, with four octets, each of which represents 8 bits. These addresses are defined by the IP protocol, which is part of the TCP/IP internetwork (OSI network) layer. There are five classes of IP addresses, A through E. Classes A, B, and C are unicast IP addresses, used to individually identify a single network interface. The class of address determines whether it has a 1-octet network part (Class A), 2-octet network part (Class B), or 3-octet network part (Class C). Class D addresses are multicast addresses, used to allow one packet to be sent, with many hosts receiving a copy of the packet. Class E addresses are reserved for research use.

IP defines the concept of a network number or network address, which is a number that represents an individual IP network. The network number has binary 0s in all host bit positions. Each IP network also has a network broadcast address, used to send packets to all hosts in a single IP network. The broadcast address for each network has all binary 1s in the host bits.

Subnetting provides a method of subdividing an IP network into smaller and more useful subsets, called subnets. Subnetted addresses include the network portion, plus a subnet field and a host field. The subnet field and the host field are created from the original host portion for the entire network. Computers know the format of these subnetted addresses based on the subnet mask, which defines which bits comprise the combined network and subnet parts, and which bits are the host part. Then, Class A, B, and C format rules identify the network part of the addresses.

The Internet requires that all IP addresses used when sending packets through the Internet be unique. These globally unique IP addresses are called public IP addresses because they are appropriate for use on the public Internet. Private networks that are not connected to the Internet may use any host addresses, as long as each host address within the private network is unique. RFC 1918 reserves several specific IP networks for use inside private internetworks, including 1 Class A, 16 Class B, and 256 Class C networks. Private addresses—addresses inside the private networks—are discarded by routers and are not routed on the Internet backbone.

A more extensible and scalable version of IP, IP version 6 (IPv6), is now available in many standard products, including Cisco routers. IPv6 uses 128-bit addresses rather than the 32-bit addresses currently used in IPv4. IPv6 will eventually replace IPv4, although the migration may take decades.

IP addresses can be assigned to hosts by using static configuration or dynamic configuration. Today, the most popular method to dynamically assign IP addresses is to use the Dynamic Host Configuration Protocol (DHCP). For some addresses, such as those used by servers or networking devices, it makes more sense to statically configure the addresses so that they never change.

To forward IP packets over a LAN, a host must know both the destination IP address and destination MAC address. Before sending a packet over a LAN, a host must encapsulate the packet in an Ethernet frame, with the frame having the destination MAC address of the next device that needs to receive the packet. TCP/IP defines the Address Resolution Protocol (ARP) to dynamically learn these MAC addresses. A variation on ARP called proxy ARP can be used to allow a host to learn the MAC address of a router on the LAN. Today, most hosts simply send ARP messages to find their default gateway's MAC address when they need to send packets to another network or subnet.

Check Your Understanding

Complete all the review questions listed here to test your understanding of the topics and concepts in this chapter. Answers are listed in Appendix A, "Answers to Check Your Understanding and Challenge Questions."

1. What transport layer protocol does TFTP use?

   A. TCP

   B. IP

   C. UDP

   D. CFTP

2. Which of the following is a basic service of the transport layer?

   A. Provides reliability by using sequence numbers and acknowledgments

   B. Segments upper-layer application data

   C. Establishes end-to-end operations

   D. All answers provided are correct.

3. Which of the following protocols operate(s) at the TCP/IP internet layer?

   A. IP

   B. ICMP

   C. ARP

   D. All answers provided are correct.

4. Which of the following is a true statement about the OSI model and TCP/IP model?

   A. TCP/IP combines the OSI presentation, transport, and session layers into its application layer.

   B. TCP/IP combines the OSI data link and physical layers into its network access layer.

   C. TCP/IP is more complex because it has more layers.

   D. When the TCP/IP transport layer uses UDP, it provides reliable delivery of packets. The transport layer in the OSI model never does.

5. How do routers use the TCP/IP internet layer forward packets from the source to the destination?

   A. By using a routing table

   B. By using ARP responses

   C. By referring to a name server

   D. All the answers provided are correct.

6. If a device does not know the MAC address of a device on an adjacent network, it sends an ARP request looking for what?

A. The default gateway's MAC address

B. The destination host's MAC address

C. The default gateway's IP address

D. The destination host's IP address

7. What are the two parts of an IP address that are not subnetted?

A. Network part and host part

B. Network part and MAC part

C. Host part and MAC part

D. MAC part and subnet mask

8. What internet layer protocol is used to map a known IP address to an unknown MAC address?

A. UDP

B. ICMP

C. ARP

D. RARP

9. Which of the following initiates an ARP request?

A. A device that can locate the destination IP address in its ARP table

B. The RARP server in response to a malfunctioning device

C. A diskless workstation that needs to learn its IP address

D. A device that cannot locate the destination MAC address in its ARP table

10. Which of the following best describes an ARP table?

A. A way to reduce network traffic by providing lists of shortcuts and routes to common destinations

B. A way to route data within networks that are divided into subnetworks

C. A protocol that performs an application layer conversion of information from one stack to another

D. A table in RAM that maps IP addresses to MAC addresses

11. Which of the following best describes an ARP reply?

A. A message sent by a device to a source in response to the source's ARP request.

B. The shortest path between the source and the destination

C. The updating of ARP tables through intercepting and reading messages traveling on the network

D. The method of finding IP addresses based on the MAC address, used primarily by RARP servers

12. Imagine a packet that passes through several routers from source computer to destination computer. The routers and hosts only use Ethernet. What happens to the destination MAC address of the Ethernet frames as they pass from one host or router to the next?

A. The destination MAC address stays the same from router to router.

B. Each router changes the destination MAC address to the MAC address of the next router in the path to the destination device.

C. The router nearest the source computer provides the MAC address of the destination computer.

D. The router nearest the source computer does a RARP to learn the destination computer's MAC address.

13. Which of the following does *not* describe the TCP/IP protocol stack?

A. It maps exactly to the OSI reference model's upper layers.

B. It supports all standard physical and data link protocols.

C. It transfers information in a sequence of packets.

D. It reassembles packets into complete messages at the receiving location.

14. How are the OSI and TCP/IP models similar?

A. Both have seven layers.

B. They have identical application layers.

C. Both have comparable transport and network layers.

D. Both use only circuit-switched technology.

15. Which of the following is not a function of the TCP/IP internet layer?

A. IP defines an addressing scheme for networks and hosts.

B. ICMP provides control and messaging capabilities.

C. ARP determines the data link layer address for known IP addresses.

D. UDP provides connectionless exchange of packets with guaranteed delivery.

16. Which of the following are protocols found at the TCP/IP transport layer?

A. TCP and IP

B. TCP and UDP

C. UDP and ARP

D. ARP and DHCP

Challenge Questions and Activities

These questions require a deeper application of the concepts covered in this chapter and are similar to the style of questions you might see on a CCNA certification exam.

1. In the process of routing, what header and/or trailer is discarded by a router?

   A. IP header

   B. IP trailer

   C. OSI Layer 2 header and trailer

   D. OSI Layer 3 header and trailer

2. What is the valid range of the first octet of Class A, B, C, D, and E network addresses, respectively?

   A. 0–127, 128–191, 192–223, 224–239, 240–255

   B. 1–126, 128–191, 192–223, 224–239, 240–255

   C. 1–127, 128–191, 192–223, 224–239, 240–255

   D. 1–128, 129–192, 193–224, 224–240, 241–256

Routing Fundamentals and Subnets

Objectives

Upon completion of this chapter, you should be able to answer the following questions:

- What are the two main functions of routers?

- What is the purpose of routed protocols, such as IP?

- What is the function of IP as a connectionless versus connection-oriented networking service?

- What are the steps of data encapsulation in an internetwork as data is routed to one or more Layer 3 devices?

- What are the fields in an IP packet header?

- What process do routers use to accomplish path selection and switching functions to transport packets through an internetwork?

- What are the differences between static and dynamic routing?

- What are the differences between distance vector and link-state routing protocols, including convergence?

- What are several common metrics used by routing protocols?

- What are some of the purposes and benefits of subnetting?

- How is a subnet mask determined?

- How is a resident network calculated through the ANDing process?

Key Terms

This chapter uses the following key terms. You can find the definitions in the Glossary.

path determination   page 393

routed protocol   page 394

routable protocol   page 394

IP routing table   page 395

Time to Live (TTL) field   page 401

Point-to-Point Protocol (PPP)   page 403

unreliable protocols   page 408

connectionless   page 408

connection-oriented   page 408

IP header   page 409

connected subnets   page 411

Routing Information Protocol (RIP) page 413, 418

convergence   page 414

metric   page 415

hop count   page 416

bandwidth   page 416

delay   page 416

Border Gateway Protocol (BGP)   page 418

Enhanced Interior Gateway Routing Protocol (EIGRP)   page 418

continues

continued

Interior Gateway Protocol (IGP)   page 418

Open Shortest Path First (OSPF)   page 418

Intermediate System-to-Intermediate System (IS-IS)   page 418

interior routing protocols   page 418

exterior routing protocol   page 418

Exterior Gateway Protocol (EGP)   page 418

autonomous system (AS)   page 418

distance vector   page 419

link state   page 419

hybrid   page 419

routing updates   page 421

periodic updates   page 421

triggered update   page 421

subnet   page 425

subnet number   page 425

subnet address   page 425

subnet mask   page 425

static-length subnet masking (SLSM)   page 427

subnet broadcast address   page 434

assignable IP address   page 434

subnet zero (zero subnet)   page 435

broadcast subnet   page 435

resident subnet   page 443

Routers have two main functions:

- Collectively, routers perform end-to-end delivery of IP packets from the sending host to the receiving host. To do so, routers receive packets, decide to which router or host to send the packets next, and forward them.

- Routers maintain a routing table with the best routes to reach each possible destination, typically through the use of dynamic routing protocols.

This chapter begins with a major section covering the two main functions of routers. The first section includes a detailed description of the forwarding (routing) process. The second section then focuses on the basics of routing protocols and how to learn the relative location of each IP network and subnet, which allows the forwarding process to send the packets via the best paths through the internetwork. Finally, because routing and IP addressing are so intricately related, the chapter closes with a discussion of the details of IP subnetting.

IP Routing (Forwarding)

Most computers send and receive data with computers that are not on the same Ethernet switch. Often, the other computer is in another building, or even in another city, state, or country. That is almost always true when surfing the Internet, for instance.

Layer 2 devices, such as LAN switches, can forward data on only Ethernet links. LAN switches cannot connect to WAN links, because those links use physical and data link standards that are different from those used by Ethernet. However, routers, by design, can connect to multiple types of physical networks. More importantly, routers understand how to forward IP packets over a large variety of physical network types. In fact, the term *internetwork* refers to how routers interconnect different physical networks into one cohesive communication infrastructure.

Collectively, routers can receive IP packets sent by computers and send the packets over any physical network, working together to deliver the packets to the correct destinations. To make it all work, routers must forward packets from one physical network to the next, collectively forwarding the packet from the source host to the destination host. This forwarding process is called IP routing or *IP forwarding*. To do so, a router examines incoming packets, looks at the destination IP address, and decides out which interface to forward the packet.

The IP routing process relies on each router knowing how to route IP packets based on its IP routing table. For routing to work well, a router's IP routing table needs to be complete, listing all possible destinations to which the router might need to forward packets. Routers use routing protocols, such as RIP and EIGRP, to dynamically learn the required IP routes. (The process of learning routes is also sometimes called **path determination**.) The second major section of this chapter, "Routing Protocols," discusses the details of how IP routing protocols work. The rest of this section focuses simply on the IP routing (forwarding) process, assuming that the routers' IP routing tables have already been filled with useful routes.

A Brief History of Some Confounding Terms

Before getting into the routing coverage, a couple of troublesome terms need to be defined. The online course refers to IP as both a ***routed protocol*** and a ***routable protocol***.

The term *routable protocol* evolved from discussions comparing protocols such as IP, which can be routed by routers, with other, similar protocols, such as NetBEUI, that cannot be routed by routers. In that case, someone might have said, "IP is routable, but NetBEUI is nonroutable." So, the terms *routable protocol* and *nonroutable protocol* were born.

The term *routed protocol* refers to the protocol that defines what is being routed, or forwarded, by a router. To appreciate this term, remember that in the 1990s, most corporate networks included products from several networking models. For instance, many networks used products that implemented the Novell NetWare model. NetWare defines a Layer 3 protocol called Internet Packet Exchange (IPX), which, similar to IP, includes a packet header and logical addressing that could be grouped for easy routing. Routers can be configured to route the packets defined by IPX. So, IPX is called a *routable protocol*, and because of that, IPX, like IP, is also called a *routed protocol*. Other routed protocols include packets from other networking models, such as AppleTalk, Vines, DECnet, and XNS.

Table 10-1 summarizes the key terms that describe routing and routing protocols, along with a brief reminder of their meaning.

Note

The terms Layer 2 forwarding—the equivalent of LAN switching—and Layer 3 forwarding—the equivalent of routing—are commonly used today because of technology called multilayer switching (MLS). MLS is covered in the Networking Academy CCNP curriculum.

Table 10-1　Routing-Related Terms and Their Meaning

Term	Meaning
Routing	The process of receiving packets, deciding where to forward them next, and forwarding them.
Forwarding/Layer 3 forwarding	Has the same meaning as *routing*.
Routed protocol	A protocol, such as IP, that defines a packet that can be forwarded by a routing process.
Routable protocol	Has the same meaning as *routed protocol*.
Routing protocol	A protocol used between routers so that they can dynamically learn routes to add to their routing tables.
Path determination	Depending on the context, it can mean the process of matching the routing table (as done during the routing of a packet), or it may refer to how a routing protocol learns and adds routes to a router's routing table.

For the duration of this chapter, IP routing will be referred to as either IP routing or IP forwarding, and the terms routed protocol, routable protocol, and path determination will not be used further.

Routing Between Two Connected LAN Subnets

As mentioned many times in Chapter 9, "TCP/IP Protocol Suite and IP Addressing," IP addressing rules exist in part to make IP routing more efficient. To begin the discussion of IP routing, a brief review of IP addressing rules, particularly the grouping of IP addresses into networks, is needed. Figure 10-1 shows an internetwork, with just enough details to explain the points.

Figure 10-1   Addresses and Interfaces Used in a Simple Two-LAN, No-WAN Network

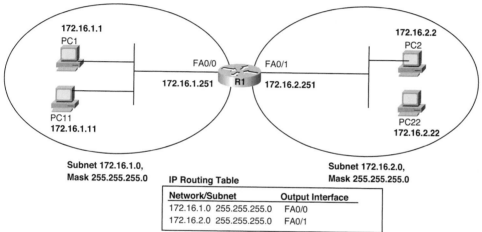

Note

All examples in this chapter use subnetting. The subnetting is simple, using a mask of 255.255.255.0 and Class B networks such as 172.16.0.0. This means that the addresses in each subnet have the same value in the first three octets.

Figure 10-1 shows two IP subnets—172.16.1.0 and 172.16.2.0—with a single router separating them. The router has an interface physically attached to each of the two LANs, with each interface having an IP address from each subnet assigned to it.

Figure 10-1 also shows the basic components of the IP routing table for router R1. The **IP routing table** holds the information on which the router bases its forwarding decision. It is similar to the concept of a road sign beside a road—when you drive, you might look for road signs and make decisions about which roads to take based on those signs. Similarly, routers find the routing table entry that matches the destination of a packet and use the forwarding instructions, such as the outgoing interface, for the matched entry in the routing table.

The IP routing table in Figure 10-1 holds two entries, one for each of the IP subnets. The grouping of IP addresses into IP networks allows the router to have just these two routing table entries, allowing many IP networks and subnets to be added to the internetwork without straining the router. Each LAN could have a few hundred hosts, but the router would need only these two routing table entries.

The IP routing process uses network layer (Layer 3) logic, but routers also use data link protocols for forwarding packets. Additionally, hosts must be involved in the routing process in addition to routers. The next three sections examine how routing works, first from a network layer perspective, and then from a data link layer perspective, and finally from a host computer's perspective.

IP-Centric Perspective

Routers perform the internal process of routing using a large number of very small steps. This section covers the most important routing steps, focusing only on the IP protocol and the forwarding of an IP packet. Figure 10-2 shows an example in which PC1 sends an IP packet to PC2.

Figure 10-2   IP Routing Logic, from IP Perspective

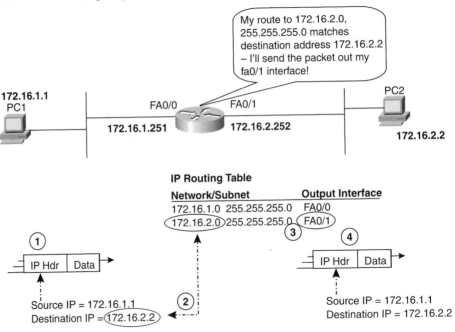

Figure 10-2 illustrates the following process:

1. PC1 sends an IP packet, with its own IP address (172.16.1.1) as the source IP address and PC2's IP address (172.16.2.2) as the destination IP address.

2. After receiving the packet, R1 compares the destination address (172.16.2.2) to the IP routing table, finding the subnet (172.16.2.0) in which the destination resides.

3. The matching entry in the IP routing table tells R1 out which interface to forward the packet.

4. R1 forwards the IP packet out interface FA0/1, with no changes to the source and destination IP address.

The process is indeed relatively simple. It needs to be simple, because routers need to forward hundreds of thousands, or even millions, of packets per second.

Network Access Layer Perspective

Figure 10-3 shows several more details of the same sample flow shown in Figure 10-2. This time, it includes the details of how the Ethernet LANs are used to deliver the IP packets.

Figure 10-3   IP Routing Logic, Including the Data Link Layer Perspective

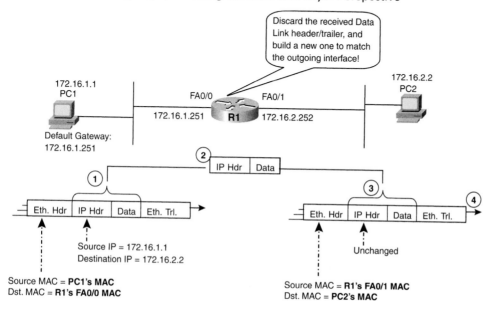

The following list explains the process shown in Figure 10-3 (the routing steps outlined in Figure 10-2 are ignored in this explanation):

1. PC1 sends an IP packet to its default gateway (R1, 172.16.1.251) by sending the packet inside an Ethernet frame. The Ethernet frame's destination MAC address is R1's MAC address on the interface attached to that same LAN (R1's FA0/0 interface's MAC address).

2. After receiving the packet, R1 discards the Ethernet header and trailer, because they are no longer needed.

3. Before forwarding the packet out interface FA0/1, R1 encapsulates the IP packet into another Ethernet frame. It has a new Ethernet header and trailer, not the old ones. This new header's destination MAC address is PC2's MAC address so that the frame is delivered to and processed by PC2.

4. R1 forwards the Ethernet frame out interface FA0/1, with no changes to the source and destination IP address, but with the new Ethernet header and trailer.

In effect, routers use the network access protocols—the equivalent of the OSI data link and physical layers—to deliver IP packets to the next destination. However, once the IP packet makes it to the next router or host, the data-link header and trailer have completed their work, so they are discarded.

The function of network access protocols is similar to the function of the postal service. When the postal service delivers a letter to the destination address, no single vehicle drives the letter from the sender's house to the recipient's house. The postal service may use small and large trucks, planes, trains, boats, or whatever to move the letter through the system. Likewise, a router uses the physical network to which it connects to deliver the packet to the next router. That next router might use a different kind of physical network to pass the packet on to the next router. This process continues until the packet is delivered to the right destination.

IP Routing: Host Perspective

The logic used by a host computer when it needs to send IP packets is important yet often overlooked. Even the examples used so far in this chapter have ignored the logic used by the host, PC1, simply starting the discussion with "PC1 sends…." This section pauses to focus on the simple but important routing logic used by typical host computers.

First, an application on the PC must need to send some data. For review, Figure 10-4, which you see frequently in the online curriculum, details the five steps of data encapsulation.

Figure 10-4   The Five Steps of Data Encapsulation

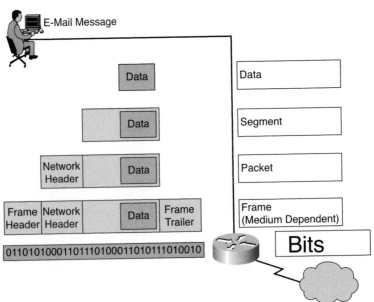

Note

In keeping with the same theme as a popular mnemonic for the OSI model layers, the mnemonic "Dozens (of) Sausage Pizzas—Full Belly" might be helpful for memorizing the five data encapsulation steps (data, segment, packet, frame, bits).

Figure 10-4 represents a few important underlying points. First, the terms listed on the right are very important, particularly *packet*, which refers to the Layer 3 header and encapsulated data, and *frame*, which refers to the data-link header and trailer and encapsulated data. Figure 10-4 also reminds us that the sending and receiving hosts process the data using all layers of the protocol model.

Next, consider that when a host needs to send a packet, it must make a small but important decision about where to send the packet, as follows:

1. If the destination IP address is on my same IP network/subnet, send the packet directly to that host.

2. If the destination IP address is not on my same IP network/subnet, send the packet to my default router.

To decide which of the two options to use, a host must be able to determine which host IP addresses are on its attached IP network or subnet. To do that, a host must examine its IP address and subnet mask using logic that is explained in the later section "Determining the Subnet in Which a Host Resides." In Figure 10-5, PC1 (172.16.1.1) wants to send a packet to PC2 (172.16.2.2) again. PC1 knows that the range of IP addresses that could exist on its local LAN is 172.16.1.1 through 172.16.1.254. (172.16.1.0 is the subnet number, and 172.16.1.255 is the subnet broadcast address, both of which are reserved.) So, PC1 sends the packet to its default gateway.

Figure 10-5   Host Routing Logic

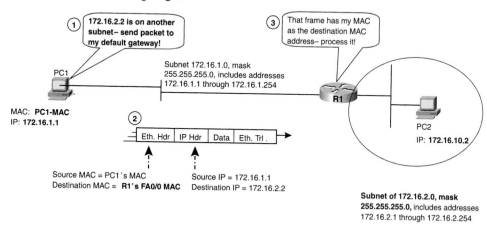

Figure 10-5 points out the process by which a host delivers a packet to a nearby router. The following list describes the process:

1. The router compares the destination address (172.16.2.2) to its connected subnet and determines that the destination is on a different subnet. So, PC1 sends the packet to its default gateway.

2. PC1 puts the IP packet in an Ethernet header, with R1's MAC address as the destination address.

3. The router processes as a received frame only if the frame is sent to the router's unicast MAC address or if it is a broadcast/multicast frame. Because the frame is addressed to R1's MAC address, R1 processes the frame.

When PC1 decides to send a packet to its default gateway, its logic includes the use of the MAC address associated with the default gateway, as learned using ARP, and as discussed in Chapter 9.

Brief Review of Routing So Far

Before getting to the last several details about IP routing, let's review the main steps of IP routing covered so far:

1. When a host decides to send a packet to another host on the same network/subnet, the sending host sends the packet directly to that other host.

2. When a host decides to send a packet to another host on a different network/subnet, the sending host sends the packet to its default gateway.

3. Regardless of which of the first two steps it uses, the sending host can use ARP to learn the correct MAC address to which to send the encapsulating Ethernet frame.

4. The router processes a received data-link frame only if the frame is addressed to the router or is a multicast/broadcast frame.

5. If a packet is sent to the router inside a data-link frame, the router discards the data-link header and trailer upon receipt of the packet.

6. The router compares the destination IP address of the packet to its IP routing table, using the matched routing table entry to tell the router how to forward the packet.

7. The router encapsulates the packet in another data-link header and trailer based on the outgoing interface.

8. The router forwards the frame out the outgoing interface.

The next section describes a few more details of the IP routing process and shows several examples with more routers and with WAN links.

A Deeper Look at Routing

This chapter has introduced some of the core concepts related to the process of routing or forwarding IP packets. This section explores that process in more depth, including coverage of several small, simple tasks and a few relatively complicated tasks.

Details of Routing in a Single Router

This section describes the rest of the steps taken by a single router when routing an IP packet. When a router receives a frame, before extracting the encapsulated packet, the router must decide if the frame experienced any errors during transmission. Ethernet, as well as other data-link protocols in use today, includes a *Frame Check Sequence (FCS)* field in the data-link trailer. Any networking device, including a router, can perform a math operation on the received frame's FCS field to determine if the frame experienced any errors. If a router determines that the frame experienced errors, the router simply discards the frame. If the frame did not experience any errors, the router attempts to route the packet.

Note

The online curriculum occasionally refers to the Ethernet FCS field as a *cyclic redundancy check (CRC).*

Before forwarding the packet, the router must decrement the *Time to Live (TTL) field* and possibly discard the packet. The TTL field is an 8-bit field in the IP header that is used to prevent packets from being forwarded indefinitely when routing loops exist. For example, two routers could have incorrect routes such that R1 sends a packet to R2, and R2 sends it right back. The packet would go back and forth forever, consuming the link's bandwidth, if not for the TTL field. Routers prevent packets from looping forever by decrementing the TTL field in each packet by 1 each time the packet is forwarded by a router. When a router decrements a packet's TTL field to 0, the router discards the packet.

The IP Header Checksum field holds an FCS-like field, but it applies only to the IP header. The value of this field is derived by applying a math function to the entire IP header. However, because routers change the TTL field each time they forward a packet, routers must recompute the IP Header Checksum field each time a packet is forwarded.

Figure 10-6 shows the detailed steps used by a router when forwarding a single packet. The specific values in the figure reflect the same familiar packet sent by PC1 (172.16.1.1) to PC2 (172.16.2.2). The following list describes the process illustrated in Figure 10-6:

1. Use the received frame's FCS field to determine if the frame had errors during transmission; if so, discard the frame.

2. Examine the incoming frame's destination (Layer 2) address; process the frame only if it was sent to this router or is a broadcast/multicast frame.

3. De-encapsulate the IP packet by discarding the frame header and trailer.

4. Decrement the IP header's TTL field by 1; if decremented to 0, discard the packet.

5. Recalculate the header checksum.

6. Make the routing decision by comparing the destination IP address in the packet with the IP routing table. If a match of the routing table is found, forward the packet based on the matched route, as detailed in the next steps. If not, discard the packet.

7. Find the destination data-link address for the new data-link header (in this case by checking the ARP cache to find the entry listing PC2's IP and MAC addresses).

8. Encapsulate the IP packet in a new data-link frame, based on the outgoing interface.

9. Send the frame out the outgoing interface.

Figure 10-6   Detailed Routing Steps in a Single Router

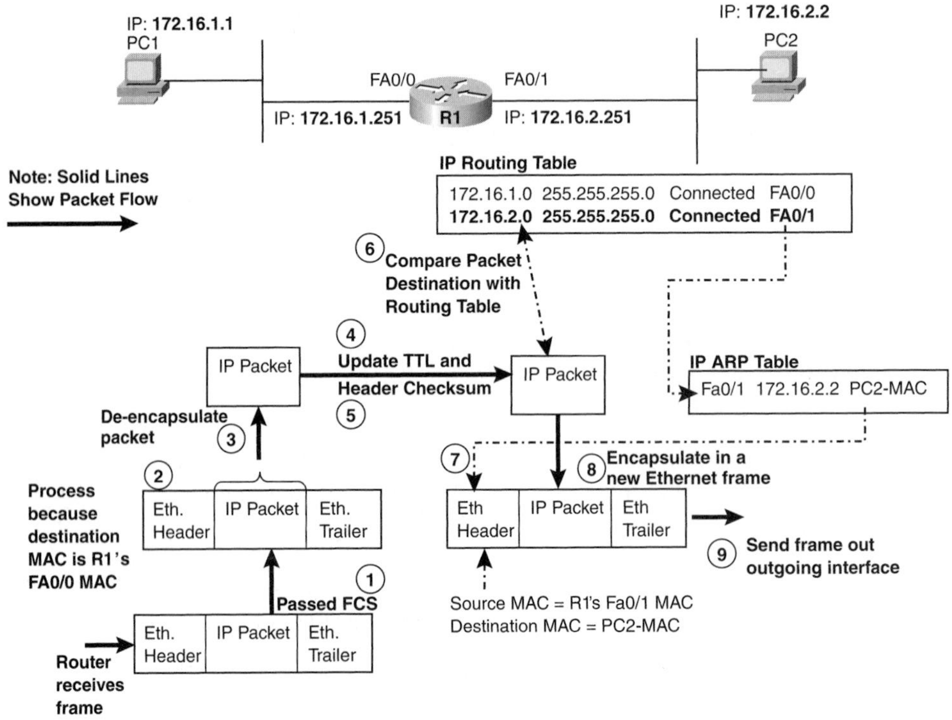

Step 6 deserves a little more explanation than what is in the preceding list. Routing tables list IP network numbers and subnets, along with the subnet mask. Routers, hosts, and even humans can look at a network/subnet and its mask and determine the range of IP addresses in that subnet or network. For example, subnet 172.16.2.0, mask 255.255.255.0, means "all hosts that begin with 172.16.2." So, a packet sent to 172.16.2.2 matches the entry shown in Figure 10-6. The section "IP Subnetting," later in the chapter, covers the many details of subnet masks and how they can be used to determine which IP addresses are in which subnet—a process used continually by routers.

The internal routing process may seem to be a lot of work when examining such a detailed example. However, router vendors such as Cisco Systems have developed many ways to improve the internal processing of these steps. As a result, inexpensive branch-office routers can perform this process tens of thousands of times per second, and core routers in the Internet can do these steps millions of times per second.

Perspectives on WAN Routing

Although the Figure 10-6 example shows all LANs, the same concept happens with WANs as well. Routers always strip old data-link headers and trailers and then add new headers and trailers, even with WAN interfaces. When using some WAN types, such as Frame Relay, routers must also have Layer 3-to-Layer 2 mapping information, similar to an ARP cache, to be able to put the correct data-link addresses in the newly created data-link headers.

Figure 10-7 shows an example of routing over a point-to-point WAN link, with PC1 sending a packet to PC3. R1's configuration shows that its S0/0/0 interface has been configured to use a data link layer protocol called *Point-to-Point Protocol (PPP)*. So, R1 adds the appropriate PPP header and trailer to the packet before forwarding it to R2.

Figure 10-7   Encapsulations Used When Routing PC1 to PC3 over a WAN

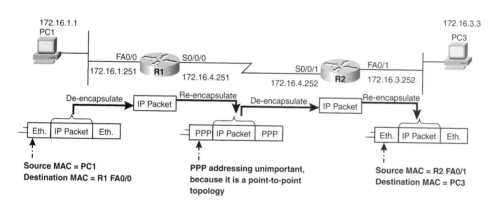

As it turns out, with point-to-point WAN topologies, there is no need for any Layer 3-to-Layer 2 mapping information. PPP and other WAN data link layer protocols are covered in the Cisco Networking Academy CCNA 4 course.

 The packet tracer configuration file NA01-1007 uses a configuration that mostly matches Figure 10-7. The simulation area shows pings of PC3 by PC1. Clicking the routers in simulation or real-time mode shows the routing tables.

IP Routing: Working with Layer 2 Protocols

Although you do not need to know the details of the underlying data-link and physical networks to understand many aspects of IP routing, you do need to know how IP uses data link layer protocols to pass IP packets to the next router or host. This section focuses on several of the issues and concepts related to IP routing and its use of Layer 2 protocols.

Importance of Layer 3-to-Layer 2 Mapping

The natural routing logic of routers calls for sending packets to either another router or, once the packet is at the last router, the destination host. As part of that process, routers always discard the incoming frame's data-link header and trailer and build new data-link headers and trailers. The new header holds information specific to the outgoing interface and a vitally important piece of information: the destination data-link address of the next device that needs to receive the IP packet.

Routers need to have Layer 3-to-Layer 2 mapping information to put the right destination data-link address into a new frame header. Figure 10-8 shows a sample internetwork that focuses on the Layer 3-to-Layer 2 address mapping, focusing on the IP ARP cache on PC1 and two routers, R1 and R2. In this figure, PC1 sends a packet to PC3, with the frames listed below the internetwork pointing out several details about the life of this packet.

Figure 10-8   Use of the ARP Cache in Routing

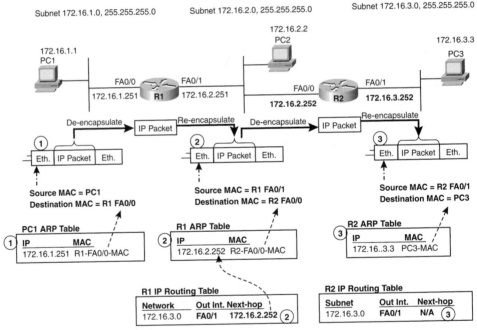

Note

The explanations in this list assume a complete ARP cache. If the PC or router were missing a needed ARP cache entry, the PC or router would use an ARP broadcast to learn the information.

The following list corresponds to the process illustrated in Figure 10-8:

1. PC1 wants to send a packet to 172.16.3.3, so the IP packet's destination IP address is 172.16.3.3. However, to get R1 to receive and process the frame, PC1 looks in its ARP cache, finds the entry matching its default gateway (172.16.1.251), and uses the listed MAC address as the destination MAC address of the frame.

2. After R1 has received the frame, de-encapsulated the packet, and decided to send it to 172.16.2.252 (R2) next, R1 must build the new Ethernet header. R1 first looks for

172.16.2.252 in its ARP cache and then uses the listed MAC address as the destination of the frame.

3. After R2 has received the frame, de-encapsulated the packet, and noted that the destination IP address (172.16.3.3) is on a directly connected network, R2 must build the new Ethernet header. Knowing that the destination is located on a directly connected network, R2 looks in its ARP cache for IP address 172.16.3.3 (PC3) and uses the listed MAC address as the destination of the frame.

Although this example shows the importance of Layer 3-to-Layer 2 address mapping on Ethernet LANs, the same kind of information is needed for other types of data links, including most every other type of LAN, and Frame Relay in the WAN.

Comparing Routing and Switching Logic

Chapters 6 through 8 focused on Ethernet LANs, with Chapter 8 covering Ethernet switching. Chapters 9 and 10 have focused on IP and routing, mostly ignoring switching. In real networks, both routers and switches work together to forward data through a network. This section provides a summary example that shows the logic on switches and routers in the same internetwork. The sample internetwork shown in Figure 10-9 uses the same topology as shown in Figure 10-8, but with the LAN switches shown. Again in this case, PC1 sends an IP packet to PC3.

Figure 10-9   Comparing Routing and Switching Logic

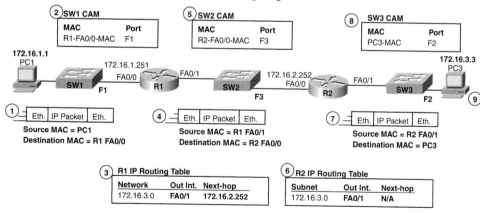

Note

In Figure 10-9, the routing tables and CAMs show only the entries required for PC1 to send packets to PC2

The following list explains the process illustrated in Figure 10-9. The explanations assume a complete ARP cache. If at any point the needed entry is not found, the PC or router uses an ARP broadcast to learn the information.

1. PC1 sends a packet to destination IP address 172.16.3.3 (PC3). PC1 uses R1's FA0/0 interface's MAC address as the destination MAC address. (This step is identical to Step 1 in the previous example.)

2. SW1 receives the frame and makes a forwarding decision based on its CAM. The decision causes SW1 to forward the frame out port F1 so that it reaches R1.

3. R1 receives the frame and, seeing its own MAC as the destination, processes the packet. R1's route to reach subnet 172.16.3.0 references next-hop address 172.16.2.252, so R1 uses its ARP cache entry for 172.16.2.252 to determine the destination MAC address to use.

4. R1 eventually builds the new data-link header and sends the frame, with R2's FA0/0 MAC address as the destination.

5. SW2 forwards the frame based on its CAM entry, out port F3, so the frame makes it to R2.

6. R2 receives the frame and, seeing its own MAC as the destination, processes the packet. R2's route to reach subnet 172.16.3.0 shows no next-hop IP address, meaning it is directly connected to R2. R2 uses its ARP cache entry for the true destination of the packet, 172.16.3.3, to determine the destination MAC address to use.

7. R2 eventually builds the new data-link header and sends the frame, with PC3's MAC address as the destination.

8. SW3 forwards the frame based on its CAM entry, out port F2, so the frame makes it to PC3.

9. PC3 receives and processes the frame.

Although the example has a lot of steps, it helps to consider Steps 2, 5, and 8 individually, because they represent the logic on the three switches. The logic is short and sweet: "Here comes a frame. Let me make a filtering/forwarding decision." The logic is concerned with only the Ethernet header. The routers, as mentioned at Steps 3, 4, 6, and 7, have more work to do. In fact, many of the routing process details shown in Figure 10-6 are omitted from the explanations.

 Packet Tracer   The packet tracer configuration file NA01-1009 uses a configuration that mostly matches Figure 10-9. The simulation area shows pings of PC2 and PC3 by PC1. Clicking the routers and switches in simulation or real-time mode shows the respective routing and switching tables, reinforcing the concept of the switching tables showing only local MAC addresses and the routing tables showing subnets of the entire internetwork.

Comparing the Benefits of Routing and Switching

The vast majority of networking devices used for forwarding data in today's enterprise networks are routers and switches. Although routers and switches provide some similar functions and benefits, some differences certainly exist; otherwise, both types of devices would not be needed. Several chapters of this book have already covered some of the differences. For example, switches provide a large number of ports for cabling each end-user computer, whereas routers do not. However, LAN switches today are mostly Ethernet-only LAN switches, with no support for other types of LANs or, more importantly, WANs—all functions provided by routers.

This section does not attempt to provide an exhaustive list of all the comparison points between routers and switches, but rather points out a few perspectives not made elsewhere in the book.

Routers create multiple LAN broadcast domains, because routers do not forward broadcasts. This one fact has many implications. LAN switches do not have any visibility beyond a router, because they do not learn any MAC addresses on the other side of a router. For example, switch SW1 in Figure 10-9 could not possibly know the MAC addresses to the right of router R1. So, switches can be thought of as local devices, forwarding frames on only one side of a router. Routers, however, can and must have visibility throughout the entire internetwork to be able to forward packets from end to end.

Routers provide the performance benefits of making broadcast domains smaller, as mentioned in Chapter 8, "Ethernet Switching." Interestingly, limiting broadcast domains also allows for greater security. Some tools used by people who attack computer networks take advantage of broadcasts, and routers naturally stop those broadcasts. Also, routers provide more sophisticated security tools than do switches; in particular, the access control lists (ACLs) used by routers are more powerful than those used by switches. (ACLs are covered in the Networking Academy CCNA 2 course.)

Table 10-2 lists some of the main comparison points between routers and switches.

Table 10-2   Comparing Routers and Switches

Feature	Router	Switch
Relative speed	Slower	Faster
OSI layer used for the forwarding decision	Layer 3	Layer 2
Type of address forwarding is based on	IP	MAC
Separates interfaces into different broadcast domains?	Yes	No
Separates interfaces into different collision domains?	Yes	Yes
Security	Stronger	Weaker

Important Characteristics of IP

Before concluding this first major section of the chapter, this section explains two important characteristics of the IP protocol: it is unreliable, and it is connectionless. Before you consider the implications of these characteristics, a quick definition of *protocol* may be helpful:

A protocol defines messages, often in the form of headers, plus the rules and processes by which these messages are used to achieve some stated purpose.

IP defines an IP header, as well as rules for sending IP headers and IP packets using routing, and rules for IP address assignment—all examples of things listed in the formal definition of protocols.

IP Is Unreliable

In the world of networking, protocols that do not attempt to recover lost data are referred to as *unreliable protocols*. This term does not mean that the protocols are bad or work poorly—the Internet works with IP as the most important protocol, for instance, and it works pretty well. In networking, the term *unreliable* means that a protocol does not attempt to perform any error recovery of data that the protocol discards. The detailed routing steps explained in the previous sections of this chapter mentioned several cases in which the router discards the packet, but they never mentioned any effort by the router to somehow recover the lost packets. So, IP is an unreliable protocol in networking terms.

Although unreliability in networking terms is not a bad characteristic, you need to realize which protocols will attempt to recover lost data, and which will not. Today, when an application wants reliability—which to networking really means error recovery by resending lost data—one of two things happens:

- The applications uses the TCP transport layer protocol, which performs error recovery. This option is more common.

- The application protocol is reliable, performing the work needed to resend lost data.

Also note that some applications do not require reliability, so they do not use TCP, and the application protocol does not bother with error recovery, either.

IP Is Connectionless

This section covers the concepts behind the terms *connectionless* and *connection-oriented*. Table 10-3 lists the key points contrasting these terms, with some explanations following.

Table 10-3   Defining Connectionless and Connection-Oriented

Term	Meaning	Examples
Connectionless	The sender and receiver do not pre-arrange for communication to occur	IP, Ethernet, UDP
Connection-oriented	The sender and receiver must pre-arrange for communication to occur—otherwise, the communication fails	TCP, Frame Relay

A few real-life analogies help define these differences. The postal system, as used by the general populace, is connectionless. To send a letter, you do not need to contact the person to whom you mail the letter—you just put his address on the letter and send it. With IP, the host sending a packet does not need to contact the destination host ahead of time.

A telephone call is connection-oriented. You cannot just pick up the phone and say "Hey, Gary" and expect your buddy Gary to start talking. You first have to pre-arrange to talk to Gary by calling his phone number, waiting for his phone to ring, and having him actually agree to talk by picking up the phone and not hanging up on you.

(The online curriculum equates the term connection-oriented with the term circuit switching. A circuit-switching protocol typically has many attributes, one of which is that it is connection-oriented. However, the terms connection-oriented and circuit switching do not mean the exact same thing. Similarly, the terms connectionless protocol and packet switching do not mean exactly the same thing.)

Full IP Header

Some of the more detailed discussion of IP routing requires a deeper knowledge of the *IP header*, which is shown in Figure 10-10.

Figure 10-10 IP Header

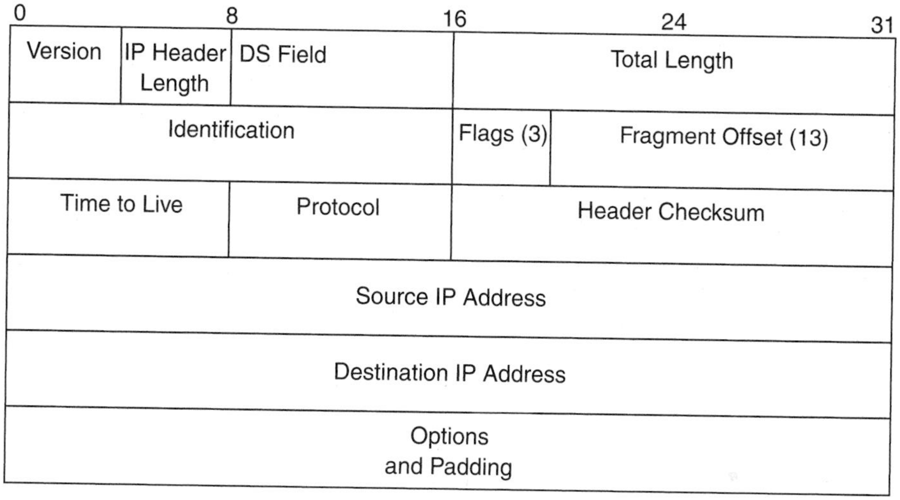

Note

For the purposes of IP routing, pay particular attention to the Time to Live (TTL) field and Header Checksum field.

Table 10-4 describes the fields inside the IP header. The table can be a bit overwhelming; it is included here for reference.

Table 10-4   IP Header Fields

Field	Meaning
Version	IP version. Most networks use IPv4 today, with IPv6 becoming more popular. The header format reflects IPv4.
Header Length	Defines the length of the IP header, including optional fields. Because the length of the IP header must always be a multiple of 4, the header length is multiplied by 4 to give the actual number of bytes.
DS Field	Differentiated Services Field. This byte was originally called the Type of Service (ToS) byte, but it was redefined by RFC 2474 as the DS Field. It is used to mark packets for the purpose of applying different quality-of-service (QoS) levels to different packets.
Total Length	Identifies the entire length of the IP packet, including the data.
Identification	Used by the IP packet fragmentation process. If a single packet is fragmented into multiple packets, all fragments of the original packet contain the same identifier for the original packet to be reassembled.
Flags	3 bits used by the IP packet fragmentation process.
Fragment Offset	A number set in a fragment of a larger packet that identifies the fragment's location in the larger original packet.
Time to Live	A value used to prevent routing loops. Routers decrement this field by 1 each time the packet is forwarded; once it decrements to 0, the packet is discarded.
Protocol	Identifies the contents of the data portion of the IP packet. For example, protocol 6 implies that a TCP header is the first thing in the IP packet data field.
Header Checksum	A value used to store an FCS value, whose purpose is to determine if any bit errors occurred in the IP header (not the data) during transmission.
Source IP Address	The 32-bit IP address of the sender of the packet.
Destination IP Address	The 32-bit IP address of the intended recipient of the packet.
Options	IP supports additional header fields for future expansion via optional headers.
Padding	If the optional headers do not use a multiple of 4 bytes, padding bytes are added, composed of all binary 0s, so that the header is a multiple of 4 bytes in length.

Other than a few references in the final major section, "IP Subnetting," this concludes the specific coverage of IP routing. However, you will continue to see routing examples throughout the rest of the chapter, because both "IP Subnetting" and the next section address concepts that work directly with IP routing.

Routing Protocols

Routers forward IP packets based on the contents of their respective routing tables. Before routers can forward packets correctly, they must somehow add the correct entries to those routing tables. This section introduces the concepts related to how routers learn routes.

The most common way for a router to learn routes is to use an IP routing protocol. When a collection of routers uses the same IP routing protocol, the routers send messages to each other. Those messages are specific to a particular routing protocol and are defined in standards documents or by a vendor. These messages include information about the available networks and subnets and information about the network topology. The routers can then process the information in the messages, called routing protocol updates, and as a result, each router can add routes to its respective IP routing tables.

This section defines how routers learn the routes in their IP routing tables, with a detailed look at the IP routing protocol features. The section concludes with a comparison of different routing protocols.

Note

The terms network and subnet can be used interchangeably for the majority of explanations in this chapter. Rather than keep repeating both terms, this section simply uses the word subnet.

How Routers Learn IP Routes

The vast majority of IP routes in an average IP router are learned via a routing protocol. However, two other popular methods for learning routes also exist. All three methods are introduced next.

Learning Connected Routes

Subnets to which a router's interfaces are connected are called *connected subnets*. Routers automatically add routes to their IP routing tables for directly connected subnets, assuming that the router has been configured correctly and the interface is working. Cisco routers simply add those connected routes to their IP routing tables.

Figure 10-11 shows a familiar sample internetwork, with the IP routing tables of R1 and R2. The routing tables contain connected IP routes only at this point.

Figure 10-11 Connected Routes Only, on R1 and R2

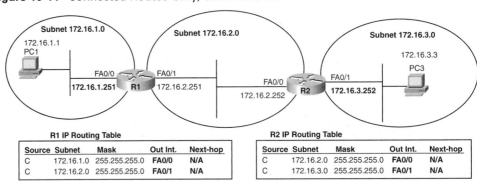

Figure 10-11 shows a conceptual view of the IP routing tables in R1 and R2. The fields in the routing table need some explanation, mainly because the focus of this section is how to add entries to this table. Keep in mind that the routers were able to learn the entries in each table only because the routers are connected to these IP networks. The following fields make up the table:

■ **Source**—This column refers to how the router learned the route—in other words, the source of the routing information. "C" is shorthand for "connected."

■ **Subnet/Mask**—These two fields together define a set of IP addresses, either an IP network or IP subnet.

■ **Out Int.**—The abbreviation for "output interface," this field tells the router that to send packets to the subnet listed in the routing table entry, it should forward the packets out this interface.

■ **Next-hop**—Short for next-hop router, this field is meaningless for routes to connected subnets. For routes in which the packet is forwarded to another router, this field lists the IP address of the router to which this router should forward the packet.

Static Routes

Routes can be added to routers' IP routing tables via the router configuration. For example, router R1 in Figure 10-11 needs a route to reach subnet 172.16.3.0, which is on the right side of the figure. R1 could be configured with the **ip route 172.16.3.0 255.255.255.0 172.16.2.252** configuration command, and the following entry would be added to R1's routing table:

    S 172.16.3.0 255.255.255.0 Fa0/1   172.16.2.252

Comparing the command from the previous paragraph with the routing table entry, three of the five details in the routing table entry were actually entered into the command. The "S" was not entered in the command; it refers to the source of this route being a static configuration command. The output interface was chosen by R1 because FA0/1 is the interface that R1 would use to send packets to neighboring router 172.16.2.252.

Basics of Learning Routes with Routing Protocols

The general idea behind routing protocols is pretty simple. Each router sends messages to the routers attached to the same subnets. The messages essentially list all the routing information each router knows. In turn, each router sends messages listing all the new routes they know. Eventually, all routers learn all the routes. It is sort of like living in a neighborhood where everyone gossips all the time—as soon as something happens, it is only a matter of time until everyone in the neighborhood knows about it.

Figure 10-12 shows an example of how a simple routing protocol called *Routing Information Protocol (RIP)* advertises and learns routes. R2 knows a connected route to 172.16.3.0, so RIP then advertises this route to R1.

Note

The static route suggested in the previous section has been deleted at this point so that RIP can instead learn the route to network 172.16.3.0.

Figure 10-12 Connected Routes on R1 and R2

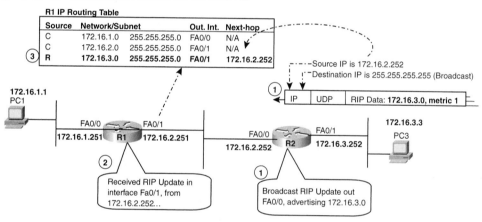

The steps in Figure 10-12 are explained in the following list:

1. R2 sends a RIP update message that includes the subnet number, 172.16.3.0. The message itself is broadcast onto the LAN so that any and all routers on the LAN can learn about this route.

2. R1 receives the broadcast and considers its contents. At this point, R1 does not have a route to network 172.16.3.0, so this must be R1's best available route, because it is R1's only available route.

3. R1 adds a route to network 172.16.3.0 to its routing table. R1 uses the interface on which it heard the RIP update as the outgoing interface of the route—namely, R1's FA0/1 interface. The underlying logic is that R1 should be able to successfully send packets to that neighboring router out the same interface in which the routing protocol message was received. Finally, R1 lists the next-hop IP address the of the router that sent the message, taken from the source IP address of the routing update.

Not all routing protocols follow the same details in how they work, but in the most basic sense, they work the same: neighboring routers tell each other about the routes they already know.

Routing Protocol Features

The TCP/IP model includes a large variety of routing protocols. Why so many? Well, TCP/IP has enjoyed a long life, so over time, some newer routing protocols were created to improve upon the old ones. In some cases, certain routing protocols were created to provide features that were not a part of other routing protocols, making them possibly better, or at least different.

Network engineers must choose the right routing protocol(s) to use in their internetworks. While this course does not get into enough detail to fully analyze the options, the following list outlines some of the general considerations used when choosing which routing protocols to use:

- **Robust metric**—Different routing protocols use different metrics. Some metrics make more realistic choices about which routes are best, considering link bandwidth and delay.

- **Router processing overhead**—Some routing protocols consume more CPU and memory than other routing protocols, with the most CPU and memory used by link-state protocols. The processing load created by routing protocols in part determines the scalability of the routing protocol.

Note

Flapping refers to an interface that fails, recovers, and repeats the process frequently.

- **Stability**—A routing protocol should be able to react to unusual situations, like protocol errors or flapping links, and keep the routing table entries as stable as possible.

- **Rapid *convergence***—Convergence is the process by which routers recognize that something has occurred that changes some routers' routes, react to the event, and find the best current routes. The time required for this to occur is called *convergence time*. Rapid convergence is one of the most important features of routing protocols.

- **Implementation effort**—Some routing protocols require more planning and work before deploying the routing protocol in larger networks, whereas others can simply be enabled with little overhead and planning.

- **Standards support**—Some routing protocols are defined in RFCs, making them open standards, and some are Cisco-proprietary, namely IGRP and EIGRP. Cisco-proprietary routing protocols require the use of Cisco routers.

The upcoming topics give a little more technical detail behind some of the items on this list. The topics include metrics, interior versus exterior routing protocols, the underlying routing protocol algorithms, and what it means to support variable-length subnet masks (VLSMs).

Using Metrics to Pick the Best Routes

Besides simply learning routes, routing protocols must be able to choose between competing alternative routes. A router can learn of multiple routes to reach the same subnet when redundancy exists in the network topology, as shown in Figure 10-13.

Figure 10-13   R1 Learns Multiple Routes for 172.16.3.0

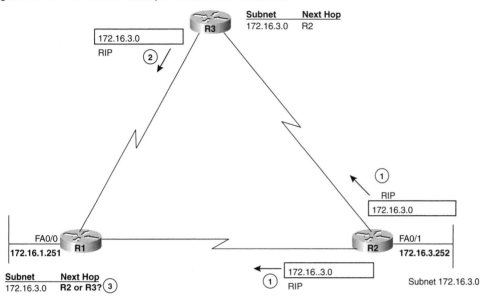

R2 advertises its route for subnet 172.16.3.0 to both R1 and R3. R3 then also advertises the route to R1, so R1 now learns a route to the same subnet, but via two paths through the internetwork.

From R1's perspective, which route is better? Routing protocols determine the best route using something called the *metric*. The root word of metric is meter, which is a generic word for some kind of measurement. A routing protocol's metric allows a router to measure how good each competing route is and then pick the best route.

RIP and the Hop Count Metric

RIP is a good routing protocol to use as an example for learning because the metric, *hop count*, is simple. The hop count metric represents how many routers sit between a router and the destination subnet. Figure 10-14 shows RIP with the metric information included.

First, follow the lower path in Figure 10-14. R2 advertises a metric 1 (one hop) route for 172.16.3.0 directly to R1. At the same time, R2 advertises a metric 1 (one hop) route to R3. R3 then advertises a route for 172.16.3.0 to R1, but before doing so, R3 adds 1 to the metric.

After R1 learns of both routes, R1 has two competing routes—a one-hop route through R2, and a two-hop route through R3. R1 then chooses the lower-metric route through R2.

Note

The RIP metric shown in the advertised RIP Updates represents the sender's metric to reach a subnet, plus 1. For example, R2's route to 172.16.3.0 is 0, because no routers separate R2 from that IP network—but R2 advertises a hop count of 1.

Figure 10-14 R1 Learning One Metric 1 and One Metric 2 Route

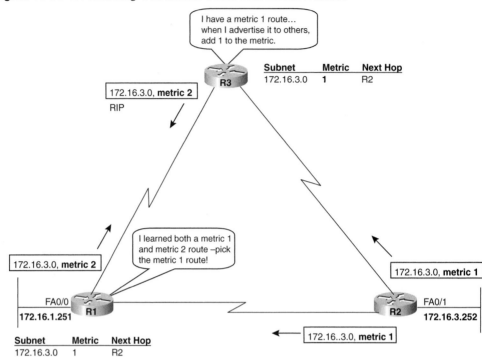

Other Metric Components

RIP's use of hop count makes it a good candidate for learning about routing protocols, but it is not a terribly good metric. For example, in Figure 10-14, suppose the lower link—the link between R1 and R2—were a relatively slow link. Using RIP, R1 would still pick the one-hop route over the slow link, which may not actually be the best path.

The Cisco-proprietary Interior Gateway Routing Protocol (IGRP) and Enhanced IGRP (EIGRP) solve this problem by using a much more robust metric. Their metric is calculated based on up to four variables:

Caution

Cisco highly recommends that both IGRP and EIGRP use only bandwidth and delay to compute their metric. Using reliability or load can cause routers to quickly change routes, possibly even every second, causing an effect called *route flapping*.

- *Bandwidth*

- *Delay*

- Link loading

- Link error rate (called reliability)

By default, both IGRP and EIGRP use only bandwidth and delay.

Figure 10-15 shows a sample network in which EIGRP chooses the longer hop-count route that is perceived to be faster.

Figure 10-15   EIGRP's Use of Constraining Bandwidth

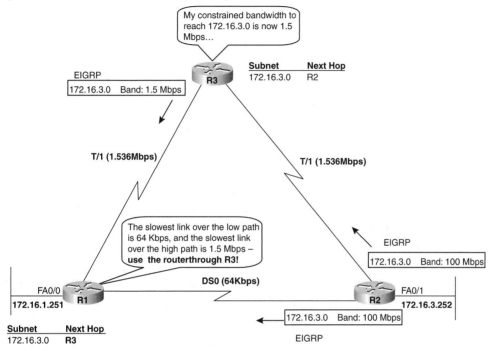

IGRP and EIGRP think of bandwidth in terms of the constraining bandwidth. In this case, the better of R1's possible routes has a slowest link of T1 (1.5 Mbps), whereas the worst route has a constraining link of 64 Kbps.

Additionally, some routing protocols may use a few other metric components. For example, OSPF uses a more generic metric concept, called cost, which refers to a cost associated with each link. Some routing protocols have used a number of clock ticks as defined on the original IBM PCs, with a clock tick being 1/18 of a second. The following list summarizes the key components of metrics covered here:

- **Hop count**—Used by RIP and others
- **Bandwidth, delay, load, reliability**—Used by IGRP and EIGRP
- **Cost**—Used by OSPF
- **Ticks (clock ticks)**—Used by Novell IPX

Finally, all the routing protocols covered so far are Interior Gateway Protocols (IGP), except the last routing protocol described in this section: **Border Gateway Protocol (BGP)**, which differs significantly from all the IGPs, as it should, given its role of exchanging routes for the entire Internet. The concepts behind IGPs, and Exterior Gateway Protocols (EGP), are explained in the next section. The current version (BGP V4) supports VLSM and CIDR, both important tools for conserving the IPv4 address space. BGP does not fit the IGP mold regarding metrics or routing algorithms; rather, by default, BGP uses a metric that counts the number of autonomous systems in each possible route, picking the lowest number of autonomous systems.

Table 10-5 summarizes the routing protocols and their metrics. Note that for all metrics, lower values mean a route is better.

Table 10-5   Routing Protocol Metrics

Routing Protocol	Metric
Routing Information Protocol (RIP)	Hop count.
Enhanced Interior Gateway Routing Protocol (EIGRP)	By default, a computation based on bandwidth and delay of the route; can also include link loading and link reliability.
Interior Gateway Routing Protocol	The same principle as EIGRP, with a slightly different computation.
Open Shortest Path First (OSPF)	Assigns a cost to each interface and uses the cumulative cost of all links in a route. Costs may be set, or they may default as an inverse function of link bandwidth (in other words, the faster the link, the lower the cost).
Intermediate System-to-Intermediate System (IS-IS)	Uses the term metric, but the metric works like OSPF's cost metric, except that no default values are assigned.
Border Gateway Protocol (BGP)	Many options, but by default, uses the number of autonomous systems.

Interior and Exterior Routing Protocols

Most IP routing protocols today are considered to be *interior routing protocols*. One routing protocol, BGP, is considered to be an *exterior routing protocol*. Oddly enough, because routers used to be called gateways, the terms *Interior Gateway Protocol (IGP)* and *Exterior Gateway Protocol (EGP)* are also used. The definitions for each are as follows:

- **IGP**—A routing protocol that was designed and intended for use inside a single *autonomous system (AS)*

- **EGP**—A routing protocol that was designed and intended for use between different autonomous systems.

These definitions use another new term: autonomous system. An AS is an internetwork under the administrative control of a single organization. For instance, an internetwork created and paid for by a single company is a single AS. An internetwork created by a single school system is a single AS. Other examples include large divisions of a state or national government, where different government agencies may be able to build their own internetworks. Each ISP is also a different AS (or, in some cases, more than one AS, for technical reasons).

In short, an AS is defined more by the bounds of the organizational chart for a business or institution. Figure 10-16 shows four different autonomous systems, each represented as a cloud. Note that the two enterprise autonomous systems each use a different IGP routing protocol inside their internetworks (EIGRP and OSPF). Between each AS, BGP, the only viable EGP routing protocol today, is used.

Figure 10-16   Comparing IGPs and EGPs

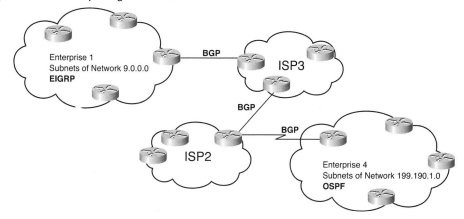

Routing Protocol Algorithms

Each routing protocol defines messages that are sent between adjacent routers to learn about routes. To decide which routes the adjacent routers can learn, each routing protocol must define rules to determine what information is included in the messages and how the routers should process the information. The part of a routing protocol that defines how a router should process the information it learns from these routing protocol messages is called a routing protocol's algorithm.

IGP routing protocols typically use either a *distance vector* algorithm, a *link-state* algorithm, or a combination of the two, called a *hybrid* algorithm. This section introduces each type.

Distance Vector Algorithms

Distance vector routing protocols have only a limited view of an internetwork. The best way to appreciate that limited view is with a diagram; the top of Figure 10-17 shows an actual network topology that uses RIP, a distance vector protocol. The bottom of the figure shows router R1's limited perspective of the topology, based on vectors. The figure focuses on R1's route to reach subnet x.

Figure 10-17   RIP's Distance Vector Perspective

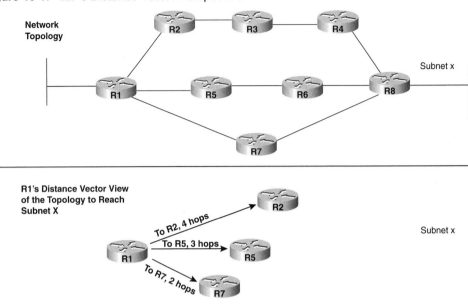

RIP learns about three routes to reach subnet x, with the metrics differing in each case. The only thing that RIP on R1 knows is that it can reach subnet x over three routes, conceptually represented in the bottom half of Figure 10-17 as vectors. The vectors' lengths in the figure represent the metric, which in RIP's case is hop count. As with all routing protocol metrics, smaller is better, so RIP would pick the route with the shortest vector—in other words, the route with the smallest metric.

Note

RIP and IGRP are IGPs that are also distance vector routing protocols.

Note that RIP has no idea about the topology of the network beyond the neighboring router to which it can forward packets. Also, the routing updates do not include information about the additional topology. The updates include only the subnet number and a metric.

Link-State Algorithms

Link-state routing protocols use quite different logic compared to distance-vector routing protocols. Link-state protocols advertise information about the entire topology. So, in Figure 10-17, R1 would have enough information to build the mathematical equivalent of the topology shown at the top of the figure. In fact, all routers exchange topology information until they all have an identical set of information about the topology, in something called a *topology database*.

For example, OSPF sends link-state advertisements (LSAs) in its routing updates. These LSAs describe each router and link in the internetwork, and they are flooded throughout the internetwork so that all routers have the same information in their topology databases. Once a router has an LSA describing each router and each subnet in the internetwork, it runs some pretty fancy math against the topology database. This math, called the Dijkstra shortest path first

(SPF) algorithm, processes the database to find all routes to reach each subnet, and then pick the "shortest" path—the path with the lowest metric.

Note

OSPF and Integrated IS-IS are IGPs that use link-state algorithms.

Hybrid Algorithms

EIGRP, which is an IGP, uses both distance-vector concepts and link-state concepts. Distance-vector protocols require less overhead and much less computation than link-state protocols, but link-state protocols have other benefits, including the ability to converge quickly when the network topology changes. EIGRP takes the best of both algorithms by providing very fast convergence in most cases without the CPU drain of running the complicated math of the SPF algorithm.

Routing Protocol Updates

Routing protocols define messages that routers send to each other to exchange routing information. These messages are generically called *routing updates*, or simply updates. The basic idea of a routing update is not too difficult to grasp. For example, in Figure 10-15, R2 was connected to subnet 172.16.3.0, so it had a directly connected route. R2 then sent a routing update to R1, so R1 could learn about a route to reach network 172.16.3.0. Routing updates differ slightly depending on the routing protocol. This section points out some of the key differences.

Some routing protocols send periodic updates, and some do not. The term *periodic update* means that once during every time period, a router sends a routing update to its neighbor. These periodic updates allow the router receiving the update to know that the sending router is still up and working. Some routing protocols do not use periodic updates, instead relying on other methods to determine whether a neighboring router is still up and working.

When sending updates, some routers send *full updates*, and some send *partial updates*. Full updates include all the routes that a router would normally advertise, even if nothing has changed, whereas partial updates include only information about changed routes. For example, if a router could advertise routes for three subnets, with a full update, it would always advertise all three routes in every routing update—even if the routes had remained up and working for the last several months. Partial updates use less overhead in the network, because partial updates include only information about changed routes.

When something occurs to change the network topology, routers may need to change their routes. So, when one router that normally sends periodic updates notices a change in topology, that router has a choice: send an update with the new information immediately, or wait until the next regular time to send an update. Routers that send the update immediately are said to be sending a *triggered update*, with the term "trigger" referring to the topology change that caused or triggered the router to send the update.

All these concepts related to how updates work will make more sense in the CCNA 2 course, when you get a chance to configure routers and see them working and watch the routing protocols work.

Classless and Classful Routing Protocols

The actual routing update messages include the network and subnet numbers that are being advertised. However, with some routing protocols, specifically RIP Version 1 and IGRP, the subnet mask is not included in the routing update.

Other than being trivia for an assessment question, you may wonder what difference it makes whether the update lists the subnet mask. Well, routing protocols that do not include the subnet mask in routing updates do not support an important subnetting feature called variable-length subnet masking (VLSM). This section describes VLSM to help you understand classless and classful routing protocol concepts. You'll learn a little more about VLSM in the "IP Subnetting" section later in this chapter. Also note that VLSM is covered in detail in the CCNA 3 course.

VLSM provides a great deal of flexibility when subnetting a single Class A, B, or C network. VLSM simply means that different subnet masks can be used on different subnets of the same Class A, B, and C network. This allows network engineers to reduce the number of wasted IP addresses, which is particularly important when using public IP network numbers.

The terms *classless routing protocol* and *classful routing protocol* also relate to the issue of VLSM support. The following two statements summarize the terms related to VLSM support while defining the terms classful and classless routing protocol:

A classful routing protocol does not send subnet masks in routing updates, so it cannot support VLSM.

A classless routing protocol does send subnet masks in routing updates, so it does support VLSM.

Note

The online curriculum refers to classful/classless routing protocols using the term *classless routing*, which instead refers to how a router uses a default route.

(Many references in networking confuse the concepts of classless/classful IP addressing, classless/classful IP routing, and classless/classful routing protocols. The previous definitions pertain to routing protocols. The Networking Academy CCNA 3 curriculum introduces classless routing, which relates to the use of the router **ip classless** command. The third variation of the terms classless/classful pertains to IP addressing and was covered briefly in Chapter 9.)

Comparing Routing Protocols

Thus far in the "Routing Protocols" section, you have learned the concepts of routing protocols and have seen specific examples of how routing protocols work. However, you have not learned many details about the individual routing protocols. This final section about routing protocols collects and compares the core concepts of each IP routing protocol.

RIP is an RFC-standard distance-vector routing protocol that uses hop count as its metric. RIP has been around a long time, starting as a Xerox-proprietary standard (part of Xerox Network Systems [XNS] Protocol) and then evolving into an IP standard in the 1980s. The original standard, later dubbed RIP Version 1 (RIP V1), converged slowly and did not support VLSM. Later, RIP Version 2 (RIP V2) was created, speeding convergence somewhat, adding VLSM support, and adding other features as well. However, RIP V2 did not change the RIP V1 limit on hop count: a valid RIP route can have at most 15 hops, with a 16-hop route being considered invalid.

Cisco introduced Interior Gateway Routing Protocol (IGRP) in part to address the deficiencies of RIP V1. IGRP was hugely successful. As a Cisco-proprietary routing protocol, IGRP's success helped Cisco gain market share in the router marketplace in the late 1980s and early 1990s. IGRP is a distance vector protocol, with its metric being calculated with a mathematical function that by default is based on bandwidth and delay.

The next routing protocol to hit the market was Open Shortest Path First (OSPF). OSPF was the first link-state protocol available to IP, solving the convergence problems of RIP and IGRP by converging very quickly, while also adding VLSM support. OSPF had the typical negatives of link-state protocols—namely, the higher overhead and the additional design work required when implementing the protocol. The metric is a generic value called cost, but by default the cost works based on bandwidth, giving lower-cost values to faster links.

Cisco later improved IGRP as a new protocol, appropriately named Enhanced IGRP (EIGRP). EIGRP changed IGRP in some significant ways, using both distance-vector concepts and link-state concepts. This resulted in EIGRP's ability to converge very fast, but without nearly as much overhead as link-state protocols. The parts of IGRP that were already well designed, such as the robust metric, remained unchanged (except for multiplying the metric formula by 4096 to allow better metrics for super-high-speed links). EIGRP almost sounds too good to be true with its low overhead, fast convergence, and little work required to plan and implement. The only real catch with EIGRP is that it is Cisco-proprietary, meaning that internetworks that use another vendor's routers as well as Cisco routers need to use another routing protocol—at least in the parts with the other vendor's routers.

BGP differs from the other routing protocols in that it is designed to exchange the large number of routes needed for routing in the Internet. As an exterior gateway protocol, BGP differs significantly from all the IGPs. Table 10-6 lists the routing protocols, summarizing some of these key points for reference.

Note

IGRP has been completely replaced by EIGRP, to the point that Cisco no longer includes IGRP in the latest Cisco IOS software releases.

Note

RIP is covered in more depth in the CCNA 2 curriculum.

Table 10-6   Comparison of Routing Protocols

Routing Protocol	Algorithm	VLSM Support?	Fast Convergence?	Metric	IGP/EGP	Standard?
RIP V1	Distance vector	No	No	Hops	IGP	Yes
IGRP	Distance vector	No	No	Bandwidth, delay	IGP	No
OSPF	Link-state	Yes	Yes	Cost	IGP	Yes
EIGRP	Hybrid	Yes	Yes	Bandwidth, delay	IGP	No
IS-IS	Link-state	Yes	Yes	Metric	IGP	Yes
RIP V2	Distance vector	Yes	No	Hops	IGP	Yes
BGP	—	Yes	—	Various	EGP	Yes

Over time, some routing protocols may go away, others might be added, and others may be improved. Today, most enterprises use either EIGRP or OSPF as their IGP. Both of these IGPs scale very well and converge very fast, especially compared to the alternatives. BGP, being both excellent and the only option, is the predominant EGP routing protocol today.

This concludes the focus on routing protocols. Next, this chapter looks at the concepts and mechanics of IP subnetting.

 Lab 10.2.9   Small Router Purchase

The purpose of this lab is to introduce the variety and prices of network components in the market. This lab looks specifically at small routers used by telecommuters when working from home.

IP Subnetting

Subnetting is one of the most important topics covered in the Networking Academy CCNA curriculum, and it may well be the most difficult. Chapter 9 introduced the concepts. This section dives into the details of subnetting. The CCNA 2 course solidifies the concepts covered here by requiring that you apply these concepts when implementing IP internetworks using routers. The CCNA 3 course goes further by introducing how to do subnetting using VLSM. In short, subnetting will be an important part of your work if you're continuing to the next several Networking Academy CCNA courses.

This section briefly recaps the concepts of subnetting and then dives into the details of subnetting with the following major topics:

- How to determine the number of subnets required for a given internetwork topology, and how to determine a subnet mask that reserves at least that many subnets

- How to find out the subnet numbers, and usable IP addresses in each subnet, when using a particular IP network and subnet mask

- Given an existing IP address and subnet mask, how to determine the subnet in which the address resides

A Brief Review of Subnetting

The act of subnetting takes a single Class A, B, or C network and breaks it into smaller subdivisions called subnets. So, to be able to look at a diagram of an internetwork and decide how many subnets are needed, you need to have some basic rules about subnets fresh in your mind:

- IP hosts on the same LAN—specifically, in the same broadcast domain—should use IP addresses in the same IP subnet.

- The two router interfaces on either end of a point-to-point leased line should use IP addresses in the same subnet.

- Hosts on different LANs that are separated by at least one router should use IP addresses in different IP subnets.

- IP addresses in an internetwork should be unique.

Besides these four rules, you need to understand the following terms before getting into the details of subnetting:

- *Subnet*—A sequential group of IP addresses that have the same value in the network and subnet parts of the addresses.

- *Subnet number*—A dotted-decimal number that represents a particular IP subnet. Also called *subnet ID* or **subnet address**.

- *Subnet mask*—A dotted-decimal number that helps identify the structure of IP addresses. The mask represents the network and subnet parts of related IP addresses with binary 1s and the host part of related IP addresses with binary 0s.

The next section tackles the first part of subnet design: picking the subnet mask based on the number of subnets needed and the number of hosts per subnet.

Determining the Number of Required Subnets and the Resulting Subnet Mask

To determine what subnet mask to use in a single Class A, B, or C network, a network engineer must come up with a subnetting plan, often called a *subnetting scheme*. The subnetting scheme defines the structure of the subnetted IP addresses in that network, the subnet mask, the list of possible subnet numbers, and the range of IP addresses that can be assigned to hosts in each subnet. To come up with these details, the engineer starts by answering the following questions:

- How many subnets are required for a particular internetwork?

- What is the largest number of hosts needed in the largest subnet?

- How many subnet bits does the subnet mask need to support (at least) that many subnets?

- How many host bits does the subnet mask need to support (at least) that many hosts per subnet?

- What subnet mask(s) support(s) the required number of subnet and host bits?

This section explains how to answer these questions, along with the binary and shortcut processes to find the valid subnet mask(s). Mastering this chapter's subnetting coverage, for most people, requires significant work. The key to success is willingness to practice. To that end, many of the remaining sections in this chapter refer to practice problems in Appendix C, "Extra Practice." For maximum benefit, stop and take the time to work the practice problems and understand the answers before you move on to the subsequent section. Also, ask your instructor for additional practice problems.

Determining the Number of Subnets and Hosts

Because hosts separated by one or more routers are in different subnets, network engineers need to decide just how many subnets are needed for a particular internetwork. The planned network topology determines the number of required subnets to some degree, with some topics outside the scope of the Networking Academy CCNA curriculum also determining the number of subnets. However, for many simple internetworks, the number of required subnets can be easily determined from network diagrams such as Figure 10-18, which shows three small internetworks, with the subnets circled.

Figure 10-18 Small Internetworks and Their Subnets

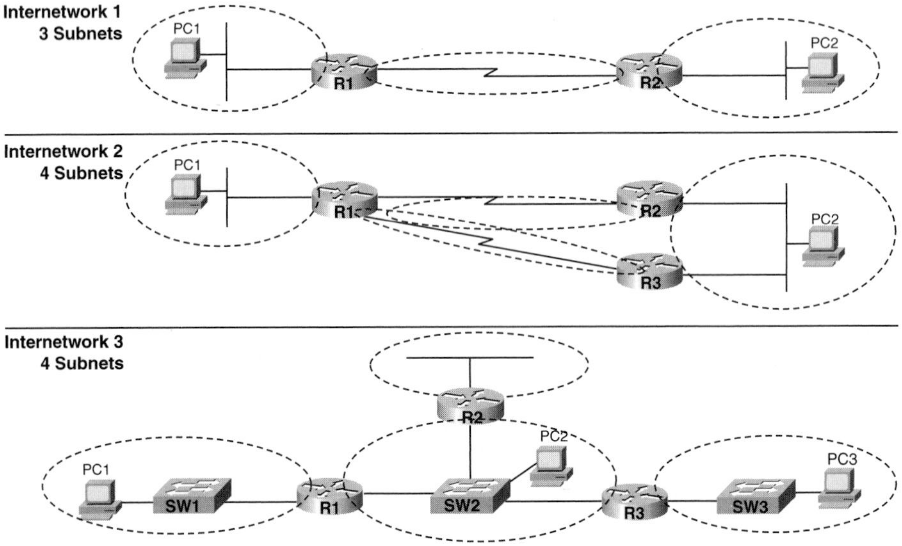

Note

The rules about the number of required subnets also apply to the number of unsubnetted IP networks required if no subnetting is used. For example, internetwork 1 could use three IP networks (unsubnetted) or three subnets of a single classful IP network.

The point of Figure 10-18 is to provide a few examples of how to look at an internetwork and determine the number of required subnets. First, examine internetwork 1 at the top of the figure. Two LAN broadcast domains exist, so, per the first rule listed in the section "A Brief Review of Subnetting," each broadcast domain requires a separate subnet. The single point-to-point WAN link also requires a separate subnet, totaling three subnets needed for the first internetwork in Figure 10-18.

The second internetwork in Figure 10-18 shows a topology that may cause you some confusion, particularly the single subnet needed for the LAN on the right. Although two routers connect to the LAN on the right, only a single subnet is needed for that LAN, because it is still a single broadcast domain. Also, remember that the definitions for subnetting state that all interfaces not separated from each other by a router are in the same subnet, so R2's and R3's interfaces, as well as PC2's NIC, are not separated from each other by a router. The left-side LAN and the two point-to-point links each require a subnet, totaling four subnets for internetwork 2.

The third internetwork shows only LANs. With LANs, each broadcast domain requires a subnet, and there are four broadcast domains.

Determining the largest number of hosts in the largest subnet takes a little more work than finding the number of required subnets. In real life, it requires a detailed knowledge of all devices that will attach to each LAN, and some ability to predict the future. Many engineers know the number of LAN-attached devices from planning the physical installation of the LAN switches and cabling plant. They then add some percentage to that for growth.

For the purposes of this book, the number of IP addresses needed in the largest subnet will be assumed. So, for the rest of this chapter, the problem statement will start with the assertion that "*x* subnets and *y* hosts are needed."

This chapter assumes the use of a single subnet mask throughout the entire subnetted Class A, B, or C network. This practice is sometimes called *static-length subnet masking (SLSM)* to contrast it with VLSM, in which the mask can be different in different parts of the same IP network. When you use SLSM, the number of hosts in the largest subnet determines how large the host field in the addresses must be. However, to take advantage of VLSM, an engineer would have to determine the number of hosts in each subnet.

Note

Appendix C has several practice problems related to this section, under the heading "Determining the Number of Required Subnets Based on a Network Diagram."

Determining the Number of Subnet and Host Bits in the Mask

The process of subnetting a Class A, B, or C IP network never changes the size of the network part of the addresses. Instead, it reduces the size of the host part to create a subnet part of the addresses. Figure 10-19 shows the concept for Class A, B, and C addresses.

Figure 10-19 Structure of Subnetted IP Networks

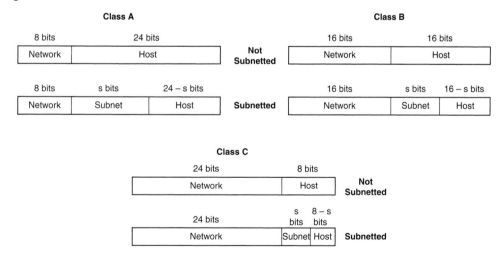

As you can see, in each case, the Network field remains at 8, 16, or 24 bits for Class A, B, and C networks, respectively. Nothing in the subnetting process changes the size of the network part of the addresses.

To create the subnet field, the host field is shortened, in a process often called borrowing bits or loaning bits. In Figure 10-19, borrowed bits, which comprise the subnet part of the address structure, are shown as being s bits long. In this book, the variable s represents the number of subnet bits, and h represents the number of host bits.

Finding the Number of Subnet and Host Bits in the Mask

To find the number of required subnet bits and host bits in the structure of a subnetted address, some simple math is required. The steps can be summarized as follows:

How To

Step 1 Find the number s such that $2^s - 2$ => the number of required subnets.

Step 2 Find the number h such that $2^h - 2$ => the number of required hosts.

Note

In the CCNA 3 course, you learn about *classless addressing*, in which the number of subnets is 2^s instead of $2^s - 2$. The formula for the number of hosts per subnet always is $2^h - 2$, even with classless addressing.

These formulas are based on a couple of key points. First, using n bits, 2^n different numbers exist, so this part of the formula defines the maximum number of hosts or subnets that can be numbered with n bits. However, with classful IP addressing (as is assumed throughout CCNA courses 1 and 2), two reserved subnets of each IP network cannot be used. Also, in each subnet, two host addresses are also reserved. So, both formulas subtract 2 at the end.

Reminder About the Powers of 2

Finding the number of subnet and host bits in the mask, once you know the required number of subnets and hosts, is an exercise in remembering the powers of 2. Table 10-7 lists the powers of 2, from 2^0 through 2^{15}.

Table 10-7   Powers of 2, 2^0 Through 2^{15}

2^0	2^1	2^2	2^3	2^4	2^5	2^6	2^7	2^8	2^9	2^{10}	2^{11}	2^{12}	2^{13}	2^{14}	2^{15}
1	2	4	8	16	32	64	128	256	512	1024	2048	4096	8192	16,384	32,768

It never makes sense to have a subnet field of 1 bit or a host field of 1 bit, because $2^1 - 2 = 0$, meaning no subnets or hosts would be reserved. As such, when subnetting, the subnet part must include at least the first 2 bits in the original unsubnetted host part, and the host part must include at least the last 2 bits of the original unsubnetted host part.

Memorizing the table is not vital, but memorizing the powers of 2 through 2^{10} is practical because you will refer to these numbers often. However, it may be practical to simply keep handy and use a short reference like Table 10-7; through repetition, you will naturally memorize the lower numbers in the list. Also, when subnetting, you may need numbers as high as 2^{22}. In those rare cases, multiplying a power of 2 by 2 gives you the next power of 2—possibly a better plan than trying to memorize all the powers of 2 up to 2^{22}.

Examples: Finding the Number of Required Subnet and Host Bits

This section explains sample problems in which you must find the number of subnet and host bits to meet a set of requirements. Table 10-8 lists the requirements for four different sample problems that will be referenced in the upcoming pages. Each problem lists the number of subnets and hosts required and the number of subnet and host bits required in each case.

Table 10-8   Four Practice Problems: Finding the Number of Subnet and Host Bits

Problem Number	Required Number of Subnets	Required Number of Hosts	Minimum Number of Subnet Bits in Mask	Minimum Number of Host Bits in Mask
1	200	200	8	8
2	5	15	3	5
3	12	3000	4	12
4	100	100	7	7

The last two columns can be determined by comparing the previous two columns' values with the powers of 2 (as in Table 10-7), remembering to subtract 2 from the values of the powers of 2. For example, in Problem 1, 126 ($2^7 - 2$) is less than 200, so 7 subnet bits is not enough; however, 254 ($2^8 - 2$) is greater than 200, so 8 subnet bits will be enough. In fact, 8 subnet bits will supply 54 subnets (254 – 200) more than the design requires.

Problem 2 shows a case that causes people a small amount of trouble when they forget the "minus 2" part of the formula. The number of required hosts per subnet is 15, so 4 host bits is not enough, because 14 ($2^4 - 2$) is less than 15. If the "minus 2" is ignored, 4 host bits would appear to be enough, because 16 (2^4) must be greater than or equal to the number of required hosts, or 15 in this case.

After you determine the minimum number of subnet and host bits in the mask, you must determine the actual subnet mask. The subnet mask will be configured, or learned with the Dynamic Host Configuration Protocol (DHCP), by the hosts and networking devices in the internetwork so that they, too, know the structure of the IP addresses. The next section covers how to find the subnet mask using binary math. The section following it also shows how to find the subnet mask, but without using any binary math.

Note

Appendix C has several practice problems related to this section, under the heading "Determining the Required Number of Subnet and Host Bits."

Determining the Subnet Mask: Binary Version

Before doing the math, it is important to understand a few very important facts about the values of subnet masks:

- A subnet mask represents the combined network and subnet parts of an address structure with binary 1s.

- A subnet mask represents the host part of an address structure with binary 0s.

Note

This process finds the mask that uses the smallest number of subnet bits to meet the requirements.

Finding the Subnet Mask with the Minimum Number of Subnet Bits

To construct the subnet mask, you just need to write down a 32-bit binary number with 1s for the network and subnet bits and 0s for the host bits. The following formalized process does just that:

Step 1 Write down 8, 16, or 24 binary 1s, depending on whether the network being subnetted is a Class A, B, or C network, respectively. These bits represent the network bits.

Step 2 Going left to right, write down an additional s binary 1s, with s being the number of subnet bits.

Step 3 Write down binary 0s for the rest of the bits; these represent the host bits.

Step 4 Convert this 32-bit binary number, 8 bits at a time, back to decimal.

Step 4 in this process represents one of the biggest problems for people new to subnetting. So, it is worth doing a few examples, with one showing the pitfall at Step 4.

Assume Class B network 128.1.0.0 is being subnetted using Problem 1 from Table 10-8, which requires 8 subnet bits and 8 host bits. The following lines show the bits of the subnet mask, recorded per Steps 1–3 in the process:

11111111 11111111	*11111111*	00000000
Step 1	Step 2	Step 3

To create the mask, the preceding number should be converted, 8 bits at a time, back to decimal. Chapter 1, "Introduction to Networking," covered the math, so it will not be repeated here. Also, Appendix B has a binary-decimal conversion chart that you can use. In this case, the mask is 255.255.255.0.

Next, consider Problem 2 in Table 10-8, in which Class C network 192.168.9.0 is being subnetted, with a need for three subnets with five host addresses each. The following lines show the bits of the subnet mask, recorded per Steps 1–3 in the process:

11111111 11111111 11111111	*111*	00000
Step 1	Step 2	Step 3

In this case, the mask has 24 binary 1s for the network part, 3 binary 1s to represent the subnet part, and 5 binary 0s to represent the host part. The tricky part is in the conversion—the conversion always uses 8 bits at a time, even when those 8 bits may contain both subnet and host bits. For example, the first three octets each convert to 255. The last octet, composed of 3 subnet bits and 5 host bits, is converted as one entity—in other words, 11100000 is converted. This subnet mask comes out to be 255.255.255.224.

Finding All Possible Subnet Masks That Meet the Requirements

The process already presented in this section enables you to find the subnet mask that has the least number of subnet bits and still meets the stated requirements. However, the requirements may allow one of multiple different subnet masks to work. For example, if a Class B network needs 7 subnet bits in its mask, and 7 host bits, three different subnet masks would work. Figure 10-20 shows details.

Figure 10-20   Options for Subnet Masks - Class B Network, Requires 7 Subnet and 7 Host Bits

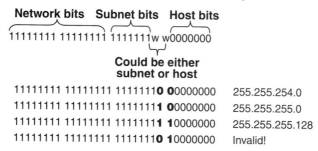

Two bits—the last one in the third octet and the first one in the fourth octet—could be used as a subnet or host bit. The reason is that the requirements state that only 7 subnet and 7 host bits are required, but there are 16 bits in which to place the subnet and host part of the mask. Figure 10-20 uses "w" (for "wildcard") to represent the 2 bits that could be either a subnet or host bit.

Figure 10-20 shows the three valid subnet masks that meet the requirements, plus one mathematical possibility that is invalid as a subnet mask. The reason that one value is invalid is explained by the following description of the requirements of a subnet mask:

> A subnet mask must begin with a number of consecutive 1s, and once a single digit is listed as binary 0 (going left-to-right), all the remaining digits must be 0s.

So, to find the possible subnet masks, write down, left-to-right, binary 1's for all network and subnet bits. Then, starting at the far right, and moving left, write down zero's for all the required host bits. Then, any remaining yet-to-be-written bits can be 0's or 1's, as long as the above requirement is met.

Table 10-9 summarizes the original four problems listed in Table 10-8, but with a particular IP network listed, and the resulting wildcard mask.

Note

Wildcard as used here is not an official term; it is just a term used by the author to explain the idea.

Table 10-9   Four Practice Problems: Subnet Masks Listed

Problem Number	Network	Number of Subnet Bits	Number of Host Bits	Mask
1	128.1.0.0	8	8	255.255.255.0
2	192.168.9.0	3	5	255.255.255.224
3	172.31.0.0	4	12	255.255.240.0
4	130.10.0.0	7	7	255.255.254.0, 255.255.255.0, or 255.255.255.128

Note

Appendix C has several practice problems related to this section, under the heading "Determining the Subnet Mask." The answers, which you can access by visiting this book's website (http://www.ciscopress.com /title/1587131641), show how to use both the binary and shortcut methods.

Determining the Subnet Mask: Shortcut Version

The binary process for finding the subnet mask works in all cases. The process shown in this section uses no binary math, but it works only in cases in which the number of subnet bits is 8 or less. (A shortcut like the one shown here can be used with longer subnet fields; the process here is kept simpler, with 8 or fewer subnet bits to ensure that the patterns used are obvious.)

The process listed here resembles the process covered in the online curriculum and uses the same underlying math. However, the shortcut process described here uses slightly different terminology. Many texts and courses use some variation on this process, and your instructor may even have her own variation that you may use in class.

Finding the Subnet Mask

The shortcut process to find the mask, given a classful network and a number of subnet bits (8 or fewer), works as follows:

Step 1 Write down the default Class A, B, or C mask (255.0.0.0, 255.255.0.0, or 255.255.255.0, respectively).

Step 2 Identify the default mask's interesting octet, which is the first octet of value 0 when reading left-to-right. (In other words, octet 2 for Class A, octet 3 for Class B, and octet 4 for Class C). This is the octet holding all the subnet bits, given the assumption of 8 or fewer subnet bits.

Step 3 Using a subnet mask shortcut table like Table 10-10, replace the interesting octet's 0 value with the correct value from the table.

The first two steps should be pretty easy to do after memorizing the default masks for each class of network. The third step is the one that requires some explaining. To do Step 3, you need a copy of Table 10-10.

Table 10-10   Subnet Mask Shortcut Chart

Powers of 2 (Increment)	128	64	32	16	8	4	2	1
Mask Value	128	192	224	240	248	252	254	255
Number of Subnet Bits	1	2	3	4	5	6	7	8

For Step 3, use Table 10-10 per this process:

a. Find the number of subnet bits, listed in the last row.

b. Use the value in the Mask Value row, right above that number of subnet bits, as the new value of the subnet mask's interesting octet.

For example, using Problem 2 from Tables 10-8 and 10-9, network 192.168.9.0 is subnetted with a need for 3 subnet bits. So, the first two steps call for writing down the default mask for Class C networks, with the interesting octet (Step 2) shown as a bold octet—octet 4 in this case:

255.255.255.*0*

The number of subnet bits is 3, so, using Table 10-10, the mask's interesting octet should be the number above it, 224. The subnet mask in this case would then be

255.255.255.*224*

(Shown in Table 10-10, a shorter version of writing the subnet mask has been developed, called prefix notation, or sometimes "slash" notation. Because subnet masks represent the number of combined network/subnet bits as binary 1s, this notation represents a mask by its number of consecutive binary 1s. For example, a mask of 255.255.255.0 would be /24.)

Finding the Mask, with Slightly Less Memorization

If you like this process, memorizing the values in Table 10-10 would be very helpful, but you do not necessarily have to memorize all of it. A popular variation on the process relieves you of having to memorize the values in the Mask Value row of Table 10-10.

For this slightly different process, you use the same subnet mask shortcut chart but leave out the Mask Value row. Instead, you use the row labeled Powers of 2. You need to memorize the powers of 2 for several other areas of the exam anyway, so using this process enables you to rely on information that you should already know at exam time. In this variation, you find the number of subnet bits listed in the Number of Subnet Bits row of Table 10-10, and then add all the powers of 2 in the Powers of 2 row, from left to right, up through the column stating the number of subnet bits. Figure 10-21 shows an example, with 3 subnet bits.

Figure 10-21 Finding the Subnet Mask Using the Powers of 2

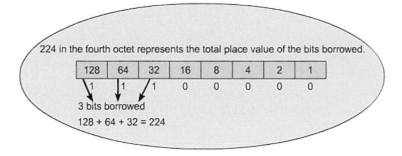

Tip

Remember, no calculators or filled-in charts or notes can be used on the assessments or the CCNA exams.

Note

Appendix C has several practice problems related to this section, under the heading "Determining the Subnet Mask." The answers show how to use both the binary and shortcut methods.

Determining the Subnet Numbers and Assignable IP Addresses in Each Subnet

So far in this section on subnetting, you have learned about the first steps that a network engineer takes when planning the installation of a new internetwork. Network engineers determine the number of required subnets from looking at the drawings and determine the maximum number of hosts in the largest subnet from other planning information. Then, the engineer picks the IP network number to be subnetted. Finally, the engineer determines a static-length subnet mask that will support at least the required number of subnets and the required number of hosts per subnet.

At this point in the progression, the engineer needs to determine the actual subnet numbers that are available with this subnetting scheme. Once the subnet numbers are identified, the engineer can make a list of the IP addresses in each subnet that can be assigned to hosts in those subnets. As mentioned in Chapter 9, some of those addresses may be statically configured, which is typical of servers, router interfaces, and end-user hosts that seldom move around. Also, the engineer will likely configure a DHCP server that assigns some of the IP addresses in each subnet.

Note

The online curriculum uses the term *major network* to refer to an unsubnetted Class A, B, or C network.

For this next major step to work, the engineer begins with a classful IP network number and a subnet mask. From that information, the engineer creates a table that lists the subnet numbers and the range of valid assignable IP addresses in each subnet. The following sections identify both the binary and shortcut processes to find that information. But first, a few details need to be reviewed.

Terminology and Background

Regardless of whether you use binary or decimal shortcuts to find the subnet numbers, you need a good grasp of several terms, including a few new terms, before diving into the math. One key term, *subnet number*, was defined earlier in this chapter in the section "A Brief Review of Subnetting." Keep in mind that some networking resources, including the online course, refer to the subnet number as a subnet identifier, or subnet ID for short.

- **Subnet number**—The numerically lowest number in a subnet, it is a dotted-decimal number that represents a particular IP subnet.

- *Subnet broadcast address*—The highest numerical value in a subnet. Packets sent to this address are routed to the destination subnet, at which point the packet is sent inside a Layer 2 broadcast frame so that all hosts in the subnet receive the frame. It is also useful for finding the range of assignable IP addresses in a subnet.

- *Assignable IP address*—An IP address that may be assigned to an interface. This term specifically excludes reserved IP addresses in a subnet, such as IP subnet numbers and subnet broadcast addresses.

- **Network broadcast address**—The numerically largest IP address in any single IP network.

- *Subnet zero (zero subnet)*—The numerically smallest subnet number in any subnetting scheme, characterized by a value of all binary 0s in the portion of the subnet number. With classful IP addressing, this subnet is one of the two reserved subnets that should not be used.

- *Broadcast subnet*—The numerically largest subnet number in any subnetting scheme, characterized by a value of all binary 1s in the subnet portion of the subnet number. Its name is derived from the fact that this subnet's broadcast address is identical to the network-wide broadcast address. With classful IP addressing, this subnet is one of the two reserved subnets that should not be used.

Defining these terms early may be helpful, but some of them make sense only in context. The next four sections point out the use of these terms in the context of finding the important details about subnetting.

Finding the Subnet Numbers—Binary

The key to understanding the binary process to find the subnet numbers revolves around these three facts that are true about all subnet numbers:

- The network part of every subnet number is identical to the network part of the IP network number that is being subnetted.

- The host part of every subnet number is all binary 0s.

- The subnet part of a subnet number varies from subnet to subnet to identify different subnets.

Seeing an example of what these rules mean can be very helpful. Figure 10-22 shows an example using Problem 1 from Tables 10-8 and 10-9, which uses Class B network 128.1.0.0 and subnet mask 255.255.255.0.

Figure 10-22   Finding Subnets in Binary—128.1.0.0, 255.255.255.0

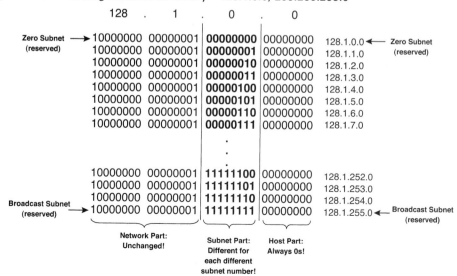

Figure 10-22 shows the binary and decimal versions of several of the possible subnets; however, because there are 256 possible subnet numbers, with two of these reserved, the figure does not show them all. The network part—the first two octets in this case—remains the same in all 256 subnets. The host bits—the last 8 bits—are always binary 0s, and the subnet part is different for each subnet.

Figure 10-22 also points out the first and most obvious example as to the meaning of the term *zero subnet*, which is also called *subnet zero*. The name zero subnet comes from the fact that the zero subnet's subnet field is all binary 0s. In Figure 10-22, the first listed subnet, 128.1.0.0 in decimal, shows eight binary 0s in the subnet field. So, it is the zero subnet.

The zero subnet is significant when working with subnetting for two main reasons:

- The decimal value of the zero subnet is identical to the classful IP network number.

- With classful IP addressing (as covered in the Networking Academy CCNA 1 and 2 courses), the zero subnet is reserved and should not be used.

Although Figure 10-22 shows a completed example, it does not show the process used to create the details. The generic process is as follows:

Step 1 Calculate 2^s, where s is the number of subnet bits.

Step 2 Write down the binary version of the classful IP network number.

Step 3 Note that the classful IP network number is the same number as the zero subnet and should not be used.

Step 4 Draw two vertical lines down the length of the page, separating the network and host parts of the 32-bit binary number.

Step 5 Copy down the network and host bits on multiple lines until you have a total of 2^s lines of binary, with all but the first one (the zero subnet) not having any bits listed in the subnet part.

Step 6 Starting with the second row, add 1 in binary to the previous subnet field. This causes each successive subnet field to have a different value. Do this through the end of the list, which should end with a subnet field of all binary 1s.

Step 7 Note that the last entry—the one with all binary 1s in the subnet field—is the broadcast subnet and is reserved.

Step 8 Convert the 32-bit numbers, an octet at a time, back to decimal to have the subnet numbers in decimal.

That is a lot of steps, but much of it is just organization to get to Steps 6 and 7, where the fun part begins. Figure 10-23 shows another example, using the details of Problem 2 in Table 10-9. In this case, Class C network 192.168.9.0 is used, with mask 255.255.255.224, which implies 3 subnet bits.

Figure 10-23 First Five Steps for Finding Subnets of 192.168.9.0, Mask 255.255.255.224

```
3 Subnet bits:                          Subnet Part:
2ˢ = 8                                   3 bits

                    Network Part: 24 bits      │ Host Part:
                                               │ 5 bits

Zero Subnet ──→  11000000 10101000 00001001 │000│00000
(reserved)       11000000 10101000 00001001 │   │00000
                 11000000 10101000 00001001 │   │00000
                 11000000 10101000 00001001 │   │00000
                 11000000 10101000 00001001 │   │00000
                 11000000 10101000 00001001 │   │00000
                 11000000 10101000 00001001 │   │00000
                 11000000 10101000 00001001 │   │00000
```

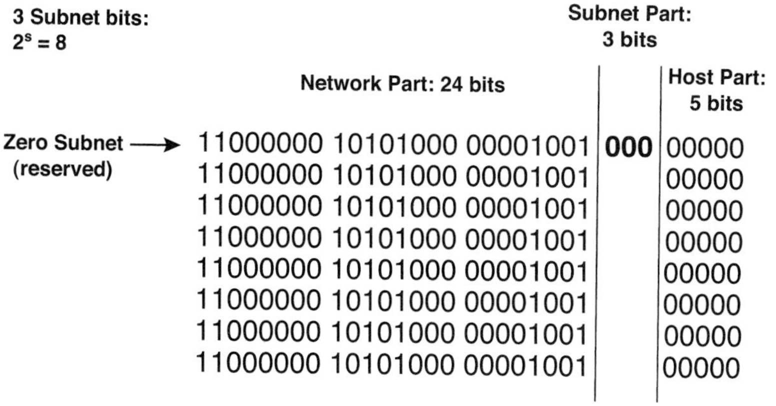

Figure 10-23 shows the completion of the first five generic steps of the binary process to find all subnets. The first line lists the binary equivalent of the network number, which is also the zero subnet. Then, vertical lines separate the network, subnet, and host parts of the subnet numbers. Remember, the problem statement suggested a need for 3 subnet bits and 5 host bits. Note that the subnet and host parts are both totally inside the fourth octet. Finally, the network and host parts were copied down for all eight numerically possible subnets.

The first time Step 6 is used, binary 1 is added to binary 000, yielding 001. The next iteration calls for adding 001 to 1, yielding 010. Figure 10-24 shows the completed addition steps, which completes the list of subnet numbers.

Figure 10-24 All Steps for Finding Subnets of 192.168.9.0, Mask 255.255.255.224

```
3 Subnet bits:                          Subnet Part:
2ˢ = 8                                   3 bits

                    Network Part: 24 bits      │ Host Part:
                                               │ 5 bits

Zero Subnet ──→  11000000 10101000 00001001 │000│00000  192.168.9.0   ←── Zero Subnet
(reserved)       11000000 10101000 00001001 │001│00000  192.168.9.32        (reserved)
                 11000000 10101000 00001001 │010│00000  192.168.9.64
                 11000000 10101000 00001001 │011│00000  192.168.9.96
                 11000000 10101000 00001001 │100│00000  192.168.9.128
                 11000000 10101000 00001001 │101│00000  192.168.9.160
                 11000000 10101000 00001001 │110│00000  192.168.9.192
Broadcast   ──→  11000000 10101000 00001001 │111│00000  192.168.9.224  ←── Broadcast
subnet                                                                      subnet
(reserved)                                                                  (reserved)
```

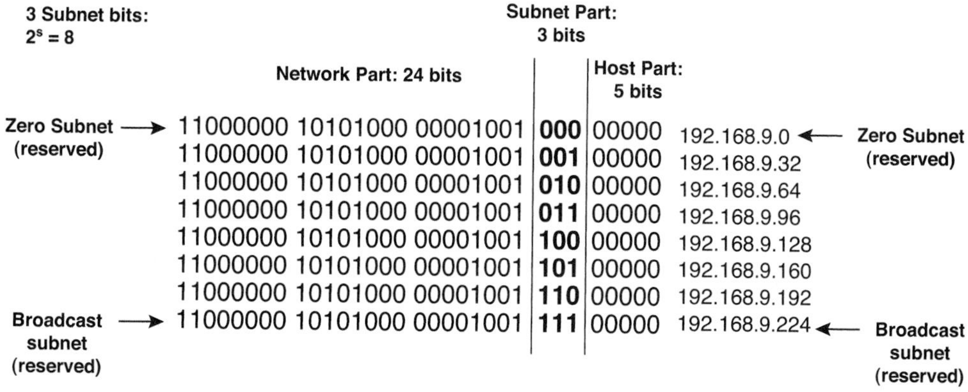

Note

Appendix C has several practice problems related to this section, under the heading "Determining the Subnet Numbers Given an IP Network and Subnet Mask." The answers show how to use both the binary and shortcut methods.

Finding the Subnet Broadcast Address: Binary

Finding the subnet numbers is a very important process as an end to itself. Finding each subnet's broadcast address is not all that important by itself, but finding these broadcast addresses is valuable in that they can be used to help find the range of valid assignable IP addresses in a subnet.

Finding the broadcast address of each subnet, using binary, is easy if you have already built the information as shown in Figure 10-24. To do so, just use the following logic:

Step 1 In each binary subnet number, change all the host bits to binary 1.

Step 2 Convert these new numbers back to decimal, 8 bits at a time (even if an octet is partly subnet and partly host).

These steps are not difficult by themselves, but to be complete, Figure 10-25 repeats the same example of Figure 10-24, with the bits changed and broadcast addresses listed.

Figure 10-25   Finding the Broadcast Addresses of Each Subnet, Network 192.168.9.0, Mask 255.255.255.224

```
11000000 10101000 00001001 |000|11111   192.168.9.31
11000000 10101000 00001001 |001|11111   192.168.9.63
11000000 10101000 00001001 |010|11111   192.168.9.95
11000000 10101000 00001001 |011|11111   192.168.9.127
11000000 10101000 00001001 |100|11111   192.168.9.159
11000000 10101000 00001001 |101|11111   192.168.9.191
11000000 10101000 00001001 |110|11111   192.168.9.223
11000000 10101000 00001001 |111|11111   192.168.9.255
```

Finding the Range of Valid Addresses

While finding the subnet numbers and broadcast addresses of a network is important, the goal may often be to discover the valid assignable IP addresses in each subnet. Once the subnet numbers and corresponding broadcast addresses are listed, finding the range of valid assignable addresses is easy—and it requires no binary math. The simple steps are as follows:

Step 1 To find the smallest of the assignable IP addresses in a subnet, add 1 to the fourth octet of the subnet number.

Step 2 To find the largest of the assignable IP addresses in a subnet, subtract 1 from the fourth octet of the subnet broadcast address.

That's it. To complete the example of 192.168.9.0, mask 255.255.255.224, Table 10-11 lists the ranges.

Table 10-11   Range of Valid Assignable IP Addresses for Problem 2

Subnet	Lowest IP Address	Highest IP Address	Broadcast Address
192.168.9.0*	192.168.9.1	192.168.9.30	192.168.9.31
192.168.9.32	192.168.9.33	192.168.9.62	192.168.9.63
192.168.9.64	192.168.9.65	192.168.9.94	192.168.9.95
192.168.9.96	192.168.9.97	192.168.9.126	192.168.9.127
192.168.9.128	192.168.9.129	192.168.9.158	192.168.9.159
192.168.9.160	192.168.9.161	192.168.9.190	192.168.9.191
192.168.9.192	192.168.9.193	192.168.9.222	192.168.9.223
192.168.9.224*	192.168.9.225	192.168.9.254	192.168.9.255

*These subnets are reserved and should not be used.

Note

Appendix C has several practice problems related to this section, under the heading "Determining the Broadcast Addresses and Ranges of Assignable Addresses." The answers show how to use both the binary and shortcut methods.

Finding Subnets and Broadcast Addresses Using Shortcuts

Learning the binary process to find subnets and broadcast addresses can result in a better understanding of the structure of IP addresses and the true meaning behind the mechanics of subnetting. However, using binary can also be maddening and time-consuming. This section shows how to find the subnets and broadcast addresses without binary math.

The shortcut hinges on a regular pattern in the actual subnet numbers and broadcast addresses. You may have seen those patterns in Table 10-11, where each successive subnet is 32 more than the previous subnet, and each successive broadcast address is also 32 more than the previous broadcast address.

Although the pattern may be obvious to see in a completed example like Table 10-11, it may not be so easy to see how to start with a network number and subnet mask and come up with the actual subnet numbers and subnet broadcast addresses. This section formalizes the process. The process requires that you gather four key facts about each such problem:

- The zero subnet number, which is always equal to the classful network number.

- The broadcast subnet's broadcast address, which is always equal to the network-wide broadcast address.

- The number of subnet bits.

- The *increment*, which is the amount by which one subnet number varies from the previous subnet number. It is equal to $2^{(8-S)}$, where *s* is the number of subnet bits.

Finding the first item, the zero subnet, is obvious. To find the network-wide broadcast address, the IP network number is used, but it is changed. For Class A addresses, the last three octets of

Note

This process assumes 8 or fewer subnet bits, as do the similar shortcut processes in the online curriculum; the process can be expanded to use wider subnet fields.

the network number are changed to 255; for Class B, the last two octets are changed to 255; and for Class C, the last octet is changed to 255. For example, with network 10.0.0.0, the network-wide broadcast address is 10.255.255.255. For 192.168.9.0, the network-wide broadcast address is 192.168.9.255. The third and fourth items in the list are relatively easy to find. The number of subnet bits can be determined as described earlier in the section "Finding the Number of Subnet and Host Bits in the Mask." The fourth item in the list, the increment, is very important, and it's easy to calculate.

Armed with these facts, a decimal process can be used to find all subnets and broadcast addresses without using any binary math. The process runs as follows:

Step 1 Create a table similar to Table 10-12, with the number of empty rows being 2^S, one row for every numerical subnet. (If that table is too big to draw, just leave some lines for the first several subnets and the last several subnets.)

Step 2 Write down the zero subnet in the first empty row's subnet column.

Step 3 Write down the network-wide broadcast address in the last row's broadcast address column.

Step 4 Decide which octet holds all the subnet bits. (Remember, this process assumes at most 8 subnet bits.) For Class A networks, this is the second octet; for Class B networks, the third octet; and for Class C networks, the fourth octet.

Step 5 To find the subnet numbers, take the previous subnet number and add the increment to the octet where the subnet bits sit.

Step 6 To find the broadcast addresses, take the later broadcast address and subtract the increment from the octet where the subnet bits sit.

Although this process may seem long and difficult, with a little practice, using this process will become second nature and allow you to find the answers relatively quickly. Table 10-12 shows an example with network 192.168.9.0, mask 255.255.255.224, completed through Step 3 of the preceding process. Note that per Step 1, Table 10-12 has 8 (2^3) mostly empty rows. Also, Step 4's results are not listed in the table, but the fourth octet is the octet that increments during this process.

From here, you can derive the subnets by taking the zero subnet and adding the increment of 32 ($2^{(8-S)} = 2^{(8-3)} = 2^5 = 32$, in this case) to the fourth octet. So, the next subnet would be 192.168.9.32, the next 192.168.9.64, and so on, until the list looks like the first column of Table 10-11.

Table 10-12   Subnetting Shortcut Table

Subnet	Lowest IP Address	Highest IP Address	Broadcast Address
192.168.9.0			
			192.168.9.255

To find the broadcast addresses, the process starts at the bottom of the table and works upward. Start with 192.168.9.255 and subtract the increment from the fourth octet, resulting in 192.168.9.223, and write it in the next row above. The next one would be 32 less again, or 192.168.9.191, and should be recorded one row higher again as well.

At the end of the process, the first and last rows will match the completed Table 10-11. At that point, the first and last IP addresses can be filled in easily, as covered in the section "Finding the Range of Valid Addresses."

It is easy to make assumptions about this process with only a single example. So, the next example uses Class B network 172.31.0.0, mask 255.255.240.0. In this example, the following facts feed into the process:

- The zero subnet is 172.31.0.0.

- The network-wide broadcast address and the broadcast subnet's broadcast address are 172.31.255.255.

- The number of subnet bits is 4.

- The increment is $2^{(8-4)}$, or 16.

- The number of rows in the table is 2^4, or 16.

- The subnet bits are in the third octet, so this is the octet that changes from subnet to subnet and broadcast address to broadcast address.

Table 10-13 shows a shortcut table, with the starting points in bold, and the filled-in portions of the subnet numbers and broadcast addresses.

Table 10-13   Subnetting Shortcut Table—172.31.0.0, Mask 255.255.240.0, Increment 16

Subnet	Lowest IP Address	Highest IP Address	Broadcast Address
172.31.0.0			172.31.15.255
172.31.16.0			172.31.31.255
172.31.32.0			172.31.47.255
172.31.48.0			172.31.63.255
172.31.64.0			172.31.79.255
172.31.80.0			172.31.95.255
172.31.96.0			172.31.111.255
172.31.112.0			172.31.127.255
172.31.128.0			172.31.143.255
172.31.144.0			172.31.159.255
172.31.160.0			172.31.175.255
172.31.176.0			172.31.191.255
172.31.192.0			172.31.207.255
172.31.208.0			172.31.223.255
172.31.224.0			172.31.239.255
172.31.240.0			**172.31.255.255**

Note

Appendix C has several practice problems related to this section, under the heading "Determining the Subnet Broadcast Addresses and Ranges of Assignable Addresses." The answers show how to use both the binary and short-cut methods.

The middle two columns are left as an exercise. To find the first assignable address, just add 1 to the subnet number's fourth octet. To find the last assignable address, just subtract 1 from the broadcast address.

(A variation on this process allows you to use addition to find the broadcast addresses. First, find the zero subnet's broadcast address by adding the increment, minus 1, to the zero subnet number's interesting octet. Then, start at the top of the chart and add the increment to the broadcast addresses to get the next-lower entry in the table.)

Determining the Subnet in Which a Host Resides

The coverage of subnetting in this chapter so far has used the perspective of an engineer designing and implementing a new internetwork. In some cases, however, you will need to look at an internetwork that has already been implemented and gain an understanding of the subnetting scheme in that internetwork.

One of the most common activities when working with an established internetwork is to figure out the subnet in which a host resides—in other words, its *resident subnet*. For example, the IP address 192.168.9.99, when using mask 255.255.255.224, is a part of subnet 192.168.9.96. Being able to determine the subnet number is important for many reasons, including the fact that IP routing tables hold lists of IP subnets and networks.

This section explains how to determine the resident subnet of an IP address.

Finding the Resident Subnet: Binary

To find the subnet number using binary math, use the following process:

Step 1 Convert the IP address and mask to binary, writing the IP address first and the subnet mask directly below it.

Step 2 Perform a bitwise Boolean AND of the two numbers.

Step 3 Convert the resulting 32-bit number, 8 bits at a time, back to decimal.

The first and last steps are basic decimal-to-binary and binary-to-decimal conversions that have been covered before. The second step requires the use of Boolean logic on two 32-bit numbers. Remember, a Boolean AND (also called a logical AND) means that 2 bits are compared. If they are both 1s, the result is 1; otherwise, the result is 0. A bitwise Boolean AND means to take two equal-length binary numbers and AND the first bit of each number, then AND the second bit of each number, then the third, and so on, for all 32 bits.

Table 10-14 shows an example in which the resident subnet of 192.168.9.99, mask 255.255.255.224, is found. Note that it is impossible to know the subnet in which an address resides without knowing both the address and the subnet mask.

Table 10-14   Using a Bitwise Boolean AND to Find the Subnet Number

	First Octet	Second Octet	Third Octet	Fourth Octet
IP Address 192.168.9.99 (Step 1)	11000000	10101000	00001001	01100011
Mask 255.255.255.224 (Step 1)	11111111	11111111	11111111	11100000
AND Result— Subnet Number (Step 2)	11000000	10101000	00001001	01100000
Decimal Subnet Number	192.168.9.96			

Just to make sure the process is clear, examine the first 3 bits of each binary number—110 in the address and 111 in the mask. The first bits of each number are 1 and 1, so the Boolean AND yields a 1. The second bit of each number is also a 1, with the AND again yielding a 1. However, the third bits are 0 and 1, yielding a 0 for the third bit of the result. The final result of the AND between all 32 bits is the resident subnet number.

Finding the Resident Subnet: Shortcut

After you have perfected finding all the subnets of a single IP network, finding the resident subnet without using binary is easy. The following process gives the steps, again starting with an IP address and subnet mask:

 Step 1 Write down the Class A, B, or C network number in which the address resides.

Step 2 Using the process defined earlier in this chapter in the section "Finding Subnets and Broadcast Addresses Using Shortcuts," discover all subnet numbers of the Class A, B, or C network, using the stated subnet mask.

Step 3 Compare the IP address to the subnet numbers, finding the subnet number that is closest to the IP address but still less than the IP address. That is the resident subnet.

For example, Table 10-11 lists the subnets of network 192.168.9.0, mask 255.255.255.224. Using 192.168.9.99, mask 255.255.255.224, as an example again, the table lists subnets 192.168.9.0, 192.168.9.32, 192.168.9.64, 192.168.9.96, 192.168.9.128, and so on. Subnets 192.168.9.96 and 192.168.9.128 are the two closest subnet numbers to 192.168.9.99, but 192.168.9.96 is the one that is less than 192.168.9.99—so 192.168.9.96 is the resident subnet number.

For one other example, consider 172.31.211.88, mask 255.255.240.0. Table 10-13 already lists all the subnet numbers. Subnets 172.31.208.0 and 172.31.224.0 are the two closest subnet numbers, with 172.31.208.0 being the one smaller than 172.31.211.88, making 172.31.208.0 the resident subnet number.

Note

Appendix C has several practice problems related to this section, under the heading "Finding the Resident Subnet." The answers show how to use both the binary and short-cut methods.

 Lab 10.3.5   Basic Subnetting

This lab exercise is broken into four parts. The first part provides a basic overview of the subnetting and the ANDing processes. The last three parts are exercises in which Class A, B, and C networks, are subnetted.

Summary

IP is both connectionless and unreliable in networking terms. *Connectionless* means that IP does not attempt to pre-arrange any details before sending data—it just sends the packets. *Unreliable* means that IP does not attempt to recover IP packets that may be discarded or lost. Application protocols can choose to perform error recovery—in other words, be reliable in networking terms—by using TCP, or by the application protocol performing the error recovery itself.

Protocols at each layer of the OSI model add control information to the data as it moves through the network. Because this information is added at the beginning and end of the data, this process is referred to as encapsulating the data. Layer 3 adds network, or logical, address information to the data, and Layer 2 adds local, or physical, address information.

Layer 3 routing uses logic by which a packet is delivered from the sending host to a router. Then, the router can deliver it to another router, and that one in turn to another, and so on, until the packet reaches a router connected to the same subnet as the destination host. The last router sends the packet to the destination host.

To send the packets, routers use a wide variety of network access layer protocols, such as Ethernet. When Ethernet is used, the hosts and routers send the IP packets inside Ethernet frames. These frames pass through Ethernet devices, such as switches, using the same rules covered in earlier chapters of this book.

Routers can know IP routes based on static configuration, based on being directly connected to a subnet, or by using routing protocols. Routing protocols learn all the routes to each subnet, choosing the best routes for the IP routing table based on the metrics of each route. These dynamic routing protocols use routing update messages to communicate with one another and maintain their routing tables. When the network topology changes, the time required before all routers have changed to use the now-best routes to each subnet is called convergence time.

Interior Gateway Protocols (IGPs) differ from Exterior Gateway Protocols (EGPs) in that IGPs work within an autonomous system, whereas EGPs work to exchange routing information between different autonomous systems. IGPs can use distance vector logic, which means that a router learns only a limited amount of topology information about a route—specifically, a metric (distance) and a next-hop router (directional vector). IGPs can also use link-state logic, which means that the router knows all routers and links, and the current state (up or down) of each link, from which the router can determine the best current routes. One routing protocol, EIGRP, uses both distance-vector and link-state logic, so it is sometimes called a hybrid routing protocol.

The 32-bit subnet mask helps define the structure of an IP address. The default subnet mask for a Class A address is 255.0.0.0. For a Class B address, the subnet mask always starts out as 255.255.0.0, and a Class C subnet mask begins as 255.255.255.0.

The process of subnetting requires the use of subnet masks that define a three-part structure of IP addresses:

- The original network address, either one, two, or three octets long, based on the IP network class rules

- The subnet address, made up of the bits borrowed, represented by the extra binary 1s in the subnet mask

- The host address, made up of the bits left after borrowing some for subnets, represented as binary 0s in the subnet mask

Routers use subnet masks to determine the subnetwork portion of an address for an incoming packet. Often, routers perform a Boolean AND, sometimes called logical ANDing, to find the subnet number. Routers need to determine the subnet number, because the IP routing table holds a list of subnet numbers, and the router needs to determine which routing table entry matches the destination of each packet.

Check Your Understanding

Complete all the review questions listed here to test your understanding of the topics and concepts in this chapter. Answers are listed in Appendix A, "Answers to Check Your Understanding and Challenge Questions."

1. How many bits are in an IPv4 address?

   A. 16

   B. 32

   C. 64

   D. 128

2. What is the maximum decimal value of each octet in an IPv4 address?

   A. 32

   B. 255

   C. 256

   D. 128

3. What does the network part of an IP address specify?

   A. The network to which the host belongs

   B. The identity of the computer on the network

   C. Which node on the subnetwork is being addressed

   D. Which networks the device can communicate with

4. What does the host number designate in an IP address?

   A. The identity of the computer on the network

   B. Which node on the subnetwork is being addressed

   C. The network to which the host belongs

   D. Which hosts the device can communicate with

5. What is the resident subnet of host 192.168.73.121, given a subnet mask of 255.255.255.224?

   A. 192.168.0.0

   B. 192.168.73.32

   C. 192.168.0.96

   D. 192.168.73.96

6. What is the result of converting the decimal number 192.5.34.11 to its binary form?

    A. 11000000.00000101.00100010.00001011

    B. 11000101.01010111.00011000.10111000

    C. 01001011.10010011.00111001.00110111

    D. 11000000.00001010.01000010.00001011

7. What is the result of converting the binary IP address 11000000.00000101.00100010.00001011 to its decimal form?

    A. 190.4.34.11

    B. 192.4.34.10

    C. 192.4.32.11

    D. None of the above

8. What portion of the Class B address 154.19.2.7 is the network port?

    A. 154

    B. 154.19

    C. 154.19.2

    D. 154.19.2.7

9. What portion of the IP address 129.219.51.18 represents the network?

    A. 129.219

    B. 129

    C. 14.1

    D. 1

10. Which of the following addresses is an example of a broadcast address on subnet 123.10.0.0 with a subnet mask of 255.255.0.0?

    A. 123.255.255.255

    B. 123.10.255.255

    C. 123.13.0.0

    D. 123.1.1.1

11. How many host addresses can be used in a Class C network?

    A. 253

    B. 254

    C. 255

    D. 256

12. What is the minimum number of bits that can be borrowed to form a subnet?

A. 1

B. 2

C. 3

D. 4

13. How many bits are in a subnet mask?

A. 16

B. 32

C. 64

D. 128

14. Performing the Boolean AND function as a router would on the IP addresses 121.8.2.5 and 255.0.0.0, what is the network/subnetwork address?

A. 121.8.1.0

B. 121.8.0.0

C. 121.8.2.0

D. 121.0.0.0

15. With a Class C address of 197.15.22.33 and a subnet mask of 255.255.255.224, how many bits have been borrowed to create a subnet?

A. 1

B. 2

C. 3

D. 4

16. Performing the Boolean AND function as a router would on the IP addresses 172.16.2.120 and 255.255.255.0, what is the subnet address?

A. 172.0.0.0

B. 172.16.0.0

C. 172.16.2.0

D. 172.16.255.0

17. Which of the following best describes one function of Layer 3, the network layer, in the OSI model?

A. It is responsible for reliable network communication between nodes.

B. It is concerned with physical addressing and network topology.

C. It determines which is the best path for traffic to take through the network.

D. It manages data exchange between presentation layer entities.

18. What function allows routers to evaluate available routes to a destination and to establish the preferred direction in which to forward a packet?

   A. Data linkage

   B. Path determination

   C. SDLC interface protocol

   D. Frame Relay

19. How does the network layer forward packets from the source to the destination?

   A. By using an IP routing table

   B. By using ARP responses

   C. By referring to a name server

   D. By referring to the bridge

Challenge Questions and Activities

The questions and activities in this section require a deeper application of the concepts covered in this chapter. The questions listed here are similar in both difficulty and style to what you might see on a CCNA certification exam, whereas the activities are similar to the exams only in that they require applying detailed concepts to a particular scenario.

Use Figure 10-26 to answer Question 1 that follows.

Figure 10-26 Topology for Challenge Question 1

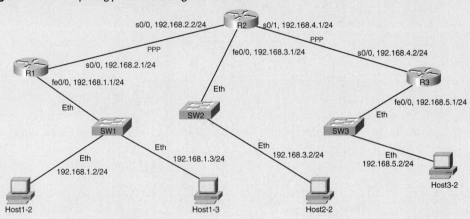

Table 10-15 shows the configuration of three host computers in Figure 10-26. Use the information from this table and Figure 10-26 to troubleshoot.

Table 10-15 Challenge Question 1 Host Settings

	Host1-2 Configuration	Host1-3 Configuration	Host2-2 Configuration
IP Address	192.168.1.2	192.168.1.3	192.168.3.2
Subnet Mask	255.255.255.0	255.255.255.0	255.255.255.0
Default Gateway	192.168.3.1	192.168.1.1	192.168.3.1

1. Host2-2 can ping Host3-2. Host1-2 can ping Host1-3 but cannot ping Host3-2. Why can't Host1-2 successfully ping Host3-2?

   A. Host3-2 is on a different subnet.

   B. Host1-3 has the incorrect default gateway configured.

   C. Host1-2 has the incorrect default gateway configured.

   D. Host3-2 has the incorrect default gateway configured.

Use Figure 10-27 to answer Question 2.

Figure 10-27 Topology for Challenge Question 2

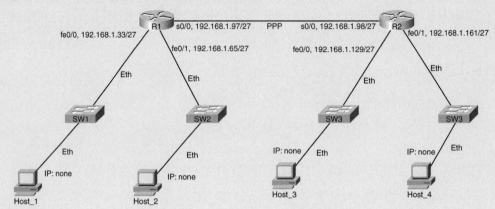

Table 10-16 shows the configuration of three host computers in Figure 10-27. Use the information from this table and Figure 10-27 to troubleshoot.

Table 10-16   Challenge Question 2 Host Settings

	Host_1 Configuration	Host_3 Configuration	Host_4 Configuration
IP Address	192.168.1.35	192.168.1.130	192.168.1.194
Subnet Mask	255.255.255.224	255.255.255.224	255.255.255.224
Default Gateway	192.168.1.33	192.168.1.129	192.168.1.161

2. Host_4 cannot ping Host_1. Why?

A. Host_4 has the wrong default gateway configured.

B. Host_4 has a host address that is out of range for the subnet.

C. The link between R1 and R2 has addresses from the same subnet.

D. Host_1 has the wrong subnet mask.

 If you have not yet done so, you may want to load the enterprise-broken-1 Packet Tracer configuration mentioned back in Chapter 1. This Packet Tracer configuration shows a sample internetwork with some problems. Chapter 1 suggested that the problems may be too difficult after just covering the first chapter, but you should now have the skills to find and fix the problems with that configuration.

CHAPTER 11

TCP/IP Transport and Application Layers

Objectives

Upon completion of this chapter, you should be able to answer the following questions:

- What are some functions of the TCP/IP transport layer?

- How does flow control affect data transmission?

- What are some of the processes of establishing a connection between peer systems?

- How does windowing affect data transmission?

- How does acknowledgment affect data transmission?

- What are the TCP/IP transport layer protocols, and what purpose do they serve?

- What TCP protocols are often used for network management purposes?

- What is the format of the TCP and UDP headers?

- What are TCP and UDP port numbers, and how are they used?

- What are the TCP and UDP well-known port numbers?

- What TCP protocols are often used for network management purposes?

Key Terms

This chapter uses the following key terms. You can find the definitions in the Glossary:

Transmission Control Protocol (TCP)   page 455

User Datagram Protocol (UDP)   page 455

flow control   page 456

window   page 456

three-way handshake   page 458

SYN   page 458

ACK   page 458

forward acknowledgment   page 460

expectational acknowledgment   page 460

segmentation   page 461

in-order delivery   page 461

Source Port   page 463

Destination Port   page 463

Sequence Number   page 463

Acknowledgment Number   page 463

Header Length   page 463

Reserved   page 463

Flags   page 463

Window   page 463

Checksum   page 463

Urgent   page 463

Options and Padding   page 463

continues

continued

Data   page 463

Length   page 464

port numbers   page 464

destination port number   page 465

dynamic port numbers   page 465

well-known ports   page 465

registered port numbers   page 467

Domain Name System (DNS)   page 469

Hypertext Transfer Protocol (HTTP)   page 469

Simple Mail Transfer Protocol (SMTP)   page 469

Post Office Protocol version 3 (POP3)   page 469

File Transfer Protocol (FTP)   page 469

hostname   page 470

domain name   page 470

top-level domain   page 470

GET request   page 471

hyperlink   page 472

SMTP server   page 473

SMTP client   page 473

Trivial File Transfer Protocol (TFTP)   page 475

Simple Network Management Protocol (SNMP)   page 475

Telnet   page 475

Network Management System (NMS)   page 476

SNMP agent   page 476

This chapter continues the discussion of TCP/IP by delving deeper into several TCP/IP protocols. The first major section explains the functions of the two popular TCP/IP transport layer protocols: TCP and UDP. The second major section covers a wide range of application layer protocols.

The TCP/IP Transport Layer

The TCP/IP transport layer includes several protocols, most notably the *Transmission Control Protocol (TCP)* and *User Datagram Protocol (UDP)*. Although both protocols provide services to applications, TCP provides several more functions. However, those extra functions come at a price—specifically, more header overhead—and TCP's features might slow down the rate of data transfer. You can think of TCP as a luxury car and UDP as an economy car. Both types get you where you need to go, but the luxury car has cooler features and is more comfortable. However, it comes with a higher price tag. Similarly, TCP provides many great features, but it requires more overhead than UDP.

Note

The name TCP/IP is created by combining the names of the two most popular protocols: TCP and IP.

Although TCP in particular provides a wide variety of functions, the main goal of the transport layer can be summarized as follows:

> To provide the service of taking data from one application process on one computer and delivering that data to the correct application process on another computer.

Contrasting the transport and internet layers, the internet layer delivers data (packets) from one computer to another, but it does not think about which application sent the data or which application on the receiving computer needs the data. For example, if you have five web-browser windows open, the internet layer delivers the data to the computer, but the transport layer works to ensure that each browser gets the data destined for it and not one of the others.

Table 11-1 lists the most important features of TCP and UDP, and it notes which features are supported by each transport layer protocol.

Table 11-1   Comparing TCP and UDP

Transport Layer Feature	TCP	UDP
Flow control and windowing	Yes	No
Connection-oriented	Yes	No
Error recovery	Yes	No
Segmentation and reassembly of data	Yes	No
In-order delivery of data	Yes	No
Identifying applications using port numbers	Yes	Yes

This section covers the topics shown in Table 11-1, as well as including a reference to the contents of the TCP and UDP headers. Note that all the topics in this section apply only to TCP, except for the final topic which applies to both TCP and UDP.

Flow Control and Windowing

When a host sends data using TCP, the receiving host can control how fast each TCP sender sends the data over time. This process is called *flow control*.

Receivers use flow control for many reasons. First, the receiver needs time to process the received data. The receiving host also has a finite amount of memory, so if data keeps arriving before the receiving host can process the previously received data, it might run out of memory. For example, a receiving host may run out of memory in part because of the speed of today's high-speed LANs, or it could happen if one host receives data from many other TCP senders at the same time. Regardless, a receiving host needs a way to tell the sending host(s) to slow down.

This section describes two forms of flow control: dynamic sliding windows and withholding acknowledgments.

Flow Control Through Dynamic Sliding Windows

Note

Segments do not have to have 1000 bytes of data; the example uses 1000-byte-long segments simply to make the math more obvious.

The receiver tells the sending host how many bytes the sending host can send before it receives an acknowledgment—a value called a *window*. When the sending host sends an entire window's worth of data, it must wait on an acknowledgment, thereby slowing its rate of sending data. Figure 11-1 shows an example. (In the figure, each arrowed line represents a segment with 1000 bytes just to keep Figure 11-1 less cluttered.)

Figure 11-1   Dynamic Windowing

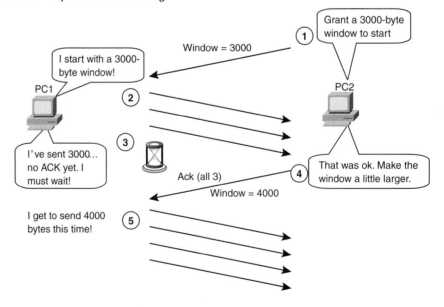

The process illustrated in Figure 11-1 is explained as follows:

1. PC2 sends a segment to PC1 in which the Window field in the TCP header is set to 3000. This means that PC2 grants PC1 the right to send 3000 bytes to PC2.

2. PC1 sends PC2 3000 bytes via three 1000-byte segments.

3. PC1 has sent all 3000 bytes, but it has not received any acknowledgments; therefore, it must wait.

4. PC2 sends PC1 an acknowledgment, and this time, it grants a slightly larger 4000-byte window.

5. PC1 sends four 1000-byte segments.

This example shows a classic case of dynamic windowing. The receiver, PC2 in this case, grants a window to PC1. PC1 can send the number of bytes in the window before it receives an acknowledgment. The process works well to protect the receiver's memory in particular. For example, if PC2 had 100 KB of memory that it could use for a particular TCP connection, PC2 would know to never increase its window to more than 100 KB for fear of not having enough space to store the data.

Flow Control Through Withholding Acknowledgments

After a sending host has sent one window worth of bytes, it must wait to send more. Knowing that, the receiver can choose to wait to send acknowledgments, which effectively prevents the sender from sending more data. Figure 11-2 shows an example, similar to Figure 11-1.

Figure 11-2   Withholding Acknowledgments

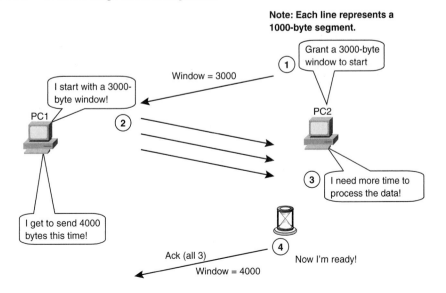

Note

The window is sometimes called the granted window because of the process described in Step 1.

Note

The TCP RFCs use the term *octet* instead of byte, with the term octet being a generic reference to 8 bits.

Note

If the receiver can process the data quickly enough, it keeps increasing the window until a state is reached in which the sender keeps sending segments and gets acknowledgments before exhausting the window. As a result, the sending host would not have to slow down.

The first two steps exactly match Figure 11-1. At Step 3, PC2 has received all 3000 bytes but needs more time to process the data. So, instead of immediately acknowledging receipt of the segments, PC2 waits until it can catch up on the work and then sends an acknowledgment at Step 4. Note that PC2 does not increase the window size at Step 4 because it is already having difficulty processing 3000 bytes at a time.

This process of withholding acknowledgments is sometimes referred to as *start/stop flow control*. In effect, the receiver puts up a stop sign for the sender by withholding the acknowledgment. Although simple, this method does not work as well as simply using well-chosen dynamic window sizes.

Establishing and Terminating TCP Connections

By definition, connection-oriented protocols use messages, events, or other prearranged settings on the communicating devices before they allow any end-user communication to occur. TCP is a connection-oriented protocol in part so that it can assign initial values to the window and sequence number values shown in Figures 11-1 and 11-2. TCP also allows two computers to agree to many other settings before the hosts attempt to send any end-user data.

TCP uses a process called a ***three-way handshake*** to create a new TCP connection and to initialize the various numbers used to control and manage a TCP connection. The three-way handshake is simply three TCP segments that use two of the TCP flags found in the TCP header. The flags are called synchronize (*SYN*) (pronounced "sin") and acknowledge (*ACK*). Figure 11-3 shows an example of the three-way TCP connection-establishment flow.

Figure 11-3   Three-Way TCP Connection Establishment

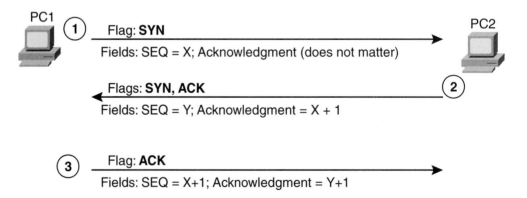

First, note the bold SYN and ACK flags shown in Figure 11-3. The three segments have the following flags set:

1. The first segment has a SYN flag set but does not have the ACK flag set. This means that the SYN bit in the TCP header is set to binary 1, and the ACK flag is set to binary 0.

2. The second segment has both SYN and ACK set.

3. The third (and ongoing) segments have only the ACK bit set.

The first message in a TCP connection is the only segment that can have just the SYN flag set. The second message is the only segment that can have both SYN and ACK set. The third (and ongoing) segments have the ACK bit set, but not the SYN bit, which essentially means that the Acknowledgment field is now valid and the TCP connection was correctly established. After the third segment is sent, data can be sent using this TCP connection.

After a connection is established and the data is sent, the application can choose to keep the connection alive or terminate it. For example, after loading a web page, most web browsers terminate the TCP connection. TCP supports several variations on terminating the TCP connection. The most common is a four-way termination flow, which uses another flag called the finished (FIN) flag.

TCP Error Recovery (Reliability)

TCP is a reliable protocol—at least as far as networking terminology is concerned. In networking, reliable protocols perform error recovery, which means that they ensure that all the data eventually gets to the receiver, even if some data is lost in transit. Figure 11-4 shows an example of how a TCP receiver tells the TCP sender that all the data was received.

Figure 11-4   TCP Acknowledgments with No Error Recovery Needed

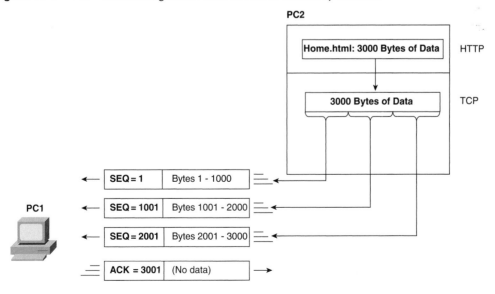

TCP uses two TCP header fields—Sequence Number and Acknowledgment Number—to signal the other computer as to whether a segment was received. The sequence number keeps track of all the bytes sent over a TCP connection by numbering the first byte of data inside each segment.

For example, the first segment's sequence number of 1 represents the first byte of the 1000 bytes of data in the first segment. The first byte of the second segment is the 1001st byte of data sent by PC2 to PC1; therefore, when PC2 sends its next segment, it sets the sequence number to a value of 1001 because the previous segment's bytes were essentially numbered 1 through 1000.

TCP acknowledges the receipt of data by using the Acknowledgment field of the TCP header. The Acknowledgment field identifies the next byte a host expects to receive. For example, PC1's Acknowledgment field of 3001, set in the next segment sent by PC1 back to PC2, means that PC1 expects PC2 to send it a segment starting with byte number 3001 next. In other words, PC1 expects PC2's next segment to have a sequence number of 3001. The practice of acknowledging data by stating the next byte expected to be received, rather than identifying the last byte received, is called a *forward acknowledgment* or *expectational acknowledgment*.

TCP performs error recovery by having the receiving host send an acknowledgment that implies some data was lost. Figure 11-5 shows an example in which TCP recovers from an error.

Figure 11-5   TCP Error Recovery

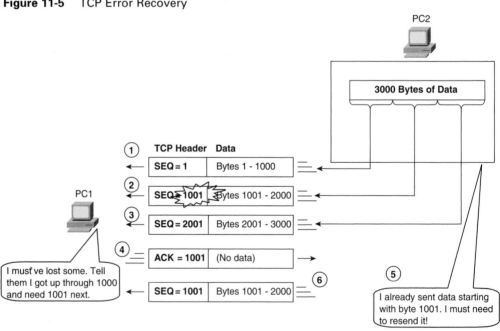

The key to this example is the logic implied at PC1 and the acknowledgment number in the segment labeled Step 4. The first three steps show the same first three segments shown in Figure 11-4, but in this case, the second segment is lost or destroyed during transmission. PC1 then signals that the segment was lost by sending a segment with the acknowledgment set to 1001. Literally, this setting means that PC1 acknowledges the receipt of the first segment.

However, PC1 knows that PC2 will receive this acknowledgment and decides to resend the lost segment because, as shown in Step 5's logic bubble, PC2 knows that it sent more data—data that apparently, according to the acknowledgment in Step 4, never arrived.

Several variations of error recovery exist besides this example. For example, to combat losing an acknowledgment in transit, the sending host sets a timer when it sends each segment. If the segment is not acknowledged within a certain amount of time, the sender cannot be sure if the segment made it across the internetwork; therefore, it resends the segment.

Note

The online course uses the phrase *positive acknowledgment with retransmission* to describe the processes shown in Figure 11-4 and Figure 11-5.

Segmentation, Reassembly, and In-Order Delivery

Figures 11-4 and 11-5 showed another of TCP's many features, namely *segmentation*. TCP segmentation refers to the process of TCP accepting a large chunk of data from the application protocol and breaking it into pieces that are small enough to be appropriate for transmission through the internetwork. For example, in Figures 11-4 and 11-5, PC2 segments 3000 bytes of application layer data into three parts. PC2 then puts a TCP header in front of each chunk, which creates three different TCP segments. In fact, the term segment was chosen to describe the TCP header and its data because of this segmentation process.

As with IP packets, the size or length of a segment is limited, typically depending on the types of data-link protocols used to forward the segment. For example, most end-user hosts reside on Ethernet LANs. Ethernet frames allow 1500 data bytes in the data field of a frame. The data field of an Ethernet frame holds the IP header and TCP header, followed by the TCP data field. Because the IP and TCP are each 20 bytes long, the data portion of a TCP segment is typically limited to 1460 bytes. The maximum length of the TCP data field is referred to as the maximum segment size (mss).

TCP on the receiving computer reassembles the data into its original form. At the same time, the receiver also guarantees that the data will be in order. For example, if a single 3000-byte file was broken into three segments for transmission, but they were assembled in the incorrect order on the receiving side, the file becomes useless. So, TCP provides a guarantee of *in-order delivery*.

Because of IP routing, a TCP receiver can receive data out of order. Figure 11-6 shows a classic case of how TCP segments can be reordered while being forwarded through an IP internetwork, and how the receiving TCP stack simply puts the data back in its original order. The routing logic hinges on the fact that when multiple routes exist to reach the same subnet, and the routing protocol metrics tie, the routers can load-balance packets over several routes. However, one route might be faster or less congested than the other route, which makes the packets arrive in a different order than the order in which they were sent.

Figure 11-6 TCP Providing In-Order Delivery

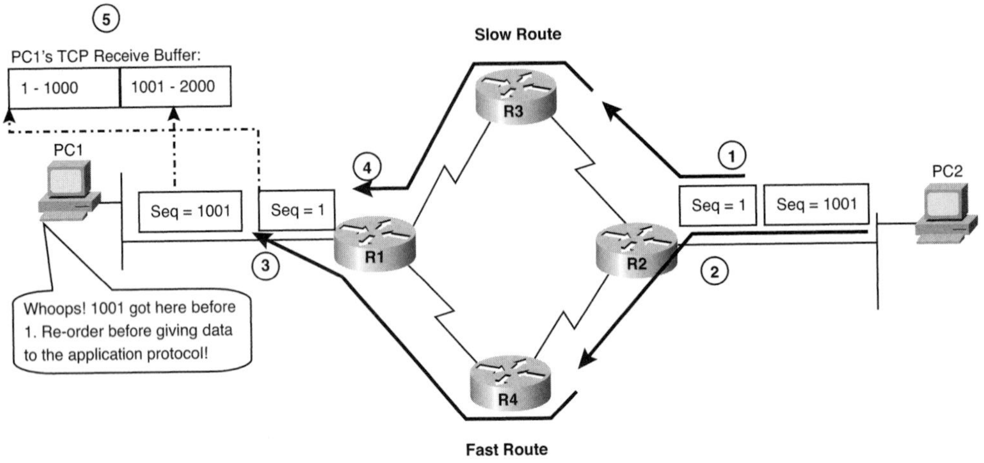

This concept becomes clearer when using the exact steps outlined here:

1. PC2 sends two segments. The first segment (sequence number 1) is routed over the slow high route.

2. Router R2 sends the second segment (sequence number 1001) over the fast low route.

3. The second segment sent arrives before the first segment, so PC1 copies the segment into a memory buffer.

4. The first segment sent arrives next.

5. The first segment sent (sequence number 1) should be in front of the segment with sequence number 1001, so PC1's TCP software stores this data in the correct order in its memory buffer.

TCP and UDP Header Reference

Similar to many other networking protocols, TCP and UDP use a header to hold important information for performing their tasks. For example, TCP needs the ACK and SYN flags used for connection establishment, and the Sequence Number and Acknowledgment Number fields to perform error recovery. Figure 11-7 shows the contents of the TCP and UDP headers.

Of particular importance, the first two fields in each header are identical. The one function performed by both TCP and UDP—namely, the use of port numbers to identify application processes—is implemented by using the Source Port and Destination Port fields at each header's beginning. Beyond those fields, TCP has a much longer header (20 bytes versus 8 bytes) so that it has all the fields required to implement the much larger number of features than UDP.

Figure 11-7   TCP and UDP Headers

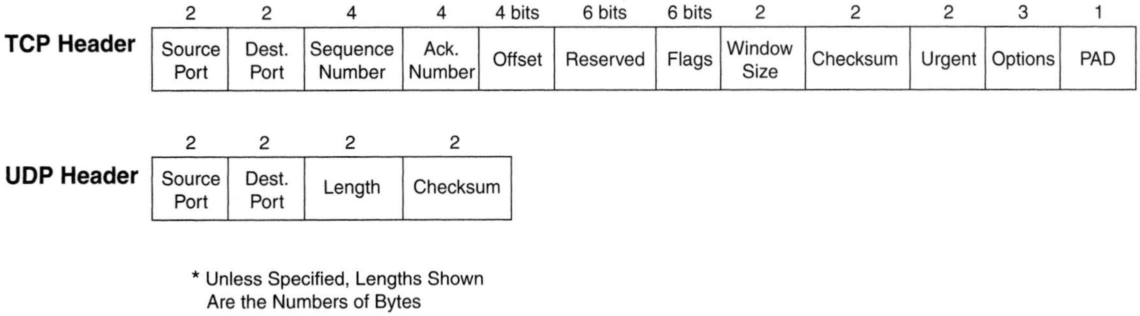

	2	2	4	4	4 bits	6 bits	6 bits	2	2	2	3	1
TCP Header	Source Port	Dest. Port	Sequence Number	Ack. Number	Offset	Reserved	Flags	Window Size	Checksum	Urgent	Options	PAD

	2	2	2	2
UDP Header	Source Port	Dest. Port	Length	Checksum

* Unless Specified, Lengths Shown
Are the Numbers of Bytes

Table 11-2 describes the TCP header fields.

Table 11-2   TCP Header Fields

Field	Meaning
Source Port	Identifies the application process on the sending computer that sent the data.
Destination Port	Identifies the application process on the receiving computer for which the data is intended.
Sequence Number	Identifies the first byte of the sent data for the purposes of allowing the receiver to acknowledge receipt of the data and to reorder data as necessary.
Acknowledgment Number	Set in a sent TCP segment, this number notes the sequence number of the next byte the host expects to receive. The Acknowledgment Number field recognizes lost packets and flow control.
Header Length	Number of sets of 4 bytes in the TCP header, which allows the receiving host to easily find the end of the TCP header and the data's beginning.
Reserved	Reserved for future use.
Flags	Each bit has different meanings to signal some function. For example, connection establishment uses the SYN and ACK flags.
Window	As set in a sent segment, Window signifies the maximum amount of unacknowledged data the host is willing to receive before the other host must wait for an acknowledgment. Used for flow control.
Checksum	Frame Check Sequence (FCS)-like field that can confirm that no errors occurred in the TCP header.
Urgent	Used to point to the sequence number of sent data for which the sender requests an immediate (urgent) acknowledgment from the receiver.
Options and Padding	Additional headers used to expand the protocol in the future. It is seldom used today.
Data	Holds the data as supplied by the application layer protocol.

Table 11-3 describes the UDP header fields.

Table 11-3   UDP Header Fields

Field	Meaning
Source Port	Identifies the application process on the sending computer that sent the data.
Destination Port	Identifies the application process on the receiving computer for which the data is intended.
Length	Number of octets in the UDP segment, including the data.
Checksum	FCS-like field that can confirm that no errors occurred in the UDP header.

Identifying Application Processes Using Port Numbers

The one function performed by both UDP and TCP is providing a means to identify the specific application process that sends the data, and the application process that needs to receive the data. For example, your PC might simultaneously use two web browsers, an e-mail client, and File Transfer Protocol (FTP) software or an instant-messaging application. Each item is considered as a different application process.

When your PC receives an IP packet, it must determine to which application process it must give the data. To make this determination, TCP and UDP use *port numbers*. Figure 11-8 shows an example with Keith's PC running four application processes. Each application uses a different local port number, each identifying a different application process.

Figure 11-8   Using Port Numbers to Identify the Correct Application Process

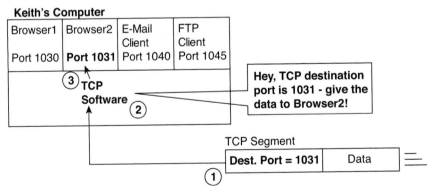

Figure 11-8 shows the steps by which Keith's computer receives a segment and decides to which application process to give the data, as follows:

1. An IP packet with a TCP segment inside of it arrives at the PC. Because it is a TCP segment, IP gives the segment to the TCP software inside the computer.

2. TCP examines the ***destination port number*** in the header. The destination port number identifies the application process on the destination (or receiving) computer (Keith).

3. Based on a value of 1031 in the Destination Port Number field, the PC's TCP software gives the data to Browser2.

The port numbers shown in Figure 11-8 are called ***dynamic port numbers*** because the host computer dynamically picks which port number to use for each application process. A host typically dynamically allocates port numbers of value 1024 (2^{10}) through 65,535 ($2^{16} - 1$), which is the largest possible port number. When the host starts a new application process (for example, the user opens a new browser window), the host allocates a dynamic port number that the computer is not already using for another process. By allocating unique port numbers, the process shown in Figure 11-8 can work well.

Figure 11-8 also provides a good backdrop from which to explain a few variations in terminology related to TCP. First, the process shown in the figure is sometimes called *multiplexing TCP connections*, or simply *multiplexing*. The term multiplexing originated in the world of networking, but with TCP, it refers to sending segments from multiple connections to a computer, with the TCP software on that computer choosing the right application based on the port number. Additionally, and as mentioned earlier in the section titled "Establishing and Terminating TCP Connections," when an application uses TCP to connect to an application on another computer, that application creates a TCP connection. Sometimes, the term *conversation* is used instead of connection.

Note

TCP/IP RFCs suggest dynamic port numbers from 49,152 through 65,535, but in practice, most hosts use dynamic port numbers beginning at 1024.

In some cases, a single application uses multiple ports at the same time. A unique port number is needed for each TCP or UDP connection. For example, when downloading a web page, a browser can open several TCP connections, which use several port numbers.

Connection to Servers: Well-Known Ports

Most TCP/IP applications use a client/server model for communications. In the client/server model of a computer, a client is software that needs some service, and the server is the software that provides the service. For example, a web browser is a client because it needs to display information for the end user, and the web server is a server because it supplies that information.

Servers cannot use dynamic port numbers because the clients that use the server must know ahead of time what port number the server uses. Servers must wait and listen for segments sent by any and all clients, and the clients need to know the port number that a particular service uses.

To allow servers to work well, TCP/IP defines one or more ***well-known ports***, each reserved for use by a specific application protocol. When a client connects to a server, the client already knows what well-known port the server should be using. Figure 11-9 shows an example of this concept, with a web browser connecting to a server at Hypertext Transfer Protocol's (HTTP's) well-known port of 80.

Figure 11-9   Client Connecting to Well-Known Port of a Web Server (80)

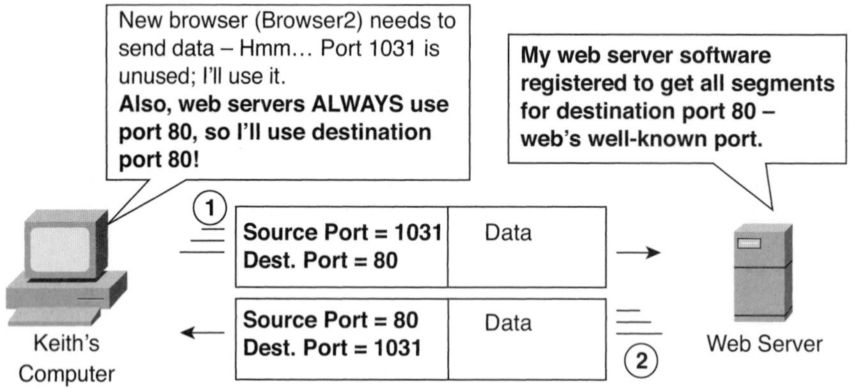

Web browsers know that the well-known port for web servers—more specifically, for the HTTP protocol—is port 80. Figure 11-9 illustrates the following points:

1. Keith's browser sends the segment as shown, with a destination port of 80.

2. The segment has a source port of 80 because it comes from the web server, and the destination port matches the port used by browser2 on Keith's computer.

Many of the most common application protocols use well-known ports, as listed in Table 11-4.

Note

FTP uses a different well-known port for control purposes (port 21) than the actual transfer of files (port 20).

Table 11-4   Popular Applications and Their Well-Known Port Numbers

Port Number	Protocol	Application
20	TCP	FTP data
21	TCP	FTP control
23	TCP	Telnet
25	TCP	Simple Mail Transfer Protocol (SMTP)
53	TCP, UDP	Domain Name System (DNS)
69	UDP	Trivial FTP (TFTP)
80	TCP	HTTP (WWW)
110	TCP	Post Office Protocol version 3 (POP3)
161	UDP	Simple Network Management Protocol (SNMP)

(The term *server* can mean "single high-powered computer." In this chapter, server means "TCP/IP software application," one that uses port numbers. An individual physical server might run many TCP/IP servers or services. So, the server hardware, running multiple TCP/IP software services, like web servers [which serve web pages], FTP servers [which serve files], and the like, needs to use port numbers to differentiate the different applications).

Comparing Well-Known, Dynamic, and Registered Ports

The Internet Assigned Numbers Authority (IANA [www.iana.org]) assigns the values for well-known ports and the values for a similar concept called **registered port numbers**. The difference between well-known and registered ports is that registered ports are assigned to servers that the average end user can start. Well-known ports are used only for applications typically controlled by IT staff. For example, instant-messaging applications, voice applications, and video applications—all of which an average end user can start—technically must have one side of a connection act as a server, so these applications use registered port numbers. However, web services, FTP services, and e-mail services, which are usually controlled by IT staff in a typical company, use well-known port numbers.

Table 11-5 summarizes the three overall categories of uses of port numbers. It also shows the reserved port number ranges.

Table 11-5   Uses of Port Numbers

Type of Port	Range of Values	Purpose
Dynamic	1024 – 65,535[1]	Allocated by clients for each new application process
Well-known	0 – 1023	For high-privilege processes, used so that all clients know the correct port number to which to connect
Registered	1024 – 49,151[2]	Equivalent to well-known ports in concept, but used specifically for nonprivileged application processes

[1] IANA formally suggests that dynamic ports start at 49,152. However, in practice, hosts typically use dynamic port numbers that begin at 1024. The CCNA 1 course also states that they begin at 1024.

[2] The online curriculum states that registered port numbers are simply 1024 and greater, whereas IANA specifically restricts the highest value to 49,151.

Both TCP and UDP use port numbers, as described in this chapter. However, whereas TCP has many features, UDP's only significant feature is its use of port numbers to identify application processes.

Most operating systems (OSs) include commands that display the port numbers used on that computer. For example, Microsoft OSs support the **netstat –an** command to display the currently used TCP and UDP port numbers. To force a TCP connection to become active, open a browser and browse a web page. Then, use the **netstat –an** command to view the TCP connection, along with the port number used on your PC and the web server.

The TCP/IP Application Layer

This section, which concludes this final chapter of the Cisco Networking Academy Program CCNA 1 course and this book (hoorah!), briefly covers several application layer protocols. The TCP/IP application layer performs the same functions as defined in the top three layers of the Open Systems Interconnection (OSI) model. At the TCP/IP application layer, application protocols define the format of the data being transferred (for example, binary or ASCII text); any required encryption; the protocol rules for transferring data; and combinations of messages, which are called *dialogues* or *sessions*, that must all be sent and received before a transaction can be considered complete.

Many people confuse the application layer with the applications themselves. Application software, like a web browser or e-mail client, typically implements application layer protocols. However, these protocols are only part of the application software. For example, the application layer protocols define nothing about the user interface. Figure 11-10 uses an e-mail client to show the general distinction.

Figure 11-10   Distinction Between an E-Mail Application and E-Mail Application Layer Protocols

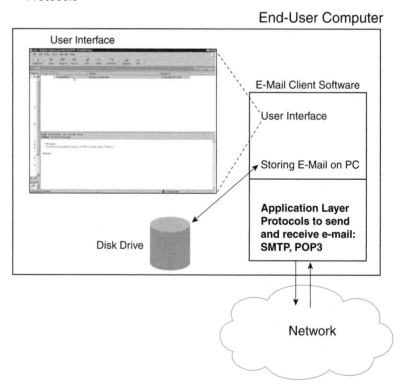

Figure 11-10 shows the main features of an e-mail client. The client provides a graphical interface for the user and stores e-mails on the PC's disk drive. It also implements e-mail protocols, such as SMTP and POP3, to send and receive e-mails.

This section covers the basic concepts about a handful of application layer protocols. Today, the protocols are grouped based on whether they are mostly used by end users or network engineers.

Application Protocols Used by End Users

This section covers the following TCP/IP application layer protocols:

- *Domain Name System (DNS)*—Resolves names into IP addresses.

- *Hypertext Transfer Protocol (HTTP)*—Transfers files from web servers to web browsers.

- *Simple Mail Transfer Protocol (SMTP)* and *Post Office Protocol version 3 (POP3)*—Send and receive e-mail, respectively.

- *File Transfer Protocol (FTP)*—Stores and retrieves files.

This section explains each of these application layer protocols in more detail.

Name Resolution Using DNS

Most people do not easily remember IP addresses, but they do remember names, especially if the names remind them about the topic at hand. For example, you might see an advertisement on TV that mentions a website. The website isn't listed as 192.168.9.3, although if correct, it works; instead, a hopefully memorable name is listed, such as www.cisco.com.

DNS was designed to allow people to use memorable names and let computers use numeric IP addresses. To make that work, when a person enters a name into an application, the computer uses a DNS resolution request to find the corresponding IP address. For example, the PC in Figure 11-11 reaches www.cisco.com using a web browser, but the PC ends up sending a packet to destination IP address 198.133.219.25, the IP address of the www.cisco.com web server.

Figure 11-11 illustrates the following process:

1. The PC finds the hostname inside the Universal Resource Locator (URL).

2. The PC requests name resolution from a DNS server to find the IP address of the server whose hostname is in the URL.

3. The DNS supplies the IP address that the web server uses.

4. The PC can send packets (like those containing HTTP GET requests) to that IP address.

Figure 11-11   DNS Resolution After Inserting a URL into a Web Browser

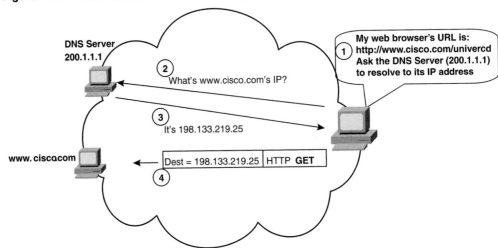

The names that DNS uses follow a particular format, one that is familiar even to those not involved in the IT world. The name itself, such as www.cisco.com, is generically called a *hostname*; these names can include alphabetic, numeric, and some special characters. The part that identifies the organization (in this case, the cisco.com part) is called a *domain name*. The last part (.com, in this case) is called a *top-level domain*.

A name's high-level domain states something about its nature. For example, .com means "commercial," .gov means "government," and .edu means "education." Table 11-6 lists some of the more common high-level domains.

Table 11-6   Common High-Level DNS Domains

Domain	Description
.us	United States, typically local or state government
.uk	United Kingdom
.com	Commercial enterprise
.edu	Educational institution
.gov	Government (typically U.S. government)
.org	Nonprofit organization
.net	Internet service provider (ISP) or another network service provider
.mil	U.S. military

World Wide Web and HTTP

Most every TCP/IP application layer protocol uses a client/server model. With web services, the web browser is the client, and…well, the term web server says it all.

Web-browser software displays information in a window of the PC's video display. That information can be simple text, graphics, video, or animation. The browser can also play audio. Today, the most popular browser software is Internet Explorer (by Microsoft), but Netscape and Mozilla Firefox are other popular web browsers.

Web-server software stores information that the web server wants to make available to web browsers. For example, Cisco Systems has a website (Cisco.com) that lists tons of information on its products and services. Cisco has many physical computers that run web-server software, and the expectation is that many Cisco customers will use web browsers to connect to the web-server software and look at the Cisco web pages.

Note

The term server can refer to server hardware or server software. This chapter focuses on the functions of server software.

Web servers use HTTP to transfer the files that make up a web page, sending the files from the server to the browser. The following general process occurs when the browser first requests a particular web page:

1. The browser asks the web server to send one file that contains instructions and displayable content.

2. The browser displays the file's contents.

3. The browser also looks at the instructions inside the first file, which might tell it to get more files from the web server.

4. The browser asks the web server for the additional files.

5. The browser displays the additional content, which might also include instructions to download other files.

6. The browser continues to look for instructions to download other files that are part of the web page until all files are downloaded and displayed.

Figure 11-12 depicts the flow and logic of how the web browser transfers files. As shown in Figure 11-12, HTTP uses a *GET request*, which identifies the file that the browser needs from the server. The server obliges and sends the file. In this case, the first file (home.html) holds instructions that tell the browser to ask for two additional files.

The term HTTP is derived from the first type of file supported by a web browser—a file with Hyper Text Markup Language (HTML) text and instructions. Original web browsers needed to download HTML files exclusively, and to do so, they needed a protocol to transfer the HTML files. So, the name HTTP is derived from the idea of a protocol to transport hypertext.

To load a web page, a user must somehow imply what Universal Resource Locator (URL) needs to be loaded. The URL, commonly referred to as a web address, identifies a web page that needs to be displayed. URLs can simply be entered in the browser or implied by a user clicking a *hyperlink*. A hyperlink is the part of a web page that includes a hidden URL. When a user clicks the hyperlink's text or object, the browser loads that URL.

Figure 11-12   HTTP Transfers Three Files

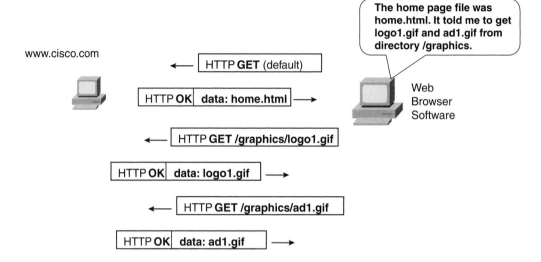

A URL itself has structure. In fact, the DNS name is a major part of a URL. For example, the following URL is the home page for Cisco documentation:

http://www.cisco.com/univercd

As with all URLs, the portion of the text between the double slash and single slash (www.cisco.com, in this case) is the DNS hostname. The part after the single slash can represent many things (in this case, it implies a directory on the server and the default web page in that directory).

Lab 11.2.4   Protocol Inspector, TCP, and HTTP

In this lab, you get a basic overview of how to use Protocol Inspector or some other network traffic analysis tool. The lab allows you to look at TCP and HTTP operations by capturing the segments sent as part of a web browser downloading a web page.

E-Mail Protocols: SMTP and POP3

E-mail works much like the postal system. When you send a letter, you give the letter to the postal system by putting it where a postal worker will pick it up. The postal system then delivers the letter. The postal workers do not actually give the letter to the person it was sent to. Instead, the postal worker puts the letter in the recipient's mailbox, and the recipient then checks the mail and gets the letter. In effect, the postal system delivers the letter to a mailbox, and then the recipient must take action to get the mail from the mailbox.

E-mail follows this same nitpicky system. Figure 11-13 shows an example of PC1's user sending an e-mail to PC2's user.

Figure 11-13 Process of Sending an E-Mail

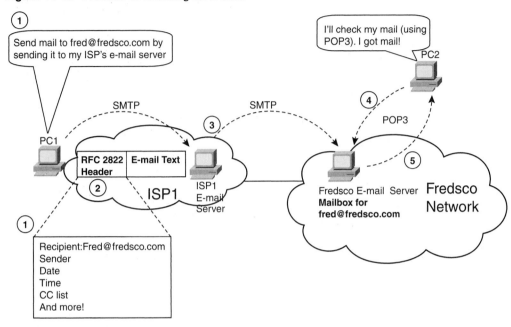

In this case, PC1's user sends an e-mail to e-mail address fred@fredsco.com, which is the e-mail address of PC2's user. Figure 11-13 illustrates the following process:

1. PC1's user types an e-mail and clicks **Send**. The e-mail software encapsulates the e-mail in a header that includes familiar information, such as the intended recipient, the sender, the subject line, and other information.

2. PC1, which is a home-based user who uses an ISP named ISP1, sends the e-mail to its *SMTP server* using SMTP. In this case, PC1 is an *SMTP client*.

3. The ISP1 SMTP server views the recipient's e-mail address and decides that the e-mail must be sent to the SMTP server at fredsco.com. So, ISP1's e-mail server uses SMTP to send the e-mail to Fredsco's SMTP server.

4. Some time later—and it could be a long time—the user at PC2 (Fred) decides to check his e-mail. To do so, PC2 uses POP3 to request e-mail from the Fredsco e-mail server.

5. The server replies and sends the e-mail to PC2 using POP3.

The first three steps in this example deliver the e-mail to the recipient's e-mail mailbox, and the last two steps define how the recipient can get the e-mail. SMTP defines the first part of the process. However, a different protocol (typically POP3, but sometimes IMAP4) retrieves the e-mail from the mailbox.

In fact, in some cases, the physical server used for sending e-mail is a different server than the one used for checking e-mail. If you look at the configuration settings on an average e-mail client application, such as Microsoft Outlook, you can see a separate place to refer to the out-going e-mail server (SMTP) and incoming e-mail server (usually, POP3).

The last particularly important point from Figure 11-13 is that most SMTP servers are config-ured so that they accept e-mails from only hosts inside the same internetwork, not from other internetworks. SMTP has poor security, so many internetworks simply allow their own users to send e-mail using that server, but no one else. For example, PC1 is connected to ISP1, so PC1 is allowed to send its e-mail to the ISP1 SMTP server. Had PC1 attempted to directly send the e-mail to the Fredsco.com SMTP server, the security rules at Fredsco.com would have rejected the attempt, because PC1 is not an internal user of the Fredsco.com network. These types of restrictions help reduce the amount of spam e-mail.

File Transfer Protocol

File Transfer Protocol (FTP) supports file transfers, with the basic flows working like a ware-house. In this analogy, the FTP server acts as the warehouse, with FTP clients storing files in the warehouse and retrieving copies of those files. Figure 11-14 shows this basic concept.

Figure 11-14   Storing and Retrieving Files from an FTP Server

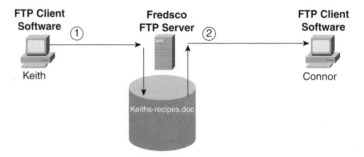

Figure 11-14 illustrates the following process:

1. Keith uses FTP client software to store a file (Keiths-recipes.doc) on the FTP server.

2. Later, Connor uses FTP client software to retrieve a copy of the Keiths-recipes.doc file.

At no time did Keith and Connor send or receive packets to or from each other, much like end-user PCs do not directly send data to each other when sending e-mail.

When a client connects to an FTP server, FTP uses two separate TCP connections: the control and data connections. One connection, using well-known port 21 on the FTP server, sends con-trol information, such as commands through which the user sets the data transfer mode (binary or ASCII). A connection using well-known port 20 is used for the actual data transfer.

Note

By Telnetting to an SMTP server using destination port 25 (which is the SMTP port number), you can usually get a message or two back that verify that the server works. For example, the **telnet smtp.example.com 25** command attempts a Telnet to the SMTP server at example.com. The same can be attempted using the POP3 well-known port of 110.

Application Protocols Often Used for Network Management

This section covers three application layer protocols that network engineers primarily use to manage internetworks:

- *Trivial File Transfer Protocol (TFTP)*—Works similarly to FTP, but with some benefits when used on networking devices.

- *Simple Network Management Protocol (SNMP)*—Allows management software (the client) to query networking devices (the servers) to manage and control the networking devices.

- *Telnet*—Allows a client to emulate a terminal. It allows a user to sit at one computer (the Telnet client) and use a remote computer (the Telnet server) through a text-based interface.

Next, this section explains each of these application layer protocols.

TFTP

TFTP performs the same general functions as FTP. Both use a warehouse-style model that enables clients to store and retrieve files from a server.

So, why does the world need both FTP and TFTP? Well, the reasons relate to the choice of the term "trivial" in TFTP's name. TFTP server software requires a few lines of software code. Many specialized devices, such as routers and switches, particularly in years past, needed to conserve every bit of permanent storage space. FTP is highly functional, but it takes many lines of software code. TFTP allows devices, such as routers and switches, to transfer files without consuming too much permanent storage space.

TFTP's negative is that it has few functions, so it is a useful tool for IT professionals, but not end users. For example, TFTP does not allow the TFTP client to change directories to look for files on the server. TFTP also does not support basic username and password security.

Most network engineers use a Telnet client package and a TFTP server package on their PCs. Many freeware and shareware Telnet clients and TFTP servers can be found at http://www.tucows.com. PumpKIN (http://kin.klever.net) and Solarwinds (http://www.solarwinds.net) are two useful TFTP servers, and you can download both of them for free.

SNMP

Imagine that you work for a large company, and your job is to monitor the health of its large enterprise internetwork. When you get to work each day, you sit in front of a large-screened PC. On the screen, a diagram of the U.S. shows all the company's locations. One city is high-lighted in red, so you click that site. A new and more detailed diagram appears that shows the routers, switches, and hosts at that site. The screen shows a WAN link, which is colored red and blinking, meaning that it is down. The screen also notes that your PC has already contacted the provider, listing information about the trouble ticket opened with that provider. With a few clicks, you confirm that the site's alternate router to the rest of the internetwork is up and working, meaning that the users are still able to work right now. You take a break and pour a cup of coffee.

The *Network Management System (NMS)* software can perform all these tasks—and more. NMSs provide a user interface for network-operations staff. The information shown on the screen is gathered by using SNMP. The NMS can sit anywhere on the internetwork as long as it can send and receive IP packets with the devices in the internetwork. The NMS then uses SNMP to get information from the networking devices.

For example, Figure 11-15 shows an NMS sending an SNMP GET request to a router to learn that router's current IP routing table and another SNMP GET request to a switch to learn its current content-addressable memory (CAM).

Figure 11-15 NMS Using SNMP GETs to Retrieve Information from SNMP Agents

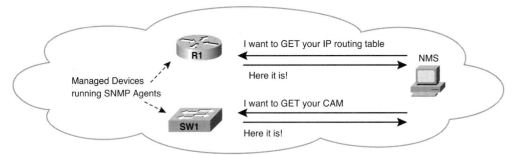

For the process shown in Figure 11-15 to work, two important types of components must exist in the network: the NMS and a managed device. A managed device supports the capability to receive SNMP GET requests and reply to them, as shown in the figure. A managed device— typically, networking devices, hosts, and servers—needs to run software called an *SNMP agent*, which actually performs the work of accepting and replying to SNMP messages.

Telnet

Telnet, which loosely stands for *terminal emulation over a network*, allows a user to sit at one computer and access another IP host by using Telnet client software. (The other host must run Telnet server software.) After it connects to the other host, the user at the Telnet client (called the *local host*) can issue commands that are executed on the other IP host (called the *remote host*). This model basically works like a dumb terminal accessing a mainframe or minicomputer in the old days, with Telnet providing the same function over an IP network.

Anyone proceeding on to the CCNA 2 course will become familiar with Telnet because it is the primary tool with which to remotely access, monitor, and control routers and switches. Figure 11-16 shows an example. In the figure, PC1 Telnets to router R2, which happens to be at another site on the other side of a WAN link. The window at the bottom of Figure 11-16 shows the Telnet client user interface on PC1, with the command being executed, and the output seen on the screen created by router R2.

Figure 11-16   Telnet Client Accessing a Router

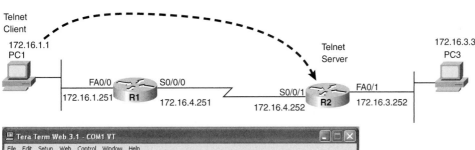

Cisco routers and switches come with built-in Telnet servers, which makes the process in Figure 11-16 convenient. When connecting, the client specifies the IP address or hostname of the remote device and the terminal type. (The terminal type simply implies the basic terminal characteristics, such as the width and height of the window.) Once connected, anything typed in the window is sent to the remote host, and any replies from the remote host are displayed in the Telnet client window. For example, Figure 11-16 shows the Telnet client user issuing a **show ip route** command with router R1 replying with the contents of that router's IP routing table.

Application Protocol Summary

Although many other application protocols exist, the protocols mentioned in this section represent the mainstream of end-user application protocols and the protocols used for network management. These protocols share a common feature: They all use a TCP/IP transport layer protocol (either TCP or UDP) to send their data from client to server and vice versa. The following statements summarize which application layer protocols—at least the ones mentioned in this chapter—use which transport protocols:

- **TCP**—HTTP, SMTP, POP3, FTP, and Telnet

- **UDP**—DNS, TFTP, and SNMP

UDP does not provide error recovery, so it might be disconcerting to see three key application protocols using UDP. However, TFTP implements error recovery at the application layer. DNS

Note

DNS uses TCP for a function beyond the scope of this book. For name resolution as described here, it uses UDP.

and SNMP either use a timeout mechanism that allows them to resend a request or they allow the user to repeat the action to attempt the same operation again.

Summary

The primary duty of the transport layer, which is OSI model Layer 4, is to take data from one application process on one computer and deliver the data to the correct application process on another computer. To differentiate between different application processes, the transport layer (both TCP and UDP) identifies data from upper-layer applications based on their port numbers.

UDP essentially provides only the basic delivery and identification of applications using port numbers. TCP provides several additional functions, including reliability (error recovery), flow control, segmentation and reassembly, and in-order data delivery. To do so, TCP uses connection-oriented logic, establishing connections dynamically using a three-way handshake.

TCP numbers the first byte of each segment with a sequence number and acknowledges receipt of data by using an acknowledgment number. This process allows the receiving host to tell the sender to re-send data. The sequence numbers allow the receiver to notice when data is received out of order so it can arrange the data in the correct order before giving it to the application.

Flow control ensures that a transmitting node does not overwhelm a receiving node with data. The simplest method of flow control used by TCP involves a "not ready" signal through the receiver withholding its acknowledgments until it is ready to receive more data. TCP also uses dynamic windowing, which is a more efficient process by which the receiver grants the sender the right to send a set amount of data before requiring an acknowledgment.

The term *positive acknowledgment with retransmission* refers to the process of explicitly acknowledging received data, with the sender resending any unacknowledged segments.

Connection-oriented TCP provides a wide range of functions, but UDP has some advantages over TCP. The connectionless UDP uses less overhead (an 8-byte header versus TCP's 20 bytes), and UDP does not slow down because of flow control.

The following application layer protocols are used popularly by end users or network engineers:

- **DNS**—Used in IP networks to translate names of network nodes into IP addresses
- **FTP**—Transfers files between networks
- **HTTP**—Delivers HTML documents to a client application, such as a web browser
- **SMTP**—Provides e-mail services
- **SNMP**—Monitors and controls network devices and manages configurations, statistics collection, performance, and security
- **Telnet**—Used to log in to a remote host that runs a Telnet server application and then to execute commands from the command line

Check Your Understanding

Complete all the review questions listed here to test your understanding of the topics and concepts in this chapter. Answers are listed in Appendix A, "Answers to Check Your Understanding and Challenge Questions."

1. When talking with an individual whose primary language differs from yours, you might need to repeat your words and speak slowly. Repeating your words can be compared to _____, and the need to speak slowly can be compared to the _____ functions of the transport layer.

    A. Reliability; flow control

    B. Flow control; reliability

    C. Transport; acknowledgment

    D. Flow control; transport

2. Which of the following TCP/IP protocols is connection-oriented, resends anything not received, and divides outgoing messages into segments?

    A. IPX

    B. TCP

    C. UDP

    D. SPS

3. What does the Window field in a TCP segment indicate?

    A. Number of 32-bit words in the header

    B. Number of the called port

    C. Number used to ensure correct sequencing of the arriving data

    D. Number of octets that the device is willing to accept from the device on the other end of the TCP connection

4. Which of the following transport protocols exchanges datagrams without guaranteed delivery?

    A. UDP

    B. TCP

    C. IRQ

    D. LLC

5. What do TCP and UDP use to differentiate between different conversations that simultaneously cross a network?

    A. Port numbers

    B. IP addresses

    C. MAC addresses

    D. Route numbers

6. How does TCP initiate a connection between the source and the destination before data transmission?

   A. Two-way handshake

   B. Three-way handshake

   C. Four-way handshake

   D. Holton functions

7. What is the range of port numbers used by most computers for dynamic port numbers used by clients?

   A. Below 255

   B. Between 256 and 512

   C. Between 256 and 1023

   D. Above 1023

8. With TCP transmission, what occurs if a segment is not acknowledged in a certain time period?

   A. UDP takes over the transmission.

   B. The virtual circuit is terminated.

   C. Nothing happens.

   D. Retransmission occurs.

9. Which answer best describes flow control?

   A. A method of managing limited bandwidth

   B. A method of connecting two hosts synchronously

   C. The capability of the receiving host to control how fast a TCP sender sends data over time

   D. A method of checking data for viruses before transmission

10. What is the purpose of TCP in the TCP/IP protocol stack?

   A. Closely maps to the OSI reference model's upper layers

   B. Supports all standard physical and data-link protocols

   C. Transfers information from one application on one host to another application on some other host in a sequence of datagrams

   D. Recovers data by performing path selection

11. Which of the following is one of the protocols found in the TCP/IP transport layer?

    A. FTP

    B. UDP

    C. Telnet

    D. DNS

12. What is the purpose of port numbers?

    A. Allows a host to multiplex received segments, selecting the correct application process to which to give received data.

    B. Source systems use them to keep a session organized.

    C. End systems use them to assign end users dynamically to a particular session, depending on their application use.

    D. Source systems generate them to predict destination addresses.

13. Why is the TCP three-way handshake used? (Select two correct answers.)

    A. To establish a connection between end devices before data transmission begins

    B. To determine how much data each station can accept without an acknowledgment

    C. To synchronize SYN numbers

    D. To change binary **ping** responses into information in the upper layers

14. What does a dynamic TCP Window field do?

    A. It makes the window larger so that more data can come through at once, which results in more efficient bandwidth utilization.

    B. The window size slides to each section of the datagram to receive data, which results in more efficient bandwidth utilization.

    C. It allows the window size to be adjusted dynamically by the receiving host during the TCP session, which results in more efficient bandwidth utilization.

    D. It limits the incoming data so that each segment must be sent one by one, which is an inefficient utilization of bandwidth.

15. UDP segments use what kind of protocols to provide reliability, if at all?

    A. Network layer protocols

    B. Application layer protocols

    C. Internet protocols

    D. Transmission Control Protocols

16. If you have two web browsers open on your computer and packets are received for both, how does your computer know which packets belong to which web-browser window?

   A. Each web browser has a different IP address.

   B. The hosts HTTP software tracks the URL of the GET requests from each browser, and looks for that URL in the HTTP messages coming back to the host from the server.

   C. Each web browser uses a different MAC address.

   D. Each web browser uses a different port number.

17. Which of the following is an example of a client/server application?

   A. E-mail

   B. Spreadsheet

   C. NIC

   D. Hard-drive utilities

18. The client side of the client/server relationship is which of the following?

   A. Located on a mainframe computer

   B. Requestor of services

   C. The provider of services

   D. Always located on the server

19. Which of the following best describes DNS?

   A. It translates the name of a network node into a numeric IP address.

   B. It is the same as the name you give your primary server.

   C. It represents the specific location where your LAN is located.

   D. It is an IP address used to represent a print server.

20. The .com top-level domain is typically assigned to which of the following?

   A. Governments

   B. Nonprofit organizations

   C. Internet service provider companies

   D. Corporations

21. During a Telnet connection, the Telnet server is responsible for which of the following?

   A. Initiating the Telnet connection

   B. Processing commands input from the Telnet client computer

   C. Client-side Telnet application

   D. Client-side printing

22. At which three layers of the OSI model does Telnet primarily work?

    A. Application layer, session layer, and transport layer

    B. Presentation layer, session layer, and transport layer

    C. Data link layer, transport layer, and presentation layer

    D. Application layer, presentation layer, and session layer

23. What well-known port(s) does FTP use?

    A. 23

    B. 67 and 68

    C. 80

    D. 20 and 21

24. Which of the following is used to remotely observe and manage networking devices and to gather information about them?

    A. SMTP

    B. SNMP

    C. SNTP

    D. TFTP

Challenge Questions and Activities

These questions require a deeper application of the concepts covered in this chapter and are similar to the style of questions you might see on a CCNA certification exam.

1. Ethernet frames should be no more than 1500 bytes in length. Under that assumption, what is the maximum size of the data portion of a TCP segment over Ethernet?

   A. 1460 bytes

   B. 1480 bytes

   C. 1484 bytes

   D. 1492 bytes

2. The three-way TCP handshake process includes the use of SYN and ACK bits. In which of the three segments of this process are both the SYN and ACK bits set?

   A. Segment one

   B. Segment two

   C. Segment three

   D. Segments two and three

Answers to Check Your Understanding and Challenge Questions

Chapter 1

Check Your Understanding

1. C

A modem modulates (converts from digital to analog) a signal it sends and demodulates (converts from analog to digital) a signal it receives. It connects to a telephone line and does not replace the connection to a LAN hub.

2. B

The motherboard is the main circuit board of a computer. A PC subsystem includes things such as the power supply and disk drives. The backplane is the large circuit board that contains expansion slots. The computer memory is a board of small chips that plug into a slot on the motherboard.

3. A, C, and D

Mozilla Firefox, Internet Explorer, and Netscape are popular web browsers. Adobe Acrobat creates PDF files. Windows Media Player is an application that plays audio and video files.

4. B

A network interface card (NIC) is a printed circuit board that provides network communication. NICs connect to LANs, not WANs. NICs are used with other types of networks, such as Token Ring. Each NIC has a unique data link layer address.

5. D

Before you install a NIC, you need knowledge of how the NIC is configured, how to use the NIC diagnostics, and the ability to resolve hardware resource conflicts.

6. C

The binary numbering system is based on powers of 2. The octal numbering system (not covered in this chapter) is based on powers of 8, hexadecimal is based on powers of 16, and ASCII is used for the numeric representation of characters such as letters.

7.

Term	Definition
Bit	Smallest unit of data in a computer
Byte	Unit of measurement that describes the size of a data file, the amount of space on a disk or another storage medium, or the amount of data being transferred over a network
kbps	Standard measurement of the rate at which data is transferred over a network connection
MB	Approximately 8 million bits

8. C

The largest decimal value that can be stored in 1 byte is 255. This is the sum of the place values of an 8-bit counter (128, 64, 32, 16, 8, 4, 2, 1). The other answers are too large or too small.

9. B

The decimal number 151 is 10010111 in binary. The bits that are turned on are in the 128, 16, 4, 2, and 1 columns (128 + 16 + 4 + 2 + 1 = 151). The decimal equivalent of 10100111 is 128 + 32+ 4 + 2 + 1, which equals 167. The decimal equivalent of 10101011 is 128 + 32 + 8 + 2 + 1, which equals 171. The decimal equivalent of 10010011 is 128 + 16 + 2 + 1, which equals 147.

10. C

The binary number 11011010 in decimal is 218 (128 + 64 + 16 + 8 + 2 = 218). The binary equivalent of decimal number 186 is 10111010 (128 + 32 + 16 + 8 + 2 = 186). The binary equivalent of decimal number 202 is 11001010 (128 + 64 + 8 + 2 = 202). The binary equivalent of decimal number 222 is 11011110 (128 + 64 + 16 + 8 + 4 + 2 = 222).

11. A

The binary number 0010000100000000 is 0x2100 in hexadecimal. The 0x means it is a hex number. Break the binary number into 4-bit segments to solve: 0010 = 2, 0001 = 1, 0000 = 0, and 0000 = 0. Assemble all the parts into a single answer: 0x2102. 0x2142 is 0010000101000010 in binary. 0x0082 is 0000000010000010 in binary. 0x0012 is 0000000000010010 in binary.

12. A

The hexadecimal number 0x2101 is 0010000100000001 in binary. The binary number 0001 0000 0001 0010 is 0x1012 in hex. The binary number 0100 1000 0000 1000 is 0x4808 in hex. The binary number 1000 0000 1000 0100 is 0x8084 in hex.

13. A and C

The **ping** command tests a device's network connectivity. **Ping** does not discover IP addresses of intervening routers; **traceroute** (**tracert**) does. Pinging 127.0.0.1 verifies that the TCP/IP protocol stack and the NIC transmit/receive functions are working properly.

Challenge Activities

Activity 1-1: The activity requested that you try to describe the subnets used in the Packet Tracer network shown in the enterprise-working configuration. The following figure shows the network with the subnets described.

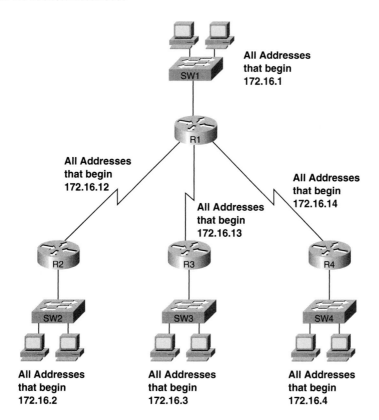

Finding the complete answers requires a deeper understanding of subnetting, as covered in Chapter 10. However, by examining the IP addresses configured for each device, you can note that the first three octets of the IP addresses on each LAN are the same (172.16.1, 172.16.2, 172.16.3, and 172.16.4). The WAN links also use subnets, as shown in the figure, although the text has not yet explained how that works.

Activity 1-2: This activity provided you with an opportunity to troubleshoot several problems. This activity is truly a challenge, because the text has not provided many examples of the types of things needed to solve the four problems in this Packet Tracer configuration. However, this chapter does mention everything you need to know to solve the problems.

The following list details the symptoms that you might have found by trying to ping each device from every other device:

- PC11 cannot ping other computers besides the ones on the same LAN.

- PC21 cannot ping other computers besides the ones on the same LAN.

- PC31 cannot ping any other computers.

- PCs on the LAN near R4 can ping only each other; they cannot ping any computers in any other part of the network.

Finding the root cause of these problems might simply be too advanced compared to how much of the class you have covered so far. However, the following list describes the reasons behind these four problems:

- PC11 has the wrong subnet mask (255.255.0.0). The mask defines how much of the IP addresses must be the same. The mask used on each computer on the same LAN needs to be the same. As a result, PC11 cannot ping other computers besides the ones on the same LAN.

- PC21's configuration for its default gateway references the wrong IP address (172.16.1.254). Instead, it needs to reference an IP address of a router on the same subnet (in this case, 172.16.2.254).

- PC31's IP address should begin with 172.16.3 to match the other IP addresses in the same subnet. However, its IP address begins with 172.16.4.

- Router R4 does not have any routes to reach the other subnets in this network.

Chapter 2

Check Your Understanding

1. B

The sending (source) computer encapsulates data and places it on the wire as bits. When a destination computer receives the bits, it performs several steps of de-encapsulation to convert the bits back into the original data and give the data to the application.

2. C

Each computer needs its own modem to connect to the Internet service provider.

3. B

The Media Access Control (MAC) address is "burned in" to a network card. This is also known as a "hardware address" or "physical address."

4. C

A star topology has all nodes directly connected to one central networking device, such as a hub or switch. A bus topology has nodes arranged in a line, a ring topology has nodes arranged in a circle, and a mesh topology has devices directly connected to most, if not all, other devices.

5. B

TIA and EIA are acronyms for Telecommunications Industry Association and Electronic Industries Alliance.

6. A and B

Local-area networks (LANs) operate in a limited area, provide access to high-bandwidth media, and provide full-time connectivity to local services. A LAN does not directly connect to the Internet, but rather connects to a networking device, such as a router, which then connects to the Internet. Access VPNs connect traveling and home-based workers to a corporate network.

7. A

A wide-area network (WAN) connects LANs that are separated by a large geographic area.

8. C

A metropolitan-area network (MAN) spans an area such as a city or a suburb.

9. D

Storage-area networks (SANs) enable concurrent access of disk or tape arrays, providing enhanced system performance. They also provide a reliable disaster recovery solution and are scalable. They *maximize* system and data availability.

10. B

A Virtual Private Network (VPN) uses encryption to offer secure connectivity over a shared public network infrastructure.

11. B

An intranet (intra = inside) VPN links various locations of a company over a shared infrastructure.

12. B

It is sometimes desirable for a company to give business partners, customers, and employees secure access to the inside network from the outside. An extranet (extra = outside) is used to do this.

13. B

As data moves down through the layers, various headers (and sometimes trailers) are added. This process is called "encapsulation."

14. D

The Open System Interconnection model has seven layers (the TCP/IP model has *four* layers).

15. D

The OSI model was created by an independent body to ensure interoperability between equipment from different manufacturers. It provides details on how networking devices and software operate at the different layers.

16. B

For many students, a mnemonic (a phrase that uses the first letter of each word as a prompt for the layer name) helps them remember the correct order. Here is an example: Please Do Not Take Sausage Pizza Away.

17. B

The data link layer handles physical (MAC) addressing, network topology, and network access. The physical layer defines the electrical, mechanical, procedural, and functional specifications for activating, maintaining, and deactivating the physical link between end systems. The transport layer segments data given to it by the session layer into smaller chunks, because the network has restrictions on the size of a single packet sent over the network. The network layer provides connectivity and path selection between two host systems.

18. D

Encapsulation is the process of wrapping data from a higher adjacent layer in a particular protocol header. For example, a network header is added to a segment it receives from the transport layer.

19. B

A packet is constructed at the network layer and is passed to the data link layer for encapsulation. The protocol data unit (PDU) for the data link layer is the frame, so the packet is encapsulated into a frame.

20. B

The transport layer deals with reliability, flow control, and error correction. The application layer is responsible for handling protocols such as e-mail. The internet layer handles logical addressing and path selection. The network access layer provides the physical link to the medium.

21. D

Cables have a maximum distance over which they can reliably transmit a signal. This distance can be extended by putting a repeater at the end of a network segment and attaching another cable. The repeater cleans up the weak incoming signal and sends a fresh signal out the other port.

22. C

Bridges are Layer 2 devices and use MAC addresses to make decisions. Routers are Layer 3 devices and use IP addresses to make decisions.

23. B

Switches, like hubs, are used as the center of a star topology. They also have multiple ports. In addition, they use the destination MAC address of incoming frames to make filtering and flooding decisions. Switches are considered Layer 2 devices because they use MAC (Layer 2) addresses to make filtering and forwarding decisions.

24. C

A router is a Layer 3 device. The Layer 3 protocol data unit (PDU) is a packet.

25. B

Encryption uses a mathematical algorithm to make data incomprehensible to anyone who is not authorized to view it. A key is generated by the algorithm, and the receiver of the data uses the key to de-encrypt the data.

Chapter 3

Check Your Understanding

1. D

Electrical current flows easily through conductors; semiconductors control the flow of electricity; insulators make it difficult for electrical current to flow.

2. B

Attenuation is the weakening of a data signal caused by cable resistance and outside factors, such as interference from electrical devices.

3. A

Volt is the unit of measure for voltage; ampere is the unit of measure for current; ohm is the unit of measure for resistance.

4. D

When a circuit has electrons flowing through it, it is said to be closed. An open circuit has no electrons flowing. Voltage is the force that drives the electrons through the circuit (electro-motive force).

5. D

Ethernet over UTP cable has a maximum allowed cable length of 100 meters.

6. B

The TIA/EIA-568-B wiring standard uses eight wires to make four pairs.

7. C

Category 5 and Category 6 UTP cabling use RJ-45 connectors. Telephones use RJ-11 connectors, which look similar, but are smaller.

8. C

Coaxial cable can run longer distances before a repeater must be installed. STP and UTP must have a repeater installed every 100 meters. 10BASE2 can run 185 meters, and 10BASE5 can run 500 meters. Coaxial cable is thicker than STP and UTP, so it is more difficult to install. It is also more expensive. STP and UTP now have faster data transfer rates than coax cable.

9. C

Twisting the wires provides for a cancellation effect, which reduces noise on the cable.

10. D

The Telecommunications Industry Association/ Electronic Industries Alliance (TIA/EIA) guidelines include several standards, such as the TIA/EIA-568-B standard used for LAN cabling.

11. B

Full duplex over fiber-optic cabling is achieved by using two strands of fiber. The receive (Rx) interface on one device is connected to the transmit (Tx) interface on the other device, and vice versa.

12. D

Because fiber-optic cable uses light instead of electricity to transmit a signal, it is not susceptible to EMI. It is more expensive to install than copper-based networks and is difficult to install. While it is an industry standard for some applications, it is not commonly available at your neighborhood electronics store.

Challenge Questions and Activities

1. D

The cable from the serial port on Host1 to the console port on Router1 is a rollover cable. At the computer end is a DB9 adapter, and an RJ-45 adapter is at the router end. The cable plugs into the console port on the router.

The cables from Switch1 to Host1 and from Router1 to Switch1 are both straight-through cables.

The cable from Router1's Ethernet port to Router2's Ethernet port is a crossover cable.

Chapter 4

Check Your Understanding

1. D

Fiber-optic cable has a core of glass fiber and uses LEDs or lasers to transmit a signal. The light is reflected by the cladding, so it does not escape the core and can travel for long distances. Because fiber-optic cable is not affected by electromagnetic or radio frequency interference, it is less susceptible to noise than other types of networking media, such as copper or wireless.

2. A

Attenuation is the loss of signal strength. In copper cabling, it can be caused by impurities in the copper and improper installation of the cable ends (impedance mismatches). In optical fiber, it can be caused by impurities in the glass, microbends in the core, and improperly installed cable ends.

3. A

Crosstalk occurs when cabling is poorly terminated. It happens when the wire pairs are untwisted too much and the signal on one wire is picked up by a neighboring wire. The other answers contribute to interference, but are not crosstalk.

4. C, E, and F

Ten tests are specified for testing copper cable. They are wire map, insertion loss, near-end crosstalk (NEXT), power sum near-end crosstalk (PSNEXT), equal-level far-end crosstalk (ELFEXT), power sum equal-level far-end crosstalk (PSELFEXT), return loss, propagation delay, cable length, and delay skew.

5. A, B, and E

Three distinct kinds of crosstalk are near-end crosstalk (NEXT), far-end crosstalk (FEXT), and power sum near-end crosstalk (PSNEXT).

6. B and C

Sine waves describe repetitive motion. They repeat the same pattern at regular intervals and have continuously varying x- and y-axis values.

7. D

UTP cable is the least expensive to install. It costs less per linear foot and is less expensive to terminate.

8. D

A common use of a cable-testing device is to do wire mapping. By connecting a device to both ends of the cable, a map is displayed that can be used to determine the pinout of the cable.

9. D

The TIA/EIA-568-B standard specifies ten tests for copper cabling use in a high-speed Ethernet LAN.

10.

Term	Definition
Near-end crosstalk	Crosstalk signal measured from the same end of the link
Far-end crosstalk	Crosstalk occurring farther from the transmitter
Power sum near-end crosstalk	Measures the cumulative effect of NEXT
Attenuation	Decrease in signal amplitude over the length of a link
Insertion loss	Combination of impedance discontinuities on a communications link and signal attenuation
Wire map	Ensures that no open or short circuits exist in the cable

Chapter 5

Check Your Understanding

1. C, D

An Ethernet switch filters frames based on destination MAC addresses and creates separate collision domains. It functions most like a high-speed multiport bridge.

2. B

Switches are typically located on the same floor as the workstations that are connected to them. Speeds that were once attainable only with fiber-optic cable are now achievable with copper cable, so UTP cabling is preferred because it is cheaper to install.

3. B and D

Switches typically have a large number of physical ports, or jacks, to which Ethernet cables from various other devices can be connected. Hubs supplied that same function in years past. Bridges separate LANs into different collision domains but typically have only two ports. Repeaters simply extend LAN segment lengths, also typically with only two ports on a repeater.

4. D

Some earlier networking devices, such as NICs and routers, did not have an RJ-45 jack for connecting an Ethernet network because they did not have an internal transceiver. Instead, they used an external transceiver that included an AUI connector.

5. A

Crossover cables connect devices that are identical, such as a switch to a switch. (Note that some current Cisco devices use a process called Auto-mdix to automatically detect the pinout of a cable. This makes it possible to use a straight-through cable to connect a switch to a switch.)

6. A

Although a wireless AP is similar to both a hub and a switch in that it provides a central point of connectivity, it is most like a hub because it creates a shared medium. Switches create separate collision domains.

7. D

A router is the best device for connecting to WANs. Its Ethernet interfaces provide LAN connectivity, and its serial interfaces provide WAN connectivity.

8. B

WANs use serial data-transmission methods through protocols such as HDLC, PPP, and Frame Relay.

9. D

A data communication equipment (DCE) device provides the clocking rate for a serial connection. Most often, the DCE is a CSU/DSU that connects to a customer's router.

10. D

A data terminal equipment (DTE) device is the router that is at a business location. It receives clocking information from a CSU/DSU that is also on the premises.

11. B

DSL operates over telephone lines. A DSL modem connects to the line by using an RJ-11 connector.

12. C

A router connects to an external CSU/DSU with a serial cable. A network engineer must select a cable with ends that match the serial port on the router and the serial port on the CSU/DSU. Several types are available.

13. B

A rollover cable connects a terminal to a console port on a router or a switch. The cable has a pinout where pin 1 is connected to pin 8, pin 2 to pin 7, pin 3 to pin 6, and pin 4 to pin 5. The end of the cable at the terminal is connected to a DB-9 adapter. (Note that some premanufactured cables have a DB-9 connector already molded on one end of the cable and an RJ-45 connector on the other end.)

Chapter 6

Check Your Understanding

1. B

The portion of the IEEE 802.3 standard that performs OSI data link layer functions is called Media Access Control (MAC). The IEEE 802.2 standard defines functions in the upper sublayer of IEEE standard Ethernet, called Logical Link Control.

2. B

The lower portion of Layer 2, the MAC sublayer, and Layer 1, the physical layer, map to the IEEE 802.3 standard.

3. A and D

Logical Link Control (LLC) can identify the type of data inside a frame's data field. It can also control the mutual transmissions between two devices on a LAN to perform error recovery. This last function is rarely used, however. LLC does not verify MAC addresses, and because it is part of Ethernet, token passing is not used.

4. B

The first six hexadecimal numbers in a MAC address are used to identify the manufacturer of a NIC, and they are called the Organizationally Unique Identifier (OUI). The last six hexadecimal numbers in a MAC address identify that particular NIC.

5. C

MAC addresses are 48 bits long. They are 12 hexadecimal numbers long, and it takes 4 bits to represent a hexadecimal number. (Hexadecimal = base16, and 2^4 = 16, so 4 bits are required per hexadecimal number.) Twelve hexadecimal numbers times 4 bits each equals 48 bits.

6. B

The access method used by Ethernet is carrier sense multiple access with collision detection (CSMA/CD). It controls access and senses collisions on a single network. CSMA/CA (collision *avoidance*) is used with wireless networking and is similar to Ethernet CSMA/CD. TCP/IP is a suite of protocols used to support communication between networks.

7. C

The Media Access Control (MAC) address is burned into memory on the NIC. Transceivers are adapters that connect to the AUI port of a device and provide a port for connecting a medium (an RJ-45 connection, for example). The computer basic input/output system (BIOS) is a set of startup instructions for a computer. Complementary metal-oxide semiconductor (CMOS) is a material used in computer chips.

8. A

Because Ethernet is a broadcast medium, every device must examine every frame it receives. If the destination MAC address does not match the MAC address on the NIC, the device ignores the frame.

9. D

The Ethernet header contains the preamble and Start Frame Delimiter fields, which signal when a new frame is being sent on the LAN. The Ethernet header also includes the source and destination MAC address fields, which identify the sending and receiving NICs. Finally, the Ethernet trailer includes the FCS field, which is used to detect whether the frame experienced any transmission errors."

10. C

Media Access Control is a set of rules that determines which computer in a shared-medium environment is allowed to transmit. It does not capture and release data, nor is it a formal byte sequence that has been transmitted.

11. B

The sending NIC performs some polynomial math calculations, called a cyclic redundancy check (CRC), with the frame as input. It puts the results of that CRC formula into the FCS field. The receiver runs the same CRC math on the received frame. If the results do not match the FCS field in the received frame, the frame has errors and is discarded. IEEE 802.2 LLC can be used to request retransmission of lost or in-error frames, but it is not used by most higher-layer protocols today.

12. B

Collisions occur when two stations listen for traffic, hear none, and transmit simultaneously. Other nodes are not informed when one node places a frame on the network; they just listen for traffic before they transmit. Jitter is analog distortion that can result in data loss, but it is not a source of collisions.

13. D

Logical Link Control (LLC), addressing (MAC addresses), and Media Access Control (access and collision detection) are all important functions of the data link layer.

14. C

Deterministic protocols, such as Token Ring, use a token-passing scheme to allow a host to send data. A host "captures the token" and sends its data, and the token is released to the next host. No collisions occur with a deterministic MAC protocol. Hubs are Layer 1 devices that have no bearing on the number of active users. Deterministic protocols are not used to limit access of users, but rather to give all users equal access.

Challenge Questions and Activities

1. B and D

Computers that connect to a switch via full duplex are in their own collision domains.

Therefore, full duplex can be used, and CSMA/CD is not necessary and is turned off. Computers that connect to the hubs are forced to connect at half duplex, because hubs do not support full duplex. The links between the hubs and the switch are half duplex, again because hubs do not support full duplex.

2. C

Ethernet IEEE 802.3 frames have a 7-byte Preamble and a 1-byte Start Frame Delimiter (SFD). A DIX frame has an 8-byte Preamble. These two types of Ethernet are compatible (they can be used on the same network).

Activity 6-1: Some of the terms are source (MAC address), destination (MAC address), Type (field), Logical Link Control (LLC), and checksum. Ethernet IEEE 802.3 includes the LLC information.

Chapter 7

Check Your Understanding

1. B

The 5-4-3 rule is used when implementing a network with hubs (or repeaters) and 10BASE5, 10BASE2, and 10BASE-T networks. There can be no more than five cable segments and, four hubs (or repeaters), and only three segments can have hosts attached. The design's purpose is to ensure that CSMA/CD works correctly by making sure collisions are heard in a reasonable amount of time. The cabling and hubs (or repeaters) delay a signal, so limiting the number of segments and devices ensures that the collision fragment can propagate the network in a timely manner.

2. C

Thick Ethernet has a maximum transmission distance of 500 meters. See Table 7-1 for details on this and other 10-Mbps Ethernet distances.

3. C

This answer stems from the 5-4-3 rule. Assuming bridges and switches are not used, 10-Mbps Ethernet networks can have no more than five segments separated by four repeaters (or hubs), and no more than three of the segments can have devices attached. Bridges and switches separate a LAN into different collision domains, with the 5-4-3 rule applying to each collision domain, as covered in Chapter 8.

4. C

Fast Ethernet has a transfer rate of 100 Mbps. When used with switches in full-duplex mode, it can simultaneously support 100 Mbps transmitting and 100 Mbps receiving.

5. C and D

The Gigabit Ethernet 1000BASE-X standard includes these two fiber-optic specifications:

1000BASE-SX and 1000BASE-LX. Refer to Table 7-6 for details.

6. D

1000BASE-SX (short distance) Ethernet uses a shortwave laser as a light source and transmits over multimode fiber (MMF). 1000BASE-LX uses single-mode fiber (SMF) and requires a more expensive long-wave laser as a transmitter.

7. B

The preferred backbone medium on large campuses is 1000BASE-LX because it supports transmission distances of up to 5000 meters. 1000BASE-SX is used inside single buildings and supports transmission distances of up to 220 meters. 100BASE-T is commonly used from the wiring closet to the desktop. The 1000BASE-CX standard was designed for use between switches inside wiring closets.

8. C

802.3ae is the IEEE standard for 10GigE.

9. A

If 1000BASE-T is used in half-duplex mode, Gigabit hubs are a requirement, and no one sells them. Instead, 100BASE-T is connected through switches with Gigabit interfaces that support full duplex.

10. C

1000BASE-SX Ethernet is used for short distances within buildings. It uses MMF-optic cable and has a maximum transmission distance of 220 m.

Challenge Questions and Activities

Activity 7-1: The following table lists the common names of the Ethernet standards, the type of cabling (media) used by each, and the speeds.

Network Type	Media Type	Transmission Rate
10BASE5	Thick coax	10 Mbps
10BASE2	Thin coax	10 Mbps
10BASE-T	UTP Cat3	10 Mbps
100BASE-TX	UTP Cat5	100 Mbps (full duplex: 200 Mbps)
100BASE-FX	MMF	100 Mbps (full duplex: 200 Mbps)
1000BASE-SX (Gigabit)	MMF	1000 Mbps (full duplex: 2000 Mbps)
1000BASE-LX (Gigabit)	MMF	1000 Mbps (full duplex: 2000 Mbps)

| 1000BASE-T (Gigabit) | UTP Cat5e | 1000 Mbps (full duplex: 2000 Mbps) |
| 10GBASE-various (10 Gigabit) | SMF or MMF | 10 Gbps (full duplex: 20 Gbps) |

Activity 7-2: Straight-through cables connect dissimilar devices. For example, they connect a switch to a router or a computer to a switch.

Crossover cables connect similar devices, such as a switch to a switch or a computer to a computer. You can make a crossover cable by using the straight-through wire order on one end of the cable and switching the orange and green pairs on the other end.

Chapter 8

Check Your Understanding

1. D

   The purpose of microsegmentation is to reduce collisions. It does this by enabling dedicated access between hosts, enabling both directions of concurrent transmission via full duplex, and increasing the capacity of each workstation by eliminating collisions.

2. B

   LAN switches use MAC addresses to make forwarding decisions. Routers use IP addresses, which consist of a network portion and a host portion.

3. D

   Full-duplex includes two paths for data transmission (simultaneous send and receive) from 10 Mbps to 1 Gbps, doubles bandwidth between nodes, and provides collision-free transmission.

4. C

   The three types of switching methods are store-and-forward (receive the entire frame on one port before sending it out another), cut-through (start sending the frame out the correct port as soon as the destination MAC address is read), and fragment-free (make sure the frame is 64 bytes long so that a collision fragment is not forwarded).

5. B

   A network can have redundant (multiple) paths from a source to a destination. If more than one path is active at the same time, a broadcast frame can loop around the network and cause a broadcast storm. STP puts a redundant path in a blocked state and stops the potential for loops. If the primary path goes down, STP dynamically activates the secondary path.

6. D

The five possible states of an STP port are blocking, listening, learning, forwarding, and disabled.

7. C

Bridges are Layer 2 devices and use MAC addresses to make forwarding decisions. Routers are Layer 3 devices and use IP addresses to make forwarding decisions.

8. A, B, and D

Bridges operate at Layer 2 of the OSI model, are more intelligent than hubs (OSI Layer 1 devices), and build and maintain address tables. Bridges use the address tables to make forwarding decisions.

9. A

Microsegmentation is the process of giving every host its own switch port. This dedicated segment reduces the number of collisions in the network (all devices use full duplex).

10. B

LAN switches are sometimes called "multiport bridges." They are faster than bridges, because they use hardware to make forwarding decisions instead of using only software. Switches offer higher bandwidth with lower latency. Most modern NICs on the hosts do not need to be replaced.

11. A

A collision domain is the network area bounded by Layer 2 devices such as bridges and switches. (Note: Routers, which are Layer 3 devices, are also boundaries of collision domains.)

12. C

A repeater extends a collision domain by increasing the network's physical reach. More devices are likely added, increasing the chances of a collision. Because repeaters are Layer 1 devices, they forward all traffic.

13. B

Segmentation is the process of using bridges, switches, and routers to break up collision domains.

Challenge Questions and Activities

1. F

Collision domain boundaries are set by both Layer 2 devices (bridges and switches) and Layer 3 devices (routers). Each switch port defines a collision domain. Six switch ports have devices connected, so there are six collision domains.

The hubs are Layer 1 devices and have no bearing on the number of collision domains. They do, however, extend the collision domain from the switches to the hosts.

2. B

Only Layer 3 devices (routers) define broadcast domain boundaries. There are two connections to ports on the router, so there are two broadcast domains. A broadcast forwarded by SW1 is not forwarded by the router to SW2.

Chapter 9

Check Your Understanding

1. C

Trivial File Transfer Protocol (TFTP) uses the User Datagram Protocol (UDP).

2. D

The transport layer provides reliability by using sequence numbers and acknowledgments. It takes large "chunks" of data and breaks them into smaller, more manageable segments. It also establishes end-to-end connectivity from host application to host application.

3. D

Internet Protocol (IP), Internet Control Message Protocol (ICMP), and Address Resolution Protocol (ARP) all operate at the TCP/IP internet layer.

4. B

TCP/IP combines the OSI data link and physical layers into its network access layer. It also combines the OSI application, presentation, and session layers into its application layer. It has fewer layers than the OSI model. Last, UDP does not provide reliable transport.

5. A

Routers are Layer 3 devices that make their routing decisions by looking at network layer addresses. They keep a routing table that lists which networks can be reached through which interfaces.

6. A

When the destination host is on a different subnet, the PC will attempt to send the packet to its default gateway, or default router. The PC knows the IP address of the default gateway, either through static configuration or DHCP; however, the PC must learn the MAC address of the default gateway using ARP.

7. A

An Internet Protocol (IP) address has two parts when subnetting is not used: the network part and the host part.

8. C

Address Resolution Protocol (ARP) is used to map a known IP address to an unknown Media Access Control (MAC) address.

9. D

A device must have both the destination IP address and the destination MAC address to send a frame. If the ARP table does not contain a listing that maps the destination IP address to a MAC address, the device must initiate an ARP request. A diskless workstation that knows its MAC address but needs to learn its IP address uses Reverse Address Resolution Protocol (RARP) to do so.

10. D

ARP tables are stored in the device's memory (in RAM). They map known IP addresses to known MAC addresses. When the device is turned off, the contents of the table are lost and must be rebuilt when the device is turned on again.

11. A

An ARP reply is made in response to an ARP request (no surprise there!). An ARP request is a broadcast to MAC address FF.FF.FF.FF.FF.FF. All devices on the LAN check to see if the included IP address in the request belongs to them. If it does not, they ignore the request. If it does, the device sends an ARP reply directly to the device that made the ARP request, giving its MAC address.

12. B

As a frame is passed from router to router, each router removes the frame header and trailer. It then re-encapsulates the packet with the appropriate header and trailer for the Layer 2 protocol on the next link. This new header includes the MAC address of the next router (next hop) on the path to the destination computer. Only the last router in the path uses the destination computer's MAC address.

13. A

The TCP/IP protocol stack maps best to the OSI model's lower layers. The TCP/IP application layer maps to three of the OSI layers: application, presentation, and session. The TCP/IP transport layer maps to the OSI transport layer, the TCP/IP internet layer maps to the OSI network layer, and the TCP/IP network access layer is a combination of the OSI data link and physical layers.

14. C

The OSI model has seven layers; TCP/IP has four. The application layer of the TCP/IP model includes three of the OSI layers: application, presentation, and session. TCP/IP and OSI have comparable transport and network (internet) layers and describe packet-switched technology.

15. D

TCP/IP provides many functions, including an IP addressing scheme, Internet Control

Message Protocol (ICMP) messaging and control, and ARP requests and replies to supply MAC addresses for known IP addresses. UDP does not provide guaranteed delivery of packets (datagrams) and is not part of the Internetwork layer.

16. B

The transport layer includes UDP and TCP protocols.

Challenge Questions and Activities

1. C

The Layer 2 (data link) header and trailer are discarded by a router as it moves the packet from link to link. The frame is de-encapsulated at each router interface and re-encapsulated with the next Layer 2 protocol header and trailer as it is placed on the link toward the destination.

2. B

The A through E class ranges are 1–126, 128–191, 192–223, 224–239, and 240–255. Network "0" is not used in Class A because it is reserved (it was originally defined as a broadcast address), and 127 is not used because it is the local loopback network address (the localhost is 127.0.0.1).

Chapter 10

Check Your Understanding

1. B

IPv4 addressing (still more common than IPv6) has four octets of 8 bits each for a total of 32 bits.

2. B

Each octet of an IP address has 8 bits, which allows binary numbers 00000000 through 11111111—the equivalent of 0 through 255 in decimal.

3. A

The network part of an IP address specifies the network to which the host belongs. The host part of an IP address identifies the specific host.

4. B

The host part of an IP address identifies which node (host) on the subnetwork is being addressed. The network part of an IP address specifies the network to which the host belongs.

5. D

You can find the answer by converting the address and mask into binary, performing a bit-wise Boolean AND, and converting it back to decimal. Alternatively, the decimal shortcuts in this chapter could be used, with the fourth octet being the interesting octet, with an increment of 256 – 224 = 32. So, the subnet number would begin with 192.168.73, with the last octet being a multiple of 32 closest to .121, but not larger than –96 in this case.

6. A

Beginning with the first octet on the left, each octet is converted separately as follows:

192 = 128+64 = 1+1+0+0+0+0+0+0

5 = 4+1 = 0+0+0+0+0+1+0+1

34 = 32+2 = 0+0+1+0+0+0+1+0

11 = 8+2+1 = 0+0+0+0+1+0+1+1

7. D

Beginning with the first octet on the left, each octet is converted separately as follows, as far as needed:

11000000 = 126+64 = 192 , so answer A can be eliminated.

00000101 = 4+1, so answers B and C can be eliminated.

None of the dotted-decimal answers are correct.

8. B

Class B addresses use the first two octets for the network part. The network part is 154.19.

9. A

It is necessary to determine this address class by knowing the range of addresses for each class. The range for Class A's first octet is 1–126, for Class B's first octet is 128–191, and for Class C's first octet is 192–223. From this information, you can determine that the given address is a Class B address (129 is between 128 and 192). A Class B network address uses the first two octets as its network part, so 129.219 represents the network.

10. B

This is a Class A address, because the first octet is in the range of 1–126. The default sub-net mask for a Class A network is 255.0.0.0. The given mask indicates that all bits in the second octet were used for subnetting, so the subnet number will increment by 1 (subnet 0 = 123.0.0.0, subnet 1 = 123.1.0.0, subnet 2 = 123.2.0.0, and so on). The broadcast address for a subnet has all binary 1s in the host portion of the address. The address 123.10.255.255 meets that requirement. Here is the address in binary:

01111011.00001010.11111111.11111111

11. B

A Class C network has only one octet available for host addresses. There are $2^h - 2$ usable addresses in the subnet (the first and last addresses are reserved and cannot be used). Because 8 host bits are available, the number of useable host addresses is $2^8 - 2$, which equals 254.

12. B

Use the $2^s - 2$ formula to find the number of usable subnets. (The value s is the number of bits used for subnetting.)

$2^1 - 2 = 0$, so borrowing 1 bit for subnetting leaves you with no usable subnets.

$2^2 - 2 = 2$, so borrowing 2 bits for subnetting leaves you with two usable subnets.

$2^3 - 2 = 6$, but this is not the minimum number you can borrow.

$2^4 - 2 = 14$, but this is not the minimum number you can borrow.

13. C

A design goal of a network is to have fewer collisions so that network throughput is increased. One method of reducing collisions is to reduce the number of broadcasts. If you reduce the number of devices in a collision domain, there should be fewer collisions. Subnetting allows you to increase the number of broadcast domains by spreading the range of IP addresses over several router ports (only routers define broadcast domains).

14. B

An IPv4 subnet mask has the same number of bits as an IPv4 address: 32.

15. D

It is necessary to first convert the IP address to binary and to then align the subnet mask (in binary) directly beneath it. After that, do the Boolean ANDing (0+0 = 0, 0+1 = 0, 1+0 = 0, 1+1 = 1).

	01111001.00001000.00000010.00000101
AND	11111111.00000000.00000000.00000000
equals	01111001.00000000.00000000.00000000
which is	121.0.0.0 in dotted decimal.

16. C

The default Class C subnet mask is 255.255.255.0. The 224 in the fourth octet indicates the value of the bits used for subnetting. That value (224) is 11100000, which means that three bits were borrowed for the subnet part of the address.

17. C

It is necessary to first convert the IP address to binary and to then align the subnet mask (in binary) directly beneath it. After that, do the Boolean ANDing (0+0 = 0, 0+1 = 0, 1+0 = 0, 1+1 = 1).

          10101100.00010000.00000010.01111000

AND   11111111.11111111.11111111.00000000

equals   10101100.00010000.00000010.00000000

which is   172.16.2.0 in dotted decimal.

18. C

Routers use the network layer information, specifically the IP destination address, to determine the best path for routing traffic. They do this by comparing the destination network address to a routing table that includes viable paths to the network.

19. B

The process of evaluating available routes is called path determination.

20. A

Routers use the network layer information, specifically the IP destination address, to determine the best path for routing traffic. They do this by comparing the destination network address to an IP routing table that includes paths to the destination network.

Challenge Questions and Activities

1. C

Host1-2 and Host1-3 can successfully ping each other because they are on the same subnet. No traffic has to go through a router. When Host1-2 tries to ping Host2-2 or Host3-2, the packets must be sent to R1 for forwarding. The packets should be sent to the IP address of the Ethernet interface on R1: 192.168.1.1 (also known as the "default gateway"). Host1-2 has the incorrect IP address in its configuration, and the packets are not processed by the router.

2. B

The default gateway for Host_4 is 192.168.1.161. The subnetwork address is 192.168.1.160, and the subnetwork broadcast address is 192.168.1.191. The address given to Host_4 (192.168.1.194) is not from the same address range as the subnetwork to which it is connected.

Chapter 11

Check Your Understanding

1. A

Retransmitting segments to achieve reliability because they were not successfully received is similar to repeating your words. Slowing your rate of speech is similar to using flow control so that you do not overwhelm the receiver.

2. B

TCP is connection-oriented, divides data into segments, and resends segments that are not received.

3. D

The Window field indicates how many octets (bytes) the device is willing to accept before acknowledgment.

4. A

UDP exchanges datagrams without guaranteed delivery.

5. A

TCP and UDP use port numbers to track different conversations crossing the network. The conversations might be with a single device (only one IP and MAC address) or with multiple devices (several IP and MAC addresses).

6. B

TCP uses a three-way handshake to synchronize the connection before data can be sent. The first segment has only the SYN bit set, the second segment has both the SYN and ACK bits set, and the third and ongoing segments have only the ACK bit set. TCP also uses a four-way handshake to terminate the TCP connection.

7. D

Port numbers ranging from 0–1023 are well-known port numbers. Numbers above 1023 are available for dynamic assignment, although IANA formally recommends that hosts use dynamic ports of 49,152 and above.

8. D

TCP starts a timer when a segment is sent. If an ACK is not received before the timer expires, the segment is retransmitted.

9. C

The receiving device uses flow control. This device must both receive and process incoming segments. If it is overwhelmed by the rate of data coming from the sending device, it uses flow control, which tells the sending device to slow down.

10. C

TCP's primary job is to transfer data from one application process, on one computer, to another application process, on another computer—also with guarantees that the data will arrive, and in order.

11. B

The TCP/IP transport layer includes TCP and UDP.

12. A

Port numbers identify the application process that sent (source port) or should receive (destination port) the data in a TCP or UDP segment or datagram. The port numbers allow easy identification of the application processes sending and receiving the data.

13. A and B

Port numbers identify the application process that sent (source port) or should receive (destination port) the data in a TCP or UDP segment or datagram. The port numbers allow easy identification of the application processes sending and receiving the data.

14. C

The TCP window field is a receiving TCP host's primary means of performing flow control. By increasing and decreasing the granted window size, as listed in the Window field of a TCP header, the receiver can allow the sender to send as fast as is possible without sending the data too fast for the receiver to process it.

15. B

UDP does not provide reliability by itself. It relies on application layer protocols for reliability.

16. D

Both browsers on the host make requests to the web server on destination port 80 but use different source ports. When segments are sent from the web server to the host, they use source port 80 and the destination port that was originally assigned dynamically to each of the web browsers on the host.

17. A

E-mail is a client/server application. Client software is installed on the user's computer; server software is installed on a server (usually, a powerful computer with much memory and storage space) where mail is stored and later retrieved by the client software.

18. B

The client software is installed on the local user's computer. It requests services from the server.

19. A

DNS translates the name of a network node, such as Cisco.com, into an IP address (in this case, 198.133.219.25). Although you are most familiar with this process when typing URLs into web browsers, DNS also works with the **ping** and **tracert** commands.

20. D

The .com top-level domain is an abbreviation for company, which is typically assigned to corporations.

21. B

Telnet allows a user to remotely log in to a computer or networking device. The local computer, which acts as the telnet server, displays information on its screen, and its keyboard is used for input. The remote computer is responsible for processing any input from the local computer.

22. D

Telnet works at the application layer of the TCP/IP model, which is the equivalent of the OSI model's application, presentation, and session layers.

23. D

FTP uses port 20 to transfer data and port 21 to control information.

24. B

SNMP remotely observes and manages networking devices. It gathers the information and displays it for the network operator.

Challenge Questions and Activities

1. A

The IP header and the TCP header are each 20 bytes long, so no more than 1460 bytes are left for data.

2. B

The SYN bit is set in the first segment from host 1 to host 2. The SYN and ACK bits are both set in segment 2 from host 2 to host 1. The ACK bit is set in the third segment from host 1 to host 2.

Decimal to Binary Conversion Table

Decimal Value	Binary Value	Decimal Value	Binary Value
0	0000 0000	23	0001 0111
1	0000 0001	24	0001 1000
2	0000 0010	25	0001 1001
3	0000 0011	26	0001 1010
4	0000 0100	27	0001 1011
5	0000 0101	28	0001 1100
6	0000 0110	29	0001 1101
7	0000 0111	30	0001 1110
8	0000 1000	31	0001 1111
9	0000 1001	32	0010 0000
10	0000 1010	33	0010 0001
11	0000 1011	34	0010 0010
12	0000 1100	35	0010 0011
13	0000 1101	36	0010 0100
14	0000 1110	37	0010 0101
15	0000 1111	38	0010 0110
16	0001 0000	39	0010 0111
17	0001 0001	40	0010 1000
18	0001 0010	41	0010 1001
19	0001 0011	42	0010 1010
20	0001 0100	43	0010 1011
21	0001 0101	44	0010 1100
22	0001 0110	45	0010 1101

Decimal Value	Binary Value	Decimal Value	Binary Value
46	0010 1110	76	0100 1100
47	0010 1111	77	0100 1101
48	0011 0000	78	0100 1110
49	0011 0001	79	0100 1111
50	0011 0010	80	0101 0000
51	0011 0011	81	0101 0001
52	0011 0100	82	0101 0010
53	0011 0101	83	0101 0011
54	0011 0110	84	0101 0100
55	0011 0111	85	0101 0101
56	0011 1000	86	0101 0110
57	0011 1001	87	0101 0111
58	0011 1010	88	0101 1000
59	0011 1011	89	0101 1001
60	0011 1100	90	0101 1010
61	0011 1101	91	0101 1011
62	0011 1110	92	0101 1100
63	0011 1111	93	0101 1101
64	0100 0000	94	0101 1110
65	0100 0001	95	0101 1111
66	0100 0010	96	0110 0000
67	0100 0011	97	0110 0001
68	0100 0100	98	0110 0010
69	0100 0101	99	0110 0011
70	0100 0110	100	0110 0100
71	0100 0111	101	0110 0101
72	0100 1000	102	0110 0110
73	0100 1001	103	0110 0111
74	0100 1010	104	0110 1000
75	0100 1011	105	0110 1001

Decimal Value	Binary Value	Decimal Value	Binary Value
106	0110 1010	136	1000 1000
107	0110 1011	137	1000 1001
108	0110 1100	138	1000 1010
109	0110 1101	139	1000 1011
110	0110 1110	140	1000 1100
111	0110 1111	141	1000 1101
112	0111 0000	142	1000 1110
113	0111 0001	143	1000 1111
114	0111 0010	144	1001 0000
115	0111 0011	145	1001 0001
116	0111 0100	146	1001 0010
117	0111 0101	147	1001 0011
118	0111 0110	148	1001 0100
119	0111 0111	149	1001 0101
120	0111 1000	150	1001 0110
121	0111 1001	151	1001 0111
122	0111 1010	152	1001 1000
123	0111 1011	153	1001 1001
124	0111 1100	154	1001 1010
125	0111 1101	155	1001 1011
126	0111 1110	156	1001 1100
127	0111 1111	157	1001 1101
128	1000 0000	158	1001 1110
129	1000 0001	159	1001 1111
130	1000 0010	160	1010 0000
131	1000 0011	161	1010 0001
132	1000 0100	162	1010 0010
133	1000 0101	163	1010 0011
134	1000 0110	164	1010 0100
135	1000 0111	165	1010 0101

Decimal Value	Binary Value	Decimal Value	Binary Value
166	1010 0110	196	1100 0100
167	1010 0111	197	1100 0101
168	1010 1000	198	1100 0110
169	1010 1001	199	1100 0111
170	1010 1010	200	1100 1000
171	1010 1011	201	1100 1001
172	1010 1100	202	1100 1010
173	1010 1101	203	1100 1011
174	1010 1110	204	1100 1100
175	1010 1111	205	1100 1101
176	1011 0000	206	1100 1110
177	1011 0001	207	1100 1111
178	1011 0010	208	1101 0000
179	1011 0011	209	1101 0001
180	1011 0100	210	1101 0010
181	1011 0101	211	1101 0011
182	1011 0110	212	1101 0100
183	1011 0111	213	1101 0101
184	1011 1000	214	1101 0110
185	1011 1001	215	1101 0111
186	1011 1010	216	1101 1000
187	1011 1011	217	1101 1001
188	1011 1100	218	1101 1010
189	1011 1101	219	1101 1011
190	1011 1110	220	1101 1100
191	1011 1111	221	1101 1101
192	1100 0000	222	1101 1110
193	1100 0001	223	1101 1111
194	1100 0010	224	1110 0000
195	1100 0011	225	1110 0001

Decimal Value	Binary Value
226	1110 0010
227	1110 0011
228	1110 0100
229	1110 0101
230	1110 0110
231	1110 0111
232	1110 1000
233	1110 1001
234	1110 1010
235	1110 1011
236	1110 1100
237	1110 1101
238	1110 1110
239	1110 1111
24	1111 0000
241	1111 0001
242	1111 0010
243	1111 0011
244	1111 0100
245	1111 0101
246	1111 0110
247	1111 0111
248	1111 1000
249	1111 1001
250	1111 1010
251	1111 1011
252	1111 1100
253	1111 1101
254	1111 1110
255	1111 1111

Extra Practice

This appendix contains a variety of practice problems. These problems reinforce processes and math formulas used to analyze many of the basic features of networking.

The practice problems in this appendix are organized based on the chapters that explain the related processes or formulas used to solve the problems. Table C-1 lists the general types of problems found in each major section of this appendix and the corresponding chapter in which you can find more information.

Table C-1 Types of Problems Found in Appendix C

Type of Problem	Corresponding Chapter
Converting to and from binary, decimal, and hexadecimal numbers	1
Calculating the data transfer time	2
Determining the scope of collision domains, broadcast domains, and locations in which full duplex can be used	8
Assessing IP address structure, identifying the class of an IP address, and determining the size of the network and host parts of the address	9
Analyzing and calculating information about subnetting	10

Chapter 1 Practice Problems

Like most types of math problems, the key to mastering the process of converting to and from binary, decimal, and hexadecimal numbers is practice. This section lists several practice problems for converting numbers between different formats. The four types of problems related to Chapter 1, and posed in this appendix, are as follows:

- Converting an 8-bit binary number to a decimal number
- Converting a decimal number to an 8-bit binary number
- Converting an 8-bit binary number to a hexadecimal number
- Converting a hexadecimal number to an 8-bit binary number

Converting an 8-bit Binary Number to a Decimal Number

Convert the 8-bit binary numbers listed in Table C-2 to their decimal equivalents.

Table C-2   Binary-to-Decimal Conversion Problems

Problem Number	Binary	Decimal Value
1	01010101	
2	10101010	
3	11100011	
4	11110000	
5	00001111	
6	11000000	

Converting a Decimal Number to an 8-bit Binary Number

Convert the decimal numbers listed in Table C-3 to their 8-bit binary equivalents. Note that you should include any leading 0s in the binary number, resulting in an 8-bit number as the answer for each problem. The reason for including the leading 0s is that this math is most often used when converting IP addresses from decimal to binary, and that process requires that each of the four decimal numbers in an IP address be converted to an 8-bit number, including leading 0s.

Table C-3   Decimal-to-Binary Conversion Problems

Problem Number	Decimal Value	Binary
1	255	
2	128	
3	200	
4	9	
5	100	
6	248	

Converting an 8-bit Binary Number to a Hexadecimal Number

Convert the 8-bit binary numbers in Table C-4 to their 2-digit hexadecimal equivalents. Use leading 0s as needed so that all answers show a 2-digit hex number.

Table C-4   Decimal-to-Binary Conversion Problems

Problem Number	8-bit Binary Number	2-digit Hex Number
1	01010101	
2	10101010	
3	11100011	
4	11110000	
5	00001111	
6	11000000	

Converting a Hexadecimal Number to an 8-bit Binary Number

Convert the hexadecimal numbers in Table C-5 to their 8-digit binary equivalents. Use leading 0s as needed so that all answers show an 8-digit binary number.

Table C-5   Hexadecimal-to-Binary Conversion Problems

Problem Number	2-digit Hex Number	8-bit Binary Number
1	F0	
2	0E	
3	AB	
4	07	
5	7A	
6	AA	

Chapter 2 Practice Problems

This section provides extra practice problems related to the math covered in Chapter 2. In Chapter 2 you learned how to use the data transfer time calculation to determine how long it would take to transfer a file of a certain size. The calculation uses several variables, including the following:

- The size of the file

- The constraining link bandwidth

- In some cases, a throughput estimate

Essentially, you can calculate the theoretical fastest download time by using the following formula, where S is the size of the file in bits and BW is the bandwidth of the slowest link in the path between two points:

$$T = S/BW$$

Alternately, a more realistic measurement substitutes a throughput speed of something less than the constraining bandwidth speed to more accurately reflect that a single file transfer must compete with other traffic. In the following formula, P is the throughput speed in bits per second:

$$T = S/P$$

Figure C-1 shows a sample internetwork that will be used for the problems in this section. It shows two PCs that will transfer a file, with three links. Each link is labeled with a letter (A, B, and C), with the problems stating the link speed of each of the links.

Figure C-1   Sample Internetwork for Data Transfer Time Calculation Problems

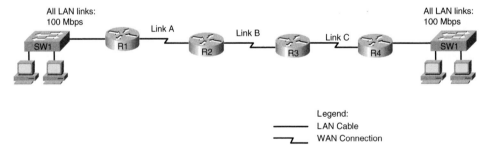

Determine the data transfer time for the problems in Table C-6 by determining the constraining link speed and then calculating the time. Note that the file sizes are listed in bytes, not bits. For these problems, you should calculate the theoretically best transfer time, assuming that the file transfer can use all the bandwidth available in the internetwork.

Table C-6   Data Transfer Time Problems—Theoretical

Problem Number	Link A's Bandwidth	Link B's Bandwidth	Link C's Bandwidth	File Size	Transfer Time
1	1.5 Mbps	768 kbps	512 kbps	10 MB	
2	256 kbps	768 kbps	256 kbps	5 MB	
3	64 kbps	512 kbps	512 kbps	200 MB	

Now determine the data transfer time for the problems in Table C-7, using throughput instead of bandwidth. Note that the throughput is shown in the problems as a percentage of the constraining link's bandwidth.

Table C-7   Data Transfer Time Problems—Using Estimated Throughput

Problem Number	Link A's Bandwidth	Link B's Bandwidth	Link C's Bandwidth	File Size	Throughput as Fraction of Constraining Link Bandwidth	Transfer Time
1	1.5 Mbps	768 kbps	512 kbps	10 MB	1/2	
2	256 kbps	768 kbps	256 kbps	5 MB	1/3	
3	64 kbps	512 kbps	512 kbps	200 MB	1/4	

Chapter 8 Practice Problems

Chapter 8 covers the concepts of and differences between collision domains and broadcast domains and explains cases in which a link can be allowed to use full-duplex logic. So, this appendix provides two practice problems for identifying the collision domains, broadcast domains, and links that could use full duplex. Using Figures C-2 and C-3, identify each individual collision domain and broadcast domain and note each link that is allowed to use full duplex.

Figure C-2   Problem 1 for Identifying Collision Domains, Broadcast Domains, and Full-Duplex Links

Figure C-3   Problem 2 for Identifying Collision Domains, Broadcast Domains, and Full-Duplex Links

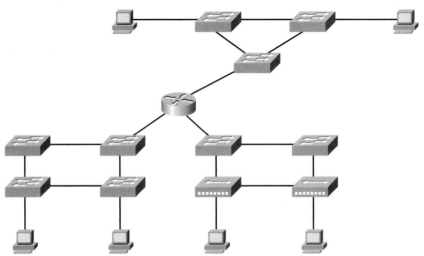

Chapter 9 Practice Problems

This section includes three different types of problems:

- Dissecting the structure of an IP address, specifically the size of the network and host parts, assuming that subnetting is not in use. This process will be referred to as dissecting an IP address.

- Determining basic facts about an IP address, including whether it is from the range of private IP addresses. You also need to determine whether the address is reserved or can be legally assigned for use as an IP address for a host, again assuming that subnetting is not in use.

- Dissecting the structure of an IP address, this time assuming that subnetting is used, which means each address has three parts (network, subnet, and host). However, the subnet masks used in each case are simple and should not require any binary math to find the answers.

Dissecting Unsubnetted IP Addresses

When analyzing IP addresses, it is important to be able to identify the parts of an IP address, both with and without subnetting. For the problems in Table C-8, first determine the class of IP address. Then, record its Class A, B, or C network number, the size of the network part of the address, and the size of the host part of the address. (No subnetting is used for the addresses shown in this table.) The first problem's answers are provided, to serve as an example.

Table C-8   Dissecting Unsubnetted IP Addresses

Problem Number	IP Address	Class	Network Number	Number of Octets in the Network Part	Number of Octets in the Host Part
1	10.1.1.1	A	10.0.0.0	1	3
2	200.20.200.200				
3	128.28.2.2				
4	191.240.1.1				
5	224.1.1.1				
6	100.1.1.1				
7	192.191.2.2				
8	150.1.4.4				

Determining Whether Addresses Are Private and Valid

Next, examine the IP addresses shown in Table C-9. None of these addresses are subnetted. Identify the class of each address, whether the address can be assigned for use on an IP host, and whether the address is a private IP address.

Table C-9   Determining Whether Addresses Are Valid and Private and Identifying Their Address Classes

Problem Number	IP Address	Class of Address	Assignable to an IP Host?	Part of a Private Network?
1	192.168.0.0			
2	128.1.255.255			
3	239.1.1.1			
4	9.1.1.1			
5	172.32.0.255			
6	193.1.1.1			
7	223.223.223.0			
8	245.1.1.1			

Dissecting a Subnetted Address That Uses a Simple Mask

Table C-10 ends the practice problems for Chapter 9 by repeating problems similar to those shown in Table C-8, but with simple subnetting applied to the IP address. Complete the empty cells for each of the problems shown in Table C-10. The first problem's answers are provided, to serve as an example.

Table C-10   Dissecting Subnetted IP Addresses

Problem Number	IP Address	Mask	Class	Subnet Number	Number of Octets in the Network Part	Number of Octets in the Subnet Part	Number of Octets in the Host Part
1	10.1.1.1	255.255.0.0	A	10.1.0.0	1	1	2
2	200.20.200.200	255.255.255.0					
3	128.28.2.2	255.255.255.0					
4	191.240.1.1	255.255.255.0					
5	99.1.1.1	255.255.255.0					
6	100.1.1.1	255.255.0.0					
7	192.1.2.2	255.255.255.0					
8	150.1.4.4	255.255.255.0					

Chapter 10 Practice Problems

Chapter 10 covers many details related to subnetting. This appendix includes practice problems related to most aspects of subnetting. The problems are listed in the same order in which they are covered in Chapter 10, with the problems covering the following topics:

- Determining the number of required subnets for an internetwork, based on a diagram of the internetwork

- Determining the minimum number of subnet and host bits required in the structure of an IP address to support the maximum number of required subnets and hosts per subnet

- Determining the subnet mask(s) that supports the stated maximum number of subnets and hosts per subnet

- For a chosen IP network and mask, determining all the subnets of that network

- For a chosen IP network and mask, determining the subnet broadcast address for each subnet and the range of assignable addresses in each subnet

- For a given IP address and mask, determining the resident subnet

Determining the Number of Required Subnets, Based on a Network Diagram

Determining the number of required subnets, based on a network diagram, is an important skill when planning for the number of subnets. Examine Figure C-4 through Figure C-7 and determine the number of required subnets for each figure. You may want to circle each portion of the internetworks in the figures that must be in the same subnet.

Figure C-4   Problem 1 for Determining the Number of Required Subnets

Figure C-5   Problem 2 for Determining the Number of Required Subnets

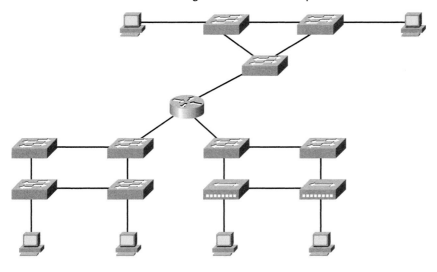

Figure C-6   Problem 3 for Determining the Number of Required Subnets

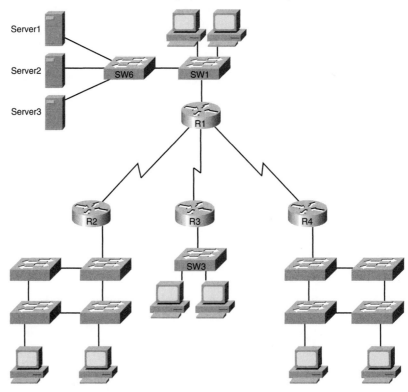

Figure C-7   Problem 4 for Determining the Number of Required Subnets

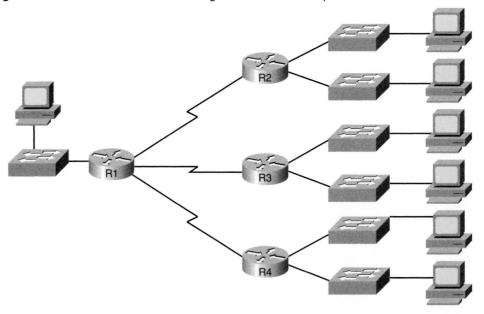

Determining the Required Number of Subnet and Host Bits

Another important skill is to be able to determine the number of subnet and host bits required in a subnet mask to meet the requirements for a certain maximum number of subnets and a maximum number of hosts per subnet. For the CCNA 1 course, the number of subnets allowed when using s bits for the subnet field is $2^s - 2$. (The CCNA 3 course covers classless addressing concepts that show how two other subnets can be made available, making the formula 2^s.) The formula for the number of hosts per subnet is always $2^h - 2$, even with classless addressing.

For the problems in Table C-11, determine the number of required subnet and host bits to meet the stated requirements. The "Maximum Number of Subnets Needed" column defines the largest number of subnets that a particular internetwork needs. To solve the problem, you must determine the minimum number of subnet bits that allows all the subnets to be created. For example, in Problem 2, the internetwork needs at most 200 subnets; to support 200 subnets, a minimum of 8 subnet bits required because 7 subnet bits would provide for only $2^7 - 2$, or 126, subnets, whereas 8 subnet bits would provide for $2^8 - 2$, or 254, subnets. Although the answer of "8 subnet bits" provides for more than 200 subnets, the least number of subnet bits meets the requirement.

Similarly, the "Maximum Number of Hosts Needed per Subnet" column lists the largest number of host IP addresses needed in any subnet. The answer must list the minimum number of host bits that provides enough host addresses.

Table C-11   Determining the Number of Subnet and Host Bits Required

Problem Number	Classful Network Being Subnetted	Maximum Number of Subnets Needed	Maximum Number of Hosts Needed per Subnet	Minimum Number of Required Subnet Bits	Minimum Number of Required Host Bits
1	10.0.0.0	4000	4000		
2	128.1.0.0	200	200		
3	192.168.2.0	10	10		
4	172.30.0.0	200	100		
5	200.1.1.0	50	2		
6	150.1.0.0	255	200		

Determining the Subnet Mask

After you have determined the number of required subnet and host bits for a particular set of subnetting requirements, you need to determine what subnet mask meets those requirements. In Table C-12, an engineer has already determined the number of subnet bits and host bits required in the mask for several designs. For these problems, determine the subnet mask that meets the requirements. If more than one mask works, determine two masks: one that supports the maximum number of subnets while still meeting the requirements, and one that supports the maximum number of hosts while still meeting the requirements.

Note that Table C-12 does not show the answers to Table C-8's problems.

Table C-12   Determining the Subnet Mask, Given a Set of Requirements

Problem Number	Classful Network Being Subnetted	Minimum Number of Required Subnet Bits	Minimum Number of Required Host Bits	Only Possible Mask, or Mask That Supports the Maximum Number of Subnets	Mask That Supports the Maximum Number of Hosts per Subnet (as Needed)
1	10.0.0.0	12	12		
2	128.1.0.0	10	6		
3	200.1.1.0	5	3		
4	192.168.2.0	3	4		
5	172.30.0.0	7	7		
6	150.1.0.0	4	4		

Determining the Subnet Numbers of a Single Network When Given a Subnet Mask

After you have determined the Class A, B, or C network number to use for a new internetwork, and have decided on the subnet mask to use, you must then determine the actual subnet numbers. As usual, the answer can be found using binary math and decimal shortcuts. Using Chapter 10 as a reference, find the subnet numbers of the networks shown in Table C-13, using the listed masks.

Table C-13   Determining the Subnets of Particular Networks Using a Static-Length Mask

Problem Number	Network	Mask
1	10.0.0.0	255.255.0.0
2	172.16.0.0	255.255.252.0
3	192.168.8.0	255.255.255.192

Note that the next section's problems ask you to find the range of valid assignable IP addresses in each subnet for these same three problems. Feel free to work on the problems in the next section at the same time that you work on this section.

Determining the Subnet Broadcast Addresses and Range of Assignable Addresses

Another type of problem when working with subnetting is to determine the range of assignable IP addresses in a subnet. To find the range, it is useful to first find the subnet broadcast address, because the assignable IP addresses are the numbers that sit between the subnet number and that subnet's broadcast address.

Table C-14 lists the same three IP networks and masks as in Table C-13. For these three problems, continue your work by determining the range of valid addresses and the broadcast address for several subnets. In cases for which the number of subnets is large, just find the answers for the first two or three subnets and the last two or three subnets.

Table C-14   Determining the Range of Assignable Addresses in Each Subnet

Problem Number	Network	Mask
1	10.0.0.0	255.255.0.0
2	172.16.0.0	255.255.252.0
3	192.168.8.0	255.255.255.192

Finding the Resident Subnet

The last type of problem offered in this appendix is most useful when analyzing an existing internetwork. In such cases, it may be important to be able to look at an IP address and mask, and identify the subnet number. Table C-15 lists several problems that supply an IP address and a mask. For these problems, determine the subnet number in which that IP address resides.

Table C-15   Determining the Resident Subnet

Problem Number	IP Address	Mask	Resident Subnet
1	10.1.2.3	255.255.0.0	
2	172.16.100.2	255.255.254.0	
3	192.168.8.201	255.255.255.252	
4	192.168.19.177	255.255.255.240	
5	172.30.200.200	255.255.248.0	
6	200.1.1.180	255.255.255.192	

Glossary

1s digit   In decimal math, the right-most digit of a number.

10s digit   In decimal math, the second digit from the right in a multidigit number.

100s digit   In decimal math, the third digit from the right in a multidigit number.

10BASE2   An IEEE standard for Ethernet (IEEE 802.3) that uses thin coax cabling with each device connecting to the coax using a T-connector, which is attached to the cable. 10BASE2 limits the length of a single segment to 185 meters.

10BASE5   A 10-Mbps baseband Ethernet specification (IEEE 802.3) using standard (thick) 50-ohm baseband coaxial cable. 10BASE5, which is part of the IEEE 802.3 baseband physical layer specification, has a distance limit of 500 m (1640 feet) per segment.

10BASE-T   An Ethernet standard (IEEE 802.3a) that uses UTP cabling to connect each device to a hub.

100BASE-FX   A Fast Ethernet standard (IEEE 802.3u) for 100-Mbps Ethernet using multimode optical cabling.

100BASE-TX   A Fast Ethernet standard (IEEE 802.3u) for 100-Mbps Ethernet using two-pair UTP cabling.

1000BASE-LX   Generally called long-reach Gigabit Ethernet, it is an IEEE standard (IEEE 802.3z) for Gigabit Ethernet based on single-mode fiber, which is designed to support long cabling distances.

1000BASE-SX   Generally called short-reach Gigabit Ethernet, it is an IEEE standard (IEEE 802.3z) for Gigabit Ethernet based on multimode fiber, which is designed to support short cabling distances.

1000BASE-T   An IEEE standard (IEEE 802.3ab) for Gigabit Ethernet based on four-pair UTP cabling.

1000BASE-X   Refers to all fiber-based Gigabit Ethernet standards.

5-4-3 rule   A rule for network design using 10BASE2 and 10BASE5 repeaters and/or 10BASE-T repeaters and hubs. This rule states that between any two devices on a LAN, there can be at most 5 cable segments (counting the segment to which they are attached), 4 repeaters/hubs, and 3 LAN segments with end-user devices attached to them.

5-4-3-2-1 rule   Expands the 5-4-3 rule, with the 2 referring to the number of segments with no end-user devices on them. The 1 refers to the fact that the combined network is 1 collision domain.

access link   A term used in Cisco campus LAN design that refers to an Ethernet cable that connects an end-user device to an access layer switch.

access point (AP)   A WLAN device that communicates with other devices, typically PCs with wireless NICs, using radio waves. The AP also connects to the wired LAN, which provides wireless users with access to the wired LAN.

access switch   A Cisco campus network design term that refers to typically small switches that sit in wiring closets near end-user devices. The end-user devices connect to the access switch, allowing the devices to communicate with other devices attached to the network.

access VPN   A VPN created to allow individual users to access an enterprise network, typically from home, when traveling, or from wireless hotspots.

ACK   A flag in the TCP header that signifies whether the Acknowledgment field in the TCP header is meaningful.

acknowledgment number   Set in a sent TCP segment, this number notes the sequence number of the next byte this host expects to receive. It is used to recognize lost packets and flow control.

active hub   A LAN hub that has electrical power, which allows it to regenerate and repeat electrical signals.

active scanning   In WLANs, a process by which a wireless NIC sends probe messages to find the best AP.

Address Resolution Protocol (ARP)   A TCP/IP Layer 3 protocol that allows a host that knows another IP address on the same LAN to dynamically discover that other host's MAC address.

ad-hoc mode   One of two modes for a wireless NIC (the other being infrastructure mode) in which the NIC purposefully attempts to associate with other wireless NICs instead of an AP.

adjacent layer interaction   Refers to how a protocol from one layer of a networking model provides some service to another protocol that sits at the next higher adjacent layer in the model. This interaction occurs on one computer.

algorithm   The logic or process that a computer program uses to make decisions. In networking, many protocols use algorithms, including STP and all IP routing protocols.

alternating current (AC)   The continual reversing of electrical current in opposite directions over a conducting material transmission medium.

American National Standards Institute (ANSI)   A U.S. government–accredited standards body that develops U.S. standards, often working as the U.S. representative with international standards bodies.

American Registry for Internet Numbers (ARIN)   The organization to which IANA assigns the right and responsibility to assign IP addresses to organizations in the U.S.

ampere (amp)   A unit of measurement for electrical current.

amplitude   For continuous wave-like signals, such as sound, light, and analog electrical signals, it is the maximum absolute value of the signal's power.

analog signal   An energy signal in which the waveform varies similarly, or analogous, to a natural waveform such as sound or electromagnetic radiation.

antistatic strap   A device that discharges static electricity away from a person's body so that the person can work on computer electronics with less chance of harming the electronics through static discharge.

AppleTalk   A networking model developed by the Apple Computer Corporation. Cisco routers can be configured to route AppleTalk packets.

application layer   The top layer of both the OSI and TCP/IP models. In OSI, this layer defines the interface to application processes. In TCP/IP, this layer performs functions similar to the top three layers of the OSI model.

application-specific integrated circuit (ASIC)   A computer chip that is designed for a specific purpose as opposed to general purposes. For example, LAN switches use ASICs to perform certain functions, such as forwarding frames, so that the process works quickly.

ARP broadcast   An ARP message sent to the LAN broadcast (FFFF.FFFF.FFFF) MAC address. The message is sent by a host to request that another host—a host that uses the IP address listed in the ARP broadcast—respond with its MAC address.

ARP reply   An ARP message sent in response to an ARP broadcast, which lists the MAC address of the host that sends the ARP reply.

ARP request   See ARP broadcast.

ARP table   A list of information learned via ARP—specifically, a list of IP addresses, their corresponding MAC addresses, and the interfaces on which the information was learned with ARP.

ASCII-(American Standard Code for Information Interchange)   Defines a standard for binary values that represent the text characters stored by a computer.

assignable IP address   An IP address that can be assigned to an interface. This term specifically excludes reserved IP addresses in a subnet, such as IP subnet numbers and subnet broadcast addresses.

associate   In WLANs, the process by which a wireless NIC sends messages to an AP to form an agreement that allows that NIC to use the AP.

asymmetric switching   In LAN switches, a reference to cases in which a frame is forwarded, or switched, when the incoming and outgoing interfaces use different speeds.

Asynchronous Transfer Mode (ATM)   A networking technology that implements the lower two layers of the OSI model. Today, ATM is mainly a WAN technology, using SONET for the underlying physical links.

asynchronous transmission   Specifically for Ethernet at 10 Mbps, the Ethernet devices do not send any electrical signal when idle; in fact, long periods might pass without any electrical signals on the wires.

attachment user interface (AUI)   A 15-pin connector first used with 10BASE5 Ethernet LANs. AUI connectors are sometimes used with older Ethernet NICs and router interfaces as well.

attenuation   The effect on any energy wave in which the wave degrades to a lower power level over time.

audio speaker   A device external to a PC through which the computer can play sounds.

Automatic Medium-independent Crossover (Auto-mdix)   Allows switches to detect if a cable with the wrong pinouts is mistakenly used between switches, and then reverse the interface's logic to make the cable work correctly.

autonegotiation   A process defined by IEEE 802.3x that describes how Ethernet NICs and switch ports can automatically negotiate the speed and duplex settings used on an Ethernet link.

autonomous system (AS)   A term used with routing protocols that refers to an internetwork that is in the control of one company, organization, school, or government divi-

sion. For example, a single company is typically a single AS, and a school system is typically a single AS.

auxiliary port (aux port)   A physical port on most Cisco routers designed to allow out-of-band access to the router. An external modem can be cabled to the aux port and a phone line attached to the modem. Then, the network engineer can use a PC and modem to call the router and log in to that router, even if the IP network is broken.

B channel   In ISDN, Bearer (B) channels are separate groups of bandwidth that can transmit data to different sites. For example, a BRI line, with two B channels, can concurrently have connections to two sites, sending and receiving 64 Kbps of data with each remote site.

backbone level   Links between the hubs/switches in the LAN core. These switches do not have links to end-user devices; they connect to only other hubs/switches.

backbone link   In LANs, a link between two switches that is used to forward frames between major sections of the LAN.

backplane   On a PC, a large circuit board that contains sockets for expansion cards.

bandwidth   In networking, a measurement of the speed of bits that can be transmitted over a particular link.

Base 10   The decimal numbering system. *See also* decimal numbering.

Base 16   The hexadecimal numbering system. *See also* hexadecimal numbering.

Base 2   The binary numbering system. *See also* binary numbering.

baseband   A transmission method that uses the entire medium's bandwidth to transmit a single signal. It is used by most Ethernet types.

Basic Rate Interface (BRI)   A type of ISDN line composed of two 64-Kbps B channels and one 16-Kbps signaling (D) channel.

beacon   In WLANs, a beacon is a message sent by an AP for which wireless NICs listen. Wireless NICs can then learn of the presence and signal strength from each AP and choose an AP to which the NIC will associate.

binary numbering   A system that uses two digits, 0 and 1, which computers use. This is the Base 2 numbering system.

binary-to-decimal conversion chart   A chart, like in Appendix B, that lists binary numbers and their corresponding decimal values.

bit (binary digit)   The smallest unit of information on a computer, with each bit's value being either a binary 0 or 1. Short for "binary digit."

bits per second (bps)   A unit of measurement of the number of bits that can be transmitted in 1 second.

bit-time   The time required to send a single bit over some transmission medium. The time can be calculated as 1 / *speed*, where *speed* is the number of bits per second sent over the medium.

blocking state   An interface state defined by the IEEE 802.1D STP. *See also* STP blocking state.

Border Gateway Protocol (BGP)   A routing protocol designed to exchange routing information between different autonomous systems. As such, BGP is an Exterior Gateway Protocol (EGP).

bridge   In Ethernet, a Layer 2 device that receives an electrical signal in one port, interprets the bits, and makes a filtering or forwarding decision about the frame. If the bridge forwards a frame, the bridge regenerates the electrical signal as well.

bridge protocol data unit (BPDU)   Refers to the messages defined by the IEEE 802.1D STP. STP was first created for use by LAN bridges.

bridging table   A general term for the table a LAN bridge uses for its forwarding/filtering decisions. The table holds a list of MAC addresses and the port out which the bridge should forward frames for those frames to reach the correct destination. Also called a CAM table when referring to the bridge table on Cisco LAN switches.

broadband   A transmission method by which devices send multiple electrical signals over the same medium. The term refers to the use of a broad number of frequencies or bandwidths.

broadcast   In Ethernet, a frame that is sent to the broadcast MAC address (FFFF.FFFF.FFFF).

broadcast address   In Ethernet, a special Ethernet address (FFFF.FFFF.FFFF) used as a destination MAC address to cause a frame to be sent to all devices on an Ethernet LAN. Alternatively, in IP, each subnet has a single broadcast address, which is more commonly called the subnet or directed broadcast address. *See* subnet broadcast address.

broadcast domain   A set of LAN interfaces (including NICs and network device interfaces) for which a broadcast frame sent by any one device is forwarded to all the other interfaces in that same broadcast domain.

broadcast frame   In Ethernet, a frame sent to the broadcast MAC address of FFFF.FFFF.FFFF. A broadcast frame should be forwarded to all devices on the same LAN.

broadcast medium   A transmission medium whose operations mean that any data sent by any device using the medium is received by all other devices on the medium.

broadcast storm   An event in which LAN broadcasts are continually forwarded in loops throughout a LAN. This consumes most—if not all—LAN bandwidth, making the LAN generally unusable.

broadcast subnet   The numerically largest subnet number in any subnetting scheme, characterized by a value of all binary 1s in the subnet portion of the subnet number. Its name is derived from the fact that this subnet's subnet broadcast address is identical to the network-wide broadcast address. With classful IP addressing, this subnet is one of the two reserved subnets that should not be used.

buffer   In fiber-optic cabling, refers to a part of an optical cable that provides physical protection to the glass fibers inside the buffer.

buffering   The process of how a bridge or switch prevents collisions. Bridges and switches store, or place into a buffer, each received LAN frame, waiting until the output interface is idle before forwarding the frame.

building block   In Cisco campus LAN design, this term refers to the combined distribution and access layer switches in a single building. Cisco suggests using a similar design in each building and creating a campus LAN by connecting the building LANs (called building blocks) to core LAN switches.

burned-in address (BIA)   Another name for the MAC address that is permanently assigned to a LAN NIC. The address is burned into a chip on the card. *See also* Media Access Control (MAC) address.

bus   A collection of circuits through which data is transmitted from one part of a computer to another. The bus connects all the internal computer components to the CPU. The ISA and the PCI are two types of buses on PCs.

bus topology   A physical network topology that looks like a bus route in that the electrical signal passes the entire length of a cable, and each device receives the electrical signal. Alternately, a logical network topology that causes all devices on the network to receive a copy of the same electrical signal regardless of the physical topology.

byte   8 bits; used by many low-level operations on computer processors.

cable   A strand of plastic, insulation, and encapsulating wires or optical media for the purpose of protecting the media and for convenience when installing the media.

cable modem   A device that can send and receive data over a CATV cable.

cable router   A single device that acts both as a cable modem and an IP router.

capacitor   An electronic component that stores energy in the form of an electrostatic field. It consists of two conducting metal plates separated by an insulating material.

carrier sense multiple access with collision avoidance (CSMA/CA)   A WLAN access mechanism, similar to CSMA/CD, but by which the devices first request the right to send, which hopefully avoids collisions.

carrier sense multiple access with collision detection (CSMA/CD)   The algorithm used by Ethernet devices to reduces collisions by making each device wait for the LAN to be idle before sending a frame. If collisions occur, the sending devices detect the collision, wait, and retry.

Category 3   A name for a type of UTP cabling as defined by the EIA and TIA. This cabling type was commonly used for telephone lines and the original 10BASE-T LANs.

Category 4   A name for a type of UTP cabling as defined by the EIA and TIA. This cabling type was commonly used for Token Ring LANs.

Category 5   A name for a type of UTP cabling as defined by the EIA and TIA. This cabling type was originally specified for 100BASE-T LANs.

Category 5e   A name for a type of UTP cabling as defined by the EIA and TIA. This cabling type meets higher testing standards than Category 5 and is an acceptable medium for 1000BASE-T.

Category 6   A name for a type of UTP cabling as defined by the EIA and TIA. This cabling type meets the highest UTP cabling standards to date.

CATV   An acronym for cable TV.

CD-ROM drive   An optical drive that can read information from a CD-ROM. This can also be a CD-RW drive, a DVD drive, or a combination of all three in one drive.

cell   In WLANs, a small area in which a wireless AP's radio transmission can be heard well enough so that a wireless NIC can communicate with the AP.

central processing unit (CPU)   The microchip on a computer that performs the primary computations and instructions.

channel service unit/data service unit (CSU/DSU)   A device that connects to a WAN circuit on one side and a serial cable on the other, with the serial cable typically connecting to a router. The CSU/DSU understands how to perform physical (Layer 1) signaling on WAN circuits.

Checksum   An FCS-like field in the TCP header that can confirm that no errors occurred in the TCP header.

circuit switching   A process by which a networking device forwards bits based on a connection called a circuit. For example, twentieth-century telephone networks created a circuit between two phones when a phone call was placed; the switching equipment forwarded the binary representation of a voice based on where the circuit was routed when the call was established.

cladding   A portion of a fiber-optic cable that surrounds the core to reflect light back into the core and prevent the light from escaping.

Class A   A class of unicast IP networks whose first octet ranges from 1 to 126 (inclusive). Addresses in a Class A network have the same value for the first octet.

Class B   A class of unicast IP networks whose first octet ranges from 128 to 191 (inclusive). Addresses in a Class B network have the same value for the first two octets.

Class C   A class of unicast IP networks whose first octet ranges from 192 to 223 (inclusive). Addresses in a Class C network have the same value for the first three octets.

Class D   A class of IP addresses whose first octets range from 224 to 239 (inclusive); used for IP multicasting.

Class E   A class of IP addresses whose first octets range from 240 to 255 (inclusive); used for experimental purposes.

classful address   A unicast IP address that is considered to have three parts: a network part, a subnet part, and a host part. The term classful refers to the fact that the classful network rules are first applied to the address, and then the rest of the address can be separated into a subnet and host part to perform subnetting.

classful network   A Class A, B, or C IP network, as defined by the classful rules that state that Class A networks have a one-octet network part, Class B networks have a two-octet network part, and Class C networks have a three-octet network part.

classful routing protocol   A routing protocol that does not send subnet masks in routing updates, so classful routing protocols cannot support variable-length subnet masking (VLSM).

classless addressing   A unicast IP address that is considered to have two parts: a prefix and a host part. The term classless refers to the fact that the classful network rules are not applied to the address.

classless routing protocol   A routing protocol that sends subnet masks in routing updates, so classless routing protocols support variable-length subnet masking (VLSM).

client   In networking, a computer that relies on some other computer to supply a service. For example, a computer that wants to store files on another computer, look at web-based content on another server, or print documents on another computer's printer is a client.

client/server model   A method of networking between computers in which end-user computers are clients that need some service, such as a place to store and print files. Other computers act as servers to provide those services.

clocking   On WAN links, the process by which one device on the link trusted to maintain the timing at which the devices encode and decode bits on the link. In normal cases, the telco provides clocking to the CSU/DSU on each link, and the CSU/DSU provides clocking to the routers.

cloud   In networking, a symbol used when drawing network diagrams that represents a part of the network whose details can be ignored for the purposes of the diagram.

collision   In Ethernet LANs, an event in which two or more devices send a frame onto the same collision domain so the electrical signals of the multiple frames overlap, which destroys any ability for other devices to correctly interpret the frame's bits.

collision attempt limit   In CSMA/CD with Ethernet, this refers to the maximum number of times (16) that a device can attempt to resend a frame after it initially experiences a collision. After this number of attempts, the NIC then tells the software that asked the NIC to send the frame that the frame cannot be sent.

collision back-off limit   In CSMA/CD with Ethernet, the back-off timer is doubled for each failed attempt to resend a collided frame. The collision back-off limit defines the maximum value to which the timer can grow.

collision back-off timer   In the CSMA/CD algorithm, devices that send frames that later collide with another frame must wait before trying to send the frame again. The devices use their back-off timer to determine how long to wait.

collision domain   A set of LAN interfaces (including NICs and network device interfaces) for which a frame sent out any two of these interfaces at the same time, causing a collision.

collision fragment   An electrical signal that results from the overlapped collided signals on an Ethernet LAN.

collision jam size   The number of bits (32) in the jam signal used by Ethernet NICs and the CSMA/CD algorithm.

COM port   A physical connector on a PC that can be used for a wide variety of serial communications functions. The COM port can be used with a rollover cable to connect to a Cisco router or switch console port. Along with a terminal emulator on the PC, the COM port allows a person to log in to the router or switch.

compact disk (CD)   A storage device that can be used to store various binary digital data, including digital music. Used by computers to store data.

computer hardware   Physical components, such as processors, RAM, disk drives, video displays, keyboards, and so on, that, when combined correctly, provide a physical capability to run software.

computer software   Instructions that can be executed on computer hardware with the intent of performing some function that is useful to the computer's user.

concentrator   A term referring to LAN hubs, specifically because of their role as a place to connect cables from many end-user devices.

conductor   Any material through which electrical current passes relatively easily.

connected subnet   From a router's perspective, a subnet to which a router has connected one of its interfaces. Routers learn their initial IP routes based on being connected to these subnets.

connectionless   Any communication in which the sender and receiver do not prearrange for communications to occur.

connection-oriented   Any communications in which the sender and receiver must prearrange for communications to occur; otherwise, the communication fails.

connector   In networking, a reference to a molded plastic and/or metal end to a cable that can be inserted into a socket.

Content Addressable Memory (CAM) table   Refers to a Cisco switch's MAC address table. This term refers to the fact that the table is stored in CAM, which is memory hardware that allows fast table lookups.

convergence   A process by which routers recognize that something has occurred that changes some routers' routes, react to the event, and find the now currently best routes. The time required for this to occur is called convergence time. Rapid convergence is one of the most important features of routing protocols.

copper conductor   Copper, usually in the form of a wire, that easily passes electrical current.

copper wire   A long, thin strand of copper.

core   In an optical cable, the center of the cable over which the optical signal passes. The core is made of glass-like material called silica (silicon dioxide).

core link   In Cisco campus LAN design, an Ethernet link between two core switches.

core switch   In Cisco campus LAN design, a switch whose role is to forward frames between buildings (building blocks). Core switches typically connect to the distribution switches at each building but do not directly connect to any end-user devices or server farms.

Coulomb's Law   A physics law that states that like electrical charges repel each other, and opposite electrical charges attract each other.

crossover   A general reference to swapping the transmit and receive media in a cable. Also popularly used to refer to Ethernet crossover cables.

crossover cable   A UTP cable in which some pairs of twisted-pair wires are crossed when comparing the RJ-45 connectors on either end of the cable. 10BASE-T and 100BASE-T crossover cables connect the pair at pins 1 and 2 on each end to pins 3 and 6 on the other end. 1000BASE-T crossover cables also cross the pairs at pins 4 and 5 and pins 7 and 8.

crosstalk   Noise created on one wire as a result of current flowing over a nearby wire.

cut-through switching   A method of internal processing by LAN switches. The switch looks at the destination MAC address as soon as the first part of an incoming frame arrives, and then the switch starts sending the frame out the output interface even before the entire frame is received on the input interface.

cyclic redundancy check (CRC)   Occasionally used to refer to a Frame Check Sequence (FCS). *See also* Frame Check Sequence (FCS).

D channel   A portion of the bandwidth in an ISDN line used for call setup and tear-down.

data communications equipment (DCE)   A device that supplies clocking to another device.

Data field   The field in a frame, packet, segment, or other data structure defined by some networking protocol that holds the data as supplied by a protocol defined at the next higher layer in the protocol model.

data flow   This term is a generic reference to the process of how networking devices encapsulate, de-encapsulate, and forward data.

data link layer   Layer 2 of the OSI model. Provides transit of data across a physical link by defining the rules about how the physical link is used. To do so, the data link layer is concerned with physical (as opposed to logical) addressing, network topology, network access, and error notification.

data terminal equipment (DTE)   A device that receives clocking from another device and adjusts its clock as needed.

data transfer time   A phrase used in the online curriculum that refers to a simple math problem that calculates the time required to download a file. The time might be theoretical, based on the constraining link bandwidth, or more realistic by estimating the actual (lower) throughput.

DCE cable   A WAN cable that a router uses when the router is supplying clocking, thereby acting as data communications equipment.

decimal numbering   A numbering system that uses the ten digits (0 through 9) used by humans. It is the Base 10 numbering system.

decimal-to-binary conversion chart   A chart, like in Appendix B, that lists decimal numbers and their corresponding binary values.

DECnet   A proprietary networking model created by the Digital Equipment Corporation (DEC). Cisco routers can be configured to route DECnet packets.

decrypt   A process by which encrypted data is fed into a mathematical formula, along with a secret key, to re-create the data in its original unencrypted form.

de-encapsulation   A process by which a computer, after it receives data over some transmission medium, examines the headers and trailers at each successive higher layer, eventually handing the data to the correct application.

default gateway   On a computer, a reference to an IP address on the same subnet, with that IP address being the IP address of a router. When the computer needs to send a packet to another subnet, it sends the packet to its default gateway. Also known as default router.

delay   *See* latency.

delay skew   In cables that have multiple wire pairs, the wires differ slightly in length. Delay skew refers to the difference in time for electricity to travel over the shortest and longest wire pair; too much delay skew can make data transmission over the cable difficult or even impossible.

demodulate   The process of receiving an analog electrical signal and interpreting the received signal as a series of binary digits. One of the two functions of a modem.

Department of Defense (DoD)   A division of the U.S. government in charge of the military. A DoD research project created the early TCP/IP protocols.

Destination Media Access Control (MAC) Address   The field in an Ethernet header that lists the MAC address to which a frame has been sent.

Destination Port   A field in a TCP or UDP header that identifies the application process on the receiving computer for which the data is intended.

destination port number   The value of the destination port field in a TCP or UDP segment.

Destination Service Access Point (DSAP)   A 1-byte field in the IEEE 802.2 header that is used to specify the type of data encapsulated behind the 802.2 header.

detector   In optical transmission, detectors receive the incoming light signal and convert the light into electrical energy, which is, in turn, interpreted as a binary 0 or 1.

deterministic   Refers to whether the performance of a device, attached to a particular type of LAN, can be accurately predicted (determined). Token Ring LANs are deterministic, but Ethernet LANs are nondeterministic.

DHCP reply   A message, typically sent by a DHCP server in response to a DHCP request, that supplies an IP address and other information to a DHCP client. Also known as DHCP acknowledgment.

DHCP request   A DHCP message, sent by a DHCP client, requesting that a DHCP server lease an IP address to the client.

DHCP server   A computer that supplies a DHCP service, which means that the server can assign IP addresses to clients.

digit   When writing any number via a series of symbols, a single one of those symbols. For example, 2 is one digit in the number 123.

digital signal level 0 (DS0)   The smallest single unit of transmission in the T-carrier system; runs at 64 Kbps.

digital signal level 1 (DS1)   Another member of the T-carrier system, with 24 DS0s plus 8 kbps of overhead for a total bandwidth of 1.544 Mbps. Also called a T1.

digital signal level 3 (DS3)   Another member of the T-carrier system, with 28 DS1s plus overhead for a total bandwidth of 44.736 Mbps. Also called a T3.

digital signal   An energy signal that looks like a square wave with a constant power state that then immediately changes to some other power state. Digital signals are often used to transmit data.

digital subscriber line (DSL)   A class of technologies that allow digital transmission on normal phone lines, outside the range of frequencies usually used for voice, which allows concurrent voice calls and data transmission. Typically used as an Internet access technology.

digital transmission   A style of transmission or an encoding scheme in which discrete voltage/light frequency levels are used, with transitions to alternate voltage/light frequency occurring as quickly as the signal can change. The resulting graph shows a square waveform.

digital video disk (DVD)   A storage device that can store various binary digital data, including audio and video. Computers can use it to store data.

direct current (DC)   A type of electrical current flow in which the current always flows in one direction over a particular conductor.

Direct Sequence Spread Spectrum (DSSS)   A physical layer transmission standard used in the IEEE 802.11 and 802.11b WLAN standards.

directly connected network   *See* connected subnet.

disabled state   An interface state defined by the IEEE 802.1D STP. *See also* STP disabled state.

disk drive   *See* hard disk drive.

distance vector (DV)   A type of routing protocol algorithm that advertises each IP subnet along with a numeric metric that describes how far away each subnet is from the router sending the route advertisement.

distribution switch   A Cisco campus network design term that refers to switches that do not attach to end-user devices but that distribute traffic between different access switches and the rest of the network.

DIX V2   The final 10BASE5 standard, as defined by Digital Equipment Corporation (DEC), Intel, and Xerox, before letting the IEEE take over the development of Ethernet standards.

DNS server   A server that has a list of hostnames and corresponding IP addresses, intended for receiving requests from end-user devices and responding with the IP address that corresponds to the name listed in the DNS request.

domain name   A name, as defined by DNS, that uniquely identifies a computer in the Internet. DNS servers can then respond to DNS requests by supplying the IP address that is used by the computer that has a particular domain name. This term also refers to the part of a domain name that identifies a single company or organization, such as cisco-press.com.

Domain Name System (DNS)   An Internet-wide system by which a hierarchical set of DNS servers collectively hold all the name-IP address mappings, with DNS servers referring users to the correct DNS server to successfully resolve a DNS name.

dotted decimal   A convention for writing IP addresses, with four decimal numbers, ranging from 0 to 255 (inclusive), with each octet (each decimal number) representing 8 bits of the 32-bit IP address. The term originates from the fact that each of the four decimal numbers are separated by a period (or dot).

DSL   *See* digital subscriber line (DSL).

DSL access multiplexer (DSLAM)   A device that connects to a local phone line, inside the telco switching office, that separates the data transmitted by DSL from the voice transmitted as analog signals.

DSL modem   A device that can send and receive digital signals over a phone line by using DSL technology.

DSL router   A device that acts as both a DSL modem and an IP router.

DTE cable   A serial WAN cable that routers use to connect to an external CSU/DSU. Routers use DTE cables when, as normal, the router acts as a DTE.

dual ring topology   A ring topology that uses two rings to provide a failover path in case one cable fails.

Dynamic Host Configuration Protocol (DHCP)   A protocol used for the purpose of dynamically assigning IP addresses to hosts.

dynamic port number   Using values between 1024 and 65,535, these ports are allocated by clients for each new application process.

E/1 circuit   A WAN circuit provided by a telco that runs at 2.048 Mbps. E/1 circuits are popular in some parts of the world, particularly Europe. Other parts of the world use T/1 circuits.

Echo reply   An ICMP packet sent by any IP host in reaction to the receipt of an Echo request. The **ping** command expects to receive this packet from a computer to which it sent an Echo request.

Echo request   An ICMP packet that the **ping** command sends to test connectivity.

electrical current   Movement of electrical energy in a particular direction.

electromagnetic (EM)   A term referring to both electrical and magnetic energy. Both types of energy affect the other, with electrical energy creating magnetic fields and magnetic energy creating electrical currents.

electromagnetic interference (EMI)   The physics process by which an electrical current creates magnetic fields, which in turn causes other electrical currents in nearby wires. The induced electrical currents can interfere with proper operation of the other wire.

electromagnetic spectrum   Refers to the different energy wavelengths and frequencies. The spectrum is described by various categories based on those wavelengths (for example, infrared and microwave).

electromotive force (EMF)   Another term for voltage, it is the force that causes electrons to leave their orbits and create an electrical current.

Electronic Industries Alliance (EIA)   An association of companies in the electronics industry that often works in conjunction with the TIA to define the standards for many networking cables, including most electrical and optical LAN cables.

electrons   Subatomic particles that have negligible mass but have a negative charge that is equal in strength to a proton's positive electrical charge.

electrostatic discharge (ESD)   The process by which free-floating electrons (static electricity) jump to an electrical conductor.

element   In chemistry, a material whose atomic makeup is composed of a single type of matter.

e-mail server   Software whose function is to interact with client e-mail software on end-user computers, as well as other e-mail servers, for the purpose of forwarding and holding e-mail. An e-mail server is like a local post office, where you can send mail and where they hold letters or packages for you until you retrieve them.

e-mail software   Software on an end-user computer that provides a user interface to the user for creating, sending, and receiving e-mail. The software typically implements popular TCP/IP application layer protocols, such as SMTP and POP3.

encapsulation   The process by which a computer adds networking headers and trailers to data from an application for the eventual transmission of the data onto a transmission medium.

encoding   The process of changing the energy levels transmitted over some networking medium to transmit bits over that medium.

encoding scheme   A set of rules that define the energy levels and transitions required to transmit bits over a transmission medium.

encrypt   A process by which data, oftentimes a packet, is fed into a mathematical formula along with a secret number (called an encryption key). The resulting value, which is called an encrypted packet, is sent through a network.

end-user   A person using a computer that connects to a network.

end-user level   Links (Ethernet cables) between a hub/switch and the end-user device (typically, a PC).

Enhanced Interior Gateway Routing Protocol (EIGRP)   A popular Cisco-proprietary IP routing protocol that uses a robust metric, converges quickly, and is used inside a single organization.

enterprise network   A network created for and owned by a single autonomous entity, such as a corporation, government agency, or school system.

equal-level far-end crosstalk (ELFEXT)   Pair-to-pair ELFEXT is expressed in dB as the difference between the measured FEXT and the insertion loss of the wire pair whose signal is disturbed by the FEXT. ELFEXT is an important measurement in Ethernet networks using 1000BASE-T technologies.

error detection The process of discovering if a frame experienced any bit errors during transmission. Typically, this process uses the data-link trailer's FCS field, and the receiving device discards any frames that experienced errors.

error recovery The networking function of noticing when packets are not successfully delivered to the destination computer so the sender resends the lost packets.

EtherChannel The use of multiple Ethernet links between two switches, with the switches combining the links into a single logical link. The switches then load-balance traffic over the link. Without an EtherChannel, only one of the parallel links would be useable because of STP.

Ethereal A networking analysis tool from Ethereal Software, which is available for free download and use (http://www.ethereal.com).

Ethernet A LAN standard, first created by Xerox, and later standardized by IEEE 802.3, 802.2, and many other standards. It provides a vast array of speeds, media, and features.

Ethernet header The overhead data added to the beginning of a Layer 3 packet when the packet is encapsulated by Ethernet before sending a frame onto a network.

expansion card A computer card that can be placed into an available expansion slot inside a PC.

expansion slot An opening in a computer, usually on the motherboard, where an expansion card can be inserted to add new capabilities to the computer.

expectational acknowledgment With protocols like TCP that acknowledge data, the process of sending an acknowledgment number that identifies the next byte that the receiver expects to receive, rather than identifying the last byte that the receiver received. Also called forward acknowledgment.

extended star topology A network topology with a central location, connected to multiple other locations, with the other locations in turn being connected to even more locations. It is essentially a hierarchical topology but typically is drawn with the central site in the center, with the rest of the topology radiating outward in all directions.

Exterior Gateway Protocol (EGP) An obsolete IP routing protocol that exchanged routes between different autonomous systems.

exterior routing protocol Any routing protocol that is designed to exchange routing information between different autonomous systems.

external modem A PC modem located outside the PC, typically connected to the PC by a serial port.

extranet VPN A VPN created for sites of multiple different organizations.

F connector The round connector used on the end of coaxial cables for CATV systems and cable modems.

far-end crosstalk (FEXT) Crosstalk that occurs at a cable's far end.

Fast Ethernet One of several types of Ethernet. This type sends data faster than the original Ethernet (100 Mbps versus 10 Mbps), so when it was created, it was named "Fast" Ethernet.

Fast Link Pulse (FLP) A set of 33 Normal Link Pulses (NLP) that encode data between two devices on an Ethernet LAN. The autonegotiation process uses the data in the pulses.

Federal Communications Commission (FCC) A U.S. government agency that performs many roles, including regulating any products and standards that might radiate EM energy. The FCC ensures that different products do not cause harmful interference to other types of products.

Fiber Distributed Data Interface (FDDI) A LAN standard, defined by ANSI X3T9.5, that specifies a 100-Mbps token-passing network using fiber-optic cable, with transmission distances of up to 2 km. FDDI uses a dual-ring architecture to provide redundancy.

fiber optic Refers to the glass fibers inside certain cables over which light is transmitted to encode 0s and 1s.

fiber-optic cabling A networking cable that contains transmission media made of strands of very pure glass fibers. Networking devices send light over the glass fibers to communicate.

field   In networking, this term generically refers to a subset of a header or trailer that has been defined for some specific purpose. For example, IP headers include a Source IP Address field and a Destination IP Address field, as well as other fields.

file   A collection of bits and bytes on a computer, stored together, that comprise a larger cohesive entity (for example, a single document, a single spreadsheet, a single graphics image, a single video, or a single MP3 audio file).

File Transfer Protocol (FTP)   A robust protocol used to transfer files.

filtering (Ethernet)   In Ethernet, the process performed by a bridge or switch when it decides that it should not forward a frame out another port.

FIN flag   A 1-bit field inside each TCP header that is set to binary 1 in TCP segments that are used to terminate an existing TCP connection.

fixed-function router   A router whose physical interfaces cannot be removed and replaced with other interfaces.

flag   An individual bit in the TCP header, with each bit having a different meaning. For example, TCP connection establishment uses the SYN and ACK flags.

Flash card   A removable storage medium that computers, routers, switches, and other devices can use to store digital data, which is data that is not lost when the disk does not have power.

flooding   A process used by a switch or bridge to forward broadcasts and unknown destination unicasts. The bridge/switch forwards these frames out all ports except the port on which the frame was received.

floppy disk   A type of removable computer storage device, rectangular in shape. The term "floppy" comes from the original floppy disks, which had outer plastic covers that easily bent.

floppy disk drive   A device that can read and write to floppy disks.

flow control   A process by which computers and networking devices can increase and decrease the rate at which data is being sent; this is done to regulate the flow of traffic, which hopefully improves overall network performance.

forward acknowledgment   *See* expectational acknowledgment.

forwarding (Ethernet)   In Ethernet, the process performed by a bridge or switch when it decides that it should forward a frame out another port.

forwarding/Layer 3 forwarding   *See* routing.

forwarding state   An interface state defined by the IEEE 802.1D STP. *See* STP forwarding state.

fragment-free switching   A method of internal processing by LAN switches. The switch looks at the destination MAC address as soon as that part of an incoming frame arrives. Then it starts sending the frame out the output interface, even before the entire frame is received on the input interface. Unlike cut-through switching, however, fragment-free switching waits until the first 64 bytes of a frame have arrived before forwarding the frame. This ensures that the frame did not experience any normal collisions.

frame   Refers to the bits sent over a network, specifically including the data-link header, trailer, and any data encapsulated by the header and trailer.

Frame Check Sequence (FCS)   A field in the trailer of many data link layer protocols, including Ethernet. The FCS field determines if the frame experienced any bit errors during transmission. If it did, the frame is discarded.

Frame Relay   A WAN technology that allows each site to connect to some nearby Frame Relay switch, with logical circuits called permanent virtual circuits (PVC), allowing a router to directly send data to other sites over the single physical access link.

Frame Relay access link   Refers to the physical medium between a customer site and a device in a service provider's Frame Relay network.

framing   The process of creating a frame.

frequency   For continuous wave-like signals, such as sound, light, and analog electrical signals, the number of times in 1 second that the repeating waveform can be completed. The equation is 1 / period.

Frequency Hopping Spread Spectrum (FHSS)   A physical layer transmission standard used in some of the earliest WLAN standards.

full duplex   Networking transmission logic in which the devices on either end of a transmission medium are both allowed to send data at the same time.

full mesh   A physical topology in which all devices are connected to all other devices. Also, a logical topology in which all devices can directly send data to each other.

gateway   Normally, a relatively general term that refers to different kinds of networking devices. Historically, when routers were first created, they were called gateways.

GET request (HTTP)   An HTTP command by which a browser can request that the server send it a web object (file).

GET request (SNMP)   An SNMP message by which a network management system (the SNMP client) can request information from the device being managed (an SNMP agent).

gigabit (Gb)   One billion bits.

Gigabit Ethernet   Ethernet that transmits data at 1,000,000,000 (one billion) bits per second.

gigabyte (GB)   One billion bytes.

ground   The electrical reference to the Earth; electricity flows to the Earth if a conductive path to ground exists.

half duplex   Networking transmission logic in which the devices on either end of a transmission medium cannot both send data at the same time.

hard disk   A magnetic medium, typically circular, onto which bits can be stored as magnetic charges.

hard disk drive   A device that reads and writes data on a hard disk. The primary storage device in most computers.

hardware address   Another name for MAC address. *See also* Media Access Control (MAC) address.

header   The overhead bytes added to data, by some networking protocol, so that protocol can interact with other computers and networking devices that implement the same protocol. The header is typically shown to the left of the end-user data so that English-language readers, who read from left to right, see the header first. The header is transmitted on the media before the end-user data. *See* same layer interaction; trailer.

header length   A field in the TCP header that states the number of sets of 4 bytes in the TCP header. This allows the receiving host to easily find the end of the TCP header and the beginning of the data.

Hertz (Hz)   A unit of measurement that means a number of cycles through some repeating event (per second).

hexadecimal numbering   A system that uses 16 digits (0 through 9 and A through F). Mainly used to make working with binary easier, because each hexadecimal digit represents four binary digits. This is the Base 16 numbering system. Also called hex.

hierarchical physical topology   A network topology with a central location, connected to multiple other locations, with the other locations in turn being connected to even more locations. These topologies are essentially an extended star design, but they are typically drawn with the central site at the top of the figure, branching downward in a diagram.

high-speed WAN interface card (HWIC)   A removable interface card in a router whose interfaces connect to WAN circuits at speeds up to 8 Mbps.

hop count   A popularly used routing protocol metric that represents the number of routers that exist between a router and a particular subnet.

host   In TCP/IP, any computer that has an IP address. In some cases, this term includes only computers that use IP addresses. This implies that networking devices, such as routers and switches, that have IP addresses are not also hosts.

host address   An IP address used by an IP host.

host bits   The bits in an IP address that are the host part of the address.

host part   The part of a 32-bit IP address that identifies an individual host inside a single subnet.

hostname   A text name, useful for end users, that represents an IP address. DNS servers can be used to resolve the name into the IP address it represents.

hub   In Ethernet, a Layer 1 device that receives an electrical signal in one port, interprets the bits, and regenerates a clean signal that it sends out all other ports of the hub. Typically, it also supplies several ports, which are oftentimes RJ-45 jacks.

hybrid   A term that refers to hybrid routing algorithms, which are the algorithms used by EIGRP. EIGRP is a combination of some distance-vector and link-state routing protocol algorithms.

hyperlink   An icon, graphic, or text on a web page that corresponds to some (hidden) URL. When a user clicks the icon, graphic, or text, the browser retrieves the web page at the hidden URL.

HyperTerminal   A terminal emulator from Hillgraeve, Inc. (http://www.hillgraeve.com) that was formerly shipped as part of most Microsoft operating systems. HyperTerminal is available for free download and can be used to access routers and switches through its console ports.

HyperText Markup Language (HTML)   A convention for how to store text and instructions in a file on a web server so that when it is downloaded to a web browser, the browser displays the correct text, colors, font sizes, and other formatting information. It is the original format used for web content.

Hypertext Transfer Protocol (HTTP)   Defines the commands, headers, and processes by which web servers and web browsers transfer files.

IEEE 802.1D   The IEEE standard for STP.

IEEE 802.2   The IEEE standard for the upper half of the data link layer of Ethernet, Token Ring, and some other LAN standards. This standard is often called Logical Link Control (LLC).

IEEE 802.3   The original IEEE standard for Ethernet, based mostly on DIX V2, but with some changes to the Ethernet header.

IEEE 802.3a   The IEEE standard for 10BASE2 Ethernet.

IEEE 802.3ab   The IEEE standard for Gigabit Ethernet using UTP cabling.

IEEE 802.3ae   The IEEE standard for 10 Gigabit Ethernet using optical cabling.

IEEE 802.3i   The IEEE standard for 10BASE-T Ethernet.

IEEE 802.3u   The IEEE standard for both fiber- and UTP-based 100-Mbps Fast Ethernet.

IEEE 802.3x   The IEEE standard for Ethernet autonegotiation.

IEEE 802.3z   The IEEE standard for Gigabit Ethernet using optical cabling.

IEEE 802.5   The IEEE standard for Token Ring LANs.

IEEE (Institute of Electrical and Electronics Engineers)   An organization of professionals that does many things, including defining many LAN standards.

ifconfig   A command on some operating systems, including Linux and UNIX, that allows the user to change the IP address, mask, default gateway, and other settings.

IGP   *See* Interior Gateway Protocol.

impedance   Refers to several things that all reduce the flow of electricity over a conductor, including resistance, but also including capacitance and inductance.

infrared (IR)   Part of the electromagnetic spectrum, IR is visible light that can be used for some forms of communication. It works well when a line of sight exists between the devices, and it is commonly used in TV remote controllers.

infrastructure mode   One of two modes for a wireless NIC (the other being ad-hoc mode) in which the NIC purposefully attempts to associate with an AP instead of other wireless NICs.

in-order delivery   A feature of TCP in which the TCP receiver reorders any data received out of order so that the receiving application always receives its data in the same order that the sending application sent the data.

input/output (I/O) device   A device external to the computer that takes input from a human user and supplies information back to that computer user. Examples include a keyboard, mouse, and display.

insertion loss   The combination of the effects of signal attenuation and impedance discontinuities on a communications link.

insulator   Material that resists the flow of electrical current more than other materials.

integrated circuit (IC)   A device made of semiconductor material. It contains many transistors and performs a specific task. The primary IC on the motherboard is the CPU. ICs are often called chips.

Integrated Services Digital Network (ISDN)   A technology used by telcos to provide digital transmission services over two-wire (one-pair) local telephone circuits to the home, as well as over four-wire circuits. Each single ISDN line has a signaling (D) channel and multiple Bearer (B) channels that can be used to send data.

intelligent hub   A LAN hub that has electrical power, which allows it to regenerate and repeat electrical signals. Intelligent hubs also typically can be managed remotely by SNMP or can allow engineers to log in to the hub.

interesting octet   A term used in some Cisco Press books, but not throughout the industry, as part of a shortcut technique used to find the answers to subnetting problems without using binary math.

interframe spacing   A time period between Ethernet frames that allows fairness with the CSMA/CD algorithm. Without a space between frames—in other words, without some time with no frames being sent—a NIC might always listen for silence, never hear silence, and therefore never get a chance to send a frame.

Interior Gateway Protocol (IGP)   Any routing protocol designed to be used between routers inside the same AS. RIP, IGRP, EIGRP, and OSPF are all examples of IGPs.

Interior Gateway Routing Protocol (IGRP)   A Cisco-proprietary IP routing protocol that uses a robust metric, distance-vector logic, but that has been superseded by the much faster converging EIGRP.

interior routing protocol   *See* Interior Gateway Protocol (IGP).

Intermediate System-to-Intermediate System (IS-IS)   A routing protocol created for the OSI networking model. It was later expanded to exchange both OSI and IP routes.

internal modem   A PC modem located inside the PC.

International Organization for Standardization (ISO)   An international standards body that defines many networking standards. Also, the standards body that created the OSI model.

Internet   The network that combines enterprise networks, individual users, and ISPs into a single global IP network.

Internet access link   Refers to any transmission medium or service with which a company or home user connects to an ISP.

Internet Architecture Board (IAB)   An organization that oversees the development of the TCP/IP model.

Internet Assigned Numbers Authority (IANA)   An organization that assigns the numbers important to the proper operation of the TCP/IP protocol and the Internet, including assigning globally unique IP addresses.

Internet connection   A network connection that allows bits to pass from a subscriber (which could be an individual or an enterprise) to some ISP.

Internet Control Message Protocol (ICMP)   As part of the TCP/IP Internet layer, ICMP defines protocol messages used to inform network engineers of how well an internetwork is working. For example, the **ping** command actually sends ICMP messages to determine whether a host can send packets to another host.

Internet Engineering Task Force (IETF) The standards body responsible for the development and approval of TCP/IP standards.

Internet Explorer A popular web browser from Microsoft.

Internet layer A layer of the TCP/IP networking model. This layer includes the IP protocols, as well as ARP and ICMP.

Internet Packet Exchange (IPX) A proprietary network layer protocol defined by the NetWare protocol.

Internet Protocol (IP) One of the protocols of the TCP/IP network model. It defines the concepts of logical addressing and routing.

Internet service provider (ISP) A company that helps create the Internet by providing connectivity to enterprises and individuals, as well as interconnecting to other ISPs to create connectivity to all other ISPs.

internetwork A combination of many IP subnets and networks, as created by building a network using routers. The term internetwork is used to avoid confusion with the term network, because an internetwork can include several IP networks.

intranet VPN A VPN created for sites inside a single organization.

ions An atom that has too many or too few electrons as compared with the number of protons, thereby giving it an electrical charge.

IP address A 32-bit number, written in dotted-decimal notation, used by the IP to uniquely identify an interface connected to an IP network. It is also used as a destination address in an IP header to allow routing, and as a source address to allow a computer to receive a packet and to know which IP address to send a response to.

IP header The header defined by the IP; used to create IP packets by encapsulating data supplied by a higher layer protocol (such as TCP) behind an IP header.

IP network A collection of IP addresses that have the same value in the network part of the addresses.

IP network number A number that represents an IP network. The IP network number cannot be used as a host IP address. All IP network numbers have the network's value in the network part of the number and all 0s in the host part.

IP routing A process in which a router receives a packet, compares the destination IP address packet's to the router's routing table, finds the best matching route, and forwards the packet based on the instructions in that matched route.

IP routing table A table held by a router that lists subnet and network numbers, along with details of how that router should forward packets destined for those subnets and networks. The table's entries can include the outgoing interface and the next-hop router's IP address.

IP version 4 (IPv4) The version of the IP protocol upon which the majority of the TCP/IP internetworks are built.

IP version 6 (IPv6) A newer version of the IP protocol to which all TCP/IP hosts might eventually migrate; however, the migration might be slow. IPv6 includes a new addressing structure that uses 128-bit IP addresses.

ipconfig A command on many Microsoft PC operating systems that displays IP configuration information, including the IP address, subnet mask, default gateway, and DNS IP address.

IPv4 *See* IP version 4 IPv4.

IPv4 address depletion The global phenomenon by which the finite 32-bit IPv4 address space was quickly being assigned in the 1990s because of the phenomenal growth of the Internet. Without strong solutions, the IPv4 address space would have been completely assigned, stifling Internet growth. Address depletion was solved by several short-term solutions, such as NAT and CIDR, and in the long term by migrating to IPv6.

IPv6 See IP version 6 (IPv6).

jack In networking, a reference to an opening in hardware, with a particular shape, that allows a connector with the matching shape to fit into the opening.

keyboard A device external to a PC on which a user can type to give input to a computer.

keyboard port A port designed to connect a keyboard to a PC.

kilobit (kb) 1000 bits.

kilobits per second (kbps) A unit of measurement of the number of times 1000 bits can be transmitted in 1 second. 1 Kbps = 1000 bps.

Kilobyte (KB) 1000 bytes.

known unicast An Ethernet frame whose destination address is a unicast MAC address, with that MAC address being listed (known) in a switch's MAC address table.

L2PDU A generic term referring to a frame. The 2 refers to OSI Layer 2. PDU stands for protocol data unit, which is a generic term for any message sent by some networking protocol.

L3PDU A generic term referring to a packet. The 3 refers to OSI Layer 3. PDU stands for protocol data unit, which is a generic term for any message sent by some networking protocol.

L4PDU A generic term referring to a segment. The 4 refers to OSI Layer 4. PDU stands for protocol data unit, which is a generic term for any message sent by some networking protocol.

LAN address Another name for MAC address. *See* Media Access Control (MAC) address.

LAN cable Describes any cable used in a LAN.

LAN switch A networking device that provides several functions, including a place to connect cables from end-user computers and the efficient forwarding of data frames between the connected computers. Switches also support Spanning Tree Protocol as well as VLANs.

laser An acronym for "light amplification by stimulated emission of radiation," lasers transmit light at a very spe-cific and small band of wavelengths. Lasers can be used for digital transmission of data, particularly when long distances are needed.

latency The time that passes while some event occurs. In networking, latency typically refers to the time that occurs between when something is sent in a network until it is received by another device.

layer When speaking of networking models, a layer is a general type of protocol placed into a category.

Layer 1 device A networking device whose main function relates to OSI Layer 1. Ethernet hubs and repeaters are examples of Layer 1 devices.

Layer 2 device A networking device whose main function relates to OSI Layer 2. Ethernet bridges and switches are examples of Layer 2 devices.

Layer 3 device A networking device whose main function relates to OSI Layer 3. Routers are examples of Layer 3 devices.

Layer 3-to-Layer 2 mapping A generic term for the need to have some way to know the Layer 2 address used by a device using a particular Layer 3 address. For example, IP ARP allows an IP host to learn a device's Layer 2 MAC address based on that device's IP (Layer 3) address.

Layer x PDU (LxPDU) Refers to the PDU with which a Layer x protocol is concerned. x matches a layer of the OSI model. For example, an IP packet is an L3PDU.

Layer x protocol Describes a protocol as being similar in function to the functions defined by a particular OSI layer. The x might be any OSI layer (1 through 7).

leading zero In a multidigit number, the existence of one or more 0s at the beginning of the number. In most math operations, these digits are unnecessary, so they are not written; with some binary operations, particularly when working with converting IP addresses between binary and decimal, the leading 0s are necessary.

learning state An interface state defined by IEEE 802.1D STP. *See* STP learning state.

leased line A WAN service in which a company leases a transmission medium between two points. Also called leased circuit.

Length field A field in many headers in networking protocols that defines the length of the frame, packet, segment, or part of the frame, packet, or segment.

light emitting diode (LED) A semiconductor device that emits light when a current passes through it. LEDs are commonly used as indicator lights and are used to transmit data over optical cables.

lightning bolt Refers to the style of line used to represent WAN connections when drawing network diagrams. The line style has a jagged part in the middle, much like an animated version of a lightning bolt.

link A generic term, often used for WANs and sometimes LANs, that describes a transmission medium.

link state A type of routing protocol algorithm in which the routing protocol advertises all the details of each link in the network, each router, and the state (up/down) of each link. The routers can then create a mathematical model of the network, calculate the best path to reach each subnet, and add routes to their routing tables.

Linux A popular operating system for PCs.

listening state An interface state defined by the IEEE 802.1d STP. *See* STP listening state.

local-area network (LAN) A network created for devices located in a limited geographic area, through which the company owning the LAN has the right to run cables. The network cables are relatively short (from tens of meters to a few kilometers in length).

logical addressing Generically, a term that refers to a networking address scheme in which the addresses do not directly identify a piece of hardware; considered somewhat opposite of physical addressing. With IP, a reference to the fact that IP addresses are logical in that the IP address assigned to a NIC on a PC follows certain rules for address assignment such that if the hardware were to move to another part of the network, the IP address must change. This implies that IP addresses are not tied to the physical hardware, so they are called logical addresses.

logical bus topology A network topology whose logic and data flow resemble a bus route. *See also* bus topology.

logical full mesh Refers to the transmission logic, often found in Frame Relay, in which all devices may send and receive data directly to and from each other. *See also* full mesh.

Logical Link Control (LLC) The IEEE 802.2 standard that defines the upper sublayer of the Ethernet Layer 2 specifications (and other LAN standards).

logical partial mesh Refers to the transmission logic, often found in Frame Relay, in which only a subset of the devices can directly send and receive data to and from each other. *See also* partial mesh.

logical star topology A network topology whose logic and data flow resemble a star. *See also* star topology.

loopback circuit Ethernet NICs use a loopback circuit to be able to recognize collisions. As an Ethernet NIC transmits on one twisted pair and receives on another, the NIC cannot sense a collision on the attached cable. So, the NIC includes wiring that passes the transmitted electrical signal back to the receive circuitry on the NIC. That way, the NIC can sense when a collision has occurred.

loopback IP address A special reserved IP address, 127.0.0.1, that can be used to test TCP/IP applications. Packets sent to 127.0.0.1 by a computer never leave the computer or even require a working NIC; instead, the packet is processed by IP as the lowest layer and is then sent back up the TCP/IP stack to another application on that same computer.

MAC address See Media Access Control (MAC) address.

MAC address table On a bridge or switch, a table that lists all known MAC addresses, and the bridge/switch port out which the bridge/switch should forward frames sent to each MAC address.

mainframe A relatively large and complex computer. Mainframes became part of the mainstream computing in the 1980's.

maximum transmission unit (MTU)   The largest IP packet size allowed to be sent out a particular interface. Ethernet interfaces default to an MTU of 1500 because of Ethernet's limitation that the data field of an Ethernet frame should be limited to 1500 bytes, and the IP packet sits inside the Ethernet frame's data field.

maximum untagged frame size   In Ethernet, the maximum size of a frame, specifically under the assumption that no VLAN trunk tags have been added to the frame.

media   Plural for medium. See medium.

Media Access Control (MAC)   Refers to the lower of the two sublayers of the IEEE standard for Ethernet. It is also the name of that sublayer (as defined by the IEEE 802.3 subcommittee).

Media Access Control (MAC) address   A 48-bit-long (12 hex digit) address assigned to a NIC or another LAN interface when the NIC or interface is manufactured.

medium   In networking, any material or space over which data can be transmitted. For example, an Ethernet cable with copper wire conductors is a networking medium.

megabit (Mb)   1 million bits.

megabits per second (Mbps)   A unit of measurement of the number of times 1,000,000 bits can be transmitted in 1 second. 1 Mbps = 1,000,000 bps.

megabyte (MB)   1 million bytes.

megahertz   1 million Hertz. *See* Hertz (Hz).

memory chip   Integrated circuits (chips) that can store binary data, typically for reference by a CPU. Also called RAM chips. The contents of this memory is lost when the computer loses power.

metric   With routing protocols, the metric is the objective measurement of how good a particular route is.

Metro Ethernet   Use of Ethernet as a MAN/WAN technology by which a service provider uses Ethernet between a customer site and the provider.

metropolitan-area network (MAN)   A network with a geographic size between a LAN and a WAN. Typically used by service providers to create a high-speed network in a major metropolitan area where many customers might want high-speed services between large sites around a city.

microphone   A device that takes sound waves as input and produces the equivalent analog electrical signal.

microprocessor   A silicon chip that contains a CPU. A typical PC has numerous microprocessors, including the main CPU.

microsegmentation   A practice of putting a single end-user device off each switch port instead of connecting multiple devices by having a hub attached to the switch port. This results in each collision domain consisting of a single end-user device and the one switch port, which in turn allows full-duplex operation.

minicomputer   A computer smaller than a mainframe but larger and more powerful than a PC. Minicomputers became part of mainstream computing in the 1970s.

minimum frame size   In any data-link protocol, the protocol might require that frames be within a maximum and minimum frame size. Ethernet requires that all frames be at least 64 bytes in length.

modem   A networking device that modulates an analog electrical signal to encode bits over an analog medium, with the receiving modem demodulating the received signal back into bits. The word modem combines the terms modulate and demodulate.

modular router   A router whose physical interfaces can be physically removed from the router and replaced with other interfaces.

modulate   The process of taking binary digits and changing a transmitted analog electrical signal to encode bits over an analog medium. One of the two functions of a modem.

motherboard   A computer's main circuit board. The motherboard is crucial because it is the computer's nerve center. Everything else in the system plugs into it, is controlled by it, and depends on it to communicate with other system devices.

mouse   A device external to a PC. The user can move a pointer on the screen, and click buttons on the mouse, to give the computer input about what actions the user wants to take.

mouse port   A port designed to connect a mouse to a PC.

Mozilla Firefox   A popular web browser from the Mozilla foundation.

MT-RJ connector   A connector sometimes used on optical cables. The connector has the same shape as an RJ-45 connector, but with both the transmit and receive fibers inside the single connector.

multicast frame   An Ethernet frame sent to a destination MAC address whose high-order bit set to 1. By design, these frames should be forwarded to all devices on the LAN that want to receive a copy of multicast frames sent to that specific multicast MAC address.

multicast packet   An IP packet sent to a destination IP address that begins with a number between 224 and 239 (inclusive). The network should forward and copy multicast packets so that all IP hosts that want to receive a copy of packets sent to that multicast address receive a copy.

multimode fiber   One of two types of optical cables (single-mode being the other). Multimode fiber cables allow multiple angles of incidence, or modes, of light into the cable, which means that the light bounces around inside the cable more so than with single-mode cables.

multiport bridge   Another name for a LAN switch. This term refers to the fact that bridges and switches use the same basic forwarding, filtering, address learning, and STP logic, but switches have lots of physical ports, or interfaces, whereas bridges typically have only a few ports.

multiport repeater   An Ethernet repeater with more than two ports. Another name for a hub.

name resolution   The process by which a computer sends a DNS request to a DNS server, with a name in the request, and the DNS server(s) reply with the IP address that corresponds to that name.

near-end crosstalk (NEXT)   Crosstalk that occurs on the end of the cable near the transmitting device. As a result, the signal causing the crosstalk has not attenuated much, making the resulting crosstalk stronger and more disruptive.

negative voltage   A method to measure voltage and imply the direction of current flow is the opposite of the positive voltage flow.

Netscape browser   A popular web browser.

NetWare   The name of a proprietary networking model defined by the Novell Corporation. Cisco routers can route packets defined by NetWare's Layer 3 protocol: IPX. NetWare is also the name of a server OS from Novell.

network access layer   The lowest layer of the TCP/IP model; most closely matches Layers 1 and 2 of the OSI model.

network address   A dotted-decimal number used by the IP protocol to identify an entire classful Class A, B, or C network. Also called a network number or network id.

Network Address Translation (NAT)   An IP feature that helped prevent IPv4 address depletion. NAT allows many hosts to use private IP addresses, while representing each TCP connection or UDP flow from multiple computers as if they all were from the same computer that uses a single public IP address.

network analyzer   A type of software and/or hardware tool that can attach to some network media, capture all frames and packets passing over the media, and display/interpret the data. Network analyzers help network engineers troubleshoot network problems.

network bits   Refers to the bits in an IPv4 address that must be the same value for all hosts in the same classful IP network. Class A addresses have 8 network bits, class B addresses have 16 network bits, and Class C addresses have 24 network bits.

network broadcast address   The numerically largest IP address in any single IP network.

network engineer   A person responsible for the planning and implementing of a network.

Network File System (NFS)   A distributed file system protocol suite, developed by Sun Microsystems, that allows remote file access across a network.

network ID   A dotted-decimal number used by the IP protocol to identify an entire classful Class A, B, or C network. Also called a network number or network address.

network interface   A relatively generic term that refers to any physical interface connected to a network, with that interface also being used to send and receive IP packets. PC NICs and router physical interfaces are examples of network interfaces.

network interface card (NIC)   A computer card, typically used for LANs, that allows the computer to connect to some networking cable. The NIC can then send and receive data over the cable at the direction of the computer.

network layer   Layer 3 of the OSI model.

network layer protocol   Any protocol that performs functions similar to those defined in the OSI network layer (Layer 3).

network management system (NMS)   A collection of software that monitors and troubleshoots internetworks.

network model   A structured definition of protocols and standards that includes a large variety of networking functions, organized into different layers, which when fully implemented allows multiple computers to communicate with each other. The two models covered in this book are the TCP/IP model and the OSI model.

network number   *See* network address.

network operating system (NOS)   A computer operating system that is specifically designed for the purpose of acting as a server. NOSs have special features that allow better performance and management of the functions typically performed by servers.

network part   The first one, two, or three octets of a classful IPv4 address based on whether the address is in a Class A, B, or C network, respectively.

network topology   A general term referring to what a network looks like when it is drawn as a diagram.

networking device   A computer with a specific purpose to help create a network.

networking model   A definition of networking protocols and standards into different categories, called layers, along with definitions of which sets of standards and protocols need to be implemented to create products that can be used to create a working network.

neutrons   Subatomic particles with a mass equal to a proton, but they have no charge.

next-hop router   In an IP routing table entry, the next-hop router field identifies the IP address of the next router to which packets should be sent. This information allows the router to correctly forward the packet.

NIC address   *See* Media Access Control (MAC) address.

noise   In networking, a general term referring to any energy signal on a transmission medium that is not part of the signal used to transmit data over that medium.

nondeterministic   A reference to whether the performance of a device, which is attached to a particular type of LAN, can be accurately predicted (determined). Token Ring LANs are deterministic, but Ethernet LANs are nondeterministic.

Normal Link Pulse (NLP)   Electrical signals that are sent over Ethernet UTP cables to determine whether the device on the other end of the cable is still up and operational. Thirty-three NLPs are combined into a single Fast Link Pulse (FLP) to perform Ethernet autonegotiation.

nslookup   A command on many computer operating systems that performs DNS name-resolution requests to test and troubleshoot network problems.

nucleus   The center of an atom or molecule; composed of protons and neutrons.

numeral   A symbol that represents the concept of a number.

octet   Refers to a single decimal number of the four decimal numbers that comprise a dotted-decimal IP address. They are called octets because each decimal number represents 8 bits.

ohm   The unit of measurement of electrical resistance.

Ohm's law   The relationship among voltage, resistance, and current is voltage (V) equals current (I) multiplied by resistance (R). In other words, V = I * R.

open networking model   A networking model defined by a standards body, resulting in open documents that any company can read, interpret, and use to implement products that conform to that networking model.

Open Shortest Path First (OSPF)   An openly defined IP routing protocol that uses link-state logic.

Open Systems Interconnection (OSI) model   A networking model that was meant to unify the networking world by replacing a multitude of proprietary networking models with a cohesive and comprehensive open standard networking model. Today, it is used as a reference for how networking models work and for its many common terms used throughout networking.

operating system (OS)   Software that runs on a computer, controlling the actions taken by the computer hardware. Microsoft Windows XP and Linux are two popular PC OSs.

Optical Carrier 1 (OC-1)   The smallest unit of transmission in the SONET architecture; runs at 51.84 Mbps.

Optical Carrier 3 (OC-3)   A SONET standard that is effectively three times the speed of an OC-1, which is roughly 155 Mbps.

optical media   A type of transmission media that uses thin strands of glass fibers, often called fiber optics. Network devices transmit light on the fibers to encode 0s and 1s.

Options and Padding   Additional headers used to expand a protocol in the future.

Organizationally Unique Identifier (OUI)   The first half of a MAC address. Manufacturers must ensure that the value of the OUI is a value that the manufacturer has registered with the IEEE. This value is meant to identify the manufacturer of any Ethernet NIC or interface.

Orthogonal Frequency Division Multiplexing (OFDM)   A method of transmitting and processing radio signals used for the relatively fast 802.11a and 802.11g WLAN standards.

oscilloscope   An electronics testing and measurement device that graphs voltage levels over time.

outer jacket   A part of a networking cable (generally, the outermost part).

outgoing interface   A field in a router's IP routing table that tells the router that, to send packets to the subnet listed in the routing table entry, the router should forward the packets out this interface.

packet   When used generically, this term refers to end-user data along with networking headers and trailers that is transmitted through a network. When used specifically, it is end-user data, along with the network or Internet layer headers, any higher layer headers, but no lower layer headers or trailers.

packet switching   The process by which a networking device forwards a collection of bits, known as a packet, based on an address in a header included in the packet. IP networks use packet switching.

Packet Tracer   A software tool from Cisco Systems, created for use by Cisco Networking Academy Program, that can demonstrate the basics of how the flow of traffic works in networks.

parallel port   A PC interface that can transfer more than 1 bit at a time. It connects external devices, such as printers.

partial mesh   A physical topology in which only some devices connect to each other, oftentimes with all devices connecting to a central site device. Also, a logical topology in which not all devices can directly send data to each other.

passive hub   A LAN hub that does not have electrical power and therefore cannot regenerate an electrical signal. As a result, passive hubs do not extend cabling distances in LANs.

passive scanning   A practice in WLANs by which a wireless NIC does not send probe messages; instead, it prefers to wait on Beacon messages from APs and then chooses to which AP the NIC should associate.

path determination   Depending on the context, it can mean the same thing as routing or the same thing as a routing protocol does.

peer-to-peer model   A model or convention for how computers communicate by which a single computer might act as a client in some cases, and as a server in other cases, which makes each computer essentially a peer with the other computers.

period   The time between each repeating wave, measured in seconds. Short for time period.

periodic updates   A feature of some IP routing protocols by which they send routing updates, which contain routing information, at a regular time interval or period.

permanent virtual circuit (PVC)   In Frame Relay, a name for the logical transmission path between two devices connected to a Frame Relay service.

personal computer (PC)   A relatively small computer meant for use by one person at a time.

photodiode   An electro-optical component used in digital transmission systems that use optical cabling. The photodiode receives light on the cable and converts the light into a comparable electrical voltage, which can then be interpreted as bits.

physical bus topology   A network topology whose physical structure resembles a bus route. *See also* bus topology.

physical full mesh   Refers to the physical transmission paths in which all devices may send and receive data directly to and from each other. *See also* full mesh.

physical layer   Layer 1 of the OSI model. This layer defines the electrical, mechanical, procedural, and functional specifications for activating, maintaining, and deactivating the physical link between end systems. Such characteristics as voltage levels, timing of voltage changes, physical data rates, maximum transmission distances,

physical connectors, and other similar attributes are defined by physical layer specifications.

physical partial mesh   Refers to the physical connection in which only a subset of the devices can directly send and receive data to and from each other. *See also* partial mesh.

physical star topology   A network topology whose physical structure resembles a star. *See also* star topology.

pin   In a networking cable, the conducting material in a connector that, when the connector is inserted correctly into a jack or connector, touches another conducting surface, thereby allowing the flow of electricity.

ping   A command on many computer operating systems and network devices that sends ping requests (ICMP requests) to another IP address, with the host with that IP address (hopefully) sending a response, which verifies whether the network is properly working.

pinout   Refers to conventions and standards that define which wires in a cable should connect to each pin on the connectors on both ends of a cable. For example, a UTP cable used for Ethernet, using a straight-through cable pinout, connects the wire at pin 1 on one end with pin 1 on the other end the wire at pin 2 on one end with pin 2 on the other and so on.

p-intrinsic-n diode   A more formal name for photodiode. *See also* photodiode.

plastic coating   The thin covering on each copper wire that protects the wire from being broken and provides a small amount of protection from EM interference.

plug-and-play   A hardware-installation process on a computer in which the computer's operating system automatically recognizes the existence of new hardware and adds the correct operating-system software settings for the new hardware to work.

plug-in   In a web browser, an application the browser uses, inside the browser window, to display some types of content. For example, a browser typically uses a plug-in to display video.

point-to-point leased line   Refers to a leased line with emphasis that the line extends between two points. Routers typically connect to the ends of a leased line.

Point-to-Point Protocol (PPP)   A data-link protocol used on WAN links between two routers or between any two devices or points.

point-to-point WAN link   A WAN link that connects two devices—and two devices only—essentially connecting two points in a network.

port   In networking, this term is used in several ways. With Ethernet hub and switch hardware, port is simply another name for interface, which is a physical connector in the switch into which a cable can be connected. With TCP and UDP, a port is a software function that uniquely identifies a software process on a computer that uses TCP or UDP. With PCs, a port may be a physical connector on the PC, like a parallel or USB port.

port number   The actual values of the 16-bit numbers, typically shown in decimal, used as ports by the TCP and UDP protocols. *See also* port.

positive voltage   A method to measure voltage and imply the direction of current flow relative to an electrical circuit.

Post Office Protocol version 3 (POP3)   A protocol that allows a computer to retrieve e-mail from a server.

power connector   A connector that allows a power cord to be connected to the computer to give electrical power to the motherboard and other computer components.

power sum equal-level far-end crosstalk (PSELFEXT)   A LAN cabling test that checks the combined effect of ELFEXT from all wire pairs.

power sum near-end crosstalk (PSNEXT)   A LAN cabling test that measures the cumulative effect of NEXT from all wire pairs in the cable.

power supply   The component that supplies power to a computer by taking AC current from a power cord and converting it to 5 to 12 volts DC to power the computer.

preamble   The first 7 bytes of an IEEE standard Ethernet frame or the first 8 bytes of a DIX V2 Ethernet frame. With IEEE Ethernet framing, the eighth byte is the Start Frame Delimiter (SFD).

prefix   In IP subnetting, a term that refers to the portion of a set of IP addresses whose value must be identical for the addresses to be in the same subnet.

presentation layer   Layer 6 of the OSI model. Defines data formats and conversions. For example, it specifies the particular ASCII character code, whether data is text or binary, and the like.

printed circuit board (PCB)   A thin plate on which chips (integrated circuits) and other electronic components are placed. Examples include the motherboard and various expansion adapters.

printer   A device external to a PC on which the computer can print information that the user requests.

private IP address   Defined in RFC 1918, an IP address that does not have to be globally unique because the address exists inside packets only when the packets are inside a single private IP internetwork. Private IP addresses are popularly used in most companies today, with NAT translating the private IP addresses into globally unique IP addresses.

probabilistic   *See* deterministic.

processor   The microchip on a computer that performs the primary computations and instructions.

propagation delay   The time required for energy to pass over a networking medium from one end to another. The time required varies based on the medium, with the speed typically varying between 65 percent and 75 percent of the speed of light in a vacuum.

proprietary networking model   A networking model defined by a single networking product vendor, typically without any outside assistance, and with the capability to dictate changes to the model without notifying competitors.

protocol   A written specification that defines how products should perform a certain task, typically in networking, and typically regarding logic or information as it is transmitted through a network. Each protocol defines messages, often in the form of headers, plus the rules and processes by which these messages are used to achieve some stated purpose. A standards body approves and accepts these specifications.

protocol data unit (PDU)   A generic term from OSI that refers to the data, headers, and trailers about which a particular networking layer is concerned.

protocol suite   Another term for network model. *See* network model.

Protocol Type field   A field in a header, oftentimes a data-link header, that identifies the type of network layer protocol header that is encapsulated inside a frame.

protons   Subatomic particles that have a positive electrical charge.

proxy ARP   A process that uses the exact same ARP messages as normal ARP, but by which a router replies instead of the host listed in the ARP request. When a router sees an ARP request that cannot possibly reach the intended host, but for which the router knows a route to reach the host, the router acts on that host's behalf and responds to the ARP request with the router's own MAC address listed in the ARP reply.

public IP address   An IP address that has been registered with IANA or one of its member agencies, which guarantees that the address is globally unique. Globally unique public IP addresses can be used for packets sent through the Internet.

queuing   The process of holding frames or packets in memory until the interface out which the frame or packet needs to be sent becomes available.

queuing delay   How long a frame or packet sits in a queue in a switch or router waiting for its fair chance to be sent out the interface.

radio frequency (RF)   A portion of the electromagnetic spectrum that happens to have good performance characteristics for one-way and two-way communications. RF waves have some ability to pass through some materials and bounce off part of the Earth's atmosphere, which makes these waves useful for radio stations to broadcast music.

random-access memory (RAM)   Also known as read-write memory, RAM can have new data written to it and can have stored data read from it. RAM is the main working area, or temporary storage, used by the CPU for most processing and operations. A drawback of RAM is that it requires electrical power to maintain data storage. If the computer is turned off or loses power, all data stored in RAM is lost unless the data was previously saved to disk. Memory boards with RAM chips plug into the motherboard.

read-only memory (ROM)   A type of computer memory in which data has been prerecorded. After data has been written onto a ROM chip, it cannot be removed and can only be read. A version of ROM known as EEPROM (electronically erasable programmable read-only memory) can be written to. The basic input/output system (BIOS) in most PCs is stored in EEPROM.

redundancy   In LANs, redundancy refers to when a LAN design has more than one physical path between any two parts of the complete LAN. Redundant Ethernet LANs require the use of STP to ensure that frames do not needlessly loop around the redundant parts of the LAN.

regenerate   In digital transmission, the process of creating a clean exact signal based on interpreting a received degraded signal. A feature of an Ethernet repeater.

registered jack 45 (RJ-45)   A popular modular connector that is used on many networking cables, including UTP Ethernet cables with eight pin positions.

registered port number   Using values between 1024 and 49,151, these numbers are equivalent to well-known ports in concept, but they are specifically used for nonprivileged application processes.

repeat   In digital transmission systems, this term refers to the process of receiving a degraded form of what started life as a square waveform, interpreting the waveform, and regenerating the original waveform for transmission on some other medium.

repeater In Ethernet, a Layer 1 device that receives an electrical signal in one port, interprets the bits, and regenerates a clean signal that it sends out the other port of the repeater.

Request For Comments (RFC) A document that defines TCP/IP protocols.

Reserved In networking headers and trailers, fields that have not yet been defined for any specific purpose by any protocol and are available for new protocols to use.

resident subnet The subnet of which an IP address is a member.

resistance An electrical property of any material by which the material opposes or reduces the flow of current through the material.

resistor An electronic component that is made of material that opposes the flow of electrical current.

return loss A LAN cabling test that checks the noise created when a signal is reflected toward the transmitter because of impedance discontinuities. These reflections, or echoes, then interfere with the signals traveling in that same direction.

Reverse ARP (RARP) An old protocol used by hosts to dynamically learn an IP address that the host could use. RARP does not dynamically assign a mask, default gateway, or any other information, and it is not typically used at all today.

reversed pair fault A LAN cabling fault that occurs when the wires in a single pair have been reversed. For example, a straight-through cable typically connects a wire to pin 1 on each end and the other wire in that same pair to pin 2 on each end. A reversed pair fault connects a wire with pin 1 on one end to pin 2 on the other, and the other wire in that same pair to pin 2 and pin 1, respectively.

right-of-way A legal term that refers to many things, but for networking, it refers to the right to install cabling and other equipment in public spaces. For example, WAN service providers have the right to enter the utility trenches underneath streets and install cables.

ring topology A physical network topology in which one device connects to the second, the second to the third, and so on, with the last device closing the loop and connecting to the first device. Also, a logical topology for which data goes in a loop from device to device.

RJ-11 A cabling connector with six pins, with the same overall shape as an RJ-45 connector, that is popular in common telephone cables.

RJ-45 A rectangular cabling connector with eight pins, often used with Ethernet cables.

rollover cable A UTP cable pinout that specifies that the wire at pin 1 of an RJ-45 connector on one end of the cable connects to pin 8 on the other end; the wire at pin 2 connects to pin 7 on the other end; pin 3 to pin 6; and pin 4 to pin 5. This cable is used for Cisco console cables for routers and switches.

round-trip time The time required for some networking PDUs to be sent and received, and a response PDU to be sent and received. In other words, the time between when a device sends data and when the same device receives a response.

routable protocol *See* routed protocol.

routed protocol A protocol that defines a packet that can be forwarded by a router (for example, IP).

router A network device, typically connected to a range of LAN and WAN interfaces, that forwards packets based on their destination IP addresses.

routing The process by which a router receives an incoming frame, discards the data-link header and trailer, makes a forwarding decision based on the destination IP address, adds a new data-link header and trailer based on the outgoing interface, and forwards the new frame out the outgoing interface.

Routing Information Protocol (RIP)   An old IP routing protocol that uses distance-vector logic and hop count as the metric, with relatively slow convergence.

routing protocol   A protocol used between routers so they can learn routes to add to their routing tables.

routing table   A list that a router holds in memory for the purpose of deciding how to forward packets.

routing update   A message sent by a router, as defined by each routing protocol, with these messages including various kinds of routing information.

same layer interaction   Refers to how a protocol from a layer of a networking model creates some kind of header, and possibly trailer, for the purpose of communicating some information to the same protocol on another computer in the network.

SC connector   A connector used on fiber-optic cables.

screened twisted-pair (ScTP)   A type of STP cabling that omits the per-pair shielding as compared with a true shielded twisted-pair cable.

segment, LAN concepts   A collision domain, which is a section of a LAN that is bound by bridges, routers, or switches.

segment, LAN (physical)   In a LAN using a bus topology, a segment is a continuous electrical circuit that is often connected to other such segments with repeaters.

segment, TCP   When used with TCP, the term segment (verb) refers to the work TCP does to accept a large piece of data from an application and break it into smaller pieces. Again with TCP, used as a noun, segment refers to one of those smaller pieces of data.

segmentation   In TCP, the process of taking a large chunk of data and breaking it into small-enough pieces to fit within a TCP segment without breaking any rules about the maximum amount of data allowed in a segment.

semiconductor   A material that allows a small amount of easily controlled electrical current.

Sequence Number   Part of the TCP header that lists a number associated with the first byte of the data inside the TCP segment. TCP error recovery uses this number for the receiver to determine if a segment was lost in transit so that the receiver can ask the sender to resend the segment.

serial cable   A cable that routers use when connecting a router serial interface to an external CSU/DSU.

serial interface   A multipurpose physical interface on a router that is used to connect to serial WAN links. Serial interfaces can be configured to use many different data-link protocols, including HDLC, PPP, and Frame Relay, and it can support many types of serial cables.

serial port   A PC interface used for serial communication in which only 1 bit is transmitted at a time. The serial port can connect to an external modem, plotter, or serial printer. It can also connect to networking devices, such as routers and switches, as a console connection.

server   This term can refer to computer hardware that is to be used by multiple concurrent users. Alternatively, this term can refer to computer software that provides services to many users. For example, a web server consists of web server software running on some computer.

server farm   A set of servers (hardware) that sit in the same location.

service provider   A somewhat generic term for any company that provides service to another, particularly some form of network connection. Examples include WAN service providers and Internet service providers.

Service Set Identifier (SSID)   A name assigned to one or more wireless LANs. All APs that together create a single wireless LAN use the same SSID. Wireless users can then choose the SSID, or network, to connect to.

session layer   Layer 5 of the OSI model. This layer establishes, manages, and terminates sessions between two communicating hosts. The session layer provides a service to the presentation layer by synchronizing the dialogue between the two hosts' presentation layers and manages their data exchange.

shared bandwidth   Refers to the effect caused on an Ethernet LAN that uses hubs. With hubs, only one device can send at a time, meaning that all devices on the LAN must share the bandwidth.

shared medium   In some Ethernet LANs, the medium must be shared. For example, a 10BASE2 or 10BASE5 Ethernet LAN shares the coaxial cable and its use. The term shared medium refers to cases in which the medium must be shared by using some protocol, like the CSMA/CD protocol on Ethernet LANs. Wireless LANs also use a shared medium, and use the CSMA/CA algorithm to share the medium.

shield   A generic word for any cabling component that prevents unwanted interference from outside energy sources. Shields also help prevent wires inside the shield from interfering with transmissions on other fiber-optic cables.

shielded twisted-pair (STP)   A type of network cabling that includes twisted-pair wires, with shielding around each pair of wires, as well as another shield around all wires in the cable.

Simple Mail Transfer Protocol (SMTP)   Defines the process by which e-mail can be forwarded and then held for later retrieval by the intended recipient.

Simple Network Management Protocol (SNMP)   An application protocol typically not used by end users; instead, it is used by the network management software and actual networking devices to allow a network engineer to monitor and troubleshoot network problems.

single-mode fiber   One of two types of optical cables (multimode being the other). Single-mode fiber cables allow only a single angle of incidence, or mode, of light into the cable, which means that the light travels mostly down the center of the cable, allowing longer cabling distances than with multimode cabling.

single ring topology   A ring topology that use a single ring.

slot time   The minimum time a NIC or interface can take to send an entire frame. Slot time, then, implies a minimum frame size.

SMTP client   Software that implements SMTP for the purpose of sending e-mail to an SMTP server.

SMTP server   Software that implements SMTP for the purpose of receiving e-mail sent by an SMTP client.

SNMP agent   Software that responds to an SNMP request from an SNMP management station, supplying information about the configuration and status of the device.

socket   In networking, can refer to a physical jack (*see* jack) or a feature relating to how an application program communicates with the TCP or UDP protocol on a computer.

SONET (Synchronous Optical Network)   Defines the physical layer details of high-speed communications, beginning at 51.84 Mbps and going up to 40 Gbps and more, using optical cabling. Most of the world's telcos have extensively installed SONET facilities at Layer 1.

sound card   A PC expansion board that handles all sound functions.

sound wave   The vibrations that propagate through the air when something makes a noise.

Source MAC Address   A field inside an Ethernet frame that lists the MAC address of the device that sent the frame.

source port   A field inside a TCP or UDP header that identifies the application process on the sending computer.

Source Service Access Point (SSAP)   A 1-byte field in the IEEE 802.2 header that specifies the upper layer protocol on the sending computer that generated the data sent inside a frame.

Spanning Tree Algorithm (STA)   The underlying logic (algorithm) that STP uses.

Spanning Tree Protocol (STP)   A protocol, defined in IEEE 802.1d, that defines how bridges and switches can dynamically determine how to allow a redundant LAN design while preventing frames from unnecessarily looping through the LAN.

speaker   A device that takes analog electrical signals and produces the equivalent sounds waves.

split-pair wiring fault   A wiring fault in which the two wires in a single pair are incorrectly used to connect two different transmission circuits.

spread spectrum   The use of a range, or spread, of radio frequencies when transmitting data using WLANs.

square wave   A waveform in which the values change quickly over time, which gives the impression of right angles shown in a graph.

ST connector   A type of optical cabling connector.

standards   Written specifications that define how products should perform a certain task. A standards body approves and accepts the specifications.

star topology   A physical network topology that looks like a star in that a device sits in the center with cables radiating from the center. Alternately, a logical network topology in which data flows from a central device out toward other computers and devices.

Start Frame Delimiter (SFD)   The eighth byte of an IEEE standard Ethernet frame. It follows the IEEE standard 7-byte preamble.

start/stop flow control   A method of controlling how fast data is sent in a network by allowing the receiver to tell the sender to stop and start back up again.

static electricity   Free-floating electrons that are not currently attached to any atom or molecule. This electricity can flow onto electronic equipment and damage it.

static length subnet masking (SLSM)   The practice of using a single subnet mask for all subnets of a single classful IP network.

static route   An entry in an IP routing table that was created because a network engineer entered the routing information into the router's configuration.

storage-area network (SAN)   A network between computers and external storage devices that allows the computers to share the data stored on the disks and to have concurrent access to the same disks.

store-and-forward switching   A method of internal processing by LAN switches. The switch must receive the entire frame before it sends the first bit of the frame. *See* cut-through switching; fragment-free switching.

STP blocking state   An interface state defined by the IEEE 802.1d STP in which the interface does not process received frames or send frames out this interface.

STP disabled state   An interface state defined by the IEEE 802.1d STP in which the interface has failed or has been administratively disabled. No frames are received or forwarded on the interface, and it is not a current candidate to be placed into a forwarding state.

STP forwarding state   An interface state defined by the IEEE 802.1d STP in which the interface can freely send and receive Ethernet frames.

STP learning state   An interface state defined by the IEEE 802.1d STP. This state is used as an interim state while a switch learns new CAM entries based on newly received frames. The switch does not forward frames in this state.

STP listening state   An interface state defined by the IEEE 802.1d STP. This state is used as an interim state while a switch waits for its CAM entries to time out. The switch does not forward frames in this state.

STP topology   Refers to a subset of a LAN topology—specifically, the ports that are in an STP forwarding state.

straight-through cable   A UTP cable pinout that specifies that the wire at pin 1 of an RJ-45 connector on one end of the cable connects to pin 1 on the other end; the wire at pin 2 connects to pin 2 on the other end; pin 3 to pin 3; and so on. Ethernet LANs use straight-through cable pinouts for cables connecting PCs to hubs or switches.

subnet   A group of IP addresses that have the same value in the first part of the IP addresses, for the purpose of allowing routing to identify the group by that initial part of the addresses. IP addresses in the same subnet typically sit on the same network medium and are not separated from each other by any routers; IP addresses on different subnets are typically separated from one another by at least one router.

subnet address   Another term for subnet number. *See* subnet number.

subnet bits   The bits in an IP address that exist after the network bits but before the host bits.

subnet broadcast address   The highest numerical value in a subnet. Packets sent to this address are routed to the destination subnet, at which point the packet is sent inside a Layer 2 broadcast frame, so that all hosts in the subnet receive the frame. It is also useful for finding the range of assignable IP addresses in a subnet.

subnet mask   A dotted-decimal number that helps identify the structure of IP addresses. The mask represents the network and subnet parts of related IP addresses with binary 1s and the host part of related IP addresses with binary 0s.

subnet number   A dotted-decimal number that represents a particular IP subnet. Also called subnet ID or subnet address.

subnet zero (zero subnet)   The numerically smallest subnet number in a classful IP network, characterized by a value of all binary 0s in the subnet portion of the subnet number. With classful IP addressing, this subnet is one of the two reserved subnets that should not be used.

subnetting   The process of taking a classful IP network and subdividing it into smaller groups called subnets. It is the process of creating subnets.

Subnetwork Access Protocol (SNAP)   A 5-byte–long IEEE-defined header that solved a problem with the short 1-byte IEEE 802.2 DSAP field. The DSAP field was intended for use as a protocol type field, but it was too small. The SNAP header includes a 2-byte–long protocol type field. The SNAP header can then be included after the IEEE 802.2 header to have a better (longer) type field.

switch   In Ethernet, a Layer 2 device that receives an electrical signal in one port, interprets the bits, and makes a filtering or forwarding decision about the frame. If it forwards, it sends a regenerated signal. Switches typically have many physical ports, oftentimes RJ-45 jacks, whereas bridges traditionally have two ports.

switched bandwidth   Used mainly in contrast with "shared bandwidth," switched bandwidth refers to the fact that LAN switches do not have to share the bandwidth on one switch port with devices on other switch ports. So, a switch with 24 100-Mbps interfaces has effectively 2400 Mbps of switched bandwidth. *See also* shared bandwidth.

switched LAN   A LAN created by using LAN switches.

switching table   A general term used for the table used by a LAN switch for its forwarding/filtering decisions. The table holds a list of MAC addresses and the associated switch port. Switches look for each frame's destination address in the table and then forward the frame out the associated interface.

symmetric switching   In LAN switches, a reference to cases in which a frame is forwarded, or switched, when the incoming and outgoing interfaces use the same speed. It is the opposite of asymmetric switching.

SYN   A flag in the TCP header used only in the first two segments of the three-way TCP connection establishment sequence.

synchronization   A process used by two devices on either end of a transmission medium by which one end watches the incoming signal and continuously adjusts its clock based on the changes in the incoming signal. This process allows the devices to communicate even if the devices' clocks run slightly slower or faster than the other device.

Synchronous Transport Signal 1 (STS-1)   The electrical equivalent of SONET OC-1. *See* Optical Carrier 1 (OC-1).

system unit   The main component of the PC system. It includes the case, chassis, power supply, microprocessor, main memory, bus, expansion cards, disk drives (floppy, CD hard disk, and so on), and ports. The system unit does not include the keyboard, the monitor, or any other external devices connected to the computer.

T/1 circuit   A DS1. *See* digital signal level 1 (DS1).

T3   A DS3. *See* digital signal level 3 (DS3).

TCP/IP   *See* Transmission Control Protocol/Internet Protocol (TCP/IP).

telco Short for telephone company.

telecommunications carrier (T-carrier) A WAN specification in the U.S. and some other parts of the world that defines the structure and speeds of many typical WAN transmission media.

Telecommunications Industry Association (TIA) An electrical standards body that defines the standards for many networking cables, including most electrical and optical LAN cables.

Telnet Defines the protocols that allow a user on one computer to remotely access another computer, enter commands, and have those commands execute on the other computer. It is commonly used by network engineers to remotely access routers and switches.

Telnet client Software that provides a terminal emulator, with the emulator using Telnet protocols to communicate with a Telnet server, so the user of the Telnet client can log in and issue commands on the Telnet server.

terabit (Tb) One trillion bits.

terabits per second (Tbps) A unit of measurement of the number of times 1,000,000,000,000 bits can be transmitted in 1 second. 1 Tbps = 1,000,000,000,000 bps.

terabyte (TB) One trillion bytes.

terminal A simple old computing device that had a video screen, a keyboard, and very little processing logic.

Thicknet A common term for 10BASE5 Ethernet, referring to the fact that 10BASE5 cabling is thicker than the coaxial cabling used for 10BASE2 (Thinnet).

Thinnet A common term for 10BASE2 Ethernet, referring to the fact that 10BASE2 cabling is thinner than the coaxial cabling used for 10BASE5 (Thicknet).

three-way handshake Refers to the three TCP segments that must flow between two hosts to create a TCP connection.

throughput Refers to the real actual data transfer rate between two computers at some point in time. Throughput is impacted by the slowest-speed link used to send data between the two computers, as well as a myriad of variables that might change during the course of a day.

TIA/EIA-T568-A A standard that defines the color of the individual wires in a UTP cable and the pin positions they should use inside an RJ-45 connector.

TIA/EIA-T568-B A wiring standard from the TIA and EIA. This standard defines rules and requirements for unshielded twisted-pair (UTP) cabling and requirements for how to use the pins on the connectors on the ends of the cables.

Time to Live (TTL) field A field in the IP header that prevents a packet from indefinitely looping around an IP internetwork. Routers decrement the TTL field each time they forward a packet, and if they decrement the TTL to 0, the router discards the packet, which prevents it from looping forever.

token passing A process used with some LAN technologies by which access to the LAN is managed using a token. A device can send only when it has claimed the use of the token. The token, which is a small frame, is passed around the LAN to give each device an opportunity to have the right to send a frame.

Token Ring A LAN standard developed by IBM, standardized in IEEE 802.5 and 802.2, that uses a logical ring and physical star topology with token-passing arbitration.

top-level domain The last part of a DNS name, which represents the highest part of the DNS naming hierarchy. .com, .org, and .us are examples of top-level domains.

tracert (traceroute) A command on many computer operating systems that discovers the IP addresses, and possibly hostnames, of the routers used by the network when sending a packet from one computer to another.

trailer Overhead bytes added to data, by some networking protocol, that help the protocol to perform its work by interacting with other computers and networking devices that implement that same protocol. The trailer is typically shown to the right of the end-user data so that English-language readers (who read from left to right) see the trailer last; the trailer is transmitted on the media after the end-user data. *See* same layer interaction; header.

transistor A device that amplifies a signal or opens and closes a circuit. Microprocessors can have millions of transistors.

Transmission Control Protocol (TCP) Part of the TCP/IP model, TCP lets applications guarantee delivery of data across a network.

Transmission Control Protocol/Internet Protocol (TCP/IP) A network model defined by the IETF that has been implemented on most computers and network devices in the world.

transmission media/medium See media and medium.

transmission speed The number of bits per second transmitted over some transmission medium using an encoding scheme.

transmitter A piece of networking hardware that generates the correct energy signal over a networking medium to send data to another device.

transport layer Layer 4 of the OSI model or Layer 3 of the TCP/IP model. Both the OSI and TCP/IP transport layer protocols perform the same kinds of functions. This layer focuses on protocols to deliver data from an application process on one computer to the correct application process on the other computer.

transposed-pair wiring fault A problem with the pinouts of a networking cable. This fault is characterized by two main features: a wire pair is connected to completely different pins at either end of the cable, and the transposed pinouts do not serve any useful purpose.

triggered update A routing protocol update message that is specifically sent by a router in reaction to some event in the internetwork (typically, the loss of a route).

Trivial File Transfer Protocol (TFTP) A simple protocol, which can be implemented by using a small amount of software, that allows file transfer.

trunk In Ethernet LANs, trunk refers to any Ethernet link between two switches. This term can also specifically refer to a link between switches that allows traffic from multiple different VLANs to pass.

Type field Another term for Protocol Type field. *See* Protocol Type field.

unicast IP address An IP address that represents a single host IP address.

unicast MAC address A MAC address that identifies a single NIC or interface.

Universal Resource Locator (URL) A formatted string of text that identifies, at least in theory, any computing resource to a web browser. It includes the protocol, the name of another computer, and some information that identifies the location of the resource on the other computer. For example, http://www.cisco.com/univercd describes the HTTP protocol, a computer with hostname www.cisco.com, and a resource (it happens to be a web page) located in a directory or file called "univercd" on that server.

Universal Serial Bus (USB) port This PC interface lets peripheral devices, such as mice, modems, keyboards, scanners, and printers, be plugged in and unplugged without resetting the system. USB ports eventually might replace serial and parallel ports.

unknown unicast frame A frame with a unicast MAC destination address for which a switch does not have that MAC address listed in the switch's MAC address table. Switches flood unknown unicast frames.

unreliable protocol A protocol that does not perform error recovery.

unshielded twisted-pair (UTP) Refers to a general type of cable, with the cable holding twisted pairs of copper wires and the cable itself having little shielding.

uplink In campus LAN design, an Ethernet link connecting an access switch to a distribution switch.

urgent A field in a TCP header used to point to the sequence number of sent data for which the sender requests an immediate (urgent) acknowledgment from the receiver.

USB memory stick   A removable storage medium, inserted into a PC's USB port, that computers can use to store digital data—data that is not lost when the disk does not have power.

User Datagram Protocol (UDP)   A major protocol in the TCP/IP networking model. UDP is an alternative to TCP at the transport layer, providing very few functions, but with the benefit of less overhead.

variable-length subnet mask (VLSM)   A condition in which more than one subnet mask is used in different subnets of the same Class A, B, or C network.

video card   A board that plugs into a PC to give it display capabilities. Video cards typically include onboard microprocessors and additional memory to speed up and enhance graphics display.

video display   A device external to a PC that displays visual information for the user.

VINES   A proprietary networking model from the Banyan corporation. Cisco routers can route packets defined as part of the VINES networking model.

virtual private network (VPN)   Refers to the use of a public network, typically the Internet, to deliver packets that need to be treated as private. To do so, VPNs encrypt packets before they pass through the Internet.

volt   A measure of electrical potential between two points that are separated by a conductive material.

voltage   Another term for electromotive force (EMF). *See* electromotive force (EMF).

WAN circuit   A leased line. *See* leased line.

WAN connection   Generically refers to any WAN transmission medium or WAN service.

WAN interface card (WIC)   A removable card that can be installed into modular Cisco routers. WICs have different types of physical connectors that are useful for WAN connections.

WAN service provider   A company, oftentimes a telco, that provides WAN transmission services to its customers.

wattage   The unit of measurement of electrical power.

waveform   Refers to the behavior of energy signals, such as electricity and light, over time. Waveforms are often graphed, with the energy levels on the y-axis and time on the x-axis.

wavelength   For continuous wave-like signals, such as sound, light, and analog electrical signals, the length of time required for the repeating signal to complete one cycle through its pattern.

web address   Refers to a URL. *See* Universal Resource Locator (URL).

web browser   A type of software product that has a graphical window to display the contents of a website. Today, Microsoft Internet Explorer, Mozilla Firefox, and Netscape are the most popular web browsers.

web content   Text, images, animation, programs, video, and other items that can be viewed by a web browser.

web developer   A person who creates a website.

web page   A single collection of information, organized on a web server, that can be loaded into another computer's web browser upon that browser's request.

web servers   Software that makes web content available to web browsers.

website   A collection of content—text, images, animation, programs, video, and audio—that pertains to the same general subject area and has been organized together.

well-known port   Used by TCP and UDP, with values between 0 and 1023, these ports are allocated by high-privilege processes. They are used so that all clients know the correct port number to connect to.

wide-area network (WAN)   A network that connects devices in a wide geographic area that requires the use of transmission services from a WAN service provider. The service provider has the right-of-way to install cables over wide geographic areas.

Wi-Fi   A trademark of the Wi-Fi Alliance (http://www.wi-fi.org), which is a trade organization dedicated to the advancement of wireless technologies.

window   As set in a sent segment, signifies the maximum amount of unacknowledged data the sending host is willing to receive before the other sending host must wait for an acknowledgment. Used for flow control.

Window field   A field in the TCP header that allows a host to tell another host how large a window the first host will grant. *See also* window.

Windows Media Player (WMP)   A popular tool for playing audio and watching video (from Microsoft).

Windows XP   A popular operating system for PCs.

winipcfg   A command on some Microsoft PC operating systems (such as Windows 95 and Windows 98) that graphically displays IP configuration information, including the IP address, subnet mask, default gateway, and DNS IP address.

wire map   A cable test that shows the pinouts of a LAN cable.

word   A combination of a small number of bytes that a particular type of processor chip can manipulate with a single instruction. In many computer-processor architectures, a word is 4 bytes long.

workgroup level   Links between the hub/switch that attach to end-user computers and other hubs/switches in the core of the LAN.

XNS (Xerox Network Systems)   A proprietary networking model defined by Xerox. Cisco routers can route packets defined by the XNS protocol.

zero subnet   *See* subnet zero (zero subnet).

INDEX

Numerics

10-Mbps Ethernets, 269-271

100-Mbps Ethernets, 269, 278-279

    100BASE-FX, 281-282

    design, 280-281

1000BASE-LX, 283

1000BASE-SX, 283

1000BASE-T, 286-288

1000BASE-X, 283-286

100BASE-FX, 281-282

10BASE-T

    collisions, 253-254

    Ethernets, 76-77, 272

        design, 275-278

        wiring, 272-274

5-4-3 rule, 275

5-4-3-2-1 rule, 276

A

abbreviations, bits/bytes, 45

AC (alternating current), 131

access

    network access layer (TCP/IP), 340-341

    remote, history of, 23

    switches, 193

    VPNs, 90

access control lists (ACLs), 407

access points (APs), 154-155, 209-210

ACK (acknowledgment)

    flags, 458

    flow control through withholding, 457

Acknowledgment Number field, 463

ACLs (access control lists), 407

active scanning, 155

adding analog waves to digital tests, 170

Address Resolution Protocol (ARP), 327, 378-384

addresses

    BIA, 247

    broadcast, 81, 361-362

        network, 434

        searching, 438

        shortcuts, 439-442

    flooding, 302-303

    IP, 31, 353

        assignment, 353-362

        classes, 353-362

        determining assignable (in subnets), 434-444

        IP routing, 344-345

        managing, 373-384

        networking math, 362-364

        overview of, 353

        public, 370

        subnetting, 32, 364-368

        unicast, 356

        unique, 368-372

    IPv4, depletion of, 370-371

    MAC, 78

        Destination, 245

        Ethernet, 247

        Source, 245

        tables, 299

        unknown unicast frames, 304

    ranges, 438-439

    unicast, 81

    unknown unicast frames, 304

    URLs, 35

adjacent layer interaction, 114-115

administration

    IP addresses, 373

        applying ARP, 378-384

        comparing DHCP/static addresses, 377

        dynamic IP address configuration, 375-377

        static IP address configuration, 373-374

    networks, 475-476

    NMS, 476

    out-of-band, 227

agents, SNMP, 476

algorithms

    CSMA/CD, 240

    Ethernet operation, 251-257

routing protocols, 419
  distance vector algorithms, 419-420
  hybrid algorithms, 421
  link-state algorithms, 420
STA, 315
alien crosstalk, 176
alternating current (AC), 131
American National Standards Institute (ANSI), 73
American Registry for Internet Numbers (ARIN), 369
American Standard Code for Information Interchange (ASCII), 47
amperes, 130
amplitude, 22, 167
analog bandwidth, 103-104, 125
analog modems, connecting, 21-23
analog signals
  creating from digital signals, 170
  frequency-based cable testing, 169
analyzing IP address structures, 358-359
ANSI (American National Standards Institute), 73
application layer (TCP/IP), 108, 347-349, 468
  network management, 475-476
  overview, 477-478
  protocols, 469-474
application-specific integrated circuits (ASICs), 298
applications
  processes, 464-467
  TCP/IP, 25
    HTTP, 26-28
    IP, 30-34
    networking models, 28
    standards, 25
    transport layers, 29
    troubleshooting, 34-44
applying
  ARP, 378-384
  powers of 2, 362
APs (access points), 154-155, 209-210
ARIN (American Registry for Internet Numbers), 369
ARP (Address Resolution Protocol), 327, 378-384
arp command, 380
AS (autonomous system), 418
ASCII (American Standard Code for Information Interchange), 47
ASICs (application-specific integrated circuits), 298

assigning IP addresses
  analyzing structures, 358-359
  classes, 359-360
  defining classes, 356-357
  LANs, 353-356
  managing, 373-384
  network numbers, 361-362
  networking math, 362-364
  unique, 368-372
association, APs, 155
asynchronous transmission, 271
atoms, 126
attachment user interface (AUI), 195
attenuation, 132-133
  copper cabling, 175-176
AUI (attachment user interface), 195
Auto-mdix (Automatic Medium-independent Crossover), 198, 288
autonegotiation
  100-Mbps Ethernet design, 280
  duplex and speed, 257-258
autonomous system (AS), 418
auxiliary ports, 227

B

B channels, 220
back-off timers, 252
backbones
  level links, 191
  links, 280, 310
backplanes (PCs), 10
bandwidth, 97, 416-417
  analog, 103-104
  data transfer time calculations, 102-103
  LANs, 97-98
  planning, 105
  shared, 319-321
  switched, 323
  throughput, 100-101
  WANs, 98-100
Base 10 (decimal numbering), 48
  converting, 49-56
  IP addresses, 56-58
Base 16 (hexadecimal numbering), 59
Base 2 (binary numbering), 49
  converting, 49-56
  IP addresses, 56-58
baseband transmissions, Ethernets, 239

Basic Rate Interface (BRI), 220

beacons, 155

benefits of routing and switching, 406-407

BGP (Border Gateway Protocol) metrics, 418

BIA (burned in address), 247

binary numbering (Base 2), 49

    converting, 49-56, 364

    IP addresses, 56-58

binary versions, determining subnet masks, 429-431

bits, 45-46

    determining number of host/subnet, 427-429

blocking STP, 312-313

Bohr, Niels, 127

Boolean logic, 60-62

Border Gateway Protocol (BGP) metrics, 418

BPDUs (bridge protocol data units), 315

BRI (Basic Rate Interface), 220

bridge protocol data units (BPDUs), 315

bridges, 203-204

    collisions

        domains, 206

        preventing, 323-325

    Ethernet, 78-79

    Layer 2, 297-301

    multiport, 208

    tables, 299

broadband, 239

broadcast addresses, 81, 361-362

    network, 434

    searching, 438

    shortcuts, 439-442

    subnets, 365

broadcast domains

    identifying, 328-329

    Layer 2, 325-328

broadcast frames, forwarding, 304-306

broadcast subnets, 435

broadcasts, ARP, 379

browsers. *See* **interfaces; web browsers**

buffering

    fiber-optic cabling, 151

    frames, 323-325

    switches, 255

building blocks, 194

burned in address (BIA), 247

bytes, 45-46

C

cable modems, 220

cables

    10BASE-T Ethernets, 272-274

    Cat 5, 97

    connecting, 24

    copper media, 125

        digital transmission, 125-134

        LANs, 134-144

        signaling over, 172

    crossover cables, 274

        pinouts, 143-144

        UTP, 197

    Ethernets, 141, 239

    fiber-optic, 283

    LANs, 189

        connecting Ethernet devices, 200-204, 206-212

        connectors/media, 194-195

        Ethernet physical layer, 190

        PC communications models, 212-216

        selecting Ethernet types, 191-193

        UTP cable pinouts, 196-200

    length, 180

    networks, 16-17

    optical media, 146, 149-150

        comparing copper cabling, 146-147

        electromagnetic spectrum, 147-148

        fiber types, 151-152

        transmissions, 174

    pinouts, 140

    rollover cables, 144, 225

    serial cables, 217

    small networks (2 PCs/one cable), 4

    straight-through, 141, 197, 273

    testing standards, 180-182

    UTP, 76

    WANs, 216-217

        fixed/modular routers, 224-225

        layers, 217-221

        router console cabling, 225-227

        selecting DCE/DTE cables, 222-223

    wireless media, 152-157

calculating

    data transfer time, 102-103

    hosts per network, 363

CAM (Content Addressable Memory), 83, 207

    STP, 314-316

    switches, 306-307

    tables, 299, 302-303

    unknown unicast frames, 304

capacitors, 9

carrier sense multiple access collision detect (CSMA/CD), 240
  10BASE-T Ethernets, 275-276
  Ethernet operation, 251-257
carrier sense multiple access with collision avoidance (CSMA/CA), 156
Category 5 (Cat 5), 97
CATV cable connections, WANs, 220
CD-ROM drives, 11
cells, APs, 154
central processing units (CPUs), 8
channel service unit/data service unit (CSU/DSU), 218
channels
  B, 220
  D, 220
charts, conversion, 58
Cheapernets, 137
Checksum field, 401, 463
CIDR (classless interdomain routing), 371
circuits, 133-134
cladding, 151
Class D IP addresses, 359
Class E address spaces, 359
classes
  IP addresses, 353-362
  networks, 363-364
classful routing protocols, 422
classless interdomain routing (CIDR), 371
classless routing protocols, 422
client/server network models, 213-216
clock ticks, 417
clocking, 222
coaxial cables, 136, 172. *See also* **cables**
collisions, 252
  10BASE-T LANs/hubs, 253-254
  domains, 202, 254-257, 318
    bridges, 206
    identifying, 328-329
    large/long, 319-321
    small, 321-323
  fragments, 275
  preventing, 255, 323-325
commands
  arp, 380
  ip subnet-zero, 422
  ipconfig, 38, 354
  netstat –an, 467
  nslookup, 38

ping, 39, 209, 380
ping 172.16.2.21, 39
traceroute, 42
tracert, 42-44
comparing
  copper cabling and fiber-optic cabling, 146-147
  DHCP and static addresses, 377
  routing protocols, 422-424
  TCP and UDP, 455
complex analog signals, 169
components
  fiber-optic cabling, 150-151
  metrics, 416
  networks, 7
    cables, 16-17
    devices, 17-19
    hardware, 7-13
    NICs, 13-15
  WLANs, 153-155
concentrators, 202
conductors, copper media, 129-130
configuration
  10BASE-T Ethernets, 275-278
  dynamic IP addresses, 375-377
  static IP addresses, 373-374
connected subnets, 411-412
connection-oriented, defining, 408
connectionless, defining, 408
connections. *See also* **cables**
  bandwidth, 97
    analog, 103-104
    data transfer time calculations, 102-103
    Ethernet LANs, 97-98
    Ethernet WANs, 98-100
    LANs, 97
    planning, 105
    throughput, 100-101
  consoles, 144
  directly connected networks, 345
  LANs
    cabling, 189
    connectors/media, 194-195
    devices, 200-204, 206-212
    Ethernet physical layer, 190
    PC communications models, 212-216
    routing between subnets, 395-400
    selecting Ethernet types, 191-193
    UTP cable pinouts, 196-200
  networks, 3
    ASCII alpha-numeric code, 47
    binary numbering (Base 2), 49

bits/bytes, 45-46
Boolean logic, 60-62
cables, 16-17
components, 7
conversion charts, 58
converting binary to decimal, 49-51
converting decimal to binary, 51-56
converting IP addresses between decimal and binary, 56-58
decimal numbering (Base 10), 48
defining, 3-7
devices, 17-19
enterprise, 19-20
hardware, 7-13
hexadecimal numbering (Base 16), 59
home connections, 21-24
NICs, 13-15
numbering, 45
TCP/IP, 25-32, 34-38
troubleshooting tools, 38-44
servers, 465-466
TCP, 465, 458
WANs
cabling, 216-217
fixed/modular routers, 224-225
layers, 217-221
router console cabling, 225-227
selecting DCE/DTE cables, 222-223
connectors, 9
Ethernets, 194-195
power, 10
RJ-11, 14
RJ-45, 140
consoles
connections, 144
routers, 225-227
Content Addressable Memory. See CAM
convergence, rapid, 414
conversations, 465
conversion charts, 58
converting
binary numbering to decimal numbering, 49-51
decimal numbering to binary numbering, 51-58, 369
copper media, 125. See also cables
attenuation, 175-176
coaxial cabling transmissions, 172
digital transmission, 125-134
insertion loss, 175-176
LANs, 134-143, 145-146
noise, 176-177

optical media, 146-147
signaling over, 172
core component, fiber-optic cabling, 151
core switch links, 194
cost, 417
Coulomb's Law, 127
CPUs (central processing units), 8
CRC (cyclic redundancy check), 245, 401
crossover cable, 274
pinouts, 143-144
UTP pinouts, 197
crosstalk, 176-179
CSMA/CA (carrier sense multiple access with collision avoidance), 156
CSMA/CD (carrier sense multiple access collision detect), 240
10BASE-T Ethernets, 275-276
Ethernet operation, 251-257
CSU/DSU (channel service unit/data service unit), 218
currents, measuring, 130-131
cut-through switching, 309
cyclic redundancy check (CRC), 245, 401

D

D channels, 220
data communication equipment (DCE), 222-223
Data field, 463
data flow, 329-331
data link layer, 108, 217-221
data terminal equipment. See DTE
data transfer time calculations, 102-103
databases, topology, 420
DC (direct current), 131
DCE (data communication equipment), 222-223
de-encapsulation, 111-113
DEC (Digital Equipment Corporation), 237
decimal numbering (Base 10), 48
converting, 49-56
IP addresses, 56-58
decimals, converting to binary numbers, 364
default gateways, 36, 374
default routers, 374
defining
IP address classes, 356-357
networks, 3-7

delay, 416-417
  propagation, 180, 307
  queuing, 307
  skew, 180
delivery, in-order (TCP), 461
depletion of IPv4 addresses, 370-371
design
  100-Mbps Ethernets, 280-281
  10BASE-T Ethernets, 275-278
  LANs, 317
    collision domains, 318-325
    data flow, 329-331
    identifying domains, 328-329
    Layer 2 broadcast domains, 325-328
    segments, 331
  WLANs, 153-155
desktops, 13. See also PCs
Destination MAC addresses, 245
Destination Port field, 463
destination port numbers, 465
Destination Service Access Point (DSAP), 249
detecting collisions, 253-254
detectors, 285
deterministic media access, 259-260
devices
  collision domains, 318
    large/long, 319-321
    small, 321-323
  data flow, 329-331
  Ethernet, 200-204, 206-212
  I/O, 9
  identifying, 328-329
  LANs, 74-75
  Layer 1, 329
  Layer 2, 329
  Layer 3, 329
  networks, 17-19
DHCP (Dynamic Host Configuration Protocol), 349, 469
  dynamic IP address configuration, 375-377
  static IP addresses, 377
dialogues, 468
Digital Equipment Corporation (DEC), 237
Digital Signal level 0 (DS0), 98
digital signals, 170
digital subscriber line. See DSL
digital transmission using copper wires, 125-134
Dijkstra shortest path first (SPF), 420
direct current (DC), 131

Direct Sequence Spread Spectrum (DSSS), 156, 210
directed broadcast addresses, 365
directly connected networks, 345
disks, memory, 9
distance vector algorithms, 419-420
distribution switches, 193
DIX Ethernet, 237
  frames, 246-247
  Type field, 250
DNS (Domain Name System), 349, 469
  name resolution, 35-36
domains
  broadcast (Layer 2), 325-328
  collisions, 202, 254-257, 318
    bridges, 206
    large/long, 319-321
    preventing, 323-325
    small, 321-323
  identifying, 328-329
  names, 470
  top-level, 470
downloading web pages, 26-28
drives
  CD-ROM, 11
  floppy disk, 11
  hard disk, 12
DSAP (Destination Service Access Point), 249
DSL (digital subscriber line), 220
  connecting, 23-24
DS0 (Digital Signal level 0), 98
DSSS (Direct Sequence Spread Spectrum), 156, 210
DTE (data terminal communication), 222-223
duplex settings, autonegotiation, 257-258
Dynamic Host Configuration Protocol (DHCP), 349, 469
  name resolution, 35-36
dynamic IP address configuration, 375-377
dynamic port numbers, 465
dynamic ports, 467
dynamic sliding windows, flow control through, 456-457

E

e-mail, TCP/IP application layer, 472-474
E/1 circuits, 221
effort, implementation, 414
EGP (Exterior Gateway Protocol), 418-419
EIA (Electronic Industries Association), 73, 134

EIGRP (Enhanced IGRP), 416

electrical currents, creating, 128

electricity
circuits, 133-134
currents, 130-131
units of measurement, 132
voltage, 130
wattage, 131

electricity, static, 128

electromotive force (EMF), 130

electromagnetic (EM) energy, 148, 209

electromagnetic interference (EMI), 147

electromagnetic spectrum, 147-148

electrostatic discharge (ESD), 128

Electronic Industries Alliance (EIA), 73, 134

electrons, 126

elements, atoms, 126

ELFEXT (equal-level far-end crosstalk), 180

EM (electromagnetic) energy, 148, 209

EMF (electro-motive force), 130

EMI (electromagnetic interference), 147

encapsulation, 111-112, 243

encrypted packets, 89

end-user level links, 191

Enhanced IGRP (EIGRP), 416

enterprise networks, 19-20

equal-level far-end crosstalk (ELFEXT), 180

errors
link error rates, 416
recovery, 29, 459-461

ESD (electrostatic discharge), 128

Ethernets, 237
10-Mbps, 269-271
100-Mbps, 269, 278-279
100BASE-FX, 281-282
design, 280-281
10Base-T, 76-77, 272
10BASE-T
design, 275-278
wiring, 272-274
bridges, 78-79
cabling, 141
devices, 200-204, 206-212
frames, 80, 247-248
framing, 242
DIX, 246-247
encapsulation, 243
IEEE 802.3 fields, 244-245

Gigabit, 282-283
1000BASE-T, 286-288
1000BASE-X, 283-286
future of, 288-290
headers, 249-250
history of, 237
hubs, 76-77
LANs, 74-75
bandwidth, 97-98
connectors/media, 194-195
LLC, 248-249
MAC addresses, 247
NICs
installing, 15
searching, 14
operation, 251
autonegotiation, 257-258
CSMA/CD, 251-257
MAC processes, 259-260
physical layer, 190
repeaters, 75-76
standards, 238-242
switches, 206-208, 297
CAM, 306-307
internal processing, 307-309
Layer 2 bridging, 297-306
STP, 310-316
timing, 272
Type fields, 250
types, 191-193
WAN bandwidth, 98-100

expansion slots, 10-12

expectational acknowledgments, 460

extended shared media, 319

extended star topologies, 95

Exterior Gateway Protocol (EGP), 418-419

Extranets, VPNs, 90

F

far-end crosstalk (FEXT), 179

Fast Link Pulse (FLP), 258, 280

FCC (Federal Communications Commission), 156

FCS (Frame Check Sequence), 240, 401

FDDI (Fiber Distributed Data Interface), 281

features, routing protocols, 414-419

Federal Communications Commission (FCC), 156

FEXT (far-end crosstalk), 179

FHSS (Frequency Hopping Spread Spectrum), 156, 210

Fiber Distributed Data Interface (FDDI), 281

fiber-optic cabling, 146-150, 283

  copper cabling

    comparing, 146-147

    electromagnetic spectrum, 147-148

  signaling over, 172

  types, 151-152

Fibre Channel, 286

fields

  Acknowledgment Number, 463

  Checksum, 401, 463

  Data, 463

  Destination Port, 463

  Flags, 463

  Header Length, 463

  IEEE 802.3, 244-245

  IP headers, 410

  Length, 246

  Options, 463

  Padding, 463

  Reserved, 463

  Sequence Number, 463

  Source Port, 463

  TTL, 401

  Type, 246, 250

  Urgent, 463

  Window, 463

File Transfer Protocol (FTP), 348, 464

  TCP/IP application layer, 474

filtering, 78, 203, 298-301

firewire, 10

fixed routers, 224-225

Fixed-Function Cisco 2503 routers, 224

flags

  ACK, 458

  SYN, 458

Flags field, 463

flapping, route, 416

flooding unicast addresses, 302-303

floppy disk drives, 11

flow control, 456-457

FLP (Fast Link Pulse), 258, 280

Fluke Network Inspector, 288

foil twisted-pair (FTP) cables, 138

formats

  MAC addresses, 247

  subnetted IP addresses, 366-367

forward acknowledgments, 460

forwarding, 78, 203, 298-301

  bridges, 205

  broadcasts, 304-306

  frames, 307-309

  IP routing, 393

    full IP headers, 409-411

    Layer 2 protocols, 403-407

    overview of, 394

    reliability of, 407-409

    routing between LAN subnets, 395-400

    routing single routers, 401-402

    WANs, 403

  multicasts, 304-306

  states, 317

  store-and-forward switching, 308

fragment-free switching, 309

fragment collisions, 275

Frame Check Sequence (FCS), 240, 401

frames, 112-113

  broadcast, 304-306

  buffering, 323, 325

  forwarding, 307-309

  multicast, 304-306

  queuing, 323-325

  switches

    Layer 2 bridging, 297-306

    operations, 297

  troubleshooting, 401

  unknown unicast, 304

framing (Ethernet) , 80, 242, 247-248

  DIX, 246-247

  encapsulation, 243

  IEEE 802.3 fields, 244-245

frequencies, 22, 148

Frequency Hopping Spread Spectrum (FHSS), 156, 210

frequency-based cable testing, 167

  analog signals, 169-170

  waves, 167-168

FTP (File Transfer Protocol), 464

  TCP/IP application layer, 474

FTP (foil twisted-pair) cables, 138. *See also* **cables**

full duplex, CSMA/CD, 254-257

full IP headers, 409-411

full mesh topologies, 95-96

future of Ethernets, 288-290

G–H

gateways, 36, 274

Gigabit Ethernets, 282-283
  1000BASE-T, 286-288
  1000BASE-X, 283-286
  future of, 288-290

half duplex
  10BASE-T Ethernets, 275-276
  CSMA/CD, 254-257

hard disk drives, 12

hardware, 7-13

Header Length field, 463

headers
  Ethernets, 249-250
  full IP, 409-411
  IEEE 802.3 Ethernet, 244
  references, 462-463

Hertz (Hz), 22

hexadecimal numbering (Base 16), 59

hierarchical physical topologies, 95

high-speed MAN services, 85

higher utilization (large collision domains), 321

history
  of Ethernets, 237
  of networks, 71-72
  of remote access, 23

home connections
  analog modems, 21-23
  cable modems, 24
  DSL modems, 23-24

hop counts, 415-417

hostnames, 470

hosts
  calculating, 363
  determining number of, 426-429
  local, 476
  parts, 356
  remote, 476
  resident subnets, 442-444
  TCP/IP, 340

HTTP (Hypertext Transfer Protocol), 25-29, 348, 471

hubs, 18, 201-202, 209
  10BASE-T Ethernets, 275-276
  collisions, 253-254
  Ethernet, 76-77
  types of, 202

hybrid algorithms, 421

hyperlinks, 472

Hyperterminals, 226

Hypertext Transfer Protocol (HTTP), 25-29, 348, 471

Hz (Hertz), 22

I

I/O (input/output) devices, 9

IAB (Internet Activities Board), 340

IANA (Internet Assigned Numbers Authority), 369

IC (integrated circuit), 9

identifying domains, 328-329

IE (Internet Explorer), 26

IEEE (Institute of Electrical and Electronic Engineers), 73, 135
  802.1D, 313-315
  802.2, 249
  802.3 fields, 244-245
  802.3ab, 287
  802.3ae, 289
  802.3z, 282
  Ethernets
    OSI model, 240-242
    types of, 238-239
  frames, 246-247
  Type field, 250

IETF (Internet Engineering Task Force), 73, 340

IGP (Interior Gateway Protocol), 418-419

IGRP (Interior Gateway Routing Protocol), 416

impedance, 132-133, 176

implementation of effort, 414

in-order delivery, TCP, 461

increments, 439

infrared (IR), 209

infrastructure mode (WLANs), 154

input/output (I/O), 9

insertion loss, 175-176, 180

installing Ethernet NICs, 15

Institute of Electrical and Electronic Engineers (IEEE), 73, 135

insulators, copper media, 129-130

integrated circuit (IC), 9

Integrated Services Digital Network (ISDN), 220

interactions, layers, 114-115

interesting octets, 432

interfaces, 78
AUI, 195
BRI, 220
FDDI, 281
IEEE 802.1D STP states, 313-314
NICs, 13-15
serial, 217-219
switches, 299
TCP/IP, 340-341
WICs, 218
Interior Gateway Protocol (IGP), 418-419
Interior Gateway Routing Protocol (IGRP), 416
internal processing, switches, 307-309
International Organization for Standardization (ISO), 106
International Telecommunications Union (ITU), 73
Internet Activities Board (IAB), 340
Internet Assigned Numbers Authority (IANA), 369
Internet connections, 3-7, 368-372
Internet Engineering Task Force (IETF), 73, 340
Internet Explorer (IE), 26
Internet Protocol. *See* IP
Internet service provider. *See* ISP
internetwork layer (TCP/IP), 341-345, 393
intranets, 89-90
IP (Internet Protocol)
addresses, 31, 353
assignment, 353-362
classes, 353-362
determining assignable (in subnets), 434-444
managing, 373-384
networking math, 362-364
overview of, 353
public, 370
subnetting, 32, 364-368
unicast, 356
unique, 368-372
packets, 343
private networks, 371-372
routing, 25, 31, 34, 343
full IP headers, 409-411
IP addresses, 344-345
Layer 2 protocols, 403-407
overview of, 394
reliability of, 407-409
routing, 342, 395-403
subnetting, 424
determining assignable IP addresses, 434-444
overview of, 424-425
schemes, 425-433

TCP/IP internetworking layer, 30-34
troubleshooting, 34-36, 38
ip subnet-zero command, 422
ipconfig command, 38, 354
IPv4 (Internet Protocol version 4)
address spaces, 359-360
depletion of, 370-371
IPv6 (Internet Protocol version 6), 372
IR (infrared), 209
ISDN (Integrated Services Digital Network), 220
ISO (International Organization for Standardization), 106
ISP (Internet service provider)
analog modems, 21-23
cable modems, 24
DSL modems, 23-24
ITU (International Telecommunications Union), 73

J–K

jack punch down, RJ-45, 200

keyboards, ports, 10

L

L3PDU (Layer 3 protocol data unit), 242
LANs (local-area networks)
ARP, 378-384
bandwidth, 97-98
cabling, 189
connecting Ethernet devices, 200-204, 206-212
connectors/media, 194-195
Ethernet physical layer, 190
PC communications models, 212-216
selecting Ethernet types, 191-193
UTP cable pinouts, 196-200
collisions, 253-254
copper cabling, 134-144
design, 317
collision domains, 318-325
data flow, 329-331
identifying domains, 328-329
Layer 2 broadcast domains, 325-328
segments, 331
devices, 74-75
Ethernet, 74-75
IP addresses, 353-357
speed limitations, 289
STP, 310-312
blocking, 312-313

CAM, 314-316
states, 313-314
subnets, 395-400
switches, 82, 208, 298, 323
WLANs, 153-157
laptops, 13
large collision domains, 319-321
large networks (Internet), 4, 7
latency, 307
Layer 1
data flow, 329-331
devices, 329
Layer 2
bridging, 297-306
broadcast domains, 325-328
data flow, 329-331
devices, 329
protocols, 403-407
Layer 3, 404
data flow, 329-331
devices, 329
Layer 3 protocol data unit (L3PDU), 242
layers
application (TCP/IP), 347-349, 468
interactions, 114-115
internetwork (TCP/IP), 341-345
network access (TCP/IP), 340-341
OSI, 107-109, 328-329
physical (Ethernet), 190
TCP/IP
internetworking, 30-34
overview of, 350-352
transport, 29
transport (TCP/IP), 345-347, 455-467
WANs, 217-221
learning
IP routes, 411-413
states, 314-317
leased circuits, 84
leased lines, point-to-point, 83-84
LED (light emitting diode), 9
length, cabling, 180
Length field, 246
light emitting diode (LED), 9
limitations of LANs, 289
link-state advertisements (LSAs), 420
link-state algorithms, 420
links
access switches, 193
backbone, 191, 280, 310

core switches, 194
end-user level, 191
error rates, 416
hyperlinks, 472
LLC, 190
loading, 416
point-to-point WAN, 216
uplinks, 193
workgroup level, 191
listening states, 314-316
LLC (Logical Link Control), 190, 248-249
loading links, 416
local hosts, 476
local-area networks. *See* LANs
logic, routing and switching, 405-406
logical bus topologies, 91-92
Logical Link Control (LLC), 190, 248-249
long collision domains, 319-321
long distances (LX), 283
loopback circuits, 254
loopback IP addresses, 360
LSAs (link-state advertisements), 420
LX (long distances), 283

M

MAC (Media Access Control), 78
addresses
Ethernets, 247
tables, 299
unknown unicast frames, 304
Destination addresses, 245
Ethernet processes, 259-260
Source addresses, 245
mainframe computers, 71
management
IP addresses, 373
applying ARP, 378-384
comparing DHCP, 377
dynamic IP address configuration, 375-377
static IP address configuration, 373-374
networks, 475-476
NMS, 476
out-of-band, 227
MANs (metropolitan-area networks), 85
mapping
Layer 3-to-Layer 2, 404
wire maps, 180

masks (subnet), 61-62, 367-368

    SLSM, 427

    VSLM, 422

mathematics (networks), 45, 362-364

    ASCII alpha-numeric code, 47

    binary numbering (Base 2), 49

    bits/bytes, 45-46

    Boolean logic, 60-62

    conversion charts, 58

    converting binary to decimal, 49-51

    converting decimal to binary, 51-56

    converting IP addresses between decimal and binary, 56-58

    decimal numbering (Base 10), 48

    hexadecimal numbering (Base 16), 59

maximum transmission unit (MTU), 416

measurement

    currents, 130-131

    resistance, 133

    units of, 132

    voltage, 130

media. *See also* **cables**

    copper, 125

        digital transmission, 125-134

        LANs, 134-146

    Ethernets, 194-195

    optical, 146-150

        comparing copper cabling, 146-147

        electromagnetic spectrum, 147-148

        fiber types, 151-152

    shared, 319

    wireless, 152-157

Media Access Control. *See* **MAC**

memory

    CAM, 207

        switches, 306-307

        tables, 299-303

    disks, 9

    RAM, 8

    ROM, 8

Metcalfe, Robert, 237

metrics

    components, 416

    hop count, 415

    robust, 414

    routes, 414-418

metropolitan-area networks (MANs), 85

microprocessors, 8

microsegmentation, 323

minicomputers, 71

MLS (multilayer switching), 394

MMF (multimode fiber), 286

models

    client/server, 213

    OSI, 106-109

    peer-to-peer, 213

    TCP/IP networking, 28, 110, 339-340

        application layer, 347-349

        de-encapsulation, 113

        encapsulation, 111-112

        frames, 112-113

        internetwork layer, 341-345

        layer interactions, 114-115

        network access layer, 340-341

        overview of, 349-352

        packets, 112-113

        PDUs, 112-113

        segments, 112-113

        transport layer, 345-347

modems

    analog, 21-23

    cable, 24, 220

    DSL, 23-24

modular routers, 224-225

motherboards, 9

mouse, ports, 10

Mozilla Firefox, 26

MTU (maximum transmission unit), 416

multicast frames, forwarding, 304-306

multilayer switching (MLS), 394

multimeters, voltage measurement, 130

multimode fiber (MMF), 286

multimode fibers, 151-152

multiplexing, 347, 465

multiport bridges, 208

multiport repeaters, 77, 202

N

names

    bits/bytes, 45

    domains, 470

    resolution, 35-36, 469

    transmission rates, 46

nanometer (nm), 148

NAT (Network Address Translation), 371-372

near-end crosstalk (NEXT), 178-180

Netscape, 26

netstat –an command, 467

Network Address Translation (NAT), 371-372

Network File System (NFS), 348

network interface cards. *See* NICs

Network Link Pulses (NLPs), 258

Network Management System (NMS), 476

network operating system (NOS), 215

networks

    access layer (TCP/IP), 340-341

    application layer (TCP/IP), 347-349

    bandwidth, 97

        analog, 103-104

        data transfer time calculations, 102-103

        Ethernet LANs, 97-98

        Ethernet WANs, 98-100

        LANs, 97

        planning, 105

        throughput, 100-101

    broadcast addresses, 434

    classes, 363-364

    components, 7

        cables, 16-17

        devices, 17-19

        hardware, 7-13

        NICs, 13-15

    connections, 3

    copper

        digital transmission, 125-134

        LANs, 134-143, 145-146

    defining, 3-7

    directly connected, 345

    enterprise, 19-20

    home connections, 23

        analog modems, 21-22

        cable modems, 24

        DSL modems, 23-24

    hosts, 363

    internetwork layer (TCP/IP), 341-345

    LANs

        cabling, 189

        connecting Ethernet devices, 200-204, 206-212

        connectors/media, 194-195

        Ethernet physical layer, 190

        PC communications models, 212-216

        selecting Ethernet types, 191-193

        UTP cable pinouts, 196-200

    large (Internet), 4, 7

    management, 475-476

    MANs, 85

    math, 362-364

    numbering, 45

        ASCII alpha-numeric code, 47

        binary numbering (Base 2), 49

        bits/bytes, 45-46

        Boolean logic, 60-62

        conversion charts, 58

        converting binary to decimal, 49-51

        converting decimal to binary, 51-56

        converting IP addresses between decimal and binary, 56-58

        decimal numbering (Base 10), 48

        hexadecimal numbering (Base 16), 59

    numbers, 361-362

    overview of, 71

        broadcast/unicast addresses, 81

        Ethernet bridges, 78-79

        Ethernet frames, 80

        Ethernet hubs/10Base-T, 76-77

        Ethernet LANs/LAN devices, 74-75

        Ethernet repeaters, 75-76

        history of, 71-72

        LAN switches, 82

        need for protocols/standards, 73-74

    parts, 356

    private IP, 371-372

    SANs, 86-87

    small (two PCs/one cable), 4

    TCP/IP, 25

        de-encapsulation, 113

        encapsulation, 111-112

        frames, 112-113

        HTTP, 26-28

        IP, 30-34

        layer interactions, 114-115

        networking model, 110

        overview of, 349-352

        packets, 112-113

        PDUs, 112-113

        segments, 112-113

        standards, 25

        transport layers, 29

        troubleshooting IP, 34-38

        troubleshooting tools, 38-44

    topologies, 91

        extended star, 95

        full mesh, 95-96

        hierarchical physical, 95

        logical bus, 91-92

        partial mesh, 95-96

        physical bus, 91-92

        physical star, 91-92

        ring, 94

    transport layer (TCP/IP), 345-347

    unique IP addresses, 368-372

VPNs, 87-88
   intranets, 89-90
   types of, 90
WANs, 83
   cabling, 216-217
   fixed/modular routers, 224-225
   layers, 217-221
   point-to-point leased lines, 83-84
   router console cabling, 225-227
   routers, 85
   selecting DCE/DTE cables, 222-223
   wired, 154

neutrons, 126

NEXT (near-end crosstalk), 178-180

next-hop routers, 345, 412

NFS (Network File System), 348

NICs (network interface cards), 13-15, 135
   Ethernet, 211-212

NLPs (Network Link Pulses), 258

nm (nanometer), 148

NMS (Network Management System), 476

noise, 171
   attenuation, 175-176
   cabling testing standards, 180-182
   coaxial cabling transmissions, 172
   copper/fiber-optic cabling, 172
   optical cabling transmissions, 174
   sources of, 176-177
   types of crosstalk, 178-179

nondeterministic media access, 259-260

NOS (network operating system), 215

nslookup command, 38

number of required subnets, determining, 425-433

numbering

numbers
   ARIN, 369
   IANA, 369
   networks, 45, 361-362
      ASCII alpha-numeric code, 47
      binary numbering (Base 2), 49
      bits/bytes, 45-46
      Boolean logic, 60-62
      conversion charts, 58
      converting binary to decimal, 49-51
      converting decimal to binary, 51-56
      converting IP addresses between decimal and binary, 56-58
      decimal numbering (Base 10), 48
      hexadecimal numbering (Base 16), 59

port application processes, 464-467
   subnets, 434-437

O

octets, 432

OFDM (Orthogonal Frequency Division Multiplexing), 156

Ohm's law, 132

open networking models, 106

operating systems, NOS, 215

operations
   Ethernets, 251
      autonegotiation, 257-258
      CSMA/CD, 251-257
      MAC processes, 259-260
   switches, 297
      CAM, 306-307
      internal processing, 307-309
      Layer 2 bridging, 297-306
      STP, 310-316

optical media, 146-150
   cabling transmissions, 174
   copper cabling
      comparing, 146-147
      electromagnetic spectrum, 147-148
   fiber types, 151-152

options, 10-Mbps Ethernets, 272

Options field, 463

organization, WLANs, 155-157

Organizationally Unique Identifier (OUI), 247

Orthogonal Frequency Division Multiplexing (OFDM), 156

OSI model, 106
   devices, identifying, 328-329
   Ethernets, 240
      comparing standards, 241-242
      IEEE 802.2 standards, 240
      IEEE 802.3 standards, 240
   layers, 107-109

OUI (Organizationally Unique Identifier), 247

out-of-band management, 227

outer jackets, fiber-optic cabling, 151

P

packets, 112-113, 399
   encapsulation inside Ethernet frames, 243
   encrypted, 89
   IP, 343

Padding field, 463

parallel ports, 10

partial mesh topologies, 95-96

parts (network/host), 356

passing tokens, 259

passive scanning, 155

paths
determination, 394
internal processing, 310

PCB (printed circuit board), 9

PCMCIA (Personal Computer Memory Card International Association), 12

PCs (personal computers), 9
backplane, 10
communications models, 212-216
history of, 72
home connections
analog modems, 21-23
cable modems, 24
DSL modems, 23-24
small networks (2 PCs/one cable), 4

PDUs (protocol data units), 112-113

peer-to-peer network models, 213-214

performance, broadcast domains, 326-328

periodic updates, 421

periods, 22
waves, 167

permanent memory, 9

permanent virtual circuits. See PVCs

Personal Computer Memory Card International Association (PCMCIA), 12

personal computers. See PCs

phone lines
analog modems, 21-23
DSL modems, 23-24

physical bus topologies, 91-92

physical network topologies, 91

physical layer, 108
Ethernet (LAN cabling), 190
WANs, 217-221

physical star topologies, 91-92

ping 172.16.2.21 command, 39

ping command, 39, 209, 380

pinouts
cabling, 140
crossover-cable, 143-144
Ethernets, 141
selecting, 145

TIA/EIA-568-A, 142
UTP cable, 196-200

planning bandwidth, 105

plug-ins, web browsers, 28

point-to-point leased lines, 83-84

Point-to-Point Protocol (PPP), 403

point-to-point WAN links, 216

POP3 (Post Office Protocol version 3), 472-474

ports, 78
auxiliary, 227
dynamic, 467
keyboards, 10
mouse, 10
multiport repeaters, 77
numbers, 464-467
parallel, 10
registered, 467
serial, 10
switches, 299
USB, 10
well-known, 465-467

Post Office Protocol version 3 (POP3), 472-474

power connectors, 10

power sum equal-level far-end crosstalk (PSELFEXT), 180

power sum near-end crosstalk (PSNEXT), 179-180

powers of 2, 428
applying, 362

PPP (Point-to-Point Protocol), 403

Preamble, 245, 271

presentation layer, 108

preventing collisions, 255, 323-325

printed circuit board (PCB), 9

private IP networks, 371-372

probabilistic, 259

processes, application, 464-467

processing internal switches, 307-309

processors
CPUs, 8
microprocessors, 8

propagation delay, 180, 307

protocol data units (PDUs), 112-113

protocols
Ethernets, 248-249
Internet layer, 341
need for, 73-74
routing, 411
algorithms, 419-421
classful, 422

classless, 422
comparing, 422-424
routers leaning IP routes, 411-413
selecting, 414-419
updates, 421
standards, 25
TCP/IP
application layer, 469-474
network management, 475-476
overview, 477-478
protons, 126
proxy ARPs, applying, 378-384
PSELFEXT (power sum equal-level far-end crosstalk), 180
PSNEXT (power sum near-end crosstalk), 179-180
public IP addresses, 370
purchasing LAN switches, 208
PVCs (permanent virtual circuits), 96

Q–R

queuing
delay, 307
frames, 323-325

radio frequencies (RFs), 209
radio frequency interference (RFI), 147
RAM (random-access memory), 8
ranges, searching addresses, 438-439
rapid convergence, 414
RARP (Reverse Address Resolution Protocol), 375
rates, transmission names, 46
read-only memory. *See* **ROM**
Realtime tab, 39
reassembly, TCP, 461
recovery, TCP errors, 459-461
redundancy, 280
references, headers, 462-463
registered jack 45 (RJ-45) connectors, 140, 200
registered ports, 467
reliability, 417
IP routing, 407-409
TCP error recovery, 459-461
remote access, history of, 23
remote hosts, 476

repeaters, 200
Ethernet, 75-76
multiport, 202
replies, ARP, 380
requests, ARP, 379
Requests For Comments (RFCs), 340
Reserved field, 463
resident subnets, 442-444
resistance, 132-133
resistors, 9
resolution
DNS, 35-36
names, 469
return loss, 180
Reverse Address Resolution Protocol (RARP), 375
reversed-pair fault, 181
RFCs (Request For Comments), 340
RFI (radio frequency interference), 147
RFs (radio frequencies), 209
ring topologies, 94
RIP (Routing Information Protocol), 327, 413-415
RJ-11 connectors, 14
RJ-45 (registered jack 45) connectors, 140, 200
robust metrics, 414
rollover cables, 144, 225
ROM (read-only memory), 8
routable protocols, 394
routed protocols, 394
routers
console cabling, 225-227
default, 374
default gateway, 36
fixed, 224-225
Fixed-Function Cisco 2503, 224
IP, 34
learning IP routes, 411-413
modular, 224-225
next-hop, 345, 412
processing overhead, 414
routing single, 401-402
serial interfaces, 217-219
WANs, 85
routes
flapping, 416
IP, 411-413
metrics, 414-418
static, 412

routing
  CIDR, 371
  IP, 31, 34, 343, 393
    full IP headers, 409-411
    IP addresses, 344-345
    Layer 2 protocols, 403-407
    overview of, 394
    reliability of, 407-409
    routing between LAN subnets, 395-400
    routing single routers, 401-402
    WANs, 403
  protocols, 411
    algorithms, 419-421
    classful, 422
    classless, 422
    comparing, 422-424
    routers learning IP routes, 411-413
    selecting, 414-419
    updates, 421
  switching
    benefits of, 406-407
    logic, 405-406
  tables, 395
Routing Information Protocol (RIP), 327, 413-415

S

same layer interaction, 115
SANs (storage area networks), 85-87
scanning, 155
schemes, subnet, 425-444
ScTP (screened twisted-pair) cables, 138. *See also* **cables**
searching
  address ranges, 438-439
  broadcast addresses, 438
  Ethernet NICs, 14
  resident subnets, 443-444
  subnets, 435-442
segmentation, 321, 346
  TCP, 461
segments, 74, 112-113, 323, 331
selecting
  DCE/DTE cables, 222-223
  Ethernet types (speeds), 191-193
  pinouts, 145
  routing protocols, 414-419
  UTP cable pinouts, 196-200
semiconductors, copper media, 129-130
sending frames over Ethernets, 247-248
Sequence Number field, 463

sequence numbers, 30
serial cables, 217
serial interfaces, 217-219
serial ports, 10
servers, 213
  connections, 465-466
  web, 26
Service Set Identifier (SSI), 155
session layer, 108
sessions, 468
SFD (Start Frame Delimiter), 240, 245, 271
shared bandwidth, 319-321
shared media, 319
shielded twisted-pair (STP) cables, 135-138. *See also* **cables**
shielding, 136, 172
short distances (SX), 283
shortcuts
  broadcast addresses, 439-442
  determining subnet masks, 432-433
  resident subnets, 444
shortest path first (SPF), 420
signals
  analog
    creating digital signals from, 170
    frequency-based cable testing, 169
  collisions, 252
  noise, 171
    attenuation, 175-176
    cabling testing standards, 180-182
    coaxial cabling transmissions, 172
    copper/fiber-optic cabling, 172
    optical cabling transmissions, 174
    sources of, 176-177
    types of crosstalk, 178-179
simple analog signals, 169
Simple Mail Transfer Protocol (SMTP), 348, 472-474
Simple Network Management Protocol (SNMP), 349, 475-476
sine waves, 168
single routes, routing in, 401-402
single-mode fiber (SMF), 151-152, 286
sizes of networks, 7
skew, delay, 180
SLSM (subnet-length subnet masking), 427
small collision domains, 321-323
small networks (two PCs/one cable), 4
SMF (single-mode fiber), 151-152, 286

SMTP (Simple Mail Transfer Protocol), 348, 472-474

SNAP (Subnetwork Access Protocol), 250

SNMP (Simple Network Management Protocol), 349, 475-476

Source MAC address, 245

Source Port field, 463

Spanning Tree Algorithm (STA), 315

Spanning Tree Protocol. *See* **STP**

spectrums, spread, 210

speed
    100-Mbps Ethernet design, 280-281
    autonegotiation, 257-258
    Ethernets, 191-193, 239
    LAN limitations, 289
    WANs, 221

SPF (shortest path first), 420

split-pair wiring fault, 182

spread spectrum, 210

square waves, 168

SSI (Service Set Identifier), 155

STA (Spanning Tree Algorithm), 315

stability, 414

standards
    1000BASE-T, 286-288
    1000BASE-X, 283-286
    cabling testing, 180-182
    Ethernets, 238-242
    need for, 73-74
    support, 414
    TCP/IP, 25
    TIA/EIA-568-A, 142
    WLANs, 155-157

Start Frame Delimiter (SFD), 240, 245, 271

states
    forwarding, 317
    learning, 314-317
    listening, 314-316
    STP, 313-314

static electricity, 128

static IP addresses
    configuration, 373-374
    DHCP, comparing, 377

static routes, 412

static-length subnet masking (SLSM), 427

storage area networks (SANs), 85-87

store-and-forward switching, 308

STP (shielded twisted-pair) cables, 135-138. *See also* **cables**

STP (Spanning Tree Protocol), 310-312
    blocking, 312-313
    CAM, 314-316
    states, 313-314
    topologies, 315

straight-through cables, 141, 273
    UTP pinouts, 197

strengthening material, fiber-optic cabling, 151

structures, IP addresses, 358-359

subnets, 364-368
    broadcast, 435
    connected, 411-412
    IP, 32, 424
        determining assignable IP addresses, 434-444
        overview of, 424-425
        schemes, 425-433
    LANs, 395-400
    masks, 61-62, 427
    numbers, 434-438
    resident, 442-444
    searching, 439-442
    VSLM, 422
    zero, 435-436

Subnetwork Access Protocol (SNAP), 250

support, standards, 414

switched bandwidth, 323

switched LANs, 323

switches
    10BASE-T Ethernets, 276-278
    access, 193
    buffering, 255
    collisions, 323-325
    core links, 194
    cut-through switching, 309
    distribution, 193
    Ethernet, 206-208, 297
        CAM, 306-307
        internal processing, 307-309
        Layer 2 bridging, 297-306
        STP, 310-316
    fragment-free switching, 309
    interfaces, 299
    LANs, 82, 208, 298
    ports, 299
    store-and-forwarding switches, 308

switching
    MLS, 394
    routing
        benefits of, 406-407
        logic, 405-406
    tables, 207, 299

SX (short distances), 283

SYN flags, 458

synchronization, 222

system units, 12

T

T/1 circuits, 221

tables

ARP, 380
bridging, 299
CAM, 83, 299-307
MAC address, 299
routing, 34, 395
switching, 207, 299

tabs, Realtime, 39

TCP (Transmission Control Protocol), 346, 455

application processes, 464-467
connecting, 458
error recovery, 29, 459-461
header references, 462-463
in-order delivery, 461
multiplexing, 465
reassembly, 461
segmentation, 461
UDP, 455

TCP/IP (Transmission Control Protocol/Internet Protocol), 25, 339

application layer, 468
  network management, 475-476
  overview, 477-478
  protocols, 469-474
HTTP, 26-28
IP, 30-34
models, 339-340
  application layer, 347-349
  internetwork layer, 341-345
  network access layer, 340-341
  overview of, 349-352
  transport layer, 345-347
networking model, 28, 110
  de-encapsulation, 113
  encapsulation, 111-112
  frames, 112-113
  layer interactions, 114-115
  packets, 112-113
  PDUs, 112-113
  segments, 112-113
standards, 25
transport layer, 29, 455
  application processes, 464-467
  connection TCP, 458

  flow control, 456-457
  header references, 462-463
  in-order delivery, 461
  reassembly, 461
  segmentation, 461
  TCP error recovery, 459-461
  windowing, 456-457
troubleshooting
  IP, 34-38
  tools, 38-44

telco, 219

Telecommunications Industry Association (TIA), 73, 134, 273

Telnet (Terminal Emulation), 348, 476

temporary memory, 8

terminals, 71

terminating TCP connections, 458

terminology

MANs, 85
networks, 71
  broadcast/unicast addresses, 81
  Ethernet bridges, 78-79
  Ethernet frames, 80
  Ethernet hubs/10Base-T, 76-77
  Ethernet LANs/LAN devices, 74-75
  Ethernet repeaters, 75-76
  history of, 71-72
  LAN switches, 82
  need for protocols/standards, 73-74
SANs, 86-87
topologies, 91
  extended star, 95
  full mesh, 95-96
  hierarchical physical, 95
  logical bus, 91-92
  partial mesh, 95-96
  physical bus, 91-92
  physical star, 91-92
  ring, 94
VPNs, 87-88
  intranets, 89-90
  types of, 90
WANs, 83
  point-to-point leased lines, 83-84
  routers, 85

testing

cables, 180-182
frequency-based cable, 167
  analog signals, 169-170
  waves, 167-168
multimeters, 130

TFTP (Trivial File Transfer Protocol), 348, 475

Thicknets, 137

Thinnets, 137

three-way handshakes, 458

throughput versus bandwidth, 100-101

TIA (Telecommunications Industry Association), 73, 134, 273

TIA/EIA-568-A standard, 142

ticks, 417

time periods, waves, 167

Time to Live (TTL) fields, 401

timers, back-off, 252

timing (Ethernet), 272

tokens, passing mechanisms, 259

tools, troubleshooting, 38-44

top-level domains, 470

topologies
    databases, 420
    networks, 91
        extended star, 95
        full mesh, 95-96
        hierarchical physical, 95
        logical bus, 91-92
        partial mesh, 95-96
        physical bus, 91-92
        physical star, 91-92
        ring, 94
    STP, 315

traceroute command, 42

tracert command, 42, 44

transfers, data transfer time calculations, 102-103

transistors, 9

Transmission Control Protocol. *See* **TCP**

Transmission Control Protocol/Internet Protocol. *See* **TCP/IP**

transmission rates, 46

transmitters, 285

transport layer, 29, 108, 345-347, 455
    application processes, 464-467
    connecting TCP, 458
    flow control, 456-457
    header references, 462-463
    in-order delivery, 461
    reassembly, 461
    segmentation, 461
    TCP error recovery, 459-461
    windowing, 456-457

transposed-pair wiring fault, 182

triggered updates, 421

Trivial File Transfer Protocol (TFTP), 348, 475

troubleshooting
    cable testing standards, 180-182
    frames, 401
    IP, 34-38
    noise, 171
        attenuation, 175-176
        coaxial cabling transmissions, 172
        copper/fiber-optic cabling, 172
        optical cabling transmissions, 174
        sources of, 176-177
        types of crosstalk, 178-179
    TCP error recovery, 459-461
    tools, 38-44

trunks, 280, 310

TTL (Time to Live) fields, 401

Type field, 246, 250

types
    of crosstalk, 178-179
    of current, 131
    of Ethernets, 191-193, 238-239
    of fiber-optic cabling, 151-152
    of hubs, 202

U

UDP (User Datagram Protocol), 346, 455
    header references, 462-463
    TCP, 455

unicast IP addresses, 81, 356
    flooding, 302-303

unique IP addresses, 368-372

units, transmission rates, 46

Universal Resource Locator (URL), 35, 471

Universal Serial Bus (USB), 10

unknown unicast frames, 304

unreliable protocols, 408

unshielded twisted-pair. *See also* **UTP**

updates
    periodic, 421
    routing protocols, 421
    triggered, 421

uplinks, 193

Urgent field, 463

URL (Universal Resource Locator), 35, 471

USB (Universal Serial Bus), 10

User Datagram Protocol (UDP), 346, 455
  header references, 462-463
  TCP, 455
UTP (unshielded twisted-pair) cables, 76, 137-146. *See also*
cables
  cable pinouts, 196-200

V

valid addresses, searching range of, 438-439
Virtual Private Networks. *See* **VPNs**
VLSM (variable-length subnet masking), 422
voltage, 130
VPNs (Virtual Private Networks), 87-88
  intranets, 89-90
  types of, 90

W

WANs (wide-area networks), 71, 83
  bandwidth, 98-100
  cabling, 216-217
    fixed/modular routers, 224-225
    layers, 217-221
    router console cabling, 225-227
    selecting DCE/DTE cables, 222-223
  interface cards (WICs), 218
  point-to-point leased lines, 83-84
  routers, 85
  routing, 403
wattage, 131
wavelengths, 148
waves, frequency-based cable testing, 167-168
web browsers, 26
  plug-ins, 28
web pages, downloading, 26-28
web servers, 26
well-know ports, 465-467
Wi-Fi alliance, 157
WICs (WAN interface cards), 218
wide-area networks. *See* **WANs**
wildcards, 431
Window field, 463
windowing, 456-457
wire maps, 180
wired networks, 154
wireless LANs. *See* **WLANs**

wireless media, 152-157
wiring. *See also* **cables**
  10BASE-T Ethernets, 272-274
  copper media, 125
    digital transmission, 125-134
    LANs, 134-143, 145-146
WLANs (wireless LANs), 12, 153-157, 209-210
workgroup level links, 191
workstations, 215
WWW (World Wide Web), TCP/IP application layer, 471

X–Z

Xerox, 237
XNS (Xerox Network System) protocol, 422

zero subnets, 435-436

Notes

Notes

Cisco Press

SAVE UP TO 30%

Become a member and save at **ciscopress.com**!

Complete a **user profile** at ciscopress.com today to become a member and benefit from **discounts up to 30% on every purchase** at ciscopress.com, as well as a more customized user experience. Your membership will also allow you access to the entire Informit network of sites.

Don't forget to subscribe to the monthly Cisco Press newsletter to be the first to learn about new releases and special promotions. You can also sign up to get your first **30 days FREE on Safari Bookshelf** and preview Cisco Press content. Safari Bookshelf lets you access Cisco Press books online and build your own customized, searchable electronic reference library.

Visit **www.ciscopress.com/register** to sign up and start saving today!

The profile information we collect is used in aggregate to provide us with better insight into your technology interests and to create a better user experience for you. You must be logged into ciscopress.com to receive your discount. Discount is on Cisco Press products only; shipping and handling are not included.

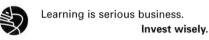

Learning is serious business.
Invest wisely.

Continue Your Studies with these Recommended Titles

1-58720-156-9

Your First Introduction to Key Networking Topics

Voice over IP First-Step
ISBN: 1-58720-156-9

Wireless Networks First-Step
ISBN: 1-58720-111-9

Network Security First-Step
ISBN: 1-58720-099-6

CCNA Exam Preparation

CCNA Certification Library
ISBN: 1-58720-095-3

CCNA Command Quick Reference
ISBN: 1-58713-159-5

**CCNA Flash Cards and Exam
Practice Pack**, Second Ed.
ISBN: 1-58720-079-1

CCNA Video Instruction Pack
ISBN: 1-58720-168-2
Available May 2006 on ciscopress.com

1-58720-095-3

Your Guide to a Successful IT Career

The IT Career Builder's Toolkit
ISBN: 1-58713-156-0

1-58713-156-0

Illustrated Reference Books Make Learning Simple

Home Networking Simplified
ISBN: 1-58720-136-4

Learn the basics of home networking, from connecting to the Internet to connecting your computers

Internet Phone Services Simplified
ISBN: 1-58720-162-3
Available April 2006

Shows how to integrate Internet phone services into the home, subscribe to a service, install equipment, and troubleshoot potential issues

Home Network Security Simplified
ISBN: 1-58720-163-1
Available June 2006

Describes the fundamentals of home network security and shows how to design security strategies

Wireless Home Networking Simplified
ISBN: 1-58720-161-5
Available August 2006

Shows how to design a wireless home network

1-58720-136-4

ciscopress.com

Learning is serious business.   **Invest wisely.**

CISCO SYSTEMS

Register this Book for Exclusive Content

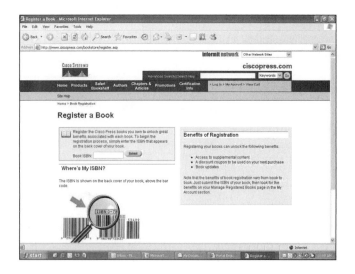

Gain access to the following benefits when you register *Networking Basics CCNA 1 Companion Guide* on ciscopress.com.

n **Packet Tracer** configuration files for activities described in the book

n **Answer Key** to Appendix C, "Extra Practice Problems"

n PDF chapter from *Network Security First-Step* and *Voice over IP First-Step*

n Coupon code for **35% off** Cisco Press titles, including *CCNA Certification Library*, *CCNA Flash Cards and Exam Practice Pack*, Second Ed., and *Cisco CCNA Network Simulator*.

To register this book, go to **www.ciscopress.com/bookstore/register.asp** and enter the book's ISBN located on the back cover. You'll then be prompted to log in or join ciscopress.com to continue registration.

After you register the book, a link to the supplemental content will be listed on your My Registered Books page.

ciscopress.com

Learning is serious business. **Invest wisely.**